EUROPE

ASIA

Ainu

s Beag

Vasilika

AFRICA

Itugao

Ibo

Nuer

pelle

Tiv

Manu

Ashanti

Azande

Banyoro

Kapauku

Yoruba

Mbuti

Arapesh

Alorese

Tiwi

Trobriand

Barotse

Yir Yoront

Bushman

INDIAN

Swazi

OCEAN

Arunta

AUSTRALIA

Anthropology

Holt, Rinehart and Winston, Inc.

New York
Chicago • San Francisco
Atlanta • Dallas
Montreal • Toronto

Anthropology

William A. Haviland

University of Vermont

A Leogryph Book

Design: **Ladislav Svatos**
Line art: **Vantage Art, Inc.**
Photo editing: **Robert Morton**
Production services: **Cobb-Dunlop**
Cover Photo: **Anthony Howarth from Woodfin Camp**

Copyright © 1974 by Holt, Rinehart and Winston, Inc.
All rights reserved
74 75 76 77 78   032   10 9 8 7 6 5 4 3 2
Printed in the United States of America
Library of Congress Catalog Card Number: 74–1641
ISBN: 0-03-011476-4

Contents

Contents

Contents

Contents   xiii

Contents

Contents

Contents

Preface

Purpose of the book

This text is designed for introductory anthropology courses at the college level. It treats the four divisions of anthropology—physical and cultural anthropology, linguistics and prehistoric archeology—and presents the key concepts and terminology germane to each.

The aim of the text is to give the student an overview of the principles and processes of anthropology, as well as to familiarize him with those subjects he can expect to meet should he pursue the subject in advanced courses. Because there are many ways to teach anthropology effectively and because anthropologists in general are a pragmatic group, willing to draw on any theoretical approach that offers insights into human behavior, the text draws from the research and ideas of a number of schools of anthropological thought. Therefore, the student will be exposed to a mix of such approaches as evolutionism, historical particularism, diffusionism, functionalism, French structuralism, structural functionalism, and others.

Each author has his own ideas about the way a textbook should be written and how the material should be presented. Some prefer to present only the most basic information about the subject with a minimum of graphic material and student aids. Such a design, it is felt, allows the teacher great latitude in the classroom: it is up to him to fill in the details and enrich the text with examples and other explanatory materials. Other authors think the best texts are those that attract the student's attention with extensive, lavish photographs and other graphics, study questions, projects, sample tests, and the like. Each of these methods has its merits. However, this text takes an eclectic approach, choosing the best from both methods. The book attempts to evoke a maximum of student understanding by presenting anthropology as interestingly as possible: clarity of expression in defining ideas and concepts; an orderly presentation of material; abundant colorful examples to illustrate concepts; numerous photographs and other graphic material including six full-color portfolios; suggested annotated reading lists and up-to-date original studies at the end of each chapter; a glossary; and a comprehensive bibliography with 500 entries.

Advantages   In addition to covering the basics of both physical and cultural anthropology, the book is designed to integrate rather than separate the physical and cultural areas so there is a "feedback" of information, a continuous back-and-forth reference between the two subdisciplines. Thus, in chapters devoted primarily to physical anthropology, references are made and examples given to illustrate how particular developments in man's physical evolution affect his cultural development; similarly, in the chapters on cultural anthropology, references to physical anthropology explain why certain cultural characteristics prevail.

Another advantage of this text is that each chapter has been developed as a self-contained unit of study. This method of organization facilitates student comprehension and gives the teacher greater freedom, enabling him to assign readings from the text in accordance with his own particular pedagogical method and sequence of presenting the material. Finally, each chapter itself has been organized into easily digestible segments by the liberal use of subheads, numbered entries, and other dividing techniques.

**Organization
of the book**   The book has been divided into seven parts.

Part 1   **The study of man,** defines anthropology, explains how it relates to other disciplines and the importance of its contributions to man's knowledge of the world around him. Chapter 1 presents the principal goals of anthropology and defines each of its four subdivisions; Chapter 2 is a history of the discipline. Chapter 3 considers some of the concepts of biology and evolution and relates these to man, thus setting the stage for the upcoming section, which studies man's evolution.

Part 2   **The evolution of man,** contains five chapters devoted to an illumination of physical anthropology. Chapter 4 discusses the evolution of man's closest animal relatives, the primates, and compares their behavior to that of man. Chapters 5 through 7 document the archeological and paleontological evidence for man's existence on earth over the past two million years, illuminating the major trends in human evolution that have made man such a distinctive animal. Chapter 8 considers how the variations, or the so-called races of man, came into existence and the implications of this variation on human behavior and culture today.

Part 3 **The archeological record,** is devoted to a cultural consideration of modern man's beginnings. Chapter 9 presents the principal methods and theories of archeology. Chapters 10 through 12 detail the course of man's cultural evolution from the Paleolithic era, when he first became a social being, through the time when he began producing his own food, up to the rise of civilization in the Old and New Worlds.

Part 4 **Culture and man,** covers the ways man communicates, behaves, and lives in groups. Chapter 13 defines culture and discusses its importance; Chapter 14 examines language, the vehicle by which culture is transmitted, and thus introduces linguistics as a sub-division of anthropology; and Chapter 15 raises the question of the relationship between culture and personality, thus introducing the student to psychological anthropology.

Part 5 **The formation of groups,** deals with the ways culture accomplishes the organization of groups, which themselves are necessary for the cooperative behavior on which human life depends. The chapters describe marriage and the family, kinship patterns, and other forms of social organization necessary for group living.

Part 6 **Social integration,** deals with the things groups do, and the ways different groups are integrated into larger social units. Chapters 20 through 22 describe economics, politics, and other kinds of social controls. Other chapters examine the integrative roles of religion and art.

Part 7 **Change and the future,** looks at the dynamics of culture change and concludes with some speculations on the future of man from an anthropological viewpoint.

Outstanding features of the book

1. Readability

The purpose of a textbook is to transmit and register ideas and information, to induce the readers to see old things in new ways and to think about what they see. A book may be the most elegantly written, most handsomely designed, most lavishly illustrated text available on the subject, but if it is not interesting, clear, and comprehensible to the student, it is valueless as a teaching tool.

To aid readability, this text is carefully structured, each section within the book and each chapter within each section organized so that the material is presented to the student in segments, each clearly separated from the other. It is easier for the student to grasp and retain the material if it is presented as a series of discrete "quanta," rather than as a continuous flow of information.

The readability of the text is also enhanced by the writing style. The book is designed to present even the most difficult concepts in prose that is alive, energetic, and easy to retain. Where technical terms have been necessary, they are always italicized, carefully defined in the text, and defined again in the glossary in simple, clear language.

Because much learning is based on analogy, numerous and colorful examples have been utilized to illustrate, emphasize, and clarify anthropological concepts. Wherever possible, there is a cross-cultural perspective, comparing cultural practices in other societies with those of the student's own culture. Many educators feel that this practice makes ideas easier to grasp because it renders them more familiar. For example, in the chapter on sex and marriage, the marriage system and sex roles practiced in our own country are compared with those practiced by non-Western peoples. Additionally, the text points out how the communes organized by the disenchanted young of this country are really attempts to recreate the kinship networks found in small-scale societies. Thus, from such examples, the student can perceive the nature of a cultural entity, such as marriage; he can also see its varieties, its processes, and the way it relates to his own culture and existence.

2. Original studies

A special feature of this text is the Original Study that follows each chapter. These studies, which consist of selections from case studies and other original writings of anthropologists, are the actual writings of men and women working in anthropology today. Each study is integrally related to the material in the chapter it follows, and often sheds additional light on some important anthropological concept or subject area found in the chapter. The studies represent an attempt to keep the student abreast of current research and discoveries in the field and to enable him to experience almost first-hand some of the excitement generated by new anthropological ideas and discoveries. Thus, at the end of Chapter 16, which covers patterns of subsistence, there is an original study dealing with the technology of the Guayaki in making tools for food-getting. Other studies focus on the synthesis of known data through new points of view; an example is the study in Chapter 2 by Wendell H. Oswalt.

3. Illustrations

Sociologists, anthropologists, and other social scientists have discovered that, under the influence of television, visual material is gaining increased importance as a teaching tool in today's classroom. Accordingly, this text uses numerous illustrations and other graphic materials. The illustrations have been chosen to supplement and emphasize the text and to clarify for the student concepts that are not easily rendered into words. A number of the illustrations are unusual in that they are not the "standard" anthropological textbook photographs; each has been chosen because it complements the text in some distinctive way. For example, the photos on pages 220–221 depict a number of ancient artifacts that display methods of cultivation and domestication. The line drawings, maps, charts, and tables were selected especially for their usefulness in illustrating, emphasizing, or clarifying certain anthropological concepts and should prove valuable teaching aids.

The six full-color portfolios, designed to stimulate the student's eye and mind, encompass the prehistoric megaliths of Europe, ancient art of the old world, art of the Precolumbian New World, the culture of the Persian Nomads, the world of the Eskimo hunter-gatherer, and the American Indian. Each portfolio has a definite theme and includes a text that explains the illustrations and makes some important anthropological point. For example, the portfolio on the American Indian contains, in paintings by European and American artists and in the words of a Seneca Indian chief, a capsule history of the cultural contact between the Indians and the white man.

4. Summaries and Suggested readings

At the end of each chapter is a summary containing the kernels of the most important ideas presented in the chapter. The summaries, which are numbered and so broken down into easy-to-cope-with units, provide handy reviews for the student. Also following each chapter is a list of suggested readings which will supply the inquisitive student with further information about specific anthropological points which may interest him. Each reading is fully annotated and provides information as to the content, value, and readability of the book. The books suggested are oriented either toward the general reader or toward the interested student who wishes to explore further the more technical aspects of some material.

5. Glossary and Bibliography

An extensive glossary at the end of the book provides the student with a complete anthropological dictionary in miniature. The glossary defines all the important terms used in the text, in clear, understandable language. The bibliography at the end of the book is a complete reference tool in itself; it contains a listing of 500 books, monographs, and articles from scholarly journals and popular magazines.

6. Supplement

Teachers will find the accompanying Instructor's Manual helpful in arranging their curricula. The Manual contains suggestions on topics for class discussions, subjects for student term papers, and sample questions for objective and essay-type examinations.

Acknowledgments

So far as acknowledgments are concerned, I owe a large debt to those anthropologists under whom I was privileged to study at the University of Pennsylvania: Robbins Burling, William R. Coe, Carleton S. Coon, Loren Eiseley, Robert Ehrich, J. Louis Giddings, Ward H. Goodenough, A. Irving Hallowell, Alfred V. Kidder II, Wilton M. Krogman, Froelich Rainey, Ruben Reina, and Linton Satterthwaite. They may not always recognize the final product, but they all contributed to it in important ways.

I also owe a debt to a number of anthropologists with whom I have worked, discussed research interests, or the field in general. Particularly influential here have been Warren W. Caldwell, Ann Chowning, Lucian and Jane Hanks, Frederika de Laguna, Evon Z. Vogt, and Gordon R. Willey.

And I owe a debt to my colleagues at the University of Vermont: Louise Basa, Paul J. Magnarella, William E. Mitchell, Stephen and Carroll Pastne, and A. Peter Woolfson. They all, at one time or another, helped me with specific problems connected with this book. Neither they, nor any of the other anthropologists mentioned here, should be held responsible for any defects in this book.

I also wish to acknowledge my debt to a number of nonanthropologists who helped with this book. To begin, David Boynton of Holt, Rinehart and Winston talked me into this project, and I have valued his friendly advice on a number of matters. I have also profited from his broad knowledge of anthropology and anthropologists. Caroline Latham, and all the people at Latham Publishing Enterprises, helped immensely with research, writing, and selection of illustrations.

The greatest debt of all is owed my wife and children, for having put up with my preoccupation with this book for the past several months.

part 1

The study of man

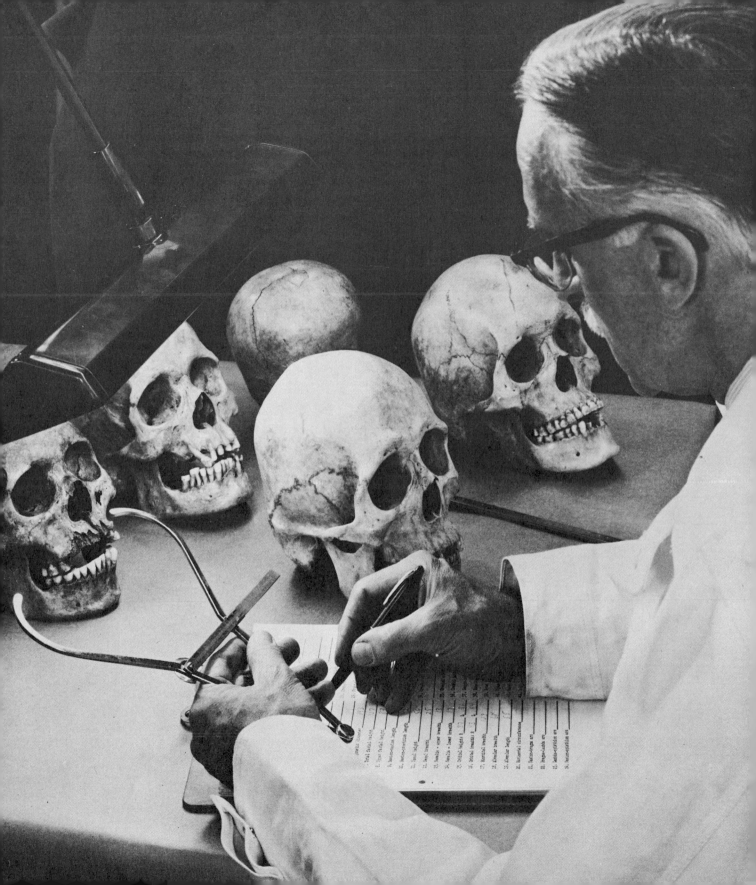

The aims
of anthropology

For as long as man has been on earth, he has wondered about who he is, where he came from, and why he acts the way he does. It would seem that much of human history has resulted from man's efforts to answer these basic questions. Because of the limits of his knowledge and technology, man, throughout most of his history, has been unable to accumulate an extensive and reliable body of data concerning his own behavior and background. Hence, he has relied on bodies of myth and folklore to answer these questions. Anthropology, as it has emerged over the last two hundred years, is the scientific approach to answering man's questions about himself.

Simply stated, anthropology is the study of man and his cultures. The anthropologist, unlike the botanist or the zoologist, is concerned primarily with a single species—*Homo sapiens,* or man, his ancestors, and near relatives. Because the anthropologist is himself a member of the species which he studies, it is sometimes difficult for him to achieve the same level of objectivity with which, for example, the botanist might pursue his work. Nevertheless, the anthropologist endeavors to study man from an objective and scientific viewpoint. His goal is to arrive at a realistic and unbiased understanding of human diversity.

Development of anthropology

The discipline of anthropology is, in its modern form, a relatively new one. If men have always wondered about themselves and their origins, why then did it take such a long time for a systematic discipline of anthropology to appear?

The answer to this is as complex as man's history. In part, the question of anthropology's slow growth may be answered by reference to the limits of man's technology. Throughout most of his history, man has been highly restricted in his geographical wanderings. Without the means of traveling to distant parts of the world, man's observation of cultures and peoples far from his own was a difficult—if not impossible—venture. Extensive travel was usually the exclusive prerogative of a few; the study of foreign cultures was not likely to flourish until adequate modes of transportation and communication could be developed.

A significant element that contributed to the slow growth of anthropology was the failure of European man to recognize the common humanity that he shares with people everywhere. Those societies which did not subscribe to the fundamental cultural values of the European were regarded as "savage" or "barbarian." It was not until the late eighteenth century that a significant number of Europeans considered the odd behavior of foreigners to be at all relevant to an understanding of themselves. This awareness of human diversity cast doubts on the traditional biblical mythology, which no longer adequately "explained" things. From the reexamination that followed came the awareness that the study of "savages" is a study of mankind.

Anthropology and the social sciences

It would not be correct to infer from the foregoing that men did not make any serious attempts to analyze their behavior before the eighteenth century. Anthropology is not the only discipline concerned with the study of man. In this respect, it shares its objectives not only with the other social sciences but with the physical sciences as well. The anthropologist does not think of his findings as something quite apart from those of

Figure 1-1. *Early anthropologists were not concerned about the stratification and positioning of the artifacts they found. This site, "La Grange," is in France.*

the psychologist, the economist, the sociologist, or the biologist; rather he welcomes their contributions to the common goal of understanding man, and he gladly offers his own findings for their benefit. The anthropologist does not expect, for example, to know as much about the role of the public schools of San Francisco as does the sociologist, or the value of the American dollar as the economist, but as a synthesist he may be better prepared to understand the relationship of these elements in analyzing the overall system of American education than any of his fellow social

Figure 1-2. *Charles Dawson searches sifted gravel for Piltdown Man fragments. Piltdown Man, hypothesized as the "missing link," was proved a hoax in 1953.*

scientists. And, going one step further than other social scientists, the anthropologist treats man not only as a social being but as a biological organism as well. Because he looks for the broad basis of human behavior without limiting himself to any single aspect of that behavior, the anthropologist is able to acquire an extensive overview of the complex biological and cultural organism that is man.

The social science to which anthropology has most often been compared is that of sociology. It is true that both anthropology and sociology are concerned with the functioning of man within a social context, and that both attempt to understand the habits and customs of people of various cultural backgrounds. Anthropology, however, is concerned with formulating universal laws of social behavior, based on a study of all aspects of man's behavior and not merely on specific examples. Furthermore, the anthropologist looks at the whole of humanity and does not limit himself to the study of Western man; anthropologists have concluded that to understand human behavior, all humans must be studied. Perhaps more than any other feature, the concentration on non-Western societies has distinguished anthropology from the other social sciences.

The emphasis which anthropology places on areas not generally studied by social scientists, such as prehistoric man or non-Western cultures, has often led to findings that dispute previous beliefs arrived at on the basis of Western studies. Because the findings of the anthropologist have often challenged the conclusions of the sociologist, the psychologist, and the economist, anthropology has traditionally played the constructive role of devil's advocate to the social sciences.

The discipline of anthropology

The discipline of anthropology may be divided into two fundamental areas. Essentially, **physical anthropology** is concerned primarily with man as a biological organism, whereas **cultural anthropology** deals with man as the animal of culture. Both these aspects of anthropology, of course, are closely related, and each contributes significantly to our knowledge of the other; we want to know how biology does and does not influence culture.

Physical anthropology

At one time, anthropologists dealt almost exclusively with the measuring of the differences in human body size and form (a method known as anthropometry). As the sciences of biology and genetics developed, however, anthropologists found other means to study human populations and the mechanisms that have made them what they are. Physical anthropology emerged as that branch of anthropology which focuses on man as a biological organism.

One of the chief concerns of the physical anthropologist is the evolution of man. Whatever distinctions man may claim for himself, he is a mammal—specifically, a primate—and, as such, subject to the same natural laws of behavior and physical change as any other living mammal. Through the analysis of fossils, and the observation of other living primates, the physical anthropologist tries to trace man's ancestry and to understand his relationship to other living things.

Another concern of the physical anthropologist is the study of human variation. Although we are all members of a single species, we differ from each other in many obvious and not so obvious ways. We differ not only in such visible traits as the color of our skin or the shape of our noses, but also in such biochemical factors as our blood types and our susceptibility to certain diseases. Where once the work of the anthropologist was limited to body measurements and the rough classification of human types, the modern physical anthropologist applies his knowledge of genetics and biochemistry to achieve a fuller understanding of the variations of mankind and the ways in which men have adapted to their various environments.

Figure 1-3. *Dr. Malcom McKenna studies this fossil under a laboratory light. Precision instruments aid the study of fossils, which is at the heart of physical anthropology.*

Cultural anthropology

Because there is no culture without man the animal, the work of the physical anthropologist provides an invaluable framework for the cultural anthropologist. In order to understand the work of the cultural anthropologist, it is first necessary to clarify what we mean when we refer to culture. In ordinary usage, we might refer to an individual as being "cultured" if he is well mannered, well read, skilled in several languages, and able to chat knowledgeably about art and music. While these abilities certainly reflect upon the individual's knowledge of his culture, they do not confer upon him the exclusive right to "culture" as that term is employed by the anthropologist. When we speak of culture, we refer to man's learned behavior, passed on from generation to genera-

tion by nonhereditary means. Culture is the way of life of an entire people. The manifestations of culture may vary in complexity from place to place, but no man has more culture in the anthropological sense than any other.

Cultural anthropology may be broken down into the areas of archeology, linguistics, and ethnology. Although each of these areas has its own special interests, all are dealing with cultural data. The archeologist, the linguist, and the ethnologist may take different approaches to the subject, but each is primarily concerned with gathering data that may be useful in explaining the various cultures of man, and the way that these cultures have developed and adapted.

Figures 1-4 and 5. *Dr. Gale Sieveking carries artifacts from the High Lodge site.*
Volunteers, half of them students, use basic tools in helping Dr. Sieveking.

Archeology. Due to the intangible nature of ideas, much of man's past survives only in the form of things which he once made. The area of anthropology concerned with finding and studying the material remains of earlier cultures is called archeology. The archeologist studies the tools, pottery, and other enduring relics that remain as the legacy of long-extinct cultures.

The archeologist serves in many ways as the historian of anthropology, reconstructing the events of man's past. However, unlike the historian, who is concerned only with the past 5000 years during which men have left written records of their accomplishments, the archeologist is also concerned with the millions of years in which man developed culture without the benefit of the written word. By studying what ancient man left us, the archeologist gathers evidence of the ways in which cultures grow, change, and interact with one another. Scientists cannot experiment with humans, as they can with other animals, to see what may happen in certain circumstances. But they can formulate hypotheses—for example, about cultural change in given conditions—and then test these archeologically by investigating situations where those conditions actually occurred. Although the destructive forces of time have obliterated much of the valuable evidence of man's prehistory, archeologists continue the search for the earliest roots of man's culture.

Linguistics. Perhaps the most distinctive feature of man is his ability to speak. Man is not alone in his use of symbolic communication. Studies have shown that the sounds made by some other animals—especially by apes—may serve functions comparable to that of speech in men; yet, no other animal has developed so complex a system of symbolic communication as has man. Ultimately, it is man's languages that allow him to preserve and transmit his culture from generation to generation.

The branch of cultural anthropology that studies man's languages is called linguistics. Linguistics may deal with the description of a language (the way it forms a sentence or conjugates a verb) or with the history of languages (the way languages develop and influence each other with the passage of time). Both approaches shed valuable information, not only about the ways in which people communicate, but about the ways in which they understand the external world as well. The colloquial language of Americans, for example, includes a number of slang words, such as "dough," "greenback," "dust," "loot," and "bread," to identify what a Papuan would recognize only as "money." Such situations help identify things which are considered of special importance to a culture. Through the study of linguistics, the anthropologist is better able to understand how people perceive themselves and the world around them. In his analysis of language, the anthropological linguist makes a significant contribution to our understanding of man and his prehistory.

Ethnology. As the archeologist studies cultures of the past, so the ethnologist studies cultures of the present. While the archeologist must count on the mercy of time in his pursuit of data, the ethnologist is able to study cultures from first-hand experience. It has been observed with some validity that "the ethnographer is an archeologist who catches his archeology alive."[1]

[1]Clyde Kluckhohn, *Mirror for Man: A Survey of Human Behavior and Social Attitudes* (Greenwich, Conn.: Fawcett Publications, 1970).

The heart of the ethnologist's approach is field work. Whenever possible, the ethnologist lives among the people whom he is studying. By eating their food, speaking their language, and personally observing their habits and customs, the ethnologist is able to understand a society's way of life to a far greater extent than any "armchair anthropologist" ever could; he learns a culture by learning how to behave acceptably himself in the society in which he is doing field work. The ethnologist does not rely upon library research; he is a dynamic investigator. He tries to become a participant-observer in the culture which he is studying. This does not mean that he must eat human flesh to study cannibals. By living among cannibals, the ethnologist may understand the role of cannibalism in the overall cultural scheme. He must be a meticulous observer in order to be able to get a broad overview of a culture without placing undue stress on any of its component parts. Only by discovering how all social institutions—political, economic, religious—fit together can he begin to understand the cultural system.

Every society is a complex system of interrelated elements, and often the ethnologist will be more interested in one aspect of a culture than another. For example, he may be especially interested in the religious practices of a particular group of people. As a trained anthropologist, however, he almost invariably discovers that each aspect of a culture is tied in with nearly every other aspect. That is, he discovers that the culture's religious beliefs are reflected not only in people's overt religious rituals, but in the food they eat, the games they play, the structure of their families, and the ways in which they go about fulfilling their daily needs as well. Christians celebrating Lent, for example, may follow certain dietary restrictions, may observe certain religious holidays by going to church and attending mass, and may refrain from playing music or dancing. The ethnologist may stress certain aspects of a people's behavior, but the complex nature of culture makes it almost impossible to isolate any single feature for exclusive study. By cross-cultural comparisons of cultures which survive today, the

The study of man ● part 1

Figure 1-6. *Cultural anthropologists often study a society by trying to live as its people do. Here, Dr. Napoleon Chagnon is eating a sweet fruit, known as the Surinam cherry, with Yąnomamö Indian tribesmen.*

ethnologist is able to arrive at valid conclusions concerning the nature of culture everywhere.

Anthropology and the scientific method

The chief concern of the anthropologist is the objective and systematic study of mankind. If the anthropologist were to pursue his work in a subjective or haphazard fashion, we might classify him along with the poet or the philosopher as a serious but unscientific investigator of the human condition. However, this is not the case. Anthropology has been called a social or a behavioral science by some, a life science by others, and no science at all by still others. Can the work of the anthropologist properly be labeled scientific? What exactly do we mean by the term science?

Science is a method by which data can be gathered and formulated into consistent laws of behavior. These laws may be laws which seem to regulate natural phenomena—as do the laws of physics—or they may be laws which seem to explain human behavior—as do the laws of psychology. In either case, certain fundamental principles of scientific investigation must be observed if the resulting conclusions are to be considered valid. The goal of any science is to arrive at a coherent system of verifiable theories.

The scientist begins with an **hypothesis,** or tentative assumption intended to explain the relationship between certain phenomena. By gathering various kinds of data which seem to support his generalizations, and, equally important, by showing why alternative hypotheses may be eliminated from consideration, the scientist arrives at a system of validated hypotheses, or **theory.** A theory will then be exposed to constant reexamination, and it may be revised or discarded if contradictory data should be discovered. The scientist does not think of any theory as being beyond challenge.

Methodological approaches

In order to arrive at a valid set of theories concerning human behavior, the cultural anthropologist employs the scientific method in gathering and analyzing his data. He may follow either of two procedures in order to explain cultural phenomena: he may analyze a particular culture in which he has done field work, or he may arrive at an hypothesis based on a comparative study of more than one society. In analyzing a single society, the anthropologist may consider one particular characteristic of a culture, examining it both in relationship to other features of the culture and in an historical context as well. If he is employing the comparative method, he may observe the occurrence of a particular characteristic in various societies, and then develop an hypothesis to explain why the characteristic appears in some cultures and not in others. In both cases, he is willing to submit his theories to rigorous tests and challenges. The goal of the cultural anthropologist is to accumulate data that may be used to formulate verifiable theories of culture.

Anthropological research may be classified as nonhistorical or historical; that is, the anthropologist may study one or more contemporary

Figure 1-7. *Anthropology is finding more and more use for scientists from the hard sciences like geology, botany, and zoology. Geophysicist Jack Evernden became involved with anthropology through his work with potassium argon dating. Here, in a laboratory at the University of California at Berkeley, Dr. Evernden uses devices capable of detecting fractions of a billionth of an ounce of material. These devices enable him to measure accumulations of argon gas in volcanic rock. The measurements are used to date the rock, and the resulting information is used to date groups of extinct species found with the rock.*

cultures, or he may study the development of a culture throughout the course of its history. The ethnographer, who analyzes a single society on the basis of his field work, may provide valuable data based on in-depth, first-hand observation;

although specific cases are essential to build up the corpus of data needed for cross-cultural study, the consideration of a single society is generally insufficient for the testing of an hypothesis. Without some basis for comparison, the hypothesis grounded on a single case may be no more than an historical coincidence. A single case may be adequate, however, to refute a theory which had previously been held as universally valid. Margaret Mead's discovery in 1928 that Samoan adolescents grow up virtually stress-free was sufficient ground for rejecting the theory that adolescence is invariably accompanied by psychological stress.

Explanations of cultural phenomena may be generated and tested by the comparison of ethnographic data for several societies found in a particular region. Nonhistorical, controlled comparison provides a broader context for understanding cultural phenomena than does the ethnography of a single culture. The anthropologist who undertakes such a comparison may be more confident that the conditions he believes to be related really are related, at least within the region which he is investigating; however, an explanation which is valid in one region is not necessarily valid in another.

Ideally, anthropological theories would be generated on the basis of world-wide comparisons. The cross-cultural researcher examines a world-wide sample of societies in order to discover whether or not theories proposed to explain cultural phenomena seem to be generally applicable. Because his sample is selected at random, it is probable that the conclusions of the cross-cultural researcher will be valid; however, the greater the number of societies that are being examined, the less likely it is that the investigator will have a detailed understanding of all the societies encompassed by his study. The cross-cultural researcher depends upon the ethnographer for his data. It is difficult for any single individual personally to perform in-depth analyses of a broad sampling of human cultures throughout the world.

The alternative to studying contemporary cultures in their present state is the historical analysis of society, referred to as ethnohistory. Ethnohistorical data are based, not only upon the reports of earlier anthropologists, but upon the accounts of explorers, missionaries, and traders as well. Accordingly, the historical researcher sometimes must depend upon incomplete, inaccurate, or unclear data. Nevertheless, the analysis of historical sequences is a valuable approach to understanding the phenomenon of cultural variation. By examining the conditions believed to have caused certain phenomena, we can discover whether or not those conditions truly predate those phenomena. Historical research and archeologists' field studies are valuable means of testing and confirming theories of culture.

Anthropology and contemporary life

It should not be assumed that anthropology is a static discipline. To the contrary, anthropological phenomena are in a constant state of flux. Looking at our own culture, we can easily see the alteration of traditional values and institutions. Changing sexual roles, new attitudes towards the wedding ritual, and new alternatives to the traditional forms of marriage and the family are just a few examples of the fundamental changes readily apparent in our own culture. New areas of research are being opened to the anthropologist all the time; yet, at the same time, many opportunities seem to be rapidly disappearing. The plundering of valuable archeological sites for financial or political gain, for example, casts a veil of urgency over the work of the anthropologist. While human greed destroys that which remains of ancient Mayan and Cambodian civilizations, environmental pollution makes the work of the anthropologist more difficult every day. Modern anthropology is a demanding and full-time discipline requiring concerned and well-trained individuals. Anthropology is the systematic study of man and his works, past and present. Younger than most of the social sciences, anthropology is

Figure 1-8. *Junius Bird scrutinizes some recently acquired artifacts. Certain anthropologists spend much time studying artifacts. The functions artifacts served, and the engravings etched upon them, reveal much about their makers and users.*

rapidly gaining in sophistication and respectability. It intends not to replace the work of the economist, the political scientist, the psychologist, and the sociologist, but rather to supplement and expand upon that work. As his tools and his methods become more efficient, the anthropologist grows ever closer to achieving his ultimate goal of creating a valid science of man.

☐

PERHAPS THE SUMERIANS WERE RIGHT

Actually, the first Ph.D. in anthropology was granted less than one hundred years ago. It may be that anthropology has made false starts or involved itself in silly games and infantile diversions, but it is also true that it has been a slum-child of the sciences bereft of manpower and living on the table scraps of the more prosperous disciplines. From the beginning the efforts of anthropology have been scattered across the cultures of the earth and the several million years of human history. Instead of a massive assault on some single human problem, anthropologists have skirmished against a host of questions.

The rise of anthropology vaguely corresponds with the colonization and development of the "underdeveloped" nations. It corresponds with the rape and destruction of the archaeological record and the deliberate destruction of countless peoples and their ways of life. At the moment of its founding anthropology faced the problem of a disappearing subject matter. Early in this century, Franz Boas said to Robert Lowie, "Here is a hundred dollars, go study the Navajo." Lowie set out knowing only that the Navajo lived somewhere to the west of New York. Here was no chance to formulate significant theoretical questions or to develop methodology. Here was only a chance to find some old people and say, "What was it like when you were young?" So it went and so it goes today. Archaeologists snatch their data from the teeth of bulldozers; cultural anthropologists work with remnants of peoples not yet destroyed.

Out of the frantic attempts of these ethnographers have come written records concerning hundreds of cultures that no longer exist or exist in altered form. At this very moment, Brazilian soldiers and frontiersmen are completing the extermination of unstudied Indian tribes of the Amazon Basin; the mountain peoples of Southeast Asia are perishing in wars they never sought and do not understand, and in California a bulldozer is destroying the last fragile records of a vanished tribe. In a few unthinking moments of history many of the cultures and works of man constructed over centuries have been destroyed. But much has been saved, and the laden bookshelves of almost any library bear testimony to the hero's task the ethnographers performed. So long as there are human beings, so long as they care about others, this monumental contribution of an infant science will remain one of the great treasures of humanity. There are still cultures to be studied and archaeological sites to be excavated, but will we get to them in time?

The ethnographic record, the books and articles written by anthropologists, missionaries, and explorers, contains much information about our own and other people's cultures. Out of the comparison of these materials, out of an awareness of the similarities and differences among the peoples of the world, the concept of culture has gradually emerged. If there is some great discovery in anthropology, some great contribution to human wisdom, then it is the discovery of culture. Of course, human beings have always been aware of culture, but they have often attributed a sacred quality to their own. One's own way of life has always seemed right and proper, perhaps a gift from the Creator to be preserved as a sacred trust. Even where men have not been convinced of their superiority to other men, they have seen their own cultures as right for them and other cultures as right for other people.

Brought up in a culture regarded by its members as god-given, biologically inherited, and infinitely superior to all others, the early anthropologists struggled slowly toward the truth: Cultures are invented by ordinary men and passed on to others by means of processes of cultural transmission. Cultures may be sacred because they are beautiful or because they represent sincere, triumphant, human work. Beyond that, they are no more sacred than an eggbeater, a telephone, or any other human work. Historically, anthropologists did not begin to use the term social heredity in definitions of culture until the 1920s, and learning appeared frequently in definitions of cultures in the late thirties and early forties.

In the abstract, the idea that ways of life are simply the product of messages handed down across the generations seems innocuous enough. In fact, the view of culture as natural, rather than supernatural, is as revolutionary and as hard to believe as the idea that the earth is round and circles the sun or the idea that human beings evolved by natural processes from other animals. In our daily life we act as though the earth were flat, we speak of sunrise and sunset, and we separate the artificial from the natural. When an ethnographic film shows us Bushmen hunting, warfare in New Guinea, or an Australian aboriginal initiation, we snicker in the back rows. Here are people who do not know how to act properly, crazy people doing crazy things. Do we not recognize that we are equally crazy and that our own customs are equally absurd or, if you like, equally rational? Perhaps we do know it in a way, but we are not prepared to act upon it. The idea that everything we think of as right or wrong was just an idea thought up by some wise man or fool several centuries ago is as repugnant as it is revolutionary and subversive.

Imagine that it is Sunday in Cicero Falls. The minister, a recent convert to anthropology, has decided to express his respect for God in the manner of the ancient Sumerians. He strips off his ornaments and clothing and delivers his sermon in the nude. As anthropologists we are inclined to say, "so what," but as citizens of Cicero Falls we are outraged. Who decided that it was good to wear clothing in a church with the thermostat set at eighty? Who decided that it is wrong to eat dog meat, that cultural transmission can occur in a lecture hall, that "shit" is a dirty word, that only women wear skirts, that you should sleep with the same woman all of your life, or that it is uncomfortable to sit on the floor? Anthropology tells us that these are all arbitrary conventions constructed by men and quite likely to change. Such conventions may, of course, be useful and adaptive in one way or another, but should we not examine them? Perhaps, after all, the Sumerians were right.

Summary

1.

Anthropology is the study of man and his cultures. The anthropologist is concerned not only with any one aspect of man but with man as a totality. Anthropology is a synthesizing science, combining the perspectives of sociology, economics, psychology, biology, and other physical and social sciences. Although both anthropology and sociology attempt to understand the habits and customs of people of various cultural backgrounds, anthropology is far more concerned with formulating universal laws of social behavior and is not limited in perspective to Western cultures.

2.

The two major fields of anthropology are physical anthropology and cultural anthropology. Physical anthropology is concerned with tracing the evolutionary development of the human animal and studying biological variation within the species. The physical anthropologist approaches his subject through the analysis of the fossil record, observation of living primates, and a knowledge of anatomy, genetics, and biochemistry. The cultural anthropologist studies man's culture; the way of life of an entire people. There are three subfields of cultural anthropology: archeology, linguistics, and ethnology. The archeologist recovers and studies the relics of cultures past and reconstructs man's cultural history. Linguistics is that branch of anthropology which specializes in the study of the structure and history of languages. Ethnology is that specialized branch of cultural anthropology concerned with the study of contemporary cultures.

3.

The chief concern of the anthropologist is the objective and systematic study of mankind. The anthropologist employs the method of other scientists by beginning with an hypothesis, or assumed explanation, and using his data to test his hypothesis and ultimately arriving at a theory—a system of validated hypotheses. The data used by the anthropologist may be field data of one society or comparative studies of numerous societies.

Suggested readings

Fried, Morton H. *The Study of Anthropology.* New York: Thomas Y. Crowell Co., 1972.
This is a nuts-and-bolts discussion of anthropology as a way of life and study. A modest, how-to volume addressed to undergraduates and potential graduate students. Fried delineates the character of anthropology in the United States, as well as how to get into the profession.

Oliver, Douglas Z. *Invitation to Anthropology.* Garden City N.Y.: Natural History Press, 1964.
This guide to the basic concepts of anthropology is seen by the author as an outline of what ideally he would like all high school graduates to know about the anthropological profession. This slim volume is neither a textbook nor a substantive introduction, but a brief overview of the field.

Pelto, Pertti J. *The Nature of Anthropology.* Columbus, Ohio: Charles Merrill Books, Inc., 1966.
Designed to provide a basic perspective of anthropology, this work outlines the scope, character, and history of the discipline. Methods of anthropological research and a summary of significant research are described. A discussion of the fundamental concepts of anthropology and problems for the future concludes the book.

Smith, Allan H. and Fischer, John L. *Anthropology.* Englewood Cliffs, N.J.: Prentice-Hall, Inc., 1970.
Anthropology is part of the Behaviorial and Social Science Survey Series of the Social Science Research Council. It is a comprehensive review and appraisal of the current state of the discipline. Approximately one half of the book deals with the concerns of anthropology as a behavioral and social science in the four major subfields of social and cultural anthropology, archeology, linguistics, and physical anthropology. The remainder of the volume deals with the training of anthropologists and recommendations for the future.

The development
of anthropology

Travelers have always been fascinated by the seeming strangeness in the behavior and beliefs of people in other places. Marco Polo, perhaps the most famous traveler of the thirteenth century, wrote to his Italian relatives of his amazement at the manners and morals of the Chinese court; the Spanish conquistadors were perplexed by the customs of the New World civilizations they eventually destroyed; modern travelers leave their 747 with camera in hand, ready to record on film the landmarks of their destination and the dress of its inhabitants. Underlying this widespread curiosity about the culture of other peoples is an equally widespread desire to understand the meaning and significance of physical and cultural variety. Although people have been asking the same basic questions about the differences between cultures for a very long time, the answers which have been proposed in the past have differed dramatically from those which are now offered. Most of what we now believe to be true of the development of mankind was discovered in the last one hundred years, and much of it only in the last few decades. The history of anthropology's development as a science is closely tied to the changing views of man's cultural history.

Historical background

The story of modern anthropology really begins around the middle of the nineteenth century. Before that time, European thought was dominated by the traditional teachings of the Bible and the Christian Church. According to these authorities, all things in the universe, ranging from the lowly rocks to the heavenly angels, fit into some predetermined niche in the Great Chain of Being. Furthermore, according to this view, the entire world and every species of plant and animal in it were created by God in one masterful stroke some six thousand years previously. Challenging these long entrenched ideas was no small task, and it was not until the close of the eighteenth century that a number of courageous men dared to take up the questions of human progress and the perfection of man's condition on earth.

The eighteenth and early nineteenth centuries

The eighteenth century was an era of many exciting discoveries for European man. Extensive sea voyages were uncovering a great deal of information which seemed to challenge the traditional views concerning the origins and diversity of plant and animal life forms. As the age of discovery made the global survey of man a reality, major advances in science, philosophy, and technology rapidly altered the European's perception of the world. The concept of a world in equilibrium was giving way to the concept of a world in progress.

As advances in chemistry and physics were beginning to stir public faith in scientific inquiry and analysis, important archeological breakthroughs challenged some of Europe's most established beliefs. In the early nineteenth century, Jacques Boucher de Perthes, a French customs official and amateur archeologist, discovered some flint tools along with the bones of extinct elephants in the Somme Valley. Despite the strong evidence uncovered by him that men had actually lived on earth long before the date provided by the Bible for the Great Flood, Boucher de Perthe's findings were largely ignored for many years. Most scholars were not yet prepared to accept such a radical departure from the traditional view of the Creation.

Even the most determined traditionalists, however, were finding it difficult to ignore the mounting evidence of man's long history on earth. The discovery of stone implements in Danish peat bogs confirmed an earlier theory that man had endured through sequential ages of stone, bronze, and iron. Later excavations uncovered artifacts which predated even the Stone Age. By the time Charles Lyell published his geological evidence that the earth was considerably older than the Bible stated, it was difficult for any but the most stubborn to be contented with the biblical version of the Creation. Before the nineteenth century, there was little reason to believe that the orderly appearance of new living types had taken any more time than the duration of the recorded history of mankind. By the middle of the century, the principle of geological succession had made it nearly impossible for any educated person not to believe otherwise.

As the geologists and archeologists increasingly turned toward an evolutionary view of man, po-

litical and economic theorists too began to discuss man's behavior in less static terms. Men of such different visions as Karl Marx and John Stuart Mill were analyzing man's institutions in terms of his development from the primitive to the modern. At the same time, evolution was the dominant theme of such early anthropologists as J. F. McLennan and J. J. Bachofen. As far back as the eighteenth century, the notion of human progress was becoming the guiding light for anthropological thought.

The first half of the nineteenth century represented, for the most part, less a departure from the beliefs of the previous century than a culmination of those beliefs. It was at this time, for example, that the theory of racial determinism was proposed to account for the differences between various cultures. According to this theory formulated before the development of modern genetic science, the differences between people were attributable mainly to their varying "racial" backgrounds. The Hottentots, for example, were considered to be one step above the apes, but that step was judged to be a very small one. Although the influence of the environment on human culture was conceded, racial determinism was based on the premise that heredity is the main factor in determining a culture's potential for achievement. Meanwhile, theories of psychic unity were formulated in order to explain the many similarities between cultures. These theories held that the human mind was essentially the same all over the world and that all people began to develop their cultures with the same psychological potential. In keeping with the eighteenth century belief in the doctrine of progress, both the racial determinism and psychic unity theories assumed that man and his cultures changed and developed with the passage of time.

Evolutionism

The concept of evolutionism was already an important aspect of anthropology before the appearance of Charles Darwin's theory. Europe of the early nineteenth century was in a state of

Georges Cuvier   Charles Lyell   Jacques Boucher de Perthes

Figure 2-1. *Zoologist Georges Cuvier, geologist Charles Lyell, and amateur archeologist Jacques Boucher de Perthes furthered anthropological studies. The study of ancient man has depended on men from a variety of scientific disciplines.*

dynamic change. As science and industry developed and the continent continued to be torn by war, class struggles, and technological changes, interest was focused more than ever before on the human condition. The time was right for a science of man.

Charles Darwin.   Among the most important events in the history of modern science was the appearance, in 1859, of Charles Darwin's *The Origin of Species.* Darwin's work represents the first formal statement of the theory of evolution. Although Darwin himself was concerned primarily with the way in which various species develop through biological evolution, his ideas gave new impetus to the concepts of cultural evolution which had been roughly developed by earlier anthropologists. Although Darwin commented only briefly on the evolution of man himself, the

implication of his theory was obvious and far-reaching.

Anthropological evolutionism

The anthropological evolutionists believed that society and culture developed in a regular sequence of predictable stages. By studying social evolution, they hoped to develop a science of culture that could formulate universal laws of human behavior and cultural development. In looking for such laws, the evolutionists tended to emphasize the similarities among cultures rather than the differences. Although they did not completely deny the importance of the exchanging of cultural traits between societies, they believed that isolated societies tend to develop similar tools and institutions independently in the

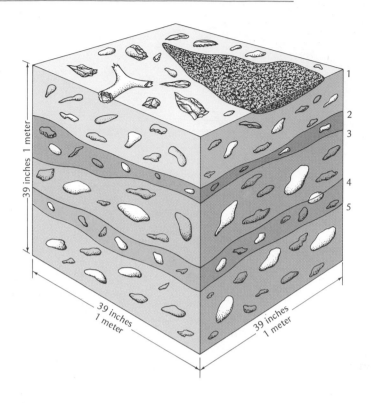

Figures 2-2, 3, and 4. *Stratigraphy is now a valuable aid to anthropologists. Archeological sites are dug slowly with concern for the location of fossils and artifacts. Upon the opening of an archeological site, such as the one in Figure 2-2 at High Lodge, trenches are dug to establish strata. Determinations are made as to how the site relates to previous geological data and age calculations. At a site where humans have lived, such as the one in Figure 2-3 at Nippur, stratigraphy reveals floor levels. At Nippur, 12 floor levels have been unearthed, with artifacts sticking out at each level. Archeological sites are broken down into square meter segments. Measurements are taken to establish the position of each fossil and artifact relative to the position of each other object. The cubic meter in Figure 2-4 contains hand tools, animal bone, and the remains of a hearth. Such graphic representation helps piece a site together.*

course of time. The process whereby cultures develop similar features without cultural exchange is called **independent invention.**

Because they believed that all societies passed through the same stages of evolution in a fixed sequence, the evolutionists held that contemporary primitive cultures closely resembled an early stage through which their own culture had once evolved. Victorian society was imagined to be the highest stage of the sequence through which less "civilized" societies were still evolving. Therefore, the evolutionists believed that the behavior of the "savages" could be compared to that of the early Europeans, and their method is referred to as the **comparative method.** An important feature of this method was the belief that the behavior of people within a culture can be explained by reference to conditions earlier in their history which no longer prevail. The rule requiring marriage to outsiders, for example, was thought of as being left over from a hypothetical stage of cultural evolution in which women were kidnapped from outside groups to provide wives for the men of the tribe. Although the kidnapping is no longer practiced, the rules requiring marriage to outsiders may remain.

Among those individuals most important in formulating the evolutionist position were Lewis Henry Morgan, Sir Edward Tylor, and Herbert Spencer.

Lewis H. Morgan. In *Ancient Society* (1877), Lewis H. Morgan defined savagery, barbarism, and civilization as the three basic stages of social evolution. By associating certain specific attributes to each of these stages, Morgan intended to create a complete scheme of characteristics that would define the various evolutionary stages. He associated the use of bows and arrows and the gathering mode of subsistence, for example, with savagery; whereas the domestication of animals he viewed as a feature of barbarism.

Sir Edward B. Tylor. The English anthropologist Sir Edward B. Tylor also attempted to describe the evolution of culture in his work, *Primitive Culture*

(1871), but his focus was primarily on the development of religion and not on technology. According to Tylor, religion generally evolves from animism (the belief in spirits, ghosts, and souls) to polytheism (the belief in numerous deities) to monotheism (the belief in a single God). At its most advanced stage, Tylor claimed, religion is associated with morality; questions of right and wrong are related to the idea of God. Tylor concluded that these progressive stages of development were the result of increasing rationality on the part of man.

Herbert Spencer. Tylor's approach was closely paralleled in the writing of Herbert Spencer, although Spencer's emphasis was considerably different. In *Principles of Sociology* (1896), Spencer traced the supposed evolution of marriage from polygamy through monogamy, stressing the evolution of society towards increased specialization and complexity. Like Morgan and Tylor, Spencer envisioned the evolution of culture as taking place in distinct and definable stages.

What the nineteenth century evolutionists were attempting to establish was a scheme for the historical progression of cultural forms. In seeking out universal cultural laws, the evolutionists hoped to explain the similarities and differences between cultures. Although the work of the evolutionists was an important step toward finding natural causes for cultural developments, their basic belief that all cultures pass through identical stages of development often led them to excessively generalized and overly simplified conclusions.

Reactions to evolutionism

As the nineteenth century drew to a close, many anthropologists were beginning to voice their objections to the methods and findings of the evolutionists. Until that time, little actual ethnological data had been available, and the conclusions reached by such men as Tylor and Morgan were generally based not on first-hand experience but rather on the frequently unreliable accounts given by travelers, missionaries, and colonial officials. Furthermore, the evolutionists were frequently guilty of forcing their essentially unreliable data to fit certain preconceived schemes.

Franz Boas. Among the first to voice his objection to the "arm-chair" school of anthropology was a German-born anthropologist named Franz Boas. Boas maintained that it was necessary to gather as much data as possible about individual cultures before any general laws of cultural development could be stated. He suggested that the anthropologist should study each culture thoroughly, both in its present and historical forms, while carefully recording his findings in detail. By placing great emphasis on fieldwork, Boas was attempting to set higher standards of research for anthropology. Boas demonstrated his approach by directing his attention to the fading American Indian cultures before they were lost to study and analysis forever.

In gathering data on Indians of the United States and Canada, Boas discovered many facts which did not seem to correspond to the generalized schemes of cultural behavior described by the evolutionists. He found, for example, that clans among the Northwest Indians resulted from village fission, whereas among the Navajo they resulted from the fusion of separate groups. Simple geometric designs did not necessarily represent the degeneration of what once had begun as a naturalistic design. Masks were used by different tribes for quite varied religious purposes. Boas upheld that the same factors could hardly account for similar developments among different cultures. He formulated the thesis that each culture is unique and that similarities between cultures are best explained by the assumption that cultural exchange has taken place. In this thesis—known as **historical particularism**—Boas was voicing his objection to the evolutionists' attempts to formulate one grand scheme of cultural development without adequately considering the diversity of human cultures.

Boas objected not only to the methods of the

Figure 2-5. *Franz Boas was a prominent cultural anthropologist. He led the opposition against predetermined evolutionism. Boas stressed that an individual cultural trait must be studied in the context of its society.*

evolutionists, but also the manner in which their findings were evaluated. Generally speaking, the evolutionists thought of non-Western people as savages and freely made value judgments based on European cultural standards. Tylor, for example, although among the most liberal of his contemporaries, wrote of the "stupidity and unpractical conservatism and dogged superstition" of certain contemporary "primitive" societies. Boas denied that any society was any more rational, logical, or civilized than any other. His thesis that a culture must be judged according to its own standards and values rather than those of the investigator is known as **cultural relativism.** Relativism, as opposed to the belief that one's own culture is inherently superior to any other, represented a tremendously liberating philosophy at that time.

Boas' work represents a major step forward for the field of anthropology. As developed by Boas' students, ethnography, a detailed description of a society's culture, concerned itself with the exact recording of all the characteristics of each individual culture, interpreted as closely as possible according to the viewpoint of the native. This approach gave long overdue recognition to the validity of the world's various cultures, but it failed to stress the discovery of general laws of cultural behavior and development. Although Boas recognized the search for universals as a valid ideal, the collection of data became the primary function of the anthropologist, and the search for the laws of culture was temporarily abandoned.

The diffusionists

While the students of Boas pursued their work in America, several related movements were gathering strength in Europe. In opposition to the evolutionists, some European anthropologists argued that all culture began in one or more specific areas, from which it then spread throughout the world. The belief that all cultures share a common origin is known as **diffusionism.**

The most extreme form of diffusionism was proposed by a small group of British anthropologists that included Grafton Elliot Smith and W. J. Perry. These men argued that all cultural traits were originally developed in Egypt and subsequently spread throughout the world in waves of emigration. "Primitive" cultural forms, therefore, were thought of as being no more than degenerate forms of the original Egyptian civilization. The emphasis of these British diffusionists was on the inherent uninventiveness of mankind. They believed that all cultures on earth were merely a reflection of the one great original civilization that flourished thousands of years ago. In stressing the degenerate nature of all "primitive" non-western societies, the extreme diffusionists proved themselves to be nearly as biased as the evolutionists.

Most advocates of diffusionism, however, did not assume such an extreme position. The largest faction of diffusionists included such German anthropologists as Fritz Graebner, Father Wilhelm Schmidt, and Martin Gusinde. These men believed that culture originally arose in several areas, called culture circles, from which it gradually spread out. Similarities between cultures were believed to be the result of the overlapping of culture circles; accordingly, the more ways in which cultures resembled each other, the greater were the chances of an historical relationship. These German diffusionists are known as the *Kulturkreise* (culture circle) school.

Meanwhile, similar schools of thought, based largely on the theories of Boas and his students, were developing in America. Rather than asserting that cultural traits diffused from a few select areas, members of these schools associated various traits with certain geographical environments which they referred to as **culture areas.** After mapping out and classifying the tribal groups of North and South America, they proposed a law of diffusion stating that cultural traits tend to spread out in all directions from their center of origin; therefore, the relative age of cultural traits could be determined by their geographical distribution. Those traits which have spread farthest

from their center of origin were assumed to be the oldest. The larger the area, the older the trait. Taking tepees as an example, we can infer that they represented quite an old trait, for by the time the white man had penetrated the American continent, the American Indian tepee was a widespread form of housing, adapted to a number of varied environments. In the Far West, tepees were made of cedar bark; the Plains Indians made theirs of hides; and the Indians of the Northeast made theirs of birchbark. By the time a trait has reached its marginal area of diffusion, it will probably have been replaced at its point of origin, wherever this may be, by another trait. Taking an analogy from zoology, we find, for example, that marsupials, which once occupied the ecological niche today filled by placental mammals, are to be found nowadays only in certain geographical fringe areas of the world, such as in Australia and Oceania.

The main problem with the culture area concept and the related age-area hypothesis, however, was that they tended to be no more than simplified versions of environmental determinism, or the belief that the form of a culture can be explained entirely in terms of its general environment. Such a belief by itself became increasingly unacceptable to twentieth century anthropologists.

Diffusionism, then, did not prove to be a satisfactory framework for anthropology. None of the

Figures 2-6, 7, 8, 9, and 10. *Masks are an important part of many people's culture. The double face mask in Figure 2-7 is from an African tribe on the Ivory Coast; the other masks are from North American Indian tribes. Masks serve a variety of functions. They have been used in birth, marriage, and death ceremonies, in governing, and to symbolize power. The mask is strongly associated with social control.*

diffusionist approaches could adequately account for the primary origin of cultural traits. How, for example, did the original culture of Egypt develop? By maintaining that the development of culture happened only once and then spread outward, the extreme British diffusionists still retained much of the faulty cultural scheme proposed by the evolutionists. Diffusionism, like evolutionism, ultimately failed to provide all the answers.

The functionalists

An important school of anthropology which arose in opposition to the extreme evolutionist and diffusionist positions was known as **functionalism.** Although the functionalists shared Boas' emphasis on intensive field work and the detailed collection of data, their approach differed from that of Boas and the diffusionists in one very significant respect: the functionalists were not concerned with the historical approach to the study of culture. Dissatisfied with the far-fetched reconstructions of the past offered by both the evolutionists and the diffusionists, members of the functionalist school reacted by abandoning all such efforts. Rather, they emphasized the study of contemporary cultures without drawing any analogies to the past.

The functionalists maintain that each of the traits within a culture has a specific function which serves to hold the social system together and that the structure of a society is determined by the way in which it fulfills those functions. The work of the anthropologist, as envisioned by members of this school, was to study the ways in which various cultural institutions function to solve the problem of maintaining the system. Although the evolutionists had also recognized the interrelationship between culture traits, they focused primarily on tracing the origin and development of those traits. The functionalists denied the importance of historical background and limited themselves to the study of twentieth century cultures.

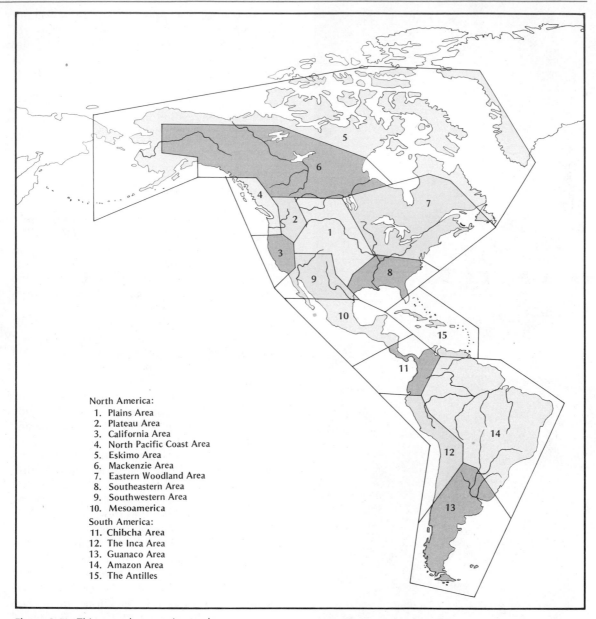

Figure 2-11. *This map shows various culture areas of North and South America; within each numbered area the tribes share many adaptive culture traits.*

North America:
1. Plains Area
2. Plateau Area
3. California Area
4. North Pacific Coast Area
5. Eskimo Area
6. Mackenzie Area
7. Eastern Woodland Area
8. Southeastern Area
9. Southwestern Area
10. Mesoamerica

South America:
11. Chibcha Area
12. The Inca Area
13. Guanaco Area
14. Amazon Area
15. The Antilles

A. R. Radcliffe-Brown. One of the major theoreticians of the functionalist school was A. R. Radcliffe-Brown. He interpreted ceremonies, myths, and legends as an expression of a society's collective emotions, an idea which he borrowed from the French sociologist Émile Durkheim. To Radcliffe-Brown, ceremonies served to regulate individual conduct and promote a feeling of solidarity among the members of a group. According to this functionalist view, the significance of a revivalist meeting, for example, lies in the fact that it serves to bring people together; its religious value is secondary. He viewed societies as composed of a system of customs, and he discussed customs in terms of their relation to other customs. But the question remains: why did a particular custom arise in a society in the first place? In his study of the Andaman Islanders, an island people living off the Indian subcontinent, Radcliffe-Brown voiced his objection to the search for cultural origins, arguing that it is possible to discover natural laws of society by analyzing the interrelation of customs within contemporary societies. Although he invoked the idea of "psychic unity" so dear to nineteenth century evolutionists (he spoke of "universal psychological processes"), Radcliffe-Brown ultimately declared that anthropology should limit itself to the description of existing societies.

Bronislaw Malinowski. Another major theoretician of the functionalist school was the Polish-born anthropologist Bronislaw Malinowski. Malinowski argued that people everywhere share certain biological and psychological needs and that the ultimate function of all cultural institutions is to fulfill those needs. Everyone, for example, needs to feel secure in his relationship to the physical universe. Therefore, when his science and technology are inadequate to explain certain natural phenomena—such as eclipses or earthquakes—man develops religion and magic to account for those phenomena and to restore his feeling of security. The nature of the institution, according to Malinowski, is determined by its function.

Unlike Radcliffe-Brown, Malinowski did not entirely reject the question of cultural origins; rather, he argued that the origin of cultural traits could be discovered by the analysis of the trait's function within a given society. Malinowski outlined three fundamental levels of needs which he claimed had to be resolved by all cultures.

1) A culture must provide for biological needs, such as the need for food and procreation.
2) A culture must provide for instrumental needs, such as the need for law and education.
3) A culture must provide for integrative needs, such as religion and art.

If the anthropologist could analyze the ways in which a culture fills these needs for its members, Malinowski believed that he could also deduce the origin of cultural traits.

The functionalist approach represented another step forward for anthropology. It was functionalism which finally emphasized the analysis of relationships within cultures and the ways in which cultures function to fill the needs of its members. Yet the functionalists failed to account adequately for the origin of cultural phenomena. Despite Malinowski's claim, the relationship between traits and their functions does not seem to be a directly causal one. Cultural traits and functions affect each other, but they do not seem to have a strict cause and effect relationship. Furthermore, the functionalist approach fails to adequately explain the similarities and differences between cultures. Why does a culture choose one institution to fill a function when a different institution might fill that same function? The functionalists, for example, tried to explain kinship systems in terms of a cohesive function. This explanation begs the issue; ultimately, every aspect of a society can be explained in terms of function. Yet such questions as why a kinship system arose remain unanswered. It is like explaining the function of an organ of the human body without ever asking what part of the body it helps to maintain. Although the functionalists served an important role in pointing out many of the oversimplifications proposed by the evolutionists and diffusionists, they did not offer acceptable alternatives to historical analysis.

Recent trends

Just as the schools of Boas, the diffusionists, and the functionalists appeared in response to the inherent weaknesses in the theories of the evolutionists, later anthropologists have searched extensively for suitable alternatives to the weaker theories of their predecessors. Whereas the general tendency of the counter-evolutionists was either to abandon or postpone the search for universal laws of culture, later theorists have tended to resume interest in that search. At the same time, they have been attempting to develop more precise means of studying and measuring cultural phenomena.

Structuralism

One important theory of culture is that of the French structuralists. Led by Claude Lévi-Strauss, the structuralists think of culture as an expression of the underlying structure of the human mind. This approach is another step away from that of the evolutionists, in that it is concerned primarily in analyzing societies through the observations of the members of the society.

Claude Lévi-Strauss.   In his writings, Claude Lévi-Strauss has argued that human behavior within a cultural framework is a surface representation of an individual's underlying mental structures, or ideas. The structuralists analyze the psychological structure of a society by examining the beliefs and ideas of its members. Lévi-Strauss' studies have centered around the concept of polarity, explaining cultures in terms of a complex system of oppositions. The spatial arrangement of a Trobriand village, for example, presents a series of concentric rings which are said to reflect a series of symbolic polarities. Moreover, the village

Figure 2-12. *Claude Lévi-Strauss is the most prominent advocate of French structuralism, an approach to analyzing cultures. He concentrates on the origins of societal systems, and looks to a culture for its underlying rules of thought.*

is divided into central and peripheral, sacred and profane areas. The central area may be inhabited only by bachelors, whereas married couples must dwell in the periphery.

Ethnosemantics

Ethnosemantics—sometimes referred to as cognitive anthropology or the "new ethnography"—takes the approach of Lévi-Strauss a step further. The goal of the ethnosemanticists is to arrive at a description of a culture as a member of that culture would see it, free from the biases of the outsider. An Englishman describing American football to a fellow countryman would probably do so in terms familiar to themselves; most likely he would describe the game in terms of rugby, a somewhat similar game widely played in England. The description, however, would fall short of conveying to an Englishman exactly what the American game consists of, since it would be described in terms of another game. Football would probably emerge as a caricature of rugby.

The way languages categorize colors has been a subject investigated by the ethnosemanticists. They have grouped societies in terms of the number of colors they perceive. Some societies, for instance, think only in terms of black and white, whereas others think in terms of upward to eleven color categories. If one knows the number of color terms in the language, one can predict with a fair amount of certainty what those colors will be. All languages have terms to describe black and white; the other colors to be added, listed in order, are red, yellow, green, blue, brown, gray, orange, pink, and purple. Most technologically simple societies have very few terms for colors; the number of terms increases with the complexity of a society because color naming is apparently of relatively little use to societies living close to nature. The inference is that such societies reflect the first stages of abstract color naming.

The approach of the ethnosemanticists clearly has its roots in the cultural relativism of Boas and his students. Because they rely on data obtained from a small number of individuals, however, the ethnosemanticists sometimes limit the validity of their work. The data they obtain is based on ideal situations as the ideal is perceived by a small percentage of the population.

Taken alone, both structuralism and ethnosemanticism display significant limitations as approaches to the study of culture. In conjunction with other approaches, however, these schools represent a valuable contribution to anthropology.

Neo-evolutionism

The main thrust of anthropology during the first half of the twentieth century had been a reaction against the generalizations proposed by the nineteenth century evolutionists. In the late 1940s, however, several anthropologists—most notably Leslie White and J. H. Steward—called for a revival of the search for universal laws of culture and cultural development. This school of modern anthropology is referred to as **neo-evolutionism.**

Leslie White. According to Leslie White's system of analysis, all culture consists of three essential components. He refers to these components as the techno-economic, the social, and the ideological. White defines the techno-economic aspect of a culture as the way in which the members of the culture deal with their environment, and it is this aspect which then determines the social and ideological aspects of the culture. In effect, White combines the principles of economic and environmental determinism. Because White considers the manner in which a culture adapts to its environment to be the most significant factor in its development, his approach has been labeled the **cultural materialist** approach. In *The Evolution of Culture* (1959), White stated his basic law of evolution, that culture evolves in proportion to the increased output of energy on the part of each individual, or to the increased efficiency with which that energy is put to work. In other words, culture develops in direct response to technological progress. Unlike the historical particularists, White concentrates primarily on the similarities between cultures in an attempt to arrive at universal cultural laws. White's position is weakened, however, by his failure to account for the fact that technological "progress" may occur in response to purely cultural stimuli. In this respect, his theories are heavily influenced by eighteenth century notions of human progress.

Julian H. Steward. Because Julian H. Steward too is concerned primarily with the response of a culture to its environment, he might also be labeled a neo-evolutionist. Unlike White, however, Steward is concerned with the evolution of specific cultures rather than with the examination of culture in general. Whereas White is concerned with the general categories of culture, Steward is concerned with the comparison of specific historical sequences. His approach, a blending of evolutionism and historical particularism, involves the identification of recurrent developments which can be used as the basis of valid cultural laws.

Because it views evolution as a sequence of steps generally applicable to all cultures, White's theory has been referred to as general evolution. Steward's theory that each culture adapts differently in response to unique environmental pressures, on the other hand, has been labeled specific evolution. Steward himself referred to his approach as **cultural ecology**—that is, the interaction of specific cultures with their environments. Initially, Steward was struck by a number of similarities in the development of urban civilizations in both Peru and Mesoamerica and noted that certain developments were paralleled in the urban civilizations of the Old World. He identified the constants and abstracted from them his laws of cultural development. Steward proposed three fundamental procedures for cultural ecology:

1) The interrelationship of a culture's technology and its environment must be analyzed. How effectively does the culture exploit available resources to provide food and housing for its members?

2) The pattern of behavior associated with a culture's technology must be analyzed. How do members of the culture go about performing the work that must be performed for their survival?

3) The relationship between those behavior patterns and the rest of the cultural system must be determined. How does the work they do to survive affect the people's attitudes and outlooks? How is their survival behavior linked to their social activities and their personal relationships?

Steward's method incorporates the best features of the functionalist approach and calls for scientific observation of the ways in which environmental and cultural phenomena are related, stressing cultural systems as wholes rather than individuals within the culture. In cultural ecology, the first concern is the culture's adaptation, and other aspects of the cultural system are determined from that basis. Like White, Steward argues that the environment is the chief determining factor of culture.

The future

It should not be concluded from our discussion of the foregoing approaches that the field of anthropology is split into a number of warring factions. With few exceptions, anthropologists have shown a great willingness to draw on any theoretical tool, no matter which theoretical "school" gave birth to that particular tool. The primary concern of modern anthropology is that of cultural evolution and the search for general laws that govern the way cultures form, develop, and adapt to changes in the physical and social environment, but this search is being carefully conducted within the context of rigorous field research and sound data. At the same time, there is a wide-spread interest in the interrelationship between culture and environment, tying anthropology to the natural as well as to the social sciences. This combination of concerns holds great promise for the continued growth of our understanding of human behavior.

Original study

TRAVELERS AND ENCYCLOPEDISTS

It is customary to credit Herodotus (c. 484–c. 425 B.C.) as fathering history and anthropology, and I do not dispute either of these claims. He begins by stating, "What Herodotus the Halicarnassian has learnt by inquiry is here set forth; in order that so the memory of the past may not be blotted out from among men by time . . ." In the era of Herodotus "history" meant inquiry or research and by extension information resulting from inquiry; by the second century B.C., however, the word had come to mean the particular kinds of descriptions recorded by Herodotus. *Histories* by Herodotus is primarily an account of the Greco-Persian War, with the additional presentation of related and unrelated information ranging topically from anthropology to zoology; about one-ninth of this work is devoted to ethnographic data. Herodotus personally visted Egypt and much of the Near East and the quality of his description of Egyptian homelife speaks for itself.

But concerning Egypt I will now speak at length, because nowhere are there so many marvellous things, nor in the whole world beside are there to be seen so many works of unspeakable greatness; therefore I shall say the more concerning Egypt.

As the Egyptians have a climate peculiar to themselves, and their river is different in its nature from all other rivers, so have they made themselves customs and laws of a kind contrary to those of all other men. Among them, the women buy and sell, the men abide at home and weave; and whereas in weaving all others push the woof upwards, the Egyptians push it downwards. Men carry burdens on their heads, women on their shoulders. Women make water standing, men sitting. They relieve nature indoors, and eat out of doors in the streets, giving the reason, that things unseemly but necessary should be done in secret, things not unseemly should be done openly. No woman is dedicated to the service of any god or goddess; men are dedicated to all deities male or female. Sons are not compelled against their will to support their parents, but daughters must do so though they be unwilling.

Everywhere else, priests of the gods wear their hair long; in Egypt they are shaven. With all other men, in mourning for the dead those most nearly concerned have their heads shaven; Egyptians are shaven at other times, but after a death they let their hair and beard grow. The Egyptians are the only people who keep their animals with them in the house. Whereas all others live on wheat and barley, it is the greatest disgrace for an Egyptian so to live; they make food from a coarse grain which some call spelt. They knead dough with their feet, and gather mud and dung with their hands. The Egyptians and those who have learnt it from them are the only people who practise circumcision. Every man has two garments, every woman only one. The rings and sheets of sails are made fast elsewhere outside the boat, but inside it in Egypt. The Greeks write and calculate by moving the hand from left to right; the Egyptians do contrariwise; yet they say that their way of writing is towards the right, and the Greek way towards the left. They use two kinds of writing; one is called sacred, the other common.

2 chapter ● **The development of anthropology**

The brevity, clarity, and scope of this passage is striking. Admittedly we would prefer to know more about each topic discussed, but what is more important in the present context is that this description has a calm and studied objectivity. To Herodotus the Egyptians were different from the Greeks, but they were not quaint or bizarre. In his accounts of them he usually described what he had seen or heard. His record of the esoteric Egyptian embalming practices, for example, could only have been obtained through lengthy and systematic interviews, and the same is true of his discussion of their religion, to which he gives an ethnological perspective by comparisons with Greek ideas. On the basis of this Egyptian material, Herodotus should be credited with fathering ethnography.

The 1492 voyage of Christopher Columbus is not only a watershed in the history of exploration, but an ethnographic landmark as well. The original letter in which Columbus reported the results of his first adventure is not known to exist, but an approximation of the primary text is available from copies. Two of the eight printed pages of text are devoted to Indians of the Caribbean, and those met on the island of Haiti are described in the following words.

The people of this island, and of all the other islands which I have found and of which I have information, all go naked, men and women, as their mother bore them, although some women cover a single place with the leaf of a plant or with a net of cotton which they make for the purpose. They have no iron or steel or weapons, nor are they fitted to use them, not because they are not well built men and of handsome stature, but because they are very marvellously timorous. They have no other arms than weapons made of canes, cut in seeding time, to the ends of which they fix a small sharpened stick. And they do not dare to make use of these, for many times it has happened that I have sent ashore two or three men to some town to have speech, and countless people have come out to them, and as soon as they have seen my men approaching they have fled, even a father not waiting for his son. And this, not because ill has been done to anyone; on the contrary, at every point where I have been and have been able to have speech, I have given to them of all that I had, such as cloth and many other things, without receiving anything for it; but so they are, incurably timid. It is true that, after they have been reassured and have lost their fear, they are so guileless and so generous with all they possess, that no one would believe it who has not seen it. They never refuse anything which they possess, if it be asked of them; on the contrary, they invite anyone to share it, and display as much love as if they would give their hearts, and whether the thing be of value or whether it be of small price, at one with whatever trifle of whatever kind it may be that is given to them, with that they are content. I forbade that they should be given things so worthless as fragments of broken crockery and scraps of broken glass, and ends of straps, although when they were able to get them, they fancied that they possessed the best jewel in the world. . . . And I gave a thousand handsome good things, which I had brought, in order that they might conceive affection, and more than that, might become Christians and be inclined to the love and service of their highnesses and of the whole Castilian nation, and strive to aid us and to give us of the things which they have in abundance and which are necessary to us. And they do not know any creed and are not idolators; only they all believe that power and good are in the heavens, and they are very firmly convinced that I, with these ships and men, came from the heavens, and in this belief they everywhere received me, after they had overcome their fear. And this does not come because they are ignorant; on the contrary, they are of a very acute intelligence and are men who navigate all those seas, so that it is amazing how good an account they give of everything, but it is because they have never seen people clothed or ships of such a kind.

What is most significant about this ethnographic sketch is the author's attitude of objectivity, which resulted in a report unadorned with embellishments and exaggeration. At the same time we miss details and note that most of the account deals with cultural dimensions which need only have been seen to be described. One would gather that Columbus had an attitude toward the people which would have led to a competent account if he had been interested enough to compile it.

Source:
From *Other Peoples, Other Customs: World Ethnography and its History* by Wendell H. Oswalt. Copyright © 1972 by Holt, Rinehart and Winston, Inc. Reprinted by permission of Holt, Rinehart and Winston, Inc.

Figure 2-13. *Indians depicted as cannibals.*

Summary

1.

Evolutionism grew out of a period of important advances in science, philosophy, and industrial technology during the first half of the nineteenth century. Darwin's *On the Origin of Species* was the first formal statement of the theory of biological evolution and provided the first model for anthropology. The evolutionists of nineteenth century anthropology employed the concepts of adaptation and natural selection from biological evolution and conceived of society as developing in a regular sequence of predictable stages. Lewis H. Morgan defined three basic stages of cultural evolution: savagery, barbarism, and civilization, all characterized by specific technological attributes. Sir Edward Tylor focused upon the development of religion, postulating three basic stages: animism, polytheism, and monotheism, each resulting from increasing rationality in human concepts. Herbert Spencer's *Principles of Sociology* traced the evolution of marriage forms from polygamy through monogamy. The nineteenth century evolutionists were attempting to discover universal laws of cultural behavior in a single progression of stages through which all cultures passed or must pass.

2.

Franz Boas was the major theoretician of the historical particularist school of the twentieth century. He objected to the general lack of ethnographic data and the ethnocentric values employed by the evolutionists in formulating laws of cultural behavior and development. Boas emphasized the careful study of individual cultures and collection of ethnographic data, and in doing so he observed cultural phenomena which did not correspond to the generalized schemes of the evolutionists. This led him to conclude that each culture was unique in its development and that similarities between cultures were due only to diffusion. The historical particularists abandoned the search for universal cultural laws and stressed the collection of data.

3.

Diffusionism is the belief that all cultural traits spread throughout the world from one or more points of common origin. It was the primary movement in early twentieth century European anthropology. Grafton Elliot Smith and W. J. Perry were major proponents of the extreme diffusionists and argued that all cultural traits originated in Egypt. Fritz Graebner and Father Wilhelm Schmidt were representative of the *Kulturkreise* school in Germany. Less extreme than the English diffusionists, they contended that culture arose in several areas and spread throughout the world from these "culture circles." The culture area school developed contemporaneously in America, arguing that specific cultural traits were found in association with particular types of environment. This school developed the diffusionist theory that cultural traits spread within these culture areas and that the relative age of each trait could be calculated from their distance from their points of origin.

4.

The functionalists, unlike the evolutionists, were interested in the function of specific cultural traits in maintaining a social system rather than in the origin of those traits. A. R. Radcliffe-Brown argued that it was possible to discover universal cultural laws by analyzing the function of specific cultural traits in societies, and proposed the existence of universal psychological processes as responsible for such laws. Bronislaw Malinowski proposed three levels of fundamental human needs which every culture has to fill—

biological, instrumental, and integrative—and argued that the origin of cultural traits could be discovered by the analysis of their function within a given society.

5.
The French structuralists, led by Claude Lévi-Strauss, proposed a model of cultural behavior whereby culture was a surface representation of the underlying structures of the human mind. They approached their analyses through the examination of the conscious beliefs and ideas of individuals within a culture. The ethnosemanticists attempted to analyze cultural phenomena by studying the intentions, goals, and values of individuals within the cultural system according to linguistic models.

6.
The neo-evolutionists revived the search for universal laws of cultural phenomena and development. Leslie White proposed that all culture is composed of three components: the techno-economic, the social, and the ideological. The way a culture utilized its environment is the significant factor in its development. White proposed a model whereby cultures evolved in proportion to increased utilization of energy by the system. Unlike White's approach to the evolution of culture in general stages, labeled general evolution, Julian Steward was interested in specific deviations from those stages, an approach called specific evolution. Steward was the founder of an approach now known as cultural ecology in which cultural phenomena are analyzed in terms of their interaction with the environment.

Suggested readings

Eiseley, Loren *Darwin's Century: Evolution and the Men Who Discovered It.* Garden City, New York: Doubleday, 1958.
Eiseley traces the development of evolutionary ideas in biology from the seventeenth through the nineteenth centuries. Darwin's thought is examined in relation to his predecessors and contemporaries; minor evolutionary theoreticians are also discussed. Footnotes and a bibliography present a wide range of primary, as well as secondary sources.

Harris, Marvin *The Rise of Anthropological Theory: A History of Theories of Culture.* New York: T. Y. Crowell, 1968.
One of the most recent histories of anthropological theory, this book traces the development of the profession as a science. Harris takes a very definite stand in support of the cultural-materialist approach and criticizes his colleagues from this point of view. Because of the opinionated nature of the book, it has been the focus of much controversy in the field, but still stands as one of the most exciting histories of the field ever written.

Hays, H. R. *From Ape to Angel: An Informal History of Social Anthropology.* New York: Putnam, 1964.
The focus of this book is on personalities and anecdotes. It is written in a lively, readable style meant for the general public. It is an informal history of the science. The book is divided into four sections: the Classical Evolutionists, the Critical Reaction, Diffusion and Sociology, and Psychological Insight and Social Responsibility.

Hodgen, Margaret T. *Early Anthropology in the Sixteenth and Seventeenth Centuries.* Philadelphia: University of Pennsylvania Press, 1964.
In an attempt to explore the antecedents of anthropological theory, this book considers the heritage of Renaissance, Medieval, and Classic Grecian social philosophy in anthropology.

Lowie, Robert H. *The History of Ethnological Theory.* New York: Holt, Rinehart and Winston, 1937.
This book is devoted only to that part of anthropology which concerns culture, and indicates the course of theoretical progress from evolutionary precedents to the time of its publication. It is a classic in its field.

Penniman, T. K. *A Hundred Years of Anthropology.* New York: Humanities Press, 1965.
Penniman outlines developments in prehistory and technology in the Old World. Following this is a good survey of physical anthropology by J. S. Weiner and by Beatrice Blackwood. Only the section by Weiner has a bibliography. Penniman's approach is comparative and analytic, with a tolerance for all methods.

Stocking, George W., Jr. *Race, Culture and Evolution: Essays in the History of Anthropology.* New York: Free Press, 1968.
A collection of essays which, unlike most such collections, is intended to be read as one book. Stocking presents a unique approach to the history of anthropological theory. This is not a retrospective justification of present methods but a historical account of the development and progress of a social science. Each idea is presented as reasonable within its own period and not attacked with the hindsight of numerous generations.

Biology
and evolution

A common component of the mythology of all cultures is the legend that explains the appearance of man on earth. For example, the Nez Perce Indians of the American northwest believe that mankind is the creation of Coyote, one of the animal people that inhabited the earth before man. Coyote chased the giant beaver monster, Wishpoosh, in an epic chase whose trail formed the Columbia River. When Coyote caught Wishpoosh, he killed him and dragged his body to the river bank. Ella Clark retells the legend:

With his sharp knife Coyote cut up the big body of the monster.

"From your body, mighty Wishpoosh," he said, "I will make a new race of people. They will live near the shores of Big River and along the streams which flow into it."

From the lower part of the animal's body, Coyote made the people who were to live along the coast. "You shall live near the mouth of Big River and shall be traders.

"You shall live along the coast," he said to others. "You shall live in villages facing the ocean and shall get your food by spearing salmon and digging clams. You shall always be short and fat and have weak legs."

From the legs of the beaver monster he made the Klickitat Indians. "You shall live along the rivers that flow down from the big white mountain north of Big River. You shall be swift of foot and keen of wit. You shall be famous runners and great horsemen."

From the arms of the monster he made the Cayuse Indians. "You shall live along Big River," Coyote said to them. "You shall be powerful with bow and arrows and with war clubs."

From the ribs he made the Yakima Indians. "You shall live near the new Yakima River, east of the mountains. You shall be the helpers and the protectors of all the poor people."

From the head he created the Nez Perce Indians. "You shall live in the valleys of the Kookooskia and the Wallowa rivers. You shall be men of brains, great in council and in speech-making. You shall also be skillful horsemen and brave warriors."

Then Coyote gathered up the hair and blood and waste. He hurled them far eastward, over the big mountains. "You shall be the Snake River Indians," said Coyote. "You shall be people of blood and violence. You shall be buffalo hunters and shall wander far and wide."

It is interesting to speculate about the influence of such persistent myths on modern scientific explanations of the same sequence of events. One of the most striking similarities lies in the way both myth and science try to explain the relationship between an organism's form and function and the environment in which it lives.

Adaptation

The term **adaptation** refers to the possession of certain anatomical, physiological, and behavioral characteristics that permit organisms to survive in the special environmental conditions in which they are generally found. Anyone who has ever looked carefully at the plants and animals that survive in the deserts of the western United States can cite many examples of adaptations. For example, some desert plants have roots close to the surface of the soil, enabling them to soak up the slightest bit of moisture; many have special organs for the storage of water; their leaves are coated with wax or covered with needles to prevent excessive evaporation of water from the pores of the leaf. Desert animals are also adapted to their environment. The kangaroo rat can survive without drinking water; many reptiles live in burrows where the temperature is lower; most animals are nocturnal, or active only in the cool of the night.

Natural selection

Many of the stories traditionally offered to explain the observable cases of adaptation rely heavily on the intentionality of a world creator. The legend of Coyote and Wishpoosh is one such example; the early nineteenth century scientific belief that God created each animal separately to occupy a specific place in a hierarchical ladder of being is another. Certainly it is hard to escape the impression that such a neat fit between organism and environment is the result of some careful planning or foresight. The modern scientific explanation, however, makes any such direction of the

Figures 3-1 and 2. *These moths, both of the same species, illustrate the principle of adaptation. Their coloration is used as camouflage. The dark moth's color is an adaptation to a sooty industrial area.*

universe unnecessary; it postulates that adaptation is the natural outcome of the process of natural selection.

Natural selection refers to the evolutionary process through which factors in the environment exert a pressure that selects some individuals and not others to reproduce the next generation of the group. In other words, instead of a completely random selection of individuals whose inheritance factors will be passed on to the next generation, there is a selection by the forces of nature.

In the popular press, natural selection is often equated with the survival of the fittest, in which the weak and the unfit are eliminated from the population by disease, predation, or starvation. Obviously, the survival of the fittest has some bearing on natural selection; one need hardly point out that the dead do not reproduce. But there may be many cases in which individuals survive but do not reproduce. They may be incapable of attracting mates, or they may be sterile, or they may produce offspring that do not survive after birth. For example, dairy farmers often notice that certain cows in the herd, although they are perfectly healthy individuals, simply never calve. This is an instance of natural selection at work, leading to different rates of reproduction for different types of individuals within any group.

The case of sickle-cell trait

One of the best studied examples of adaptation through natural selection in man can be seen in the inheritance of the trait of sickling red blood cells. Sickle-cell trait is caused by the inheritance of an abnormal form of hemoglobin in the red blood cells. Under certain low-oxygen conditions, this hemoglobin variant causes the cells to take on a characteristic sickled shape and crack when entering small blood vessels. In its severe form, called sickle-cell anemia, this condition causes early death. Sickle cell first came to the attention of geneticists when it was observed that most of

the Americans suffering from the trait are black and few are white. Investigation traced the abnormality to a group of Africans that live in a clearly defined belt throughout central Africa.

Geneticists were curious to know why such a deleterious inheritance factor remained in the population. According to the theory of natural selection, any change or mutation that is harmful will tend to disappear from the group, since the individuals that inherit the abnormality will be less likely to reproduce. Why, then, had this seemingly harmful condition remained in the central African population?

The answer to this mystery began to emerge when it was noticed that the areas in which sickle-cell anemia is prevalent are also areas in which falciparum malaria is very common. Moreover, it was discovered that similar hemoglobin abnormalities are found in residents of southern Italy and Sicily, as well as in certain Asiatics, all of whom also live in regions where falciparum malaria is common. Further research established that the abnormal hemoglobin was associated with an increased ability to survive the effects of the malarial parasite; it seems that the effects of the abnormal hemoglobin were less injurious than the effects of the malarial parasite. Under such conditions, natural selection worked against those with normal hemoglobin who succumbed to malaria, and in favor of those who had sickle-cell trait but were also resistant to malaria.

This example also points out how specific adaptations tend to be; the abnormal hemoglobin was an adaptation to the particular parts of Africa in which the malarial parasite flourished. When Africans adapted to that region moved to America, where falciparum malaria is unknown, what was previously an adaptive characteristic became an injurious one. Where there is no malaria to attack those with normal hemoglobin, the abnormal hemoglobin becomes comparatively disadvantageous. Although the rates of sickle-cell trait are still relatively high among American blacks, (about 10 percent show the sickling trait) geneticists predict that within the next several generations, selection pressure will have worked against

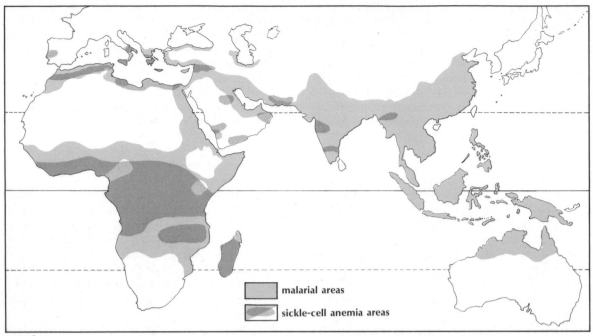

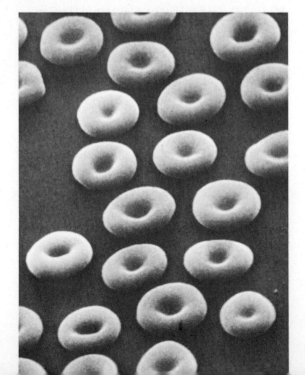

Figures 3-3, 4, and 5. *Sickle-cell trait is an adaptation of the blood to combat malaria. The sickling gene and malaria are mostly found in the same parts of the world. Sickle-cell anemia withdraws oxygen from red blood cells, leaving them sickle-shaped. In America, where malaria is not a problem, sickle-cell anemia strikes many blacks who receive it hereditarily.*

malarial areas

sickle-cell anemia areas

the extreme form of this condition (anemia), causing a noticeable decrease in the number of individuals that display it.

Heredity

As the example of sickle-cell anemia shows, adaptive traits can be passed from one generation to the next through the mechanisms of heredity. It is upon this inheritance of adaptations that the process of natural selection depends. Our knowledge of the mechanisms of heredity is fairly recent; most of the fruitful research into the molecular level of inheritance has taken place in the past two decades. Although certain aspects remain puzzling, the outlines by now seem reasonably clear.

The transmission of genes

Biologists call the actual units of heredity **genes,** a term that comes from the Greek word for birth. The presence and activity of genes were originally deduced rather than observed; no one knew what genes were but everyone knew what they did. Modern technological advances, such as the invention of the electron microscope and the technique of X-ray diffraction, have made the nature of this unit much clearer.

DNA. It is now generally agreed that genes are actually portions of molecules of deoxyribonucleic acid, or **DNA.** DNA is a complex molecule with an unusual shape, rather like the spiral staircase in the leg of the Eiffel Tower. The way that smaller molecules are arranged in this giant molecule is actually a code that contains information to direct the synthesis of proteins. It is at this level that the development of certain traits really occurs; the code, for example, directs the formation of the protein that colors the iris of the eye, thus determining eye color; it also directs the formation of the hemoglobin molecule in red blood cells. Recently there has been great progress in cracking the genetic code, in a series of events as exciting as any spy story.

DNA molecules have the unique property of being able to produce exact copies of themselves. Thus a copy can be made and passed to another organism; as long as there are no errors made in the replication process, the new organism will be almost exactly like the original.

Genes. A gene is a unit of the DNA molecule that directs the development of a single observable or identifiable trait. When we speak of the gene for blue eyes, we are referring to the portion of a DNA molecule that contains the genetic code for the proteins that gives eyes their characteristic color. A gene, then, is not really a separate structure, as had once been imagined, but a location, like a dot on a map. It is estimated that human DNA contains at least 10,000 different genes.

Chromosomes. DNA molecules do not float freely about in our bodies; they are located on structures called **chromosomes** found in the nucleus of each cell. Chromosomes are probably nothing more than long strands of DNA, covered with some kind of protective protein coating. The chromosomes of most cells can easily be seen under a conventional light microscope. Each kind of organism has a characteristic number of chromosomes, which are usually found in pairs. For example, the body cells of the fruit fly each contain 4 pairs of chromosomes; those of humans contain 23 pairs; those of some brine shrimp have as many as 160 pairs. The two chromosomes in each pair contain genes for the same traits: the two in pair A, for instance, might both contain genes for eye color. But the genes are not necessarily the same: one might be a gene for brown eyes and the other a gene for blue eyes. Genes that are located on paired chromosomes and are coded for different versions of the same trait are called **alleles.**

Cell division. In order to grow and maintain good health, the body cells of an organism must divide and produce new cells. Cell division is initiated when the chromosomes replicate, forming a second set that contains an exact duplicate of each chromosome in the nucleus. This set then separates from the original set, is surrounded by a membrane, and becomes the nucleus that directs the activities of a new cell. This kind of cell division is called **mitosis,** and it produces new cells that have exactly the same number of chromosome pairs as did the parent cell.

When new individuals are produced through sexual reproduction, it involves the merging of two cells, one from each parent. If two regular body cells, each containing 23 pairs of chromosomes, were to merge, the result would be a new individual that had 46 pairs of chromosomes; such an individual, if it lived at all, would surely be a monster. But this increase in chromosome number never occurs, because the sex cells that join to form a new individual are the product of a different kind of cell division, called **meiosis.** Although meiosis begins like mitosis, with the replication of the original chromosomes, it proceeds to divide that number into four new cells rather than two. Thus each new cell has only half the number of chromosomes found in the parent cell. Human eggs and sperm, for example, have only 23 single chromosomes, whereas body cells have 23 pairs, or 46 chromosomes.

The process of meiotic division has important implications for genetics. Since chromosome pairs are separated, two different types of new cells will be formed; two of the four new cells will have the first chromosome and the two will have the second. Of course, this will not make any difference if the original pair was identical, or **homozygous.** For example, if both genes of the original pair contained the gene for blue eyes, then all new cells will have the blue gene. But if the original pair was **heterozygous,** or consisted of one blue and one brown gene, then half of the new cells will contain the blue gene and the other half will contain only the brown gene; the offspring have a 50–50 chance of getting either gene. It is impossible to predict any single individual's genotype, but a statistical average can be established.

Patterns of inheritance

What happens when a child inherits the gene for blue eyes from one parent and the gene for brown eyes from the other? Will the child have blue eyes, brown eyes, or some shade midway between the two? Many of these questions were answered, in the nineteenth century, by the meticulous observations of an Austrian monk, Gregor Mendel, who worked with garden peas to determine the way various traits are inherited.

Mendel discovered that certain genes are able to mask the presence of others; one gene will be **dominant** whereas its allele is **recessive.** The gene for brown eyes, for example, is dominant to the gene for blue eyes. An individual whose eye-color genes are heterozygous, with one brown (B) and one blue (b) gene, will have brown eyes. Thus the heterozygous condition (Bb) will show exactly the same physical characteristic, or **phenotype,** as the homozygous brown (BB), even though the two have a slightly different genetic composition, or **genotype.** Only the homozygous recessive genotype (bb) will show the phenotype of blue eyes.

The dominance of one gene does not mean that the recessive allele is lost or in some way blended. A brown-eyed heterozygous parent (Bb) will produce sex cells containing both brown and blue genes. Certain recessive genes, such as the gene for albinism in humans, can be handed down for generations before they join with another recessive in the process of sexual reproduction and show up in the phenotype. The presence of the dominant gene simply renders the recessive gene inactive.

All of the traits that Mendel studied in garden peas showed this dominant-recessive relationship, and so for some years it was believed that this was the only relationship possible. More recent studies, however, have indicated that patterns of inheritance are not always so simple. In some cases, neither gene is dominant; they are both codominant. An example of codominance in human heredity can be seen in the inheritance of blood types. Type A is produced by one gene;

Gregor Mendel

Figure 3-6. *Gregor Mendel discovered and described the laws of inheritance in 1865. He conducted breeding experiments with garden peas, and carefully recorded the results. His laws, emphasizing dominant and recessive genes, are valid for many of man's traits.*

Type B is produced by an allele. A heterozygous individual will have a phenotype of AB, since neither allele can dominate the other.

The inheritance of blood types points out another complexity of heredity. The number of alleles is by no means limited to two; certain traits seem to have three or more allelic genes. Of course, only one allele can appear on each of the pairs of chromosomes, so each individual is limited to two alleles. There is a third allele for blood group inheritance, a gene for Type O blood. Type O is recessive to both the A and B alleles.

Another relatively recent discovery is the fact that dominance need not always be complete. This is the case with the alleles for normal and abnormal hemoglobin. The homozygous dominant condition (HH) produces only normal molecules of hemoglobin; the homozygous recessive condition (hh) produces such a high level of abnormal molecules that the individual generally dies of anemia before adulthood. The heterozygous condition (Hh) produces some normal and some abnormal molecules; the presence of the abnormal molecules confers resistance to the malarial parasite and the presence of a certain level of normal molecules usually insures viability. The normal is dominant to the abnormal, but the dominance is incomplete, and therefore the recessive gene is not completely inactive. It is now believed that many instances in which phenotypes appear to indicate complete dominance may show incomplete dominance on the molecular level.

Population genetics

At the level of the individual, the study of genetics suggests the way that certain traits are transmitted from one generation to the next and enables a prediction about the chances that any given individual will display some phenotypic characteristic. At the level of the group, the study of genetics takes on additional significance, revealing mechanisms that support evolutionary interpretations of the diversity of life.

A key concept in genetics is that of the **population,** or a group of similar individuals that can and does interbreed. It is on the population level that natural selection takes place, so that some members of the population produce more than their share of the next generation, and other individuals produce less than their share. Thus, over a period of generations, the population shows a measure of adaptation to its environment due to this evolutionary mechanism.

The stability of the population

By and large, the characteristics of any given population remain remarkably stable. For example, generation after generation, the green frogs in Farmer MacDonald's pond look much alike, have the same calls, exhibit the same behavior when breeding. Another way to look at this remarkable consistency is to say that the **gene pool** of the population—the total number of different genes and alleles—remains the same.

The relative stability of the gene pool of a population is not only easy to observe; it is also easy to understand. Mendel's experiments with garden peas, and all subsequent genetic experiments as well, have shown that, although some genes may be dominant to others, the recessive gene is not lost or destroyed. A homozygous individual has a 50 percent chance of passing on to the next generation the dominant gene; he also has a 50 percent chance of passing on the recessive allele. The recessive gene may again be masked by the presence of a dominant gene in the next generation, but it is there nonetheless, and will be handed on again.

Since no gene is ever "lost" in the process of reproduction, the frequency with which certain genes occur in the population will remain exactly the same from one generation to the next. This principle was worked out in 1908 by G. H. Hardy, an English mathematician, and G. Weinberg, a German physician, and is therefore known as the **Hardy-Weinberg Law.** It demonstrates algebraically that the percentage of individuals that are homozygous for the dominant gene, homozygous for the recessive allele, and heterozygous, will remain the same from one generation to the next, no matter how random mating takes place.

The nature of DNA itself is also a factor for stability in the gene pool. Mistakes in replicating genetic material are rare; in an overwhelming majority of cases, the new strands of DNA are exactly like the old ones. Moreover, in the rare cases that mistakes are made, the DNA in living cells possesses a self-correcting ability to cut out the sections of the molecule that are wrong.

Another stability factor is the fact that heterozygous individuals sometimes are larger, stronger, and have more survival advantages than dominant or recessive homozygotes. The superiority of the heterozygote may serve to retain a consistent level even of deleterious genes. This stability factor, called balanced polymorphism, is probably responsible for the retention of the gene for abnormal hemoglobin in certain African populations; although homozygous recessive individuals die before they can reproduce, the frequency of that gene remains the same because of the superior survival ability of the heterozygotes.

Factors for change

According to the principle of the Hardy-Weinberg Law, there could never be any adaptive change in a population, since every generation would have exactly the same gene frequencies as the one preceding it. But the Hardy-Weinberg Law makes a number of assumptions that are not necessarily the case in real life. It assumes that mating is random, whereas it often happens that geographical, physiological, or behavioral factors separate certain members of a population from the others. It assumes that the population is a large one, large enough for statistical averages to express themselves, whereas it sometimes occurs —on islands, for example—that a population is quite small. Most importantly, it assumes that no mutations on the gene level will occur, introducing new genes into the population, whereas it is known that such mutations do take place. Thus the Hardy-Weinberg Law is not an ironclad rule, and change in the gene pool does indeed take place.

Mutation.   The most important source of change is mutation of genes. Although mutation is normally a rare occurrence, the large number of genes in each individual sex cell, the large number of sex cells produced (the human male ejaculates hundreds of millions of sperm cells at a single time), and the large number of individuals in a population mean that there will always be new mutant genes.

Geneticists have calculated the rate at which various types of mutant genes appear. In the human population, they run from a low of about 5 mutations per million sex cells formed, in the case of a gene abnormality that leads to the absence of an iris in the eye, to a high of about 100 mutants per million, in the case of a gene that causes a form of muscular dystrophy. The average is about 30 mutants per million.

Research with viruses and bacteria suggested that certain factors can increase the rate at which mutations occur. These include certain chemicals, such as some dyes and also some antibiotics; some chemicals used in the preservation of food are currently suspected of having this property. Another important cause of increased mutation rates is irradiation. The ultraviolet rays of sunshine may be a mutation-causing agent; so may X-rays. Radioactive rays have the same mutation-causing effect, as was so sadly demonstrated by the high rates of mutations found in the children of survi-

Figure 3-7. *There are albinos, like this Hopi Indian girl, among all human populations. Albinism occurs relatively frequently among certain American Indian tribes.*

vors of the bombings of Hiroshima and Nagasaki.

Genetic research studies with corn have shown that certain genes appear to have the function of causing mutations in seed color and plant size. It is speculated that such mutator genes may also occur in human DNA. This might explain why some mutations appear so frequently. The presence of these mutator genes has been likened to a fail-safe mechanism for preserving the variability of the gene pool; even if offspring with the mutator gene are selected against, the mutation will not disappear from the gene pool but will simply recur, as a result of the mutator gene's action.

Genetic drift. Each individual is subject to a number of chance events that determine life or death. For example, an individual squirrel in good health and possessed of a number of adaptive traits may be killed in a forest fire; a genetically superior baby cheetah may not live longer than a day because its mother is unable to provide its food, whereas the weaker offspring of a mother with superior hunting abilities may survive. In a large population, such accidents of nature are unimportant; the accidents that preserve individuals with certain genes will be balanced out by the accidents that destroy them. However, in small populations, such averaging out may not be possible. A forest fire that kills 100 squirrels is not significant if the total population is 10,000; but if the population consists of only 200 individuals, the death of half that number may result in the loss of certain traits, and the increased frequency of others, regardless of their survival value.

The effect of chance events on the gene pool of small populations is called **genetic drift.** Genetic drift is thought to be an important factor in causing the often bizarre characteristics found in isolated island populations. It is also thought to have been an important factor in human evolution, because many early hominids probably consisted of relatively small populations.

Gene flow. Another factor that brings change to the gene pool of a population is **gene flow,**

Figures 3-8, 9, and 10. *Charles Darwin based his theory of evolution on natural selection. This process saw characteristics of an organism that helped the organism survive being perpetuated and slightly refined with each succeeding generation. While on his voyage with the H.M.S. Beagle, Darwin stopped at the Galapagos Islands. He noted that each island environment had its own specially adapted form of finch.*

or the introduction of new genes from nearby populations. Gene flow occurs when previously separated groups are once again able to interbreed, as for example when a river that once separated two populations of small mammals changes course. Migration of bands of individuals may also lead to gene flow. This has been observed in several North American rodents that have been forced to leave their territory due to changes in environmental conditions. Gene flow has been an important factor in human evolution, both in terms of the early hominid groups and also in terms of current racial variation. For example, the last 400 years have seen the establishment of a new phenotype throughout much of Latin America as a result of the introduction, into the gene pool of the Indians native to the area, of new genes from both the Spanish colonists and the Africans that the Europeans imported as slaves.

Natural selection. The factors for change listed above may produce gradual change in the population, but that change would not necessarily make the population better adapted to its biological and social environment. Genetic drift, for example, often produces strange characteristics that have no survival value; mutant genes may be either helpful or harmful to survival. It is the action of natural selection that makes evolutionary change adaptive. Natural selection reduces the frequency of the genes for harmful or maladaptive traits within the population and increases the frequency of the genes for adaptive traits.

This change in the frequency with which certain genes appear in the population is actually a very slow process. For example, one researcher in the area of sickle-cell trait has estimated that it will take 2000 years to bring about a 5 percent reduction in the frequency of the gene for sickle-cell within the American population. Yet given the great time span involved—life on earth is thought to have existed for three to four billion years—even such small and slow changes will have a significant cumulative impact on both the genotypes and phenotypes of any population.

Discussions of the action of natural selection typically focus on anatomical or structural changes, such as the evolutionary change in the type of teeth found in primates; ample evidence (fossilized teeth, for example) exists to interpret

The study of man ● part **1**

such changes. By extrapolation, biologists assume that the same mechanisms work on behavioral traits as well. It seems reasonable that a hive of bees capable of communicating the location of nectar-bearing flowers would have a significant survival advantage over those that must search for food by trial and error. Natural selection of behavioral and social traits was probably a particularly important influence on hominid evolution, since in the primates, social mechanisms began to replace physical structures for food-getting, defense, and mate attraction.

Many anthropologists point out the close parallel between biological and cultural evolution, and therefore they postulate that a process of natural selection continues to work on cultural traits within a society. Traits of a culture that enable an increased percentage of its people to survive and reproduce will become fixed in the social group; traits that are disadvantageous will be eliminated. Since the adoption of cultural traits is to some extent a matter of choice, cultural evolution is much more rapid than biological evolution. Man cannot choose to have a larger brain, even though he recognizes that such a brain would have adaptive value; he can, however, choose to live in a social structure that facilitates sharing of available knowledge among all members of the group.

Evolution of populations

One of the most evident consequences of the process of natural selection is the increased adaptation of a population to its environment. This kind of evolutionary change can be seen as a kind of refinement of the organism. As it moves from the rather generalized prototype to the more and more specialized versions, it becomes better and better adapted; each new "model" replaces the old, in a process somewhat analogous to the yearly changes in General Motors cars. Of course, there is a certain danger in this increased adaptation. If the environment changes for some reason, those organisms that are best adapted to the old environment will have the greatest difficulty surviving in a new environment. It is thought that such changes took place a number of times during the course of vertebrate evolution; one of the most dramatic examples was the sudden extinction of the dinosaurs. In such cases, it is usually the more generalized organisms that survive; later they may give rise to a new line of specialists.

But not all evolution is a linear progression from one form to a more specialized form of the same type. Evolution may also be **divergent,** or branching. Divergent evolution is probably responsible for much of the diversity of life to be observed today. Evolution may also be **convergent,** when two dissimilar forms develop greater similarities. Convergent evolution is thought to take place in circumstances where an environment exerts similar pressures on several different organisms.

Because evolution can take so many different courses, it is often difficult to reconstruct the sequence of events that led to the emergence of any given group or species, especially in view of the fact that evidence, such as fossil remains, is often so fragmentary and incomplete. The story of hominid evolution is particularly confusing, since it appears to consist of relatively rapid sequences of divergent, convergent, and linear evolution.

Speciation

Both linear and divergent evolution can result in the establishment of a new **species.** The term species is often defined as a population or group of populations that is mechanically capable of interbreeding. Thus the green frogs in Farmer MacDonald's pond are the same species as those in nearby Farmer Gray's pond, even though it may be the case that the two populations never actually do interbreed; in theory, they are capable of it if they are brought together. This definition is not altogether satisfactory, because isolated populations are often in the process of evolving into different species, and it is hard to tell exactly when they become separate. For example, all dogs supposedly belong to the same species, but a male Saint Bernard and a female Chihuahua are not capable of producing offspring; even if they could somehow manage the feat of copulation, the Chihuahua would die trying to give birth to such large pups. On the other hand, Alaskan sled dogs are able to breed with wild wolves, even though they are theoretically different species; the very thought of a wolf copulating with most other breeds of dog, however, is ridiculous. Although all species definitions are relative rather than absolute ones, the modern concept of species puts more stress on the question of whether breeding actually takes place in the wild than on the more academic question of whether it is technically feasible.

Subgroups within species that are quite capable of interbreeding but only rarely do are called **races.** Evolutionary theory suggests that species evolve from races through the gradual accumulation of differences in the gene pool of the separated groups.

Isolation mechanisms

Certain factors, known as **isolation mechanisms,** serve to separate breeding populations, creating first divergent races and then divergent species. Some isolation mechanisms are geographical, preventing gene flow between members of separated populations as the result of traveling individuals or bands. Anatomical structure can also serve as an isolation mechanism, as we saw in the case of the Saint Bernard and the Chihuahua. Other physical isolation factors include early miscarriage of the offspring; weakness or presence of maladaptive traits that cause early death in the offspring; or, as in the case of the mule, sterility of the hybrid offspring.

Isolation mechanisms may also be social rather than physical. Speciation due to this mechanism is particularly common among birds. For example, cuckoos (birds that do not build nests of their own but lay their eggs in other birds' nests) attract mates by mimicking the song of the bird species whose nests they borrow; thus cuckoos that are physically capable of mating have different courtship behavior, which effectively isolates them.

Social isolation mechanisms are thought to have been the most important factor in speciation during hominid evolution. They continue to play a part in the maintenance of racial barriers. Although mating is physically possible between any two humans of the opposite sex, the awareness of social and cultural differences often makes the idea distasteful, perhaps even unthinkable; this isolation is due to the force of the culturally implanted concept of a significant difference between "us" and "them." Yet, as evidenced by the blending of races that has taken place in many parts of the world, man is also capable of reasoning away social isolation mechanisms that would, in the case of other animals, lead separate races to evolve into separate species. Such speciation is very unlikely in *Homo sapiens.*

Original study

THE PROCESS
OF CHANGE

There is no longer any doubt about the fact of evolution as the central process of nature. Organic evolution is a general principle of biology, applying equally to all forms of life. Among biologists who have considered the evidence there is overwhelming acceptance of the thesis that man evolved in the same way that other animals did. In their evolution species often progressively diverge with time from other related species. In his development, man in this way left behind him some of those traits that are more or less common to other advanced organisms that populate this globe. Man also has acquired traits that distinguish him from the rest of the animal world.

By *evolution* is meant any change in hereditary endowment continuing through successive generations of time. It is a lawful change in the genetic composition of the members of a population. It consists of all the ways in which some inherited qualities develop and permeate the species while others decline or fail to be preserved. Both processes may go on simultaneously with different traits in the same population, while still other hereditary features may persist and pass unmodified from generation to generation. Ordinarily the term "evolution" is used for continuous changes that have gone on for many generations, but this process is the accumulation of changes going on from fathers and mothers to sons and daughters. In essence, evolution is the accumulation of genetic changes between successive parents and offspring. The differences one can see between a father and his son provide living evidence of the evolution that has been proceeding throughout many generations. If it were not for such differences between parent and child, however slight they may be, there could be no evolution.

A child sometimes resembles one of his grandparents but not his father or his mother. Whatever degree of resemblance he demonstrates to earlier ancestors must have come to him through his parents, but the extent to which the genetic makeup of an earlier ancestor will be communicated to him cannot be predicted. No one knows in what member of a large family a noteworthy physical feature of a grandfather will reappear or whether it will reappear at all. Such a hereditary trait may occur in only some of the offspring, express itself to various degrees, or become modified. The process of evolution is continuous change with time. It may vary in rate, however. Indeed, when there are no changes whatever in environment or habits and when members of the population do not mate with those of other populations, one may see merely small chance fluctuations in physical characteristics from generation to generation without continuing evolution in any direction. In nature there are instances of so-called living fossils, such as the opossum and the horseshoe crab, that have remained almost the same over millions of years. In man, however, especially in the last several centuries, increased population mobility and far-reaching changes in living conditions must have accelerated the rate of evolution. Human evolution has probably never been faster than now. at least in respect to features that adapt us to modern living conditions.

Sexual reproduction ensures that each successive generation differs from the last. The relatives of a newborn infant sometimes say, "He is the image of his father." At most, however, the child merely resembles one of his parents. One never sees a child who is identical in every feature to either parent. Photographs show that individuals look quite different from the way either of their parents appeared at the same age. Variation is present among members of a family and among families and groups. Such variation is both the cause and the result of the feedback mechanism of evolution. That is, evolution largely depends on some rather than other kinds of variation, but it is in turn responsible for ever-diverging types and increasing ranges of variation. Nevertheless, differences within a foreign family or group, the basic kind of variation, may be difficult to see. To some observers, "All Chinese look alike." This is because the features in which the Chinese differ from our own group of people are so strikingly evident that one may fail to notice the individual differences which exist among the Chinese—variations that they find perfectly adequate for identifying their acquaintances. For example, the skinfold of the eyelid that gives the almond-eyed appearance to the Chinese has innumerable variations and individual differences. We have plenty of visible proof for the fact that evolution is at work among us to produce cumulative effects of group differentiation. Such evidences consist of observations of what happens within the family and the population and what has happened between species over long spans of time. Unlike some other scientific principles, however, the large number of factors entering into most evolutionary events makes it difficult to predict what future organisms will be like. But for the past, the salient conditions are known or can be inferred, and evolution provides the explanation.

Source:
From *Physical Anthropology* by Gabriel Ward Lasker. Copyright © 1973 by Holt, Rinehart and Winston, Inc. Reprinted by permission of Holt, Rinehart and Winston, Inc.

Summary

1.
Natural selection refers to the evolutionary process through which factors in the environ-ment exert pressure that selects some individuals and not others to reproduce the next generation of the group.

2.
The inheritance of the trait that produces a disease known as sickle-cell anemia is one of the best studied examples of adaptation through natural selection. Sickle-cell trait is an adaptation to life in regions in which a kind of malarial parasite flourishes; in these regions, sickle-cell trait plays a beneficious role. But in other parts of the world, the sickling trait is injurious. This disease has remained in certain populations because it confers upon the individuals suffering from it a resistance to a form of malaria.

3.
The unit of heredity is known as the gene. It directs the development of a single observable or identifiable trait. A gene is a unit of DNA (deoxyribonucleic acid), a complex molecule in the shape of a spiral staircase. The way that smaller molecules are arranged in this giant molecule is actually a code that contains information to direct the synthesis of proteins. DNA molecules have the unique property of being able to produce exact copies of themselves; thus a copy can be made, passed on to another organism, and the new organism will be almost exactly like the original.

4.
Chromosomes are cell structures that contain DNA. Each kind of organism has a charac-teristic number of chromosomes, usually found in pairs. Man has 23 pairs. Chromosomes are gene-carrying structures. Genes that are located on paired chromosomes and are coded for different versions of the same trait are called alleles.

5.
There are two types of cell division: mitosis and meiosis. In mitosis, the chromosomes of one cell reproduce a set of duplicate chromosomes which then separate, forming a new cell identical to the original one. Meiosis occurs only in organisms which reproduce sexually and involves the merging of two parent cells. Meiosis begins with the replication of original chromosomes, but these are divided into four cells, each containing 23 single chromosomes.

6.
The Austrian monk Gregor Mendel studied the mechanism of inheritance with garden peas. He discovered that certain genes are able to mask the presence of others. They are called dominant. The allele of a dominant is recessive. The gene for brown eyes, for example, is dominant to the gene for blue eyes.

7.
The phenotype refers to the physical characteristics of an organism, whereas the genotype refers to its genetic composition. Two organisms may have the same phenotype, but different genotypes.

8.

A key concept in genetics is that of population, or a group of similar individuals that can and does interbreed. Natural selection takes place on the population level. The total number of different genes and alleles in a population is called the gene pool. The frequency with which certain genes occur in a population remains the same from one generation to another. The principle whereby this stability is maintained was worked out by scientists G. H. Hardy and G. Weinberg in the Hardy-Weinberg Law.

9.

The most important source of genetic change is mutation. Mutation is normally a rare occurrence, but some factors, such as certain chemicals or radioactive substances, can increase the mutation rate.

10.

The effect of chance events on the gene pool of small populations is called genetic drift. Genetic drift may have been an important factor in human evolution, because many early hominids probably consisted of relatively small populations. Another factor that may bring change to the gene pool of a population is gene flow, or the introduction of new genes from nearby populations. Gene flow occurs when previously separated groups are once again able to breed.

11.

Natural selection is the force that makes evolutionary change adaptive. It reduces the frequency of genes for harmful or maladaptive traits within a population and increases the frequency of genes for adaptive traits.

12.

Evolution is the process whereby an organism changes into a new form from a previous form. Evolution is not necessarily a linear progression. It may be divergent, or branching; or convergent, when two dissimilar forms develop greater similarities.

13.

A species is a population or group of populations that is mechanically capable of inter-breeding. The concept of species is relative rather than absolute; whether breeding takes place in the wild or not is more important than the academic question of whether it is technically feasable or not. Subgroups within species that are quite capable of interbreeding but only rarely do are called races.

14.

Isolation mechanisms serve to separate breeding populations, often creating divergent races and then divergent species. Isolating mechanisms can be physical, such as a geographical barrier, or social, such as the caste system.

Suggested readings

De Beer, Sir Gavin R. *Atlas of Evolution*. London: Nelson, 1964.
A magnificently illustrated and lucidly written book dealing with the principles and processes of evolutionary change.

Harris, G. A., et al. *Human Biology: An Introduction to Human Evolution, Variation and Growth*. New York: Oxford University Press, 1964.
This work represents an attempt to synthesize, at an introductory level, present knowledge of the biological organization of past (and present) human populations. The first section of the book covers evolutionary theory, the history of the primates, the fossil evidence for human evolution, and anthropogenesis. The second is concerned with the principles of human genetics as applied to family and population studies, and the third with systematic descriptions of human variation. These are followed by a section on the nature of human growth and the factors which determine it, varieties of human physique and other constitutional traits. Finally, the ecology of human populations is considered with particular reference to climate, nutrition, and disease.

Levine, Robert Paul *Genetics*. New York: Holt, Rinehart and Winston, 1968.
Substantially revised and updated, this book authoritatively analyzes the nature, transmission, and function of genetic material. In this edition, protein synthesis and its regulation form the subject matter of two entirely new chapters.

Merrell, David J., ed. *Evolution and Genetics: The Modern Theory of Genetics*. New York: Holt, Rinehart and Winston, 1962.
The theory of evolution, with discussion of evidence ranging from geographical distribution to biochemical factors, is fully presented in a book that also outlines the modern theory of the mechanism of evolution and explains the operation of evolutionary forces.

Salthe, Stanley N. *Evolutionary Biology*. New York: Holt, Rinehart and Winston, 1972.
An erudite, challenging, often philosophical synthesis of evolutionary thought. The author's approach is universal, drawing from all fields of knowledge.

Savage, Jay M. *Evolution*. New York: Holt, Rinehart and Winston, 1969.
Using evolution as the central, unifying concept of biology, the author focuses on the changes in biological organization produced by the interaction of genetic variation and environmental selection. The entire treatment develops from a generalized statement of the Modern Synthetic Theory of Evolution and is based on current knowledge of genetics. Problems are interspersed throughout the body of the text, and bibliographies appear at the end of each chapter.

part 2

The evolution of man

portfolio one

The mute stones speak

Among the most fascinating monuments of early man's urge to build greatly are the megaliths of Europe. Begun as early as 4000 B.C. (long before the time of the pyramids in Egypt), they have a history of over 2000 years. Essentially, they comprise five types of structure whose remains are mostly stone, but which may have originally included wood: menhirs, huge, single standing stones; tombs, mainly composed of several standing stones with a large capstone surmounting; alignments of standing stones, sometimes in very long rows; circles of large stones, often connected at their tops by stone lintels; and apsidal temples, principally found in Malta.

Probably the best known megalithic monument is Stonehenge, which stands majestically and mysteriously on Salisbury Plain in Wiltshire, England. Celebrated in legend as early as the sixth century, Stonehenge was considered a marvel by Richard the Lion Hearted. Geoffrey of Monmouth, the twelfth century chronicler, told that "Giants of old did carry them from the furthest ends of Africa" and set them up in Ireland, from whence Merlin, King Arthur's magical aide, transported them to Britain, ". . . and laid down the stones so lightly as none would believe . . ." There was, he wrote, "not a stone that lacketh in virtue of witchcraft." And indeed, Stonehenge's presence has cast its spell on many. James I's architect Inigo Jones discerned the "rarity of its invention" and declared it "elegant in order." He believed it a work of Roman times; others insisted it was the work

Stonehenge, Wiltshire, England.

A trilithon at Stonehenge.

Passage grave, County Sligo, Eire.

Carronmore, megalithic tomb, County Sligo, Eire

Stone circle, Scotland.

Pentre Ifan dolmen, Wales.

Stone circle, Isle of Lewis, Hebrides, Scotland.

Callanish stone circle, Isle of Lewis, Hebrides, Scotland.

of Druids, those holy men of the Celts. Some argued that
Stonehenge was built in the time of Adam and Eve and ruined
in the flood; others, even as late as 1880, concluded that
it was the work of the people of Atlantis!

Recent archeology has unlocked much of the story of
Stonehenge, as it has of similar monuments, like the stone
circle of Callanish in Scotland's Hebrides. From radiocarbon
dating of organic material buried in the ditches and rings
of holes at Stonehenge, it is known that the work was begun
about 2500 B.C. and may have continued to 2000 B.C., roughly
the same time as the Minoan culture was flourishing in Crete
and about the same time as the construction of the great
pyramids. Geologists have revealed that the stones which
comprise the circle (80 or more weighing up to five tons each)
come partly from a site in Wales—some 240 miles by sea and
land from the Salisbury Plain—and partly from an area
about 20 miles north of Stonehenge. Simply gathering the
materials for the work must have been a herculean feat.
Inspired in part by folklore, other investigators have
speculated about the "why" of Stonehenge, asserting that it
may have been an astronomical observatory of some kind, in
addition to its clear function as a burial ground and
ceremonial meeting place. Just imagine, says astronomer
Gerald Hawkins, the impressive power demonstrated if the high
priest should call his people together in the stone circle
one night late in June and announce that he will call the
sun from below the earth to rise above *that* stone there—
and, behold, it rises on command. Hawkins, aided by a
computer, has determined a convincingly large number of
correlations between Stonehenge stone placements and sight
lines and the major events and movements of the sun and moon,
including especially eclipses, which apparently the
arrangement of stones could accurately predict. The degree
of sophistication we must ascribe to the builders of
Stonehenge thus increases dramatically.

But perhaps most importantly, Stonehenge, the dolmens
of Ireland and Wales, and the circles of Scotland, stand as
signs of early man's connection with the earth, with the
forces of nature which he urgently needed to comprehend and
which he profoundly embraced. That force of intimacy
communicates itself over the millenia.

Photographs by Paul Caponigro

The modern primates

Man has long had a close contact with other animals. Some animals, such as dogs, horses, and cows, have lived close to man for so long that little attention is paid to their behavior. We are interested only in how well they do what they were bred for—companionship, racing, milk-giving. Domestic animals are so dependent on man that they have lost many of the behavioral traits of their wild ancestors. Except to a small child, perhaps, and a dairy farmer, a cow is not a very interesting animal to watch.

Wild animals, in contrast, have always fascinated man, especially exotic ones. Circuses and zoos attest to this fascination. In cultures very different from ours, like those of some American Indians, a man can have a special relationship with an animal in that he may think of himself as descended from it; this animal represents his "totem."

A curious feature of man's interest in animals is his desire to see them as mirror images of himself. Stories in which animals talk, wear clothes, and exhibit human virtues and vices go back to antiquity. Many children learn of Reynard the Fox, Bruin the Bear, or Bre'r Rabbit; the animals created by Walt Disney and Walt Kelley have become an integral part of our culture. Occasionally one sees on television trained apes dressed like humans eating at a table, pushing a stroller, or riding a tricycle. They are amusing because they look so "human."

Over the ages, man has trained animals to perform tricks, making them mimic his own behavior. But never did he suspect the full extent of the relationship he has with them. The close biological tie between man and the other primates is now better understood. Certain primates are studied with an entirely new purpose—to see how they socialize, how they communicate, if they can learn, if they use tools. These have long been regarded as purely human traits, but now we know that some animals do have them. Their behavior may help us understand something of the origins of human culture—and the origin of man himself.

The classification system

In order to understand man's exact place among the animals, it will be helpful to describe briefly the system used by biologists to classify living things. The basic system was devised by the eighteenth century Swedish naturalist Karl von Linné. The purpose of the Linnaean system was simply to classify the great mass of confusing biological data that had accumulated up until that time. Von Linné—or Linnaeus—classified living things on the basis of overall similarities into small groups, or species. Modern classification has gone a step further by distinguishing superficial similarities between organisms—called analogies —from basic ones—called homologies. Groups of like species were organized into a larger, more inclusive group, called **genera** (the singular term is genus). The characteristics on which Linnaeus based his system were:

1) body structure: a Guernsey cow and a Holstein cow are of the same species because they have identical body structure. A cow and a horse do not.

2) body function: cows and horses bear their young in the same way. Although they are of different species, they are closer than cows and chickens, which lay eggs, and have no mammary glands.

3) sequence of bodily growth: both cows and chickens give birth to fully formed young. They are therefore more closely related to each other than either one is to the frog, whose tadpoles undergo a series of changes before attaining adult form.

By making distinctions such as these, Linnaeus went from specific animals through larger and larger groups until he arrived at the most all-inclusive group of all: animal kingdom. Following are the categories of the Linnaean system applied to the classification of man:

Kingdom	Animalia
Phylum	Chordata
Class	Mammalia
Group	—
Order	Primates
Family	Hominidae
Genus	Homo
Species	*Homo sapiens*

Each class can be expanded or narrowed by

adding the prefix "sub" or "super." A family could thus be part of a superfamily, and in turn contain two subfamilies. When a category—such as group—is blank, it means that there is no intermediate classification necessary at that level. The mammalian class divides directly into orders without the intermediate stage of groups.

Modern taxonomy is based not only on the comparison of bones but also of blood groups, parasites, embryology, and genetic material, such as chromosomes.

The order of primates

The primate order is divided into two suborders: the **prosimians,** or "lower primates" (tarsiers, lemurs, and tree shrews); and the **anthropoids,** or "higher primates." The anthropoid suborder in turn is broken down into three superfamilies: the Ceboidea, or New World monkeys; the Cercopithecoidea, or Old World monkeys; the Hominoidea, containing the families Hominidae, or modern and extinct forms of man and Pongidae. The members of the pongid family are called the "great apes" or "anthropoid apes."

Establishing evolutionary relationships

What is the evidence pointing to the relationships among the primates? Evidence can be drawn from comparative anatomy, biochemistry, and fossil remains.

Comparative anatomy. The primates as a whole show similar developmental tendencies. The skull of the primates, if compared to that of other mammals, appears elongated from top to bottom and foreshortened from front to back. The **cranium,** or brain case, is very large, forming in turn a high, vertical forehead. The skull joins the vertebral column underneath; it does not hang forward from it. The face is located below the

Figures 4-1, 2, and 3. *Prosimians represent the earliest primate ancestors. They are nocturnal animals dwelling in trees, who depend on insects for food.*

cranium rather than in front of it. The eyes are in a frontal position, and stereoscopic vision and depth perception are possible. The well-defined eye orbit is protected from behind by a bony partition. Primate vision is extremely sharp; the higher primates have color vision whereas the lower ones lack it. The snout typical of other mammals has become flattened, possibly resulting from the diminished sense of smell; instead, primates have a face.

The primate brain is large, heavy in proportion to total body weight, and very complex. Primates, in turn, are intelligent animals that lead a complex social life.

On either side of the primate jaw (except in that of prosimians) in front, are two straight-edged, chisel-like broad teeth called incisors. Behind the incisors is a canine, which in lower mammals is large, flaring, and fanglike and is used for defense and carrying food. Among the higher primates the canine, though still large, begins to conform more to the size of the incisors. In man, incisors and canines are practically indistinguishable. Behind the canines are the premolars. Last come the molars, with four or five cusps, used mostly for grinding food. This basic pattern of dentition contrasts sharply with that of nonprimate mammals. Old World monkeys, apes,

Figure 4-4. *The hands of primates are similar. Man's hands are distinguished by well-developed thumbs, the hands of brachiating primates by long fingers.*

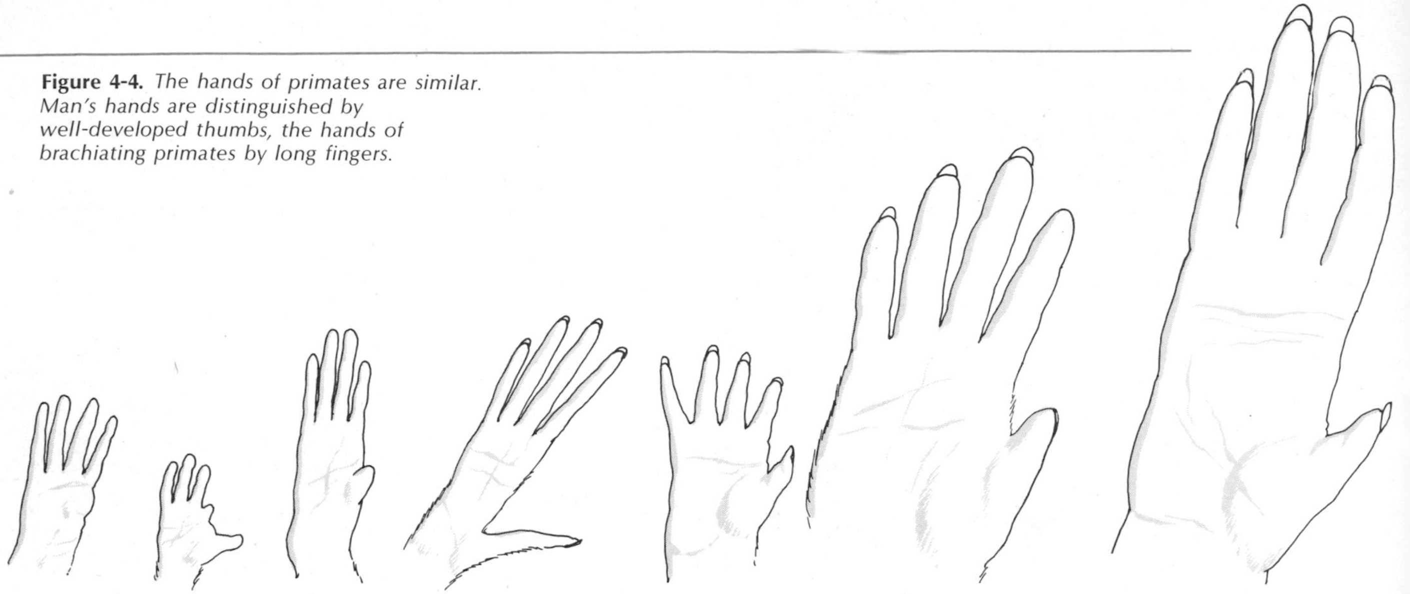

Spider monkey   Potto   Colobus   Gibbon   Baboon   Chimp   Orang

and man have two premolars and three molars. New World monkeys have three premolars and either two or three molars.

Higher primates have powerful and highly flexible limbs. In some species the forelimbs are longer and stronger than the hind limbs. The forelimbs articulate with the shoulder and can move with great freedom. This is associated with primates' ability to **brachiate**—use their arms to swing and hang among the trees. In all primates the limbs end in hands and feet of five digits, and the digits are prehensile (they are able to grasp). The thumb and the great toe are opposable to varying degrees, so food can easily be handled and branches grasped. The opposable great toe of the ape is often more opposable than the thumb and almost makes the foot resemble a hand. Modifications of the hind feet led to bipedalism and the upright or orthograde position. The digits of higher primates have flattened nails instead of claws. The lower primates have both claws and nails.

Biochemistry. There is a striking similarity in blood and protein chemistry among the higher primates, indicating close evolutionary relationship. On the basis of tests with blood proteins, it has been shown that the chimpanzee and gorilla are closest to man; next comes the orangutan; then the Old World monkeys; New World monkeys; and finally the prosimians. Investigation of the chromosomes of man and other primates has also provided further evidence of man's kinship to the apes.

Fossil remains. The work of the paleontologist is based on the comparison of fossil bones with those of living animals. Every bone carries with it the marks of its own history. Muscle attachments, for example, leave depressions and ridges; these, in turn, can be compared with those found in other fossils and on the bones of living animals. On the basis of such comparisons, a paleontologist can determine the function a bone had. It is often possible for a paleontologist to imagine what the living animal may have looked like from a study of a few fossil remains.

Most of the traits discussed in the foregoing paragraphs are present in the lower primates, and all are seen to a much greater degree in the higher

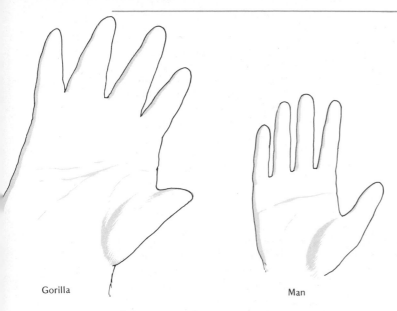

Gorilla   Man

primates. Man has perfected most traits to a degree not realized by any other species. Among the very lowest primates some traits are missing, while others are clearly present, so that the borderline between primate and nonprimate becomes blurred, and the difference is one of degree rather than kind.

Modern primates

The modern primates are mostly restricted to warm areas of the world. They are divided into two suborders, Prosimii and Anthropoidea. Prosimii are small mostly quadrupedal Old World animals; Anthropoidea include monkeys and apes. Primates are usually subdivided into seven families.

The lower primates

The prosimians, commonly called the lower primates, are thought to be the most primitive primates. They include the tree shrew, the tarsier, and the lemur. They range from Africa and Madagascar to southern and eastern Asia. They are small and resemble small rodents and insectivores in general body outline. They have long tails, and all have characteristically primate "hands" used in pairs, rather than one at a time. They move on all fours, with the forelimbs in a "palms-down" position and also cling from branches. Prosimians occupy a place between the higher primates and insectivores.

The tree shrew. The tree shrew is a small animal that lives among the upper branches of trees. Tree shrews were until very recently usually classed with the insectivores, an order of mammals that includes the moles and tree shrews. In general body outline the tree shrew is rodentlike, but in its relative brain size, flattened incisors, and "human" ears it resembles primates. The part of the brain governing vision is highly developed, whereas that governing smell is much less so. It has grasping "fingers" and "toes." In contrast to other primates, it has a rodentlike snout, and claws instead of nails. Tree shrews may represent a very early primate type.

The lemur. This arboreal, nocturnal creature may be as small as a mouse or as large as a cat. The short snout is pointed and doglike, the ears are large and pointed, the eyes big. The ring-tailed lemur looks like a raccoon. In brain structure, the lemur is clearly a primate. The prehensile digits have flattened nails, except for the second toe, which has a claw. In the anatomy of its upper lip and snout, the lemur resembles nonprimate mammals.

The tarsier. The head, eyes, and ears of this kitten-sized arboreal primate are huge in proportion to the body. The digits end in platelike, adhesive discs. The tarsier is named for the elongated tarsal or heel bone that provides leverage for it to jump six feet or more. Tarsiers are mainly insect eaters. In the structure of the nose and lips, and the part of the brain governing vision, tarsiers resemble monkeys.

The higher primates

The suborder Anthropoidea, or the higher primates, is divided into three superfamilies: the New World monkeys, the Old World monkeys, and man and the apes. The higher primates are on the whole bigger than the lower primates, and are strikingly manlike in appearance. Their facial expressions particularly bear human resemblance. The defining traits of the lower primates—large cranium, well-developed brain, acute vision, chisel-like incisors, prehensile digits—are even more apparent in the higher primates. The anthropoids generally move on all four limbs, but stand erect to reach fruit hanging in trees; some apes sometimes walk on two feet. Monkeys are highly arboreal, and New World species have prehensile tails that wrap around a tree branch, freeing the forelimbs to grasp food. Some New World monkeys brachiate; Old World monkeys almost never do.

All apes may once have been arboreal, but among modern apes, only the orangutan and the gibbon still are. The chimpanzee and the gorilla spend most of their time on the ground, but sleep in the trees and may also find food there. When on the ground, they move mostly on all fours.

New World monkeys

The New World monkeys live in forest and swamp areas of South America. They belong to the superfamily Ceboidea and are characterized by their flaring, widely separated nostrils, giving them the name of "platyrrhine" monkeys. Many are entirely arboreal, and some have long, prehensile tails by which they hang from trees. They walk on all fours with their palms down and scamper along tree branches in search of fruit, which they eat sitting upright. Spider monkeys and howlers are known to brachiate. Although they spend much of their time in the trees, they do not often swing from limb to limb by their arms and have not developed extremely long forelimbs. This distinguishes them from most of the other higher primates.

Old World monkeys

Old World monkeys belong to the superfamily Cercopithecoidea. Characterized by their closely spaced, downward pointing nostrils, they may be either arboreal or terrestrial. The arboreal species include the guereza monkey, the Asiatic langur, and the strange-looking proboscis monkey. Some are equally at home on the ground and in the trees, such as the macaques, of which there are some 50 species ranging from Gibraltar (the Barbary Ape) to Japan.

The baboon and the mandrill—terrestrial species also—live on the open African savanna. They have long, fierce faces and move on all fours in the palms-down position. Their diet consists of leaves, seeds, insects, and lizards, and they live in large, well organized troops. Because baboons have abandoned trees and live in an environment like the one in which man may have originated, they are of great interest to primatologists.

Anthropoid apes

The anthropoid apes are man's closest relatives. Their general appearance and way of life are determined by their semierect posture. In their body chemistry, the position of their internal organs, and even their diseases, they are remarkably close to man. Some are arboreal, but their great size and weight are obstacles to their swinging and jumping as freely as monkeys. The small, lithe gibbon can both climb and swing freely through the trees. Chimpanzees and gorillas climb trees, using their prehensile hands and feet to grip the trunk and branches. Their swinging is limited to leaning outward as they reach for fruit, clasping a limb for support.

Anthropoid apes, like man, have no external tail. But, unlike man, their arms are longer than their legs, indicating that their ancestors remained arboreal long after man's had become terrestrial. In moving on the ground, the apes "knuckle-walk" on the backs of their hands, resting their

The evolution of man • part **2**

weight on the middle joints of the fingers. They stand erect when reaching for fruit, looking over tall grass, or in any movement where they find the erect position more efficient. The semierect position is natural in apes because the narrow, tubular ape pelvis is unable to support the weight of the torso and limbs and because apes do not have the highly complex leg musculature that enables man to stand erect and swing his legs freely before and behind. Apes are "top heavy" because their center of gravity is placed high on their bodies.

The gibbon is found in southeast Asia and Malaya. It has a compact, slim body, disproportionately long arms and short legs and stands about three feet high. Although the gibbon's usual form of locomotion is brachiation, it can run erect, holding its arms out for balance. It resembles more a monkey in size and general appearance than it does the other apes.

The orangutan is found in Malaya, Borneo, and Sumatra. The orangutan is somewhat taller than the gibbon and much heavier, with the bulk characteristic of apes. In the closeness of the eyes and facial prominence, it looks a little like a chimpanzee, except that its hair is reddish. It has very small ears. The sparse hair, wrinkled face, and sad expression give it the look of an old man. The orang walks with its forelimbs in a fists-sideways, or a palms-down position. A shy and rather solitary animal, it is arboreal and rarely descends to the ground.

The gorilla, found in equatorial Africa, is the largest of the apes; an adult male can weigh over 400 pounds. The body is covered with a thick coat of glossy black hair, and mature males have a silvery gray upper back. There is a striking look of intelligence and dignity in the face, and like man, the gorilla focuses on things in its field of vision by directing the eyes rather than moving the head. It is mostly a ground dweller, but may sleep in trees in carefully constructed nests. Because of its weight, brachiation is limited to raising and lowering itself among the tree branches when searching for fruit. It "knuckle-walks," standing erect to reach for fruit, or to see

Figures 4-5 and 6. *Gibbons and orangutans are the southeast Asian members of the ape family. They are both brachiators who use their long arms and fingers to swing through trees.*

Figure 4-7. *Chimpanzees can both brachiate and operate on the ground. Though they find it difficult to walk slowly, they can run with ease.*

something more easily. Although gorillas are gentle and tolerant, bluffing is an important part of their behavioral repertoire.

The chimpanzee is widely distributed throughout Africa. It is probably the best known of the apes, and because it is a fast learner and a good mimic, has long been a favorite in zoos and circuses. Studies in genetics, biochemistry, and anatomy indicate it is man's closest relative. Chimpanzees forage on the ground all day, and build tree-nests at sunset.

The social behavior of primates

The physical resemblance of the higher primates to man is striking. But the most startling resemblance of all is in their social behavior. Because of their highly developed brains, higher primates behave in a manner far more complex than any other animal except man. Only recently have primatologists made prolonged close-range observations of the gorilla, chimpanzee, and baboon in their natural habitats, and we are discovering much about social organization, learning ability, and communication among our closest relatives in the animal kingdom.

The group

Primates are social animals. They live and travel in groups that vary in size from species to species. Dominant males lead, and are the central figures in the group.

Baboons live in the dry, African savanna in groups of up to 80 individuals. They have a rigid hierarchy, with the top-ranking female coming after the lowest-ranking male. Each individual knows his place, and the hierarchy is continually reinforced by such actions as grooming, or the forcible ejection of a low-ranking individual from a nest. When the baboon troop moves through open country, dominant males, mothers, and in-

The evolution of man ● part **2**

fants stay in the center of the formation, while other adults and adolescents lead, flank the sides, and take up the rear. Such formation affords protection to the more vulnerable members of the troop. The strict hierarchy of the baboon troop maintains order and thus assures safety and survival.

The gorilla group is led by a mature, silver-backed male, and consists of younger, black-backed males, females, young, and sometimes other silver-backs. As with chimpanzees and baboons, there are more females in the group than males. Group hierarchy is far harder to detect among gorillas, as it is among chimpanzees. Both these species tolerate considerable independence among individuals. The group's social structure is not nearly as rigid as that of baboons.

Gorillas and chimpanzees forage on the ground, and when the leader signals that it is time to move on, the group falls into a single file. In the absence of the dominant male, or in the case of subgroups that have formed for the day, a senior animal becomes the leader. Among gorillas, individuals join or leave the group for a day, several days, or even several months. Large groups may split up for the day and keep in touch by periodic calling to each other.

Gorilla groups are in the main quite stable, but chimpanzee groups are much more transitory. Lone chimpanzees have their own forest paths, come and go alone, and may join other chimpanzees occasionally, as when food is plentiful.

Individual interaction

One of the most notable primate activities is grooming, the ritual cleaning of another animal's coat to remove parasites, shreds of grass, or other matter. The grooming animal deftly parts the hair of the animal being groomed with two fingers, and with the thumb and forefinger of the other hand removes any foreign object, often eating it. Among gorillas, grooming is mainly hygienic; but among chimpanzees and baboons it is a gesture of friendliness, submission, appeasement, or

Figures 4-8 and 9. *Chimpanzees and gorillas are the African members of the ape family. Baron Hugo van Lawick took the top photo of chimps studied by Jane Goodall.*

closeness. Embracing, touching, and jumping up and down are forms of greeting behavior among chimpanzees. Touching is also a form of reassurance.

Gorillas, though gentle and tolerant, are also aloof and independent, and there is little individual interaction between them. Gestures of friendship between adults are rare, and usually quite restrained. Friendship or closeness between adults and infants is more evident. Among baboons, chimpanzees, and gorillas the mother-infant bond is the strongest and most long-lasting in the group. A new infant baboon is an object of tremendous interest to the group, and shortly after birth, mother and infant are surrounded by attention. The adults lip-smack, and touch the infant with their fingers or mouths. The whole group is solicitous about the mother, and tolerant of the infant's behavior for months. The new mother aligns herself with a dominant male, who protects her from animals which may threaten mother or infant. This grouping of adult male, adult female, and child may be a forerunner of the human family.

Among gorillas and chimpanzees, the mother-infant bond is especially strong and may last as long as four years. Gorilla infants and young juveniles share their mother's nests and have been seen sharing nests with mature, childless females. Zoologist George Schaller observed one such relationship as well as one in which a gorilla infant went "visiting" another infant its own age and the infant's mother daily for weeks.[1]

Sexual interaction between adults is fairly uniform among the three foregoing species of apes. Little interest is expressed in the female until she is in estrus—the time of sexual receptivity characterized by swelling and reddening of the genitals. During this time the female frequently presents, or backs up to the male in a crouching position. The male may ignore her or mount her and copulate. Among baboons, the dominant male will form an exclusive bond with a mature female in full estrus, but other females are permitted promiscuous behavior; relationships of brief duration are common.

Chimpanzees are apparently less possessive about females than are baboons, though this may have something to do with the ratio of available females to males. Primatologist Jane Van Lawick-Goodall observed an estrous female chimpanzee mounted by seven males in quick succession, none of whom sought exclusive possession. Chimpanzee courtship may be initiated either by the male or the female. In one instance, where both initiated simultaneously, the pair quickly copulated. In a second instance one partner acted indifferent, but eventually cooperated. In a third instance a female failed to arouse male interest. In a fourth instance, the male initiated courtship; the female ran away screaming, and the male, instead of pursuing, violently rocked the branches of a tree and departed.

Play

Play activity among primate infants and juveniles is probably a means of learning about the environment and testing strength (rank in the dominance hierarchy is probably based to a great degree on strength.) Chimpanzee infants mimic the food-getting activities of their mothers, "attack" dozing adults, and "harass" adolescents.

Schaller observed young gorillas do somersaults, wrestle, and play tug o' war, follow the leader, and king of the mountain. One juvenile, becoming annoyed at repeated harassment by an infant, picked it up, climbed a tree, and deposited it on a branch from which it was unable to get down. Its mother had to retrieve it.

Communication

Primates, like many animals, vocalize. They have a great range of calls that are often used together with movements of the face or body to convey a message. Observers have not yet established the meaning of all the sounds, but a good number

---

[1] George B. Schaller, "The Behavior of the Mountain Gorilla," in Irven DeVore (ed.), *Primate Behavior* (New York: Holt, Rinehart and Winston, 1965), p. 351.

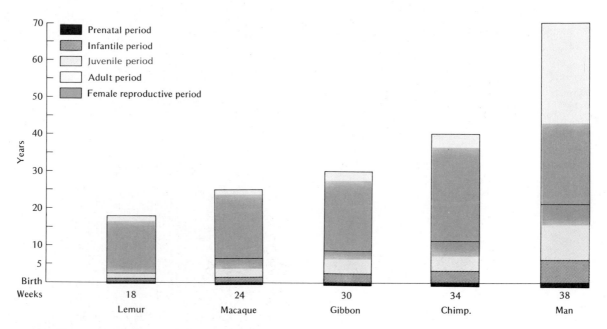

Figure 4-10. *Primates are born at earlier stages of development than other animals. Man is born at a very early stage. His larger brain size is responsible. At a later stage of development, the baby's head would be too large for the mother's pelvis.*

have been distinguished, such as warning calls, threat calls, defense calls, and gathering calls; the behavioral reactions of other animals hearing the call have also been studied. Some 20 distinct calls have been recorded for gorillas.

Primatologists K. R. L. Hall and Irven DeVore have classified numerous kinds of baboon vocalization and visual communication. The vocalizations include barking, grunting, roaring, screeching, and chattering. Most baboon sounds call attention to some gesture. Gestures of face and head include tooth-grinding, jerking of head down and forward, yawning, grinning, and lipsmacking; gestures of the body and limb include slapping the ground with hand, rearing on hind legs, shaking rocks or branches, and muzzle wiping with hand.

Tradition

Group knowledge is important for survival because it enables an animal to adapt to changing circumstances. It is important for animals to know where danger lies in order to avoid it. Primates show great adaptive ability; they learn fast as a result of their intelligent nature. In Nairobi Park, Kenya, for example, baboons are accustomed to visitors' cars; but in one recorded instance, they kept away from the vehicles for a period of eight months, following the shooting of two baboons by a person driving a car. As only a few baboons were near the shooting when it happened, one may surmise that knowledge of the incident was transmitted to other baboons by these few members of the group.

Home ranges

Primates usually move about within circumscribed areas or "home ranges." The boundaries of a range are usually carefully observed by members of a group. The ranges are of varying sizes, depending on the size of the group and on ecological factors such as availability of food. Ranges are often moved seasonally. The distance travelled by a group in a day varies; a baboon group may travel as much as twelve miles in a day. Some areas of a range are used more often than others; they are known as "core areas," and may contain water, food sources, resting places, and sleeping trees. The range of different groups may overlap, and often a tree-dwelling species will share a range with ground dwellers. In such cases, the two species are not really competing with one another for the same resources; they use the territory at different times and eat different foods.

Parental behavior

Because the primate baby is so helpless at birth, it requires the constant care and protection of its mother for a period of time. Unlike other animals, however, the primate baby must be ready at birth to go everywhere with its mother; its survival depends on the ability to remain close to her at all times. This it achieves by clinging to the mother's belly. Maternal behavior varies between species; baboon mothers, for example, remain close to the infant during the first month, not letting others approach the baby. Langurs may share some maternal responsibilities with other members of the group. Gorillas and chimpanzees are very humanlike in their care of their infants. The males of many species share in the parental responsibilities; at the least, they are attentive and protective. A study of Japanese macaques has shown that adult males may "adopt" yearlings, behaving toward their offspring with the solicitude of a mother. It is quite common for juvenile primates to assist in caring for younger children and infants; this is probably a training experience.

78

Figures 4-11, 12, 13, and 14. *Whereas a colt can stand within two hours of birth, a primate infant is helpless. Primate infants are dependent upon their mothers for food, transportation, and protection. Only in rare cases do primate mothers not care for their young. The young female baboons in the photo below seem to be learning child care from a mother with child.*

Learning

Observation of monkeys and apes has shown that their learning abilities are remarkably humanlike. Jane V. L. Goodall has seen an infant chimpanzee intently watch its mother build her sleeping nest, then build a play nest of its own.[2] She also observed a chimpanzee help itself up a steep incline by grabbing branches and pulling, as if using a bannister. Chimps are seen to hurl hard-shelled fruit against a tree trunk to break it open. One infant watched its mother copulate, and explored with its hands the genitals of the copulating pair. Experimental monkeys raised in captivity often have difficulty in copulating successfully, possibly as a result of limited learning experience in an artificial environment.

Along with learning, the ability to make and use tools is another trait chimpanzees possess in elementary form. Furthermore, they will often teach tool-making to young ones. They have been observed using stalks of grass, branches that they strip of leaves, and even sticks up to three feet long, to catch termites. They insert the stick into a termite nest, wait a few minutes, pull the stick out and eat the insects clinging to it. If the end of the stick becomes bent and unusable, the chimp breaks it off and discards it. Chimpanzees are equally deliberate in their nest-building. They test the vines and branches to make sure they are usable. If they are not, the animal moves to another site.

It is not yet known how much a chimpanzee infant must learn from first-hand observation, and how much has become part of accumulated group tradition. But much chimpanzee behavior strongly implies learning. Goodall observed an adolescent chimp climb tree A., where it caught the eye of a small monkey sitting opposite in tree B. While the monkey was thus distracted, a second adolescent chimpanzee climbed tree B., sprang on the monkey and broke its neck. Several chimpanzees then ate the monkey. Between each

[2] Jane Goodall, "Chimpanzees of the Gombe Stream Reserve," in *Primate Behavior*, Irven DeVore, ed. (New York, Holt, Rinehart and Winston, 1965) p. 448.

mouthful of meat they ate a mouthful of leaves. Chimps are normally fruit eaters, but often acquire a taste for meat.

In an experiment carried out by some Japanese primatologists, a group of Japanese macaques was fed wheat; within four hours, wheat eating had spread to the entire group of macaques living in the valley. Inventive behavior has also been observed among Japanese macaques. A group living on an island off the Japanese coast learned to clean sweet potatoes by dipping them in water by observing the female macaque who had first done it.

Aggression

Aggression is an essential element of primate social behavior, and holds the primate group together. By protecting a group's food supply, aggression insures its size and perpetuation. By providing a group with dominant leaders, aggression gives it its social structure.

Primate groups aggressively defend their home ranges and food supplies from intruders of their own species. At the same time, they usually behave in a neutral manner toward animals of other species. Aggression gives a primate group either exclusive use of an area, or dominance of the area's food supply.

Primate groups take aggressive action against predators entering their home range. Calls to alarm, prevalent among primates, normally lead to initial displays of strength and anger. Conflicts between primates and nonprimates may occur more often than is now supposed. Further studies are needed to determine how extensive such conflicts are.

Monkeys and apes fight more often with members of their own group than with members of other groups. Within a primate social group, aggressive behavior is rewarded with increased rank in the social hierarchy. A dominant male primate gets first choice of food and females, and frequent grooming by those of lower position. Should he become sick or injured, he loses his position. Those who can then dominate him will be quick to do so. A primate's position is learned as well as earned. Mothers defend their children in initial encounters, and the son of a dominant female will most likely grow up to be a dominant male.

☐

THE STUDY
OF PRIMATE BEHAVIOR

Animal behavior may be investigated in the laboratory, in artificial colonies, or under natural conditions. The kinds of knowledge gained from these different approaches supplement each other, and all are necessary if the complex roots of behavior are to be understood.

The study of the clinging reflex offers an example of this interrelationship of approaches. Harlow has shown that a baby monkey will cling to a piece of cloth; if the monkey is placed on a smooth surface it will attempt to stand, but if the cloth touches the monkey it will cling instead of trying to stand. The clinging reflex thus takes precedence over the righting reflex. This isolated fact has little meaning in the laboratory, but when free-ranging monkeys are observed the infants are seen to cling to their mothers when the group moves. In all the kinds of monkeys studied so far the clinging reflex is present at birth, and the infant monkey's survival depends on this ability to cling while its mother feeds, walks, and runs. The existence of the reflex and the infant's response to various textures can be investigated only in the laboratory, but the adaptive significance of the behavior can be appreciated only in the field. Mammals have adapted to meet the problem of the care of the newborn in many different ways: by the construction of nests, burrows, and lairs in which the young may stay; by rapid maturation so the young may keep up; by births taking place in protected locations. Most primates have adapted by the ability of the young to cling.

This behavior adaptation, reflex clinging, is essential for the survival of the species, and it must be observed to be appreciated. A newborn gibbon does not cling to a calm and sitting mother, but to one which feeds at the ends of branches that are swaying in the wind. Far above the ground, the mother may suddenly run along a branch, drop below it, taking a few violent swings, and then plunge out into the air, dropping many feet to a lower branch in a neighboring tree, landing on swaying branches or with more swings. The infant clings through these violent acrobatics, and in the flight of gibbons through giant trees the infant-mother problem is shown to be very different from the way it appears in a small cage. The strength of the clinging is essential to survival, for the mother cannot be inactive and live. The mother's hands and feet are completely involved in locomotion, and in her swings and leaps she cannot help the infant and survive herself.

The natural situation may be further complicated because the mother may be helped by other members of the group. For example, a mother baboon was seen with a newborn infant, probably only a few hours old. The infant still could not cling adequately, and its mother repeatedly helped it with one hand. The three-legged walking was difficult for the mother and she lagged behind the main body of the group of baboons and sat down every few yards. Right beside her walked an adult male. When she sat, he sat; when she started up, he started up. His actions were timed to hers, and she was never left without protection during this awkward period.

Mothers with young are centers of interest for other females, adult males, and juvenile females. The infant monkey is born into an intensely social group, and the survival of the infant depends on the adaptation and survival of the

whole group. The size and composition of this group depend on the species of primate. Its patterned behavior differs depending on the structure, physiology, and ecology of the particular species and group, but in all the monkeys and apes adaptation is by group life, and survival is only possible for a member of a group. In nature the observer sees evidence of this vital sociability in the functioning of the group, and in the laboratory Butler has shown that monkeys will work hard when the only reward is the sight of another monkey.

The behavior of the mother and of the infant monkey, and the associated behavior of the other monkeys in the group, make possible the survival of the species. Reproduction depends on breeding seasons, mating patterns, developmental physiology, and on the social structures of the group. The young are conceived, carried and born, and reared only through the coordination of a wide range of structural, physiological, and behavioral mechanisms. Behavior is an essential part of the adaptive mechanisms as seen in field studies, but much of the important adaptive behavior does not appear under normal laboratory conditions. Field studies are particularly important in discovering the actual way the adaptive behavior functions.

The social group itself is an adaptation of supreme importance. For instance, the members of a group do not necessarily learn fearful response to a particular situation from their individual experiences. Among baboons, when dominant animals give a warning cry and run, the others flee without looking for the source of the danger. The social group occupies a range, shares knowledge of local foods, paths, and dangers, and offers opportunity for play, grooming, and close association. In the group the young and females are protected, and dominance gives an order to society. For monkeys the reproductive success that is necessary for evolutionary success occurs only within the group. Field studies are particularly important to these findings because it is only under natural conditions that the functioning group may be observed.

Under natural conditions an individual animal often cannot respond promptly to motivational pressures, even when basic physiological needs are involved. For example, a thirsty baboon cannot safely leave the group and go away seeking water. When baboons are living in country where water is restricted, the whole group moves to water, and the individual can satisfy its needs only as the whole pattern of the group's activity makes this possible.

Neither individual monkeys nor the social group can wait until confronted by needs and situations (danger, thirst, hunger, sex) to respond to them; the social system must be *adapted to anticipate* both daily needs and occasional crises. A system that could meet only day-to-day problems would not survive for long, and evolution, through natural selection, builds a substantial margin of safety into the individual animals and into their way of life. The group moves more, is more exploratory, is more playful than there is any need for on the average day, but by so doing it is preparing for crises. The individual animals appear stronger and more intelligent than is necessary for normal activity, but survival requires coping with the rare event.

In field studies the primary data are the observations of the behavior of the animals. Daily activities are recorded, and, with time and luck, encounters with carnivores, diseased animals, injuries, fights, and other crises are observed. The size of a range or the number of individuals in a group may be objectively recorded, but the comparison and interpretation of the data necessarily involve subjective evaluations. Is the number of individuals in a group determined by species-specific biology, ecological factors, social factors, or by a combination of all of these? When data on the behavior of nonhuman primates are presented, the question arises whether the behavior is instinctive or learned. Behavior may, of course, be recorded without regard to this question, but it cannot be interpreted without consideration of this issue. Recent experimental work has shown that learning is far more important in the development of social behavior than anyone had imagined; monkeys reared in isolation even fail to mate normally, an activity that many thought to be purely instinctive. Actually the relative roles of inherited and environmental factors may be very different

Figure 4-15. *Psychologist Harry Harlow conducted a number of experiments to check primate response to mother surrogates. This macaque infant clung to a warm, soft terry-cloth surrogate in time of danger.*

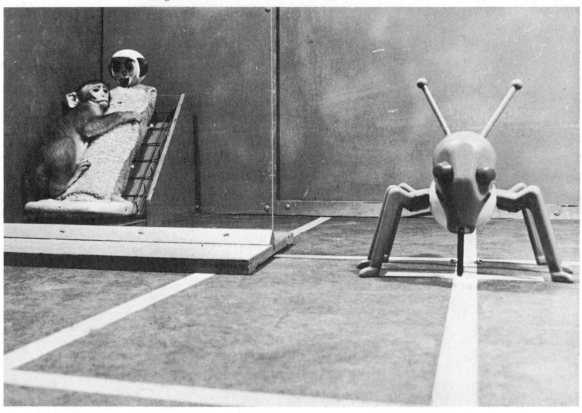

for different items of behavior. Infant clinging may be an almost purely inbuilt reflex, and adequate sexual performance may require only a minimum of childhood play, whereas food habits may be largely learned. There is much room for further experimentation and field work.

In summary, from an evolutionary point of view selection is for successful behavior. Structure, physiology, social life, all these are the result of selection, and the structure-physiology-behavior of populations of primates are adapted to each other and to a way of life. Parts of this complex are almost entirely the result of heredity with a minimum dependence on environment, whereas others are heavily influenced by learning. It is advantageous for behavior to be adaptable, to adjust to a wide variety of circumstances. What is inherited is ease of learning, rather than fixed instinctive patterns. The species easily, almost inevitably, learns the essential behaviors for its survival. So, although it is true that monkeys learn to be social, they are so constructed that under normal circumstances this learning always takes place. Similarly, human beings learn to talk, but they inherit structures that make this inevitable, except under the most peculiar circumstances.

Source:
From "The Study of Primate Behavior" by Sherwood L. Washburn and David A. Hamburg, in *Primate Behavior: Field Studies of Monkeys and Apes* edited by Irven DeVore. Copyright © 1965 by Holt, Rinehart and Winston, Inc. Reprinted by permission of Holt, Rinehart and Winston, Inc.

Summary

1.
Taxonomy is the science that studies the classification of living beings. It was founded by the Swedish naturalist Karl Von Linné—or Linnaeus. Taxonomy is based on similarities of body structure, body function, and sequence of bodily growth.

2.
The primate order embraces tree shrews, lemurs, tarsiers, monkeys, apes, and man. The first members of the order appeared about 60 million years ago during the Paleocene Epoch in the form of small squirrel-like tree shrews. Living in trees in dense tropical forests, man's first ancestors developed a number of traits which helped them adapt to their tree-dwelling way of life. Chief among these are stereoscopic vision, grasping hands, and a complex brain.

3.
The primates are characterized by having a generalized dentition, a heightening of the senses of sight and touch, a reduction in the sense of smell, increased cranial capacity, and fewer number of offspring born at a time with prolonged postnatal development.

4.
The higher primates belong to the suborder Anthropoidea. They are divided into three super-families: the New World monkeys, the Old World monkeys, and man and the apes. The New World monkeys belong to the superfamily Ceboidea (or "platyrrhine" monkeys). The Old World monkeys belong to the superfamily Cercopithecoidea (or "catarrhine" monkeys).

5.
The anthropoid apes are man's closest relatives. They are the gibbon, the orangutan, the chimpanzee, and the gorilla. Of all these, the chimpanzee is evolutionarily closest to man.

6.
The social behavior of primates is very complex. Primates are social animals, and most species live and travel in groups. Dominant males lead. Primates have elaborate systems of communication based on vocalizations and gestures. The learning ability of primates is greatly developed, and inventive behavior has been observed in several species, such as tool-making by chimpanzees.

Suggested readings

Clark, W. E. LeGros *History of the Primates,* Chicago: University of Chicago Press, 1966. This is a classic introduction to the study of fossil man by a distinguished English scholar. Man is viewed in relation to other primates and a heavy emphasis is given to the evolutionary scheme.

Jolly, Alison *The Evolution of Primate Behavior.* New York: Macmillan, 1972. In this book, Jolly attempts a survey of current knowledge about primate behavior and its relevance to human behavior. Part 1, entitled "Ecology," deals with habit and locomotion, food, predation, interspecific relations, reasons for sociability and group range, size, and structure. "Society," Part 2, discusses learning and instinct, communication, status, affiliation and sex, mothers and infants, growing up in a troop, and violence and warfare. The volume concludes with "Intelligence," with sections on primate psychology, manipulation and tools, cognition, language, social learning, and the evolution of intelligence. The bibliography is also very useful.

Lawick-Goodall, Jane van *In the Shadow of Man.* New York: Dell Publishing Co., 1971. Jane Van Lawick-Goodall's account of her 10 years of study of wild chimpanzees in Tanzania is written in a readable, informative style. The family life, sex, infant, and child-mother relations of chimps are discussed thoroughly. The correspondence of primate behavior to human life is stressed.

Romer, Alfred S. *Vertebrate Paleontology.* Chicago: University of Chicago Press, 1966. The most general appeal of vertebrate paleontology lies in the evolutionary story it presents. The material in this volume is arranged as a group-by-group treatment of the vertebrates, tracing out the various ramifications of the family tree. Knowledge of extinct vertebrates, including man and other primates, is based on preserved skeletal remains, and this study has been continually revised since its publication in 1933.

Schaller, George B. *The Year of the Gorilla.* New York: Ballantine, 1971. Schaller, who has written a scientific monograph on *The Mountain Gorilla,* describes here in popular form some of the results of his work in Africa. This is a personal book about gorillas and the way they behave. The author's simple line drawings and clear prose make this book a fine introduction to primate behavior.

Fossil primates

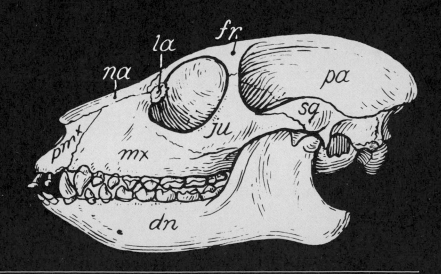

A little more than a century ago, Charles Darwin shattered the surface calm of the Victorian world with his startling theory that man is a cousin of the living apes and monkeys and is descended from their prehistoric ancestors. What would have been the public reaction, one wonders, if they had known, as we do, that one of man's earliest ancestors is thought to be a small squirrel-like tree shrew that possessed a long nose and claws and subsisted chiefly on insects?

These primitive tree shrews, like tarsiers, lemurs, monkeys, apes, and man, belong to the primate order. The fossil predecessors of modern primates date back about 60 million years. These primitive forebears of man evolved over time into different species by mutation, variation, and natural selection.

Although many of the primates discussed in this chapter no longer exist, their descendants are to be found living throughout the world. The successful adaptation of the primate line is believed to be due largely to their intelligence, a characteristic that reaches its culmination in man. Other physical traits, such as stereoscopic vision and a grasping hand, have also been instrumental in advancing the primate line.

What is the justification for studying a form of life whose history is, at best, fragmentary, and which existed millions of years ago? The study of these prehuman primates tells us something we can use to interpret the evolution of the entire primate line, including man himself. It gives us a better understanding of the physical forces that caused these primitive creatures to evolve into today's primates. Ultimately, the study of these ancient ancestors gives us a fuller knowledge of the processes through which an insect-eating, small-brained animal evolved into a toolmaker and thinker that is recognizably man.

Primate characteristics

Based on a study of both ancient and modern primates, a list of primate characteristics has been worked out.

Primate dentition

The fossil record is extremely rich in specimens of teeth and jawbones, because these structures are durable and are often the only remains of an animal to be found. Thus a whole branch of fossil study based on tooth structures, or dentition, has arisen. Dentition is most important in helping identify and classify different fossil forms; often investigators are able to infer a good deal about the total animal on the basis of only a few teeth found lying in the earth.

Primates retained less specialized teeth than other mammals, because they were arboreal, omnivorous animals. According to primatologist W. E. LeGros Clark:

> An arboreal life obviates the necessity for developing highly specialized grinding teeth, since the diet available to most tree-living mammals in the tropics, consisting of leaves, shoots, soft fruits and insects, can be adequately masticated by molar teeth of relatively simple structure.[1]

On the evidence of comparative anatomy and the fossil record, LeGros Clark has postulated the existence of an archetypal primate ancestor that possessed three incisors, one canine, four premolars, and three molars on each side of the jaw, top and bottom, for a total of 44 teeth. The incisors were used for gripping, canines for tearing and shredding, and molars and premolars for grinding and chewing food.

In the early stages of primate evolution, one incisor on each side of the upper and lower jaws was lost. This change differentiates the primates, who have two incisors, from other mammals. Moreover, the canines of most primates grew longer, forming daggerlike teeth that enabled them to rip open tough husks of fruit and other foods. In a combat situation, baboons, apes, and other primates flash these formidable looking teeth at their enemy, hoping to scare him off. Only in rare occasions, when this bluffing action fails, are teeth used to inflict bodily harm.

Other evolutionary changes in primate dentition involve the premolar and molar teeth. Over the millenniums, the first and second premolars

---

[1] W. E. LeGros Clark, *History of the Primates,* 5th ed. (Chicago: The University of Chicago Press, 1966) p. 271.

became smaller and eventually disappeared altogether, while the third and fourth premolars grew larger and more efficient by adding a second pointed projection, or cusp, thus becoming "bicuspid." The molars, meanwhile, evolved from a three-cusp pattern to the more efficient four-cusp, and even five. This kind of molar economically combined in one tooth the functions of grasping, cutting, and grinding.

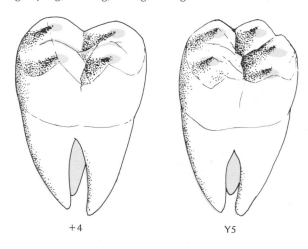

+4   Y5

Figure 5-1. *The Y5 tooth shows the Dryopithecus pattern of grooves. This pattern is found, sometimes in modified form, in gibbons, great apes, and men. The "Y" pattern leaves 3 cusps on the cheek side of the tooth, 2 on the tongue side. The +4 tooth is a modified form of the Dryopithec pattern.*

The evolutionary trend for primate dentition has generally been toward economy, with fewer, smaller, more efficient teeth doing more work. Thus man's 32 teeth are more generalized and fewer in number than those of most primates. Reduction in the number of teeth and a corresponding reduction in jaw size may have allowed for increased brain size in man.

The dentition differences between hominids and pongids are used as the basis for classification of fossil finds. Knowledge of the way the teeth fit together also indicates much about the operation of the jaws, suggesting the type of muscles needed. This in turn indicates how the skull must have been shaped to provide accommodation for the musculature. The shape of the jaws and the efficiency of the teeth also define the type of food that they were suited to deal with, indicating the probable diet of the specimen. Thus a mere jawbone can tell physical anthropologists a great deal about the animal from which it came.

Primate sense organs

The primates' adaptation to life in the trees coincided with changes in the form and function of their sensory apparatus: the senses of sight and touch became highly developed, and the sense of smell declined. When primates became arboreal, they no longer needed to live a "nose-to-the-ground" existence, sniffing close to the ground in search of food. The anthropoids have the least developed sense of smell of all land animals.

Travelling through the trees, as primates do, demands the ability to judge depth, direction, distance and the relationships of objects hanging in space, such as vines or branches. In higher primates, this ability is provided by their stereoscopic vision. Stereoscopic vision is the ability to see the world in three dimensions—height, width, and depth. It requires two eyes set apart from one another on the same plane. Each eye thus views an object from a slightly different angle, and the object assumes a three-dimensional appearance, indicating spatial relationships. Stereoscopic vision is one of the most important factors in primate evolution, for it is believed to have led to increased brain size in the visual area and a great complexity at nerve connections.

Visual acuity, however, varies throughout the primate order. Lemurs, for example, are the most visually primitive of the primates. Lacking stereoscopic vision, their eyes look out from either side of their muzzle or snout, much like a cow or a rabbit. All other primates possess stereoscopic vision. They also have a unique structure called

the *fovea centralis,* or central pit (popularly referred to as "the yellow spot"), in the retina of each eye. Like a camera lens, this remarkable feature enables the animal to focus on a particular object for acutely clear perception, without sacrificing visual contact with the object's surroundings.

Primate sense of touch also became highly developed as a result of the arboreal way of life. Primates found useful an effective feeling and grasping mechanism to prevent them from falling and tumbling while speeding through the trees. The primitive mammals from which primates descended possessed tiny tactile hairs that gave them extremely sensitive tactile capacities. In primates, these hairs were replaced by the more informative pads on the tips of the animals' fingers and toes.

The primate brain

By far the most outstanding characteristic of primate evolution has been the constantly increasing growth of the brain among members of the order. The cerebral hemispheres, the areas of conscious thought, have grown dramatically and, in all higher anthropoids, completely cover the cerebellum, which is the part of the brain that coordinates the muscles and maintains body equilibrium.

The reasons for this important change in brain size are many, but chief among them is probably the primates' arboreal existence. Paleontologist Alfred S. Romer states:

Locomotion in the trees requires great agility and muscular coordination, which in itself demands development of the brain centers; and it is of interest that much of the higher mental faculties are apparently developed in an area alongside the motor centers of the brain.[2]

An interesting hypothesis that may account for primate brain development involves the use of

[2] Alfred S. Romer, *Vertebrate Paleontology* (Chicago: The University of Chicago Press, 1945) p. 103.

the hand as a tactile organ to replace the teeth and jaws or snout. The hands assumed the grasping, tearing, and dividing functions of the snout, and the teeth and jaws grew smaller, enabling the skull and brain to expand. Certain areas of the brain became more elaborate and intricate. One of these areas is the cortex, generally considered to be the center of an animal's intelligence; it receives impressions from the animal's various sensory receptors, analyzes them, and sends responses back down the motor nerves to the proper receptor.

An animal living in the trees is constantly acting on and reacting to the environment. Messages from the hands and feet, eyes and ears, as well as from the sensors of balance, movement, heat, touch, and pain, are relayed to the cortex, individually and simultaneously. The cortex, then, must be developed to a considerable degree of complexity to receive and coordinate these impressions and to transmit the appropriate responses back. It is assumed that such development must have occurred in early primates.

The enlarged cortex not only provided the primates with a greater degree of efficiency in the daily struggle for survival, but it also gave the group a future means for the more sophisticated function of cerebration or thought. The ability to think probably played a decisive role in the primate evolution that led to the emergence of man.

The primate skeleton

The skeleton gives an animal its basic shape or silhouette, supports the soft tissues, and helps protect the vital internal organs. In primates, for example, the skull protects the brain and the eyes. A number of factors are responsible for the shape of the primate skull: changes in dentition, changes in the sensory organs of sight and smell, and increased brain size. The primate braincase (the part of the skull that contains the brain) tends to be high and vaulted. A solid partition exists in most primate species between the eye and the temple to afford maximum protection to

Figure 5-2. *As the face evolved from that of the fish, through the early mammals, all the way up to man, the progression has been toward a flatter face, more forward positioning of the eyes for better depth perception, and more overall versatility.*

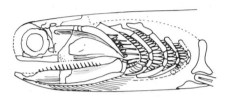

Acanthodes

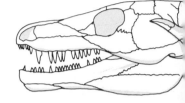

Seymouria

the eyes in their vulnerable forward position.

The foramen magnum (opening of the skull) through which the spinal cord passes and connects to the brain, is an important clue to evolutionary relationships. In primates, the evolutionary trend is for this aperture to shift forward, toward the center of the skull's base, so that it faces downward, as in man, rather than directly backward, as in dogs, horses, and other mammals. This forward shift enables the backbone to articulate at the center of the base of the skull, thereby placing the skull in a more posterior position and imparting to the animal an upright posture. The foramen magnum is an important clue in determining how far up the evolutionary ladder the specimen stands.

In most primates, the snout or muzzle portion of the skull has grown smaller as the acuity of the olfactory sense declined. The smaller snout offers less interference with stereoscopic vision; it also enables the eyes to be placed in a more frontal position. As a result, primates have more of a "true" or manlike face than other mammals. Below the primate skull and neck is the clavicle or collarbone, a holdover from primitive mammal ancestors. The clavicle serves as a strut that allows greater maneuverability of the arms, permitting

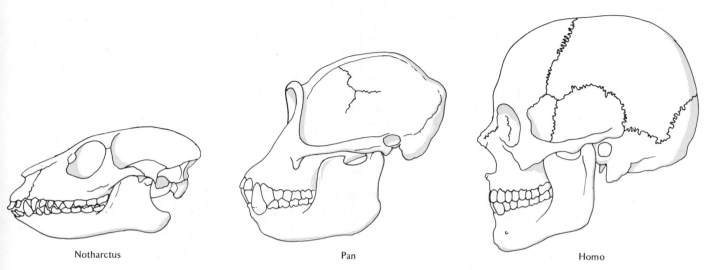

Notharctus Pan Homo

them to swing sideways and outwards from the trunk of the body. The clavicle also supports the scapula and allows for the muscle development that maintains an upright posture and erect head or shoulder blade.

Primates have also retained the characteristics, found in early mammals, of pentadactyly. Pentadactyly, which means possessing five digits, is found in many nonarboreal animals, but it proved to be of special advantage to tree-dwelling primates. Their grasping feet and hands have sensitive pads at the tips of their digits, protected by flattened nails. This unique combination of pad and nail provides the animal with an excellent grasping device for use when moving from tree to tree. The structural characteristics of the primate foot and hand make grasping possible; the digits are extremely flexible, and the thumb and big toe members are fully opposable to the other digits in most species.

Hindsight indicates that the flexible, unspecialized primate hand was to prove a valuable asset for the future evolution of this group. It was, in part, the generalized grasping hand which enabled the hominids to manufacture and utilize tools and thus speed his evolutionary advance to modern man.

Reproduction and care of young

The breeding of most mammals occurs once or twice a year, but most species of primates seem to breed continuously throughout the year. Generally, the male is ready to engage in sexual activity at any time, whereas the female's receptivity is cyclical, corresponding to her periods of estrous. This almost continuous sexual receptivity seems to have the effect of keeping the mates together, often leading to the formation of more or less stable groups, usually composed of more females than males.

One of the most noticeable adaptations to arboreal life among primates is a trend toward reduction in the size of the family, with fewer offspring born at one time to a female. The most primitive primate, the tree shrew, produces three or four young at each birth. Lemurs and marmosets, have two or three offspring. Other monkeys, apes, and man usually produce only a single offspring at a time. Natural selection may have favored single births among primate tree-dwellers because the primate infant has a highly developed grasping ability (the grasping reflex can also be seen in human infants), and more than one clinging infant would seriously encumber the mother as she moved about the trees. Moreover, a female pregnant with a large litter would be unable to lead a very active life as a tree-dweller.

Because primates bear fewer young at a time, they must take better care of them if the species is to survive. Better care usually means a longer period during which the infant is dependent upon the mother. As a general rule, the more advanced the species is, the smaller, more helpless, and immature the newborn offspring tend to be. For example, a lemur is dependent upon the mother for only a few months after birth; an ape, for two to three years; and man, for over a decade. Longer infancy is typically associated with an increase in longevity. If the breeding life of primates had not extended, the lengthened infancy could have led to a decrease in numbers of individuals.

The young of higher primate species are born with relatively underdeveloped nervous systems; moreover, they are lacking in the social knowledge that guides behavior. Thus they depend upon adults not only for protection but also for instruction, as they must learn how to survive. The longer period of dependence in higher primates makes possible a longer period of learning, which appears to be a distinct evolutionary advantage.

Dating the fossil past

Our knowledge of the evolution of primates is based largely on indirect evidence, which comes from the study of evolution through comparative anatomy, genetic comparisons, and biochemical studies. Additional evidence is provided by the science of paleontology, in which fossil remains are analyzed and the relationships of ancient and modern primates can be inferred.

The nature of fossils

Broadly defined, a fossil is any trace or impression of an organism of past geologic time that has been preserved in the earth's crust. Fossilization typically involves the hard parts of an organism; bones, teeth, shells, horns, and the woody tissues of plants are the most successfully fossilized materials. Only very rarely are soft parts of an organism fossilized.

An organism or part of an organism may be preserved in a number of ways. The whole animal may be frozen in ice, like the famous mammoths found in Siberia, safe from the actions of predators, weathering, and bacteria. It may be mummified or preserved in tarpits, peat, oil, or asphalt bogs, in which the chemical environment prevents the growth of decay-producing bacteria. It may be preserved in the bottom of lakes and sea basins, where the accumulation of chemicals renders the environment antiseptic. The entire organism may also be enclosed in a fossil resin such as amber. Specimens of spiders and insects dating back millions of years have been preserved in the Baltic area, which is rich in resin-producing conifers.

However, those cases in which an entire animal is preserved intact are rare and comprise possibly less than 1 percent of all fossil finds. The majority of fossils, generally consisting of scattered teeth and fragments of bones, are found embedded in the earth's crust as part of rock deposits. Thousands, perhaps millions of years ago, the organisms died and were deposited in the earth; they may then have been covered by sediments and silt, or sand. These materials gradually hardened and petrified, forming a protective shell around the skeleton of the organism. The internal cavities of bones or teeth and other parts of the skeleton are generally filled in with mineral deposits from the sediment immediately surrounding the specimen. Then the external walls of the bone decay and are replaced by calcium carbonate or silica.

Fossilization is most apt to occur among marine animals and other organisms that live near water, because their corpses accumulate on shallow sea or river bottoms, away from the wave and tidal action. These concentrations of shells and other organisms are covered and completely enclosed by the soft marine sediments that eventually harden into shale and limestone.

Terrestrial animals, however, are not so successfully fossilized. The bones of a land-dweller, having been picked clean and often broken by predators and scavengers, are then scattered, becoming subject to the deteriorating influence of the elements. The fossil record for many primates, for example, is poor because the acid soil of the tropical forests in which they lived decomposes the skeleton rather quickly. The records are much more complete in the case of primates that lived on the grassy plains, or savannas; here conditions are much more favorable to the formation of fossils.

Interpreting fossils. The paleontologist, or fossil hunter, is generally skilled in the techniques of geology, because a fossil is useless unless its temporal place in the sequence or strata of rocks that contain it can be determined. In addition, the paleontologist must be able to identify the fossil-laden rocks, their deposition, and other geological details.

A great deal of skill and caution is required to remove fossils from their burial place without damage. An unusual combination of tools and materials is usually contained in the kit of the paleontologist—pickaxes, enamel coating, burlap for bandages, plaster of Paris.

To remove a newly discovered skeleton, the paleontologist begins uncovering the specimen, using pick and shovel for initial excavation, then small camel hair brushes and dental picks to remove loose and easily detachable debris surrounding the skeleton. Once he has uncovered the entire skeleton (a process that may take days of backbreaking, patient labor), he covers with shellac and tissue paper any cracks that may appear on the bone to prevent damage during further excavation and handling.

Both the fossil and the earth immediately surrounding it, or the matrix, are prepared for removal as a single block. The skeleton and matrix are cut out of the earth (but not removed) and more shellac is applied to the entire block to harden it. The skeleton is covered with burlap bandages dipped in plaster of Paris. Then the entire block is enclosed in plaster and burlap bandages, perhaps splinted with tree branches, and allowed to dry overnight. After it has hardened, the entire block is carefully removed from the earth, ready for packing and transport to a museum. Before leaving the discovery area, the investigator makes a thorough sketch map of the terrain and pinpoints the find on geological maps to aid future investigators.

At the museum, the specimen is carefully uncrated. The block is cut open, and the fossil is separated from the matrix. Like the initial removal from the earth, this is a long, painstaking job involving a great deal of skill and special tools. This task may be done with hammer and chisel, dental drills, rotary grinders or pneumatic chisels, and, in the case of very small pieces, with awls and tiny needles under a microscope.

Chemical means, such as hydrochloric and hydrofluoric acid, are also used in the separation process. Some fossils require processing by other methods. For example, precise identification can be obtained by examining thin, almost transparent strips of some fossils under a microscope. Casts of the insides of skulls are made by filling the skull wall with an acid-resistant material, then removing the wall with acid. A skull may be cleaned out and the inside painted with latex. After the latex hardens, it is removed in a single piece, revealing indirect evidence of brain shape and nerve patterns. Such a cast of the internal skull is helpful in determining the size and complexity of the specimen's brain, permitting guesses about the degree of intelligence.

Rise of the primates

The early primates emerged during a tumultuous period of the earth's history, when the earth was changing radically. The surface crust was buckling and heaving, pushing huge chunks of sediment from deep in the ocean floors. New land masses were forming, and old land surfaces were being eroded and undergoing changes in vegetational covering. It was during this period that the great mountain chains—the Rockies, Andes, Alps, and Himalayas—were formed. Their formation affected the distribution of forests, grasslands and deserts.

Retreating seas revealed new land masses that became swamps. A new, mild climate favored the spread of dense, lush tropical and subtropical forests over much of the earth, including North and South America, Southeast Asia, the Middle East, and most of Africa. An enormous expansion of grasses, ivies, shrubs, and other flowering plants occurred.

With the spread of these huge belts of forest, the stage was set for the evolutionary advance from the rodentlike ground existence to the arboreal primate condition. Forests would provide our early ancestors with ecological niches, or functional positions in their habitats.

The move to an arboreal existence brought a combination of the problems of earthbound existence with those of flight. In their exploitation of space, birds have developed highly stereotyped behavior; tree-dwelling primates, on the other hand, exhibit flexible behavior in response to decision-making. The initial forays into the trees must have produced many misjudgments and errors of coordination, leading to falls that injured or killed the individuals badly adapted to arboreal life. Natural selection favored those that judged depth correctly and gripped the branches strongly. It is quite likely that the early primates that took to the trees were in some measure preadapted, with better vision and more finger-like extremities than their contemporaries.

The relatively small size of the early primates allowed them to exploit the smaller branches of trees; larger, heavier competitors, and possible predators, could not follow. The move to the smaller branches also opened up a more abundant food supply; the primates were able to gather leaves, flowers, fruits, and insects, rather than waiting for them to fall to the ground.

The exploitation of a new environment led to an acceleration in the rate of change of primate characteristics. The cumulative effect of these changes eventually led to a return to the ground, probably providing the conditions that are correlated with the appearance of the genus *Homo*.

Paleocene primates

Far back in the dawn of geologic time, a small, squirrel-like animal resembling today's tree

Figure 5-3. *Fossil primates evolved into the great apes. Faces became flatter; crania became larger to accommodate larger brains; and teeth became more generalized. Plesiadapis was an ancient rodentlike tree shrew; Smilodectes had a shorter snout, larger front portion of the brain, and more advantageously positioned eyes than Plesiadapis. Aegyptopithecus was an Oligocene ape, thought near the base of the hominoid radiation. Pliopithecus was a gibbonlike primate of the Miocene period. While its teeth, narrow snout region, and wide-set eyes are like a gibbon's, other features are like a monkey's. Proconsul was a Miocene ape of the Dryopithecus genus.*

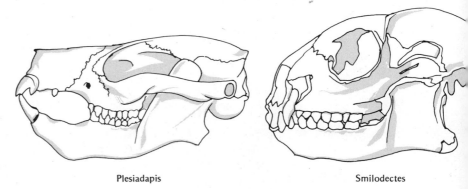

Plesiadapis   Smilodectes

The evolution of man ● part **2**

shrews scampered along the branches of trees in tropical forests. Strange as it may seem, this animal was man's first known ancestor. *Plesiadapis,* as it is called, first appeared during the Paleocene Epoch of the Tertiary Period, about 70 million years ago. It lived mostly on seeds and insects; its muzzle was long and pointed, its ears were small, its digits were flexible and suitable for grasping.

Since their survival depended on catching live food, these animals had to be quick and intelligent; the latter characteristic was reflected in their brains, which were larger than those of the tree shrews they resembled. *Plesiadapis* is known from a series of fossils from North America and Europe.

These creatures were so primitive that biologists were reluctant at first to classify them as primates. One bit of evidence came from an examination of fossilized molars, which are more like those of primates than those of moles and shrews. Moreover, the olfactory region of *Plesiadapis'* brain is noticeably smaller than the analagous area of the brain in true shrews. A final piece of evidence was that the middle ear of this creature resembled that of a lemur, another primate.

Plesiadapis is thought to resemble the tree shrews of today, the most primitive living primates. Although the tree shrew looks very much like other shrews, it differs in that it has added seeds to its diet, possesses keener vision, and has a larger visual cortex and smaller olfactory area. Yet the similarities are so great that until recently many zoologists included the tree shrews in the Order Insectivora.

Eocene primates

The Eocene Epoch, about 59 to 34 million years ago, was characterized by a warm, wet climate. Numerous new forms of primates, especially tarsiers and lemurs, emerged. Many fossil forms are known from North America, Europe, and Asia, but few from Africa. Animal fossils of North America and Europe that date from this period are very similar, because the continents were connected at this time.

Among the earliest lemurs were *Adapis* and *Notharctus.* Many fossils of *Adapis* have been discovered in France. This animal was remarkably close to the modern lemurs, especially in some specialized features of the skull, but its dentition was primitive and unlike that of the modern forms. *Notharctus* was a North American lemur; it was well adapted to grasping, leaping, and perching. By the end of the Eocene, all the North American lemurs became extinct, and the range of those in Europe, Africa, and Asia had reduced considerably.

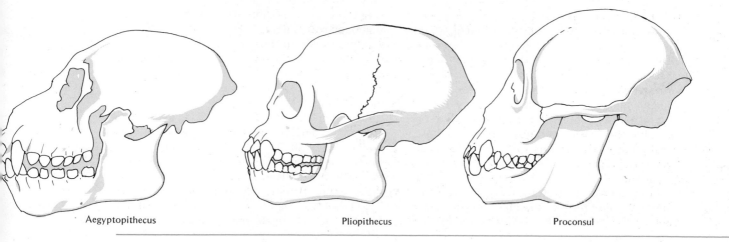

Aegyptopithecus   Pliopithecus   Proconsul

Oligocene monkeys and apes

The Oligocene Epoch occurred about 34 to 26 million years ago. Primate fossils that have thus far been discovered and definitely placed in the Oligocene era are very scant, but enough specimens exist to prove that small monkeys and primitive apes first appeared at this time. The scarcity of Oligocene primate fossils is due to the fact that the arboreal nature of primates then living restricted them to a tropical damp forest environment not conducive to fossil formation of any kind.

Two mandibles, or lower jawbones, found in the Lower Oligocene strata of the fossil-rich Fayum region of Egypt, provide science with its first evidence for the existence of Old World monkeys. The oldest of these mandibles belongs to *Parapithecus,* or "near ape," a very small primate about the size of a modern squirrel monkey. Doubts exist as to the actual function of some of the teeth on the mandible, but the fossil does reveal a primitive dentition, in the form of small canine teeth and very simple, single-cusped first premolars. All three molars present on the jaw showed a fifth cusp, which modern Old World monkeys do not have. Moreover, the two halves of the jaw met at a sharp "V" angle, a primitive characteristic unlike the smooth rounded jaw contours of later monkeys. Investigators have hypothesized that this creature possessed a relatively larger brain than the lemur and tarsier, with superior auditory and visual development.

The other mandible, found in the Fayum by paleontologist D. E. Savage, belonged to *Oligopithecus,* a small monkey about the size of a marmoset. Both *Parapithecus* and *Oligopithecus* were generalized species of monkeys whose dentition reveals a possible descent from the Eocene tarsier. It is the lack of specialization seen in these animals that leads scholars to believe they may be ancestral types from which later primates are descended.

Another primate fossil to emerge from the Fayum is *Propliopithecus,* the oldest clearly identifiable anthropoid ape. It was discovered in 1908

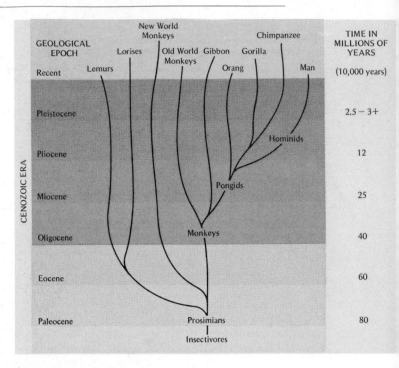

Figure 5-4. *There is still a mystery in man's evolutionary tree: where did man's true earliest ancestors diverge from the line that produced the gorilla, the gibbon, the chimpanzee, and the orangutan?*

by the German collector Richard Markgref. The only evidence for the existence of this primate is portions of a mandible. This small ape was the size of a small gibbon. The teeth of *Propliopithecus* are similar to those of an ape, and the five-cusp pattern of the molars corresponds to the molar pattern of today's anthropoid ape. In addition, the depth of the jaw is similar to that of modern apes.

One of the most exciting finds at Fayum was an almost complete skull and fragments of limb bones. Although the bones were found at the turn of the century, only recently have they been carefully studied. They belong to a species called, most appropriately, *Aegyptopithecus,* or the Egyptian Ape. It is the oldest known fossil ape (dating back about 30 million years) from this

The evolution of man ● part 2

region of Egypt, and could be a descendant of *Oligopithecus.* This fossil is interesting because it may very well prove to be a transitional form between Old World monkeys and the great apes. For example, the dentition of this fossil shows certain similarities to the teeth of great apes, whereas the skull and fragments of limbs reveal more primitive monkeylike traits. *Aegyptopithecus* is probably ancestral to *Dryopithecus.*

LeGros Clark suggests that the Oligocene fossils indicate the possibility that modern monkeys may represent an offshoot from the main line of evolution leading to apes and man. The fossil evidence of *Parapithecus* and *Oligopithecus,* and the results of comparative anatomy studies, suggest that the anthropoid apes may have descended from prosimian ancestors instead of from monkeylike ancestors, as had been previously supposed. The divergence of monkeys from the line leading to apes and man may have occurred as early as the Lower Oligocene Era.

Miocene apes

The Miocene Epoch, which succeeded the Oligocene, saw the rise, proliferation, and spread of the anthropoid ape over many parts of the Old World. The apes probably developed in the forest belt that extended from Asia westward as far as Africa.

East Africa is an area particularly rich in the fossils of Miocene apes, ranging from the size of a gibbon to that of a gorilla. At least three genera have been discovered and definitely identified as ancestors of the great apes.

The first of these fossil apes is *Pliopithecus,* which flourished in Europe, Asia, and Africa during the Miocene Epoch (about 26 to 12 million years age). Fortunately, there exists an almost complete skeleton of *Pliopithecus;* only parts of the skull are missing. From this specimen, it has been possible to determine that this small ape resembled the modern gibbon in dentition. Its limb bones, however, possess a generalized structure indicating close ties with the quadrupedal Old World monkeys. Examination of the clavicle,

breast bone, and other important structures suggests that *Pliopithecus* may have been capable of a limited degree of brachiation, or travel from limb to limb of the trees by swinging with the arms. Primates that brachiate are often relatively heavy and possess an erect posture rather than the horizontal posture characteristic of quadrupeds, such as monkeys.

The most important anthropoid fossils to be found in Africa are those of *Dryopithecus,* a somewhat larger ape that may be related to the chimpanzee and possibly the gorilla. *Dryopithecus* and "Proconsul," another fossil found in the same area, were once thought to be two different genera. However, it is now agreed by most experts that "Proconsul" was a species of the genus *Dryopithecus.*

Dryopithecus ranged over a remarkably wide geographical area: fossils of the genus have been found in Europe, Asia, and Africa. Such wide distribution indicates that these primates were very successful animals. Elwyn Simons suggests that such dispersion is due to the unbroken belt of forests, extending from Africa to southeast Asia, that provided excellent living grounds for these arboreal primates.[3]

The fossils of this early ape contain some features that are primitive and others that are much more advanced. The dentition, for example, contains features found in monkeys as well as features found in anthropoid apes and man. The molar teeth possess the advanced five-cusp pattern found in man and apes, whereas the canines are as large as those found in monkeys. The limbs of *Dryopithecus* indicate that it probably was capable of limited brachiation.

On the whole, the skull of *Dryopithecus* is not as advanced as that of living apes. The brain case is small in relation to the size of the jaw. Moreover, certain anatomical details of the nasal opening bear resemblances to Old World monkeys. The consensus among contemporary scientists places this important genus as an ancestor of pongids and perhaps also hominids.

[3]Elwyn L. Simons, "Some Fallacies in the Study of Hominid Phylogeny," *Science,* Vol. 141 (1963), pp. 879–888.

Figure 5-5. *Fossil evidence is scanty; these drawings are based on speculation. Pliopithecus was a gibbonlike primate, Oreopithecus an ape that lived in swampy regions. Yale University Professor E.L. Simons has designated Dryopithecus and Ramapithecus the only two genera among Miocene and early Pliocene hominid fossil remains.*

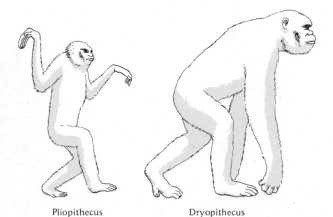
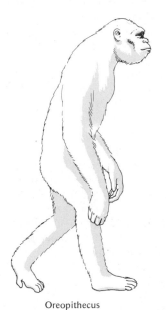

Pliopithecus   Dryopithecus   Oreopithecus   Ramapithecus

Perhaps closer to the hominid line is *Ramapithecus,* believed by E. Simons and other scientists from Yale University to be a possible ancestor of the hominids. *Ramapithecus,* whose fossil remains were discovered in the Siwalik Hills of India in 1935 by G. E. Lewis, lived during the Upper Miocene or Lower Pliocene, about 12 million years ago. Certain features of the animal's dentition, notably the small size of the canine teeth, appear to place it in the hominid line, but the shape of the palate is more characteristic of anthropoid apes. Simons, who has reconstructed the fossil jaw, states that on the basis of dentition and jaw structure, *Ramapithecus* was definitely a hominid (belonging to the family of man).[4]

The absence of large canines may be associated with a move from the savannas to high treeless plateaus; the baboons of Ethiopia, which live in a similar environment, show this same absence.

[4] E. L. Simons, "The Phyletic Position of Ramapitheous," *Postilla,* Yale Peabody Museum, No. 57 (1961).

Another possibility is that *Ramapithecus* might have defended itself in some more manlike fashion. This theory, which postulates the defensive use of tools (such as rocks and branches) rather than teeth, would place *Ramapithecus* more positively in the hominid evolutionary line. Further studies are needed, however, before positive identification of this remarkable fossil can be established.

There can be little doubt that the direct ancestors of modern anthropoid apes are found among the fossils of Miocene. It is believed that apes and man separated from a common evolutionary line sometime during the Miocene, possibly even earlier. As has been pointed out, the Miocene fossils *Dryopithecus* and *Ramapithecus* do possess some traits associated with man. Moreover, some of the Miocene apes possessed a more generalized limb structure than modern apes; this structure may have provided the basis for the development of human as well as ape limb types. A somewhat opposing view has recently been advanced by Björn Kurtén.[5] Classifying *Ramapithecus* as a hominid, he suggests that the pongids may be an offshoot of early hominids that led to an evolutionary dead end.

Another source of uncertainty about prehuman primate evolution is the debate surrounding an unusual fossil find. In 1935, the Dutch paleontologist Gustav von Koenigswald purchased in a Chinese drugstore a number of "dragon's teeth," so called by the Chinese because of their size and their supposed medicinal properties. After an examination of these teeth, von Koenigswald postulated that he had before him either the teeth of an ape or those of a giant hominid; he named his specimen *Gigantopithecus*. Today controversy still exists as to the nature of this animal, two species of which roamed the earth during the mid-Pleistocene. Was this giant a "pithecus" (ape) or was it an "anthropus" (man)?

Since von Koenigswald's fortunate purchase, many more teeth and a number of mandibles belonging to this strange genus have been discovered, many recently by Chinese scientists. The dentition and jaws possess anthropoid features, such as the massive jaw bones, as well as hominid traits, notably small canines and other dental features.

Based on the dental evidence, supposed feeding habitats, the absence of tools, and the general principle that evolution does not begin with giants but ends with them (examples being the terminal lines of such evolutionary giants as the dinosaur, mammoth, and mastodon), contemporary scientists believe that *Gigantopithecus* was an aberrant and terminal species of ape that evolved from the Dryopithecines rather than from an early hominid of giant proportions. Yet the question remains an open one. It is hoped that continuing studies combined with future fossil discoveries will provide more certain answers to the riddles of man's ancestry.

[5] Björn Kurtén, *Not from the Apes* (New York: Pantheon Books, 1972).

MAN-APES
OR APE-MEN?

More than twenty genera of extinct apes have been given different names by the paleontologists who have from time to time described these fossil remains, but the distinctions that have provided the excuse for this exuberant nomenclature have usually been based on rather trivial and unimportant characters of the teeth. The fact is that in the past we have tended to become too "hypnotized" by small variations in tooth structure, in spite of the fact that, as long ago as 1922, it was demonstrated by the German paleontologist A. Remane that individual variations in the dentition of a single species of the modern anthropoid apes are very considerable and they may far exceed the small differences on which generic distinctions among fossil apes have been claimed. Quite recently a drastic, but highly important and useful, revision of the complicated nomenclature of the large Miocene and Pliocene apes has been completed by Elwyn Simons and David Pilbeam. In place of the twenty odd generic names scattered through the literature of the subject, they recognize no more than three genera, *Dryopithecus, Gigantopithecus,* and *Ramapithecus,* of which the first contains a number of separate species. This is a most welcome simplification of the nomenclature of the fossil apes, even though it is likely that some paleontologists may regard it as an oversimplification.

The large fossil apes of Miocene age from East Africa are of particular importance, for they clearly demonstrate that these creatures were much more generalized in their anatomical structure than the large modern anthropoid apes.

They were initially given the generic name *Proconsul,* a name which has a certain air of flippancy about it because there was once a chimpanzee called Consul that used to appear on the music-hall stage and was famed for the elaborate tricks it had been trained to perform; *Proconsul* was the implied ancestor of the modern chimpanzee (which may well have been the case). The simplified nomenclature of Simons and Pilbeam has now placed these East African fossils in the genus *Dryopithecus,* recognizing three species, *D. africanus, D. nyanzar,* and *D. major,* these species varying in size from that of the pigmy chimpanzee of today to a large gorilla. We know most about the first, and smallest, of the three species; Dr. Leakey not only found its skull (incidentally the only skull of a Miocene ape so far discovered), but also some of the arm and leg bones. The skull is lightly built with no protruding brow ridges and the facial skeleton is relatively short. The canine teeth overlap in occlusion and are strongly projecting, and the front lower premolar tooth has a sectorial character. On the other hand, the incisor teeth are not enlarged as they are in the modern apes. In the upper limb skeleton the forearm is relatively short and the thumb relatively long; in other words, the upper limb shows none of the extreme specializations developed in the modern apes for brachiating habits. The thighbone is slender in build, and two of the anklebones, the heel bone, or calcaneus, and the talus show certain resemblances to those of the Old World monkeys. It has been inferred from such characters of the limb bones that *Dryopithecus africanus* was not specialized for a completely arboreal habitat, but, while it may have been an active climber, it was also able to scamper along the ground like many of the quadrupedal monkeys of today.

So generalized in structure were the limb bones that this Miocene ape might well be a representative of the ancestral stock that gave rise by divergent modifications during later geological times to the modern pongids in one direction, and to the hominids in another. That the adoption of bipedal terrestrial habits by the earliest representatives of the Hominidae must have occurred in regions of deforestation (the result of changing climatic conditions) seems very probable; further, the environment of the East African Miocene apes evidently provided possibilities of this sort, as indicated by a consideration of the fossilized fruits, seeds, and insects discovered by Dr. Leakey in the contemporary deposits. I have elsewhere made the following suggestion:

> the evolution of ground-living forms in the ancestry of the Hominidae was the result of adaptations primarily concerned, not with the abandonment of arboreal life, but (paradoxically) with an attempt to retain it. For in regions undergoing gradual deforestation they would make it possible to cross intervening grasslands in order to pass from one restricted and shrinking wooded area to another. This proposition is parallel to the interesting conjecture that water-living vertebrates initially acquired terrestrial and air-breathing adaptations in order to preserve their aquatic mode of life; for in times of drought these adaptations would make it possible to escape from dried-up rivers or pools and go overland in search of water elsewhere.

It is unfortunate that we know nothing of the limb skeleton of the dryopithecines that lived elsewhere than in East Africa, except only for a humerus and a femur found in Europe, the former very incomplete. But they are both slender and lightly built bones similar to those of *Dryopithecus africanus*. The European dryopithecine jaws and teeth are also somewhat similar, particularly in the generalized structure of the molar teeth, but they show also certain differences in minor characters. No doubt the most important fossil "ape" that has a bearing on hominid evolution is represented by the genus *Ramapithecus* of Upper Miocene or Lower Pliocene date, say ten to fifteen million years ago. I have enclosed "ape" in quotation marks because it is a matter of discussion whether it really is an ape in the sense of belonging to the evolutionary lineage of the Pongidae. On the contrary, it has been argued on the basis of the several fragmentary specimens so far discovered that it is a very primitive member of the Hominidae. If this is really so, it is the only hominid known whose remains date from pre-Pleistocene times.

The most detailed studies of *Ramapithecus* are those of Professor Simons. The fossil remains indicate that it had a wide geographical range, from India to East Africa, and perhaps as far east as China. The East African fossil consists of an upper jaw with much of the upper dentition found by Leakey in Kenya in deposits of approximately the same age as those which yielded *Ramapithecus* specimens in India. Leakey named his specimen *Kenyapithecus* on the basis of trivial differences from the Indian fossils, but, as Simons has observed, "greater differences than have been noted here typically occur among members of a single family social group within nearly all species of present day hominoids." The evidence so far available shows that *Ramapithecus* was characterized by a parabolic dental arcade; small incisors, canines, and premolars; no pronounced gap (diastema) between the upper canine tooth and the adjacent incisor tooth; and a relatively short or orthognathous facial skeleton. Simons and Pilbeam further remark that "the shallow robust mandible differs from that of *Dryopithecus* and recalls later hominids such as *Australopithecus*," and also that, since the East African dryopithecines probably range back to the Middle Miocene or even earlier, *Ramapithecus* may have had its evolutionary origin from a primitive species of *Dryopithecus*. Whether the shortened face and the small size of the front teeth of *Ramapithecus* are to be correlated with an incipient bipedalism and the development of tool-using propensities is a matter for conjecture; it is an interesting suggestion but one that is not as yet supported by objective evidence. The geographical distribution of *Ramapithecus* clearly indicates that it was a very wide-ranging species, and it is, of course, possible that its mobility over such far distances in the Old World may have been facilitated by bipedalism.

Source:
From *Man-Apes or Ape-Men? The Story of Discoveries in Africa* by Sir Wilfrid E. Le Gros Clark. Copyright © 1967 by Holt, Rinehart and Winston, Inc. Reprinted by permission of Holt, Rinehart and Winston, Inc.

Summary

1.

The first primates were arboreal insectivores, and the characteristics of all primates probably developed as an adaptation to the initial arboreal environment. While some primates no longer inhabit the trees, it is certain that these adaptations which evolved to a life in the trees were preadaptive to the exploitation of the adaptive zone now occupied by the Hominoidae. These adaptive characteristics include a generalized set of teeth, adaptive to an omnivorous diet, and fewer and smaller teeth, and a smaller jaw in the hominids. Because of these evolutionary changes in dentition, physical anthropologists can tell a great deal about an animal from the fossilized jaw bone. Other evolutionary adaptations in the primate line include stereoscopic vision, or depth perception, and an intensified sense of touch. Each of these developments had an effect upon the primate brain, resulting in a general trend towards larger size and greater complexity. There were also changes in the primate skeleton, in particular, a reduction of the snout, larger brain case, and numerous adaptations for bipedalism. In addition, changes in the reproductive pattern took place such that fewer offspring were born to each female and there was a longer period of infant dependency.

2.

A fossil is any trace of an organism of past geological time that has been preserved in the earth's crust. Fossilization typically involves the hard parts of an organism and may take place through freezing in ice, preservation in bogs or tarpits, immersion in water or embedding in rock deposits. The recovery of fossils includes excavation as well as further cleaning and preservation in the laboratory using specialized tools and chemicals.

3.

The earliest primates, as represented by Plesiadapis developed about 70,000,000 years ago and were small, arboreal creatures. In the Eocene appeared the lemurs *Adapis* and *Notharctus* and numerous species of tarsiers. The tarsiers represent an evolutionary level intermediate between lemurs and the primitive monkeys and apes.

4.

In the Oligocene appeared the most primitive known forms of Old World monkeys, represented by *Parapithecus* and *Oligopithecus. Aegyptopithecus,* also contemporary, may represent a transitional form between monkeys and apes.

5.

In the Miocene the Dryopithecines first appear, a genus ancestral to both Pongidae and Hominidae. *Pliopithecus,* the first of the fossil apes, appeared about 20 to 12 million years ago. Closer to the hominid line, *Ramapithecus* also appears in the Miocene. Although there is still controversy over the phylogenetic position of *Gigantopithecus,* most contemporary scientists believe that it was an aberrant and terminal species of ape which evolved from *Dryopithecus.*

Suggested readings

Buettner-Janush, John *Origins of Man: Physical Anthropology*. New York: John Wiley & Sons, Inc., 1966.
This introduction to physical anthropology is divided into two parts. Part I contains a discussion of evolutionary theory and systematics and descriptions of fossil man and the major groups of living primates. Man is viewed in the context of the general evolution of primates. Part II is devoted principally to *Homo sapiens'* culture, population, and genetics, and the effects of evolutionary processes on human populations.

Clark, W. E. Le Gros *The Antecedents of Man*. New York: Harper and Row, 1963.
A revision of the author's lectures on "The Palaeontology of the Primates and the Problem of Human Ancestry," this volume is an introductory text for students with no special knowledge of comparative anatomy. The interpretation of fossil material is presented in the evidence of the dentition, skull, limbs, brain, special senses, and the digestive and reproductive systems of primates.

Lasker, Gabriel Ward *Physical Anthropology*. New York: Holt, Rinehart and Winston, 1973.
A revised and enlarged edition of one of the most modern, balanced, and comprehensive texts on physical anthropology available. The selection of illustrations is especially good.

Simons, Elwyn L. *Primate Evolution*. New York: Macmillan, 1972.
This volume is a recent survey of man's place in nature. An extensive analysis of other primates is presented, followed by a consideration of what differentiates man.

Stirton, Ruben Arthur *Time, Life and Man*. New York: John Wiley, 1967.
This book is designed primarily as a text for a course in introductory paleontology, covering both plants and animals. It is written for students with little or no training in the biological and earth sciences. Most of the book deals with a chronologic presentation of the sequence of life from the Pre-Cambrian to the Pleistocene.

Early
hominids

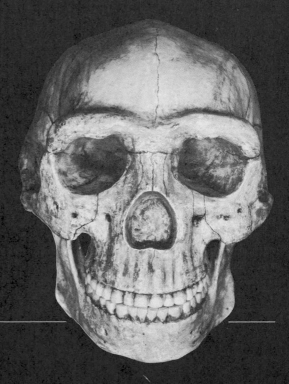

It is during the Pliocene period that we turn to look for evidence of the series of human developments that eventually led to our being able to read and understand the words of this text.

The Middle Pliocene was a watershed in the history of human evolution, for during this period man developed a number of genetic and behavioral characteristics that were to set him apart from all other animals. Among the characteristics developed by the predecessors of man at this time were: a fully erect carriage and the ability to walk erect on two feet; manipulative and dexterous hands; a greatly expanded brain; toolmaking and tool use; and possibly some kind of social organization that featured rudimentary group cooperation and division of labor.

The most outstanding fact about the development of these characteristics in man is the relatively short period of time in which they were developed. Tendencies first noticed in the apelike *Ramapithecus,* such as upright posture, were found fully developed in the man-ape *Australopithecus* ten million years later; ten million years is a mere drop in the bucket of the long eons of geologic time. The amazingly rapid advance in man's evolution during this period can be compared to the equally rapid advances in technology over the past three decades that culminated in man's landing on the moon.

Effects of environment and diet

During the late Miocene and well into the Pliocene epoch, a number of atmospheric changes took place over many areas of the earth inhabited by early hominids. The climate became increasingly cooler and drier, and the tropical forests shrank; consequently, many areas that had once been heavily forested became woodland and open savanna. The early hominid line that leads to man lived within the tropical forests or at the forest edges. With the reduction of forests, these early species found themselves spending more and more time on the ground and had to adapt to this new open environment.

Current thinking tends toward the hypothesis that the entire complex of physical and cultural changes that took place in the early hominids probably developed more or less simultaneously through a process of mutual reinforcement. Geneticist Theodosius Dobzhansky, for example, discussing whether man became a toolmaker because of his hands, or whether the hands developed as a result of toolmaking, writes:

> It is unprofitable to speculate which of the two came first; this would be akin, most likely, to asking whether the chicken or the egg came first. The two traits probably developed together reinforcing each other and conferring progressively higher adaptive advantage on their possessors.[1]

The most obvious problem facing the hominid in his new environment was that of food-getting. Food was abundant in the forest; in the savannas, however, vegetation and plant food were sparse and insufficient for the highly successful, rapidly growing hominid populations. The early hominids may have supplemented their diet first with seeds and later with a food readily available in the savannas. *Ramapithecus* and later members of the hominid stock thus became omnivorous, eaters of both plant and animal foods.

This change in diet led to several important changes in life-style. Because early hominids were omnivorous, they could easily find food and live in diverse environments; therefore, there is a rela-

[1] Theodosius Dobzhansky, *Mankind Evolving* (New Haven: Yale University Press, 1962) p. 194.

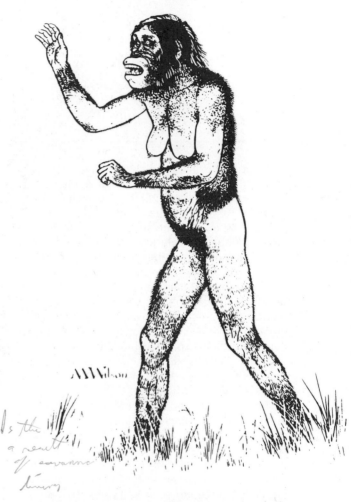

Figure 6-1a,b,c. *These drawings are artists' representations of early Australopithecines. The man at left exemplifies* A. robustus, *the larger and heavier type of this hominid genus. The other man and woman, with somewhat slighter builds, are examples of* A. africanus. *Although many of the details of such drawings are open to question, they are in accord with known fossil remains.*

tively wider geographical distribution of the early hominid species. The change of diet is correlated with a change in the dentition of these hominids. The canines used by other primates as a

The evolution of man ● part **2**

a transitional species between the quadruped and biped forms. Since no hominid fossils have been found dating from the period between the emergence of *Ramapithecus* and that of *Australopithecus,* we may assume that those hominids who did exist during the period were evolving into fully erect bipeds. *Australopithecus* is the first full biped hominid with erect posture of which we have a record.

Bipedalism, in conjunction with manipulative and dextrous hands, provided the hominids with a means of protecting themselves: it was also advantageous in other ways. For example, a fully erect biped can hold objects in the hands while running. Food does not need to be dropped and abandoned in an emergency that requires the animal's speedy departure. A biped is able to travel long distances without tiring. In addition, a biped standing erect on an open savanna is able to see further and can spot both prey and predators.

Brain reorganization and expansion

When early hominids became fully bipedal and omnivorous, the size and structure of the brain also changed. Formerly, early vegetarian hominids lived on plants and fruits; their food was around to be picked. The addition of meat to their diet made new demands on their coordination and behavior. To obtain small lizards, grubs, bugs, and eggs, they had to search more persistently and more stealthily; to catch the defenseless young of other species, they had to plan ahead and move quickly; to rob other predators of their kill, they had to cooperate in groups. Obtaining animal food presented problems that very often had to be solved on the spot. A hunter depending on stereotyped instinctual behavior alone in such a situation would have been at a competitive disadvantage; whereas a creature that could anticipate problems, dig pits, build snares, and shape stones, sticks, and bones into weapons stood a much better chance of surviving, reproducing, and proliferating.

defensive weapon became smaller. This development left the hominids defenseless on the open plain, semierect, and an easy target for keen-eyed carnivorous predators. Some investigators have concluded that the hands of these early hominids took over the weapon functions of the reduced canines, enabling the creature to throw sticks, stones, and other objects at predators, and later, to manufacture more efficient weapons from stone, wood, and bone. Similarly, it has been argued that the development of hominid bipedalism freed the hands for the later development of tool and weaponmaking.

Man stands on his own two feet

From an apelike carriage, the early hominids developed a fully erect posture; they became bipedal. *Ramapithecus* is thought to have been an incipient brachiator who sometimes walked erect,

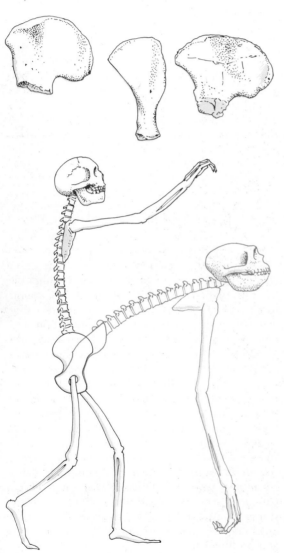

Figure 6-2. *Shown at the top of the figure are upper hip bones of* Homo sapiens, *a chimpanzee, and* Australopithecus. *The similarities of the human and Australopithecene bones are striking. The lower part of the figure shows the way that the shape of the hip bone relates to posture. On the basis of this knowledge anthropologists deduce that* Australopithecus *walked more or less upright.*

Another factor influencing brain growth was the addition of more nutritious, protein-rich meat to the diet. Vegetarian primates spend a great deal of time foraging and eating food, because plants are low in protein and a great deal of vegetation must be consumed if the animal is to remain alert and alive. Eaters of high-protein meat, however, have no need to eat as often as their vegetarian cousins. Consequently, a meat-eating hominid may have had more leisure time available to him to explore and exploit his environment; like lions and leopards, he would have time to spend lying around and playing. Such activity, coupled with the other factors mentioned here, greatly aided early hominid brain development.

The cranial capacity of the most primitive meat hunter and eater, *Australopithecus,* ranged from 450 to 580 cubic centimeters; that of *"Homo habilis"* was about 600 ccs; whereas *Homo erectus,* who hunted most widely and successfully, possessed a cranial capacity of 775 to 1300 ccs.

The earliest signs of culture: Tools

The use of tools and toolmaking, which may have arisen as a result of the need for implements to butcher and prepare meat because teeth had become inadequate for the task, also favored the development of a more efficient brain. The manufacture of tools for weapons, butchering meat, or any other purpose, requires an advanced intellect; toolmaking, like starting a fire, involves the imposition of the will on the environment in order to change it. Since tools are made in a number of shapes and sizes for a variety of purposes, such as butchering, scraping, cutting, and crushing, a toolmaker must have some preconceived idea of the kind of tool he wants to produce. The toolmaking process involves a number of steps and requires the advanced brain-eye-hand coordination found only in creatures with large, elaborate brains and superior intellects.

Biologists have found that early hominids and *Homo sapiens* are not the only animals that use tools. Sea otters use stones to crush and open clams, woodpecker finches use cactus spines to probe tree holes for insects, and chimpanzees use twigs to extract termites from their mounds. Moreover, large apes prepare nests, beavers build dams, and the enchantingly exotic bower bird builds beautiful flowery houses as part of its mating behavior. Man, however, is the only species to manufacture tools that require foresight, imagination, and standardization in form and use.

Cooperative hunting

Hominids are heavily dependent on tools for survival, and tools, in turn, are intricately involved with the hunting life-style. *Homo erectus* was a highly successful hunter, as the number of large animal bones found among his remains attests. The success of the early hunters can be attributed to a number of factors, but chief among these must be the development of cooperative hunting.

Some anthropologists believe that cooperative hunting was one of the catalysts of human development. A site in Spain has revealed that a band of *Homo erectus* used fire to drive a large herd of elephants into a swamp where they were immobilized and then killed and butchered. On the basis of archeological evidence, such as the smallness of sites, and knowledge of the methods of modern hunters and gatherers, it has been concluded that early man operated in small hunting groups, perhaps consisting of several families. Such cooperation would require planning and the use of some form of verbal communication; these traits can be seen in rudimentary form in the hunting groups of chimpanzees. A complex activity like group hunting would require a more advanced means of communication than gestures and grunts. Therefore, it is not unreasonable to assume that if early man hunted in cooperative groups and made weapons for the killing of prey as well as tools for butchering, he must have possessed speech.

Cooperative hunting also implies the sharing of food and the beginning of a sexual division of labor; this is characteristic of most meat-eating species and is known to be universal among modern hunters and gatherers. While the hominid males were away on the hunt, the females would remain behind at the base camp tending the young and foraging for fruits, vegetables, and small game. The use of the base camp is another hominid innovation. Arboreal primates rarely sleep in the same place longer than one night; when the troop moves, females and young must move with it. The wounded, aged, or infirm members who cannot move are left behind at the mercy of predators. The movable base camp thus provides a site for the females to raise the young and for the males to return with game.

The fossil evidence

The fossil evidence of hominid evolution is both sparse and tenuous. So few fossils have been found that each new addition brings changes in the general interpretive theory. Therefore, the account of hominid evolution is constantly being revised in light of new evidence, and all theories must be regarded as tentative. What is clear is that the course of hominid evolution was not smooth. Hominid lines diverge and then converge again; only in the relatively recent past was hominid evolution linear.

Australopithecus africanus: Taung and Sterkfontein fossils

In 1924, an unusual fossil was brought to the attention of Professor Raymond Dart of the University of Witwatersrand in Johannesburg; it was the cranium of an animal unlike any he had ever seen before in South Africa. Recognizing in this unusual fossil a confusing mixture of simian and hominid characteristics, anatomist Dart named his discovery *Australopithecus africanus,* or the South African ape.

Examination revealed the skull to be that of a

six-year-old male infant, now commonly called the Taung child, after its place of discovery. The skull featured a full set of milk teeth, with the first permanent molars in the process of erupting. Although apelike in overall appearance, Dart's Taung child possessed three manlike features: the canine teeth were short, the dental arcade was strikingly human, and the foramen magnum faced downward, indicating the creature was probably a biped.

Several years later at Sterkfontein, another South African site, Robert Broom, a physician and amateur fossil hunter, and his assistant, John Robinson, found other *Australopithecus africanus* remains, including a complete female skull and a large number of crude tools. Like Taung, Sterkfontein is an ancient limestone deposit believed to date back perhaps two million years.

The diet of the Taung and Sterkfontein hominids apparently consisted of fruits, nuts, and eggs; as their dentition shows, these were probably often supplemented by meat. Bones of baboons, turtles, and rodents, also found with the bones of the Australopithecenes, may have been part of their diet. Another possibility is that all of the bones, including those of *Australopithecus,* may have been dragged into the caves by leopards and other predators and that these caves were not actual living quarters for the early hominids. Anthropologist Carleton Coon points out, for example, that no primate except man has been known to live in caves, and even man rarely enters them unless he has fire or light. Caves are dark and hominids do not possess night vision; caves are clammy, damp, and uncomfortable, and they may also harbor predatory animals.[2]

Other anthropologists have been more venturesome in speculating about the diet of *Australopithecus.* They note that most of the baboon skulls were crushed, suggesting they may have been deliberately broken to extract the nutritious brains. Furthermore, the majority of the baboon skulls had been struck from the left side than from the right. This may indicate that the killers

[2]Carleton S. Coon, *The Origin of Races* (New York: Alfred A. Knopf, 1971).

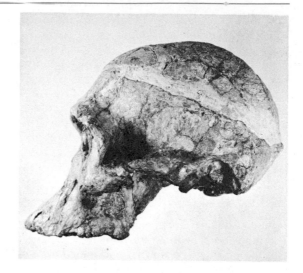

Figure 6-3,4. *These early hominid skulls are important clues to man's evolution. The one shown at the top is an* Australopithecus *specimen; the other two, found near Lake Rudolph, Kenya, by the Leakeys, are skulls of "Zinjanthropus", generally thought to be a form of A. robustus.*

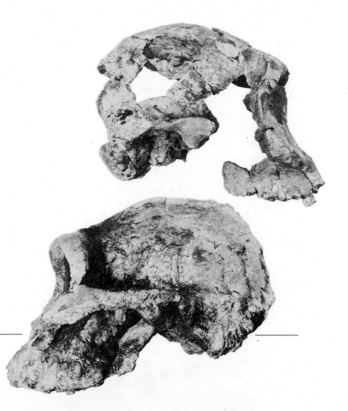

were right-handed, as are most men. It is conceivable, therefore, that the baboons were killed by Australopithecenes.

Physical traits of Australopithecus

What was *Australopithecus africanus* like, and why is he important in the story of hominid evolution? The remains of more than a hundred of these creatures have been uncovered, enabling paleoanthropologists to recreate their major features. Many *Australopithecus* specimens have been given a number of different family or generic names, but all have been placed under one of the two recongized species of Australopithecenes: *A. africanus* and *A. robustus*. An important difference between the two was one of form; the former was small and light, the later robust and heavy.

These early hominids were erect-walking primates about the size of modern pygmies. They possessed brains of moderate size, and they may have been toolmakers. Their physical appearance was most unusual by our standards: they have been described as looking like an ape from the waist up and like a man from the waist down. Their cranium was relatively low, the forehead slanted backward, and, in the *africanus* species, the brow ridge that helps give apes such massive-looking foreheads was also pronounced. The lower half of the face was chinless and accented by massive jaws. The curvature of the spine was more like that of hominids than of apes.

Much has been written about *Australopithecus'* teeth. Like modern man, *Australopithecus africanus* possessed small incisors, short canines in line with adjacent teeth, and a rounded dental arcade. The molars and premolars are larger in size but similar in form to man's teeth. The molars are unevenly worn; the upper cheek teeth are worn from the inside, and the lower cheek teeth are worn from the outside. This indicates that *A. africanus* chewed his food in hominid fashion. There is no gap between the canines and the teeth next to them on the lower jaw, a trait common in apes. Further, the large mandible is very similar to that of the later, more advanced hominid, *Homo erectus*.

Although the brain appears small and apelike and the general conformation of the skull seems nonhominid, the *Australopithecus* skull possessed a number of remarkably human features. The foramen magnum, for example, is placed forward and is downward-looking, a feature found in advanced bipedal hominids such as *Homo*. In addition, the seam joining the occipital and parietal lobes of the braincase is located to the rear of the skull, indicating that the important parietal associative areas of the cortex were somewhat expanded, as they are in *Homo*. This feature is believed to have paved the way for the later acquisition of speech.

Cranial capacity, typically used as an index of brain volume, varied among Australopithecenes from 500 to 600 cubic centimeters, which is roughly the size of the gorilla brain and about a third the size of modern man's brain. *Australopithecus,* however, was relatively small in body size, which makes the brain-body ratio closer to the hominid range. Intelligence does not depend on absolute brain capacity but upon the ratio of brain to body size. The brain of the blue whale, for example, weighs about 14 pounds, yielding a brain-body ratio of 1 : 15,000 whereas man's brain weighs about 2.7 pounds, giving him the brain-body ratio of 1 : 30.

Australopithecine fossil remains have provided anthropology with two striking facts. First, as early as three or four million years ago, this hominid ancestor of man was bipedal, walking erect. Second, hominids may have acquired their erect bipedal position before they acquired their highly developed and enlarged brain. *Australopithecus* fossils, particularly the bones of the pelvis, leg, and foot, leave no doubt that this early hominid was definitely bipedal. The shape of the spine and the number of vertebrae found in it also serve to establish bipedalism. Despite traditional emphasis on the importance of the brain, upright bipedal posture was probably more influential in man's evolutionary development. As LeGros Clark writes: "It appears, indeed, that in the process of human evolution, the expansion and elaboration of the brain followed, and were perhaps conditioned by, the perfection of the limbs for an erect mode of progression."[3]

A great deal of controversy and uncertainty exists as to the number of species included in the genus *Australopithecus*. New *Australopithecus* finds have been assigned to different "genera," to which the name *Plesianthropus, Paranthropus, Telanthropus,* and *Zinjanthropus* have been attached. Current thinking, however, tends to group all these "genera" under the single heading of *Australopithecus,* with the exception of *Telanthropus,* which is now considered to be a representative of *Homo erectus,* the earliest known true man. In an attempt to clarify the problem of classifying hominid fossils, the puzzling *Australopithecus* genus has been divided into two distinct species: *A. africanus* (*Plesianthropus*) and *A. robustus* (*Paranthropus* and *Zinjanthropus*).

Australopithecus robustus

Remains of *A. robustus* were first found at Kromdraii and Swartkrans in South Africa by Robert Broom and John Robinson in 1948 in Middle Pleistocene deposits which are about half a million years old.

A. robustus differed from *A. africanus* only in superficial aspects and shared practically all of the traits listed before. *A. robustus* was much larger than *A. africanus*, weighing perhaps 100 to 150 pounds (compared to the latter's 50 to 100 pounds). Comparison of the dentition and head shapes of the two species suggests dietetic differences. *A. robustus* ate mostly vegetable food, grinding roots, tubers, and other plant foods with its large teeth and jaws; *A. africanus*, with its smaller incisors and hominid canines, probably had a higher percentage of meat in its diet. The skull of *A. robustus* was thicker and larger than that of *A. africanus*, but the brain was about the

[3] W. E. LeGros Clark, *History of the Primates* (Chicago: The University of Chicago Press, 1963) p. 118.

same size. The *robustus* form possessed a skull cap with a simianlike sagittal crest running from front to back along the top of the skull. This feature, an example of convergent evolution in gorillas and hominids, anchors the huge muscles required to operate the powerful jaws.

A. robustus does not appear to be part of the evolutionary line leading to man. It is thought that this species had specialized too early to be an ancestor of man; some of these fossils are thought to be contemporary with early *Homo* fossils. Its evolutionary pattern reveals a tendency for the skull to remain the same size, whereas the jaw increased in size; the pattern for man is exactly the opposite. This robust species, therefore, is thought to have developed as a collateral branch of the main evolutionary line, eventually becoming extinct.

Zinjanthropus

Many hominid fossils have been found in Olduvai Gorge, a fossil-rich area near Ngorongoro Crater, on the Serengeti Plain of East Africa. Olduvai, like the Grand Canyon in America, is a huge gash in the earth, about 25 miles long and 300 feet deep, which cuts through Pleistocene and recent geological strata revealing thousands of years of the earth's history.

Beginning in 1931, Lewis and Mary Leakey worked this canyon, layer by layer, hoping to find traces of man's early hominid ancestors. In the Gorge, the Leakeys discovered crude stone implements made of pebbles rather than flaked stone, and called "pebble tools"; they date back about two million years to the Lower Pleistocene. This important find provided evidence that human culture was much older than was originally presumed.

Over the years, the Leakeys have accumulated a number of these pebble tools, and have demonstrated the existence of a pebble tool culture which they have called "Olduwan," after the Gorge. The tools bear evidence of being shaped by the human hand rather than by the erosive and

The evolution of man ● part **2**

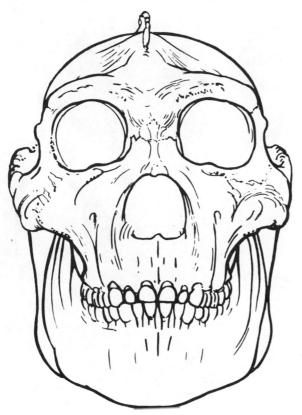

Figure 6-5. *This schematic drawing of an Australopithecine skull shows clearly the sagittal crest at the top. Some of the muscles used in chewing are attached here.*

dynamic forces of nature. Quartz choppers and other tools, for example, appear to have been produced by the primitive technique known as "percussion flaking," whereby flakes are removed from a stone core by chopping away at its surface, leaving either a one- or two-faced tool. Such tools could be used for cutting meat, scraping hides, or cracking bones to extract marrow. The Leakeys' important discovery, therefore, provides us with the first suggestion that the Australopithecenes, whose remains were later found in the same strata, might have been tool users. But some doubts remain as to the identity of the actual producer of the tools.

In the summer of 1959, the centennial year of the publication of Darwin's *The Origin of Species,* Mary Leakey made a discovery more important than the tools themselves: she found the remains of the hominid who she thought might have made the Olduvai tools. Leakey called this amazing fossil find *Zinjanthropus boisei.* At first, Leakey thought this hominid seemed a creature more advanced than *Australopithecus* and extremely close to modern man in evolutionary development. Further study, however, revealed that *Zinjanthropus,* the remains of which consisted of a skull and a few limb bones, was an East African variety of his southern neighbor, *Australopithecus.* Consequently, the designation often given this species is *Australopithecus boisei;* it is also frequently classified as a variant of *A. robustus.* Potassium argon dating places this early hominid about one and one half million years old.

The size of the teeth and certain cranial features indicate that this fossil is probably related to, if not actually descended from, *A. robustus.* Molars and premolars are enormous, as is the palate. The heavy skull, more massive even than its robust relative's, has a sagittal crest and prominent brow ridges; the brain could not have been more than 530 ccs in volume. Limb bones and cranial features indicate that *A. boisei* was a biped, but his gait was considerably different from that of modern man. For example, anthropologist P. R. Davis writes, "the muscle markings suggest that the fossil form was adapting towards bipedalism as in modern man, although musculature adaptation appears to have been less well advanced for this than the ankle joint."[4] Found with the skull and limb fragments were crude stone tools that may have been used for grinding, crushing, and butchering, as well as the remains of birds, reptiles, antelopes, and a kind of extinct pig. The bones of the larger animals had been splintered, apparently broken open to extract the marrow.

It has been suggested, by the Leakeys and others that the tools found with A. *boisei* were

[4] P. R. Davis, "Hominid Fossils from Bed I, Olduvai Gorge, Tanganyika," *Nature,* vol. 201, no. 4923, p. 968.

not produced by him, nor were the animal bones the remains of his dinner. Instead, A. boisei may have been a victim of a more advanced contemporary who created the tools, ate the animals, and possibly had the unfortunate A. boisei for dessert. That contemporary is called by some "Homo habilis"; others consider it merely a more modern version of A. africanus.

The tools found with the remains of A. robustus and A. boisei at Olduvai continue to be a problem to anthropologists. Was A. robustus a toolmaker and tool user? Many investigators agree with the Leakeys that the tools were not made by A. robustus but by the more advanced "Homo habilis." They suggest that A. robustus simply did not have the mental capacity necessary for producing tools. On the other hand, many investigators agree with LeGros Clark, who writes:

> So far as I am aware, it has never been explicitly denied that the Australopithecenes could, or did, fabricate crude implements of stone. For my part, I find the negative evidence against such a conclusion far from convincing, while the positive evidence of the association in the same deposits of stone implements mixed up with Australopithecene remains (and with no commanding evidence of the contemporaneous existence at the same sites of a more advanced hominid) is far more conclusive. In any case, as I have already remarked, if the Australopithecenes did not make and use weapons and implements of some kind, how could they possibly have survived all the hazards of the predatory animals among which they lived.[5]

"Homo habilis." Fossil remains of this hominid were discovered by the Leakeys in 1960, only a few months after and a few feet below the A. boisei find. The remains of several individuals consisted of a few cranial bones, a lower jaw, a clavicle, and the nearly complete fossil of an adult left foot. The fossils date from about 1.8 million

[5]W. E. LeGros Clark, *Man-Apes or Ape-Man?* (New York: Holt, Rinehart & Winston, Inc., 1967) p. 116.

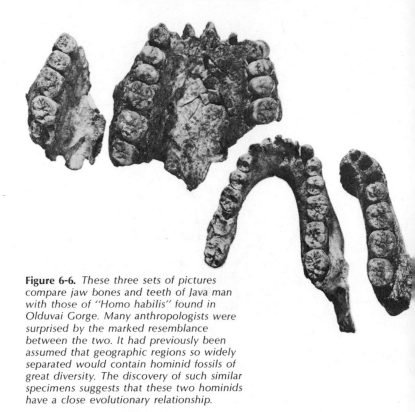

Figure 6-6. *These three sets of pictures compare jaw bones and teeth of Java man with those of "Homo habilis" found in Olduvai Gorge. Many anthropologists were surprised by the marked resemblance between the two. It had previously been assumed that geographic regions so widely separated would contain hominid fossils of great diversity. The discovery of such similar specimens suggests that these two hominids have a close evolutionary relationship.*

The evolution of man ● part **2**

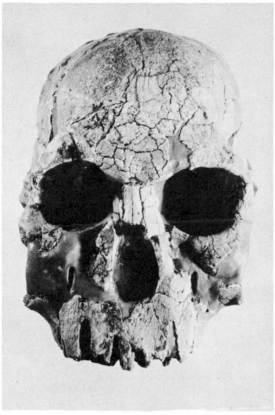

Figure 6-7a,b. *Richard Leakey, the son of Louis and Mary Leakey, discovered in the early 1970s at Lake Rudolph the skull shown here in front and side views. Leakey believes his find, over 2.6 million years old, is a third hominid type; many disagree.*

years ago and indicate generalized small bone structure; the absence of the cranial crest; a brain volume of approximately 680 ccs, the upper end of the Australopithecene range; and manlike hands and feet, which would have enabled this hominid to walk and run like a modern man. Later finds associated with *"Homo habilis"* ("able man") include a bone tool, which may have been used to work hides, and a semicircular arrangement of stones that the Leakeys have interpreted as the remains of a windbreak. Such discoveries indicate an advanced development among this unique species; *"Homo habilis"* produced a number of tools for the preparation of food, and it is probably his tools that were found earlier in the Gorge. These hominids were hunters who ranged over a wide area and operated from a base camp.

The evolutionary status of *A. boisei* and *"Homo habilis"* is a matter of controversy. Present thinking, however, postulates a line of evolutionary advance from *A. africanus* to *Homo erectus,* with *"Homo habilis"* placed in between as either a late form of *Australopithecus* or an early form of *Homo.* The robust hominid types, *A. robustus* and *A. boisei,* meanwhile, seemed to have diverged from the main line of evolution, eventually becoming extinct, perhaps because they became too specialized to survive environmental change.

Homo erectus

The remains of early members of hominid stock, notably *Ramapithecus* and *Australopithecus,* have been found in Africa, southeast Asia, and south China, indicating a wide distribution of these genera. However, no previous hominids were so widespread as *Homo erectus.* Fossils have been found in Asia, Europe, and Africa. In spite of the fact that remains of *H. erectus* have been found in so many different localities in three continents, they show very little significant physical variation. Evidence suggests, however, that the *H. erectus* of the East was culturally different than that of the West.

The remains of two different types of *Homo erectus* have been found in Asia. The two varieties, called Java Man and Peking Man, are the earliest known hominids to be in the direct line of descent of *Homo sapiens*. Of the two species, Peking Man is thought to be the more recent and more advanced. His average cranial capacity is 1000 ccs, compared to Java Man's 900 ccs. The smaller teeth, short jaw, and lack of diastema in the lower jaw of the Chinese man are further evidence of his more developed status.

Although the brain of Peking Man was slightly larger than that of his Javanese cousin, the sensory, speech, memory, and motor areas of both species indicate a capacity for language and culture. The complexity of the tools found with Peking Man give direct evidence of a relatively advanced brain development.

Java man. In 1891, the Dutch army surgeon Eugene DuBois, convinced of the existence of a missing link between man and ape, set out for Java, which he considered to provide a suitable environment for such a creature. At Trinil, Java, DuBois found what he was searching for: a fossil of a primitive kind of man, consisting of a skull cap, a few teeth, and a thighbone. Its features seemed to DuBois part ape, part man. Indeed, DuBois at first thought the remains did not even belong to the same individual. The flat skull, for example, with its enormous brow ridges and small size, appeared to be that of an ape; but it possessed a cranial capacity of 1000 ccs, larger than an ape's. The femur, or thighbone, was clearly manlike in shape and proportions, and indicated the creature was a biped. DuBois called his find *Pithecanthropus,* or "erect ape man," now commonly known as Java Man.

The scientific community of the time scoffed and did not consider DuBois' Java Man to be of human lineage. It was not until the 1920s, when other fossils of Java Man were discovered by G. H. R. von Koeningswald at Sangiran, Java, in the early Pleistocene Djetis beds, that scientists agreed both discoveries contained the remains of an entirely new genus of early man. Von Koenings-

wald found a small skull that fluorine analysis and potassium argon dating indicated to be 200,000 years older than DuBois' 500,000 year-old Trinil specimen. Significantly, the age difference indicated a long continuity of *Homo erectus* populations in Southeast Asia.

Peking man. The second variety of *Homo erectus* was found in the mid-1920s by Davidson Black, a Canadian anatomist at Peking Union Medical College. After purchasing in a Peking drugstore a few teeth sold to local inhabitants for their supposed medicinal properties, Black set out for the nearby countryside to discover the owner of the teeth and perhaps other species of early man. He found a skull encased in limestone at a place called Dragon's Hill in Choukoutien, 30 miles from Peking. Between 1929 and 1934, the year of his death, Black labored in the fossil-rich deposits of Choukoutien, uncovering fragment after fragment of the genus he had named *Sinanthropus pekinensis,* or "Chinese Man of Peking"—now called Peking Man.

After his death, Black's work was continued by Franz Weidenrich; by 1958, the remains of over 40 individuals, consisting of teeth, jaw bones, and incomplete skulls, were dug out of the limestone. World War II brought a halt to the digging, and the original Choukoutien specimens were lost during the Japanese invasion of China. Fortunately, Weidenrich had made casts of the fossils and sent them to the United States. After the war, other specimens of *Homo erectus* were discovered in Africa, Asia, and Europe.

Physical characteristics of Homo erectus. Based on fossil evidence, anatomists have reconstructed both Java and Peking populations of *Homo erectus,* revealing closely similar outward physical appearances. *Homo erectus* was short by modern standards, attaining a stature of perhaps five feet; he somewhat resembles the Australopithecenes from whom he is probably descended. He possessed an average cranial capacity of 1,000 ccs (which is within the lower range of modern man's 1000 to 2000 ccs cranial volume). The cra-

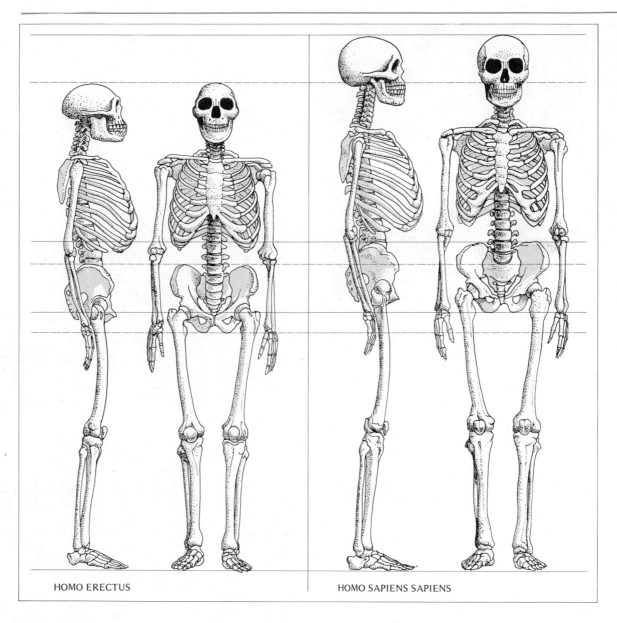

HOMO ERECTUS

HOMO SAPIENS SAPIENS

Figure 6-8a. *This drawing compares the stature and posture of* Homo erectus *with that of* Homo sapiens. *It appears that* H. erectus *was shorter, but in all other proportions these two species of the genus* Homo *seem very much the same.*

nium itself had a low vault, and the head was long and narrow. When viewed from behind, its width was greater than its height, with its greatest width at the base. The skull of modern man, when similarly viewed, is higher than it is wide, with its

Figure 6-8b. *The work of reconstructing fossil remains is painstaking and tedious. Here a Chinese anthropologist studies a skull of Peking man found at Choukoutien.*

widest dimension in the region above the ears. Moreover, the shape of the inside area of *Homo erectus'* brain showed near-human development, especially in the speech area.

Massive ridges gave this early man his simian "beetle-browed" appearance. He also possessed a retreating forehead and an underdeveloped chin. Powerful jaws with large teeth, protruding mouth, and huge neck muscles added to his rugged appearance. The limbs of this presapiens hominid were highly developed and structurally close to those of modern man. Anatomical studies of *Homo erectus'* legs and feet bones indicate that he walked and ran like modern man.

Early hominid culture

Little is known of the culture of Java Man, since little to indicate the existence of a culture of any kind has been found with his remains. The bones of Peking Man, however, tell a different, more interesting story. Discovered in the cave with

Figure 6-9. *The excavation site where Peking man was found is carefully marked off in a numbered grid system to locate fossil finds.*

The evolution of man ● part **2**

Peking Man was evidence of a number of startling developments in human evolution. Peking Man used fire for protection, warmth, and cooking; he had a burgeoning tool industry; and, apparently, he practiced cannibalism. Thousands of broken and charred bones of such animals as deer, sheep, antelope, roebuck, small hares, camels, bison, and elephants indicate that *Homo erectus* was a hunter who cooked his food. This practice may have reduced the forces of natural selection that previously favored individuals with large teeth, paving the way for reduction in tooth size, as well as supporting facial architecture.

Evidence of the human bones scattered among the animal remains at Choukoutien suggests that this hominid practiced cannibalism. The skulls had been entered via the foramen magnum, presumably to extract the nutritious brain, and the long bones of the extremities had been split to obtain the marrow.

The use of fire among *Homo erectus* has tremendous cultural importance; like tools and intelligence, it gives man more control over his environment. There may be a causal relationship between prehistoric man's use of fire and his habitation in caves. It is held that fire was used to evict and keep at bay the previous tenants of the caves, such as leopards and other large carnivores. Fire also removed the damp, clammy atmosphere of the caves and provided light as well. Moreover, because fire could harden wood to produce better spears, *Homo erectus* became a more efficient hunter.

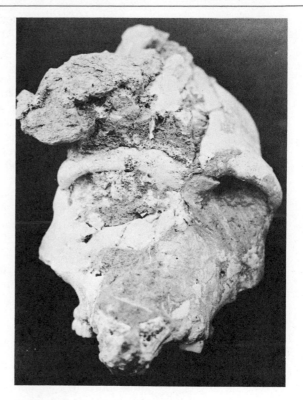

Figure 6-10. *The skulls shown in other figures were the result of many hours of patient labor. Most fossil remains look more like this when they are found; they are embedded in a matrix of rock. It takes a trained eye to recognize a fossil remain in its original condition, and it takes professional skills to remove the matrix without damage to the valuable fossilized bones.*

Original study

CULTURE AND BIOLOGY

Basically, the development or evolution of the human species has been governed by the progressive development of the cultural message, including language and material culture. Because our information concerning many aspects of this development is literally buried in the earth and because direct evidence of the use of language, the presence of particular social arrangements, the development of particular ways of doing things, or the utilization of perishable materials is generally unavailable, we can known the broad outlines but not the specific details of human evolution. During the past several million years there must have been great cultural inventions and great changes in the nature of the human genetic message. We do not know exactly when such changes took place, and we cannot speak precisely of their causes or their nature. We are certain that the various qualities leading toward humanity developed over a long period of time following an intricate process of reciprocal rather than linear causation.

Under a pattern of linear causation, a "cause" is interpreted as leading to some particular "effect." Under a pattern of reciprocal causation, there is a relationship among a variety of factors such that a change in A leads to a change in B and a change in B leads to a change in A. Thus, the progressive development of language must have facilitated the increasing use of tools.

If there was a single cause or a single beginning to the process of evolution in the human direction, it may well have been the movement of our ancestors from a forest to a grassland or savannah environment. In the new environment, with few trees to climb for safety, it appears likely that the proto-human had to rely upon vocalization, good eyesight, increasingly upright posture, and cooperation with his fellows for protection from predators. Because a developing ability to walk upright would have freed the hands for carrying things, it is possible to imagine proto-humans collecting small animals, roots, or nuts and carrying them to a safe place while using vocalizations to indicate the location of food, the presence of predators, and the direction of travel. Upright posture and increased use of the hands, eyes, and mouth presumably led to the enlargement and refinement of the brain and vice versa.

Carrying things around would contribute to the development of the human talent for thinking about things removed in time and space, a talent that is critical for the use of tools and the development of language. Upright posture combined with increasing brain size may well have led to the birth of progressively immature human infants and this must have gone hand in hand with the development of work-sharing and food-sharing human groups. The need for increased cooperation within such groups would have led to more vocalization, larger brain size, greater reliance on tools, and upright posture. Some anthropologists, perhaps more observant than others, suspect that tool use is related to the human habit of sitting upright, rather than to the habit of standing upright. If we ask which came first, increased brain size, tool use, upright posture, the beginnings of language, infant helplessness, or the development of food-sharing groups, we are at a loss to find an answer. Each small step toward humanity influenced other small steps by a process of reciprocal causation.

The development of language, the cultural message, and human social arrangements must have been quite critical to the evolution of humanity and it is therefore unfortunate that the archaeological record tells us so little about these things. Because the individual's survival and his capacity to bear viable offspring was dependent upon the capacity to cooperate with other group members, there may well have been strong social selection against individuals who were greedy, violent, uncooperative, nonverbal, or physically unattractive by whatever standards might have been in force.

Against the demonstrable necessity for love and cooperation must be placed the fact that human beings early began to kill large animals, perhaps other human beings as well, for food. At the same time that human beings were developing an improved capacity to cooperate, they were becoming the most ferocious predatory mammal on the planet. Because rules governing sexual and marital relationships, including rules forbidding sexual relationships with close relatives, are found in a wide variety of existing human cultures, it is tempting to conclude that the need to obtain sexual and marital partners outside the immediate family and often outside the immediate group might have created affiliations which served to restrict predation within the group and between the group and its immediate neighbors. The fact that human beings might well have been their own worst enemies might also have encouraged the development of defensive alliances among neighboring groups. The development of relationships both of enmity and alliance among neighboring groups of human beings could have been one of the factors in human evolution.

With the progressive refinement of the human capacity to use language and to build culture, the importance of "purely" biological factors and of adaptation to the "natural" environment in human evolution must have progressively declined. In other words, as human beings solved their adaptive problems by developing new patterns of culture or new kinds of tools and implements, their genetic message became progressively more insulated from direct effects of the natural environment. The survival and reproduction of the human individual came to depend increasingly upon his ability to function within a social environment and decreasingly upon his ability to cope individualistically with the problems of survival in nature. In modern urban societies, the "natural" environment practically disappears, although we forget it at our peril, and human biological and cultural evolution takes place almost entirely within a man-made environment. Human beings now tend to construct the forces that lead to their own biological evolution. Figuratively speaking, the automobile has replaced the tiger as an agent of natural selection.

Source:
From *Culture in Process,* Second Edition, by Alan R. Beals, George Spindler and Louise Spindler. Copyright © 1967, 1973 by Holt, Rinehart and Winston, Inc. Reprinted by permission of Holt, Rinehart and Winston, Inc.

Summary

1.
During the Middle Pliocene man developed a number of genetic and behavioral traits that were to set him apart from all other animals. These included: a fully erect carriage, the ability to walk erect on two feet; manipulative and dexterous hands; an expanded brain, toolmaking and tool use; and perhaps some kind of social organization. All these traits seem to have developed in a relatively short period of time.

2.
During the late Miocene and parts of the Pleistocene, the climate became cooler and drier; many areas that had once been heavily forested became woodland and open savanna. The early species of hominids found themselves spending more and more time on the ground; they had to adapt to this new open environment. Food-getting became a problem in this changed environment. The early hominids became omnivorous; they ate both plant and animal foods. As the early hominids became omnivorous, they could easily find food in diverse environments; therefore, their geographical distribution widened. The dentition of these early hominids also changed as a result of their changed diet. On the whole, teeth became smaller and finer; many of the defensive functions once performed by teeth were taken over by the hands.

3.
Ramapithecus was an incipient brachiator who may have at times walked erect. *Australopithecus* is the first fully bipedal hominid known. Bipedalism provided the hominid with a means of protecting itself; a biped standing erect can see far away and spot both prey and predators. Furthermore, a biped can hold objects in the hands while running; food does not have to be dropped and abandoned in an emergency that requires the animal's speedy departure.

4.
Some changes in the brain structure of early hominids were the result of their changed diet. The addition of meat to their diet made new demands on their coordination and behavior. The catching of warm-blooded prey depended on the hominid's ability to outdo their source of food. Obtaining animal food presented problems that very often had to be solved on the spot; a hunter depending on stereotyped instinctual behavior alone would have been at a competetive disadvantage in such a situation. Moreover, eaters of high-protein foods, such as meats, do not have to eat as often as vegetarians do. Consequently, a meat-eating hominid may have had more leisure time available to explore and exploit his environment.

5.
Toolmaking and use also favored the development of a more efficient brain. Toolmaking, like starting a fire, involves the imposition of the will on the environment in order to change it. It involves a number of steps requiring advanced brain- eye-hand coordination. Man, of all the toolmaking animals, is the only species to manufacture tools that require foresight, imagination, and standardization in form and use.

6.

Cooperative hunting may have been one of the catalysts of human development. Early man, such as *Homo erectus,* may have operated in small hunting groups. It is probable that he possessed speech. Cooperative hunting also implies the sharing of food and the beginning of a sexual division of labor; this is characteristic of modern hunters and gatherers. The early hominid hunters may have operated from a movable base camp.

7.

The course of hominid evolution is not clear-cut; hominid lines diverge and then converge again for most of man's evolutionary history. The few fossils found can barely provide a picture of what our ancestry was like. One of the early members of the hominid line was *Australopithecus.* Fossil remains of this four-million year old hominid were first found in two South African sites: Taung and Sterkfontein. *Australopithecus* was probably omnivorous. There are two recognized species of Australopithecines: *A. africanus* and *A. robustus.* These early hominids walked erect; they were about the size of modern pygmies. Their brains were of moderate size, and they may have been toolmakers. Their general appearance may have been like that of an apelike man. The dentition is rather manlike.

8.

In the summer of 1959, Mary Leakey discovered the remains of a hominid in Olduvai Gorge, East Africa. Leakey called this find *Zinjanthropus.* A number of pebble tools, called "Olduwan," after the Gorge, were also discovered. At first, this hominid seemed more advanced than the Australopithecines; it showed advanced physical features. It is now thought, however, that *Zinjanthropus* was an East African variety of *Australopithecus.* It is sometimes classified as *A. boisei* or as a variant of *A. robustus.* This early hominid is about one and one half million years old. *"Homo habilis,"* another hominid discovered by the Leakeys remains a controversial fossil. This hominid may have been a late form of *Australopithecus* or an early form of *Homo.*

9.

The remains of *Homo erectus* have been found in many different localities in Asia, Europe, and Africa; they show very little significant physical variation. *H. erectus* of the East was culturally different from that of the West. The Asian types of *H. erectus* are represented principally by Java Man and Peking Man; they are the earliest known hominids to be in direct line of descent of *Homo sapiens.* These hominids were short by modern standards and resembled the Australopithecines from whom they were probably descended. There is evidence that Peking Man cooked his food, had a tool industry, practiced cannibalism, and was a skilled hunter. The use of fire represents a notable cultural achievement for these early men.

Suggested readings

Brace, C. Loring Harry Nelson, and Noel Korn *Atlas of Fossil Man*. New York: Holt, Rinehart, and Winston, 1971.
The core of this Atlas consists of a series of drawings which provide a pictorial survey of all the key fossils that form the basis of our knowledge of human evolution. Each drawing highlights the diagnostic character of the fossil find to facilitate comparison and is accompanied by notes on date, geological age, place of discovery, and interpretations. Maps showing the distribution of important sites and stone tool distributions are included for each stage.

Clark, Sir Wilfred LeGros *Man-Apes or Ape-Men? The Story of Discoveries in Africa*. New York: Holt, Rinehart, and Winston, 1967.
This is an analytic narrative of the various discoveries in Africa of one of the most primitive ancestors of the human family, the "ape-man" or *Australopithecus*. Clark discusses the argument of whether these fossils represent extremely primitive ancestors of man or members of the ape family whose evolution developed parallel to man's.

Edey, Maitland, and the Editors of Life *The Missing Link*. New York: Time-Life, 1972.
This volume explains and examines the process which led to the evolution of *Australopithecus*. In addition to sections on chimpanzees, apes, and general primate behavior, a special pictorial essay on how "ape-man" lived and hunted in groups is presented.

Korn, Noel *Human Evolution*. New York: Holt, Rinehart, and Winston, 1973.
The emphasis of this shortened edition is on continuing studies of modern populations, with micro-evolutionary events studied in detail. An ecological and ethological perspective on primate and human evolution is emphasized.

Lasker, Gabriel W. *Physical Anthropology*. New York: Holt, Rinehart, and Winston, 1973.
More than a revision of the original text, this is virtually a new book, with new materials on primate behavior and human adaptation having been added. It is a balanced overview of the principal questions and areas in physical anthropology.

Pilbeam, David *The Ascent of Man: An Introduction to Human Evolution,* New York: Macmillan, 1972.
This book summarizies much of the post-1940 research on primate fossil materials. Early hominids in South Africa and East Africa from the middle and later Pleistocene form the subject of this book. This book attempts to construct and present dynamic models of human evolution by relating it to primate studies.

Simons, Elwyn L. *Primate Evolution: An Introduction to Man's Place in Nature*. New York: Macmillan, 1972.
This book is a recent survey of the fossil record of man's near relatives and some ancestors.

White, Edmund, and the Editors of Life *The First Men*. New York: Time-Life, 1972.
The story of *Homo erectus* is the subject of this book. Prehistoric man's wanderings, development of speech, and discovery of fire are discussed. The book is well-illustrated and includes special chapters on Java man and Peking man.

Homo
sapiens

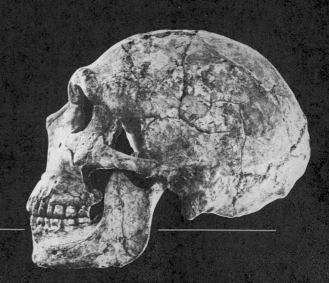

The anthropologist attempting to piece together the innumerable parts of the puzzle of human evolution must be as good a detective as he is a scholar, for the available evidence is often scant, enigmatic, or full of misleading clues. The quest for *Homo sapiens* has some of the elements of a detective story, for it contains a number of mysteries concerning the emergence of man, none of which has been completely solved to this day. The mysteries involve the appearance of the first fully sapient man, the identity of Neanderthal man, and his relationship to more modern forms.

Homo sapiens

Our early sapient ancestors must have been a hardy breed of men; for it is during the Pleistocene, an unusual geologic epoch of alternating periods of cold and subtropical warmth, that they first appear. During the Middle and Upper Pleistocene, much of the earth's surface was covered by massive ice sheets; hence this period is known as the Great Ice Age. From 600,000 to 10,000 B.C., the northernmost parts of Europe, Asia and North America experienced a number of glacial advances and retreats. In Europe, the polar ice cap moved south and vast sheets of ice, or glaciers, crunched their way down from the mountains to the lowland regions that had previously enjoyed temperate and subtropical climates.

While Europe and North Asia were experiencing the glacial and interglacial periods, the tropical parts of the world, particularly Africa and S. Asia, where *Australopithecus* and other hominids developed, underwent rainy and arid climatic changes.

It is in the Third Interglacial Period in Europe, during a break in the weather, so to speak, that we see the emergence of the first primitive *Homo sapiens*. The most outstanding characteristic of this early man was the large brain, with its average cranial capacity of 1150 to 1470 ccs. The forehead was low and sloping, the brow ridges were pronounced, but the shape of the mandible was quite close to that of modern man.

Neanderthal man appeared towards the start of the Würm glaciation; it is believed by LeGros Clark and other anthropologists that he was a descendant of the *H. sapiens* populations of the Third Interglacial Period. We do not know much about his fate in Europe because there is a 10,000

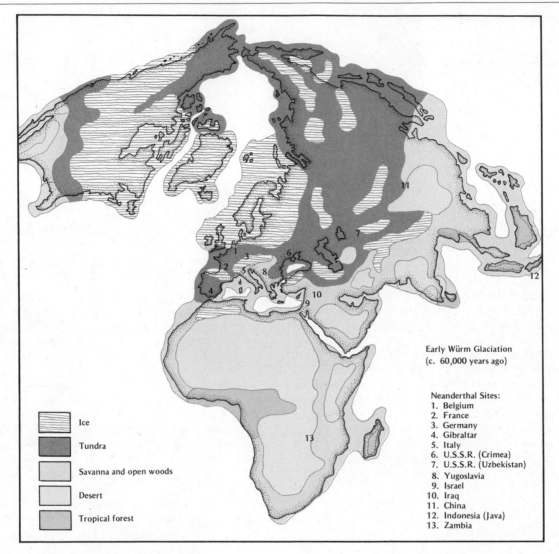

Ice

Tundra

Savanna and open woods

Desert

Tropical forest

Early Würm Glaciation
(c. 60,000 years ago)

Neanderthal Sites:
1. Belgium
2. France
3. Germany
4. Gibraltar
5. Italy
6. U.S.S.R. (Crimea)
7. U.S.S.R. (Uzbekistan)
8. Yugoslavia
9. Israel
10. Iraq
11. China
12. Indonesia (Java)
13. Zambia

Figure 7-1. *The colored areas represent land masses of the earth about 60,000 years ago; superimposed is the outline of the continents as they appear today. During the period of glaciation, the ice sheets spread to cover even a larger area than is shown here. It is interesting to note the wide variety of habitats in which Neanderthal man lived and flourished; he seems to have lived in tundra, savanna, desert, tropical forest, and even on the edge of the ice sheets.*

year gap in the fossil record. In the Near East, however, the fossil record shows transitional forms between Neanderthal and modern man.

It is not known where Cro-Magnon man came from or how he developed into modern man. His brain was not significantly larger than Neanderthal's. His resemblance to later Europeans is clear, although he was not quite as modern-looking as he has sometimes been portrayed.

The first men

Between *Homo erectus* and the first fossil indicating the presence in Europe of *Homo sapiens* is a gap of about 100,000 years. The fossils, consisting of a handful of cranial bones, were discovered in the 1930s and 1940s. The discovery of these remains of ancient man, which date back 150,000 to 200,000 years, surprised the scientific community, because it indicated that sapient man had been around much longer than had been previously thought. The skull bones belong to

Figure 7-2a. *This photo shows a rock overhang typical of the sort found in the Dordogne region of southwest France. It is in such shelters that remains of Neanderthal man have frequently been found; anthropologists speculate that a site like this one may have been continuously inhabited for 60,000 years.*

two females and represent a primitive form of *Homo sapiens;* the bones are known by the names of the places where they were found: Steinheim (Germany) and Swanscombe (England). As is the case with most transitional forms, these skulls possess both primitive and advanced characteristics. The brains are rather large for *Homo erectus* and small for *Homo sapiens.* The overall appearance of the skulls, however, is different from ours. The skulls are larger and broader with prominent brow ridges, larger face, and bigger teeth. The position of the foramen magnum and the shape of the mandible resemble those of modern forms. In addition to the finds at Steinheim and Swanscombe, other fossil remains of primitive sapiens were found at Fontechevade, France, in 1947. The incomplete skull cap remains controversial; it is shaped like that of the Neanderthals.

These early men seem to have made little cultural progress over their predecessors, *Homo erectus.* The primitive sapiens, for example, employed the kind of hand axes, scrapers, and engravers used by *Homo erectus* for thousands of years; however, the quality of the manufacture had improved. Some anthropologists believe that these early sapiens shifted their ranges southward with the advance of the vast ice sheets of the Würm glaciation. It is possible that they interbred with similar populations living in the Near East.

Neanderthal man

The discovery of Neanderthal man in 1856 was a turning point in the battle waged between science and theology over man's primate ancestry. Only three years later, with the publication of Darwin's *The Origin of Species,* the idea of man's descent from a more primitive ancestor received a formal, well-reasoned support. Many people became aware that mankind had been evolving for millions of years from a primitive ancestor into the thinking animal he is today.

The prevailing theory of human origins during most of the nineteenth century was that the entire human race was descended from Adam and Eve. Any suggestion that human beings might have had apes scampering down the family tree, or that evolution of any kind was possible, was met with derision.

The reaction to the discovery of the skeletal remains of an early man in the Neander Valley near Dusseldorf, Germany, is not difficult to imagine. The general public, learned scholars, and thinkers received the news with a great deal of doubt and distrust. Examination of the fossil skull, a few ribs, and some limb bones revealed that the individual was a human being, showing primitive and modern characteristics. The cranial capacity had reached modern proportions, but the appearance of the skull was still primitive looking. Some believed the bones were those of a sickly and deformed contemporary. Others thought the skeleton belonged to a soldier who had succumbed to water on the brain during the Napoleonic Wars. A prominent anatomist thought the remains were those of an idiot suffering from malnutrition, whose violent temper had gotten him into many scrapes, flattening his forehead and making his brow ridges bumpy.

The discovery of other skeletal Neanderthal remains between 1866 and 1910 in Europe, the Middle East, China, Indonesia, and North and South Africa led many scientists to reevaluate their thinking. Neanderthal Man was then acknowledged as a well-established, true *Homo sapiens,* rather than a deformed or aberrant specimen unrelated to man. Even as late as 1920, however, some scholars were reluctant to admit Neanderthal to the evolutionary line leading to modern man. Their opinion was based on an analysis of a Neanderthal skeleton found in 1908 near La Chapelle Aux Saintes in France. The analysis concluded that the specimen's brain was apelike and that he walked slumped like an ape.

It has since been proved by a team of American investigators that this French Neanderthal specimen was that of a middle-aged *Homo sapiens* who had suffered from malnutrition, arthritis of the spine, and other deformities. Even today, however, Neanderthals are by some scholars ex-

Figure 7-2b,c. *The limestone cliffs of the Dordogne are pocked with caves that sheltered Neanderthal man from weather and predators.*

The evolution of man ● part **2**

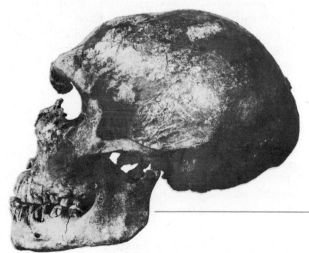

Figure 7-3,4. *The skull is of the classic type of Neanderthal; above is an early reconstruction of this type. The bones on which this reconstruction was based turned out to be those of an arthritic, and therefore the drawing is quite inaccurate.*

cluded from our ancestry, and there are those who would dispute their rightful place in the evolutionary sequence. Indeed, for many, Neanderthal is the quintessential "cave man," portrayed by imaginative cartoonists as the slant-headed, stooped, dim-witted individual, clad in animal skins and carrying a big club as he plods across the prehistoric landscape, perhaps dragging behind him an unwilling female or a dead leopard.

Classic and generalized Neanderthals. It is generally acknowledged that there are two types of Neanderthal: Classic (so called because this was the first type to be found), and General. Classic Neanderthal was typically heavier, while the generalized type was lighter and more modern in form and facial features. Moreover, the Classic Neanderthal lived in Europe; the generalized type, in the Near East.

Northern Europe was in the grip of an extremely cold and harsh climate when Classic Neanderthal appeared toward the beginning of the Wurm glaciation. A sheet of ice stretched across the continent from Scandanavia to North Germany, Southern Russia and Northern England. The Alps and other European mountain ranges were glacier-bound. Neanderthals lived along the fringes of the glaciated tundralike areas.

Much of the controversey over whether Classic Neanderthal was a *Homo sapiens* derives from the fact that he was originally seen as revealing modern as well as primitive features. For example, although he resembled modern man more closely than his predecessors in the size of his brain, he also possessed other physical features, particularly in the facial area, that seemed more primitive than that of his immediate predecessors. His brain, with an average cranial capacity of 1500 ccs was as large as, and perhaps even larger than, ours. These features notwithstanding, the Classic Neanderthal was quite varied, some looking no different than his Near Eastern contemporaries. Some anthropologists believe that Europeans today still carry some of the genes of the Classic Neanderthal.

Figure 7-5a,b. *These two views show a skull of the generalized Neanderthal type; this skull can be compared with the classic type depicted in Figure 7-4. This fossil was found in a cave on Mount Carmel in Israel; it seems amazingly modern.*

The second type of Neanderthal, the generalized form, presents a high degree of physical variation; it is, on the whole, smaller than the Classic type. There are some generalized types from the Near East who, in fact, resemble their Classic relatives. It is not unreasonable to suppose that an exchange of genes took place between populations of the generalized type and those of the Classic. Fossil evidence of the existence of this Neanderthal type has been found at Skuhl and in a cave at Mt. Carmel, both in Israel; at Shanidar, Iraq; at a site near Krapina, Yugoslavia; and in sites in the Levant. These specimens seem to have been transitional between Neanderthal and modern man.

Physical adaptations. It has been suggested that the physical differences between the two Neanderthal types arose from differences in the environment. The climate of Western Europe in which the Classic forms developed 40,000 to 80,000 years ago was a challenging one; it was bitter cold, dry, and tundralike, with frequent blizzards bringing deep snows and high drifts. The Classic Neanderthal was the first human to live in Europe under such conditions. The Classic Neanderthal's distinctive facial features may have represented an adaptation to the cold. For example, his large nose took some of the chill off the icy air he breathed. The ridges in back of the neck, prominent brow ridges, and powerful jaws may have accommodated huge muscles required to chew hides as a means of softening them in the tanning process, as Eskimos and Australian aborigines do today. The hides would have served as clothing and blankets to keep out some of the frigid cold. Moreover, the massiveness of the Classic form, particularly in the shoulders, chest, and skull, may have served to help the individual to retain body heat by reducing the body's surface area in respect to overall body size. This adaptive advantage is seen in the short, stocky builds of contemporary Eskimos.

Conversely, the smaller physical features of the generalized Neanderthaler who lived in the Mid-

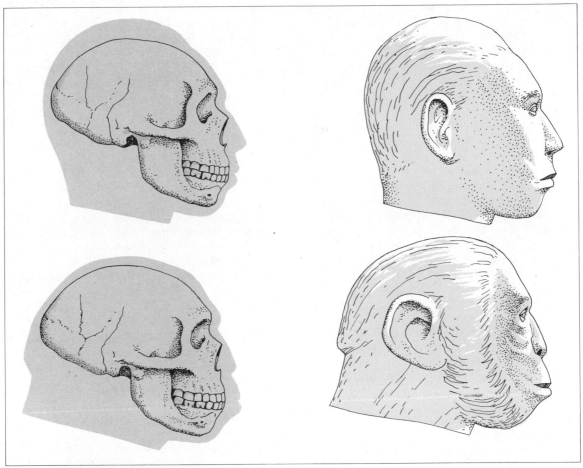

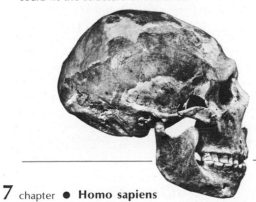

Figure 7-6a,b. *Reconstructions based on skulls, such as this classic Neanderthal, always involve guesswork. The sketch shows two ways that the fleshy parts of the face could fit the structure of this skull.*

dle East, Java, Africa and Eastern Europe, may have been due to the more temperate, less demanding climate presented by his environment.

Solo and Rhodesian man

A number of interesting fossils have been found in Java and Africa, belonging to individuals who show features common to *Homo erectus*, Neanderthal man, and modern man. For example, in Central Java, at Trinil, near Solo River, in the same area where earlier Java man was found, eleven fossil skulls with incomplete faces and teeth were unearthed in 1931. The extremely thick skulls are remarkable in that they reveal similarities to *Homo erectus* as well as to Neanderthal man. They show an average brain capacity of 1100 ccs. A number of artifacts, including fine antler and bone implements as well as crude stone tools, were also found. The advanced state of the artifacts, the large cranial volumes of the skulls, and the geologic context in which they were found indicate Solo man probably lived just before the Upper Paleolithic.

Solo man is nowadays recognized as a Neanderthaloid; his singular features are probably the result of the retention of some characteristics from earlier populations. In the face of genetic continuity, it is not unusual to find types who do not fit into any rigid category. Gene flow between local populations of the genus *Homo* probably gave rise to many distinct types.

In 1921, in the Broken Hill region of Rhodesia, South Africa, were found an almost complete skull, some postcranial bones, and the parietal and maxilla of another individual. Called Rhodesian man, this specimen shows a combination of Neanderthal and modern traits. For example, the skull possessed a cranial capacity of 1280 ccs, massive brow ridges, a prognathous (protruding) upper jaw with teeth similar to ours, and a primitive, unusually broad palate. Like Solo man, Rhodesian man probably represents a local population; in this case, his distinct features are those of an African Neanderthal. Just as modern Africans tend to look different from Europeans, so Rhodesian man looked different from Solo man and the European Neanderthals.

The enigma of the classic Neanderthal

Next to *Homo sapiens sapiens* or modern man, the Neanderthal is the best known fossil form of man. More bones have accumulated and more words have been written about Neanderthal than about any other fossil man. He lived in small bands or single family units in the open, and in caves when the weather was particularly bitter. He undoubtedly communicated by means of speech, used fire, and made tools of stone, ivory, and bone. He ate the meat that he successfully hunted, being particularly fond of the flesh of the cave bear. The eight-foot tall beast, in addition to being part of the Neanderthal diet, was also central to his spiritual life.

The Neanderthals were an advanced, fully sapient species of human being, relatively successful in eking an existence out of their impossibly cold and hostile environment. It has often been suggested that if one of these types were to be shaved, dressed in a business suit, and seated in a bus, he would differ little in appearance from his fellow passengers and would probably attract little attention. However, in any jostling match or scramble for seats, his powerful physique would give him a decided advantage over his more slightly built fellow humans. The Classic Neanderthal's hunting and living grounds were taken over by the more advanced and better adapted Cro-Magnon types, from whom it is believed modern Europeans developed.

The fate of the Neanderthals

What happened to the Classic Neanderthal? Why did such an apparently well-adapted form disappear so suddenly? No one really knows the true fate of Neanderthal man, but several interesting theories have been proposed. The first of these may be called the "environmental isolation" theory. About 40,000 years B.C., a number of climatic changes took place in Europe: the glaciers retreated, and the climate became warmer and drier. As a result, the small band/single family units of Neanderthals, who were physically and culturally overspecialized and overadapted to their bleak glacial surroundings, could not adapt to their new, warmer environment. Their world changed and they could not change with it. In addition, they were isolated by the glaciers and, unable to exchange genes with other *Homo sapiens* groups, became extinct. As F. Clark Howell notes,

> Broad areas of Europe and Asia were unfitted for human habitation. Regions such as Western and Southern Europe which were temperate during interglacial periods became, during the glacial advance, peripheral areas where, though climatic condition may not have been too congenial, there was loss of contact with other human groups because of the surrounding barriers.[1]

This theory implies that modern man is probably descended from the more successful generalized type of Neanderthal who immigrated to Europe from the Near East when the climate changed. Having lived in the temperate Near Eastern area, the general form successfully adapted to the new environment with little or no trouble. It has also been suggested that perhaps the Pre-Neanderthalers or other primitive sapiens types were the men from whom we evolved. However, no fossil evidence exists to support this last theory.

A second theory holds that since Neanderthal man was so widely dispersed over Europe, it was impossible that he should have disappeared from every place he lived. Instead, this theory holds, he interbred with the modern Cro-Magnon types from whom modern Europeans eventually evolved. For example, some anthropologists, notably Ashley Montagu, point out that some faint ancestral Neanderthal characteristics may be seen in today's Middle Eastern and European populations with their relatively prominent brow ridges, deep eye sockets, receding foreheads and chins.[2] But like all theories, it has its weak points. Howell notes, for example,

> The lack of Classic Neanderthal characteristics in Upper Paleolithic invaders make hybridization doubtful as does the fact that remains of

the two people living together have never been found. On the other hand, Mousterian artifacts still occur in some places during early blade-tool (Cro-Magnon) times, and thus "Classic Neanderthal" persistence in certain isolated refuge areas remains a distinct possibility.[3]

A third theory, advanced by Loring Brace and others, is that there was no difference between Classic and the generalized Neanderthal and that both are in the ancestry of modern man. Brace holds that the Upper Paleolithic people of Europe developed locally from Neanderthal predecessors. He believes that during the 35,000 years the Neanderthalers lived in Europe, they produced some 1200 generations. This amount of time and number of individuals were adequate for selection pressures to transform Neanderthal man into Cro-Magnon man. These pressures were essentially cultural and related to manipulatory behavior (knife wielding) in conjunction with feeding (meat eating) habits.[4]

Even today, though the theories fly and investigators dispute and disagree, it is generally admitted that the true circumstances that led to the demise of Neanderthal man will probably never be known.

Cro-Magnons: the first modern men

About 35,000 to 40,000 years ago, during the temperate period following the end of the Wurm glacial, an important change took place in Western and Southern Europe: the Neanderthal race was replaced by an Upper Paleolithic people who possessed a body structure, brain, and physical appearance similar to ours. The remains of Cro-Magnon man were first discovered in 1868 at Les Eyzies in France in a rock shelter called Cro-Magnon. Between 1872 and 1902, the fossils of

[1] F. Clark Howell, "Pleistocene Glacial Ecology and the Evolution of Classic Neanderthal Man" *Southwest Journal of Anthropology*, Vol. 8, No. 4 (1952) p. 401.

[2] Ashley Montagu, *Man: His First Two Million Years* (New York, Columbia University Press, 1969).

[3] F. Clark Howell, *ibid.* p. 404.

[4] Loring C. Brace, "The Fate of the 'Classic' Neanderthals: A Consideration of Hominid Catastrophism" *Current Anthropology* (February, 1964).

thirteen other specimens were unearthed in the caves of the Cote d'Azur near the Italian Riviera. A headless skeleton discovered in Wales has also been placed in the Cro-Magnon family.

Cro-Magnon man has suffered his share of idealization on the part of physical anthropologists; at one time he was made to look like the handsome man next door every girl wants to marry, in contrast to his Neanderthal relative, who stood just a step ahead from the ape. The fact is that the more Cro-Magnon remains that have been found, the more physical variability he has shown, as is to be expected from any human population. Therefore, it is hardly surprising to find specimens that show distinct features. In some ways, such as in the size of his brain, in the narrow nasal openings, and in the high, broad forehead, they resembled modern Europeans. But their faces, for example, were shorter and broader than those of

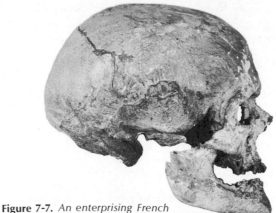

Figure 7-7. *An enterprising French businessman has built a hotel on the site of the excavation in which the first Cro-Magnon man was found. The open door of the garage leads directly to the excavation; the back wall of the hotel is the limestone cliff that sheltered early hotel-less man.*

The evolution of man ● part **2**

Figure 7-8. *To the casual eye, the skull of the Cro-Magnon man at the top left looks very like that of modern man. The artist's reconstruction of Cro-Magnon man is readily recognizable as fully human. At this point in human evolution, culture has become a more potent factor than biology; this leads to greater variation in physical characteristics.*

modern Europeans, and their brow ridges were more prominent.

Generally speaking, Upper Paleolithic man evolved a modern-looking face; the full-sized brain had already been achieved by the Neanderthals. Increased tool use among evolving *Homo sapiens* probably led to an increase in brain complexity, which in turn led to the development of more complex tool kits. The modernization of Cro-Magnon's face is the result of a reduction in the size of the teeth, and eventually of the jaw, due to the fact that specialized tools increasingly took over the cutting and softening functions once performed by the teeth. The cooking of food (as in the case of *Homo erectus*) also favored a reduction in size of the muscles involved in chewing; consequently, the bones to which these muscles were attached became finer and smaller.

Where did Cro-Magnon man come from?

The genesis and spread of Cro-Magnon man is one of the biggest mysteries of paleoanthropology. One hypothesis, which may be conveniently called the "migration theory," holds that modern man, typified by the hybrid or transitional Neanderthal specimens found at Mt. Carmel and Skuhl, developed in the Near East, migrated to Europe, and replaced the Neanderthals. With them, these modern Cro-Magnons brought a highly developed brain, more advanced tool kits, and a more complex social organization. For example, the Cro-Magnons had mastered the art of shaping flints into blades for tools and weapons, developed new and more specialized tools, lived in large, cooperative bands of several families, and were the creators of the cavepaintings found throughout Europe.

Some anthropologists find it doubtful that Upper Paleolithic man would undertake such long migrations and cite as an example that of modern hunters and gatherers, people who lead an existence similar to that of the ancient sapiens. Other anthropologists agree that Cro-Magnon replaced Neanderthal man in Europe, but doubt that he immigrated from the Near East. Instead, they propose the "theory of parallel evolution," which holds that Cro-Magnon man developed in Europe at the same time and in the same way he was developing in the Near East. In other words, the proponents of this theory agree that the Neanderthal-modern man transition took place in the Near East, but not only in the Near East. They say the origin of modern man occurred independently in many parts of the world.

While the migration theory, which emphasizes what J. E. Pfeiffer calls a "Garden of Eden" or single region of human development, tends to oversimplify a complex situation, the parallel evolution theory, it is held, depends too much on coincidence. However, many modern anthropologists, on the strength of the fossil evidence, lean toward the theory that modern man arose and developed in the Near East some 50,000 years ago, then migrated to Europe about 35,000 years ago, replacing the Neanderthalers by interbreeding with them.

A middle-ground theory holds possible that man was evolving in the same direction in all areas in response to similar selective pressures, aided by at least a minimal exchange of genes between populations, so that the genus *Homo* never fragmented into separate species.

□

WHAT WAS OUR HISTORY?

The earliest written records hardly go back six thousand years, many human groups lacking written history even today. This leaves at least two million years of human prehistory to be painfully reconstructed on the basis of those human bones, tools, and other materials which have somehow survived the ravages of time. Partly on the basis of the fossil record and partly because it could have been no other way, the earliest proto-humans must have resembled in most respects the various other primate species that exist today. Presumably, proto-humans existed in small groups vaguely resembling existing troops of baboons, chimpanzees, or gorillas.

If, in fact, human evolution was triggered by the replacement of forests by grasslands, we can imagine groups of proto-humans dispersed over the savannah regions of Africa, Southern Europe, and South Asia. Each of these groups would have constituted a breeding population, sometimes mating with members of other groups, but for the most part mating and exchanging genes within the troop. Due to chance, and the success of some individuals in producing comparatively large numbers of offspring, there is a tendency for such small groups to diverge genetically. A human or proto-human who produces ten offspring who live to produce offspring of their own will have a far greater genetic impact than will an individual who produces no offspring or only one or two. The different groups of proto-humans must, then, have had a tendency to concentrate different genes from the pool of genes available to the species as a whole.

Some of the groups of proto-humans would have occupied environments that were relatively favorable; others would have had greater difficulty in surviving. Where survival is difficult, only the lucky or gifted few survive to produce offspring. Those who survive tend to be those who possess genes which equip them to survive. In groups under stress, the rate of selection is increased and evolution proceeds comparatively rapidly. If the rate of selection is too high, the group perishes. Certain groups of proto-humans presumably evolved more rapidly than others. Because the individuals in these groups were, at least, proto-humans, their adaptation to stress must have involved simultaneous change in both genetic and cultural messages. Proto-humans may have adapted biologically or through the invention of new forms of behavior to be transmitted within the group by learning. Because a useful invention has the effect of changing the odds of survival and because genetic change in the human direction would tend to increase the ability to invent things, genetic and cultural evolution must have taken place together.

Evolution, whether genetic or cultural, often increases rates of survival and reproduction, thus leading to population increase, that is, more children survive to become adults and to produce children. A new capacity, whether it is a better brain or a sharper rock, now spreads through two mechanisms. First, the more numerous group may begin to replace less numerous groups. Second, the new trait will begin to spread from group to group as a result of intergroup mating if it is a genetic trait and as a result of imitation if it is an invented trait. Because human beings who carry sharp stones are presumably better adapted than human beings who carry dull stones, it is likely that they will be more successful

in obtaining mates and bearing offspring. An invented trait diffusing from group to group is likely to have the effect of increasing the rate of genetic mixing between neighboring human populations. Once a new genetic or invented trait has diffused or spread over the environment within which it is advantageous, the different human or proto-human populations will again begin to diverge as a result of isolation.

The course of human prehistory suggests that periods of rapid genetic and cultural evolution led repeatedly to a kind of genetic homogenization of the species so that it is unlikely that proto-humans or humans ever developed into separate species. In particular, the different breeding populations never or rarely became so different as to preclude interbreeding. Alternatively, if separate species did develop, and there is little evidence one way or another, successive genetic or cultural revolutions appear to have driven the less progressive or less human species into extinction. Although the notion of more human creatures hunting down and exterminating less human creatures has a certain genocidal appeal, the most probable and most frequent case would appear to have been the overwhelming of the less progressive groups through interbreeding. The more human creatures got the girls or the boys, as the case may have been, and, even more important, produced the larger number of viable offspring. Love is a more important means of genocide than war.

Although biological and cultural evolution must inevitably take place together, the two types of evolution differ in important ways. Minor biological changes can take place quickly as human populations merge and diverge, but major biological changes such as might be involved in the formation of a new species appear to require many generations for their fulfillment. Recognizably manlike apes appeared some three to five million years ago. *Homo erectus,* the first indisputably human form, arose at least 750,000 years ago. The first forms of *Homo sapiens,* including *Homo sapiens neanderthalensis,* appeared between 100,000 and 300,000 years ago, and *Homo sapiens sapiens,* our own form of man, developed about 35,000 years ago and appeared in all parts of the world some 10,000 to 20,000 years ago. The major stages in the development of the genus *Homo* required at least three million years. If we assume five human generations in each period of one hundred years, ten thousand years only provides time for five hundred generations. Because five hundred or even one thousand generations do not provide much time for alteration of the genetic message, we would not expect great biological change since *Homo sapiens* first spread across the world. All varieties of modern man are pretty much the same from a biological standpoint.

Source:
From *Culture in Process,* Second Edition, by Alan R. Beals, George Spindler and Louise Spindler. Copyright © 1967, 1973 by Holt, Rinehart and Winston, Inc. Reprinted by permission of Holt, Rinehart and Winston, Inc.

Summary

1.

The first European *Homo sapiens* appeared during the Third Interglacial Period of the Pleistocene Epoch. This age was characterized by marked climatic changes. The most outstanding feature of the early sapiens was his large brain. From the fossil evidence, consisting mostly of skulls, it is apparent that these early men on the whole looked more like ourselves than like their predecessors *Homo erectus*. Finds at Steinheim (Germany), Swanscombe (England), and Fontechevade (France), indicate that there was great physical variation in the populations of early man.

2.

Neanderthal man first appeared in Europe during a very cold period. This type of Neanderthal, known as Classic, shows a physical adaptation to life in a cold climate; his body is rather short and compact, somewhat resembling that of modern Eskimos. Another type of Neanderthal, known as General, lived in the Near East. He was rather smaller than the Classic types and more slender. It is probable that both types of Neanderthals interbred, for there are remains that show characteristics of both. Solo and Rhodesian man are nowadays considered local forms of Neanderthal.

3.

Several theories have been proposed to account for the disappearance of Neanderthal man. One, the "environmental isolation" theory, accounts the disappearance of the Neanderthals to their inability to adapt to a changing, warmer climate. Another theory holds that Neanderthal interbred with Cro-Magnon man, eventually becoming modern man. A third theory, advanced by Loring Brace and others, postulates that Classic and General Neanderthal were one and the same, ultimately evolving into modern man. The foregoing is purely speculative, and the fate of the Neanderthals remains a mystery.

4.

Cro-Magnon man represents our nearest predecessor. In most ways he was modern looking. The humanization of Cro-Magnon's face is the result of a reduction in the size of the teeth and the muscles involved in chewing as a consequence of the fact that he cooked most of his food. The origins of Cro-Magnon remain a mystery. Several theories have been proposed to account for the appearance of such an advanced form of *Homo sapiens*. It is reasonable to assume that hominid populations were evolving in the same direction in all areas in response to similar selective pressures, aided by some interbreeding, so that the unity of the genus *Homo* was maintained throughout the Upper Pleistocene.

Suggested readings

Constable, George, and the Editors of Life *The Neanderthals*. New York: Time-Life, 1973. Many misinterpretations of fossil remains of Neanderthal man have been made since their discovery in 1856. This part of the Time-Life Emergence of Man Series analyzes the old views in light of new evidence and discoveries. The tools, behavior, and ultimate evolution of the Neanderthal man into Cro-Magnon man is described.

Coon, Carleton S. *The Origin of Races*. New York: Alfred A. Knopf, 1963. This is a thoroughly researched, detailed history of the evolution of the races of mankind. Some of the conclusions are debatable, but the amount of information included in the book will be illuminating to the student of early man.

Howell, F. Clark, and the Editors of Life *Early Man*. New York: Time-Life, 1965. This is a magnificently illustrated survey of early man's culture and physical development. An appendix contains an annotated list of the major human fossil sites of the Old World.

Washburn, Sherwood L., and Phyllis C. Jay *Perspectives in Human Evolution—One*. New York: Holt, Rinehart and Winston, 1968. This volume is a collection of both published articles and original contributions, which includes statements on the fossil record, on behavior of man and other primates, and on psychology and development of personality.

Washburn, Sherwood L., and Phyllis C. Jay *Perspectives in Human Evolution—Two*. New York: Holt, Rinehart and Winston, 1972. This second volume of the Perspective Series includes among other selections: a summary of human evolutionary studies through 1970, three papers on the origin of language, two major review essays on primate behavior, as well as other articles on the evolution of the wrist, human skill, hyenas, and wild animals as a source of food.

Human
diversity

"What a piece of work is man," said Hamlet. "How noble in reason, how infinite in faculties, in form and moving how express and admirable, in action how like an angel, in apprehension how like a god: the beauty of the world, the paragon of animals! And yet to me what is this quintessence of dust?"

What man is to man is the province of anthropology: biology reveals what we are; anthropology reveals what we think we are. The modern anthropologist Claude Lévi-Strauss systematically describes mankind's cultures in terms of its rituals and myths. Our dreams of ourselves are as varied as our languages and our physical bodies. We are the same, but we differ. We speak English or French, our hair is curly or straight, our skin is black or white. On line in school we have size places, from tall to short, in a continuum of height. Human genetic variation is also distributed in such a continuum, with varying clusters of frequency. The significance we give our variations, the way we perceive them—in fact, whether or not we perceive them at all—is determined by our culture. For example, in many Polynesian countries, where skin color is not a determinant of social status, people really do not notice this physical characteristic; in South Africa, it is the first thing people do notice.

Variation and evolution

Many behavioral attributes—reading, for instance—are learned or acquired by living within a culture; other characteristics, such as blue eyes, are passed on physically by heredity. Environment affects both. A person growing up surrounded by books learns to read. If the culture insists that brown-eyed people watch TV and blue-eyed people read, the brown-eyed people may end up making videotapes while the blue-eyed people are writing books. These skills or tastes are acquired characteristics. Cultural changes, a surplus of drugs, steak, cornflakes, or even insufficient sleep could make a population distinct in learned behavioral characteristics, within relatively few generations.

Physical variability

Inherited physical variations are also affected by environment, but the process takes many more centuries. Man, like all living things, has adapted to environmental changes through the evolutionary process of natural selection. It seems that our species has maintained itself largely through cul-

8 chapter ● **Human diversity**

149

tural adaptations (the cooking of food and raising of crops, for instance) rather than physical changes. Moreover, there has been a constant gene flow among various human populations. Men have remained largely unspecialized animals, and the species never became extinct.

The physical characteristics of both populations and individuals are determined by genes. For any given characteristic, there are within the gene pool of *Homo sapiens* various alternative genes. In the color of an eye, the shape of a hand, the texture of skin, many variations can occur. This variability within and among individuals, found in many animal species, signifies a rich potential of new combinations of characteristics in future generations. Such a species is called **polymorphic.** Our blood types, determined by the alleles for A, B, and O blood, are an example of a polymorphic trait, a trait that may appear in any of several distinct forms. A polymorphic species faced with changing environmental conditions has within its gene pool the possibility of producing individuals with traits appropriate to its altered life. Many will die, but those whose physical characteristics enable them to survive in the new environment will reproduce, so that their genes will show up more frequently in subsequent generations. Thus mankind, being polymorphic, has been able to occupy a variety of environments.

A number of cultural and physical isolation mechanisms have served to divide the human species into geographically dispersed populations with distinct adaptive physical characteristics. An example of a cultural isolation mechanism can be seen in the nomadic life style of Paleolithic man. Features of their hunting method of subsistence included great mobility and the formation of very small (25 to 50 people) social groups. Such a way of life inevitably served to isolate local populations that would then begin to differ from one another in gene frequency. The smaller and more isolate the breeding population, the fewer its genetic variables and the more stable the combination of particular gene frequencies. Mankind is a species not only polymorphic, but **polytypic** as

well. Polytypic traits are those for which definite subspecific variations have been established. For example, a polytypic trait can be seen in the Old World distribution of skin pigment, ranging from a high frequency of genes for dark skin in the tropics to a high frequency of genes for light skin in the north. In blood type, man is polymorphic, with several distinct groups (A, B, O or AB). He is polytypic in the distribution of these types; blood group O is most frequently found among American Indian populations, group A in Western Europe, and B among Asian populations.

Adaptive advantages

The nineteenth century biologist Thomas Huxley, who once diagrammed a geographic division between populations he described as pigmented and pale, questioned whether the establishment of polytypes of skin color might indicate an accompanying trend toward specialization in the species. Huxley pointed out that the hominids' great evolutionary advantage has been their generalization; unlike many other animals, such as the mastodon or the carnivorous dinosaurs, man has not developed highly specialized adaptations to any particular climate or ecological niche. Specialization is advantageous so long as the physical and biological environment remains the same, but it is a disadvantage in periods of change—and there have been many of those in the history of the world. *Homo sapiens* maintained its genetic variability by gene flow, by random mutations, and by genetic drift. Populations combined time and again, and the resultant variability maintained man's adaptive potential. Huxley feared that in a species whose "specialty" had always been generalization the establishment of polytypes might be an ominous sign, the first step toward genuine specialization.

Huxley's questions were based on the common assumption of the nineteenth century that mankind could be divided into a number of clearly defined races. This assumption went unchallenged throughout Huxley's lifetime, but twentieth century anthropologists began to wonder whether or not the lines between different populations were really so deeply drawn. What are the "races" of mankind?

The meaning of race

Humans vary greatly in appearance and behavior, yet they recognize each other as belonging to the same group instantly. Any fertile human male can mate with any fertile human female and produce offspring. A constant gene exchange takes place, which both maintains the species' essential form and determines the range of differences within that form.

Racial classification

Early anthropologists tried to explore and define man's differences by systematically classifying *Homo sapiens* into subspecies or races. Early anthropologists emphasized classifications based on geographic location and phenotypic features such as skin color, body size, head shape, and hair texture in their racial classifications. Such classifications were continually being challenged by the presence of individuals who did not fit the categories, such as light-skinned Africans; it was assumed that these individuals were hybrids or racial mixtures. Generalized references to human types such as "Asiatic" or "Mongoloid," "European" or "Caucasoid," and "African" or "Negroid" were at best mere statistical abstractions about populations tending to have in common certain physical features; no examples of "pure" racial types could be found. These categories turned out to be neither definitive nor particularly helpful. The visible traits were found to occur not in abrupt shifts from population to population, but in a continuum that changed gradually, with few sharp breaks, from Africa to Norway. There were many variations within each group; the in-group variation was often greater than the variations between groups. In Africa, a light-skinned Kalahari Bushman might more closely resemble a person of Indian extraction than the black Nilotic Sudanese who was presumably of the same race.

The Negroid was characterized as having dark skin, thick lips, a broad nose, and kinky hair; the Mongoloid, straight hair, a flat face, a flat nose and spread nostrils; and the Caucasoid, pale skin, a narrow nose, and varied eye color and hair form. The classification then expanded to take in American Indians, Australians, and Polynesians, but even the expanded system failed to account for dramatic differences in appearance between individuals in each racial category; for example, Europeans, Arabs, and Hindus were called Caucasian.

In an attempt to encompass such variations, the schemes of racial classification multiplied. In 1926, J. Deniker classified 29 races according to texture of hair, presumably improving upon Roland R. Dixon's 1923 classification based on 3 indices of body measures. Hair texture and body build were the characteristics used for another set of racial categories proposed in 1930, and by 1947 Earnest Hooton had proposed 3 new composite races resulting from the interbreeding of "primary" races. In 1950, Carleton Coon, Stanley Garn, and Joseph Birdsell arranged races according to "functional" characteristics. Despite these classificatory attempts on the part of Western anthropologists, no definitive grouping of distinct, discontinuous biological groups was found in modern man. Definition and analysis of man's visible variations remains elusive.

Some physical variables

For a long time, physical anthropology relied heavily upon the description of visible physical characteristics of populations. Eye and skin color, hair texture, stature, girth were all carefully measured and described. The emphasis was on the differences between human beings, not on their similarities. The conclusions drawn from such data tended to be as superficial as the characteristics described themselves. Anthropological

Figure 8-1. *The faces of these children from various parts of Africa show the wide range of physical characteristics that may be found within a single racial category.*

inquiry literally went only skin deep. Physical characteristics were indiscriminately associated with cultural ones, and vice-versa, so that measurement of physical characteristics—known as anthropometry—became a discredited branch of anthropology. Certain physical "types" were believed to be related to criminal behavior, for example. Today, such anthropometrical data are interpreted in the light of other, equally relevant biological data. It is a medical fact, for example, that persons with a certain constitution are prone to coronary heart disease. Persons of different physiques do choose different occupations; there is a "bookish" type and an "outdoors" type. One does not expect a weakling to become a physical education instructor. But the relationship should not be stretched too far, because the mechanisms involved are not known, and it is suspected that many might be culturally rather than biologically determined.

Certain body types may represent an adaption to different environments. Anthropologists have observed that certain body types occur with more frequency in some parts of the world than in others. For example, there is a pronounced difference between the Eskimo body—squat, short, and compact—and that of the Sudanese Negro, whose body tends to be long, like a "beanstalk." Many anthropologists believe that the body differences represent a climatic adaptation; certain body shapes are better suited to certain living conditions than others. A person whose body is on the heavy side may suffer more from the heat of August than someone whose body is thin and light. This is due to the fact that a compact body tends to conserve more heat than a lighter one, since it has a lower surface-to-volume ratio. Thus, under arctic conditions, the Eskimo body will conserve more heat; likewise, the Negro living in hot, open country will benefit from a body that can disperse heat quickly and keep him cool. Anthropologists have also studied such body features as nose and eye shape and hair textures in relation to climate. A wide flaring nose, for example, is common in Negroids; they come from hot, damp environments in which the humidifying function

153

of the nose is secondary. Narrow noses, typical of cold-climate dwellers, are helpful in humidifying and warming cold air before it reaches the lungs. Coon, Garn, and Birdsell have proposed that the Mongoloid face exhibits features adapted to life in very cold environments. The epicanthic eye fold, a reduction of the brow-ridges, and a heavy deposition of fat around the eyes and cheeks may help to insulate the face against exposure to the cold.

Skin color. Race is most commonly associated with skin color. Perhaps this is inevitable, since skin color is such an obvious physical trait. Skin color is subject to great variation and is produced mainly by two factors: distribution of blood vessels and amount of melanin found in a given area of skin. Exposure to sunlight increases the amount of melanin in the skin; hence, the skin darkens. Some scientists believe that melanin acts to protect the skin against damaging ultraviolet solar radiation. Since the highest concentration of dark-skinned people tends to be found in the tropical regions of the world, it is thought that natural selection favors pigmented skin as a protection against the strong solar radiation of equatorial latitudes. Similarly, people living in northern latitudes tend to have lightly pigmented skins; this lack of pigmentation may be advantageous, for it enables weak ultraviolet radiation to penetrate the skin and stimulate formation of Vitamin D.

The inheritance of skin color is not well understood; but its geographical distribution, with few exceptions, tends to be continuous, like that of other human physical traits. Selective mating plays a part of influencing skin color distribution. For example, the higher the Hindu caste, the lighter its skin color will be. This skin color gradient is maintained by strict in-group marriage rules. Statistical studies have shown that there has been a similar tendency among American blacks with those of higher status choosing to marry lighter skinned males reflecting the culture's emphasis on light skin as a status symbol. It is quite

Figure 8-2. *The epicanthic eye fold characteristic of Orientals is seen in the Japanese (above), the Malays (below) and people from all parts of Asia.*

155

possible that the recent black pride movement, that places positive value on Negroid features, such as dark skins, coarse kinky hair, and broad flat noses, will lead to a reversal of this cultural selection factor.

Social significance of race

Scientific facts do not seem to change what people think about race. Racism can be viewed solely as a social problem, although at times it has been made a tool of "science." It is an emotional phenomenon best explained in terms of collective psychology. Racial conflict results from long-suppressed resentments and hostilities. The racist responds to social stereotypes, not to known scientific facts.

Racism is a social problem encountered in every society, especially in those having different racial or ethnic groups. In the Republic of South Africa, for example, "race" is defined by law; blacks live under a white police state that enforces *apartheid,* a policy of segregation and discrimination against non-European groups.

Race and behavior

The assumption that there are behavioral differences among the races of mankind remains an issue of contemporary society, not easily argued away. Throughout history, certain "races" have been attributed certain characteristics; these characteristics assume a variety of names: "national character," "spirit," "temperament," all of them vague and standing for a number of concepts totally unrelated to the biological concept of race. A common myth involves the "coldness" of the Scandinavians or the "martial" character of the Germanics or the "indolent" nature of blacks. These generalizations serve to characterize a people unjustly; not every German citizen is an advocate of genocide and not every black hates to

work. The term race has a precise biological meaning, but in the hands of the layman, the term often acquires a meaning unrelated to that given by scientists, often with unfortunate results. "Race" has been a powerful tool of politicians to justify the oppression of unwanted minorities. To date, no innate behavioral characteristic can be attributed to any group of people—what the layman would most probably term a "race"—that cannot be explained in terms of enculturation. If the Chinese happen to be especially successful mathematicians, it can probably be explained in terms of their language, pictographic and somewhat similar to ciphers in its symbolic meaning. If the American blacks on the whole have not been as successful as their fellow citizens, it is because they have been an oppressed minority lacking in opportunities. The list could go on, and all such differences or characteristics could be explained in terms of culture.

Similarly, high crime rates among certain groups can be explained in reference to culture and not biology. Individuals alienated and demoralized by poverty, injustice, and inequality of opportunity tend to display antisocial behavior more frequently than those culturally well-integrated. For example, the American Indians who have managed to compete on equal footing with other Americans have not suffered from the high rate of alcoholism and criminal behavior exhibited by Indians living under conditions of poverty in and out of reservations.

Race and intelligence

A question frequently asked is whether or not some races are inherently more intelligent than others. Intelligence tests carried on by white investigators among whites and American blacks have usually shown that whites attain higher scores. During World War I, a series of tests, known as Alpha and Beta I.Q. tests, were regularly given to draftees. The results showed that whites attained higher scores than blacks. For many people, this was proof of the white man's intellectual

ADDITION

RICKY HAS 4 DOGS AND LINDA HAS 2 DOGS.
HOW MANY DOGS DO THEY HAVE TOGETHER?

Figure 8-3. *The education television program Sesame Street, supported by public funds, was the subject of a study of its effectiveness in teaching black and white children to read and write. Some of the results are shown here.*

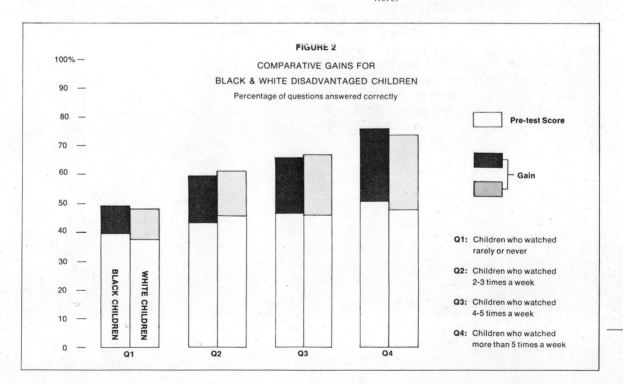

FIGURE 2

COMPARATIVE GAINS FOR
BLACK & WHITE DISADVANTAGED CHILDREN

Percentage of questions answered correctly

Pre-test Score

Gain

Q1: Children who watched rarely or never

Q2: Children who watched 2-3 times a week

Q3: Children who watched 4-5 times a week

Q4: Children who watched more than 5 times a week

BLACK CHILDREN   WHITE CHILDREN

superiority. But the evidence of the tests only showed that whites could outperform blacks in certain social situations. The tests did not measure "intelligence" per se, but the ability, conditioned by culture, of certain individuals to respond to certain socially conditioned problems. These tests had been conceived by whites for fellow middle-class whites. Persons coming from other backgrounds to meet the challenge of these tests were clearly at a disadvantage. It would be unrealistic to expect individuals from dissimilar backgrounds to respond to a problem in a similar manner.

Many large-scale intelligence tests have since been administered in this country. Notable among these is a series of tests given to a group of blacks and whites both coming from low socioeconomic backgrounds in which the blacks scored higher. It is possible that the blacks in this case came from a less deprived background than the whites. In another series of tests, this time involving literate whites from the Southern states and Northern literate blacks, blacks scored higher.

Intelligence tests however, have increasingly become the subject of controversy. There are many psychologists as well as anthropologists who believe that their use is somewhat outdated. They claim that intelligence tests are of limited use, since they are applicable only to particular cultural circumstances. Only when these circumstances are carefully met, they say, can any meaningful generalizations be derived from the use of tests.

Notwithstanding the foregoing evidence, there remains the question of whether or not there are any significant intellectual differences among races. On a purely theoretical basis, it could be assumed that just as we see a spectrum of inherited racial variations—skin color, hair texture, height—there could be a similar variation in the innate intellectual potential of different populations. It is possible that just as there are genes affecting the development of blue eyes, kinky hair, or yellow skin, there could be others affecting the development of intelligence. One person who supports that view is the American psychologist Arthur Jensen. Basing his conclusions on statistical data from tests given to American blacks and whites, Jensen believes that such intellectual differences exist.

At the present, it is impossible to separate the inherited components of intelligence from those culturally acquired. It is known, however, that human beings will develop their innate abilities and skills to the fullest only if given the opportunity. Naturally, individual differences will always exist, because no two persons are alike. But to base one's conclusions of alleged intellectual differences on unmeasurable absolutes is bound to be misleading.

HUMAN POPULATIONS AND THEIR GENETIC DIVERSITY

It is regrettable that, with the vital need for reliable information about the biological bases of differences among human populations, there is no substantive agreement among anthropologists as to even an elementary definition of the word race. No concept in physical anthropology has been the focus of more heated controversy than that of race. The record of the use of the term itself would almost constitute an intellectual history of anthropology.

Although the traditional approach that retains the concept of racial "types" is maintained by few American or Western European anthropologists, there are several other respectable positions on race.

The most widely accepted concept of race is illustrated by the population approach of Theodosius Dobzhansky, who, as a population geneticist, is interested in problems of human evolution. He sees race as an array of populations with similar distributions of hereditary characteristics, differing from other similar arrays of populations within the species. This definition is based on the acceptance of the Mendelian population as the basic unit of evolutionary change. Hence a race is viewed as a collection of populations characterized not by the absolute presence or absence of some hereditary traits but by the relative incidence of certain hereditary traits.

This definition is flexible as to where the lines that separate the races are to be drawn. One could easily distinguish the extremes—populations with profoundly different distributions of traits like blond hair or very dark skin or heavy brow ridges—but the boundaries between races are much more tenuous. From this genetic point view, they are not "real" boundaries, since populations are distributed continuously in all geographic areas, and a certain amount of gene flow between neighboring populations is assumed to occur. Stanley Garn, who has written extensively on race and has proposed several racial taxonomies, shares this point of view.

Another, more limited, opinion as to what constitutes race is that held by the serologist, William Boyd. Using a similar definition, he has restricted his classification of races to blood-group frequency. Using the distribution of the frequencies for the genes that determine the A-B-O-AB blood groups, Rh-factor compatibility, and M-N-MN blood groups, he has proposed a classification of large clusters of human populations that is in accord with the traditional Caucasoid-Negroid-Mongoloid Australoid-American Indian classification most nonanthropologists assume to be adequate. However, the layman's roughhewn taxonomy is based on "ideal" phenotype differences whereas Boyd's taxonomy rests exclusively, if narrowly, on those few characteristics for which the genetic basis is known and for which population distributions are well documented.

Julian Huxley, the British biologist, has proposed no classification nor constructed any list of races as such. Yet he does defend the reality of human races; he believes that at the close of Pleistocene there were three sharply demarcated stocks (corresponding to Caucasoid, Negroid, and Mongoloid) and that, although population expansion and migration have meanwhile attenuated the differences through hybridization, these three stocks are still discernible in modern populations.

The race concept is not taken for granted by all authorities, however, Ashley

Montagu has suggested that, in view of the kind of thinking the term "race" has engendered—"racist" attitudes about how people should be treated based on their "racial" characteristics—the term should be dropped entirely, and the term "ethnic group" be substituted. For Montagu, ethnic group means a group distinguishable by the possession of biological and cultural characteristics.

Frank Livingstone has gone even further in questioning the validity of the concept of race. Beginning with a view quite different than that of Montagu, he argues that each of the traits that make up the traditional racial "type" are distributed differently, and that the race concept is worthless as a tool in organizing or classifying what we have learned about the differences among human populations, and how these differences have arisen.

The current political atmosphere, coupled with the resurgence of American Black political and social activity, has had effects on the nature of statements concerning race. The political controversy is perhaps more responsible than anthropologists are willing to concede for spirited defenses of the concept that human populations do not differ significantly in their distribution of genes for ability, or at least, that such differences are not scientifically demonstrable.

There is no disputing that there are biological differences among human populations, and there is general agreement that genetic differences among populations are, for the most part, differences in frequency of genes, or, phenotypically, differences in the incidence of observable characteristics. The epicanthic fold of the eye, which in former days was said to be "typical" of the Mongoloid race, can be observed in low incidence among European populations, the Bushmen, and the Hottentot peoples. Its highest incidence is, of course, among East Asian populations. But what distinguishes Asian populations from other arrays of population is not the absolute presence or absence of the epicanthic fold, but rather its observed high frequency among them.

For the most part, the hereditary differences that anthropologists study probably fall into the category of relative frequency of traits that are generally present in most populations, for example, hemoglobins, haptoglobins, blood groups, and peppercorn hair form. Nevertheless, occasionally characteristics are encountered by which populations are capable of being described on an all-or-nothing basis—extremely dark pigmentation, blue eyes and blond hair, presence of lip seam, and others.

Investigation of the differences among human populations follows the lines laid down by commitment to the theory of evolution: the degree to which human populations differ from one another is the degree to which the evolutionary agencies of mutation and recombination, natural selection, gene flow, and the random fluctuation of gene frequencies in small isolated populations operate and interact to differentiate one population from another and to maintain such differences.

For all human populations, however, the major environmental factor in the ecological niche is culture itself—the sum total of patterns of social life, symbolic transaction, and technology, all of which, transmitted from generation to generation, distinguish the human species from all others. The greater part of human evolution has been evolution toward greater adaptive flexibility for cultural life. There is agreement that many of the differences in performance and ability among different population samples are obviously maintained in different cultural contexts. The major point of disagreement is the degree to which cultural differences and hereditary differences are responsible for population differences in behavior.

If the race concept is to have any substantive meaning for anthropologists, it must be couched in terms that are evolutionary, populational, and of course, genetic. A set of static categories fitting a neat taxonomic chart is useless at best and misleadingly dangerous at worst. It is the process of population differentiation that should ultimately be illuminated.

Source:
From *Human Evolution: Readings in Physical Anthropology,* Third Edition, edited by Noel Korn. Copyright © 1959, 1967, 1973 by Holt, Rinehart and Winston, Inc. Reprinted by permission of Holt, Rinehart and Winston, Inc.

Summary

1.

Many behavioral attitudes are culturally learned or acquired. Other characteristics are passed on physically by heredity. Environment affects both. Evolutionary changes occur slowly over long periods of time. Genes determine the physical characteristics of both populations and individuals. *Homo sapiens* and many other animal species are polymorphic. Their gene pools contain various alternative genes. When their environment changes, their gene pool gives them the possibility of the appropriate physical alteration to meet the change.

2.

The smaller and more isolate the breeding population, the fewer its genetic variables. Mankind is a polytypic species as well as a polymorphic one. Man has certain traits which are suited to the environment in which he lives. Men from the same environment exhibit the same traits. Within each trait typical to an environment there are variations.

3.

Man's great evolutionary advantage over other animal species is generalization. Man has not developed highly specialized adaptations to any particular climatic or ecological area. Man maintained his genetic variability by gene flow, random mutations, and genetic drift.

4.

Early anthropologists classified man according to geographic locations and phenotypic features. The presence of atypical individuals continually challenged these racial classifications. No examples of "pure" racial types could be found. The visible traits were found to occur in a worldwide continuum. No definite grouping of distinct, discontinuous biological groups has been found in modern man.

5.

For a long time, physical anthropology relied heavily on the description of visible physical characteristics of populations. Physical characteristics were indiscriminately associated with cultural characteristics. The measurement of physical characteristics—anthropometry—became a discredited branch of anthropology. Today anthropometrical data is interpreted in the light of biological data. It yields valuable information, such as the relationship between body types and climate and constitution and disease.

6.

Race is most commonly associated with skin color. Skin color is produced by two factors: distribution of blood vessels and amount of melanin in a given area of skin. Exposure to sunlight increases the amount of melanin, darkening the skin. Natural selection may act in favor of pigmented skin as a protection against the strong solar radiation of equatorial latitudes. Selective mating, as well as geographical location, plays a part in skin color distribution.

7.
Racism can be viewed solely as a social problem. It is an emotional phenomenon best explained in terms of collective psychology.

8.
Many people assume there are behavioral differences among the races of mankind. The innate behavioral characteristics attributed by these people to race can be explained in terms of enculturation. Most intelligence tests which seem to indicate whites are intellectually superior to blacks are designed by whites for whites from similar backgrounds. Blacks taking such tests are at a disadvantage. It is possible that there are genes affecting the development of intelligence. At the present, it is not possible to separate the inherited components of intelligence from those culturally acquired.

Suggested readings

Brace, C. L. and M. F. Ashley Montagu *Man's Evolution*. New York: Macmillan, 1965.
The data provided by the human evolutionary record is interpreted in terms of contemporary evolutionary theory. The emphasis is on evolutionary changes in human traits and the processes affecting such development. A good introduction for the beginning student.

Coon, Carleton S. *The Origin of Races*. New York: Alfred Knopf, 1962.
This volume traces the development of the Australoid, Mongoloid, Caucasoid, and Negroid races, using evidence from fossil man. The author's argument is that the races of mankind originated and developed separately.

Coon, Carleton S., Stanley M. Garn and Joseph B. Birdsell *Races*. Springfield, Ill.: Charles C. Thomas, 1950.
This short monograph on physical anthropology is intended as an introduction to the study of race formation. Genetic and environmental considerations are related to questions of evolutionary status. A typology of the present races of mankind concludes the work.

Korn, Noel *Human Evolution*. New York: Holt, Rinehart & Winston, 1973.
The study of modern populations is the theme of this book. Microevolutionary developments are examined in detail; an ecological and ethological approach to the study of primate and human evolution is emphasized.

Laughlin, W. S., and R. H. Osborne, eds. *Human Variation and Origins*. San Francisco: W. H. Freeman, 1967.
A collection of twenty-seven readings designed for an introductory course in physical anthropology or human biology. It is a comprehensive, integrated account of the principal aspects of human variation within and between populations. Rather than tracing the lineage of man without reference to the evolutionary processes at work, the editors stress the genetic bases and processes of adaptation. The relationships of these genetic processes with cultural behavior are also stressed, as are the effects of ecology upon the evolutionary direction of a group.

part **3**

The archeological record

Methods
of archeology

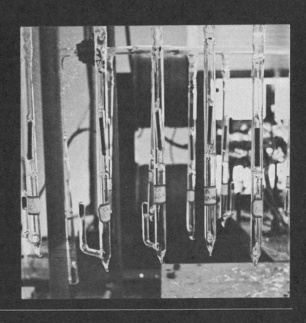

Archeology is the branch of anthropology that studies extinct cultures. Most of us are familiar with one kind of archeological material: the coin dug out of the earth, the fragment of an ancient jar, the bone of a prehistoric man or animal. The finding and cataloging of such objects was at one time the chief concern of archeologists. But the science has changed considerably over the past hundred years.

What was once a pastime of antiquarians is now a meaningful anthropological tool for the study of culture. But, writes the British archeologist and writer Leonard Cottrell:

. . . even today, a surprisingly large number of people still believe that the object of archeology is to dig 'old objects', preferably valuable ones, for collectors. But to the modern scientific excavator, the place where an object was found and the exact position relative to the site and other objects found there may be more important than the thing itself. The excavator is in search of *facts,* and a dated scrap of potsherd found in an ancient mud wall, though worthless in itself, may establish a vital date and cause the rewriting of a whole chapter of history.[1]

A rising interest in such issues has led some archeologists to portray themselves as the practitioners of a "New Archeology," in contrast to archeologists who continue as in the past to be interested mostly in the descriptive aspects of their field. The new archeologists and cultural anthropologists are not content with simply excavating, describing, and arranging in chronological order archeological data. Rather, they want to know such things as how changing subsistence patterns may have influenced forms of social organization in the past or how the development of urban living can change the social organization of a society. They are interested not merely in the scattered remains of a town but in the cultural process through which it developed and changed.

It requires much description and arrangement of raw data before an archeologist can arrive at a plausible reconstruction of the culture he is studying. Only recently has archeology reached a stage where such reconstruction is possible. Computers can process large quantities of data quickly and efficiently; these facts can then be interpreted within the framework of anthropological theory, much as the geologist uses knowl-

[1]Leonard Cottrell, *The Lost Pharaohs* (New York: Grosset & Dunlap, 1963) p. 15.

edge of geologic phenomena observable today to reconstruct earth's history.

The investigation of a buried city is, in the most literal sense, a reconstruction of the past. Fitting together the pieces of data uncovered is rather like trying to work a jigsaw puzzle without knowing what the picture is or how big it is supposed to be. Yet perhaps it is the very difficulty of the challenge that motivates the archeologist; it is, after all, a great feat to make stones speak and tell us of the unrecorded past. The following case study illustrates both the problems and the rewards of the archeologist's work.

Tikal: a case study

The ancient city of Tikal, one of the largest lowland Maya centers in existence, is situated about 200 miles by air from Guatemala City. Tikal was built on a broad limestone terrace in a rain-forest setting. Here the Maya settled in the last millenium B.C., and their civilization flourished until about A.D. 870.

Tikal covered an area of about 123 square kilometers, and its center was the Great Plaza, a large, paved area surrounded by about 300 major structures and thousands of houses. Starting from a small, dispersed population, the population of Tikal swelled to large proportions. By A.D. 550, the density of Tikal was on the order of 600 to 700 persons per square kilometer, six times that of the surrounding region.

Since 1956, Tikal and the surrounding region have been explored under the joint auspices of the University Museum of the University of Pennsylvania and the Guatemalan government. Until 1959, the Tikal Project had excavated only the major temple and palace structures found in the vicinity of the Great Plaza. It became evident, however, that in order to gain a balanced view of Tikal's development and population growth, considerable attention would have to be devoted to hundreds of small mounds, thought to be the remains of dwellings, which surround the larger

Figure 9-1a,b. *The photo is of one of the five pyramid temples standing in the center of Tikal. The structure is over 100 feet high; it was built by encasing a heap of rubble in limestone blocks held together with mortar. The temple, about 1300 years old, was built above the tomb of an important ruler. The small chamber at the top of the steps was used for religious ceremonies; it would hold only a few people at a time.*

This temple can be located on the archeological map of Tikal, just in front of the palace reservoir. Each square of the grid is one-ninth of a kilometer on all sides; this map represents only a small portion of the total site, which extends for more than 123 square kilometers. The environment of the area has changed little in the past 2000 years. It is heavily forested; the substratum is of limestone with deposits of flint. The roots of the large trees have destroyed many of the larger buildings.

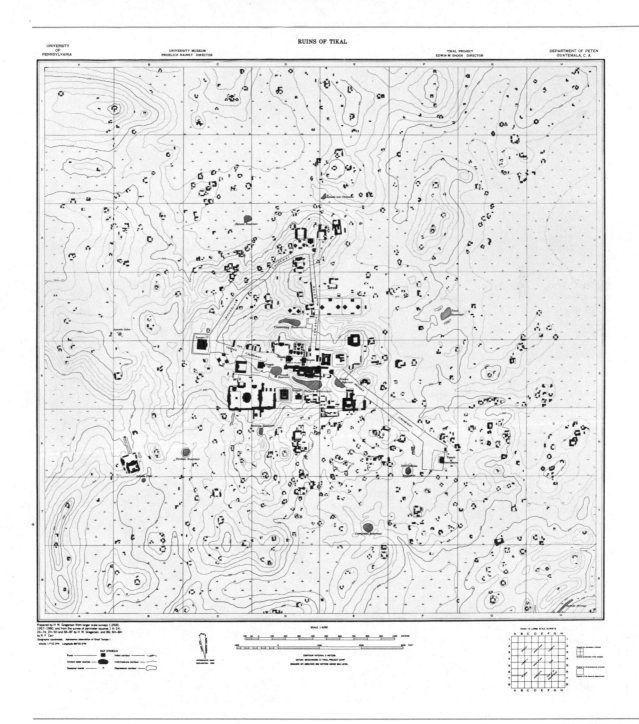

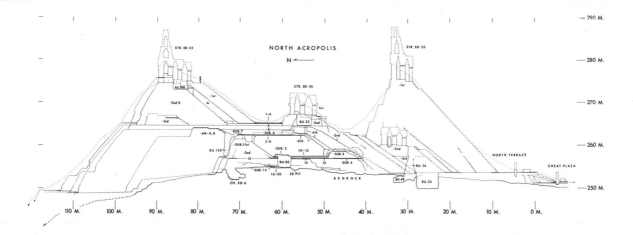

Figure 9-1c,d,e. *This drawing shows the layers uncovered by archeologists on the north acropolis of Tikal; at least 22 structures were found in this single location. The photo is taken inside a tomb excavation. The hieroglyphs on the rear wall tell the date of burial (March 18, 457) of the man for whom the tomb was built. Originally this tomb contained pottery, fine jewelry, and even two sacrificial victims. The stela drawn here (far right) also contains hieroglyphic writing, only part of which has been deciphered. This stone seems to deal with historical and calendrical matters.*

buildings. Just as one cannot get a realistic view of Washington, D.C., by looking at its monumental public buildings alone, so one cannot obtain a realistic view of Tikal without examining the full range of ruins in the area.

It became evident that a long-range program of excavating small structures, most of which were probably houses, was necessary at Tikal. Such a program would provide some basis for an estimate of the population size and density at Tikal; this information is critical to test the traditional assumption that the Maya could not have sustained large concentrations of population because their subsistence patterns were not adequate. Extensive excavation would also provide a sound basis for a reconstruction of the everyday

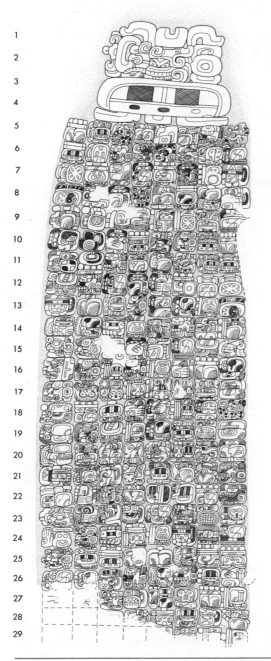

A B C D E F G H

1
2
3
4
5
6
7
8
9
10
11
12
13
14
15
16
17
18
19
20
21
22
23
24
25
26
27
28
29

life of the Maya, previously known only through a study of ceremonial remains. Moreover, the excavation might shed light on the social organization of the Maya. For example, differences in house construction and in the quality and quantity of associated remains might suggest social class differences; or features of house distribution might indicate the existence of extended families or other types of kin groups. The excavation of both large and small structures could reveal the variations in architectural structure and associated artifacts and burials; such variations might reflect the social structure of the total population of Tikal.

Surveying the site

Six square miles surrounding the Great Plaza had already been extensively surveyed by mapping crews by the time the first excavations of small structures were undertaken. Experience had shown that surface surveys were unreliable. Aerial photography is worthless in this area because the tree canopy is often one hundred feet above ground and obscures all but the tallest temples; many of the small ruins are practically invisible even to the observer on the ground. The only way to explore the region is on foot. Once a ruin is found, it is not easy to mark its exact location. To make matters worse, the survey failed to reveal the limits of the site. Ancient Tikal was far larger than the six square miles so far surveyed. More time and money were required to continue surveying the area in order to define the boundaries of Tikal. To simplify this problem, straight survey trails oriented towards the four cardinal points, with the Great Plaza as its center, were cut through the jungle, measured, and staked by government surveyors. The distribution of ruins was plotted, using the trails as a reference point, and the overall size of Tikal was estimated.

The area selected for the first excavation was surveyed in 1957 while it was still covered by forest. A map was drawn, and two years later the first excavations were undertaken. Six structures, two plazas, and a platform were investigated. The orginal plan was to strip each of the structures to bedrock, in order to obtain every bit of information possible. But three obstacles prevented this. First was the discovery of new structures not visible before exavation; second, the structures turned out to be much more complex architecturally than anyone had expected; and, finally, the enormous quantity of artifacts found then had to be washed and cataloged, a time-consuming process. Consequently, not every structure was completely excavated, and some remained uninvestigated.

Evidence from the excavation

Following this initial work, over 100 additional small structures were excavated in different parts of the site, in order to ensure that a representative sample of small structures was investigated. Numerous test pits were sunk in various small structure groups to supplement the information gained from more extensive excavations.

Excavation at Tikal revealed evidence of trade in non-perishable items. Granite, quartzite, hematite, pyrite, jade, slate, and obsidian were all imported, either as raw materials or finished products. Marine materials came from coastal areas. Tikal itself is located on a source of abundant flint, which may have been exported in the form of raw material and finished objects. The site also happens to be located between two river systems to the east and west, and so may have been on a major overland trade route between the two. Whether or not trade went on in perishable goods such as textiles, feathers, salt, or cacao is unknown. But we can safely conclude that there were full-time traders among the Tikal Maya.

In the realm of technology, there is fine stonework and monuments as well as evidence of obsidian and flint workshops. The complex Maya calendar required astronomers, and in order to control the large population, there must have been some form of bureaucratic organization. Although we do not have any direct evidence of the existence of weavers, butchers, brewers, embalmers, tailors, and other occupational specialists, we may assume their presence, given the urban character of Tikal. Tikal must have supported a population of between 40,000 to 50,000 people.

The religion of the Tikal Maya probably developed as a means to cope with the unpredictability of rains. When people are faced with problems unsolvable by technological or organizational means, they resort to magic and the supernatural. Soils at Tikal are thin, and there is no water except that which can be collected in ponds. Rain is abundant in season, but its onset tends to be unreliable. Once the wet season arrives, there may be dry spells of varying duration which can seriously affect crop productivity. To this day, the inhabitants of the region are dependent upon rain for the success of their crops.

The Maya priesthood devoted much of its time to calendrical matters; the priests tried not only to placate the deities in times of drought but also to propitiate them in times of plenty. They determined when to plant crops and were concerned with other agricultural matters. The dependence of the population of Tikal upon their priesthood for guidance in their agricultural pursuits tended to keep them in or near the city, in spite of the fact that a slash-and-burn method of agriculture required the constant shifting of plots and consequently tended to disperse the population over large areas.

As the population increased, land for agriculture became scarcer, and the Maya were forced to look for a new food source that could sustain the dense population concentrated at Tikal. From agriculture as their main form of subsistence, they turned to collecting the very nutritious fruit of the breadnut tree for food. It is not known why breadnuts became the staple diet. It may be that breadnut trees were abundant and the fruit could be easily picked. The reliance on breadnuts for subsistence relegated agriculture to a secondary role in the local economy. All the people not engaged in agriculture could then devote their time to other pursuits. A class of artisans, craftsmen, and other occupational specialists emerged to serve the needs of an elite drawn mostly from the priesthood. The arts flourished, and numerous temples, public buildings, and houses were built.

For 200 years, Tikal was able to sustain its ever-growing population. Then the pressure for food and land reached a critical point and population growth stopped. This event is marked archeologically by the pullback from prime land, the advent of nutritional problems as evidenced by the bones from burials, and by the construction of a system of ditches and embankments that probably served in the defense of the city and as a means of regulating commerce by limiting its accessibility. In other words, a period of readjustment set in, which must have been directed by an already strong central authority. Activities continued as before, but without further population growth, for another 300 years or so.

Archeological methods

The basic unit of the kind of archeological study undertaken at Tikal is the **site,** defined as a place containing archeological remains of previous human occupation. There are many kinds of sites, and sometimes it is difficult to define the boundaries of a site, for remains may be strewn over large areas. Some examples of sites are hunting campsites, in which hunters waited for game to pass; killsites, in which game was killed and butchered; village sites, in which domestic activities took place; and cemeteries, in which the dead, and sometimes their belongings, were buried.

Site location

Sites generally lie buried underground, and therefore the first task for the archeologist is that of actually finding the site he plans to investigate. Most sites are revealed by the presence of **artifacts,** by which we mean any object fashioned or

Figure 9-2a. *England's chalk downs are dotted with drawings made in prehistoric times. A favorite theme is the outline of a white horse; this photo shows the drawing of a giant. Located in Dorset, it measures over 180 feet from head to toe. Such pictures were made by simply clearing away the plant growth and revealing the chalk underneath. It is thought that the artists were contemporaries of the makers of Stonehenge, and that the pictures had ritual significance.*

altered by man—a flint chip, a basket, an axe, or a pipe. An artifact expresses a facet of man's culture; because it is man-made, archeologists like to say that an artifact is a product of man's behavior or, in more technical words, that it is a material representation of an abstract ideal. Chance may play a beneficial role in the discovery of artifacts and sites, but usually the archeologist will have to **survey** a region in order to plot the sites available to him for excavation. A survey can be made from the ground, but aerial reconnaissance, especially aerial photography, can greatly simplify the search for buried archeological remains. One recent refinement of photographic technique employs infrared film. This type of film registers

Figure 9-2b,c. *An interesting example of an archeological site best seen from the air is the Great Serpent Mound in Ohio. The mound itself is over a quarter of a mile long; it was built around 600 B.C. by Indians of the mound building Adena culture. The center of the mound served as a burial place for members of the tribe. Another archeological site revealed by aerial photography is the one near Blythe, California (right), where this drawing was found. Such portraits of giants are a common theme of prehistoric art, even in widely separated cultural areas; the animal portraits, such as the one shown above the giant, are also widespread. This site in California is virtually undetectable through a survey made at ground level.*

The archeological record ● part **3**

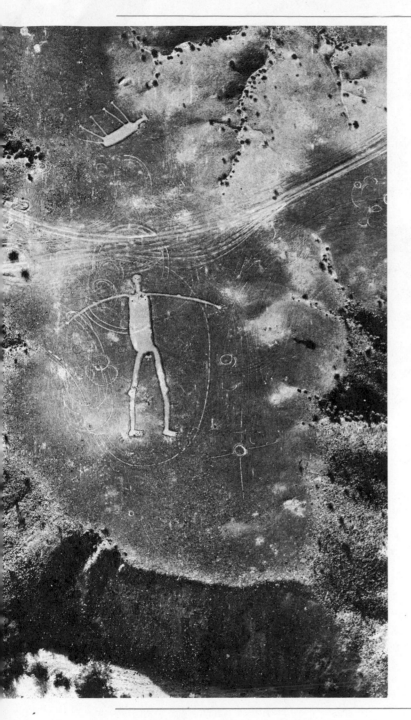

differential amounts of heat, so that the features of the landscape appear as either darker or lighter areas on the photograph, depending on the amount of heat they absorb. Archeological remains tend to absorb more heat than their surroundings, so that their shapes emerge quite clearly as dark spots on the photograph.

Many sites can be spotted by the patterns of shadows cast by irregularities of the ground surface. Such shadow patterns revealed an early Iron Age agricultural system consisting of fields separated from each other by low banks in Himmerland Province, Denmark. In another instance, an agricultural system of Romano-British peasants was revealed when flood waters from the two rivers that irrigate the region shadowed the levee of an ancient river and the boundaries of the rectangular fields.

Sites can also be spotted by **soil-marks,** or stains, that often show up on the surface of recently plowed fields. From soil-marks, many Bronze Age burial mounds were discovered in northern Hertfordshire and southwestern Cambridgeshire, England. The mounds hardly rose out of the ground, yet each was circled at its core by chalky soil-marks. Sometimes the very presence of certain chalky rock is significant. A search for Neanderthal cave sites in Europe would be simplified with the aid of a geological map showing where limestone—a mineral necessary in the formation of caves—is to be found.

Some sites may be spotted by the kind of vegetation they grow. For example, the topsoil of ancient storage and refuse pits is often richer in organic matter than that of the surrounding areas, and so it grows a distinct vegetation. At Tikal, breadnut trees usually grow near the remains of ancient houses, because these trees were used as a source of food by the Maya. An archeologist looking for the remains of houses at Tikal would do well to survey the areas in which these trees grow. A wooden monument of the Stonehenge type at Darrington, Wiltshire, was discovered from an aerial photograph showing a distinct pattern of vegetation growing where the ancient structure stood.

Documents, maps, folklore—ethnohistorical data—are also useful to the archeologist. Heinrich Schliemann, the great nineteenth-century German archeologist, was led to the discovery of Troy after a reading of Homer's *Iliad*. He assumed that the city described by Homer as Ilium was really Troy. Place names and local lore often are an indication that an archeological site is to be found in the area. Archeological surveys in North America depend a great deal upon amateur collectors who are usually familiar with local history.

Sometimes sites in eastern North America are exposed by natural agents, such as soil erosion or droughts. Many prehistoric Indian shell refuse mounds—known as middens—have been exposed by the erosion of rivers. A whole village of stone huts was exposed at Skara Brae in the Orkney Islands by the action of wind erosion upon sand dunes. And during the long drought of 1853–54, a well-preserved prehistoric village was exposed when the water level of Lake Zurich,

The archeological record ● part **3**

Figure 9-3. *These photos show work in progress at the excavation at Combe Grenal, in the Dordogne region of France. The dig is being carried out by Francois Bordes, shown here identifying a flint tool in one picture and using a level to place a string marker in another, and his wife, Denise de Sonneville-Bordes. They have found 64 levels of habitation here in this cave under its collapsed ceiling.*

Switzerland, fell dramatically. Stone quarrying revealed one of the most important Paleolithic sites in England—at Swanscombe, Kent, in which human remains thought to be about 250,000 years old were found. Ploughing often turns up bones, fragments of pots, and other archeological objects.

Conspicuous sites such as the great mounds or *tells* of the Near East are easy to spot, for the country is open. But we have seen at Tikal how difficult it is to locate ruins, even those that are well above ground, because of the dense forest that surrounds the ancient city. Thus, the discovery of archeological sites is strongly affected by local geography.

Digging a site

Once the archeologist has completed his survey, he must decide where he will dig. First of all, he asks himself the question, "Why am I digging?" Then he must consider how much time, money, and manpower he can command for such a laborious enterprise. Archeology is no longer the province of the enlightened amateur as it was decades ago, when any enterprising art collector could dig for the sake of digging. A modern dig is carefully planned and rigorously conducted; it should not only shed light on the cultural past of a people but it should also help us to understand culture processes in general.

After the site is chosen and the land is cleared, the places where the archeologist will dig must be plotted. This is usually done by means of a **grid system.** The surface of the site is divided into squares, and then each square is numbered and marked with a stake. The starting point of the grid system may be a large rock, the edge of a stone wall, or an iron rod sunk into the ground. The starting point is also known as the reference or datum point. At Tikal, this grid system is not feasible because of the large size of the ruins and the density of the vegetation. So there the plotting was done in terms of individual structures,

numbered according to the square in which they are found.

In a gridded site, each square is dug separately with great care. Trowels are used to scrape the soil, and screens are used to sift all the loose soil so that even the smallest artifacts, such as flint chips or beads, are recovered.

A technique employed when looking for very fine objects, such as fish scales or very small bones, is called **flotation.** Flotation consists of immersing soil in water and waiting for the particles to separate. Some will float, others will sink to the bottom, and the remains can be easily retrieved. If the site is stratified—that is, if the remains lie in layers one upon the other—each layer, or stratum, will be dug separately. Each layer, having been laid during a certain span of time, will contain artifacts deposited at the same time and belonging to the same culture. Culture change can be traced through the order in which artifacts were deposited. But, say archeologists Frank Hole and Robert F. Heizer, "because of difficulties in analyzing stratigraphy, archeologists must use the greatest caution in drawing conclusions. Almost all interpretations of time, space, and culture contexts depend on stratigraphy. The refinements of laboratory techniques for analysis are wasted if archeologists cannot specify the stratigraphic position of their artifacts."[2] If no stratification is present, then the archeologist digs at random. Each square must be dug so that its edges and profiles are straight; walls between squares, known as baulks, are often left standing to serve as visual correlates of the grid system.

Sorting out the evidence

An accurate reconstruction of the site is possible only if a detailed record of the dig is kept. "The excavator bears a very heavy burden of responsibility; as he excavates, he does in fact destroy the site he is investigating and, apart from the actual portable and removable objects he recovers, the essential circumstances of their find-

[2] Frank Hole and Robert F. Heizer, *An Introduction to Pre-Historic Archeology* (New York: Holt, Rinehart and Winston, 1969) p. 113.

ing will only survive in the form of his records."[3] The records include a scale map of all the features, the stratification of each excavated square, a description of the exact location and depth of every artifact unearthed, and photographs and scale drawings of the objects. This is the only way the archeological evidence can later be pieced together in order to be able to arrive at a plausible reconstruction of a culture. Although the archeologist may be interested only in certain kinds of remains, he will record every aspect of the site, whether it is relevant to his own archeological investigation or not, because such evidence may be useful to others and would otherwise be permanently lost.

After photographs and scale drawings are made, the artifacts are then cleaned—often a tedious and time-consuming job—placed in bags, and sent to the laboratory for analysis. From the shapes of the artifacts and from the traces of manufacture and wear, archeologists can usually determine their function. For example, the Russian archeologist S. A. Semenov has devoted many years to the study of prehistoric technology. In the case of a flint tool used as a scraper, he was able to determine, by examining the wear patterns of the tool under a microscope, that the prehistoric man who used it began to scrape from right to left and then scraped from left to right, and in so doing avoided straining the muscles of the hand.

Analysis of vegetable and animal remains provides clues about the environment and the economic activities of the occupants of a site. Such analysis may help clarify man's relationship to his environment and its influence upon the development of material culture, known as **technology.** For example, we know that the inhabitants of Serpent Mound, in Ontario, Canada—a mound consisting of burials and a shell midden—were there only in the spring and early summer, when they came to collect shellfish and perform their annual burial rites; apparently they moved elsewhere at the beginning of summer to pursue

[3] Stuart Piggott, *Approach to Archeology* (New York: McGraw-Hill, 1965) p. 30.

other seasonal subsistence activities. Archeologists have inferred that the mound was unoccupied in winter, because this is the season when deer shed their antlers, yet no deer antlers were found on the site. Nor were duck bones found, and so archeologists conclude that the mound was also unoccupied in the fall, when ducks stopped on their migratory route southward to feed on the wild rice growing in the region.

Dating the past

Reliable methods of dating objects and events are necessary if the archeologist is to know the sequence of events in the culture he studies. But since the archeologist deals mostly with peoples and events in times so far removed from his own, the calendar of historic times is of little use to him. So he must rely on two kinds of archeological dating: relative and absolute. **Relative dating** consists simply of designating an event or object as being younger or older than another. **Absolute dates** are dates based upon solar years, and are reckoned in "years before the present" (B.P.) or years before or after Christ (B.C. and A.D.).

Methods of relative dating. Of the many relative dating techniques available to the archeologist, **stratigraphy** is probably the most reliable. Stratigraphy (also known as Steno's Law, after the Danish doctor Nicolaus Steno) is based on the principle that the oldest layer, or stratum, was deposited first (it is the deepest) while the newest layer was deposited last (it usually lies at the top). Thus, in an archeological site the evidence is usually deposited in chronological order. The lowest stratum contains the oldest artifact, whereas the uppermost stratum contains the most recent ones.

Another method of relative dating is the **fluorine test.** It is based on the fact that the amount of fluorine deposited in bones is proportional to their age. The oldest bones contain the greatest amount of fluorine, and vice versa. The fluorine test is useful in dating bones that cannot be ascribed with certainty to any stratum within a site and cannot be dated according to the stratigraphic method. A shortcoming of this method is the fact that the rate of fluorine formation is not constant, but varies from region to region.

Relative dating can also be done on the evidence of botanical and animal remains. A common method, known as **palynology,** involves the study of pollen grains. The kind of pollen found in any geologic stratum depends on the kind of vegetation that existed at the time such stratum was deposited. Archeologists can therefore date a site by determining what kind of pollen was found associated with it.

Another method relies on our knowledge of paleontology. Sites containing the bones of extinct animal species are usually older than those in which the remains of these animals do not appear. Very early North American Indian sites have yielded the remains of mastodons and mammoths—animals now extinct—and on this basis the sites can be dated to a time before these animals became extinct, about 10,000 years ago.

Methods of absolute dating. The most important method of absolute dating is **radiocarbon analysis.** It is based on the fact that all living organisms absorb radioactive carbon (known as Carbon 14) and that this absorption ceases at the time of death. It is possible to measure in the laboratory the amount of radioactive carbon left in a given organic substance, because radioactive substances break down or decay slowly over a fixed period of time. Carbon 14 begins to decay to the stable carbon isotope known as Carbon 12 at a constant rate. The rate of decay is known as "half-life," and the half-life of Carbon 14 is 5730 years. This means that it takes 5730 years for one-half of the original amount of Carbon 14 to decay into Carbon 12. In another 5730 years, one-half of this amount of Carbon 14 will also have decayed. In 11,460 years, only one-fourth of the original amount of Carbon 14 will be present. Thus, the age of an organic substance such as charcoal, wood, shell, or bone can be measured by determining the amount of Carbon 14 that has disintegrated into Carbon 12. The radiocarbon method can adequately date artifacts and biological remains up to 50,000 years old.

Potassium-argon analysis, another method of absolute dating, is based on a technique similar to that of radiocarbon analysis. Following intense heating, as from a volcanic eruption, radioactive potassium decays at a known rate to form argon. The half-life of potassium is 1.3 billion years. Objects that are millions of years old can now be dated by measuring the ratio of potassium to argon in a given rock. Volcanic debris, such as at Olduvai Gorge, can be dated by potassium-argon analysis; thus we know when the volcanic eruption occurred.

A method of absolute dating devised in the course of studying some Pueblo Indian sites in the American Southwest is that of **dendrochronology.** It is based on the fact that in certain climates trees add a new growth-ring to their trunks every year. The rings vary in thickness, depending upon the amount of rainfall received in a year, so that such climatic fluctuation is registered in the growth-ring. By taking a sample of wood, such as a beam from a Pueblo Indian house, and comparing it with the trunk of a tree known to be as old as the artifact, archeologists can date the archeological material. Dendrochronology is applicable only to wooden objects. Furthermore, it can be used only in regions in which trees of great age, such as the giant Sequoias and the bristlecone pine, are known to grow.

Varve analysis is a method of absolute dating applicable to regions in which glaciers exist. A varve is a layer of sediment deposited by water from melting glaciers. It is composed of two layers deposited annually: one is thick and light-colored and is deposited during the summer; the other one is thin and dark and is deposited during the winter. Each varve counts for a year, so that counting varves backward from the present will build up an absolute chronology.

At Tikal, archeological dating is simplified by the presence of the very accurate Maya calendar. Most stone monuments at Tikal have dates inscribed in the Maya system, so theoretically all the archeologist has to do is to correlate these with dates in our own calendar. However, there has been some difference of opinion as to just how this calendar correlates with our own. To resolve the issue, samples from wooden lintels at Tikal, which bear Maya dates upon them, have been subjected to radiocarbon analysis. By comparing the dating reached through radiocarbon analysis with that of the Maya calendar, archeologists have correlated our calendar and that of the Maya. As a result, archeological dating at the Tikal site has been relatively accurate and can be expressed in our own dating system.

Figure 9-4a. *This photo shows some of the apparatus used by scientists in the process of analyzing and data materials collected by field archeologists. Other steps in the process of potassium-argon dating are shown on the following page.*

Preservation of archeological evidence

Preservation depends upon the nature of the archeological remains as much as upon the archeologist's digging skills. Inorganic materials such as stone and metal are more resistant to decay than organic ones such as wood and bone. Often an archeologist comes upon an assemblage—a collection of artifacts made of inorganic materials, such as stone tools, and the debris of inorganic ones long since decomposed, such as textiles or food.

Preservation is affected by climate; under fa-

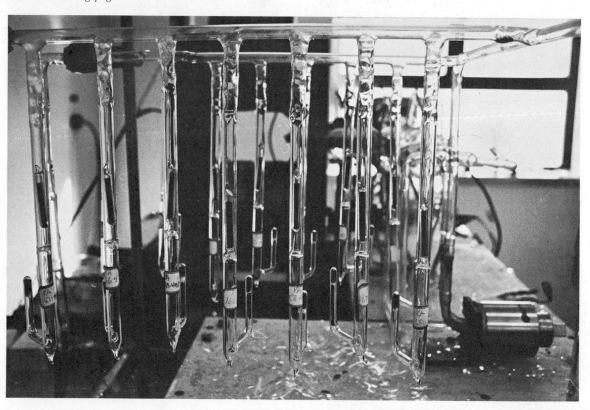

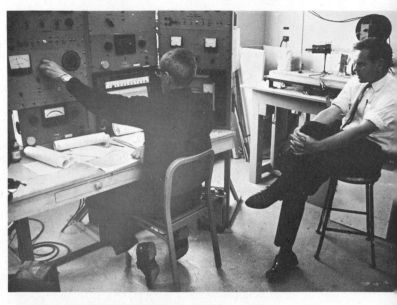

Figure 9-4b-e. *The first step is to put the rock sample in the heating machine, the large square apparatus. It is heated to 2200° F., causing it to liquify. At such high temperatures, it gives off argon gas, which is collected by the surrounding tubing. The quantity of argon given off is then measured in a mass spectrometer, the impressive machine with many dials and gauges. Argon is known to be a product of the decay of potassium, which has a half-life of 1.3 million years. Therefore the amount of argon present indicates the length of time the potassium has been decaying. The photo above shows geophysicists J. F. Evernden and G. H. Curtis in their lab in Berkeley, California.*

vorable climatic conditions, even the most perishable objects may be preserved. For example, pre-dynastic Egyptian burials consisting of shallow pits in the sand often yield well-preserved corpses. Since these bodies were buried long before mummification was ever practiced, their preservation can only be the result of rapid dessication in the very warm, dry climate. The tombs of dynastic Egypt often contain wooden furniture, textiles, flowers, and papyri barely touched by time—seemingly as fresh-looking as they were when deposited in the tomb 3000 years ago—as a result of the dryness of the atmosphere.

The dryness of certain caves is also a factor in the preservation of coprolites, or fossilized human feces. Coprolites are a source of information on prehistoric foods, and can be analyzed not only for vegetable contents but also for dietary remains. From such analysis can be determined not only what the inhabitants ate but also how the food was prepared. Because so many sources of food are available only in certain seasons, it is even possible to tell the time of year in which the food was eaten and the coprolites deposited.

Certain climates can soon obliterate all evidence of organic remains. Maya ruins found in the very warm and moist tropical rain forests of Mesoamerica are often in a state of collapse—notwithstanding the fact that they are massive structures of stone—as a result of the pressure exerted upon them by the heavy forest vegetation. The rain and humidity soon destroy almost all traces of woodwork, textiles, or basketry.

The social customs of ancient man may also account for the preservation of archeological remains. The ancient Egyptians believed that eternal life could be achieved only if the dead person were buried with his worldly possessions. Hence, their tombs are usually filled with a wealth of archeological artifacts. Many skeletal remains of Neanderthal man are known because he practiced burial, probably as a result of the fact that he too believed in the afterlife. By contrast, skeletal remains of pre-Neanderthal peoples are rare and when found usually consist of mere fragments rather than complete skeletons.

☐

A LOOK AT PREHISTORY

An interest in prehistory requires no defense. It is generally recognized that understanding man's past is an essential part of understanding his behavior at the present time and that any general explanation of human development must be answerable to the historical record.

Because the prehistorian works without written records, his methods resemble those used by paleontologists and historical geologists. Each of these disciplines seeks both to reconstruct the past and to explain the changes that can be observed in the historical record. Much of the evidence that they use consists of the remains of the past, be these geological strata, organic fossils, or the artifacts and debris of ancient cultures. Additional evidence is found in the conditions of the present, on the basis of which past conditions may be inferred. Each of these disciplines attempts to utilize many independent lines of evidence to reconstruct the past, and when the conclusions based on these different approaches converge, greater certainty in the validity of the reconstruction is achieved.

Prehistory differs from the natural sciences in that the object of its investigation is man and his works. Therefore any explanation of how changes take place must be based on a sound understanding of human behavior. This accounts for the close relationship between prehistory and the social sciences, in particular with cultural anthropology.

Prehistory is concerned with all aspects of human development. Like documentary history, it is interested in delineating and explaining social, economic, political, and demographic, as well as cultural changes. Racial and linguistic changes are also objects of interest. In this way prehistory becomes a meeting place of many disciplines, such as archeology, culture history, and historical linguistics.

The study of prehistory, either in general or in any particular region of the world, takes the form of a dialogue between the evidence, be it archeological, physical anthropological, or linguistic, and the social science theories that are used to interpret it. The discovery of new evidence frequently requires the modification of existing historical reconstruction; on the other hand, theoretical advances also permit new insights to be gained from existing data and this too results in the elaboration and modification of such reconstructions. In the case of Predynastic Egypt, the evidence, derived largely from cemeteries, is inadequate to answer many of the problems about social and political development that a growing theoretical interest in these problems has raised. Theoretical advances thus also lead archeological (and linguistic) studies to develop along wholly new lines.

Until recently, the theories that prehistorians used to interpret evidence tended to be largely informal and implicit. Methodology was concerned largely with excavation techniques and the interpretation of archeological data for site reports. This is sometimes referred to as a descriptive period. In the past few years, however, prehistorians have been paying increasing attention to making their techniques of historical reconstruction and interpretation explicit. This development is indicative of the maturation of prehistory as a discipline.

One of the earliest theoretical advances in prehistory was the recognition that race, language, and culture are independent variables, each of which must be examined separately and in terms of its own evidence. Although anthropologists have long realized that race, language, and culture each change according to their own rules and that the history of each is apt to follow a distinctive course, the tendency to think in terms of racial and ethnic stereotypes has made the application of this very difficult.

Still more difficult has been the realization that prehistoric cultures are not merely collections of traits, to be compared in terms of their overall similarities and differences, but rather systems in which each trait has played a particular role. This view, which has already gained wide acceptance, has done much to weaken the tendency to treat archeological cultures as organic bounded units. It is also permitting prehistorians to distinguish between the study of individual traits, their origin and diffusion, and the study of the development of social systems, within which cultural traits come to play a part. Related to this interest in social systems, is the increasing attention being shown to the study of prehistoric settlement patterns.

Within the context of these developments, serious attention once again is being given to the processes of cultural change. In the past, the processes of invention, diffusion, and migration were invoked in a careless and uncritical manner as explanations of culture change. Today these concepts are being reassessed and criteria are being established for distinguishing them in the archeological record.

Figure 9-5. *Excavation site at Persepolis.*

Hopefully, the theoretical developments now going on in prehistory are preparing the way for an enriched and more sophisticated understanding of man's past. Just as in the discipline of history, so in prehistory, there is no single line of investigation to be followed. Instead, all of man's achievements in all areas of human endeavor lie open for investigation. For the prehistorian, contact with these achievements is limited because prehistoric peoples cannot speak to us directly through their records. Archeological remains are not culture, they are only the products of culture. Moreover they are imperfect reflections of the culture that produced them, just as organic fossils are an incomplete version of a living animal. The interest and importance of prehistory lie not in the completeness of the records of the past, nor in the theoretical skills that are at our disposal to interpret these records. Its strength derives instead from man and his achievements both in the past and today. Imperfect as the record may be, it still leaves us with many kingdoms of the human spirit to explore.

Source:
From *Beyond History: The Methods of Prehistory* by Bruce G. Trigger. Copyright © 1968 by Holt, Rinehart and Winston, Inc. Reprinted by permission of Holt, Rinehart and Winston, Inc.

Summary

1.

Archeology is the reconstruction of past cultural systems and processes through the collection and analysis of artifacts. This is the method of the "New Archeology" as opposed to traditional archeology, which is oriented towards the description and classification of cultural artifacts. The "New Archeology" sees in the archeological record a total culture.

2.

The basic unit of study for the archeologist is the site, defined as a place containing the remains of former human occupation or presence. Archeologists generally locate sites by means of a survey of a region. Irregularities of the ground surface, unusual soil discolorations, and unexpected variations in vegetation type and coloring may indicate the presence of a site. Ethnohistorical data—maps, documents, and folklore—may provide further clues to the location of archeological sites.

3.

Once the archeologist has chosen a site, the area is divided and carefully marked with a grid system; the starting point of the dig is called the datum point. Each square within the grid is carefully excavated, and any archeological remains are recovered through employment of various tools and screens; for very fine objects, the method of flotation is employed. The location of each artifact when found must be carefully noted.

4.

Because excavation in fact destroys a site, the archeologist must maintain a thorough record in the form of maps, descriptions, scale-drawings, and photographs of every aspect of the site. All artifacts must be cleaned and classified before being sent to the laboratory for analysis. Often the shapes and markings of artifacts can determine their function, and the analysis of vegetable and animal remains may provide information.

5.

There are two types of methods for dating archeological data. Relative dating is a method of determining the age of objects relative to each other and includes the method of stratigraphy, based upon the position of the artifact in relation to different layers of soil deposits. The fluorine test is based upon the determination of the amount of fluorine deposited in bones. The analysis of floral remains (including palynology) and faunal remains is also widely employed. Methods of absolute dating include radiocarbon analysis—which measures the amount of C_{14} that has decayed into C_{12} in organic objects; potassium-argon analysis, which measures the percentage of potassium which has decayed to argon in volcanic material; dendrochronology, dating based on tree rings; and varves, or layers of sediments deposited by melting glaciers.

6.

The preservation of archeological evidence depends upon climate and the nature of the artifacts. Inorganic materials are more resistant to decay than organic ones. However, given a very dry climate, even organic materials may be well preserved. Warm, moist climates as well as thick vegetation act to decompose organic material quickly, and even inorganic material may suffer from the effects of humidity and vegetation growth. The preservation of archeological evidence is also dependent upon the social customs of ancient man.

Suggested readings

Binford, L. R. *An Archeological Perspective*. New York: Seminar Press, 1972.
A presentation of the theoretical views of the "New Archeology."

Daniel, Glyn *The Origins and Growth of Archeology*. Baltimore: Penguin Books, 1967.
An excellent, concise history of the field of archeology written by a prominent archeologist.

Willey, Gordon R., and Philip Phillips *Method and Theory in American Archeology*. Chicago: University of Chicago, 1958.
This is a combination and revision of two previously published articles. The first part is a statement of what the authors believe to be the minimal aims of archeology and the basic methods which would meet those aims. The second part concerns some theoretical considerations of New World archeology. The basic arguments of this book are that archeology and anthropology are inseparable and anthropology is more of a science than a history. The book has been particularly influential on contemporary archeological thought.

Hole, Frank, and Robert F. Heizer *An Introduction to Prehistoric Archeology*, 3rd ed. New York: Holt, Rinehart and Winston, 1973.
The best and most thorough coverage of the method and theory of archeology. It covers systematically the thinking behind archeological methods and processes, with emphasis on the latest trend towards a more scientific evaluation of the concepts of prehistory.

Michaels, Joseph W. *Dating Methods in Archeology*. New York: Seminar Press, 1973.
This is a thorough, up to date discussion of methods for dating archeological material.

Trigger, Bruce G. *Beyond History: The Methods of Pre-history*. New York: Holt, Rinehart and Winston, 1968.
A brief manual dealing with the methodology of prehistory. The book contains numerous case analyses. A whole chapter is devoted to a study of pre-dynastic Egypt. There is a selected and evaluated bibliography at the end.

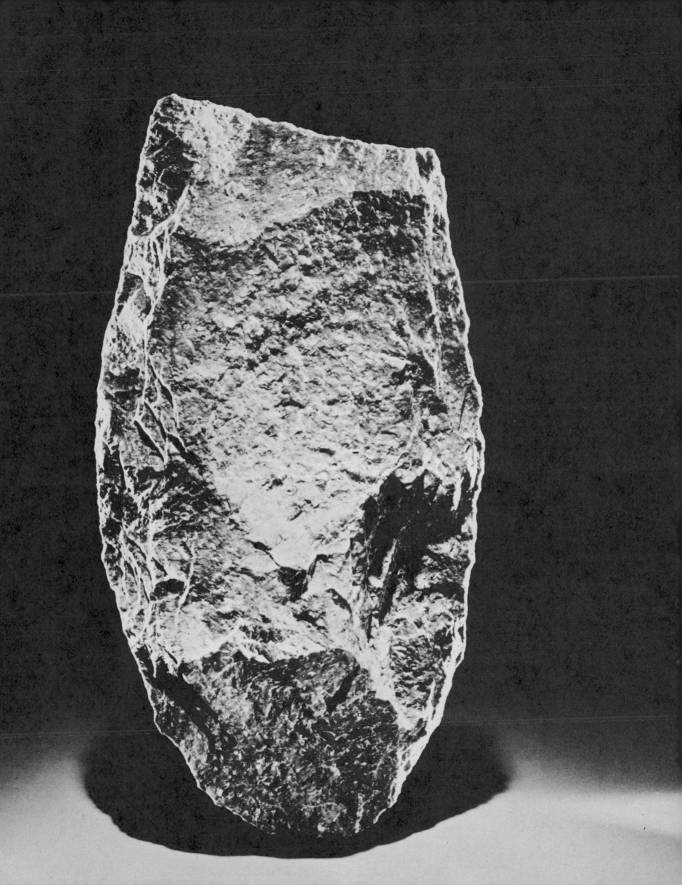

portfolio two

Art before Columbus

"All the days of my life, I have seen nothing that rejoiced my heart so much as these things, for I saw amongst them wonderful works of art, and I marveled at the subtle genius of men in foreign lands." So wrote Albrecht Durer, the great German artist, after he had seen in Belgium an exhibition of works brought back from the New World by Hernando Cortes for Emperor Charles V. Durer, like almost every viewer since, felt the power and beauty of the art that we now call "Pre-Columbian," for it was with the advent of Christian conquerors from the Old World—missionaries, soldiers, and tradesmen—that the art began to change. Prior to 1492, in its indigenous forms from Northern Mexico to the high Andes of Peru, a native art of high cultivation, great craftsmanship, and deep emotive power had flourished for over three thousand years.

It was not until the late nineteenth century, however, that Pre-Columbian art received the attention it was due. Despite the praise of Durer and others, because of its origins the art was thought "primitive," barbaric, and therefore unworthy of study. Tragically, much of it was destroyed, not because it was pagan, but because it was made of gold or turquoise or jade. Countless thousands of beautiful objects were melted down to replenish the dwindling treasury of Charles V, or broken up to decorate the jewelry of the court.

In 1892, on the four hundredth anniversary of Columbus' discovery of the New World, that event was celebrated with an exhibition of art from Mexico and Central and South America

Head of warrior wearing jaguar headdress; Las Remojadas Style.
From the American Museum of Natural History.

Wooden mask with jade; Olmec Style.
From the American Museum of Natural History.
Jade effigy axe (the "Kunz" axe); Olmec Style.
From the American Museum of Natural History.

The cache of La Venta; Olmec Style.
From the National Museum of Anthropology, Mexico City.

Nobleman; Jaina Style.
From the National Museum of Anthropology, Mexico City.

in Madrid and at the Columbian Exposition in Chicago. Pre-Columbian art was rediscovered.

The photographs on the following pages represent art from Mexico only. It was there that one of the two great generic civilizations flourished, the Meso-American; the second was the Peruvian, which built its own distinctive style. On the center-spread is a photograph of one of the great "finds" in recent New World archaeology—a ritual group of sculptures from La Venta, the important Olmec temple-city, shown exactly as they were excavated. The meaning of the group is as yet unknown, but clearly the figures express a purpose. Whether it is ritual and religious, whether this may be a trial of some kind, or perhaps simply an entertainment or contest remains to be discovered. But the images are compelling; with their down-turned "crying baby" mouths, flaring jaguarlike lips, and flexed leg stances they are uncompromising and imposing. The other objects on the same pages are also in the Olmec style, the earliest coherent period of high civilization in Mexico. The "Kunz" axe, weighing some 15 pounds, is one of the largest jade objects known in prehistoric art.

Along with jade and other stone carvings, Pre-Columbian art represents a peak of achievement in ceramics. From tiny figures, some made as whistles and some wheeled to serve as toys, to large effigy vessels and painted totems, the range of subject and style is great. On the first page of this portfolio is a ceramic figure of awesome power—a man's head encased in a jaguar mask with fierce jaws agape. Done in the Las Remojadas style, the sculpture is from central Vera Cruz, near Mexico's Gulf Coast. The elegant figure opposite is from the island of Jaina, off the Campeche coast of the Yucatan Peninsula. One of the temple-cities of the Classic Maya period, Jaina is separated from the mainland only by a narrow stretch of water and apparently served as a ritual burial ground. The figures found there, of fine clay and brilliantly glazed, are small in size but monumental in conception; they represent a peak in Pre-Columbian art.

Photographs by Lee Boltin

The earliest
cultures

Two million years ago, man was already on his way to becoming a cultured animal. Evidence from some East African sites indicates that Australopithecines were then using very crude stone tools. Exactly when man crossed the threshold of humanity is impossible to say; it can only be inferred from the evidence at hand. The archeological record shows a gradual transition from crude pebble tools to carefully manufactured large stone tools. This silent evidence of man's change is eloquent enough to the archeologist. The record is a rich one; it takes little imagination to picture the stages undergone by early man in his career as a toolmaker. The sequence of tools speaks not only of what Paleolithic man could do with his brain and hands; it also speaks of man's widening horizons as an animal of culture. Implied in this sophistication and diversification of tools is a concomitant development in man's life habits. Much importance has been placed on man's ability to make tools. The fact that other animals, such as chimpanzees, can also make tools modifies the view that toolmaking is essentially a human development. However, there is a distinction between human and nonhuman toolmaking. In human terms, "making" involves the notion of replication. Man fashions tools accord-

ing to a preconceived idea; he is able to fashion exactly the same kind of tool again when the need arises. It is the cultural tradition of toolmaking that sets man apart from his fellow creatures.

The Paleolithic era

Archeologists reconstruct past cultural systems by studying the material remains of each culture group. Through examination of the artifacts found in the earliest archeological sites, they have dated the tools found there as more than two million years old. Based on studies of cultures within this two-million-year time span, three major culture stages have been identified. These categories, intended to simplify understanding of man's cultural evolution, are the Stone Age, the Bronze Age, and the Iron Age. The Stone Age is subdivided into three stages: the Paleolithic or Old Stone Age, the Mesolithic or Middle Stone Age, and the Neolithic or New Stone Age. The Paleolithic is further divided into three periods: Lower Paleolithic, Middle Paleolithic, and Upper Paleolithic.

The earliest man-made tools are difficult to

identify. Made from pebbles, they are scarcely distinguishable from stones that have been shaped into tool-like forms by natural forces. Moreover, it takes an experienced archeologist to decide what a prehistoric tool might have been used for. Archeologists generally rely on a number of different methods in attacking the problem of tool classification. One method is to examine the wear marks scratched on tools. Scratches and other marks often indicate the direction in which the tool was used; it also may give an indication of the material being worked on. Another method is that of ethnographic analogy, which involves the comparison of similar tools found by the archeologist. However, results can sometimes be misleading; often different cultures are found to use similar objects for different purposes.

Lower Paleolithic

The earliest known Lower Paleolithic artifacts are about two million years old. Tools of this age were first found at Olduvai Gorge in East Africa; similar tools later found in the Lake Rudolph vicinity of Kenya are equally old. These early tools show striking similarities, indicating that they were probably the results of a cultural tradition of manufacturing tools according to an ideal model or pattern.

Olduvai Gorge. What is now Olduvai Gorge, a canyonlike, lava-filled depression on the arid Serengeti Plain of East Africa, was once a lake. Several million years ago, the shores of this lake were inhabited not only by numerous wild animals, but also by groups of hominids. For more than thirty years—until his recent death—archeologist Louis S. B. Leakey excavated the gorge in search of man's ancestors. There he found the remains of more than twenty individuals, including Australopithecines (of which "Zinjanthropus" is a member), "Homo habilis," and *Homo erectus*. The gorge therefore is a rich source of Paleolithic remains, and a key site providing evidence of man's evolutionary development. Among the finds is a campsite used by a hunter more than

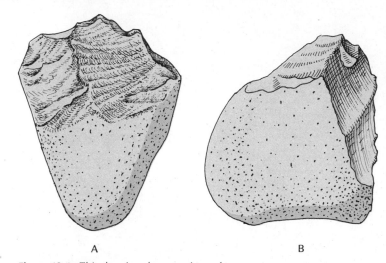

A
B

Figure 10-1. *This drawing shows a piece of flint that has simply been chipped to form a tool. The natural tendency of this hard mineral to flake when it is broken is evident; it was through careful manipulation of flaking that early man made the pebble tools found at Olduvai Gorge.*

500,000 years ago. The stone tools he used lie undisturbed, exactly as he left them, together with the bones of now extinct animals he hunted. At another spot, in the lowest level of the gorge, is a circle of stones built by some near-man about two million years ago; the circle is the only remaining evidence of what once may have been a windbreak, such as the ones built today by the Hottentots. The picture that emerges from the archeological work proceeding at Olduvai Gorge illuminates the history of mankind during a span of more than two million years.

The pebble tool tradition. The Lower Paleolithic pebble tools found at Olduvai Gorge belong to the Olduwan pebble tool tradition. The pebble tool tradition was largely based on one all-purpose generalized chopping tool. It was produced by removing a few flakes from a rock, either by using a pebble as a hammer (hammerstone) to knock off flakes, or by striking the pebble against a large rock (anvil) to remove the

The archeological record ● part **3**

flakes. This system of manufacture is called the **percussion method.** The finished product had a jagged irregular edge, efficient for cutting and chopping. The pebble tool's generalized form suggests that it served many purposes, such as butchering meat, splitting bones for marrow, and perhaps also defending the owner.

Crude as it was, the pebble tool was an important technological advance for early man; previously, he depended on found objects requiring no modification, such as bones or conveniently shaped stones. It made possible new additions to his diet, because without such tools, man could only eat animals that could be skinned by tooth or nail; therefore, early man's diet was very limited in terms of proteins. The advent of Oldowan choppers meant more than just saving labor and time; it made possible the exploitation of a whole new food source. The initial use of tools was probably the result of physical adaptation to an environment that was changing from forests to grasslands. The physical changes that adapted hominids to living in the new grassy terrain encouraged toolmaking. It has been observed that higher primates, for example, often use objects, such as sticks and stones, in conjunction with threat gestures. The change to a nearly upright bipedal posture, the increased flexibility at the shoulder, arms, and hands, and the increased size and complexity of man's brain helped man to compete with, and survive in spite of, the large predatory carnivores that shared his environment.

The African savanna is an environment with a long dry season, in which a small hominid, biologically defenseless to protect its hunting territory and ill-equipped for digging or meat-eating, had to find some way to supplement the dwindling sources of vegetable food. The use of some kind of sharp cutting tool to open the skin of an antelope, of a bashing tool to break open the long bones or shell of a tortoise, or of a pointed tool for digging, would have meant a regular and substantial increase in the quantity and variety of food consumed. The hominids also would have found these tools useful for defense.

The pebble tool tradition may well mark one of the first known times that an animal species made a cultural rather than a physical adaptation to environmental conditions. In the emerging grassland environment, early hominids had few trees to climb for protection against predators. Rather than making obvious physical adaptations towards heavier jaws, sharper teeth, or more bulk, man developed tools, thus taking a step in the process of shaping the environment at the same time that it shaped him.

Pebble tools are found at very small sites, usually on the edge of a lake or stream in the middle of a savanna region. The small size and number of tools indicate that Australopithecines lived in very small nomadic groups that moved from one temporary camp to another. Some anthropologists believe that the typical Australopithecine group contained no more than a dozen members at one time. The formation of small groups that display a high degree of mobility is also characteristic of contemporary hunter-gatherer groups.

Chellean-Acheulian tradition. There is an evolutionary continuum in the technological developments of man's early tool traditions. The Oldowan chopper, for example, became more sophisticated and developed into the Chellean hand ax. In turn, the Chellean tradition developed into the Acheulean tradition, in which the hand ax appears further perfected and finished. The earliest East African Chellean tools known are about a million years old; those found in Europe and the Near East date from about 730,000 B.C. No Chellean tools have yet been discovered in East Asia, although other traditions were in existence there.

The characteristic tool of the Chellean-Acheulian traditions is the hand ax. The earliest Chellean hand axes were manufactured from a flint core. By hitting all sides of the core with a hammerstone, the toolmaker knocked off flakes until he formed a pear-shaped tool with a pointed end and a sharp cutting edge. That the Chellean-Acheulian tradition grew out of the pebble tool tradition is indicated by an examination of the evidence discovered at Olduvai. In Bed I, the lowest level, pebble tools were found along with Australopithecine remains. In Lower Bed II, the first crude hand axes were found intermingled with pebble tools. More advanced Chellean-Acheulean hand axes appear in Middle Bed II, together with *Homo erectus* remains.

The Chellean hand axes represent a definite improvement over the general chopping and scraping tools of the pebble tool tradition. Like pebble tools, the hand axes were probably general purpose tools for food processing, hide scraping, and defense. However, they were shaped by regular blows rather than by random strikes. In this way, sharper points and more regular cutting edges were produced, and more cutting edge was available from the same amount of flint.

During this period, tool cultures begin to diversify. Besides hand axes, *Homo erectus* used tools that functioned as cleavers (these were U-shaped chopping tools); scrapers (several different types of these have been discovered, all made from flint cores); and flake tools (generally smaller tools made by hitting a flint core with a hammerstone, thus knocking off flakes with sharp edges). Many flake tools were by-products of hand ax and cleaver manufacture. Their sharp edges made them very useful. Diversification of tool cultures is also indicated by the development of chopper tool industries in Asia (contemporary with hand axes manufactured in the West) and the continuation of the more primitive pebble tool tradition in certain parts of Europe (such as in Hungary), perhaps indicating a case of culture lag.

The greater number of tool types found in the Chellean-Acheulian tradition indicates *Homo erectus* increased efficiency in exploiting the environment. The greater the range of tool types used, the greater the range of natural resources capable of being exploited in less time, with less effort, and with a higher degree of efficiency. For example, axes may have been used to kill game and dig up roots; cleavers to kill and butcher; scrapers to process hides for blankets and clothes; and flake tools to cut meat and process certain plants. Adaptation to specific regions is also in-

Figure 10-2a,b and 10-3a–e. *The great technological strides man made are shown by a comparison of top photo, an Acheulian hand ax about 400,000 years old, and bottom, a hand ax in the same tool tradition but only about 200,000 years old. The methods of manufacture shown are direct percussion with a hammerstone (10-3a and b), indirect percussion (10-3c), baton percussion (10-3d) and pressure flaking (10-3e).*

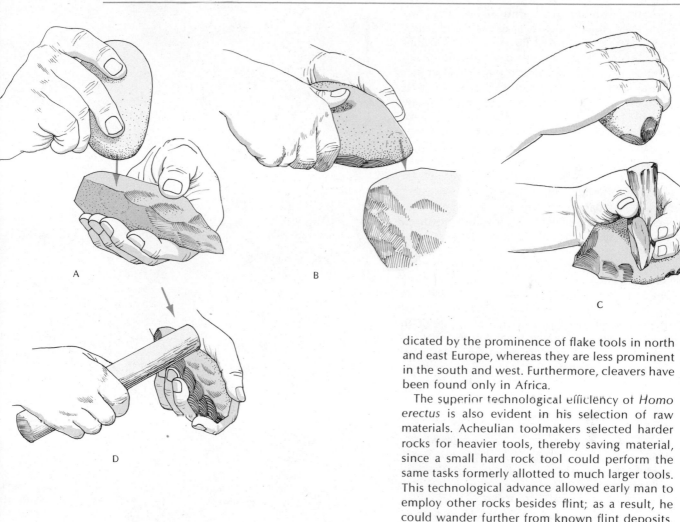

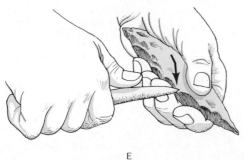

A

B

C

D

E

dicated by the prominence of flake tools in north and east Europe, whereas they are less prominent in the south and west. Furthermore, cleavers have been found only in Africa.

The superior technological efficiency of *Homo erectus* is also evident in his selection of raw materials. Acheulian toolmakers selected harder rocks for heavier tools, thereby saving material, since a small hard rock tool could perform the same tasks formerly allotted to much larger tools. This technological advance allowed early man to employ other rocks besides flint; as a result, he could wander further from known flint deposits.

Another sign of *Homo erectus'* developing technology is the evidence of fires and cooking, established by the discovery of burned stones and hearths at Choukoutien cave near Peking, China. Cooking was an extremely important cultural adaptation. When meat is cooked, it is softer and easier to skin and carve. That cooking took the place of such physical adaptations as large heavy jaws and sharp pointed canines is indicated by comparison of the dentition of the *Homo erectus* finds at Choukoutien (Peking man) with his biologically close, but non-fire-using, relative, Java man. These finds show that Java man had larger, heavier teeth. The use of fire is culturally significant for man, because it provided him with warmth and light and helped him to better survive the cold associated with his homes in caves and near lakes. Fire could also be used to scare off possible predators, including the huge cave bears that often were attracted to the same shelters as men.

During later Acheulean times, two toolmaking techniques were developed in the West which produced thinner, more sophisticated axes with straighter, sharper cutting edges. The baton method of percussion manufacture involved using a bone or antler punch to hit the edge of the flint core. This method produced shallow flake scars, rather than the crushed edge that the hammerstone method produced on the older Chellean hand axes. In later Acheulean times, the striking platform method was also used to create sharper thinner axes; the toolmakers would often strike off flakes to create a flat surface near the edge. These flat surfaces, or striking platforms, were set up along the edge of the tool perpendicular to its sides, so that the toolmaker could remove long thin flakes stretching from the edge across each side of the tool.

Levalloisian tradition. During very late Acheulean times, about 200,000 years ago, the Levalloisian technique of tool manufacture came into use. Levalloisian flake tools have been found in Africa, Europe, and even in China, where practically no hand axes have been uncovered. Some anthropologists believe that this may be a case of independent invention, since Asia is quite culturally distinct from the West. In the Levalloisian technique, the striking platform was typically made by a crosswise blow at one end of the core of a stone. Then the platform was struck, removing three or four long flakes and leaving a nodule that looked like a tortoise shell. This method produced a longer edge for the same amount of flint than the previous ones. The edges were sharper, and could be produced in less time.

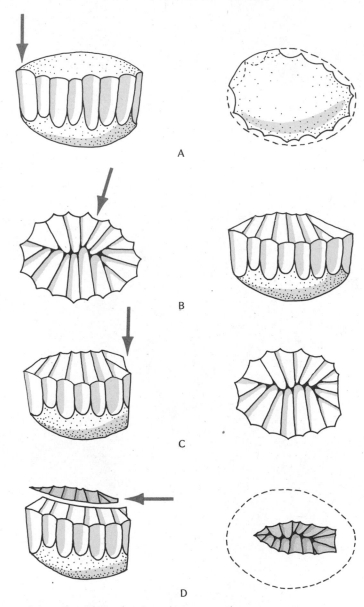

Figure 10-4. *These drawings show top and side views of the steps in the Levallois technique. 10-4a shows the trimming of the edge of the stone nucleus; b shows the trimming of the top surface; c shows the striking platform; d is the final step.*

Homo erectus was a better hunter than *Australopithecus,* because of his more advanced toolmaking and knowledge of fire. At most Acheulean sites, the most numerous animal remains are those of large herd animals, such as elephants; whereas Australopithecine sites contain only the remains of small animals and immature or crippled representatives of the larger species. *Homo erectus'* increased proficiency as a hunter seems based not just on greater technological capability, but also on an increased organizational ability reflected in his sophisticated hunting techniques. For example, excavations at Torralba and Amboina, Spain, indicate group hunting techniques were used to kill a large amount of game.

The evolution of *Homo erectus'* technology and social organization is probably most closely related to the increased size and complexity of his brain, which occurred at the same time. The decrease in the size of jaws and teeth in *Homo erectus* (and then again in his successors, the first *Homo sapiens* and Neanderthal man) is also significant. This dental reduction was made possible by the cultural adaptations of cooking and more complex tool kits, which were more efficient than any possible physical adaptation; the dental reduction in turn encouraged an even heavier reliance upon tool development, which aided the further progress of the hominids. Dental reduction also facilitated the development of language. Improvements in communication and social organization brought about by language undoubtedly contributed to man's spreading to new environments, the use of improved hunting methods, and a population increase. Evidence from tools and fossils indicates that early *Homo sapiens* were living in areas previously uninhabited by his primate ancestors.

Middle Paleolithic

The Middle Paleolithic is characterized by the emergence of Neanderthal man and by the development of the Mousterian tradition of toolmaking, which dates from about 100,000 to 60,000 B.C.; it represents a technological advance.

Mousterian tradition. The Mousterian tradition is named after the Neanderthal site of Le Moustier, France. The presence of Acheulean hand axes at Neanderthal sites is one indication that the Mousterian culture was rooted in the older Acheulean tradition. Neanderthals improved upon Levalloisian techniques; Mousterian flake tools are lighter and smaller than Levalloisian flake tools. Whereas in the Levalloisian method the toolmaker only obtained two or three flakes from the entire core, Mousterian toolmakers obtained many more smaller flakes, skillfully retouched and sharpened.

The Mousterian tool kits contained an even greater variety of tool types than the previous traditions: hand axes, flakes, scrapers, borers, notched flakes for shaving wood, and many types of points that could be attached to shafts of wood to form spears. This variety of tool types indicates that the Mousterian tool kit intensified man's exploitation of food resources and increased the availability and quality of clothing and shelter. For the first time, man could cope with the arctic conditions prevalent in Europe at this time.

The large number of Mousterian sites uncovered, as well as the pronounced differences among local tool kits, indicate that Neanderthal man's living areas were widespread. This dispersal was closely related to Neanderthal's improved hunting techniques, based on superior technology in weapon and toolmaking and an even higher degree of social organization than his predecessors. One crucial key to Neanderthal man's development was his increased brain size (about 1100–1500 ccs), approximately the same as modern man.

Many of these sites show evidence of religious beliefs and ceremonies among Neanderthals. For example, at Shanidar cave in Iraq, evidence was found of a burial accompanied by funeral ceremonies. In the back of the cave an old man was buried in a pit. Pollen analysis of the soil around his skeleton indicated that flowers had been placed below his body and in a wreath about his head. Many anthropologists interpret such burial customs as signs of a belief in an afterlife.

Neanderthal society had also developed to the point of being able to afford the luxury of concern for the individual member of the group; it appears that the disabled were often cared for by their fellows. The remains of an amputee discovered in the Shanidar cave and an arthritic man unearthed at La Chapelle attest to this fact. This means that culture was now more than just adequate to insure survival.

Most prevalent at Mousterian sites is evidence of animal cults, especially cave bear cults. For instance, in a cave in eastern Austria, seven bear skulls were found aligned in a pit. In southern France, the remains of about twenty-one cave bears were found in a pit covered by a heavy stone slab. In eastern Uzbekistan, a child's burial place was found encircled by a ring of goat skulls.

Upper Paleolithic

Archeological evidence indicates that Upper Paleolithic tool-making techniques evolved from those of the earlier Mousterian tradition. Although Upper Paleolithic cultures are associated with the remains of *Homo sapiens sapiens,* many Upper Paleolithic sites contain Mousterian flake tools of the Neanderthals. However, the typical *Homo sapiens sapiens* tool was the blade. A blade is a flint twice as long as it is wide. The toolmaker formed a cylindrical core, struck the blade off near the edge of the core, and repeated this procedure, going around the core in one direction until he finished near the center of the core. The procedure is similar to that of unwinding a roll of paper. The blade technique was a much more efficient method of tool manufacture than the Mousterian technique, because it saved much more flint.

Other efficient techniques of tool manufacture also appeared at this time. One such method was pressure-flaking, in which a bone, antler, or wooden tool was used to press off small flakes from a flint core. The advantage of this technique

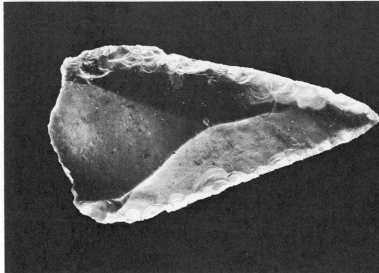

Figure 10-5a and b. *Both these photos show tools of the Mousterian tradition; they have been dated at about 50,000 to 70,000 years old. Tools like this are called points and were presumably used for a variety of functions. Points were made by removing flakes from a large flint. The numerous flakes were then touched up to become various special purpose tools.*

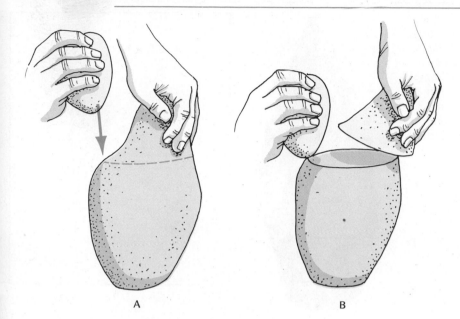

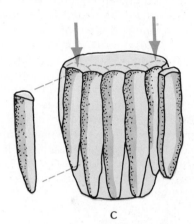

Figure 10-6. *During the Upper Paleolithic, a new technique was invented, enabling the manufacture of blades. The stone is broken to create a striking platform, then vertical pieces are flaked off the side of the flint, eventually forming a sharp-edged tool.*

A B C

was that the toolmaker had greater control over the shape of the tool than he did with percussion flaking. The Solutrean laurel leaf blades found in Spain and France are examples of this technique. The longest blade found was thirteen inches long and only about a quarter of an inch thick. Pressure-flaking also provided greater precision in retouching cutting edges for extra sharpness.

The heat treatment of raw materials before they were shaped into tools was also introduced during the Upper Paleolithic. Tools that have been treated by heating feel greasy and can be easily identified. Contemporary tests with heat treatment have revealed that untreated flints are very difficult to pressure-flake and produce very small flakes. But when flints are heat-treated, the process is much easier and longer flakes are produced.

Another Upper Paleolithic development was the invention of burins, or stone tools with chisel-like edges. They were excellent tools for carving the bone and antler increasingly available during this time. *Homo sapiens* made extensive use of the new bone and antler tools made possible by the introduction of burins. In fact, many tools, such as fishhooks and harpoons, were made exclusively from bone or antler. The atlatl, or spear-thrower, also appeared at this time. It consisted of a piece of wood with a groove in it to hold the spear. The hunter held the atlatl in his hand and used it to throw the spear. The atlatl increased the efficiency of the spear by increasing the force behind the spear throw. The bow and arrow, found in Upper Paleolithic Egypt, worked on the same principle. The bow string increased the force on the arrow and allowed it to travel farther and with greater force than if it had been thrown by hand.

Upper Paleolithic man had a greater number of tools than Neanderthal man. The highly developed Upper Paleolithic tool kit included tools for use during different seasons. In other words, cultural adaptation had become highly specific. Animal bone yards containing thousands of skeletons bear witness to the increased proficiency of group hunting during the Upper Paleolithic. Ten thousand horse skeletons were found at Solutre, France; almost one thousand mammoth skeletons were found at Predmost, Czechoslovakia.

Upper Paleolithic cultures. It becomes difficult to speak of an Upper Paleolithic culture; instead, one must make note of the many different traditions that grew out of the various environments man began to inhabit. Important Upper Paleolithic European cultures were the Aurignacian, Gravettian, Solutrean, and Magdalenian cultures, all of which were supported by the hunting of large herd animals. The Aurignacian culture dates from about 35,000 B.C. in Europe and southwest Asia. The Gravettian culture dates from about 22,000 to 18,000 B.C. and is found in Europe and southern Russia. Venus figurines, large breasted, big hipped women possibly depicting pregnancy or fertility, are characteristic of this culture. The Solutrean culture found in Spain and France lasted from about 18,000 to 15,000 B.C. The Magdalenian culture lasted from about 15,000 to 8000 B.C. and was centered in Western Europe, but occurred as far east as Russia. This culture witnessed the invention of the harpoon, the spear-thrower, and microliths; a typical tool kit of the period is illustrated in Figure 10-7.

Upper Paleolithic cultures contain the earliest remains of man's artistic behavior, including the first known cave paintings. These paintings are almost exclusively of animals and were often painted one on top of the other, indicating that they were primarily of symbolic or religio-magical significance rather than examples of art for art's sake. The original study at the end of this chapter describes several examples of Paleolithic art.

In Northern Africa, sub-Saharan Africa, Asia, and the Western hemisphere a variety of cultures existed. In Northern Africa, best known are the Aterian culture, with characteristic flaking techniques, and the Dabban culture, a blade culture. Sub-Saharan man evolved different systems because of his adaptation to heavily wooded areas. For example, the Sangoan-Lupemban tradition was characterized by core tools (hand axes, picks) which were most useful in a forest environment. Western Asia and the Middle East possessed cultures largely parallel to those of Europe. Upper Paleolithic cultural artifacts discovered in America seem to indicate in some instances a more primi-

Figure 10-7. *These drawings show a variety of tools likely to be found in the kits of Paleolithic men, along with an artist's reconstruction of the way such tools might have been used.*

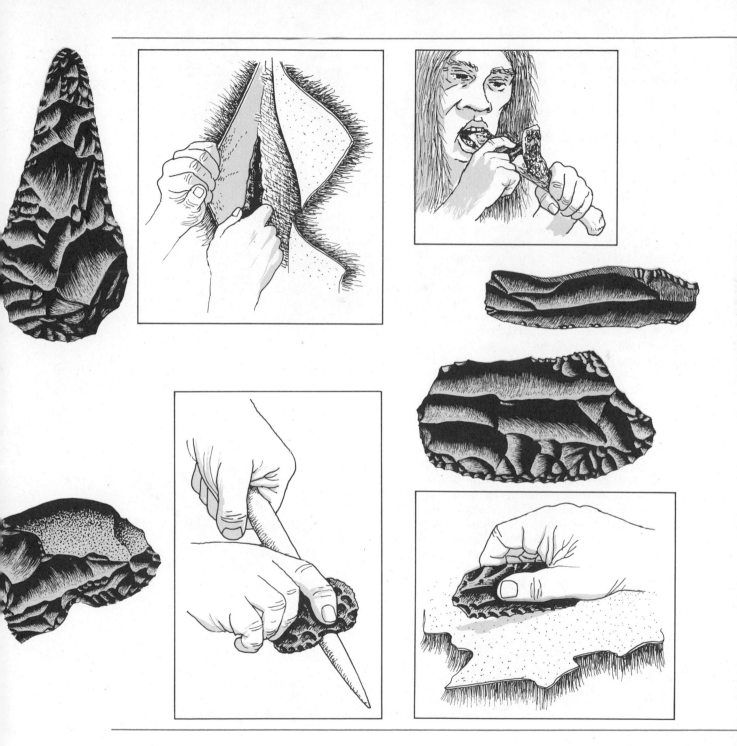

tive society, roughly comparable to the Lower Paleolithic period groups in Europe and Asia; the reasons for this cultural lag are not clear.

The Mesolithic era

By 12,000 B.C., the glacial period was ending, causing great physical changes in man's habitats. The sea levels rose; in Europe the tundras and savannas disappeared and were covered by oceans and hardwood forests. The herd animals also disappeared: some, like the reindeer, moved to colder climates; others, like the mammoths, died. Man began to collect food and to fish around lake shores, bays, and rivers. The climatic changes that occurred in Europe during the Mesolithic meant an increase in the amount of vegetable food available, with a corresponding decrease in large animal herds. So, in a sense, the European Mesolithic era marked a return to more typical hominid subsistence patterns.

Mesolithic tools

New technologies were required in the changed postglacial environment. Ground stone tools, stone tools shaped and sharpened by grinding the tool against sandstone (often using sand as an additional abrasive), were very effectively used as axes and edges. These tools were helpful in clearing forest areas and in the woodwork needed for the creation of dugout canoes and skin-covered boats. Boats first appear in Mesolithic sites, indicating that man had expanded his hunting and gathering territory to include the water. Man was then able to exploit deep water resources as well as the coastal areas.

The characteristic Mesolithic tool was the microlith, the small flint blade first manufactured in the Magdalenian culture during the later Upper Paleolithic. Microliths were small but hard and sharp. They could be mass produced because they were small, easy to make, and could be of

Figure 10-8. *The drawing above shows a Mesolithic tool consisting of a wooden or bone handle with microliths set into it. Below is a bone tool of a somewhat earlier date, fitted out for service as a harpoon. The most advanced technology is seen in the ax opposite. Made in Neolithic times, it has a smooth stone blade set in a wooden handle that gives increased leverage.*

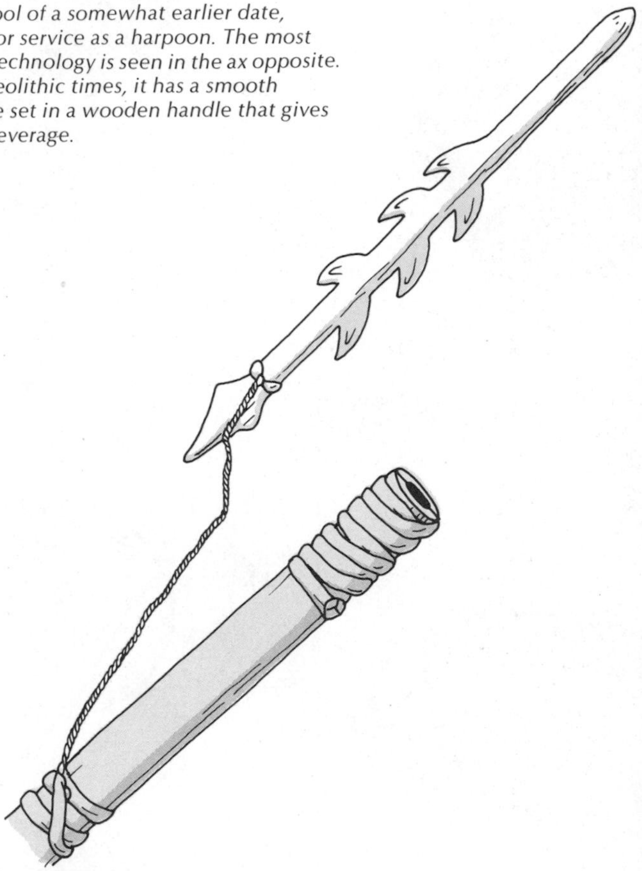

materials other than flint. Also, they could be attached to arrow shafts by using melted resin as a binder. Thus, the bow and arrow with the microlith arrowhead became the Mesolithic culture's deadliest and most common weapon.

The archeological record ● part **3**

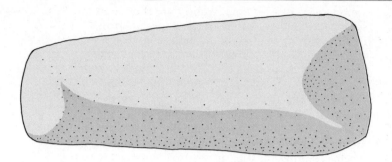

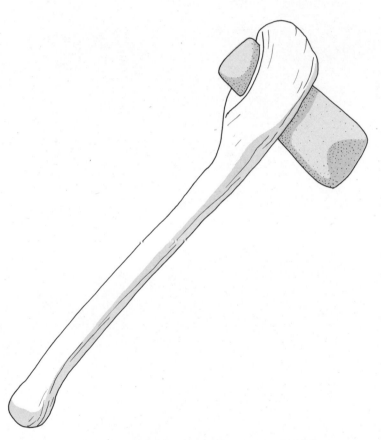

It is possible that the Mesolithic was a more sedentary period for man than earlier eras. Dwellings from this period seem better built, an indication of permanency. Indeed, this is a logical development: most hunting cultures and cultures depending on herd animals are nomadic. To be successful, one must follow the game. This is not necessary for peoples subsisting on a diet of seafood and plants, as the location of shores and vegetation remains relatively constant.

Major Paleolithic and Mesolithic trends. Certain trends stand out from the specific information anthropologists have gathered about the Stone Ages. These are general progressions that occurred from one culture to the next in most parts of the world.

One trend was towards increasingly more sophisticated, varied, and specialized tool kits. Tools became progressively lighter and smaller, resulting in the conservation of raw materials and a better ratio between length of cutting edge and weight of flint. Tools became specialized according to region and function. Instead of crude all-purpose tools, more effective particularized devices were made to better exploit the differing conditions of savanna, forest, and shore.

This more efficient tool technology enabled man to increase in population and move into more diverse environments; it also was responsible for the dropping of heavy features and physical characteristics in favor of decreased size and weight of face and teeth and the development of cranial capacity and complexity. This dependence on intelligence rather than bulk provided the key for man's increased reliance on cultural rather than physical adaptation. As the brain became modernized, conceptual thought, as evidenced in remains of religio-magical ceremonies, developed.

Throughout Paleolithic times, there appeared a trend towards the importance of and proficiency in hunting. Man's intelligence enabled him to develop tools that exceeded other animals' physical equipment; as well as the increased social organization and cooperation so important for survival and growth. This trend was reversed during the Mesolithic, when hunting lost its preeminence and was often replaced by gathering of plants and seafood.

As man grew and spread, regionalism also grew. Tool cultures developed at different times in different areas. General differences appeared between north and south, east and west. Although there are some indications of cultural contact and intercommunication, such as the obvious links between primitive and more advanced tool cultures, regionalism was a dominant characteristic of the Paleolithic era. The persistence of regionalism is probably due in large part to the need to adapt to differing environments. Paleolithic man had spread over all the continents of the world; changes in climate and environment and the exigencies of the nomadic life kept him frequently on the move. Thus Paleolithic tool kits had to be adapted to meet the requirements of many varying locations. In forest environments, men needed strong axes for working wood; on the open savanna and plains, they used the bow and arrow to hunt the game they could not stalk closely; the settlements that grew up around lakes and along rivers developed harpoons and hooks; in the subarctic regions they needed tools to work the heavy skins of seals and caribou; in the grasslands men needed tools for cutting grain and separating the usable part from the chaff. The fact that culture is first and foremost an adaptive mechanism meant that it was of necessity a regional thing.

☐

Original study

THE ART
OF EARLY MAN

Religion and art appear in the archeological record with the appearance of *Homo sapiens,* religion with Neanderthal man, and art with Cro-Magnon or modern-type man. The earliest hint of an esthetic sense in the forerunners of man comes from the Olduvai Gorge. Near the bottom of the gorge, in places where *Australopithecus* foraged more than 1,500,000 years ago, are lumps of translucent pale pink quartzite, all of them unworked and obtained from a single mineral deposit—and all apparently picked up and carried around.

Later during Acheulian times there were crude designs engraved on bone and occasional hand axes shaped far more beautifully than required for strictly utilitarian purposes. Such pieces may represent pride of craftsmanship more than art, but they show that man was expressing feelings for proportion and symmetry several hundred thousand years ago. Many factors were undoubtedly involved in the origin of art itself, for example, the use of symbols connected with death rituals. The notion that death is an apparent ending only, that part of a man lives on, demands external signs of some sort—something that will remain intact after the rituals are done.

Personal adornment was another precursor of art. There was a time before people cared enough about themselves, before they were sufficiently aware of themselves, to want to appear more attractive or add to themselves. Then something happened to bring an increasing self-consciousness, perhaps the presence of more people in larger groups, and the threat of a loss of identity. Part of the response was to color their faces and bodies, to use the personal pronoun more, and say in effect: "I am an individual; look at me. Pay attention to me. I am different, something special."

The earliest sign of the change comes from the Neanderthals, an interesting fact considering that style does not show up in their artifacts, or at least we have not learned to see style in their artifacts. There are the flowers at the grave in Shanidar, for instance. Also, Neanderthal sites commonly include natural pigments, probably to serve as cosmetics for the dead in "viewings" and burial ceremonies as well as for the living, lumps of black manganese and red ocher, some sharpened like pencils and others scratched presumably to make powder.

The new spirit flowered among Cro-Magnon people. They not only used cosmetics, but made the earliest known jewelry. They wore clothes decorated with rows of colored beads, ivory bracelets, necklaces of pierced teeth and fish vertebrae. Their more elaborate decorations were related to a general increase in the complexity of communal living, to the rise of more advanced mass-hunting methods. Jewelry may have done more than beautify. It may have helped to identify the clan or the status of people associating in groups too large for individuals to know one another by sight or name. At the same time, more complex rituals served to teach and sanctify more complex rules of behavior. This is the framework, the social context, in which art had its beginnings.

The world's first great art "movement" lasted more than 20,000 years, from Aurignacian to Magdalenian times. Some of its most spectacular products are found in underground galleries, away from natural light in the passages and chambers and niches of limestone caves, and indicate in a most vivid fashion how completely hunting dominated the attention and imagination of prehistoric man. He rarely drew people, and never anything that would be recognized as a landscape, although there are a wide variety of signs which have no obvious meaning to us. His overwhelming concern was with game animals seen as individuals, clearly defined and detached, and isolated from their natural settings.

The Les Eyzies region [of France] includes the largest cluster of art sites as well as the most striking of the lot, the famous Lascaux cave located in the woods on a plateau above the valley of the Vézère. Four boys and a dog discovered it during a walk early one September afternoon in 1940, the dog disappearing down a hole half-concealed by roots and moss and the boys scrambling after. (Boys are officially credited with the discovery of about a dozen art caves, but the unofficial count would be considerably higher, since archeologists often receive sole credit for caves they originally learned about from boys in the neighborhood.)

What they were the first to see by the wavering light of a homemade oil lamp thousands of visitors, tourists as well as archeologists and artists, have seen many times since. There is no prelude to the splendor of this gallery. The entrance leads down a short flight of stairs directly into the main hall, into a world of huge horned animals painted red and black. In a way, the first moment is the high point of the visit. You stand silent in the dark and lights are turned on and images appear as if projected on a screen, in a kind of three-dimensional panorama since the wall curves in front of you and around at the sides. For that moment, almost before the eye has a chance to look and before the ideas and questions start flowing, you take it all in at once.

Then the experience breaks into parts. The animals become individuals in a frieze along the upper wall of the hall, along an overhanging ledge formed by the scooping-out action of an ancient river. Four bulls in black outline with black curving horns dominate the assemblage; one of them, the largest cave painting yet discovered, measures eighteen feet long. Two of the bulls face one another, and five red stags fill the space between them. The frieze also includes six black horses, a large red horse, three cows, a so-called "unicorn" which is actually a two-horned creature resembling no known species, and a number of other animals which are difficult to distinguish because they are partly covered by more recently painted figures.

A small chamber, which looks like a rather uninteresting dead end until one comes closer, lies off to the side. One must step carefully at this point because there is a pit here under a domed ceiling covered with a tangle of engraved lines and crisscross patterns and unidentifiable remnants of some red and black paintings. The edge of the hole is worn smooth as if many persons had lowered themselves to the bottom in times past, perhaps by rope. (A fragment of three-ply rope has been found in the cave.)

Today an iron ladder extends into the pit. It leads to a ledge and a work unique in the records of cave art—a buffalo disemboweled by a spear through its hindquarters, a stick-figure man with a bird's head falling backward directly in front of the buffalo, a pole with a bird on it below the man, and to the left behind the man a two-horned rhinoceros. This enigmatic scene has been often and variously interpreted. François Bordes [a French archeologist] has one version which he will impart if pressed, and if you do not take him too seriously: "Let me tell you my story of this painting, a science-fiction story. Once upon a time a hunter who belonged to the bird totem was killed by a bison. One of his companions, a member of the rhinoceros totem, came into the cave and drew the scene of his friend's death—and of his revenge. The bison has spears or arrows in it and is disemboweled, probably by the horn of the rhinoceros. This is how it was."

Source:

John E. Pfeiffer, *The Emergence of Man,* revised and enlarged edition. New York: Harper & Row, 1969. Copyright 1969 by Harper & Row, Publishers, Inc. Reprinted by permission of Harper & Row.

Summary

1.

The cultural tradition of reproducing tools as the need arises sets man apart from his fellow creatures. To simplify man's cultural revolution, three major cultural stages were designated. These stages are distinguished by the materials man used to make tools: the Stone Age, the Bronze Age, and the Iron Age. The Stone Age is divided into the Paleolithic, Mesolithic, and Neolithic Ages. The Paleolithic Age is divided into the Lower, Middle, and Upper Paleolithic Periods.

2.

The earliest known Lower Paleolithic tools are about two million years old. They were first found at Olduvai Gorge. The Olduwan pebble tool tradition was largely based on one all-purpose generalized chopping tool. Lower Paleolithic men used the percussion method to make their tool. They struck the tool with a hammerstone or against a large rock to knock off flakes and form a jagged, irregular cutting edge. The tool permitted *Homo erectus* to expand his diet with animals he was previously unable to skin and cut. He also used the tool for digging and defense. The pebble tool tradition marks one of the first known times that an animal species made a cultural rather than a physical adaptation to its changing environment.

3.

The Olduwan chopper evolved into first the Chellean and then the Acheulian hand ax. These tools, the earliest of which are about a million years old, are pear-shaped, with pointed ends and sharp cutting edges. Like the chopper, they served a general purpose. During the Chellean and Acheulian periods, tool cultures began to diversify. Along with axes, cleavers, scrapers, and flake tools were developed. Further signs of *Homo erectus'* developing technology were his selection of harder rocks for heavier tools, and his use of fires for warmth and cooking. During later Acheulian times, *Homo erectus* used the baton and striking platform methods to make thinner axes with straighter, sharper cutting edges.

4.

During very late Acheulian times, about 200,000 years ago, the Levalloisian tradition of tool manufacturing arose. This technique required less time to produce tools with sharper, less sinuous edges. Evolution of man's social organization evolved together with the advances in technology. Advances in both areas were closely related to the increased size and complexity of man's brain. Improvements in communication and social organization brought about by language, improved hunting methods, and a population increase all contributed to man's spreading to new environments.

5.

The emergence of Neanderthal man and the development of the Mousterian tradition of toolmaking characterize the Middle Paleolithic Period. Mousterian flake tools were lighter and smaller than Levalloisian. Mousterian tools included hand axes, flakes, scrapers, borers, wood shavers, and spears. They increased the availability and quality of Neanderthal man's food resources, shelter, and clothing. Archeological evidence indicates that Neanderthal man engaged in religious ceremonies and cared for the disabled.

6.

Upper Paleolithic cultures evolved from the Mousterian. These cultures are associated with *Homo sapiens sapiens,* whose typical tool was the blade. The blade technique of tool-making saved much more flint than Mousterian methods. Other efficient Upper Paleolithic toolmaking techniques were pressure-flaking, heating raw materials before making them into tools, and using chisel-like stone tools called burins. Upper Paleolithic man's cultural adaptation became specific. He developed different tools for different seasons. There is no one Upper Paleolithic culture. Different environments produced different cultures. Important Upper Paleolithic European cultures supported themselves by hunting large herd animals. Upper Paleolithic cultures contain the earliest remains of man's artistic behavior.

7.

The ending of the glacial period caused great physical changes in man's habitats. Sea levels were raised, vegetation increased, and herd animals disappeared. In a sense the European Mesolithic Period marked a return to more typical hominid ways of subsistence. Ground-stone tools, used as axes and edges, answered postglacial needs for new technologies. The characteristic Mesolithic tool was the microlith, a small, hard, sharp flint blade which could be mass produced. Increased reliance on seafood and plants made the Mesolithic a more sedentary period for man.

8.

Three trends emerged from the Paleolithic and Mesolithic periods. First was a trend toward more sophisticated, varied, and specialized tool kits. This trend enabled man to increase his population and spread to new environments. It also was adaptive, leading to decreased size and weight of face and teeth and development of cranial capacity and complexity. Second was a trend toward the importance of and proficiency in hunting. This trend was reversed during the Mesolithic Period. Hunting was often replaced by gathering plants and seafood. Third was a trend toward regionalism. Man's technology and life habits begin to reflect his association with a particular environment.

Suggested readings

Bordes, François *A Tale of Two Caves.* New York: Harper & Row, 1972.
  The archeological evidence found in two French caves of the Dordogne district forms the basis of this anthropological case study. The book discusses the interdisciplinary approach and methodology employed by French anthropologists and geologists. A complete history of the research done in these caves is traced, and the information gathered on the Acheulian and Mousterian cultures is reported. Various methods used to date the findings and to understand Paleolithic societies are considered.

Clark, J. Desmond *The Prehistory of Africa.* New York: Praeger, 1970.
  This book presents an up-to-date account of the prehistoric evidence of the processes of cultural and economic change in Africa. The evidence is interpreted in light of prevailing thought. It is based on lectures given at Bryn Mawr College in 1969 and contains extensive textual notes.

Pfeiffer, John E. *The Emergence of Man.* New York: Harper & Row, 1969.
  This is a thorough survey of man's prehistory. Archeology and primatology as well as contemporary studies help round out the picture of man's development as a human being.

Semenov, S. A. *Prehistoric Technology.* New York: Barnes and Noble, 1964.
  Semenov's important study is devoted to the problems of the history of the oldest working tools. This research on the methods of manufacturing and use of prehistoric bone and stone tools illuminates the way of life of the people who employed the artifacts.

Cultivation
and domestication

During the Upper Paleolithic period, man's existence was marginal; he lived a catch-as-catch-can life, stalking herds of mammoth, bison, and reindeer, and gathering plants. About 12,000 years ago, during the period immediately following the Paleolithic, man began exchanging his nomadic hunting way of life for a more secure sedentary one. During this period, called the Mesolithic, or Middle Stone Age, man turned toward the more stable food supplies found in the rivers, lakes, and oceans. These waterways were teeming with aquatic life because of the rising seas brought about by warmer temperatures and melting glaciers. On the shores of lakes and rivers, Mesolithic men formed small permanent settlements that later developed into rudimentary farming and fishing villages.

About a thousand years later, as the Mesolithic shaded into the Neolithic, or New Stone Age, man became an established agriculturalist and pastoralist. This change in the means of obtaining food had important implications for man's development, for it meant that he was no longer the passive hunter dependent on the bounty of a capricious nature. Instead, he took matters into his own hands, prying out of nature the secrets of crop growing and animal breeding. With good reason, the Neolithic period has been called a revolutionary period in man's history.

Once man settled down and became a scientific food producer, his culture advanced rapidly. Man's social horizons expanded during the Neolithic when he started living in groups and cooperating, not only with the members inside his own group, but with those outside as well. Permanent settlements expanded into cities, and, with the growth of cities came an explosive series of inventions and discoveries. It was during the Neolithic that the basic patterns of modern life were established.

A changing way of life

In the Late Paleolithic, man was engaged in hunting, fishing, and gathering whatever nature was kind enough to provide. There is little evidence, if any, in Paleolithic remains to indicate that livestock was kept or grain cultivated. Paleolithic man followed wild herds, moving on to new areas when the old food supply was exhausted. He probably had neither the time nor the technical knowledge required to care for animals or cultivate plants; he relied solely on his muscles to acquire food and believed that magic might help to increase production of the land. But as he followed the herds or seasons, the transition that led to protecting and caring for animals and sowing, fertilizing, weeding, and watering plants may have taken place.

The Mesolithic beginnings of agriculture and pastoralism

The Mesolithic, or Middle Stone Age, may be viewed either as the final stage of the Paleolithic or as the beginning of the Neolithic. Fixed by historians as having occurred around 12,000 years ago, the Mesolithic is an important period during which man began to evolve into the social animal he is today. Faced with the environmental conditions, man shaped the patterns of his nomadic existence into a more sedentary one that offered him greater control over his food supplies and therefore an increased margin of survival.

The retreat of the glaciers in Europe brought milder climates, the return of the forests, and changes in the distribution and types of animals. The huge herds of horses, bison, reindeer, and other game no longer grazed in large herds on the open plains, easy targets for bands of hunters. Instead, the forces of natural selection drove these animals into the forest where they could move about in small groups among the dense vegetation and high trees that provided food and protective covering from their human predators. Thus, as the game became more elusive and difficult to trap, Mesolithic man improved his hunting skills. He devised ingenious snares, traps, and weapons to catch and kill the agile animals. It is held, for example, that the bow and arrow developed into a major weapon at this time in man's history.

These new climatic conditions also forced the Mesolithic hunters to turn to the rivers and sea for food. Thus, fishing became for man another major cultural adaptation to the changing world. Moreover, small settlements began developing along these riverine sources of food.

Major Mesolithic cultures

In Western Europe, two major Mesolithic cultures developed: the Azilian (southern France and Spain) and the Tardenoisian (England, Germany, and France). The most important tools used by both of these cultures were microliths, small stones, some of which bear geometric dot-and-dash designs painted in red. These microliths, about one-half inch to two inches long, are often singled out by investigators as the definitive feature of the Mesolithic Age. Most of the remains of these two European cultures are found along the edges of inland waters and swampy areas, indicating a heavy dependence on fishing for food.

In the Near East, around 11,000 years ago, the important Capsian and Natufian cultures flourished. The Capsian culture, centered mostly in various parts of North Africa, developed the microlithic tool culture later adopted by the Mesolithic hunters of Europe. The Capsians probably lived in large village settlements along lakes and rivers.

More interesting are the Natufians, a people who lived in what is now Israel and Jordan in caves, rock shelters, and primitive villages with stone-walled houses. Basin-shaped depressions in the rocks found outside these homes are thought to have been storage pits. Plastered storage pits beneath the floors of the houses were also found, indicating that the Natufians were the earliest known Mesolithic people to have stored crops. Certain tools found in the Natufian remains bear evidence that they were used to cut grain, indicating that these ancient people also may have harvested wild grain. These Mesolithic sickles, for that is what they must be, consisted of small stone blades set in straight handles of wood or bone.

The development by Mesolithic man of microliths provided him with an important advantage not found in the one-piece Upper Paleolithic tools: the small size of the microlith enabled man to devise composite tools made out of stone and wood or bone. Thus, man could make sickles,

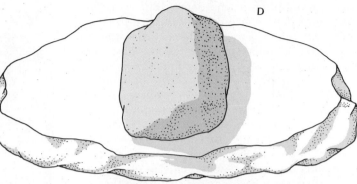

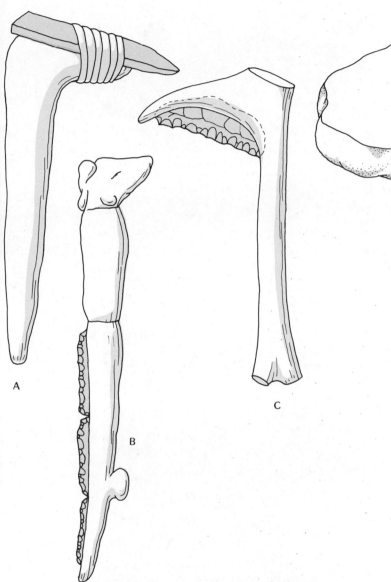

Figure 11-1. *These drawings show some of the tools with which man began to cultivate crops. Most tools were a combination of bone or wood handles and flint or in some cases bone blades. Microliths are commonly found in many agricultural tools of this period.*

harpoons, arrows, and daggers by fitting microliths into grooves in wood or bone handles. Later experimentation with these forms led to more sophisticated tools and weapons.

The Neolithic revolution

The Neolithic, or New Stone Age, was characterized by the transition from foraging for food to the domestication of animals and the cultivation of plants. It was by no means a smooth transition; in fact, it spread over many centuries and included much of the preceding Mesolithic Age.

The term "New Stone Age" is derived from the polished stone tools that are characteristic of this period. But more important than the presence of these tools is the transition from nomadism to an agricultural economy that took place at this time, representing a major change in the subsistence patterns of early man. The oldest Neolithic site containing domesticated plants and animals has been radiocarbon dated, showing it to be between 9000 and 11,000 years old.

Beginnings of cultivation and domestication

The process of cultivation among Mesolithic-Neolithic cultures did not begin with sowing.

Early forms of food production preceded the actual growing of crops and domestication of animals. For example, acorns were leached to clear them of tannin and so render them edible. Gourds were hung up to be used as hives for bees. Attempts were made to improve growing conditions; woods were burned over to improve the berry bushes; pebbles in estuaries were cleared away to improve the size and quality of plants growing there.

Prior to his attempts at cultivation, Neolithic man may have observed natural phenomena that gave him hints as to how to cultivate plants; for example, he may have noticed that hemp throve on rich soil and grew in abundance around the dwelling places of man. But at first there probably was little reliable wisdom or acquired tradition regarding cultivation. When crops were planted in quick succession, and rain was the chief method of watering, the soil was soon exhausted. Some groups simply abandoned the site and cleared another patch, and when that was exhausted, moved on again. Soon, however, new techniques for fertilization were discovered. There seems to have been a continuous use of plots, with fertility being maintained by crop rotation. In other cases, the exhausted soil was allowed to return to bush, then cleared and burned off, the ashes fertilizing the plot. Others allowed an area to return to grass and used it as pasture for their herds. The animal droppings acted as fertilizer. From observing that when a river overflowed its banks, silt was returned to the land and thereby enriched it, early man was probably led to experiment with artificial irrigation from springs and rivers.

Early man had to be ingenious in order to acquire enough food to satisfy his needs. Possibly the abundance of game and wild plant life and water and other environmental factors in certain areas accounts for his choices of animals and plants for domestication. However, bison, wild sheep, antelope, and deer existed in the New World, and no attempt was made to domesticate them. Moreover, plants were not always cultivated in the same locale where they were abundant

Figure 11-2. *These pictures tell much about the life of the early cultivators. The Egyptian wall painting (right) shows all the steps in the reaping of grain; the Greek coin depicts a field mouse sharing the harvest.*

in the wild. For example, Italy had wild olive trees, but cultivated olives were first grown in Greece; wild walnut trees and wild grapes were found in China, but the cultivated walnut came from Iran and the cultivated grape from the West. Cultivation and domestication did not necessarily occur simultaneously, but most scholars believe that domestication of animals was at least related to the growth of horticulture. In the New World, it is clear that horticulture came first. Attempts to determine the sequence of development by studying modern primitive societies have yielded no satisfactory answer. For example, some modern tribes farm without ever having owned stock, and others cultivate plants but do not breed animals.

Evidence of early cultivation.   In what ways do the remains found at ancient sites tell archeologists that the inhabitants were engaged in domestication and cultivation? Analysis of plant and animal remains at a site will usually indicate whether or not its occupants were food producers. A paleobotanist can often tell the fossil of a wild plant species from a domesticated one by a study of the husks and of the stem that holds the seed of the plant. For example, wild cereal grasses, such as barley, wheat, and maize (corn),

221

have a very fragile stem, whereas domesticated cereals have a tough stem. The structural change from a soft to a tough stem in early cultivated plants was probably an unintentional result of selection. When the wild grain stalks were harvested, their soft stems would shatter at the touch of a sickle or flail, and their seeds would be lost. It seems probable then that seeds harvested would be taken from the tough plants. Early domesticators probably also selected seeds from plants having few husks or none at all—eventually breeding them out—because husking prior to pounding the grains into meal or flour was much too time consuming. Size of plants is another good indicator of the presence of cultivation. For example, wild bean seeds and pods are much smaller than their domesticated counterparts.

Evidence of early domestication.

Domestication also produced changes in the skeletal structure of some animals. For example, the horns of wild goats and sheep differ from those of domesticated goats and male sheep (domesticated female sheep have none). Another structural change that occurred in domestication involves the size of the animal or parts of the animal. For example, certain teeth of domesticated pigs are smaller than those of wild ones.

A study of the age and sex ratios of slain animals at a site may indicate whether or not animal domestication was practiced. It has been assumed by investigators that if the age and/or sex ratios at the site differ from those in modern wild herds, the imbalances are due to conscious selection. For example, at the village of Jarmo, in northern Iraq, the ratio of male to female sheep was much higher than in wild sheep herds. It has been concluded, therefore, that the occupants of Jarmo were domesticating the sheep, slaughtering the males for food and saving the females for breeding. In another village site, the proportion of immature sheep to adults was much higher than in wild herds. It appeared, then, that the young animals were slaughtered for food, whereas the adults were used for breeding.

The theory that age and sex imbalances indicate selection by domesticators has not been proved. Hunters may have followed the same selective practices, sparing the adults and females so they would propagate the species and insure large herds for the following season.

Why man became a food producer

The consequences of cultivation and domestication are so momentous for the development of civilization that their origin should be examined carefully. What is the evidence?

Several theories have been proposed to account for this change in the subsistence pattern of early man. One major theory is the "oasis" or "desiccation" theory, based on climatic determinism. Its proponents have advanced the idea that the glacial cover over Europe and Asia caused a southern shift in the rain patterns from Europe to northern Africa and southwest Asia. When the glaciers retreated northward, so did the rain patterns. Drying resulted in northern Africa and southwest Asia, and men were forced to congregate at oases for water; because of the scarcity of wild animals in such an arid environment, early man was driven by necessity to collect the wild grasses and seeds growing around the oases. Eventually man had to cultivate the grasses to provide enough food for the community. According to this theory, domestication began because the oases attracted hungry animals, such as wild goats, sheep, and also cattle, which came to graze on the stubble of the grain fields. Man, finding them too thin to kill for food, began to fatten them up.

There is little concrete evidence to substantiate such a theory. Pollen analysis, for example, has failed to show evidence of a drastic climatic change. The theory does not explain why plant and animal domestication occurred in areas that did not dry out, such as tropical southeast Asia or South America. And it does not explain why, during droughts, sheep and goats would migrate to low-lying oases rather than to the wetter hills. Furthermore, if this theory were to be accepted, the failure of domestication to appear during the

Figure 11-3. Many kinds of domestication were attempted. The painting at the top shows Egyptians trying to domesticate wild ducks; the Sumerian relief at the bottom shows a cow at far right and the processing and storing of milk.

three earlier postglacial periods remains unexplained.

Another theory proposes that the earliest farming villages were located in the foothill regions of southwest Asia, rather than in the oases and floodplains. The proponents of this theory believe that domestication originated in areas in which the wild counterparts of the early domesticates are found in abundance. In southwest Asia, these zones were found in the hilly regions of the Fertile Crescent, the region formed by the confluence of the Tigris and Euphrates rivers, where large herds of wild goats and sheep and large stands of wild wheat and barley could be found. After people had familiarized themselves with their environment and settled down in one area, they began to domesticate the plants and animals they had previously gathered. When man had acquired enough knowledge and technological skill, he began to domesticate and cultivate. This theory proposes a cultural rather than an environmental explanation.

However, there is archeological evidence that settling down and mastering the environment does not necessarily culminate in domestication. For example, at Mureybit, in southwest Asia, storage pits and year-round occupation of stone houses indicated that its occupants had definitely settled down between 8200 B.C. and 7500 B.C. Yet the remains and artifacts indicate that the occupants were hunters and gatherers and not domesticators. Furthermore, some of the early farming villages were occupied only seasonally, not year-round.

Culture
of Neolithic settlements

A number of settlements of the Neolithic period have been excavated, particularly in the Middle East. The architectural structures and artifacts found at these sites have revealed much about the daily activities of their former inhabitants as they pursued the business of making a living.

Earliest agricultural settlements: Jarmo and Jericho

Dated about 11,000 to 9000 years ago, the earliest known sites containing domesticated plants and animals are found in the Near East. These sites occur in a region extending from the Jordan Valley eastward across the flanks of the Taurus Mountains into northern Syria and northeastern Iran, and southward into Iraq and Iran along the hilly flanks of the Zagros Mountains. The sites contain evidence of domesticated barley, wheat, goats, sheep, dogs, and pigs.

At Jarmo, a settlement in the foothills of the Zagros Mountains dating from about 7000 B.C., the inhabitants domesticated goats and cultivated barley and emmer wheat, which is somewhat like the wild wheat that grows in that area today. About fifteen dwellings, housing perhaps a hundred and fifty people, were uncovered; among the artifacts found there were mortars and pestles, and storage pits.

The dwellings were made of hard mud or adobe walls, and were divided into several rooms. Evidence indicates that the inhabitants of Jarmo cut the wheat and barley with flint sickles, ground the grain in stone troughs, and baked it in ovens or ate it as porridge out of stone bowls. The existence of trade can be deduced from the fact that some of the tools found at Jarmo were made of obsidian. This material must have been acquired in trade, since the nearest source is 300 miles away.

The earliest post-Natufian levels of the Biblical city of Jericho show many characteristics similar to those at Jarmo, although the architecture is somewhat more complex. Jericho, an oasis in Jordan, was occupied as early as 7800 B.C.; throughout the Neolithic, successive groups of people occupied the area. As a result, remains of tools, houses, clothing, and ornaments are found in horizontal strata or levels.

The earliest Neolithic level contained a village of semisubterranean houses (pithouses) of stone and adobe brick, which covered approximately eight acres. Each succeeding settlement of the city grew more complex; eventually, the city occupied an area of ten acres, surrounded by six-foot-wide heavy stone walls, parts of which are still standing today. Inside Jericho, about 3000 people lived in adobe brick houses with plastered floors built around courtyards. A village cemetery also indicates the sedentary life of these early people; nomadic groups, with few exceptions, rarely buried their dead in a single central location.

Evidence of domestic plants and animals is scant at Jericho. However, indirect evidence in the form of harvesting tools and milling equipment has been uncovered at the site. Like Jarmo, the remains at Jericho bear evidence of trade; obsidian, turquoise from Sinai, and marine shells from the coast were discovered within the city.

Comparable sites have been discovered in Iraq, Anatolia, Cyprus, and other areas of the Near East. The cultures at these sites form the basis of the development of the subsequent peasant (and later urban) communities of the Fertile Crescent.

The spread of agriculture

Agriculture seems to have spread out from southwest Asia to adjacent areas, eventually reaching eastern Europe by 6000 B.C., central Europe and the Netherlands by the end of the fifth millenium, and England late in the fourth. The Neolithic Age began independently in southeast Asia and the New World (Mexico, Peru, the Caribbean lowlands of South America) and possibly North China and other regions. But some environments were not conducive to the spread of agriculture. For example, the Russian steppes, with their heavy grass cover, were not suitable to farming without a plow, but they were ideal for herding.

Archeological evidence from southeast Asia indicates that domestication appeared there as early as, or possibly earlier than, it occurred in southwest Asia. Domesticated plants from Spirit Cave in northern Thailand have been radiocarbon dated back to the eighth millenium B.C. Because southeast Asia is hot and humid, the wheat and barley of southwest Asia could not be grown there. Instead, cultivated plants included rice, peas, beans and other legumes, as well as root crops such as yams. Conversely, plants requiring much water, such as rice, could not thrive in the dry climate of southwest Asia.

Neolithic technology

Since fewer people were needed for food production than for hunting and food gathering, some had time for inventing and manufacturing. Early harvesting tools were made of wood or bone with serrated flints inserted. Later tools were made by chipping and flaking stone, but during the Neolithic period, stone that was too hard to be chipped was ground and polished for tools. Man developed scythes, forks, hoes, and plows to replace the simple dibbles (digging sticks). Pestles and mortars were used for preparation of grain. Plows were later redesigned when man realized that domesticated cattle could be used as draft animals.

Pottery. In addition to the domestication of plants and animals, one of the characteristics of the Neolithic Age is the extensive manufacture and use of pottery. As agriculture and pastoralism developed and food supplies and leisure time increased, different forms of pottery were created for transporting and storing food, artifacts, and other material possessions. Because pottery vessels are impervious to damage by insects, rodents, and dampness, they could be used for storing small grain, seeds, and other materials. Moreover, food can be boiled in pottery vessels directly over the fire rather than by the ancient technique of cooking by burying food with hot stones. Pottery is also used for pipes, ladles, lamps, and other objects, and some cultures used large vessels for burial of the dead. Significantly, pottery remains an important container for much of mankind today.

The widespread use of pottery, which is manufactured from clay and fired, is a good indication

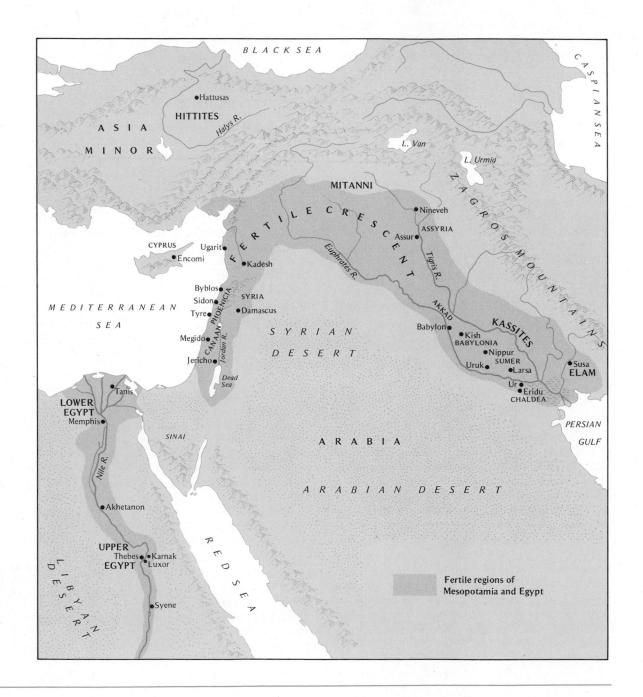

BLACK SEA

CASPIAN SEA

ASIA MINOR

HITTITES

•Hattusas

Halys R.

L. Van

L. Urmia

ZAGROS MOUNTAINS

MITANNI

•Nineveh

ASSYRIA

Assur•

CYPRUS

Ugarit•

•Encomi

•Kadesh

FERTILE CRESCENT

Euphrates R.

Tigris R.

AKKAD

KASSITES

MEDITERRANEAN SEA

Byblos•
Sidon•
Tyre•

SYRIA

•Damascus

PHOENICIA

CANAAN

Jordan R.

Megido•

Jericho•

Dead Sea

SYRIAN DESERT

Babylon•
•Kish
BABYLONIA
•Nippur
SUMER
Uruk•
•Larsa
Ur•
•Eridu
CHALDEA

•Susa
ELAM

PERSIAN GULF

LOWER EGYPT

•Tanis

Memphis•

SINAI

ARABIA

ARABIAN DESERT

Nile R.

•Akhetanon

RED SEA

LIBYAN DESERT

UPPER EGYPT

Thebes• •Karnak
Luxor

Fertile regions of
Mesopotamia and Egypt

•Syene

The archeological record • part **3**

of a sedentary community and is found in abundance in all but a few of the earliest Neolithic settlements. Its fragility and weight make it impractical for use by nomads and hunters, who use baskets and hide containers. Nevertheless, there are modern nomads who make and use pottery, just as there are farmers who lack it.

The manufacture of pottery is a difficult art, and requires a high degree of technological sophistication. To make an efficient pot requires a knowledge of clay and the techniques of firing or baking. Neolithic pots, for example, are often coarse and ill-made because of improper clay mixture or faulty firing technique.

Pottery is decorated in various ways. For example, designs can be engraved on the vessel before firing, or special rims, legs, bases, and other details may be made separately and fastened to the finished pot. Painting is the most common form of pottery decoration, and there are literally thousands of painted designs found among the pottery remains of ancient cultures.

Housing. Another outstanding Neolithic characteristic that arose as a result of agriculture and the sedentary lifestyle is the development of housing. During the Paleolithic, cave shelters, pits dug in the earth, and primitive lean-tos made of hides and tree limbs served to keep the weather out. With the Neolithic, there is evidence of dwellings that are more complex in design and more diverse in type. Some, such as the Swiss Lake Dwellings, were constructed of wood, housed several families per building, and contained doors and beds, tables and other furniture. Other more elaborate shelters were made of stone, sun-dried brick (adobe), or branches daubed with mud or clay. Monumental architecture developed in the Near East and Mesoamerica.

Figure 11-4. *Depicted here are successive stages in the manufacture of clay pottery commonly used as containers.*

Clothing. During the Neolithic, for the first time in man's history, clothing was made of woven textiles. The raw materials and technology necessary for the production of clothing came from three sources: flax and cotton came from agriculture, wool from domesticating sheep, and the

invention of the spindle for spinning and the loom for weaving arose from the inventive mind of man.

Social structure

From the evidence of artifacts and architecture found at Neolithic sites, archeologists have been able to make certain inferences about the social structure of that type of society. The absence of any large building suggests that neither religion nor government was yet an established institution able to wield real social power. Since no early Neolithic graves have been found containing tomb ornaments or burial equipment, it is believed that no person had attained the superior social status that would have required an elaborate funeral. The smallness of the villages suggests that the inhabitants knew each other very well, so that most of their relationships were probably highly personal ones, charged with emotional significance.

The general picture that emerges is one of an egalitarian society with little division of labor and probably little development of social roles. Although it is conjectured that the markings on some of the artifacts, such as hunting tools, may have had religious or magical meaning, no concrete evidence of an organized religious life has been found. The experiments in irrigation that led to successful cultivation must have required some kind of social organization, since they called for the labor of many men; but there is again no evidence that this control was provided by an organized governmental institution. Many anthropologists believe that kinship groups, such as clans, were the organizing unit for this kind of work.

The Neolithic in the New World

Hunting and food gathering were always important elements in the economy of Neolithic man

Figure 11-5. *Two kinds of decorative pottery work are shown here. The bottom photo is a bull found at the site of Sumer; it is thought that such figurines might have been used in the celebration of religious rites.*

in the New World. Apparently, early North American Indians never experienced a complete change from a hunting to a farming mode of life, even though maize was cultivated (often temporarily) where climate permitted. Agriculture developed independently of Europe and Asia; and the crops differed because of different natural conditions and cultural traits.

The Neolithic developed much later in the New World than in the Old. For example, Neolithic agricultural villages developed in the Near East around 7000 to 6000 B.C.; but similar villages did not appear in the New World until about 3400 B.C., in Mexico. Moreover, pottery, which arose in the Old World shortly after agriculture, did not develop in the New World until about 2300 B.C. Neither the potter's wheel nor the loom and spindle were used by early Neolithic man in the New World. Both pottery and textiles were manufactured by primitive manual means, and evidence of the loom and spindle does not appear in the New World until 1000 B.C.

Although the domestication of plants probably occurred around 4000 to 2000 B.C. in west central South America, the people remained nomadic for some time and only gradually became sedentary. They depended primarily on hunting for meat. The earliest animals domesticated were dogs, guinea pigs, llamas and alpacas, turkeys, bees, and ducks. Although wild sheep and bison were abundant, they were not domesticated. Neither were oxen domesticated—another reason that agriculture did not proceed at the same pace as in the Old World.

Around 2500 B.C., New World people cultivated maize, a tiny wild corn cob, having discovered that the kernels must be planted in mounds, rather than sown, as were grains in the Old World. Garden cultivation of noncereal native crops was also practiced—melons, beans, potatoes, sweet potatoes, peppers, squash, cacao, tobacco, cotton, tomatoes, pineapple, manioc or cassava, and pumpkin.

Settlements in Mexico and the Andes represent the summit of achievement among the prehistoric Americans. These cultures were based on com-

Figure 11-6. *Artifacts of the New World Neolithic period are shown here (the top photo on the opposite page is also from this cultural tradition). The meaning of the lines in the earth is not known.*

munities whose ancestors had turned from hunting and gathering to cultivation and domestication. But agriculture was only one part of a complex of ideas fundamental to the emergence of civilization, and the New World became an uneven mosaic of cultures.

Eurasian-American contacts. The artifacts found in the New World differ so greatly from those of the Old that some scholars believe there were no contacts between the two until the arrival of Columbus. However, others see evidence of Old World contacts in American prehistory. For example, the bottle gourd, domesticated in the Americas, seems to be of Old World origin; archeologists have also found a plant that may represent a hybrid crossing of Old World cotton with that of the New. Another clue to possible contact between Eurasia and the Americas is the second millenium pottery found in what is now the eastern part of the United States.

Civilization begins

Permanent settlements were an important result of Neolithic domestication and cultivation. Although there are some exceptions, evidence of sedentarism does provide clues as to the connection between man's "settling down" and his early agricultural accomplishments.

Sedentarism: the beginning of villages

There was a gradual transition among tribes from the nomadic to the sedentary way of life. At first, perhaps, a tribe lived in one area, cultivating plants until the soil was exhausted, and then moved on to new lands. Some tribes seem to have lived in a single-crop economy combined with hunting. Man's perseverance in domesticating animals that could not be driven (pigs, for example) coupled with the cultivation of fruit trees and vines resulted in the emergence of sedentarism.

Figure 11-7. *Neolithic man in the New World was sometimes a cliffdweller, as these three photos from sites in Arizona depict in vivid detail.*

Some tribes may have returned for a while to their original sites after the land had lain fallow for a time and natural regeneration had taken place. In some cases, man learned to fertilize and irrigate the soil and to crop the land. Then they began to stay not just for one season or for a lifetime, but for many lifetimes. Thus, small communities and villages arose.

There were certain problems associated with the change to sedentarism. Nomads can move from place to place to find better pastures for their herds; they can exhaust the land with one-crop farming and then find new fields. Staying in one place meant that new technologies were needed.

Urbanization and the emergence of civilization

In the more favored locales, such as the lowlands of Mesopotamia, where transport was easy and food could be accumulated and stored, villages grew into towns, and in some cases, into cities. The first cities appeared in the fertile river valleys of the Tigris and Euphrates Rivers in Mesopotamia, then in the valleys of the Nile in Egypt and the Indus in India between 4000 and 2500 B.C. As Robert Adams points out,

> The rise of cities, the second great "revolution" in human culture, was pre-eminently a social process, an expression more of changes in man's interaction with his fellows than in his interaction with his environment.[1]

Once a town or village became large enough, a new way of life developed. City life meant a more complex social organization and increased specialization of labor. Irrigation projects, for example, required the coordination of hundreds of workers.

With urbanization came a sharp increase in the tempo of human cultural development. Populations increased, writing developed, trade intensified and expanded, and the wheel, the sail, and metallurgy were invented. As social institutions ceased to operate in simple face-to-face groups of acquaintances and friends, they grew more formal and bureaucratic. City life intensified the division of labor and gave rise to the specialist. Carpenters, blacksmiths, sculptors, basketmakers, and stonecutters contributed to the vibrant life of the city.

Monumental buildings, such as royal palaces and temples, were built by thousands of men, usually slaves taken in war, and involved feats of engineering that still amaze modern architects and engineers. The inhabitants of these buildings, the ruling class composed of nobles and priests, dictated social and religious rules which were carried out by the merchants, soldiers, artisans, farmers, and other citizens.

Urbanization and its effects

A number of theories regarding the rise of cities and the by-products of urbanization have risen in recent years. Some scholars think urbanization began as the result of a need for extensive irrigation systems to increase the land's agricultural yield. In the fertile riverine deltas of the Near East, irrigation was developed to a high degree of efficiency, and large-scale irrigation works were constructed. It is held that the building of these large irrigation projects necessitated the pooling of labor of adjoining communities. This communal cooperation eventually led to the consolidation of social organization and the centralization of economic and political authority. Thus, these scholars suggest, the city was born.

However, other anthropologists point out that large irrigation projects were not the principal cause for the emergence of the city, because evidence reveals that the irrigation systems of early Mesopotamian cities were quite small and so did not require the coordination of large numbers of workers. It was not until these cities were established and growing, these scholars say, that irrigation systems grew in size and complexity. Replying to this theory, other scholars suggest that even small irrigation projects could have resulted in boundary disputes or squabbles over water rights and so required some kind of coordination or governing body with the authority to settle disputes and to sanction wrongdoers.

At present, we do not know which of these theories is correct. It is hoped that future discoveries and studies will provide us with an answer.

☐

---

[1] Robert M. Adams, "The Origin of Cities," *Scientific American,* Vol. 203 (1960), p. 153.

Original study

THE FIRST FARMERS

As hunters, individual men exercised a remarkable degree of direct control over their futures. That they required cultural devices is not questioned, but their cultural forms were uncomplicated extensions of themselves; the hunter and his ways blended into the natural setting. Each day of his adult life a man realized his successes or failures; thus he was at least a partial master of his own fate. However, when men began to farm intensively for a living, they created an unnatural landscape of cultivated fields. Then cities arose as even more bizarre environmental modifications. Like the hunter, the farmer and city dweller are at times driven by the elements and the vicissitudes of nature, but in addition, farmers and urbanites are so deeply involved in the complexities of their cultural systems that they are in a very real sense enslaved by an artificial environment built more by accident than by design.

The first seeds heralding the "revolution" sprouted in the Near East about 10,000 years ago, probably in the area ranging from Israel to southern Turkey, eastern Iraq, and western Iran. Here, along a crescent that was extremely fertile there lived peoples whose economies were based on the collection of foods as well as the hunting of animals. Among the plant products gathered were forms of barley, lentils, peas, and wheat. The region likewise supported populations of wild asses, cattle, dogs, goats, horses, and pigs. The technological products of these Near Easterners included stone-bladed sickles for cutting wild grasses as well as milling stones and mullers to pulverize seeds. On the well-watered uplands, at elevations between two and four thousand feet above sea level, wild grasses grew abundantly. The most important of these were wheat, which grew only along the hilly flanks of the crescent, and barley, which was common over a much wider area. In their natural habitat the grains of wild barley and wheat drop from the seed spikes after they have fully ripened, and they are scattered by the winds. It was essential to harvest these grasses just before the seeds dispersed. How it came to pass that the barley and wheat seeds harvested one year came to be sown the following year is unknown. Perhaps seeds accidentally were dropped on a garbage pile and sprouted the next year to produce a small but rich crop, which suggested the idea of purposeful planting to someone. In any event, by 7000 B.C. in eastern Iraq, domestic crops of barley and wheat were sown and harvested. A distinct genetic quality of the early domestic forms was that the ripened seeds remained encased in the seed spikes rather than falling to the ground. Such plants grew in the wild but were few since they did not propagate themselves effectively. However, these were precisely the genetic strains that had the greatest harvest potential for man, and because they depended on man for their effective propagation, they became the earliest known cultigens. Wheat and barley were planted at elevations lower than their natural habitat, and man no doubt learned to select the moisture-laden planting sites which were most likely to yield large harvests.

In this setting also were a group of wild animals which had greater potential as domestics than any collection of diverse species found together elsewhere in the world. The dog probably was the second animal domesticated by man, if we accept the proposition that the first was woman—who still might best be classed as in a semidomestic state. The second, or third, domestic animal was the goat, which initially was raised for its meat. Perhaps goats were first kept as pets, and their potential as a ready source of food may have been realized at this time. How goats first became tolerant of man may only be speculated. One possibility is that a newborn goat was discovered shortly after birth and that it thought "mother" when it saw a human. The baby goat may have been taken home and raised by a nursing woman in the finder's family. She may have nursed two kids at once and raised the goat in the household. Goats, and later sheep, cattle, and pigs, only became true domestics when they were successfully bred by man and assumed physical characteristics different from those of their wild cousins.

At the small settlement of Jarmo in eastern Iraq, archeologists have uncovered the remains of an early group of sedentary farmers. These people lived about 7000 B.C. in a community consisting of about twenty-five rectangular, mud-walled houses which were occupied throughout the year. Their domestic grains, barley and wheat, were supplemented by lentils, peas, and vetchling; these possibly were collected from wild plants. The people also gathered acorns, pistachio nuts, and snails for food. Dogs and goats were domestic animals, and perhaps the same was true of sheep. The other local animals were wild and were hunted. Quite obviously the economic base was broad, the diet was balanced, and food sources were reasonably dependable. It has been estimated that the average population of Jarmo was one hundred and fifty and that the site possibly occupied around three hundred years. The subsistence base reported at Jarmo probably was that of incipient farmers, a type found over much of the Near East at this time period. Around 5000 B.C. people with this way of life began to wander into the alluvial lowlands of the Tigris and Euphrates river systems. Here they settled as bottomland farmers who continued to raise barley and wheat as their primary staples but added cultivated dates to their diet as well as fish from the lowland waters. Before long, the flat alluvial farmlands were laced with canal systems designed to irrigate the plots of land needed in the expanding cultivation. The natural warmth of the area coupled with an abundant water supply and wild plants which could be productively cultivated served to carry food production far beyond anything ever before realized. This combination of conditions was critical in the emergence of a radically new form of social setting, the city. The cultural achievements necessary before large aggregates of persons could gather in cities included the establishment of a farming economy which produced dependable food surpluses year after year, the development of an effective means to store surpluses, and the establishment of a redistributing system for the products.

Source:
From *Understanding Our Culture: An Anthropological View* by Wendell H. Oswalt. Copyright © 1970 by Holt, Rinehart and Winston, Inc. Reprinted by permission of Holt, Rinehart and Winston, Inc.

Summary

1.

During the Upper Paleolithic, man led a marginal existence. But about 12,000 years ago, during the Mesolithic Age, he began to settle down. On the shores of lakes and rivers, Mesolithic men formed small permanent settlements that later developed into rudimentary farming and fishing villages. During the Neolithic, man became an established farmer and pastoralist.

2.

Two major Mesolithic cultures developed in Western Europe: the Azilian (southern France and Spain) and the Tardenoisian (England, Germany, and France). The characteristic tools of these cultures were the microliths, small stone tools. In the Near East flourished the Capsian and Natufian cultures. The Natufians, a people who lived in what is now Israel and Jordan, probably harvested wild grain.

3.

Analysis of plant and animal remains at a site will usually indicate whether or not its occupants were food producers. A wild plant, for example, usually has a soft stem, whereas a cultivated one has a tough one. Domestication produces skeletal changes in some animals. The horns of wild sheep, for example, are larger than that of their domesticated counterparts.

4.

Several theories have been proposed to account for the changes in the subsistence patterns of early man. One theory, the "oasis" or "desiccation" theory, is based on climatic determinism. Domestication began because the oasis attracted hungry animals, which were domesticated, instead of killed, by Neolithic man. Another theory holds that domestication originated in areas in which the wild counterparts of the early domesticates are found in abundance.

5.

The earliest known sites containing domesticated plants and animals are found in the Near East. At Jarmo, a settlement at the foot of the Zagros Mountains that is about 7000 years old, there is evidence not only of cultivation and domestication but also of trade. The Biblical city of Jericho, an oasis in Jordan, shows many characteristics similar to those at Jarmo, although it was more complex. It was occupied as early as 7800 B.C. At its height, Jericho occupied an area of ten acres and had about 3000 people.

6.

Agriculture seems to have spread out from southwest Asia to adjacent areas, eventually reaching Europe by 6000 B.C. Some environments were not conducive to the spread of agriculture.

7.

Another characteristic of the Neolithic Age is the extensive manufacture and use of pottery. Pottery became a necessity as the food supply increased and society became more complex. Pottery is a good indicator of a sedentary community; it is found in all but a few of the earliest Neolithic settlements. The manufacture of pottery requires a knowledge of clay and the techniques of firing or baking. Neolithic pottery is often coarse. Other characteristics of the Neolithic are the development of housing and the appearance of woven textiles.

8.

In the New World, agriculture developed independently of Europe and Asia, and the crops differed because of different natural conditions and cultural traits. There are considerable differences between the various Neolithic culture areas of the New World. Some anthropologists believe that there was some cultural borrowing between the cultures of the Old and the New Worlds.

9.

Permanent settlements were an important result of Neolithic domestication and cultivation. There was a gradual transition among tribes from the nomadic to the sedentary way of life. In favored locales, such as in the lowlands of Mesopotamia, villages grew into towns, and, in some cases, into cities. The first cities appeared in the fertile river valleys of Mesopotamia, India, and Egypt. With urbanization, a new way of life developed; population increased; writing developed; trade intensified; and new inventions, such as the wheel, drastically changed the technology of Neolithic man. Several theories have been proposed to explain the rise of cities. Some scholars think urbanization began as the result of a need for extensive irrigation systems. Others argue that it was not until these cities were established and growing that irrigation systems grew in size and complexity. At present, we do not know which of these theories is correct.

The rise of cities

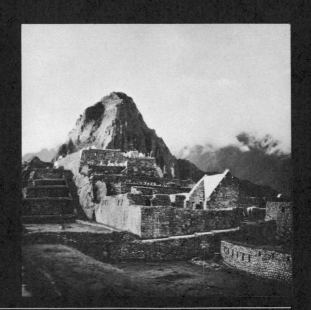

A walk down a busy city street brings us in contact with numerous activities that are essential to the well-being of our society. The sidewalks are crowded with people going to and from offices and stores. The traffic of cars, taxis, and trucks is heavy, sometimes almost at a standstill. In a brief, two-block stretch, there may be a department store, shops selling clothing, appliances, or books, a restaurant, a newsstand, a gasoline station, and a movie theater. Perhaps there will also be a museum, a police station, a school, a hospital, or a church. That is quite a number of services and specialized skills to find in such a small area.

Each of these services or places of business is dependent on others. A butcher shop, for instance, depends on slaughterhouses and beef ranches. A clothing store depends on designers and the farmers who produce cotton and wool. Restaurants depend on refrigerated trucking and vegetable and dairy farmers. Hospitals depend on a great variety of other institutions to meet their more complex needs. All institutions, finally, depend on the public utilities—the telephone and electric companies. Although interdependence is not immediately apparent to the passerby, it is an important aspect of modern cities.

The interdependence of goods and services in a big city is what makes so many products readily available to us. For instance, refrigerated air transport makes it possible to buy fresh California artichokes on the East Coast. This same interdependence, however, has undesirable effects if one service stops functioning, for example, because of strikes or bad weather. In recent years a number of major American cities have had to do without services as vital as newspapers, subways, and schools. The question is not so much "Why does this happen?" but rather "Why doesn't it happen more often, and why does the city continue to function so smoothly when one of its services stops?" The answer is that services are not only interdependent, but they are also adaptable. When one breaks down the others take over its functions. During a long newspaper strike in New York City in the 1960s, for example, several new magazines were launched, and television expanded its coverage of news and cultural events.

On the surface, city life seems so orderly that we take it for granted; but a moment's pause reminds us that the intricate fabric of city life did not always exist, and the goods so accessible to us were once simply not available.

What civilization means

This complicated system of goods and services available in such a small space is a mark of civilization itself. The history of civilization is intimately bound up with the history of cities. This does not mean that civilization is to be equated with modern industrial cities or with present-day American society. Both the ancient Athenians and the Australian aborigines of today are included in the term "civilization," but each represents a very different kind. It was in the life of the earliest cities, however, that civilization first developed. In fact, the word comes from the Latin *civis,* which refers to one who is an inhabitant of a city, and *civitas,* which refers to the community in which he dwells. Thus, the word *civilization* contains the idea of "citification," or "the coming-to-be of cities."

Cities first developed during the period called the Neolithic, or New Stone Age, which began in the Near East 10,000 to 11,000 years ago. Anthropologists once thought that during the Neolithic Age man began to use ground stone tools for the first time, but it is now known that such tools were in use earlier. The term Neolithic Age is still used; but it is now defined chiefly by the appearance of domesticated plants and animals. Prior to the beginning of the Neolithic Age man lived a more nomadic existence.

From nomad to farmer

During the Paleolithic Age, man was a hunter and food-gatherer. He lived in nomadic groups that followed large herds and hunted for food as it was needed. He gathered wild plants and grains that grew in his environs. Towards the beginning of the Mesolithic Age, about 14,000 years ago, some nomadic groups settled down in small villages, and, although they continued to hunt animals, they increasingly relied on the shellfish, fish, and wild vegetation at hand. Their settlements are known as Mesolithic preagricultural villages.

What caused this change from a nomadic hunting life to a more sedentary life of fishing and gathering plants? One theory is that the change was caused by melting glaciers and warmer climate. The melting glaciers caused the oceans to rise and flood grazing lands, and the warmer climate was favorable to the development of forests; thus, where there had once been plains, there were now inlets, bays, and abundant forests. This made hunting more difficult, so man settled down and began to rely on fish and plants for a living. During the Paleolithic and Early Mesolithic periods, man lived in small groups, probably because small nomadic groups could move faster. Once nomadic groups settled down, the population probably began to grow because there was no longer any need to restrict the frequency of births as there had been in the nomadic culture adapted for mobility.

If the birthrate began to increase during the Mesolithic Age, it did so just as climate changes were beginning to make food sources scarce. Man responded to this change by inventing better tools and utensils. The large, heavy tools of the Paleolithic era, made of a single piece of flint, were replaced by smaller, lighter tools with bone or wood handles and replaceable flint or other stone blades. These new implements enabled early man to increase the amount of wild grains harvested.

The Neolithic age

The Mesolithic Age, which ended about 10,000 years ago, saw the establishment of the first villages and the refinement of tools. It was followed by a period of even greater cultural advances—the Neolithic Age. The most important advance of the Neolithic culture was the domestication of plants

and animals. This must have happened very slowly. Man probably began by domesticating those species of grains and wild animals that most easily lent themselves to domestication.

Sites in the Near East and southwest Asia indicate that domesticated species first appeared about 10,000 years ago.[1] Excavations have actually uncovered successive layers of plant and animal remains in some Neolithic villages. The stratification of such sites shows that in the oldest, most deeply buried layers, barley remains are from wild species. In the more recent layers, wild species are found less and less frequently and are finally replaced entirely by domesticated species.

The emergence of civilization

The world's first cities sprung up in Mesopotamia, then in Egypt and the Indus Valley, between 6000 and 4500 years ago. The inhabitants

Figure 12-1. *The dry climate of Egypt helps preserve archeological sites and artifacts. The picture left shows an abandoned village of relatively recent date; the site being excavated may have looked much the same.*

Figure 12-1a. *This wall painting shows the way that Egyptian houses were constructed.*

[1] R. J. Braidwood, "The Agricultural Revolution," *Scientific American*, Vol. 203 (1960), p. 134.

of Sumer, in Mesopotamia, developed the first civilization about 5000 years ago. Finally, almost 3000 years ago, the first cities appeared in Mexico and Peru.

What characterized these first cities? Why are they called the birthplaces of civilization? The first characteristic of cities—and of civilization—is their large size and population. But the first cities were far more than expanded Neolithic villages. The changes that took place in the transition from village to city were so great that the emergence of urban living is considered by some to be one of the greatest "revolutions" in human culture.

Cities and culture change.
If someone who grew up in a small village of Maine, Wyoming, or Mississippi were to move to Chicago, Detroit, or Los Angeles, he would experience a number of marked changes in his way of life. Some of the same changes in daily life would have been felt 5000 years ago by a Neolithic village dweller upon moving into one of the world's first cities in Mesopotamia. Of course, the differences would be less extreme today. In the twentieth century, every American village, however small, is part of civilization; in Neolithic times, the cities *were* civilization, and the villages were precivilized.

There are four basic culture changes that mark the transition from precivilized village life to that of life in civilized, urban centers in Neolithic times.

Agricultural innovation.
The first culture change characteristic of life in cities—hence, of civilization itself—was an improvement in farming methods. The ancient Sumerians, for example, had an extensive system of dikes, canals, and reservoirs to irrigate their farmlands. With such a system, they could control the water resources at will; water could be held and then run off onto the fields when necessary. Irrigation was an important factor affecting the increase of crop yields. Because farming could now be carried on independently of the seasons, more crops could be harvested in one year.

The introduction of the plow in Mesopotamia about 2000 B.C. made it possible to till land whose surface was too hard for a hoe or digging stick. This led to a further increase in crop yields, and then to food surpluses. Crop surpluses were probably a factor contributing to the high population density of civilized society. Examination of Neolithic villages in southwestern Iran shows that population density increased from one to two persons per kilometer in villages without irrigation, and up to six or more persons per kilometer in villages with irrigation systems.

Diversification of labor.
The second culture change characteristic of civilization is diversification of labor. In a Neolithic village that possessed neither irrigation nor plow farming, everyone was needed in the raising of crops. The high crop yields made possible by improved farming methods and the increased population freed more and more people from farming. For the first time, a sizable number of people was available to pursue nonagricultural activities. With specialization came the expertise that led to inventing new and better ways of making things. In a Neolithic city, the majority of the population still farmed, but many of the inhabitants were skilled workers or craftsmen.

Contemporary public records indicate there was a considerable variety of such skilled workers. For example, an early Mesopotamian document from the city of Lagash lists the artisans, craftsmen, and others paid from crop surpluses stored in the temple granaries. Among them were coppersmiths, silversmiths, sculptors, merchants, potters, tanners, engravers, butchers, carpenters, spinners, barbers, cabinetmakers, bakers, clerks, and brewers.

Social stratification.
The third culture change characteristic of civilization is social stratification, or the emergence of social classes. Symbols of status and privilege appeared for the first time in the ancient cities of Mesopotamia, and people were ranked according to the kind of work they did or the family they were born into.

Figure 12-2. *The wall paintings and the sculpture found at excavation sites tell us much about the inhabitants of the city that was built there. The top photo is from an Egyptian tomb; the bottom photo was taken at Persepolis, capital of the Persian Empire.*

People whose skills freed them from the most common work—farming—were the earliest holders of status. In general, the more unusual a person's skill, and the more removed it is from the labor that the largest number of men perform, the higher is that person's social status. Status in our society may come from being a highly paid professional athlete, a movie actress, or a corporation executive. Status in a Neolithic city originally might come from being a metal worker, a tanner, a priest, or a trader. With time, certain specialists would have accumulated more wealth and influence than others. The possession of wealth, and the influence it could buy, became in itself a requisite for status.

Evidence of social stratification. How do archaeologists know that there were different social classes in ancient civilizations? There are four main ways:

1. *Burial customs.* Graves excavated at early Neolithic sites are mostly simple holes dug in the ground, containing few grave goods. Grave goods are utensils, figurines, and personal possessions placed in the grave in order that the dead person might use them in the afterlife. The paucity of grave goods in Neolithic sites indicates an egalitarian, or classless, society. Graves excavated in civilizations, by contrast, vary widely in size, mode of burial, and the number and variety of grave goods. This indicates a stratified society—one divided into social classes. The graves of important persons contain not only a great variety of artifacts made from precious metals, but sometimes, as in some early Egyptian burials, even the remains of servants evidently killed to serve their master in his afterlife.

2. *The size of dwellings.* In early Neolithic sites, dwellings tended to be uniformly small in size. In the oldest excavated cities, however, some dwellings were notably larger than others, well-spaced, and located together in one district, whereas dwellings in another part of the city were much smaller, sometimes little more

Figure 12-3. *Workers at a site in Thebes lift the wooden sarcophagus of an Egyptian nobleman from an underground tomb.*

Figure 12-4. *This painting was found inside the tomb of Tutankhamen; the baboon represents a god of the underworld.*

than hovels. In the city of Eshnunna in Mesopotamia, archaeologists excavated houses that occupied an area of two hundred meters situated on main throughfares, and huts of fifty meters located along narrow back alleys. The rooms in the larger houses often contained impressive art work, such as friezes or murals.

3. *Written documents.* Preserved records of business transactions, royal chronicles, or law codes of a civilization reveal much about the social status of its inhabitants. Babylonian and Assyrian texts reveal three main social classes— aristocrats, commoners, and slaves. The members of each class had different rights and privileges. This stratification was clearly reflected by the law. If an aristocrat put out another's eye, his eye was to be put out. Hence, the saying "an eye for an eye. . . ." If he broke another's bone, his bone was to be broken. If he put out the eye or broke the bone of a commoner, he was to pay a mina of silver.[2]

4. *Correspondence.* European documents describing the aboriginal cultures of the New World as seen by visitors and explorers also offered evidence of social stratification. Letters written by the Spanish Conquistadors about the Aztec empire indicate that they found a social order divided into several main classes. First came the nobles, and after them the commoners. Both these classes were divided into clans. Within each clan, members had higher or lower status, depending upon their degree of descent from the clan founder. Those clans considered more closely related to the nation's founder had higher status than those whose kinship was more distant. The third class in Aztec society consisted of serfs bound to the land and porters employed as carriers by merchants. Last were the slaves.

Central government. All of the characteristics of civilization already mentioned—innovations in farm technology, the growth of specialized skills, and the emergence of social classes—were really

[2]Sabatino Moscati, *The Face of the Ancient Orient* (New York: Doubleday, 1962), p. 90.

interconnected. The emergence of social classes, for instance, did not really occur until some members of civilization had left farming to take up specialized skills. And this specialization of labor, in turn, did not take place until innovations in farming techniques had produced a crop surplus that freed some people from farming.

When all three of these characteristics had reached a certain point of development, there was a need for strong organization and control. One further culture change then appeared. This was the emergence of a governing elite, a strong central authority required to deal with the many problems arising within the new cities, owing to their size and complexity. The new governing elite saw to it that different interest groups, such as farmers, craftsmen, or moneylenders, did not infringe on each others' rights or exploit each other. It ensured that the city was safe from its enemies by constructing walls and raising an army. It levied taxes and appointed tax collectors so that construction, the army, and other public expenses could be paid. It saw to it that merchants, carpenters, or farmers who made legal claims received justice. It guaranteed safety for the lives and property of ordinary people, and assured that any harm done one man by another would be justly dealt with. In addition, surplus grain had to be stored for times of scarcity, and the extensive irrigation system had to be supervised by competent, disinterested individuals. The mechanisms of government served all these functions.

Evidence of a centralized authority in ancient civilizations comes from such sources as law codes, temple records, and royal chronicles. Excavation of the city structures themselves provides further evidence. For example, archeologists believe that the cities of Mohenjo-daro and Harappa in the Indus Valley were governed by a centralized authority because they show definite signs of city planning. They are both over three miles long; their main streets are laid out in a rectangular grid pattern; and both contain city-wide drainage systems.

The governmental organization of the earliest cities was typically headed by a king and his special advisers. In addition, there were sometimes councils of lesser advisers. Formal laws were enacted and courts sat in judgment over the claims of rival litigants or the criminal charges brought by the government against an individual.

Of the many ancient kings known, one stands out as truly remarkable for the efficient government organization and highly developed legal system that characterized his reign. This is Hammurabi, the Babylonian king who lived between 1950 and 1700 B.C. He promulgated a set of laws for his kingdom, known as the Code of Hammurabi, which is important because of its thorough detail and humaneness. It prescribes the correct form for legal procedures and determines penalties for perjury, false accusation, and injustice done by judges. It contains laws applying to property rights, loans and debts, family rights, and damages paid for malpractice by a physician. There are fixed rates to be charged in various trades and branches of commerce. The poor, women, children, and slaves are protected against injustice. The Code was publicly displayed on huge stone slabs so that no one accused could plead ignorance. Even the poorest man knew his rights.

Some civilizations flourished under a ruler with extraordinary governing abilities, such as Hammurabi. Other civilizations possessed a widespread governing bureaucracy that was very efficient at every level. The government of the Inca civilization is a case in point.

The Inca empire of Peru reached its zenith in the sixteenth century A.D., just before the arrival of the Spanish. In the mid-1400s, the Inca kingdom probably did not extend more than twenty miles beyond the modern-day city of Cuzco, which was then its center. Within a thirty-year period, in the late 1400s, the Inca kingdom enlarged a thousand times its original size. By A.D. 1525, it stretched 2500 miles from north to south and 500 miles from east to west. Its population may have been as high as 16 million, composed of people of various tribes. In the achievements of its governmental and political system, the Inca civilization surpassed every other civilization of the New World. At the head of the government was the emperor, regarded as semidivine, followed by the royal family, the aristocracy, imperial administrators, the lower nobility, and the masses of artisans, craftsmen, and farmers.

The empire was divided into four administrative regions, further subdivided into provinces, and so on down to villages and families. Planting, irrigation, and harvesting were closely supervised by government agricultural experts and tax officials. Teams of professional relay runners could carry messages up to 250 miles in a single day over a network of stone roads. The Inca had neither writing, nor the wheel, nor horses; public records and historical chronicles were kept in the form of an ingenious system of colored beads, knots, and ropes. Nevertheless, Inca culture is considered a civilization because it had socially stratified cities with dense populations, a varied division of labor, and a centralized government supported by a large agricultural peasant community.

The Aztec empire, which flourished in Mexico in the sixteenth century, is another example of a civilization governed by a very efficient bureaucracy that was headed by a semidivine king. A council of nobles, priests, and army leaders chose the king from among the men of royal lineage. Although the king was an absolute monarch, the councillors, whose tasks were similar to those of U.S. presidential aides, advised him on affairs of state. A vast number of government officials oversaw various functions, such as the maintenance of the tax system, the courts of justice, management of government storehouses, and control of military training.

The making of civilization

From Mesopotamia to China to the South American Andes, we witness the enduring achievements of man's intellect: magnificent palaces built high above ground; sculptures so perfect as to be unrivaled by those of contemporary artists; engineering projects so vast and daring as to awaken in us a sense of wonder. Looking back to the beginnings of history, we can see a point at which man transforms himself into a "civilized" being; he begins to live in cities and to expand the scope of his achievements at a rapid pace. How is it, then, that man at a certain moment in history decided to become a master builder, to harness the mighty rivers so that he could irrigate his crops, and to develop a system whereby his thoughts could be preserved in writing? The fascinating subject of the development of civilization has occupied the minds of philosophers and anthropologists alike for a long time. We do not yet have the answers, but we can distinguish a number of characteristics whereby we can identify a civilization.

The characteristics of civilization

Most anthropologists are willing to define civilization in terms of six main characteristics.

Writing. Before 3000 B.C., "writing" consisted of pictures drawn or carved on stone, bone, or shell to commemorate a notable event, such as a hunt, a military victory, or the deed of some king. The earliest picture-writing—called pictographs—functioned much like historical paintings or newspaper photos. The figures in such pictures gradually became simplified and generalized and stood for ideas of things, rather than for the things themselves. Thus, a royal palace could be represented by a simple stick drawing of a house with a crown placed above it. This representation of the idea of a palace is called an ideogram. In the older pictographic writing, it would have been necessary to draw a likeness of an actual palace in order to convey the message effectively. Ideographic writing was faster, simpler, and more flexible than pictographic writing. Over the centuries the ideograms became more simplified, and, although their meaning was clear to their users, they looked less and less like the natural objects they had originally depicted.

In Mesopotamia, about 6000 years ago, a new writing technique emerged, which used a stylus to make wedge-shaped markings on a tablet of damp clay. Originally, each marking stood for a word. Since most words in this language were monosyllabic, the markings came, in time, to stand for syllables. There were about 600 signs, half of them ideograms, the others functioning either as ideograms or syllables.

There was a great need for early government to keep records of state affairs, such as accounts of their food surplus, tribute records, and other business receipts. The earliest documents appear to be just such records—lists of vegetables and animals bought and sold, tax lists, and storehouse inventories. Writing was an extremely important invention, because governments could keep records of their assets instead of simply relying upon the memory of administrators.

Monumental architecture. Giant buildings and temples, palaces, and large sculptures are usually found in civilizations. The Maya city of Tikal contained over 300 major structures, including temples, ball courts, and "palaces" (residences of the aristocracy). The Pyramid of the Sun in the pre-Aztec city of Teotihuacan is 700 feet long and over 200 feet high. Its interior is filled by more than one million cubic yards of sun-dried brick. The tomb of the Egyptian pharaoh Cheops, known as the Great Pyramid, is 755 feet long and 481 feet high. It contains about 2,300,000 stone blocks, each with an average weight of 2.5 tons. The Greek historian Herodotus reports that it took 100,000 men 20 years to build this tomb. Such gigantic structures could only be built because the considerable manpower, engineering skills, and raw materials necessary for their construction could be harnessed by a powerful central authority.

Taxation. A system of taxation enabled government to pay its administrators and craftsmen for performing state functions. Citizens and conquered peoples were usually forced to pay some form of tribute to the state.

The Assyrian government, for example, had a retinue of tax collectors who levied taxes and

Figure 12-5 *A taste for monumental architecture is often the hallmark of civilization. The giant pyramids of the Egyptians are a case in point, as are the Egyptian temples, such as the one here at Thebes, with a huge statue of a god*

dwarfing the massive temple columns. Grandiose monuments were found in the New World as well. The photo above is of the Pyramid of the Sun, at Teotihuacan, Mexico. Near it is the elaborate carving of the temple to the god Quetzalcoatl.

accepted payment in either material goods, such as grain, wool, wood, and livestock, or in silver. In addition, conscription into the army was also considered a form of taxation.

Sciences. It was within civilizations that sciences such as metallurgy, geometry, and astronomy were first developed.

Metals were in great demand for the manufacture of farmers' and craftsmens' tools, as well as for weapons. Copper, iron, and tin were separated from their ores, then smelted, purified, and cast to make plows, swords, axes, and shields. In wars over border disputes or fertile land, stone knives, spears, and slings could not stand up against bronze spears, arrowheads, swords, or armor.

Geometry was used by the Egyptians for such purposes as measuring the area of a field or staking off an accurate right angle at the corner of a building.

Astronomy grew out of the need to know when to plant and harvest crops, to hold religious observances, and to find the exact bearings on voyages. Astronomy and mathematics were used to devise calendars. The Mayans calculated that the solar year was 365 days (actually, it is $365\frac{1}{4}$ days). The Babylonians were able to calculate the exact date of the new moon.

Art. Civilization, ancient as well as modern, is characterized by a high degree of interest in the arts. Pottery, wall paintings, sculpture, and jewelrymaking flourished in the earliest cities. The division of labor created leisure, enabling people to pursue activities other than those directly concerned with survival.

Trade. Extensive trade systems were developed by early civilizations in order to obtain raw materials from which weapons, tools, fabric, and utensils could be made and ornaments could be fashioned. With these goods, an abundant crop yield and military advantage were assured, and the aristocracy could demonstrate its wealth and status. Extensive trade agreements were maintained with distant civilizations, not only to provide lux-

ury items, but to secure basic raw materials.

Boats gave greater access to trade centers; they could easily carry back to cities large loads of imports at less cost than if they had been brought back overland. A one-way trip from Egypt to the northern city of Byblos in Phoenicia only took four to eight days by rowboat. With a sailboat, it took even less.

Egyptian pharaohs sent expeditions to the Sinai Peninsula for copper; to Nubia for gold; to Arabia for spices and perfumes; to Asia for lapis lazuli (a blue semiprecious stone) and other jewels; to Lebanon for cedar, wine, and funerary oils; and to central Africa for ivory, ebony, ostrich feathers, leopard skins, cattle, and slaves.

Civilization and stress

Early cities faced urban problems strikingly similar to those found in modern America. Dense population, class systems, and a strong centralized government created internal stress. The slaves and

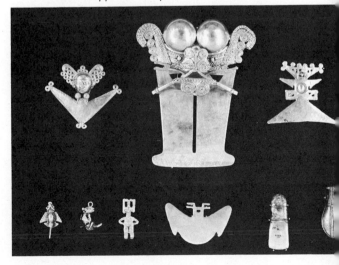

Figure 12-6. *These gold pendants were the work of master craftsmen of the New World; they were found in sites in Colombia. Only a civilization with marked division of labor could support such specialized artisans.*

the poor saw that the wealthy had all the things that they themselves lacked. It was not just a question of luxury items; the poor did not have enough space in which to live with comfort and dignity.

Evidence of warfare in early civilizations is common. Cities were fortified; documents list many battles, raids, and wars between groups; cylinder seals, paintings, and friezes depict battle scenes, victorious kings, and captured prisoners of war. Increasing population and the accompanying scarcity of good farming land often led to boundary disputes and quarrels over land between civilized states or between precivilized nomads and a state. Open warfare often developed. People tended to crowd into the walled cities for protection and to be near the irrigation system.

The class system also caused internal stress. As time went on, the rich became richer and the poor poorer. In early civilizations, one's place in society was relatively fixed. Wealth was based on free slave labor. For this reason there was little or no impetus for social reform. Records from the city of Lagash indicate that social unrest due to exploitation of the poor by the rich grew during this period. Members of the upper class received tracts of farmland some twenty times larger than those granted the lower class. An upper-class reformer, Urukagina, saw the danger and introduced changes to protect the poor from exploitation by the wealthy, thus preserving the stability of the city.

Why do civilizations develop?

Much is known about the political and economic systems, languages, and religions of many ancient civilizations; it is really a "matter of record." But there still remains much that is unknown about these civilizations, and the most intriguing mystery of all is: What caused these civilizations to develop? This question is not answered by any of the documents or artifacts excavated.

The inhabitants of ancient cities did not comment on why or how their civilization came about. They seem to have taken its existence for granted in much the same way as we do ours. They were concerned with the public affairs of their day or the personal affairs of their own lives. They did not speculate on the "why" or "how" of their civilization.

But this question—"Why do civilizations develop?"—is of great interest and importance to anthropologists. There is not, as yet, an answer to the question. But a number of theories have been proposed.

Theories of civilization's emergence

Each of the theories sees the appearance of centralized government as the point at which there is no longer any question whether or not a civilization exists. So, the question they pose is: "What brought about the appearance of a centralized government?" Or, stated another way: "What caused the transition from a small, egalitarian farming village to a large urban center in which population density and diversity of labor required a centralized government?"

Irrigation systems. The irrigation theory holds that Neolithic farmers in ancient Mesopotamia and Egypt, and later in America, noticed that the river valleys that were periodically flooded contained better soils than those that were not; but they also noted that violent floods destroyed their planted fields and turned them into swamps. So the farmers built dikes and reservoirs to collect the floodwaters and save it until it was needed. Then they released it into canals and ran it over the fields. At first, these dikes and canals, built by small groups of neighboring farmers, were very primitive. The success of this measure led to larger, more complex irrigation systems, which eventually necessitated the emergence of a group of "specialists"—men whose sole responsibility was managing the irrigation system. The centralized effort to control the irrigation process eventually blossomed into the first governing body and civilization was born.

There are several objections to this theory. Actual field studies of ancient Mesopotamian irrigation systems reveal that by the year 2000 B.C., when many cities had already flourished, irrigation was still carried out on a small scale, consisting of small canals and diversions of natural waterways. If there were state-managed irrigation, it is argued, such a system would have been far more extensive than excavations show it really was. Moreover, documents indicate that about 2000 B.C. irrigation was regulated by officials of local temples, and not by centralized government. Irrigation systems among the Indian civilizations of Central and South America (except for the Aztecs) were on a very small scale, suggesting they were built and run by families, or, at most, by small groups of local farmers.

Religion. Another theory about the possible origin of civilization is based specifically on the role religion may have played among the Maya of Tikal. It holds that the unreliable rainfall and thin soil of their harsh, tropical environment caused the Maya to depend on religion to help them overcome the difficulties faced in making a living. Thus, the desire to remain close to their priests and temples caused the Maya farmers to stay in Tikal, rather than to disperse over the countryside in small hamlets, as their slash-and-burn agriculture would normally lead them to do.

Because slash-and-burn farming would quickly have used up all the land, and because Tikal is surrounded by swamps, the increasing population had to be supported by another means. The Maya turned to the abundant breadnut tree as a staple; thus, many people were actually freed from farming to pursue other specialized tasks. As population increased and specialists multiplied, social status and acute land shortage—two characteristics of civilization—gradually made their effects felt. Hence, centralized government control was needed.

Multicrop economy. Some anthropologists believe that precivilized multicrop economies in the Old and New Worlds may have required a centralized authority to regulate the redistribution of the produce. New and Old World civilizations had a complex economy based on subsistence farming. Members of society were dependent upon each other for the wide range of food sources.

In Mexico, for example, maize was grown in almost every environment; chilis were grown in the highlands; cotton and beans were planted at intermediate elevations; certain animals were found only in the river valleys; and salt was found along the coasts.

This theory holds that some form of distribution system was necessary in order to gather and redistribute the various foodstuffs throughout the population. Redistribution must have required a centralized authority, promoting the growth of a centralized government.

☐

RULES OF LAW
IN MESOPOTAMIA

It used to be said of Hammurabi that he drew up the world's first legal code. At Susa, in Iran, explorers unearthed a diorite stele bearing his name and cuneiform inscriptions that set forth a comprehensive system of laws. This monolith, which had been carried to Susa by Elamite conquerors after one of their periodic raids on the Euphrates Valley and which may now be seen at the Louvre in Paris, is a document of enormous interest. However, we now know that though Hammurabi may have been one of the world's greatest lawgivers and administrators, he had much earlier legal documents in the Sumerian language to draw upon. For instance, there exists the code of Lipit-Ishtar, the fifth ruler of the Dynasty of Isin, who ruled a century and a half before Hammurabi.

There are thirty-eight known laws in this code, some of which seem entirely equitable by our modern standards. For instance, "If a man turned his face away from his first wife . . . [but] she has not gone out of the house, his wife which he married as his favorite is a second wife; he shall continue to support his first wife . . . If a man's wife has not borne him children but a harlot from the public square has borne him children, he shall provide grain, oil, and clothing for that harlot; the children which the harlot has borne him shall be his heirs, and as long as his wife lives the harlot shall not live in the house with his wife."

Another law code, written in Akkadian and found at Tell Obu Harmal near Bagdad, contains such practical regulations as the following: "If the boatman is negligent and causes the sinking of the boat, he shall pay in full for everything the sinking of which he caused . . . The wages of a hired man are one shekel of silver; his provender is one pan of barley. He shall work for one month . . . If an ox gores another ox and causes its death, both ox owners shall divide between themselves the price of the live ox and also the equivalent of the dead ox."

Another law, that was designed to protect the interests of a returned prisoner of war, strikes a familiar note to us today: "If a man has been made prisoner during a raid or an invasion or if he has been carried off forcibly and stayed in a foreign country for a long time, and if another man has taken his wife and she has borne him a son—when he returns, he shall get his wife back."

Still earlier codes, dating at least as far back as the celebrated Sumerian King Urnammu, have survived. But Hammurabi's much larger and more comprehensive code is one of the most important documents in human history. For here, nearly two thousand years before the codification of Roman Law, is an organized and comprehensive legal system governing most human activities. There are laws concerning marriage, divorce (including a husband's responsibility for his wife's debts), property rights, liability for military service, sale of wine, deposits and debts, murder and assault, theft, and the responsibility of professional men to their clients. The death sentence was imposed for theft, adultery, bearing false witness in cases involving the defendant's life.

Although Babylonian women did not enjoy the same social status as men, their civil rights were safeguarded under Hammurabi's code. For instance, a wife whose husband neglected her could obtain a divorce, provided she could prove she had lived a blameless life. A concubine who had borne children to

a man who sent her away was entitled to take with her whatever dowry she had brought to him, and he was obliged to give her an income from "field, garden, and movables" to support her and his offspring. It is an interesting fact that the higher the social rank of the injured party, the harsher were the penalties for crime. Some of the penalties imposed on negligent professional men seem excessive, but have a certain rough justice. If a doctor, through carelessness or inefficiency, caused his patient to lose the sight of an eye, he lost one of his own eyes. If a house fell on its owner, the builder of that house might be subject to death or at least to a heavy fine.

These rules of law as they were applied to all social classes in everyday affairs, and the numerous records of lawsuits that have survived, help to create a more intimate impression of this vanished world than can be gleaned from the physical remains of cities and temples and the lengthy chronicles of kings. But the picture would be still far from complete without permitting the ordinary men and women of Mesopotamia to speak for themselves. For this we must turn to the little cuneiform tablets on which the folk wisdom of the people was summed up in their proverbs. So many of these axioms and adages, recast in a modern idiom, would seem immediately familiar to us of the twentieth century.

> A restless woman in the house
> Adds ache to pain.

> Who has not supported a wife or child,
> His nose has not borne a leash.

> We are doomed to die; let us spend;
> We shall live long, let us save.

> Who possesses much silver may be happy,
> Who possesses much barley may be happy,
> But who has nothing at all can sleep.

> The poor man is better dead than alive;
> If he has bread, he has no salt.
> If he has salt, he has no bread,
> If he has meat, he has no lamb,
> If he has a lamb, he has no meat.

> You can have a lord, you can have a King;
> But the man to fear is the [tax collector].

Blunt, shrewd, and cynical, these are the typical complaints and observations of civilized human beings in any epoch. Here, at this very early stage of recorded history, the inevitable drawbacks of civilized life already begin to appear—the burden of taxation, the onerousness of military service, the responsibilities of wealth, the penalties of poverty, and the trials of married life.

Source:
Leonard Cottrell, *The Horizon Book of Lost Worlds*.
New York: American Heritage Publishing Co., 1962.

Summary

1.

Towards the beginning of the Mesolithic Age, about 14,000 years ago, man, heretofore a nomad, began to settle down in small villages; although these peoples continued to hunt animals, they increasingly relied on fish and the wild vegetation at hand for subsistence. Several theories have been proposed to account for this change in the life habits of Mesolithic man. One holds that a climate change caused melting glaciers to raise the sea level; consequently grazing lands were flooded. The warmer climate was favorable to the development of forests. Hunting became difficult and man turned to other food sources. The birthrate may have increased and food sources may have become scarce. Man responded to this increase by inventing new and better tools that could make obtaining food easier.

2.

The Neolithic Revolution was the result of the domestication of plants and animals. Technological innovations may have led to an increase in the food supply; as a result, some people were freed from full-time agriculture. A number of occupational specialists emerged, such as artisans and craftsmen, and metallurgy, weaving, and pottery-making became possible.

3.

Sites in the Near East and southeast Asia indicate that domesticated species first appeared about 10,000 years ago. It can be determined that domestication occurred in a region by examining animal and plant remains. Wild grain and animal species have different physical characteristics from those of domesticated species.

4.

The first cities developed in Mesopotamia, Egypt, and the Indus Valley between 6000 and 4500 years ago. There are four basic culture changes that mark the transition from pre-civilized village life to that of life in civilized urban centers: agricultural innovation, diversification of labor, social stratification, and central government. Most anthropologists are willing to define civilization in terms of six main characteristics: writing, monumental architecture, taxation, development of sciences, art, and trade.

5.

Early cities faced urban problems strikingly similar to ours. Dense population, class systems, and a strong centralized government created internal stress. Warfare was a common occurrence; cities were fortified and armies served to protect the state.

6.

A number of theories have been proposed to explain why civilizations developed. The irrigation theory holds that the effort to build and control an irrigation system required a degree of social organization that eventually led to the formation of a civilization. Another theory is based on the role religion may have played in keeping the Maya in and about the city of Tikal.

Suggested readings

Adams, Robert M. *The Evolution of Urban Society*. Chicago: Aldine, 1966.
This volume is concerned with the presentation and analysis of regularities in the two best-documented examples of early, independent urban societies. It seeks to compare systematically the institutional forms and trends of growth in both cultures. Emphasizing basic similarities in structure, it tries to suggest that both societies are variants of a single processual pattern.

Childe, V. Gordon *What Happened in History*. Baltimore, Maryland: Penguin Books, 1954.
Childe discusses the changes in material well-being and mental outlook which have taken place throughout the ages up to the break-up of the Roman Empire. It provides a brief survey of Paleolithic and Mesolithic life, Neolithic society, and of the rise of Metal Age cultures.

Clark, Grahame, and Stuart Piggott *Prehistoric Societies*. New York: Alfred A. Knopf, 1965.
This work, by two distinguished scholars, presents a view of the beginnings of human society. The discussion of the growth of human settlement and the origins of farming in the Old and New Worlds are skillfully linked by intelligent and well-written narrative to the rise of peasant communities and other issues.

Frankfort, Henri *The Birth of Civilization in the Near East*. New York: Barnes and Noble, 1968.
Ancient Mesopotamia and Egypt are the subjects of this book. Using archeological evidence, Frankfort attempts to establish the cultural innovations marking the dim boundary between prehistoric civilization and our own history. An effort is made to define the unique identity or "form" which was the central feature of each of these societies.

Lannings, Edward *Peru Before the Incas*. Englewood Cliffs, New Jersey: Prentice-Hall, 1967.
Recent archeological studies have dramatically changed our picture of the evolution of Pre-Incan civilizations. This book has two purposes: to synthesize and present publicly the new information discovered and to offer a theory of the growth of prehistoric Peruvian society.

Piggott, Stuart, ed. *The Dawn of Civilization: The First World Survey of Human Culture in Early Times*. New York: McGraw-Hill, 1961.
This is a massive work drawing on the knowledge of many scholars, such as Grahame Clark, James Mellaart, and others who have written the sections of text on the general theme of man's development as a social animal. It is profusely illustrated; there are sections dealing with ancient India, China, Mesoamerica, the Near East, and Europe. An excellent bibliography is provided.

Woolley, Sir Leonard and Jacquetta Hawkes *Prehistory and the Beginnings of Civilization*. New York: Harper and Row, 1963.
This immense two-volume work is an attempt to begin a universal interpretative history of man. Jacquetta Hawkes' portion of this first volume is on Prehistory, through the Neolithic period; she deals with art and religion, society and mind. Sir Leonard Woolley's contribution treats the beginnings of civilization, the Bronze Age, urbanization, social and economic structures, languages, science, the arts, and religion.

portfolio three

Ancient art

Although there are numerous examples of pictorial art created before man settled in cities ("civilized" himself), the great proliferation of art begins with our earliest civilizations—Sumer, Egypt, China, India, Middle America. Perhaps even the cave painters of Lascaux and Altamira and the carvers of the "Venus" figures of Willendorf and Lespugue were specialists in their craft, but in the hunter-gatherer society, art is often a propitiatory act performed by many hunters and not necessarily the work of a full time "artist." But there can be no doubt that the extraordinary bull's-head harp on the opposite page was created by someone with special skills, long training, a knowledge of another art—music and its requirements—and the ability to render the intricate legends of his time in inlaid ivory, wood and metal. The city of Ur, where the harp was found and presumably made, was one of the first cities on earth, but not so far from its prehistoric ancestors that its mythology was not filled with animals, a characteristic also of the Egyptian art that flourished at roughly the same time. The Sumerian genius included the invention of the wheel, glass, writing, bronze, the calendar, and indeed, even the city itself. On the pages following are shown a ram's head made of bronze and a tablet bearing the cuneiform, or wedge-shaped writing, with which Sumerians documented their daily business, mathematical calculations, and astronomical observations. Among Sumerian words that persist in English are alcohol, gypsum, and saffron.

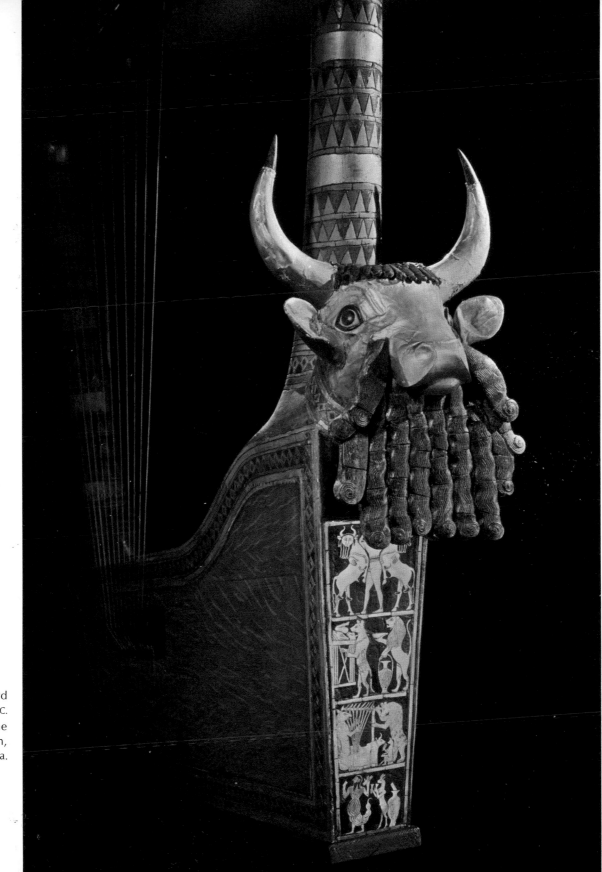

Harp, early Third
Millenium B.C.
From the
University Museum,
Philadelphia.

Ram's Head, Sumerian.
From the University Museum, Philadelphia.

Cuneiform Tablet, Sumerian.
From the University Museum, Philadelphia.

Statuette of Imhotep, Early Ptolomaic.
From the Metropolitan Museum of Art, New York.

Bracelet, Egyptian.

Miniature gold mummy-case of King Tutankhamen.

Egyptian Cat.
From the Metropolitan Museum of Art, New York.

Cycladic Idols.
Courtesy Andre Emmerich Gallery, New York.

Snake Goddess,
Palace of Knoss[e]
Crete.
From the
Boston Museum
of Fine Arts.

Following the pages of Sumerian art are two devoted
to Egypt, whose concurrent civilization is perhaps even
more spectacularly represented by art objects. In addition,
of course, since the Egyptians had access to large quantities
of stone and the Mesopotamians did not, there remain
architectural antiquities which reveal much about the life
of the times. Indeed, much of early Egyptian art has been
found in tombs as imposing as the great pyramids. The
Egyptian art shown here includes a gold and inlaid bracelet,
a bronze cat with a gold earring, a bronze statue of a scribe
(probably a wealthy landowner or nobleman, since only the
rich could write) and one of the miniature gold coffins in
the canopic chest of King Tutankhamen.

On the third double-page of illustrations are four
remarkable marble idols from the Cyclades, the Aegean islands
near the Greek mainland. The story of these islands is almost
totally unknown since little is left but some modest tombs
built of stone. Among Cycladic artifacts are a great number
of such idols, almost all nude females with arms folded across
their chest. These are presumably mother or fertility
goddesses; they resemble not only those of the Ancient Near
East and Asia Minor, but earlier objects dating back some
20,000 years to the cave-sites of Europe. Cycladic idols
were carved in an enormous range of sizes, up to life
size—the oldest life-sized nude female figures known.
Not until about the fourth century in Greece does a full-
scale female figure appear again—the nude Aphrodite, mother
of so much subsequent Western art.

Finally, in this portfolio, on the page opposite is
an example of the extraordinary art of Minoan Crete whose
rise and fall within the span of years from about 3000 B.C.
to 1100 B.C. remains an archeological mystery. The ivory
and gold goddess shown here is from the Palace of Knossos,
also known as the Palace of Minos, a structure so large and
complex that it came down in Greek legend as the Labyrinth
of the Minotaur.

Although its beauty is self-evident, much must be guessed
about the art of all the periods shown here and its creators.
It was not until Greece flourished that men began to record the
lives of their artists with regularity; it was then that the
artist truly came to be valued as a special individual.

part **4**

Culture
and man

The nature
of culture

If one were to scan a list of course offerings in a college catalog, or examine the subject classification of books in a library, one would discover that many branches of human knowledge study man himself. Moreover, it is man as he functions within the groups he forms that is so often studied. The social sciences study man in groups, as well as the interaction between individuals and groups.

A good deal of our education is thus spent studying specific aspects of our own or others' cultures. But the concept of culture itself is not usually dealt with in the course of these studies. It is not the purpose of an economics course to investigate the concept of culture. Yet, when one is studying "economics," it is not just economics one is learning, but a whole set of cultural values, assumptions, and judgments that may go largely unnoticed and unquestioned as one learns the practical foundations and application of the discipline. We may assume, for example, that individualism, political liberty, or the ideal of continual growth are values essential to the success of an economic system, whereas such values are characteristic primarily of our capitalist system and are not to be found in economic systems prevalent in other parts of the world.

Human culture, however varied, is the real object of study of the social sciences, but for the most part we are hardly aware that culture exists. Each of us tends to regard our own goals, moral values, political opinions, or attitudes to such things as war, success, freedom, and time, as being correct, based on common sense; they are "normal." We are bound to view our own society's reactions to the world as the only ones worth knowing.

We are often unaware that our responses to things we see or hear about and our judgments of others' actions are all influenced by culture. The ancient Greeks, for example, had no such notion as "Greek culture." Recognizing that their way of life differed from that of their neighbors, they thought themselves decidedly superior. It was not they but their neighbors who wore strange garments, talked strange languages, and had outlandish customs.

The concept of culture

Throughout the sixteenth to the nineteenth centuries, colonization brought European man into contact with peoples whose way of life was radically different from their own. These peoples neither read nor wrote; their clothing and housing were simple; they lacked the technology to produce fleets of ocean-going vessels, scientific instruments, or navigational charts. Because of these contrasts, it was easy for the Europeans to assume that they were superior and the newly discovered peoples were inferior.

The Europeans who arrived in foreign lands as colonizers were faced with the need to know about their subjects in order to control them; for noncolonists, there remained the fascination with exotic peoples. To this day, the fascination exerted on us by other cultures is manifest in the coverage given them in the press, television specials, and magazines.

From the observations gathered by the early Europeans, an attempt to see a people's way of life as a whole began to emerge. Marriage and child-rearing customs, economic and agricultural practices, governing and war-making behavior, religious or philosophical beliefs—all were incorporated into the concept of culture.

The first important definition of culture was proposed by the British anthropologist, Sir Edward Tylor. Writing in 1871, he defined culture as "that complex whole which includes knowledge, belief, art, law, morals, custom and any other capabilities and habits acquired by man as a member of society." This definition effectively suggests the complex nature of culture, but, as our knowledge of culture has increased, Tylor's definition has proven somewhat limited.

By the mid-twentieth century, human knowledge had so far advanced, and so many previously unknown peoples had been studied, that numerous definitions of culture were suggested at one time or another. In the 1950s, Alfred L. Kroeber and Clyde Kluckhohn examined over two hundred definitions of culture proposed by anthropologists and social scientists, in an effort to arrive at a consensus of what culture is.

They concluded that culture consists of patterns of behavior acquired and transmitted by means of symbols and artifacts—for example,

through language and art. Such patterns of behavior are based on traditional ideas and values and are characteristic of a specific human group. More recent definitions of culture tend to emphasize the abstract elements that lie behind man's observable behavior. A people's attitude toward war would be more important to an anthropologist studying culture than the material out of which these people construct their weapons. Culture, then, is not the actual observable behavior of a group of people, but an abstraction derived from it. Culture is a set of rules or standards which, when acted upon by the members of a society, produces behavior that falls within a range of variance the members consider proper and acceptable.

Culture as consensus

Culture can be seen from two closely related viewpoints. On the one hand, it may be studied strictly as that which anthropologists can observe, that is, on the **phenomenal order.** For example, an anthropologist might travel to the Southwest to watch the Navajo Indians weaving rugs. The tools they use, the designs they choose, the way the work is allocated, are all observable phenomena of the Navajo culture, or system of behavior shared by all members of a society. The Navajo culture could also be studied in another way, by trying to determine the beliefs, values, and principles of the rug makers. The anthropologist might observe that the rug serves a purpose beyond that of the purely utilitarian. It might be used in conjunction with a religious ceremony, or its designs might possess some magical significance. In trying to determine what these symbols mean to the Navajo, the anthropologist is studying the **ideational order.** It is the ideational order that is most relevant to a definition of culture, because notions of "proper" and "acceptable" behavior stem from values, and it is the abstract values that make the behavior acceptable.

Not all individuals within a culture think and behave in exactly the same way. One may find

Figure 13-1. *The top photo shows a Navajo woman spinning wool inside her hogan; at bottom her kinswoman is weaving the wool in a traditionally patterned rug.*

a group of individuals who, because of age, sex, occupation, or beliefs, share somewhat different standards. Such a group functioning within the confines of a larger culture is called a **subculture.** The degree to which subcultures are tolerated varies greatly from culture to culture.

An example of a subculture in the United States can be seen in the Amish.[1] The Old Order Amish originated in Austria and Moravia during the Reformation; today members of this order number about 60,000 and live mainly in Pennsylvania, Ohio, and Indiana. They are pacifistic, agrarian people whose lives focus on their religious beliefs. They value simplicity, hard work, and a high degree of neighborly cooperation. They dress in a distinctive, plain garb, and even today rely on the horse for transportation as well as agricultural work. They rarely mingle with non-Amish.

The goal of Amish education is to teach reading, writing, and arithmetic, and to instill Amish values in the children. They reject "worldly" knowledge and the idea of schools producing good citizens for the state. The Amish insist that their children attend school near home and that teachers be committed to Amish values. Their nonconformity to the standards of the larger culture has caused the Amish frequent conflict with state authorities, as well as legal and personal harrassment. They have resisted all attempts to force their children to attend regular public schools. Some compromise has been necessary, and "vocational training" has been introduced beyond the elementary school level to fulfill state requirements. The Amish have succeeded in gaining control of their schools and maintaining their way of life. In return, they are a beleaguered, defensive culture, more distrustful than ever of the larger culture around them.

The experience of the Amish is one example of the way a subculture is tolerated by the larger culture within which it functions. As different as they are, the Amish actually practice many values that our nation respects in the abstract: thrift, hard work, independence, a close family life. The

[1]John Hostetler and Gertrude Huntington, *Children in Amish Society* (New York: Holt Rinehart and Winston, 1971).

265

degree of tolerance accorded to them may also be due in part to the fact that the Amish are white Europeans, of the same race as the dominant culture. The American Indian subculture was treated differently by the white man. There was a racial difference; the white man came as a conqueror; and Indian values were not as easily understood or sympathized with by the larger culture. The nation was less willing to tolerate the differences of the Indians, with results that are now a matter of history, and very much a current concern.

Anthropological studies of culture

A definition of culture is not an adequate research tool for the anthropologist doing work in the field. Culture itself cannot be directly observed; only outward behavior is actually observable. In order to understand the problems of an anthropologist doing field work in a strange culture, it may be helpful to imagine the unlikely situation in which a native from the interior of New Guinea is brought for the first time into a modern urban hospital, free to explore at will. He would find rooms containing one, two, four or six very odd-looking hammocks occupied by resting or sleeping persons. He would see men and women in white going to and from the hammocks, as well as pausing at little sites in the corridors. There would be strange moving rooms that go from floor to floor. He might find eerily masked figures probing inside an apparently lifeless body. Elsewhere there would be offices, restaurants, shops, kitchens, a laundry, a pharmacy, voices filling the air from nowhere saying "Dr. Wilson, Dr. Jones, Dr. Shapiro, Dr. Anderson." The visitor would have no way of understanding any of this, and would be unable to fit any two parts together. How would he know the main purpose of the place he was in? How would he know which, of all the people he has seen, are the beneficiaries of this main purpose and which its agents? How could he distinguish which rooms and activities

Figure 13-2. *A group of Amish children walks briskly in the near-zero weather to the schoolhouse several miles away. Because of a religious prohibition against mechanized vehicles, they do not ride a school bus. The clothes the children wear also reflect the difference between the values held by the Amish and those of the dominant culture.*

Culture and man ● part **4**

are devoted to primary tasks, and which to secondary, supportive tasks? If he were to decide that the cafeteria or the laundry were the center of this place, he would be wrong. If he concluded that there was no relationship between any of the things he saw, he would be wrong again.

The anthropologist is not really in the same position as this imaginary visitor. The anthropologist goes into the field with the most advanced tools and methods of investigation available to him. Nonetheless, he will be confronted by a series of interrelated activities that at first he may not understand. What he sees may be as foreign to him as an urban hospital may be to a New Guinea tribesman. Moreover, what he sees will in reality be as cohesive and interconnected to the insider as the various departments of a hospital are to an intern. The anthropologist must try to abstract a set of rules from what he observes and hears in order to explain social behavior.

Try as he might to be objective, the anthropologist's own personal and cultural biases are bound to color his conclusions. In order to arrive at a realistic description of a culture, he should approach his subject matter from three different viewpoints. First, he must examine a people's own understanding of the rules by which their culture lives—their notion of the way their society ought to be. Second, he must determine the extent to which the people believe that they are observing those rules—how they think they actually behave. Third, he must describe the behavior he himself observes—an impartial reporter's account of the way they behave.

Anthropologist Bronislaw Malinowski encountered this problem and discovered a difference between what people do and what they say they do. The Trobriand Islanders believe that the rules of exogamy—sexual relations outside one's own group—ought to be observed.

> If you were to inquire into the matter among the Trobrianders, you would find that . . . the natives show horror at the idea of violating the rules of exogamy and that they believe that sores, diseases, even death might follow clan

incest. (But) from the viewpoint of the native libertine, *suvasova* (the breach of exogamy) is indeed a specially interesting and spicy form of erotic experience. Most of my informants would not only admit but did actually boast about having committed this offense . . .[2]

Malinowski himself believed that although such breaches did occasionally occur they were much less frequent than gossip would have it. Had Malinowski relied solely on what the Trobrianders told him, his description of their culture would have been inaccurate. There may be a variance between the way a people think they should behave, the way they think they do behave, and the way others see them behave.

Culture and society

Every human being is a member of a culture and of a society, because every human culture exists within a human society. It is within Chinese society that Chinese culture exists. But not all societies have culture. We speak of ant, or bee, or insect societies, but not of insect cultures. Bees cooperate instinctively in a way that clearly indicates a degree of social organization. Some kinds of bees live in communal hives that may contain thousands of individuals. They have specialized classes of individuals, each performing distinctive tasks such as scouting, working in the hive, feeding larvae, or removing waste materials from the hive. Social living may have arisen among animals as a mechanism ensuring the survival of the group; it is known that individuals who live in groups tend to live longer than those who live independently. In the case of the bees, social living is based purely on instinct. The bees share among themselves little more than the capacity to react to certain circumstances instinctively. Bees cannot transfer learned behavior to other bees as a person would an idea to another person, or "create" a new form of behavior.

Man, along with his fellow primates and some

---

[2] Bronislaw Malinowski, *Argonauts of the Western Pacific.*

other animal groups, possesses the instinct for social organization. A group of people from many cultures stranded over a period of time on a desert island would become a society. The members would have a common interest—survival—and would develop techniques for living and working together. Each of the members of this group, however, would retain his identity and cultural background, and the group would disintegrate without further ado as soon as its members were rescued from the island. The group would have been merely an aggregate in time and not a cultural entity. Society may be defined as a group of people occupying a territory who are dependent on each other for survival. The relationships that hold a society together are known as **social structure** or **social organization.**

British and American anthropologists have debated the relative importance of culture and society for understanding human behavior. A. R. Radcliffe-Brown, a leading exponent of the British viewpoint, was more interested in observable social relationships than in the rules that lay behind them. Essentially the conflict is a difference of emphasis. Culture and society are two closely related concepts, and an anthropologist must study both.

Society and the individual

It has been said that no man is an island. Man is eminently a social animal, and his existence is bound to the group. There are few things we can do entirely by ourselves. Individuals interact with individuals in what Ralph Linton has called patterns of reciprocity. As a member of a culture, an individual is an active part of it, but no individual is a culture by himself.

To think that individuals are merely the ingredients of society would be misleading. It is part of society's function to provide for ways whereby an individual can express his individuality. An individual is molded by his culture but not obliterated by it. But the patterns of reciprocity upon which a society operates limit the scope of an individual's activities; ultimately the role of the individual must serve some social needs. An example of one balance that must be reached between the needs of the individual and the needs of society can be seen in the social laws that regulate sexual activity. In most societies, extreme promiscuity is prohibited, because it can be disruptive to important cooperative relations between the sexes. Yet it is rare for a society to be absolutely intolerant of any promiscuous sexual activity, for such rigid regulation would limit too severely the freedom of the individual. Societal balance is achieved through a constant reorganization of priorities, the individual adjusting to the needs of the group, and the group providing an environment conducive to the expression of the individual.

Characteristics of culture

Through the comparative study of many different cultures, anthropologists have arrived at an understanding of the basic characteristics which all cultures share. A careful study of these characteristics may help us see the value and the function of culture itself.

Culture is learned

All culture is learned, not biologically inherited. Every person learns his culture by growing up in it. Ralph Linton referred to culture as man's "social heredity." The process whereby culture is transmitted from one generation to the next is called **enculturation.**

Most animals eat and drink whenever the urge arises. Man, however, eats and drinks at certain culturally prescribed times, and feels hungry as those times approach. These eating times vary from culture to culture. Similarly, an American's idea of a comfortable way to sleep will vary greatly from that of a Japanese and an African. The need to sleep is instinctual; the way it is satisfied is cultural.

Through enculturation one learns the socially appropriate way of satisfying one's instinctual needs. It is important to distinguish between the needs themselves, which are not learned, and the learned ways in which they are satisfied. Man's instinctual needs are the same as those of other animals: food, shelter, companionship, self-defense, and sexual gratification. Each culture determines how these needs will be met.

Not all learned behavior is cultural. A dog may learn tricks, but his behavior is reflexive, the result of conditioning by repeated training, not the product of enculturation. On the other hand, primates other than man are capable of forms of cultural behavior. A chimpanzee, for example, will take a twig and strip it of all leaves in order to make a tool that will extract termites from a hole. Tool-making, learned through imitation, is unquestionably a form of cultural behavior until recently thought to be exclusively human. The cultural capacity of apes, however, is obviously not nearly as well developed as that of a man. It is man's superior learning ability that makes him distinctive as a cultural animal.

Culture is shared

A second characteristic of culture is that it is shared. Ralph Linton has commented:

> Men confront nature not as isolated units but as members of organized, cooperative groups. The incorporation of the individual into the group and his training in one or another of the specialized activities necessary to the group's wellbeing has thus become the primary function of man's social heredity.[3]

Culture is a set of shared assumptions; it is the common denominator that makes the actions of individuals intelligible to the group. Because they share a common culture, people can predict each other's actions in a given circumstance and react accordingly. If a young man announces "Last

night I proposed to Sue, and we're getting engaged in June," he will be congratulated, not only for the good news of the impending marriage but also because he has acted according to the rules of society. Had he said, "Last night I asked Sue's father to trade her for my hi-fi, car, water skis, and $250 in cash," he would probably not be congratulated, because he is not acting appropriately according to his culture.

Individual behavior does not constitute culture. In every culture, there are persons whose idiosyncratic behavior has earned them the terms of "eccentric," "crazy," or "queer." Such persons are looked upon suspiciously by society and are sooner or later excluded from participating in the activities of the group. Such exclusion acts to keep the deviant behavior outside the group. Most societies have mechanisms whereby some forms of deviant behavior are incorporated into the group in an acceptable way. Among the Mohave Indians, for example, transvestitism is accepted so long as the transvestite undergoes an initiation ceremony; the person then assumes for life the role of someone of the opposite sex and is permitted to marry.[4]

Culture is based on symbols

The American anthropologist Leslie White considers that all human behavior originates in the use of symbols. Art, religion, and money involve the use of symbols. We are all familiar with the fervor and devotion that religion can elicit from a believer; a cross, an image, any object of worship may bring to mind centuries of struggle and persecution or may stand for a whole philosophy or creed. The most important symbolic aspect of culture is language—the substitution of words for objects. Stanley Salthe points out, "Symbolic language is the foundation upon which human cultures are built. The institutions of these cultures (political structures, religions, arts, economic or-

---

[3] Ralph Linton, *The Study of Man* (New York: Appleton-Century-Crofts, 1964) p. 86.

[4] George Devereux, "Institutionalized Homosexuality of the Mohave Indians," in *The Problem of Homosexuality in Modern Society*, Hendrik M. Ruitenbeek, ed. (New York: E. P. Dutton, 1963).

ganization) could not possibly exist without symbols. . ."[5]

It is through language—defined by Edward Sapir as the "purely human and noninstinctive method of communicating ideas, emotions, and desires by means of a system of voluntarily produced symbols"[6]—that man is able to transmit culture from one generation to another.

There has been much interest in the question of whether animals are capable of learning this most characteristically human form of symbolic behavior. Most animal species are not, but experiments with some apes have yielded surprising results.

Attempts to teach other primates human speech have not been successful. In a lengthy experiment in communication, the chimpanzee Viki learned to voice only a few words, such as "up," "mama," "papa." The problem of speech in other primates seems to be twofold: a lack of connection in the nonhuman primate brain between auditory and motor speech areas; and a difference in construction between the human and nonhuman primate throats.

Better results have been achieved through nonvocal methods. Chimpanzees and gorillas in the wild use specific gestures, postures, and sounds to communicate among themselves. Allen and Beatrice Gardner began teaching the American Sign Language, used by the deaf, to their chimpanzee Washoe in 1966. After 22 months, Washoe had a vocabulary of 30 signs, and her rate of acquisition was accelerating. The first signs she learned were for nouns. She was able to transfer each sign from its original referent to other appropriate objects, and even pictures of objects. Her vocabulary includes verbs, adjectives, and words like "sorry," and "please." Washoe can string signs together to produce original sentences.

The chimpanzee Sarah has learned to converse by means of pictographs—designs such as squares and triangles—on brightly colored plastic chips. Each pictograph stands for a noun or a verb. Sarah can also produce new sentences of her own. Experiments are now under way with gorillas.

Culture is integrated

For purposes of comparison and analysis, anthropologists customarily break a culture down into many discrete elements, but such distinctions are arbitrary. When an anthropologist examines one aspect of a culture, he invariably finds himself examining others as well. This tendency for all aspects of a culture to function as an interrelated whole is called **integration.**

The integration of the economic, political, and social aspects of a society can be illustrated by the Kapauku Papuans, a mountain people of western New Guinea studied by the American anthropologist Leopold Pospisil.[7] Among the status-oriented Kapauka, wealth comes from the breeding of pigs; and wealth is the key to political and legal leadership. The pigs are fed on sweet potatoes. Hence, agriculture is of prime importance. Since it is the role of women to cultivate sweet potatoes as well as to raise the pigs, there is a direct relation between women and the production of wealth. The Kapauku practice polygyny; one man possesses many wives. This makes possible the cultivation of more land and the breeding of more pigs. The increased wealth thus generated enables a man to buy more wives. Because the bride-price paid for every wife is high, the men exploit their investment to the fullest, providing as much work for the women as possible. Women cannot weed and harvest, however, until the men have cleared and drained the ground. So the more wives a man has, the more he must work.

The sweet potato can be regarded as the origin of wealth in Kapauku culture, since it makes possible the sale of pigs, the main source of income. But because only women can cultivate sweet

[5] Stanley N. Salthe, *Evolutionary Biology* (New York: Holt, Rinehart and Winston, 1972) p. 402.

[6] Edward Sapir, *Language* (New York: Harcourt Brace Jovanovich, 1949) p. 8.

[7] Leopold Pospisil, *The Kapauku Papuans of New Guinea* (New York: Holt, Rinehart and Winston, 1963).

Figure 13-3. *A group of young unmarried women takes time out for a chat during the long festivities that attend the killing of a pig among the Kapauku.*

potatoes or raise pigs, another factor in generating wealth is the possession of many wives. The men with the most wives have the most pigs and the most land under cultivation. They are also the wealthiest.

In a polygynous society, there are usually more adult women than men. The imbalance between the sexes is maintained among the Kapauku through intertribal warfare. The Kapauku will never shoot in battle at an adult female, because they consider it highly immoral. Since a part of the male population is regularly eliminated as a result of wars, the surplus of adult females tends to be maintained.

Were warfare to be eliminated in the New Guinea highlands, it would alter the ratio of males to females, disrupting the sex ratio characteristic of a polygynous society. Were an attempt made to introduce new agricultural methods that would make the labor of women unnecessary, Kapauku society would find itself with a surplus of unemployable women. The different elements of Kapauku culture—the economic, the political, and the social—are compatible with one another. The raising of sweet potatoes and pigs, the practice of polygyny, and the frequency of intertribal warfare all work together like cogs of a gear system. A culture can be compared to a machine; the parts must all be adjusted to one another or it will not run properly.

Culture and process

Culture has been more powerful than nature in shaping man as we know him today. Man's body and his culture evolved in direct response to one another. Tool using and the addition of hunting to the hominid subsistence pattern contributed to the development of the human brain, and the development of the brain in turn permitted increasing complexity both in tool making and hunting techniques. It is difficult to distinguish cause from effect in this continuing evolutionary process.

The fact that man can adapt to his environment culturally as well as physically has given him the opportunity to extend his territory beyond the natural range of other primates. By manipulating the environment, he can occupy the Arctic, the Sahara, or the moon. The social environment in which man lives is not only very complex but demands a rapid adjustment to unforeseen changes. Man adapts by changing the world, not himself, often improving it as he goes along, and he can do so in a very short time. Evolutionary changes arising from man's need to cope with change on short notice have favored behavioral plasticity and the ability to learn from experience.

Cultural adaptation

There are at least as many forms of adaptation as there are environments. The Yąnomamö people of Brazil studied by the American anthropologist Napoleon A. Chagnon provide a good example of the way man adapts to a sociopolitical environment. The Yąnomamö's adaptation to the sociopolitical environment is as important as their adaptation to nature, and it illustrates how a people must relate themselves to each other in order to survive. This adjustment affects the way they

Figure 13-4. *Anthropologist Napoleon Chagnon spent much time among the Yąnomamö of South America as he studied their culture. The photo at upper left shows the site of a village, surrounded by cleared land that has been planted with a crop of plantains. Other photos show the plantains being gathered and stored. On special occasions plantain soup is drunk from a gourd.*

are distributed over the land, their patterns of migration, and the kind of relationships they maintain with their neighbors.

The Yąnomamö are a fiercely aggressive people that inhabit jungle villages numbering 40 to 250 persons. Village life revolves around the cultivation of a plantain garden and warring against other villages. Because peace is so uncertain, a village must be prepared to evacuate, either to a new location or to the parent village, on very short notice. But since the garden is of such economic importance, abandoning it to start a new one elsewhere is seen as a formidable task, and is resisted except in the most extreme situations. Alliances are therefore made with neighboring villages, so that one village joins another's war parties, or takes in the inhabitants of another village during times of need.

The Yąnomamö are so aggressive that in a village of 100 people there is bound to be feuding and bloodshed, necessitating a split, with the dissident faction going off to establish a new garden. Although Yąnomamö try to avoid the establishment of a new garden because of the labor and uncertainty of the first harvest, their political way of life forces them to this decision frequently. Although they are an agricultural people, their choice of a garden site is based on political considerations.

It has become apparent in recent years that man's control over the environment can be pushed to the point in which he is endangered, rather than protected, by the effects of cultural evolution. Scientific control over the environment and medical control over the human body can alter, for example, the effects of natural selection. Hemophilia, or "bleeder's disease," is caused by an aberration of the sex chromosome. In the past, natural selection has operated so that most hemophiliacs were eliminated from the gene pool before they reached maturity and were able to reproduce. Today, as a result of medical advances, the life expectancy of hemophiliacs has increased; they can now live long enough to marry and reproduce, transmitting the defective gene that causes the disease to their offspring. Consequently, the number of persons affected by hemophilia has increased.

Another example of the interplay between culture and natural selection also involves medical advances. As a result of routine use of antibiotics in medical treatment, many people have become sensitized, running the risk of violent allergic reaction if the drug is administered to them; moreover some virus strains, such as certain types of gonorrhea, have developed a resistance to antibiotics.

Culture and change

All cultures change over a period of time. This might be due to the intrusion of outsiders, or to modification of behavior and values within the culture. Within our culture, clothing fashions change frequently. It has recently become culturally permissible for us to bare more of our bodies both in swimming and in dress. Along with this in recent years has come greater permissiveness about the body in photographs and movies. Finally, the sexual attitudes and practices of Americans have become more permissive in recent years. Obviously these changes are interrelated, reflecting an underlying change in attitudes toward cultural rules regarding sex.

Culture change can bring unexpected and often disastrous results. For the Yir-Yoront people of Australia, the stone ax was the main technological tool as well as one of the most important mythical symbols. The ax was a tribal totem and a symbol of masculinity. As such, it had an important place in the cosmology of the Yir-Yoront. Moreover, ax heads were an important object of trade acquired annually at ceremonial tribal gatherings. Because they were scarce, stone axes were owned only by senior men. Several decades ago, some well-intentioned missionaries provided the Yir-Yoront with steel axes. The steel axes became plentiful, so that even women and children had their own. The steel axes eliminated the need for the more primitive stone ones. As a result, the stone ax as a symbol of masculinity was destroyed; and as the steel ax could not be related

to the tribal totem, the whole ideological system of the Yir-Yoront began to disintegrate. The annual tribal gatherings dwindled, as there was no need to obtain stone heads through trade. The introduction of steel axes undermined the whole structure of Yir-Yoront society, and no substitute for the old order has yet been found.

An example of less catastrophic change can be seen in the Tiwi, a people of north Australia. An important Tiwi household consisted of the male head, his wives, offspring, cousins, nephews, uncles, sons-in-law, and all the women who came under his care either as wives of his male kin, or, in the case of orphaned female children, "wives" who were not yet old enough to have husbands. In Tiwi society, every woman was considered to be also a wife, regardless of age. And since the spirits might make her pregnant at any time, female infants were married at birth to young men of about 25, though not until puberty did they live with their husbands. For the Tiwi, wives were a form of currency, to be valued as a source of capital rather than as sexual partners. Possession of a large number of wives was the source of prestige.

When missionaries converted the Tiwi to Christianity and imposed monogamy, Tiwi men, instead of adopting the western couple family pattern, continued to head enormous households, or "camps," consisting of great numbers of women. The difference, however, is that now the head of a camp has only one wife; he is monogamous. The impact of social change has been limited to the realm of marriage. Household patterns have barely changed, and the economic structure continues to be based, as it was before the coming of the missionaries, on a large number of women and young men attached to the household; the young women gather food, the old women mind the children, and the young men go off to work.

Functions of culture

A culture cannot survive if it does not satisfy certain basic needs of its members. The extent to

Figure 13-5. *An elder of the Tiwi tribe stands near the road leading to Darwin, Australia; note the elaborate body painting.*

which a culture achieves the fulfillment of these needs will determine its ultimate success. "Success" is measured by the values of the in-group; the outsider may find the culture "unsuccessful." A culture must provide for the production and distribution of goods and services necessary for life. It must provide for biological continuity through the reproduction of its members. It must socialize new members so that they can become functioning adults. It must maintain order among its members. It must likewise maintain order between its members and outsiders. It must motivate its members to survive and engage in those activities necessary for survival.

Cultural focus. Every culture tends to emphasize certain cultural activities. In Western civilization, for example, technology occupies a prominent place; ours is a technology oriented culture. This emphasis on an area of cultural activity is known as **cultural focus.** Cultural focus is significant because it determines the things individuals value and want for themselves. To suggest to a Kapauku that his people stop raising pigs would be the equivalent of suggesting to an American engineer that the United States abandon technology and all the research, marketing, transportation, and investment that goes with it.

Evaluation of culture

It is an inextricable aspect of the process of enculturation that we all grow up thinking that our culture is the best there is. In the nineteenth century, Western man had no doubts about the fact that Western civilization (most particularly that of Victorian England) represented the peak of mankind's development. Some inquiring anthropologists, however, realized that all cultures yet studied also saw themselves as the best. This was reflected in the way the members of a society called themselves, which, roughly translated, meant "we the people," as opposed to "you subhumans." The belief that one's own culture is the best is called **ethnocentrism.**

To judge the behavior of others according to ethnocentric standards of the anthropologist's own culture is misleading. When anthropologists began to live among the so-called savages, they discovered that under the seeming strangeness was a recognizable counterpart of their own society. This led anthropologists to examine each culture on its own terms. They questioned whether or not the culture satisfied the needs and expectations of the people themselves. If the people were cannibals, for example, they asked whether or not the eating of human flesh was acceptable according to native values; why it made sense; and what were the alternatives. The idea that a culture must be evaluated according to its own standards is called **cultural relativism.** One could say, for instance, that the eating of other human beings may be acceptable to cannibals, yet it is a custom we Americans would not wish to emulate, no matter how functional it may be to some other group of people.

Both cultural relativism and ethnocentrism represent extreme viewpoints. Cultural relativism merely replaces one set of subjective standards (the anthropologist's own) with another (the culture that is studied). To be truly objective, however, the anthropologist needs a criterion for evaluation that is not derived from anyone's cultural values. A culture is essentially a system designed to insure the continued existence of a group of people. Therefore, the ultimate test of a culture is its capability of change in new circumstances. The ability of a culture to survive seems to be the best criterion by which to evaluate the success of a culture.

☐

Because we live within a unique sociocultural system, we have a tendency to assume that all of our component patterns are largely products of our own culture, having sprung from native brains. Although we acknowledge having borrowed words from the French, we tend to regard as national in origin any item now considered to be our own. One natural result of such thinking is that we feel superior to other people on the assumption that we have given them a great deal but have accepted very little in return. If such feelings are justified, they should be demonstrable with reference to something very ordinary in our lives, such as our clothing. It becomes informative, therefore, to historically consider the items of clothing worn in the United States.

The first item of apparel for a modern man is underwear. His shorts of today are derived from a similar but longer-legged undergarment worn by Europeans during the latter half of the twelfth century. Next are his trousers, a type of clothing form which originated among the riders of horses in the steppe country of Western Russia possibly as early as 3000 B.C. Trousers were popular among the Germanic peoples in the first century A.D. and probably were introduced into western Europe by these people during one of their earlier ventures westward. The modern form of trousers began to emerge in western Europe during the French revolution (1789–1795) and was developed fully by the early decades of the nineteenth century. It is of incidental note that by the early 1800s trouser cuffs had been innovated by Englishmen, who turned up the bottom of their trouser legs on rainy days. The cuffed style was introduced in the United States when a visiting Englishman was caught in the rain on his way to a wedding in New York City. Buttoned shirts, derived from a tunic style which developed into an unbuttoned shirt, emerged first in medieval Europe. The necktie may be traced back to the chin cloths which Roman orators wore to protect their throats. The neckcloths which the Croatians wore into battle may have been an idea borrowed from the Romans, but in any case the cravat was added as an item of clothing among the French and English in the 1600s. When the standing collar points began to turn down over the cravat in the 1840s, a large bow tie was used in its place. This was narrowed and became a knotted tie of the modern form in England and in the United States shortly before 1900. The double-breasted coat made its first appearance in England about 1800, and in 1890 it had dropped the tails and looked much like the sports coat of today. The belt probably came into use at the same time as trousers. Socks of felt, or perhaps they were foot bandages, were known to the ancient Greeks, whereas sewn fabric socks were worn by Roman Empire times (30 B.C.– 476 A.D.). Coarse stockings were pulled over the breeches by A.D. 1100 in England, became longer until the late 1500s, and then were shortened to below the knee and were most often made of silk or fine yarn. Finally, shoes were derived from the short Roman leather boots of the first century A.D.; however, modern forms did not begin to emerge until the time of the Crusades, when many Europeans walked much farther than they ever had before.

The clothing of a woman includes panty briefs or briefs which developed in the 1930s from longer forms of the previous decade. It was the French drawers and knickers which became shortened to panties by 1924, after which they

began to assume their modern form. The corset developed from a sleeved bodice called a kirtle worn by women in medieval Europe. The kirtle became a constricting garment when it came to be laced tightly and reinforced with sew-in strips of iron, steel, or whalebone. The corset reached from shoulder to hip during the Victorian period in England (1837–1901), but it had developed into a two-piece style in France by that time. The upper part had become known as a brassiere by 1912, and this French word was shortened to bra by 1937. The bra served as a bust-flattener in the 1920s but has since moved in the opposite direction. The lower part, called a girdle, was changed as early as 1911 when its support became less rigid and was provided by vulcanized rubber cloth rather than inserted stiffening strips of bone or metal. Undertunics were popular among Greek women about 1200 B.C., eventually came to be adopted by the Saxons, and emerged as petticoats among the sixteenth-century Venetians, from whom the French and English borrowed the idea. The modern fitted slip, cut on the bias, was developed in France during the 1920s. Blouses were worn by ninth-century English women, but they were much longer than the modern forms. Although contemporary types were a part of the garb of seventeenth-century Russian women, they were not introduced into the United States and England until about 1900. By 2000 B.C. the Semites and Babylonians wore tunics over the lower part of the body, and the Franks of Europe wore jumpers by the fifth century A.D. However, modern skirts, closely fitted and ending at the waist, did not originate until about 1800 in the United States, and they did not become popular until around 1910. The prototype of women's hose is the same as men's socks; both can be traced to the earlier socks or stockings sewn from fabric and later knitted.

Even this brief presentation illustrates that our clothing forms have a history that is much older than that of our country, and despite all of our emphasis on dress, the changes which we have made have been only stylistic in nature. "To dress American" would result in naked men and women. For all of our inventiveness we still follow the patterns set in Europe for clothing and have made no revolutionary inventions nor many lasting modifications. Thus, our cultural heritage with respect to clothing is un-American, and we would find the same to be true for many diverse aspects of our culture if we took the time to trace their origins.

Source:
From *Understanding Our Culture: An Anthropological View* by Wendell H. Oswalt. Copyright © 1970 by Holt, Rinehart and Winston, Inc. Reprinted by permission of Holt, Rinehart and Winston, Inc.

Summary

1.

Culture has been defined in numerous ways. Recent definitions of culture tend to empha-size the abstract elements derived from the actual behavior of the participants in a social system. Culture may be defined as a somewhat flexible set of rules that prescribes standards of proper and acceptable behavior within a society; it may be studied in terms of its phenomenal order—observable behavior—and in terms of the ideational order—the ideas, beliefs, values, and principles of its members. A subculture is a group functioning within the general confines of a larger culture while observing a set of rules that is somewhat different from the standard.

2.

The job of the anthropologist is to abstract a set of rules from what he observes and hears in order to explain the social behavior of a people. To arrive at a realistic description of a culture free from personal and cultural biases, the anthropologist must (a) examine a people's notion of the way their society ought to function; (b) determine how a people think they actually do behave; and (c) describe a people's observable behavior.

3.

There are generalities characteristic of all cultures. Culture is social. It cannot exist without society, which is defined as a group of people dependent upon each other for survival. Culture is learned behavior. Individual members of a society learn the accepted norms of social behavior through the process of enculturation. Culture is based on symbols. It is transmitted through the communication of ideas, emotions, and desires expressed in language. Culture is integrated so that all aspects of a culture function as an interrelated whole.

4

Culture, as adaptive behavior, has been an integral feature of the human species throughout its evolution. The increasing complexity of the human brain and increasing complexity of cultural systems have gone hand-in-hand, and the record of human evolution has been one of increasing emphasis on cultural rather than biological adaptation. Cultural behavior enables humans to adapt to a wide variety of environments and assures survival of the species.

5.

A culture must satisfy certain basic requirements of its members if it is to continue to function. It must provide for subsistence and biological continuity, enculturate new members, maintain order among its members and between its members and outsiders, and it must motivate its members to survive and engage in actions necessary to the perpetuation of the cultural system.

Suggested readings

Goodenough, Ward H. *Description and Comparison in Cultural Anthropology*. Chicago: Aldine, 1970.

The major question to which Goodenough addresses himself is how the anthropologist is to avoid ethnocentric bias when studying culture. His approach relies on models of descriptive linguistics. A large part of the book is concerned with kinship and terminology, with a discussion of the problems of a universal definition of marriage and the family. This is a particularly lucid discussion of culture, its relation to society, and the problem of individual variance.

Hewes, Gordon W. "Primate Communication and the Gestural Origin of Language," in *Current Anthropology*, vol. 14; no. 1-2, 1973: 5-12.

Hewes discusses language in primates, citing evidence from primate studies, human gestural communication, early tool use, and other sources. His basic argument is that nonhuman higher primates have the capacity for communication by means of gestural symbols. He hypothesizes that human communication systems developed out of a gestural system rather than from the vocalizations characteristic of nonhuman primates.

Keesing, Roger, and Felix Keesing *New Perspectives in Cultural Anthropology*. New York: Holt, Rinehart and Winston, 1971.

This book approaches anthropology by pinpointing the basic problems of cultural anthropology, discussing them through ethnographic examples and theoretical considerations. It also gives a very concise historical account of past theories and works.

Kluckholn, Clyde, and Alfred L. Kroeber "Culture: A Critical Review of Concepts and Definitions," in *Papers of the Peabody Museum of Archaeology and Ethnology*, vol. 47, no. 1, 1952. Cambridge, Mass.: Peabody Museum.

This paper presents varying definitions of the concept of culture. There is a semantic history of the word "culture" and its related word, "civilization," analyses of various definitions according to anthropological concepts, and indices of the definitions categorized by author and conceptual components. In addition, Kluckholn presents definitions of "culture" as employed in other countries.

Kroeber, Alfred L. *Anthropology: Culture Processes and Patterns*. New York: Harcourt Brace Jovanovitch, 1963.

This volume consists of chapters dealing specifically with matters of culture patterns and processes. The chapters are selected from Kroeber's major work, *Anthropology*.

Linton, Ralph *The Study of Man: An Introduction*. New York: Appleton-Century-Crofts, 1964.

Linton wrote this book in 1936 with the intention of providing a general survey of the field of anthropology. His study of social structure is illuminating. This book is regarded as a classic and is an important source historically.

DICTIONARIUM BRITANNICUM:

Or a more COMPLEAT

UNIVERSAL ETYMOLOGICAL

ENGLISH DICTIONARY

Than any EXTANT,

CONTAINING

Not only the Words and their Explication; but their Etymologies from the *Antient British, Teutonick, Dutch Low* and *High, Old Saxon, German, Danish, Swedish, Norman* and *Modern French, Italian, Spanish, Latin, Greek, Hebrew,* &c. each in its proper Character.

ALSO

Explaining hard and technical Words, or Terms of Art, in all the *ARTS, SCIENCES,* and *MYSTERIES* following. Together with *ACCENTS* directing to their proper Pronuntiation, shewing both the *Orthography,* and *Orthoepia* of the *English Tongue,*

VIZ. IN

AGRICULTURE, ALGEBRA, ANATOMY, ARCHITECTURE, ARITHMETICK, ASTROLOGY, ASTRONOMY, BOTANICKS, CATOPTRICKS, CHYMISTRY CHIROMANCY, CHIRURGERY, CONFECTIONARY, COOKERY, COSMOGRAPHY, DIALLING, DIOPTRICKS, ETHICKS, FISHING, FORTIFICATION, FOWLING, GARDENING, GAUGING, GEOGRAPHY, GEOMETRY, GRAMMAR, GUNNERY, HANDICRAFTS, HAWKING, HERALDRY, HORSEMANSHIP, HUNTING, HUSBANDRY, HYDRAULICKS, HYDROGRAPHY, HYDROSTATICKS, LAW, LOGICK, MARITIME *and* MILITARY AFFAIRS, MATHEMATICKS, MECHANICKS, MERCHANDIZE, METAPHYSICKS, METEOROLOGY, NAVIGATION, OPTICKS, OTACOUSTICKS, PAINTING, PERSPECTIVE, PHARMACY, PHILOSOPHY, PHYSICK, PHYSIOGNOMY, PYROTECHNY, RHETORICK, SCULPTURE, STATICKS, STATUARY, SURVEYING, THEOLOGY, *and* TRIGONOMETRY.

Illustrated with near Five Hundred CUTS, for Giving a clear Idea of those Figures, not so well apprehended by verbal Description.

LIKEWISE

A Collection and Explanation of *English* PROVERBS; also of WORDS and PHRASES us'd in our ancient Charters, Statutes, Writs, Old Records and Processes at Law.

ALSO

The Iconology, Mythology, Theogony, and Theology of the *Egyptians, Greeks, Romans,* &c. being an Account of their Deities, Solemnities, either Religious or Civil, their Divinations, Auguries, Oracles, Hieroglyphicks, and many other curious Matters, necessary to be understood, especially by the Readers of *English* POETRY.

Language
and communication

All normal humans learn to talk, and ordinarily they spend a considerable part of every day talking to each other. What are they saying? Listen to a speaker of Yoruba: *Kini se t'o ko da mi l'ohun?* A speaker of Papiàmento: *Miedu ku e machete aki den mi man?* And a speaker of Korean: *Chogi kaso kugosul posio!* What do the languages of these people on three different continents have in common?

Language is a systematic code for the communication, in **symbols,** of any kind of information. Insofar as nonhuman animals also communicate certain kinds of information systematically, we may also speak of animal language. But symbol in our definition means any kind of sound or gesture to which we ourselves have given meaning as standing for something, and not one that has a natural or biological meaning, which we call a **sign.** A tear is a sign of crying, and crying is a sign of some kind of emotional or physical state; the word "crying," however, is a symbol, a group of sounds to which we have learned to assign the meaning of a particular action, and which we can use to communicate that meaning whether or not anyone around us is actually crying.

At the moment language experts are not certain whether to give credit to animals—bees, dolphins, or chimpanzees—for the ability to use symbols as well as signs, even though these animals and many others have been found to communicate in remarkable ways. At least one famous chimp, named Washoe, has apparently been able to learn and to use some human symbols. What are the implications of this fact for our understanding of the nature and evolution of language? No certain answer can be given until further investigation of animal communication gives more facts to work with. What we can be sure of is that human language is a remarkably universal form of human social behavior, intimately related to practically everything man is and does, and that a knowledge of the workings of language is essential to any kind of work in anthropology.

The nature of language

Any human language—English, Chinese, Swahili—is obviously a means of transmitting information and sharing with others both a cultural and an individual experience. Because we tend to take language for granted, it is perhaps not so obvious that language is also a systematic code that enables us to translate our concerns, beliefs, and perceptions into symbols that can be decoded and interpreted by others. The many such codes presently in existence all over the world—an estimated 3000 different languages—may well astound and mystify us by their great variety and complexity; but basically languages are all rational systems, invented, developed, and perpetuated by man, and we should be able to figure them out, if only we have the right methods and the time.

The modern scientific study of language began as early as the seventeenth century, in the age of exploration and discovery, with the accumulation of facts: the collecting of sounds, words, and sentences from as many different languages as possible, chiefly those encountered in exotic lands by European explorers, invaders, and missionaries. The great contribution of the nineteenth century was the discovery of system, regularity, and relationships in the data, and the tentative formulation of some laws and regular principles. In the twentieth century, while we are still collecting data, we have made considerable progress in the reasoning process, testing and working from new and improved theories. Insofar as theories and facts of language are verifiable by independent researchers looking at the same materials, there may be said now to be a science of linguistics, or the study of all aspects of language.

Linguistics

The field of linguistics in general has traditionally been approached by two different methods. The **historical** study of language investigates relationships between earlier and later forms of the same language, antecedents in older languages for developments in modern languages, and questions of relationships between older languages. It is a concern of historical linguistics, for example, to identify and explain the development of early medieval spoken Latin into later medieval French and Spanish, through both natural change in the original language and the influence of con-

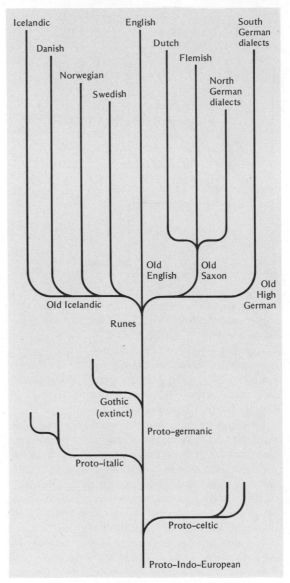

Figure 14-1. English is one of a group of languages in the modern Germanic family; this diagram shows its relationship to other languages in the same family. The root was an Indo-European language spoken by the early Aryans who spread westward over the European continent, bringing both their customs and their language with them.

tacts with the barbarian invaders from the North. The **descriptive** approach to language, on the other hand, is concerned with registering and explaining all the features of any one given language at any one time in history. A descriptive linguist concentrates, for example, on the way modern French or Spanish function now as closed systems, consistent within themselves, without any appeal to historical reasons for their development. Although Latin *ille* ("that") is identifiable as the origin of both French *le* ("the") and Spanish *el* ("the"), the descriptive linguist treats *le* and *el* only as they function in the modern language, where the meaning "that" is no longer relevant and very few people are aware that they are speaking a modern development of Latin. There is actually no ill will between historical and descriptive linguists, and presently the two approaches are recognized to be interdependent. Even a modern language is constantly changing, and it changes according to principles that can only be established historically.

Both the historical and the descriptive approaches to language are of interest to anthropology. Historical linguistics provides a means of dating (at least approximately) certain migrations, invasions, and contacts of peoples, and therefore of determining dates for the establishment of new or changed cultural groups. The concept of linguistic divergence, or the breaking up of an originally unified language with various local forms, for example, is used to identify the time at which one group of speakers of a language separated from another group. From a study of the use in rural French Canada of seventeenth-century French *icite* ("here") instead of modern French *ici,* one can date the separation of French colonists from the mother country at a specific time.

Glottochronology, also known as time-depth, introduced by linguists Swadesh and Lees, is a method of dating a more radical kind of divergence, when whole branches of language families separated from each other, such as Latin and Greek from a supposed earlier common language. Time-depth estimates rely on a complicated logarithmic formula for the number of words two languages should still have in common after they have been separated a given number of years.

Descriptive linguistics furnishes the anthropologist with both a framework for understanding, and the means to analyze, describe, and work with, the language of any people. A distinction should be made between **theoretical** and **field** linguistics, which are nevertheless interdependent and both considered to be under the general heading of descriptive linguistics. A theoretical linguist, such as the now celebrated Noam Chomsky of the Massachusetts Institute of Technology, makes a framework and a system for describing what happens in the whole encoding and sentence-making process. He hopes that his system will hold for all languages, though he may develop it in detail for only one.

The primary concern of the theoretical linguist is to answer the question of how language works rather than how to learn, use, or understand any particular language. The field linguist, on the other hand, collects raw data from speakers of a language, analyzes it, describes it in a coherent way, and typically also uses it in communicating with or about those speakers. He is a descriptive linguist by virtue of the fact that he begins by meticulously describing, to the best of his ability, and usually with special training, what is actually said in the language he is working on. He takes nothing for granted, and he learns to elicit natural responses that will illustrate every important aspect of a language. Descriptive in this sense is ordinarily opposed to prescriptive, or making a judgment about what ought to be done. For example, if the field linguist were working with a dialect group of English speakers who said consistently "he sa go tomorrow" and "I sa go next week," he would record the fact descriptively that the future for the dialect was regularly expressed by *sa;* he would not prescribe that it must or should be *shall* and that it was mispronounced or corrupted. It is the field linguist whose findings are most relevant to the concerns of anthropology, although the school of ethnosemantic anthropology, exemplified by the work of Lévi-Strauss, leans heavily on theoretical linguistics.

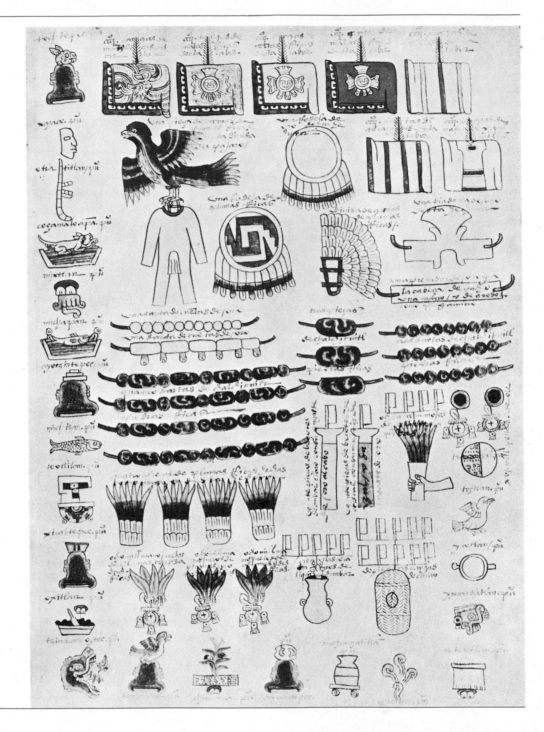

Culture and man ● part **4**

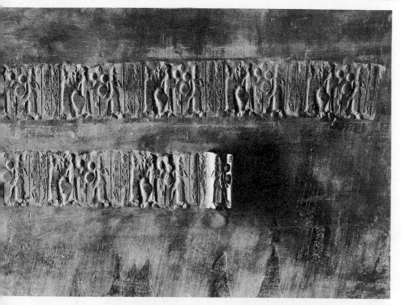

Theoretical linguistics

What happens when we talk? How do we make sentences? Current thinking highly favors the theory that most of our utterances are built up swiftly and unconsciously from basic two-part units, called in the terminology of Noam Chomsky the **deep structure**. The finished product, the complete utterance or sentence, is said to display **surface structure**, a complex web of transformed and integrated units from the deep structure. The principle is assumed to be the same for all languages, but the deep structures will differ, and the processes of getting from deep structure to surface structure should vary according to the habits, conventions, and social adaptations of different cultures. Understanding or explaining any language, according to this theory, should amount to identifying deep structure and establishing the rules whereby the deep structure is transformed into surface structure. A complete set of principles or rules should then be capable of generating or producing all possible sentences in the language. Using this terminology, Chomsky's theory is called **generative transformational grammar.**

Transformational grammar. Chomsky's theory has been widely acclaimed for bringing about a revolution in our thinking about language; indeed it provides the first consistent and logical model for a scientific description of the facts of language. The theory has been expanded, revised, and improved in detail over the past few years, and currently a considerable number of world languages are being put to a transformational analysis. Stages in the transformational process of using language have been compared to the operation of a super computer, with a series of yes-no decisions made in an elaborate program that no one has yet been able to put on paper, and with memory banks that are constantly updated and perhaps not always functioning properly. There is no doubt much truth in the analogy, considering what we do know about the functioning of the brain; but of course we have reason to believe

Figure 14-2,3. *Pictured below is a Sumerian cylinder seal. When rolled over tablets of wet clay, it produced an impression like the one shown above; the tablet was then baked or dried in the sun to make the record permanent. Opposite is a page from the Codex Mendoza, an early Spanish attempt to decipher Mexican writing, which like Sumerian was pictographic rather than syllabic.*

that emotions, biological changes, and an essential adaptability, among other things, make people somewhat different from computers.

To illustrate the theoretical process of transformational grammar in its application to a study of English, let us say for example that there is an unpleasant sensation in my head and that I want you to be aware of that fact for some reason. In encoding the message, I follow a basic pattern of English conventions in which a topic comes first (head), followed by a comment (hurt). The most important two-part unit in the deep structure will therefore be head-hurt. Because I want to identify the head in question as my own, another unit in the deep structure may be another topic and comment: head-mine. One transformational rule of English will make head-mine into my-head whenever that kind of statement is put into a larger sentence; another rule will put together the larger combination my-head-hurt; and a final rule will touch up the finished form of the utterance as my-head-hurts. The result is said to be a grammatical sentence, because it follows what we can identify as the rules or conventions of the language. Another speaker of the language can decode it effortlessly, and any native speaker could come up with the same utterance. An ungrammatical sentence would be hurts-head-my, which can be decoded with some little effort but would not ordinarily be produced by any native speaker of the language.

A practical disadvantage of transformational theory when applied to specific languages is that there turn out to be so many rules, and so many special conditions for the application of the rules, that a truly complete analysis of a moderately complex language such as English is probably humanly impossible. The computer program seems to have developed beyond the complete comprehension or control of the programmer. Furthermore, some of the simplest looking surface structures, or sentences, turn out on inspection to be enormously complicated and to require extensive and uneconomical analysis. Consequently the transformationalist has to be satisfied with a tentative and partial analysis, covering the

Figure 14-4,5. *In the photo above, the Yanomamö speak into anthropologist Chagnon's tape recorder as he carries out studies in field linguistics. The other pictures relate to another aspect of the study of communication, the study of gestures and body movements. The sequence of four photos shows two men from different villages engaging in a ritual chest-pounding duel with closed fists. The intention is at once both friendly and also threatening—a reminder that they might hurt one another but are refraining from so doing. This field of communication study is called kinesics; anthropologists have found that many subtle shades of emotion can be communicated through body movements and facial expressions. Also important is the study of proxemics, or man's use of personal space.*

main ground but always subject to further refinement.

The origins of language.   A knowledge of transformational grammar also leads to speculation about how language might have started in the first place: a computerlike brain, a versatile vocal mechanism, sounds, basic words, two-part structures, trial and error, conventions, surface structures—language. Who knows? The question of the origin of language has long been a very popular subject, and some reasonable and not so reasonable theories have been proposed: exclamations became words, sounds in nature were imitated, or people simply got together and assigned sounds to objects and actions. The main trouble with these theories, interesting and possible as some of them are, is that they account for word-making but not for sentence-making. Does transformational theory have the answer? The current attitude is generally that we have had enough speculation on the subject, that transformational theory offers some good new possibilities, and that we need to do some more work on the biological basis of language and communication before any conclusions about what might have happened can be drawn. The question of the origin of language has not been dismissed as hopeless or irrelevant: there is still the possibility of an intelligent reconstruction of the process.

The search for a truly primitive language that might show the processes of language just beginning or developing has been abandoned, no doubt permanently. Is there such a thing as a primitive language? So far, all the natural languages that have been described and studied, even among people with something approximating a Stone Age culture, appear to be highly developed, complex, and capable of expressing an immense range of experience, belief, and perceptions. At one time linguists thought they had found a truly primitive or archaic language, that of the central Australian tribe called the Arunta, described in 1930 when the tribe was on the point of extinction. The language was found to have only three vowel sounds (a, i, and u), very few consonant sounds (p, t, k, m, n, l, r, ch), no names for objects but only for states or actions, and no connective words like our prepositions or conjunctions. On the other hand, the Arunta made use of at least four hundred different gestures to supplement the spoken language. What was "missing" verbally seems to have been supplied visually. In spite of the apparent simplicity of the language, it proved to be no less difficult to learn properly, or even to describe accurately, than any other language. The truth seems to be that people have been talking on this world for an extremely long time, and every language, wherever it is, now has a long history and has developed subtleties and complexities that strongly resist any label of primitivism. What a language may or may not express is no measure of its age, but of the kind of life of its speakers, reflecting what they want or need to share and communicate.

Generalizations about language.   Important contributions to theoretical linguistics have by no means come only from recent transformational theory. Other systems of analysis and description—traditional, structural, tagmemic, and stratificational grammars, for example—have given us nearly all of the basic vocabulary of language study and many necessary insights into functions and principles. Four important general principles have been established in modern descriptive linguistics, not by any one linguist, but cumulatively, through the work and observations of many. First, language is systematic, regular, and to a large extent predictable. Second, all living language is in a state of constant growth and change, with imperceptible but steady alteration of sounds, vocabulary and structure, and often with simultaneous development toward complexity in some areas and simplicity in others. Third, the changes that occur in language are not changes that can or should be prevented or judged; the actual changing usage of people is ultimately the only basis for correctness in a language, and a grammar that describes what was or what might have been is not an accurate description of a language.

Fourth, human language is above all an oral phenomenon, and the living spoken language is not to be identified in an absolute way with written representations, which tend to be conservative and formal, reflecting a different set of conventions. All of these generalizations have, at one time or another in the past, been the subject of doubt and debate. They are presently taken for granted by every working linguist, however; they may be thought of as the tenets of modern descriptive linguistics and as the starting point for practically all current theory and practice.

Field linguistics

How can an anthropologist, a missionary, a social or a medical worker approach and make sense of a language that has not already been analyzed and described, or for which there are no immediately available materials? There are hundreds of such languages in the world; fortunately some fairly efficient methods have been developed to help with the task. It is a painstaking process to unravel a language, but it is ultimately rewarding and often even fascinating for its own sake.

The process requires first a good ear and a thorough understanding of the way speech sounds are produced. Otherwise it will be extremely difficult to write out or make intelligent use of any data. To satisfy this preliminary requirement, most people ordinarily need special training in phonetics, the study of the production, transmission, and reception of speech sounds.

Phonemes.   In order to analyze and describe any new language, an inventory of all of its sounds and an accurate way of writing them down are needed. Some sounds of other languages may be very much like the sounds of English, others may be sounds that we have never consciously produced; but since we all have the same vocal equipment, there is no reason why we should not be able, with practice, to reproduce all the sounds that anyone else makes.

The first step in studying any particular language is distinguishing the sounds that make a difference in meaning, called **phonemes,** and the sounds that are merely variations of those sounds in different contexts, called **allophones.** This is done by a process called the minimal pair test: the linguist tries to find two short words that appear to be exactly alike except for one sound, such as *bat* and *pat* in English. If the substitution of *b* for *p* in this minimal pair makes a difference in meaning, which it does in English, then those two sounds have been identified as distinct phonemes of the language and will require two different symbols to record. If, however, the linguist finds two different pronunciations, recorded tentatively as *top* and *tawp,* and then finds that there is no difference in their meaning for a native speaker, he will consider the sounds represented by *o* and *aw* as allophones of the same phoneme, and for economy of representation will use only one of the two symbols to record that sound wherever he finds it. For greater accuracy and to avoid confusion with the various sounds of our own language, the symbols of the International Phonetic Alphabet, a set of about eighty symbols, can be used to distinguish between the sounds of most languages in a way comprehensible to anyone who knows the system.

Morphemes. The process of making an inventory of sounds may of course be a long task; concurrently, the linguist may begin to collect all groups or combinations of sounds that seem to have meaning. These are called the **morphemes** of the language. A field linguist can elicit morphemes and their meanings from speakers of a language by means of pointing or gesturing, but the ideal situation is to have an informant, a person who knows enough of a common second language, so that approximate translations can be made more efficiently and confidently. It is pointless to write down data without any suggestion of meaning for it. *Cat* and *dog* would of course turn out to be morphemes, or meaningful combinations of sounds, in English. By pointing to two of either of them, the linguist could elicit *cats* and *dogs.* This tells him that there is another mean-

ingful unit, an *-s,* that may be added to the original morpheme to mean "plural." When he finds that this *-s* cannot occur in the language unattached, he will identify it as a **bound morpheme;** because *dog* and *cat* can occur unattached to anything, they are called **free morphemes.** Because the sound represented as *s* is actually different in the two words (*s* in *cats* and *z* in *dogs*), the linguist will conclude that the sounds *s* and *z* are **allomorphs** of the plural morpheme: that is, they are two varieties of the same morpheme (even though they may be two different phonemes), occuring in different contexts but with no difference in meaning.

Grammar and syntax. The next step is putting morphemes together to form phrases or sentences. This process is known as identifying the syntagms of the language, or the meaningful combination of morphemes in larger chains or strings. Proceeding slowly at first, and relying on pointing or gestures, using a method called frame substitution, the field linguist can elicit such strings as *my cat, your cat,* or *her cat,* and *I see your cat, she sees my cat.* This begins to establish the rules or principles of phrase and sentence making, the **syntax** of the language.

Further success of this linguistic study depends greatly on individual ingenuity, tact, logic, and experience with language. A language may make extensive use of kinds of utterances that are not found at all in English, and which the linguist may not therefore even think of asking for. Furthermore, certain speakers may pretend not to be able to say (or may truly not be able to say) certain things which they consider to be impolite, taboo, or inappropriate for mention to outsiders. It may even be culturally unacceptable to point, in which case the linguist will have to devise roundabout ways of eliciting words for objects.

The **grammar** of the language will ultimately consist of all observations about the morphemes and the syntax. Further work will include establishing by means of substitution frames all the **form classes** of the language: that is, the parts of speech or categories of words that work the same way in any sentence. For example, we may establish a category we call "nouns" defined as anything that will fit the substitution frame "I see a —." We simply make the frame, try out a number of words in it, and have a native speaker indicate "yes" or "no" for whether the words work. In English the words *house* and *cat* will fit this frame and will be said to belong to the same form class, but the word *think* will not. Another possible substitution frame for nouns might be "The — died," in which the word *cat* will fit, but not the word *house*. Thus we can identify subclasses of our nouns: in this case what we can call "animate" or "inanimate" subclasses. The same procedure may be followed for all the words of the language, using as many different frames as necessary, until we have a lexicon, or dictionary, that accurately describes the possible uses of all the words in the language.

One of the strengths of modern descriptive linguistics is the scientific objectivity of its methods. A descriptive linguist will not approach a language with the idea that it must have nouns, verbs, prepositions, or any other of the form classes identifiable in English. The linguist instead sees what turns up in the language and makes an attempt to describe it in terms of its own inner workings. For convenience he may, and often will, label morphemes that behave approximately like English nouns and verbs as "nouns" and "verbs"; but if he thinks that the terms are misleading, he may instead call them "x-words" and "y-words" or "form class A" and "form class B."

The methods of field linguistics are important tools for the cultural anthropologist, even when he is working with a language that has already been described. No analysis of any language is ever complete, and improvements, fresh insights, and new interpretations are always possible.

Sociolinguistics

The whole question of the relationships between language and culture is the province of **sociolinguistics,** a field that has grown out of both sociology and descriptive linguistics to become an area of almost separate enquiry. Sociolinguistics is concerned with every aspect of the structure and use of language that has anything to do with society and culture and human behavior. It is a term synonymous with both ethnolinguistics and anthropological linguistics. The field is fascinating and seemingly limitless.

Language and culture

An important sociolinguistic concern of the 1930s and 1940s was the question of whether language might indeed determine culture. Do we see and react differently to the colors blue and green, with different cultural symbolism for the two different colors, only because our language has different names for these two neighboring sections of the unbroken color spectrum? When anthropologists noticed that some cultures lump together blue and green with one name, they began to wonder about this question. The American linguist Edward Sapir first formulated the problem, and his student, Benjamin Lee Whorf, drawing on his experience with the language of the Hopi Indians, developed a full-fledged theory, sometimes called the Whorfian hypothesis. Whorf proposed that a language is not simply an encoding process for voicing our ideas and needs but rather a shaping force that guides our thinking and our behavior. The problem is a little like the old question of the chicken or the egg, and Whorf's theory about which came first has since been generally criticized as both logically unsound and not amenable to any experimentation or proof. Its primary value is that it did begin to focus attention on the relationships between language and culture.

An opposite point of view, that life fashions language, has been more recently and somewhat more rationally maintained by the British linguist Joshua Whatmough. Whatmough believes that there is nothing to show that concepts such as color, time, or space have been imposed by language, but rather that there is ample evidence that languages are creative, flexible, and adaptable to any new needs or changed perceptions of their users. If the people who make no distinction between the two colors of blue and green only had good reason to sort them out, he would argue, such as having to distinguish between a missionary's blue Ford and a doctor's green one, they could very well make their language do the job, and they might perhaps even begin to associate blue with religion and green with medicine.

Linguists are finding that although language is generally flexible and adaptable, once a terminology is established it tends to perpetuate itself and to reflect and reveal the social structure and the common perceptions and concerns of a group. For example, the English words for war and the tactics of war and the hierarchy of officers and men who fight, reflect what is obviously a reality for our culture. An observer from an entirely different and perhaps warless culture could understand a great deal about our institution of war and its conventions simply from what we have found necessary to name and talk about in our military terminology. Similarly, anthropologists have noted that in the Arabic dialects of Bedouin tribes in the Middle East there is an elaborate system of terminology for everything having to do with camels; with a certain amount of study we can determine from the naming system alone the importance of camels to the culture, attitudes toward camels (which are often treated with more care than people), and the whole etiquette of human and camel relationships. Cultural terminology is properly a concern of anthropology, and it is an example of one important area of sociolinguistics.

Kinship terms. In the same connection, considerable attention has been paid by anthropologists to the way people name their relatives in various societies: further observations on the question of kinship terms will be found in Chapter 18. In English we have terms to identify brother, sister, mother, father, grandmother, grandfather, granddaughter, grandson, niece, nephew, mother-in-law, father-in-law, sister-in-law, and brother-in-law. Some people also distinguish first and second cousin, and great aunt and great uncle. Is this the only possible system for naming relatives and identifying relationships? Obviously not. We could have separate and individual words, as some cultures do, for younger brother and older brother, for mother's sister and father's sister, and so on. What we can describe in English with a phrase, if pressed to do so, other languages make explicit from the outset, and vice-versa: some West African languages use the same word to denote both a brother and a cousin, and a mother's sister may also be called one's mother.

What do kinship terms reveal? We can certainly learn from them how the family is structured, what relationships are considered close or distant, and sometimes what attitudes to relationships may be.

Figure 14-6. *This somewhat idealized portrait of the Cherokee chief Sequoia shows him pointing to the alphabet, the result of his single-handed efforts to find a way to write the Cherokee language.*

SE-QUO-YAH

Caution is required, however, in drawing conclusions from kinship terms. Just because we do not distinguish linguistically in English between our mother's parents and our father's parents (both are simply *grandmother* and *grandfather*), does that mean that in our culture we lump them all together as faceless old people or that we treat old people badly? Some people have argued that it is so. But in France, where there is reputedly considerably more respect and concern for older relatives, perhaps even exaggeratedly so by our standards, there is no more linguistic difference between a mother's mother and a father's mother than there is in English. Kinship terms can establish the limits of so-called extended families in certain cultures, and they can define the cultural relationships between families brought together by a marriage. Other implications are still uncertain, but the area has turned out to be a rich one for investigation.

Taboo words. Another interesting concern of sociolinguistics is the matter of taboo words, obscenities, and acceptable and unacceptable language in general. Just consider, for example, the question of whether this textbook should supply at this point a list of some vigorous obscenities in English to illustrate the point. The answer is obviously that it should not, though a more formal, technical article in a journal might very well do so. What makes words socially unacceptable or inappropriate in certain contexts in certain languages? There is no universal taboo about words related to sex and excrement, as in our culture, and some cultures find our obscenities to be only a little foolish or peculiar, as we do theirs. Consider, for example, the English obscenity "bloody" or the French one, *"Sacre bleu"* (blue rite); both sound odd to American ears. By determining what may or may not be said, and when and where, we can understand a great deal about beliefs and social relationships. An interesting study has been made recently by the British anthropologist Edmund Leach of the striking relationships between animal names, verbal abuse, and cultural taboos. Leach finds a relationship, for example, between a long-standing cultural belief in the dirtiness of a dog, the fact that it is insulting in English to call someone a dog, and the fact that we may not and do not eat the dog for meat (though some cultures do). What is meat and what is not, what is insult and what is not, what is dirty and what is not: all of these are important questions that may be answered in part in language, and they are likewise matters for investigation in sociolinguistics.

Social dialects

A somewhat broader concern of sociolinguistics is the matter of social dialects. A social dialect is the language of any group of people within a larger group of people, all of whom may speak more or less the same language. Technically all dialects are languages—there is nothing partial or sublinguistic about them—and the point at which two different dialects become distinctly different languages is roughly the point at which the speakers of one are almost totally unable to communicate with speakers of the other. Boundaries may be psychological, geographical, social, or economic, and they are not always very clear. There is usually a transitional territory, or perhaps a buffer zone, where features of both are found and understood, as between central and southern China. The fact is that if you learn the Chinese of Peking you cannot communicate with the waiter in your local Chinese restaurant who comes from Canton or Hong Kong, although both languages—or dialects—are conventionally called Chinese.

In addition to the larger problem of determining dialect boundaries, and trying to determine whether linguistic differences in any given case also reflect cultural differences, there is also the problem in dialect studies of why and how people in the same community, whether it be a large American city or a small African town, can and do speak the same language in different ways. Some people are able to speak one social dialect in one situation and one in another. As a rather extreme example, in New York City presently some second-generation immigrant children from Puerto Rico are able to speak the language of their parents at home, a dialect known as Puerto Rican "Spanglish" with their contemporaries, and New York English with their teachers. The process of changing from one level of language to another, whether it be from one language to another or from one dialect of a language to another, is known as code-switching, and it has been the subject of a number of studies in sociolinguistics. Almost all of us can switch from formality to informality in our speech, and the question of why and when such things are done in various cultures is only beginning to be investigated.

Of the many other concerns of sociolinguistics today we can only mention that we also find investigations of children's languages and word games, the structure of folk tales and folk songs, bilingualism and multilingualism, pidgin languages and creoles, linguistic borrowing and innovation, formulas of address and politeness, the language of gesture and intonation, secret languages, magic languages, and myth. The list increases and has begun to duplicate many of the concerns of other fields or disciplines. It can easily be seen that almost every aspect of anthropology and sociology has a linguistic side or a relevance to linguistics. This new field of sociolinguistics proves to be not one field but many, and it is providing an opportunity for some productive cooperation and sharing between disciplines.

☐

Original study

ANIMALS, MAN, AND COMMUNICATION

Men have tried to distinguish themselves from the animals in many ways—as "featherless bipeds," as toolmakers, as the unique possessors of a soul—but perhaps it is our gift of language that most clearly sets us apart. Animals do communicate with one another. They cry, hoot, bleat, and coo, and to some degree these noises accomplish the same purposes as our language. They call infants, attract a mate, warn of danger, or cry in pain. Yet these animal noises are more like our human cries, screams, sighs, and grunts than they are like language. Language alone has an inherently meaningless set of sounds, which can be used to form a vast vocabulary; and language alone is productive of an infinite number of utterances and applicable to an infinite number of topics.

No animals speak in nature, and none can be taught to speak by man. Devoted researchers have tried to teach chimpanzees to say a few words, but after months of effort they will do little more than utter gruff noises, in a few situations where we might think a word would be appropriate. They never even come close to combining known forms into new combinations, a skill that is a crucial aspect of human speech and an ability that comes easily to every normal human child. The teeth, tongue, and larynx of a chimpanzee are adequate for speech, but his brain is not, and no amount of training can make up for this lack. All normal men on the other hand learn their first language with little direct instruction. Learn they must, but unlike the chimp they bring adequate equipment to the task.

In the several million years during which man has become differentiated from his fellow anthropoids, his brain has somehow developed a new and unique ability, an ability unknown elsewhere in the animal kingdom. Conceivably, it has been selection in favor of this ability that has brought much of man's unique development. It may even be that the expansion of the brain, a rather rapid development by usual evolutionary standards and a development that can be traced rather well through the record of fossil man, resulted from the progressive selection of ever more competent speakers. Once our barely human ancestors acquired the incipient beginnings of language, the individuals and the groups who were most skilled in speech must have had a considerable advantage when competing for limited resources. They could have cooperated more successfully, warned each other of dangers, and helped each other in time of need. Slowly but inexorably, the ever more skillful speakers would survive and pass on to their children their superior potential for speech. On the average, the better speakers probably had bigger brains, and perhaps this is why the human brain has doubled in size in the course of the last million or so years. It may even be fair to suggest that the unique character of the human brain and the trait that distinguishes it most clearly from other mammalian brains is its ability to produce language. It is hardly profitable to speculate on just how our brain accomplishes its task, but we cannot doubt that our ability to speak and the ways in which human vocal communication differs from that of our nearest nonhuman relatives rest squarely upon our biological organization.

Yet here lies a paradox, for our brains cannot produce speech without training: we must always learn our language. Any normal infant given a suitable

opportunity can learn any language, and the languages we learn are certainly diverse. We can credit our biological capacity with our general linguistic abilities, but the varied details of a man's language depend upon his unique personal experiences. In the diversity of his behavior, man is again set apart from other animals, for man alone is capable of developing and perpetuating distinct traditions, or different "cultures," whether in language or in other aspects of his behavior. Other animals have but a limited capacity to learn varied forms of behavior, and virtually no ability to teach their juniors to follow them. Behavior varies from species to species, of course, and individual diversity in behavior among members of a single species is by no means negligible, but variation from band to band or from herd to herd appears to be a very minor matter.

It is here that man is strange. Surely the diversity in the behavior of various human groups, the diversity of tradition handed down to our children, is one of our most remarkable characteristics. In the past, these differences in tradition were sometimes attributed to the diverse biological or racial characteristics of the groups or believed to be dependent in some simplistic way upon the environment in which the group lived. Such explanations can no longer be taken seriously. Caught early enough, any child can learn any language and any culture. People with the same inherent capacities learn to eat different foods, to organize different sorts of families, to construct diverse political systems, and to speak Swahili, Mohawk, or English.

Figure 14-7a,b. *These photos of baboons show the range of communication possible through posture and facial expression. The photo on the right shows one juvenile establishing dominance through use of pseudosexual posture; the other photo shows two fear postures.*

Our human potential for learning such varied behavior and for teaching our children to follow us in similar behavior must itself rest upon our uniquely human nature. It is easy to imagine that the pressures of natural selection might have produced an animal with a complex form of language that was still uniquely determined by the biological organization of the species. All members of such a species would speak exactly the same sort of language, or at least any minor variability would depend only upon the random genetic variability among the individuals. One member of such a species would not even have to be in contact with others in order to learn to talk. His speech could be a spontaneous and automatic concomitant of his biological organization, like the cries of animals or of babies, which need not be learned, though they are nonetheless used for communication. But evolution did not take this path, for each human child must learn some particular form of speech, just as he must learn some particular cultural patterns. So complex are the things he must learn, that every child, even in the most primitive of societies, must spend long years before he knows enough to behave as a responsible adult. No other species is so burdened.

The central facts of human language, then, are also the central facts of human culture: our ability to speak, like all our other human abilities, rests firmly upon our unique human inheritance. Even our peculiar ability to learn and then to perpetuate different traditions of language and culture is attributable ultimately to the kind of animal we are. The particular traditions of language or of culture that any one of us acquires result from our own individual experiences. Since language is learned so early and since it is central to so much of our other learning, it is even tempting to wonder if our ability to learn a language does not somehow lie at the core of our other human abilities. Conceivably our very ability to perpetuate varying traditions in all aspects of our culture rests in part, at least, upon our ability to perpetuate varying traditions in that most human of all our abilities, our ability to speak.

If language is so central to man, it is hardly surprising to find so much of human life mirrored in language. Not only do we give names to things, but our languages come to symbolize our social divisions, our particular position in our social organization, our attitudes, our personalities. In the perpetuation of language, in its borrowing, and in the way it changes, we see reflected the general properties of human culture. Linguists have learned much about the internal organization of language, but grammar and phonology, as they have been studied by linguists, represent only the beginning of the real complexity and importance of language. Language is so involved with the rest of our lives that it penetrates everything we do, and everything we do penetrates language. We can never hope to fully understand either language or other aspects of human behavior, without attention to both.

Source:

From *Man's Many Voices: Language in its Cultural Context* by Robbins Burling. Copyright © 1970 by Holt, Rinehart and Winston, Inc. Reprinted by permission of Holt, Rinehart and Winston, Inc.

Summary

1.
Language is a code for symbolic communication. A symbol is any sound or gesture to which we give a meaning. It is an arbitrary representation of something else. Human culture as we know it cannot exist without language.

2.
Linguistics is the science that studies all aspects of language. There are two approaches to the study of linguistics. The historical approach investigates relationships between earlier and later forms of the same language. The descriptive approach registers and explains all the features of a language at any time in history. Historical linguistics provides a means of roughly dating certain migrations, invasions, and contacts of peoples. Descriptive linguistics gives the anthropologist a framework for understanding languages and the means to analyze, describe, and work with them.

3.
Noam Chomsky has provided the first consistent and logical model for scientifically describing the facts of language. His theory is called generative transformational grammar. Chomsky holds that we unconsciously build our utterances with basic two-part units, called deep structures. Complete utterances display surface structure, a complex web of deep structure units. The principle is assumed to be the same for all languages, but the deep structures differ. Understanding a language involves identifying deep structure and establishing how deep structure becomes surface structure.

4.
Four important general principles have been established in modern descriptive linguistics. First, language is systematic, regular, and to a large extent predictable. Second, all living language is constantly growing and changing. Third, the changes that occur in language cannot and should not be prevented. Fourth, human language is primarily an oral phenomenon. Descriptive linguistics also recognizes that human language consists of more than speech; it includes also such elements as gestures and voice inflection.

5.
To analyze and describe a new language, a linguist needs an inventory of all its sounds and an accurate way of writing them down. The first step in studying a language is distinguishing the sounds that make a difference in meaning, called phonemes, from variations of those sounds, called allophones. A linguist must list all the meaningful combinations of sounds of a language. These are called morphemes. He can then put morphemes together to form phrases or sentences. Meaningful combinations of morphemes are called strings. From a study of such strings, a linguist can identify the principles which make up a language's syntax. Grammar studies the ways a language operates and is constructed.

6.
Sociolinguistics, synonymous with ethnolinguistics and anthropological linguistics, deals with the relationship between language and culture. Some linguists, such as Benjamin Lee Whorf, have theorized that language shapes culture. Others, such as Joshua Whatmough, have theorized that culture shapes language. Culture-shapes-language theories are based on evidence that language is creative, flexible, and adaptable. Though linguists have found

language flexible and adaptable, they have also found that once a terminology is established, it perpetuates itself.

7.
Anthropologists are interested in the way different societies name their relatives. Kinship terms help reveal how a family is structured, what relationships are considered close or distant, and what attitudes to relationships are held. Anthropologists are also interested in taboo words, social dialects, and code switching. A taboo word can reveal much about a society's beliefs and social relationships. A social dialect is the language of a group of people within a larger group of people, all of whom speak more or less the same language. Code-switching is the process of changing from one level of language to another.

Suggested readings

Bloomfield, Leonard *Language*. New York: Holt, Rinehart and Winston, 1933.
It is a somewhat dated standard text intended for general reader and beginning student in linguistics. An orderly survey covering a wide range of topics including meaning, syntax, phonetic and semantic change, cultural borrowing.

Burling, Robbins *Man's Many Voices: Language in its Cultural Context*. New York: Holt, Rinehart and Winston, 1970.
An investigation into the nonlinguistic factors that affect the use of language, such as kinship systems and the wider cultural context. It relies heavily on examples from South and Southeast Asia.

Carroll, John B., ed. *Language, Thought and Reality: Selected Writings of Benjamin Lee Whorf*. New York: John Wiley and Sons, 1956.
Whorf's emphasis is on the relationship between human language and human thought and the ways in which language can shape thinking. An important contribution to semantics.

Chomsky, Noam *Syntactic Structures*. The Hague: Mowton and Co., 1957. This readable introduction to Chomsky's work was the book that first established the outlines of his theory of deep structure.

Evans, Williams F. *Communication in the Animal World*. New York: Thomas Y. Crowell, 1968. This book surveys all major animal groups and reports in detail on the many systems of communication by which different creatures relate to one another and to their environment.

Gelb, Ignace J. *A Study of Writing*. London: Routledge and Kegan Paul, 1952.
The aim of this study is to lay a foundation for a new science of writing, grammatology. It attempts to establish general principles governing the use and evolution of writing on a comparative basis, and is the first systematic presentation of the history of writing based on these principles.

Gleason, H. A., Jr. *An Introduction to Descriptive Linguistics*. (rev. ed.) New York: Holt, Rinehart and Winston, 1966.
This book focuses on the descriptive approach, studying languages in terms of their internal structures. It is a lucid, well written introduction to the study of language.

Hall, Robert A., Jr. *Linguistics and Your Language*. (2nd rev. ed.) Garden City, New York: Anchor Books, Doubleday, 1960.
This is a brief popular discussion of some problems connected with language and linguistics. Emphasizes the implications of the science of language for modern society. Very interesting reading.

Hockett, Charles F. *A Course in Modern Linguistics*. New York: Macmillan, 1958.
A presentation of the generally accepted facts and principles of the field of linguistics. Hockett is influenced by Leonard Bloomfield and American linguistics in general. Contains studies on phonology, grammar, morphemic systems, phylogeny, and linguistic prehistory.

Labov, William *Language in the Inner City.* Philadelphia: University of Pennsylvania Press, 1972.
  The author argues in favor of the existence of Black English Vernacular as a dialect of English. The book studies such art forms as the ritual insult and ritualized narrative.

Premack, Ann James and David Premack "Teaching Language to an Ape" in *Scientific American:* Vol. 227:4, Oct. 1972, pp. 92–99.
  This interesting article tests the hypothesis that language is unique to the human species. It concludes that certain gestures of human speech belong to a more general system, and are capable of being understood by other primates. The program that was used to teach the chimpanzee Sarah to communicate has been successfully applied to people suffering certain types of brain damage.

Wardhaugh, Ronald *Introduction to Linguistics.* New York: McGraw-Hill, 1972.
  The book attempts to provide beginning students with a basic knowledge of the kinds of questions asked by linguists about language. Includes chapters on communication, phonetics, phonology, morphology, language change, and variation. Each chapter concludes with notes indicating further reading on the topic; it includes a glossary of terms.

Personality and culture

A wide variety of attitudes and behavior patterns can be found in cultures throughout the world. Though every individual is a unique person, his personality is largely determined by the society in which he is raised. It is difficult to give a single, all-inclusive definition of personality, but for our purposes, personality may be defined as the distinctive way a person thinks, feels, and behaves. The individual personality is largely formed through an assimilation of ways of thinking and acting that are common to the group, a process called enculturation.

How is the individual enculturated or socialized by his society? Eric Wolf, who has examined peasant societies in his book, *Peasants,* has made a number of significant observations about the social "programming" process as it occurs in both extended and nuclear families, which are the foundations of societies.[1] According to Wolf, extended families, which consist of several husband-wife-children groups, usually occur in agricultural societies where they have access to a steady, reliable source of food. In such families, group cohesion and continuity are important if

[1] Eric Wolf, *Peasants* (Englewood Cliffs, N.J.: Prentice-Hall, Inc., 1966).

the group is to survive because a large number of individuals is required to work the land. The extended family's greatest problem is to assure that its members remain within it. To do this, the family has devised a number of reinforcements, particularly in the ways it socializes its young. Thus, the extended family favors enculturation techniques that render its members dependent on it. For example, the family indulges its children with oral gratification for relatively long periods of time. This practice, according to psychological theory, assures that the individual will continue to look to his family for the fulfillment of his needs, especially his future economic needs. The family also tends to curb expressions of aggression and sexuality, hoping to teach the child to control his impulses. Such control is an important requirement for group coordination, which the structure and survival of the extended family demand. Thus, enculturation prepares the child to become a permanent member of the existing family; it also prepares for the family's future when offspring who marry will not establish their own household but reside with the family to help it produce the food it needs.

On the other hand, the smaller nuclear family, consisting of a man, woman and their offspring,

Wolf observes that enculturation techniques of the nuclear family are just the opposite of those favored by the extended family. The nuclear family tends to place less emphasis on prolonged oral dependence and to encourage displays of aggression and sexuality in its offspring. Such early training allows the individual a great deal of freedom in his relations with others and readies him to be more independent; he will need such qualities later in his struggle to make a living from an environment which does not provide a dependable, steady food supply and where the prevailing rule is "every man for himself."

Thus, an intricate interrelation exists between a society, as represented above by the family, and each of its members. Anthropologists have sought to define more precisely the nature of this relationship. Can we describe a "group personality" or a "national character" without falling into stereotyping? Do cultures assume personality characteristics deriving from particular child-raising practices? What is the status of the person who cannot adapt to the cultural norm? That part of anthropology which focusses on such questions is called psychological anthropology or, more commonly, the study of culture and personality.

Group personality

Culture, said Ruth Benedict, is personality writ large. Every society unconsciously selects from the vast variety of human potentialities certain traits which are established as normative or ideal. Those who conform to these norms are rewarded; those who deviate are punished. The result is a certain homogeneity of world view and behavior, a sort of group "personality" that forms an overall cultural orientation within which there is considerable variation. The group personality is an abstraction, not to be found in pure form in any single individual, and so it is extremely difficult to define. Yet field ethnologists are frequently struck by the feeling of personality conveyed by the group they are studying.

Cultural configuration

The Kwakiutl Indians of the Northwest Coast, when they were studied by Franz Boas at the turn of the century, were a status-dominated people who saw life as a series of rivalry situations. Great feasts called "potlatches" were regularly held, in which enormous amounts of wealth were given away or destroyed—for example, by burning great quantities of valuable oil—to affirm the status of the feastgiver or to humiliate a rival who might not be able to give away or destroy a similar amount. The host would jeer his invited rivals with songs:

I am the great chief who makes people ashamed.
I am the great chief who makes people ashamed.
Our chief brings shame to the faces.
Our chief brings jealousy to the faces.
Our chief makes people cover their faces by what he is continually doing in this world,
Giving again and again oil feasts to all the tribes.

Among the Kwakiutl, the widespread practice of obtaining supernatural power in a dream or vision became a highly competitive situation. Men sought these visions by means of hideous self-tortures. They cut strips from the skin of their arms, they struck off fingers, they went without food and water for long periods. By inflicting great pain on themselves, they sought a mental state set apart from daily living in which to achieve their vision. Through excesses of suffering, each man tried to achieve the biggest and best vision.

The Zuni Indians of the American Southwest were in many ways the opposite of the Kwakiutl. Individuals were personally restrained, slow to anger, group oriented, and generally opposed to aggression and excessive behavior. They distrusted any kind of disruption, and did not understand self-torture. They had no rites in which they sacrificed their own blood or used it for fertility. Drunkenness was repulsive to them. The old

Figure 15-1. *This blanket is typical of the type of goods distributed by the host of a Kwakiutl potlatch. Woven of mountain goat wool and bark, it features the owner's totem.*

Zuni men voluntarily outlawed liquor after it was first introduced; the rule was congenial enough to be honored.

According to Ruth Benedict, in whose book *Patterns of Culture* these tribes are described, the Kwakiutl and the Zuni represented two opposite cultural configurations. Borrowing her terms from the German philosopher Friedrich Nietzsche, she called these two fundamental modes of ideology and behavior the "Dionysian" and the "Apollonian." The Dionysian, exemplified by the Kwakiutl, is characterized by ecstatic ritual, egocentrism, and extremely individualistic behavior. The Zuni represent the Apollonian response to life. The Zuni's rule is the Golden Mean; he wants no part of excess, no disruptive psychological states; he distrusts individualism. Benedict saw cultures as comparable to great works of art, possessing internal coherence and consistency. Cultures are far more than the sum of the individuals who adhere to them, because in them are developed and elaborated traits with greater intensity and richness than any individual would be capable of, even in a whole lifetime. Each person is heir to a rich cultural heritage. The variety of cultural and individual response is summarized by a myth of the Digger Indians:

> God gave to every people a cup, a cup of clay, and from this cup they drank their life. . . . They all dipped in the water, but their cups were different.[2]

Though *Patterns of Culture* had an enormous and valuable influence in popularizing the idea of cultural variation and the influence of culture upon individual personality, the book has been severely criticized. The Apollonian-Dionysian characterization, which Benedict saw as fundamental, applies only to a few, if any, cultures in the world. More significantly, the book characterizes cultures in terms of their most obvious aspects, ignoring subtleties that may be extremely important—a tendency which is very close to stereotyping. The Kwakiutl, for example, have a delightful sense of play and humor which is sometimes displayed in farces satirizing their own potlatches. Some of the supposedly mild-mannered, pain-avoiding Zuni practice sword swallowing and ritual walking over red-hot coals. The very richness of these cultures makes any simple summary necessarily incomplete.

Growing up

In Western society, adolescence is a period of tension and stress. The no-longer-child must come to terms with biological changes, with sexual desire, and the social demands for its iniation. He may begin questioning the "truths" he has been brought up with; he may rebel against pa-

rental authority; he may come to see that injustices in the world do not correspond to the ideals he was raised to revere. Some writers believed that these conflicts arise out of the very nature of adolescence, and therefore are universal. But are they? In 1925 a young anthropologist named Margaret Mead went to Samoa to try to find the answer.

Samoan children learn that they can have their own way if they are quiet and obedient. Preference is given not to the arrogant, the flippant, the courageous, but to the quiet and demure boy or girl who "speaks softly and treads lightly." The standards of conduct are graded in this fashion: small children should keep quiet, wake up early, obey, work hard and cheerfully, play with children of their own sex; young people should work industriously and skillfully, not be presuming, marry discreetly, be loyal to their relatives, not carry tales nor be troublemakers; adults should be wise, peacable, serene, generous, anxious for the prestige of their village, and conduct their lives with all good form and decorum.

Little girls move and play together, reacting to boys with antagonism or avoidance. As they grow up, however, these groups slowly begin to break up, and boys and girls begin to play and banter together good naturedly during parties and torch-fishing excursions. A few years after puberty, the girl may take the first of a series of lovers. Liaisons may last for some time, or adolescents may slip away together into the bush. As long as there is no breach of custom, such as incest or a boy's aspiring to love an older woman, society considers these premarital relations completely natural and pays little attention to them.

Consequently, Samoans grow up with minimal sexual or social stress, in a society characterized by peaceful conformity and a tolerant attitude toward sex. The transition from childhood to adulthood is relatively smooth. Generalizing, Mead concludes that "adolescence is not necessarily a time of stress and strain, but that cultural conditions make it so. . . ."

By providing strong evidence of the effect of childhood training on the formation of the adult

[2]Ruth Benedict, *Patterns of Culture* (Boston: Houghton Mifflin, 1934) p. 21.

Figure 15-2. *Through their participation in society's culture, children learn its rules. This pair illustrates the Mauritanian custom of dressing in navy blue cloth by the age of 8.*

personality, Mead stimulated an interest in child-rearing not only as an anthropological problem, but also as a practical one. If a great deal of adolescent behavior is learned, rather than biologically induced, then in our own culture it might be possible to minimize the anxiety and antisocial behavior associated with adolescence by changing the culture. Also, the converse may be possible: by changing child-rearing practices, we may be able to change the structure of society. However, Mead cautions against thinking we can accomplish anything by simply copying the Samoans, because "unfortunately, the conditions which vex our adolescents are the flesh and bone of our society, no more subject to straightforward manipulation upon our part than is the language we speak."[3]

Development of personality

We have seen how the individual members of a society are carriers of the norms that are characteristic of the culture. But where do these norms come from in the first place? On the theory that personality is largely formed in infancy and childhood, some psychologists and psychologically oriented anthropologists have studied different societies to determine how child raising practices teach the norms to the individual child and reinforce them for the adults of the society.

Personality patterns

A person learns in childhood the patterns of behavior expected from him by the society in which he was born. Such predictable patterns of behavior are a result of cultural transmission. They provide a framework in which members of the society can make sense out of the motivations and the behavior of others.

[3]Margaret Mead, *Coming of Age in Samoa* (New York: William Morrow, 1961, 3rd ed.)

A certain minimum of cooperation is necessary for the group to survive. Whether the society chooses a culture which encourages competition and conflict or cooperation and harmony, or its own unique combination of values, the pattern of individual behavior will reflect that choice. There must be a consensus on norms and values for the group to go about its everyday round of activities. The goal of the ongoing society is to bring the individual into a general conformity with its prevailing view of the world.

Sigmund Freud. With *Totem and Taboo,* Freud expanded his theories of personality development from the psychoanalyst's couch to the vast domain of culture. In this work, he used the Oedipus complex, that is, the sexual desire of the son for his mother, which Freud saw as the most important factor in individual personality development, to explain the origins of culture and society. According to this scheme, early societies were strongly patriarchal, with the dominant man possessing exclusive sexual rights over his sisters and daughters. The sexually deprived sons rebelled, killed their father, and ate him. Overcome with guilt, the brothers then repressed their sexual desires toward their mothers, sisters and daughters. Thus came into being the incest taboo and exogamy. Through what Freud called the "racial unconscious," the sons inherited the primal guilt over the killing of the father.

Almost no anthropologist would accept this theory in its original form, because there is no evidence to substantiate it. However, one need not accept Freud's origin-of-society hypothesis in order to find in the Oedipus complex a possible basis for significant cultural norms and values. Some Freudian anthropologists, such as Geza Roheim, believe that tensions rising from the Oedipal family situation, in which the boy feels antagonistic toward his father and has to suppress his incestual desires toward his mother, are to be found in all societies, and are indeed the source of such cultural phenomena as the incest taboo and exogamy. According to Roheim, any anthro-

pologist who denies this is simply repressing his own Oedipus complex.

Bronislaw Malinowski. Bronislaw Malinowski was one of the first to challenge the universality of Freud's Oedipus complex theory with careful field research. The people of the Trobriand Islands, he pointed out, do not think of the child as belonging to his father's family. Because Trobriand society is matrilineal, the mother's elder brother functions as a child's disciplinarian and authority figure, while the father assumes the role of friend and companion to the child. Whereas the Oedipus complex is based on the triangular relationship between mother, father, and son, the true complex of relationships for the Trobriands is brother, sister and sister's son.

Whatever the final verdict on the Oedipus complex, Freud's beliefs have been accepted in other areas of psychological theory relevant to anthropology. As Edward Sapir said:

> Such relational ideas as the emotionally integrated complex, the tendency to suppression under the stress of conflict, the symptomatic expression of a suppressed impulse, the transfer of emotion and the canalizing or pooling of impulses, the tendency to regression, are so many powerful clues to understanding how the "soul" of man sets to work.[4]

Individual psychology and enculturation

Benedict and Mead emphasized the ways culture produces individual personality; Freud saw all culture as deriving from individual complexes. It remained for Abram Kardiner to seek a synthesis that would at once respect the theoretical contributions of both individual psychology and the influence of culture in the development of personality. Kardiner, a trained psychoanalyst, attempted to lift Freud's theories from their ethnocentric European matrix and enlarge the scope of

[4] Quoted in Marvin Harris, *Rise of Anthropological Theory* (New York: Thomas Y. Crowell, 1968) pp. 432.

these theories to account for cultural diversity. To do so, he rejected much of Freudian dogma, including the Oedipus complex, stages of infantile sexuality, and the emphasis on exclusively sexual aspects of human drives. What he retained was the importance of infantile experience for adult personality, and such Freudian psychological mechanisms as repression, or the suppression of unwanted feelings and emotions.

Rather than ascribing certain personality types to given cultures, Kardiner discussed the range of personalities to be found in a culture. According to this new scheme, the personality "types" described by Benedict and Mead are replaced by basic personality structures, or traits shared by nearly all group members and which are subject to wide variation even within a single society.

According to Kardiner, personalities differ because of the variation in cultural institutions. Following Malinowski's classification, Kardiner distinguishes between two kinds of institutions. Primary institutions, such as the quest for food and sexual gratification, are those which arise to fill fundamental human needs. Secondary institutions, such as government and religion, are those institutions which arise in response to needs stimulated by primary institutions. The interaction of these institutions with the personality shapes and is shaped by human culture. By explaining personality in terms of its interaction with cultural institutions, Kardiner accounts for variation of basic personality structures in different societies.

To test his thesis, Kardiner gathered from field workers the seemingly trivial details of social behavior which they might ordinarily notice but not report. The most complete source of ethnopsychological data he analyzed came from Cora Dubois' study of the Alorese culture of the South Pacific. Through their work, a correlation was discovered between the child-rearing techniques of the Alorese and the nature of their cultural institutions.

The Alorese. Alorese children were raised with a minimum of attention or affection. No effort was made during infancy to teach the child to talk. An adult might sing dance songs to soothe him, but there was no deliberate attempt to impart verbal training. The only word Dubois heard an adult direct toward a child was the repetition of its name.

Toilet training, too, was completely disregarded during the period before walking began. Adults exhibited no anger or disgust when a child soiled the carrying shawl or the body of a person caring for it. The caretaker cleaned up after the child with the most casual matter-of-factness, wiping off its buttocks with a bit of leaf, a corn husk, or a bamboo sliver.

Walking was not urged on the child. Crawling was confined to the relatively rare periods when the child was seated on a verandah, or in the living room, instead of being carried in a shawl. One child, whom Dubois watched develop, learned to stand by pulling himself up on his mother's leg in an effort to get her attention so that she would pick him up and nurse him.

Women were not merely indifferent to children, but were quite reluctant to have them. Consequently, babies received little attention even just after birth. As one informant put it, "We men are the ones who want children. Our wives don't. They just want to sleep with us."

Children were subjected to extremely severe forms of discipline. The Alorese ideal dictated that corporal punishment should only be administered by the parents, but in practice this ideal was ignored. All kinds of relatives, however distant, were almost as free as parents themselves in rapping children on the head, pulling ears, twisting mouths, tying children up, and administering other such forms of treatment.

Teasing, ridicule, and deception were also widely practiced, not only in disciplining children, but as a form of amusement, especially among young men. On one occasion, Dubois observed a man of about twenty-eight send a twelve-year-old boy to fetch a bunch of bananas he said he had left at the foot of the village. In return he promised the boy six of them. The boy raced gleefully to the indicated spot but returned saying he had not found them. He was sent off again, and when he returned the second time, he realized that he had been deceived. A group of six or seven grown men were sitting around watching the procedure and laughing heartily, to the boy's evident shame and anger.

As a result of their upbringing, the Alorese grow into aggressive and egocentric adults. This basic personality structure, induced by the lessons of early childhood, is reflected in every aspect of Alorese culture, from religion and warfare to personal relations.

One of the several formalized outlets for anger that helped to drain off the frustration and humiliations associated with the social system was a switch dance between young men. One partner stood as impassively as possible with one leg thrust forward while the other dancer, after many preliminary feints and flourishes with a rattan switch, hit him as hard as possible on the shin bone. From one to five blows were given, and then the partners changed roles.

From such data, Dubois later found it difficult to relate the personality of any individual Alorese to the supposed basic personality of the groups. The "basic" personality might be better represented as the "modal" personality. The personality which seems to characterize a culture is viewed as a statistical frequency, allowing for a wide range of individual variation. The modal personality represents the ideal, not necessarily the actual, within a given culture.

A cross-cultural approach

One way to deduce individual character and personality is to observe the way different people react to the same situation. Consider, for example, Americans who catch cold during a winter virus epidemic. One sufferer may tend to blame others for having so callously gone about in public while sick, hence giving him the disease. Another person might blame himself for having carelessly exposed himself by contact with others. Still another person might react emotionally, focusing on the different degrees of susceptibility to the dis-

Figure 15-3. *The Havasupai, Indians of the American Southwest, are gentle with children and treat them with great and obvious affection. Yet though the children are given much independence, they are also expected to learn the rules of their culture quickly and well. Adults do not intervene to save a child from the results of his errors.*

ease, saying essentially, "Why me?" Another person might blame himself for not keeping in better health. Why such various reactions to the same cold?

Anthropologist J. M. Whiting and psychologist I. L. Child suggest that the answer lies in child-rearing practices. A child's behavior is directed by means of positive and negative sanctions—that is, he is rewarded for those responses that correspond to culturally approved behavior, and he is punished for behavior that is culturally disapproved. The anxiety which the child experiences as a result of severe negative sanctions, such as spanking, may result in negative fixations, whereas excessive gratification may result in positive fixations. In other words, extreme practices during child-rearing may lend exaggerated psychological importance to certain ideas or events.

Since illness is an anxiety-causing phenomenon, a culture will tend to explain illness on the basis of the fixations established by child-rearing experiences. For this reason, Whiting and Child chose to study cultural attitudes toward illness as a key to understanding cultural fixations. Drawing data from a great number of societies, they assigned numerical values to the degree of oral, anal, sexual, dependent, and aggressive fixations. Thus they were able to correlate the effect of child-rearing techniques with each culture's approach to explaining illness.

They concluded that variations in reactions to illness among different individuals are likely to be in large part a product of general personality characteristics. But these reactions are also attributable to variations in the experience of different individuals in childhood. Such reactions are neither entirely cultural nor entirely individual.

National character

In popular thought, a national character is ascribed to the citizens of many different countries. Henry Miller epitomizes this when he says, "Madmen are logical—as are the French," suggesting that Frenchmen, in general, are overly rational. A Parisian, on the other hand, might view Americans as maudlin and unsophisticated. Similarly, we all have in mind some image, perhaps not too well defined, of the typical Russian or Japanese or Englishman. Essentially, these are simply stereotypes. But we might well ask if these stereotypes have any basis in fact. Is there, in reality, such a thing as "national character?"

Some anthropologists would answer, "yes." National character studies have focused, first, on discovering the modal characteristics of a people, and, second, on determining the child-rearing practices and education that shape such a modal personality. Margaret Mead, Ruth Benedict, and Geoffrey Gorer conducted national character studies using relatively small samples of informants. During World War II, techniques were developed for studying "culture at a distance" through intensive interviews with nationals living away from their native lands and through the analysis of newspapers, books, and photographs. By investigating memories of childhood and cultural attitudes, and by examining graphic material for the appearance of recurrent themes and values, researchers attempted to portray national character.

The Japanese

At the height of World War II, Geoffrey Gorer attempted to determine the underlying reasons for the "contrast between the all-pervasive gentleness of Japanese family life in Japan, which has charmed nearly every visitor, and the overwhelming brutality and sadism of the Japanese at war." Strongly under the influence of Freud, Gorer sought his causes in the toilet-training practices of the Japanese, which he believed were severe and threatening. He suggested that because Japanese infants were forced to control their sphincters before they had acquired the necessary muscular or intellectual development, they grew up filled with repressed rage. As adults, the Japanese were able to express this rage in their brutality in war. Another anthropologist, Weston La Barre, independently came to the same conclusions.

Neither Gorer nor La Barre was able to do fieldwork. When, after the war, the toilet-training hypothesis could be tested, it was found that the severity of Japanese toilet training was a myth. Children were not subject to severe threats or punishment. Nor were all Japanese soldiers brutal and sadistic in war; some were, but then so were

Figure 15-4. *These photos rather amusingly depict some of the stereotypes we hold of the national character of other countries. The Japanese tea ceremony and subway crowds, the French lovers and gendarmes, and the Englishman with his umbrella, bowler, and pipe are part of our mythology about these foreign countries. Yet we would surely protest foreign views of the typical American and protest the error of the stereotype.*

some Americans. Also, the fact that the postwar Japanese took the lead in the Far East peace movement hardly conformed to the wartime image of brutality.

This study was most important, not in revealing the importance of Japanese sphincters on the national character, but in pointing out the dangers of generalizing from minimal evidence and employing simplistic individual psychology to explain complex social phenomena.

The Russians

Despite severe criticism from some of their colleagues, a few anthropologists have continued their interest in the question of national character. They have both refined their techniques and expanded their sampling, with some interesting results.

One example of this sophisticated approach is the Harvard Project on the Soviet social system. Nearly 3000 Soviet citizens, who were displaced by World War II and who had decided not to return to the U.S.S.R., completed a long questionnaire. A few hundred of these were also extensively interviewed, and 51 were clinically studied in depth. What emerged from this study was one of the best portraits to date of the modal personality of a particular nation.

The strongest and most pervasive quality of the Russian personality is affiliation, or the need for interaction with other people in direct personal relationship. Unlike the average American, the Russian is liable to have a relatively small drive to achieve. Surprisingly, there are few pronounced differences between the basic attitudes of Russians and Americans in relation to authority, except that the Russians seem to have more fear of their authority figures and fewer positive expectations of them. Both Russians and Americans feel guilt and shame, but these emotions are aroused under different circumstances. An American feels guilty when he has failed to meet the formal rules of etiquette or procedural forms; the Russian does not care about formal rules, but feels guilt and shame for defects of character in interpersonal relations. In sum, the Russian personality is characterized by emotional aliveness, expressiveness, spontaneity, gregariousness, and a certain need for dependence on authority.

Objections to national character studies

Critics of national character theories have emphasized the tendency for such work to be based on unscientific and overgeneralized data. The modal personality has a certain statistical validity, they argue, but to generalize the qualities of a complex nation on the basis of such limited data is to lend insufficient recognition to the countless individuals who vary from the generalization. Further, such studies tend to be highly subjective; for example, the tendency during the late 1930s and 1940s for anthropologists to characterize the German people as aggressive paranoids was obviously a reflection of wartime hostilities and not of scientific objectivity.

It has also been pointed out that occupational and social statuses tend to cut across national boundaries. A French farmer may have less in common with a French factory worker than he does with a German farmer. The concept of national character may be a useful supplement to the concept of modal personality, but it demands a high degree of objectivity and factual investigation.

Abnormal personality

Each culture perpetuates a set of norms by encouraging some behavioral patterns and discouraging others. Such patterns vary so much from culture to culture that we may well ask whether there can be a universal standard of normalcy. The Dobuans of New Guinea and certain Plains Indian tribes furnish striking example of normal behavior radically different from ours.

Normal and abnormal behavior

The individual in Dobu whom the other villagers considered neurotic and thoroughly disoriented was a man who was naturally friendly and found activity an end in itself. He was a pleasant fellow who did not seek to overthrow his fellows or to punish them. He worked for anyone who asked him, and he was tireless in carrying out their commands. In any other Dobuan, this would have been scandalous behavior, but in him it was regarded as merely silly. The village treated him in a kindly fashion, not taking advantage of him, or making sport or ridiculing him, but he was definitely regarded as one who stood outside the normal conventions of behavior.

Among certain Plains Indians, a man, compelled by supernatural spirits, may assume woman's attire, perform woman's work, and even marry another man. Under the institution of the *berdache,* such an individual would find himself in conflict with his neighbors or the law; yet, although the *berdache* is rare among Indians, it is not looked upon as the behavior of an abnormal personality.

The standards that define normal behavior for any culture are determined by that culture itself. Obviously, no society could survive if murdering one's neighbor was looked upon as normal behavior; yet each culture determines for itself the circumstances under which murdering one's neighbor may be acceptable. What is judged to be murder in one society may be treated as justifiable homicide in another. Moral acts are those which conform to certain social standards of good and evil, and each society determines those standards for itself. Morality is thus based on culturally determined ideals.

Is this to suggest that "normalcy" is a meaningless concept as it is applied to personality? Within the context of a given culture, the concept of normal personality is quite meaningful. A. I. Hallowell somewhat ironically observed that it is normal to share the delusions traditionally accepted by one's society. Abnormality involves the development of a delusional system not sanctified by culture. The individual who is disturbed be-

Figure 15-5. *The chief of the Mossi tribe lives in a palace and is served by slaves. The slaves must dress in women's clothing to symbolize their subordinate status; this custom gives us a clue to the way the society interprets the role of women.*

cause he cannot adequately measure up to the norms of society, and yet be happy, may be termed neurotic. When his delusional system is significantly different from that of his society and in no way reflects its norms, the individual may be termed psychotic.

Culturally induced conflicts can not only produce psychosis, but can determine the form of the psychosis as well. In a culture which encourages aggressiveness and suspicion, the madman is that individual who is passive and trusting. In a culture which encourages passivity and trust, the madman is that individual who is aggressive and suspicious. Just as each society establishes its own norms, each individual is unique in his perceptions. Many anthropologists see the only meaningful criterion for personality evaluation as the correlation between personality and social conformity.

However, the situation may not be so simple. Some radical psychologists, notably R. D. Laing, are questioning the sanity of society itself. We might well ask how a society which, for example, systematically pollutes its own air and water and poisons its own food with pesticides, can act as the arbiter of sanity. It has been suggested that some of the behavior which society calls "mad" may rather be a sane response to an insane society. In any case, the purely relativist viewpoint may be too easy an answer to an enormously complex question.

Current trends in personality studies

Culture and personality studies have come a long way since the descriptive studies of Ruth Benedict and Margaret Mead were considered important explanations of the ways culture and personality interacted. Benedict divided all cultures into Apollonian and Dionysian types, while Mead considered child-rearing practices of the highest importance in explaining cultural behavior and personality. Although the work of these anthropologists has come under heavy fire for being impressionistic rather than scientific and not susceptible of replication, their theories have contributed much to the realization that human behavior is relative. The theory of cultural relativity resulting from the study of many societies undermined the ethnocentrism common to all social groups. Anthropologists have established that cultures are indeed different and that their members possess personalities reflecting these differences.

Current studies in culture and personality go far beyond the traditional ethnographic descriptive approach of Benedict, Mead, and others. In his book, *Culture And Personality,* Anthony Wallace points out that current investigators are combining Freudian pyschoanalytically based theories with biological and social variables to discover, analyze, and explain the laws of cultural dynamics. Thus, current culture and personality studies are examining human genetic and ecological processes; these processes are entirely independent of culture, but they are the cause of change in the human biological system upon which culture depends. Further, Wallace points out, culture and personality studies are being broadened to include more than the study of motivation and affect and their causes; more attention is being given to the cognitive processes of the mind, which are the basic mechanisms responsible for such cultural expressions as language, myth and art.

☐

Original study

HABITUATION AND EDUCATION

Into every culture and every civilization, year after year, hordes of uncultured "barbarians" descend in the form of newborn babies. In every society, a major —indeed, an overwhelming—amount of social energy must be spent in making cultured creatures out of this human plasm. Babies, whatever their potential may be, have few inborn abilities. They can grasp (a newly born baby can support its own weight by its grasp), but probably have to learn to utilize the capacity. They have to be taught to suck—for some, learning takes a minute or two, for others as much as a day or two. Some children are brighter than others, and the difference begins to show very early in life.

It is one of the characteristics of human beings that their children remain helpless for a very long period. Horses can walk and run a few hours after birth. Apes mature in about a third of the time that it takes human beings to mature. Even elephants, whose period of gestation is almost twice that of human beings, and whose life span is only a little shorter, are self-sufficient within about three years. Under minimal conditions, the human being requires ten or twelve years to become self-sufficient; under most conditions of culture, some fifteen years or so; and under our own system, with its complex material culture and vast need for training and education, somewhat longer than that.

Human beings, whether they are a few days old, a few years old, or a few decades old, have many needs because of the sheer fact that they are animals. Some of these needs, if left unfulfilled, will lead to the death of the animal. They must be fed, they must have a certain environmental temperature, and they need at least a certain minimal contact with others. If human babies are left without human contact, they die—even if their other needs are well attended.

Babies, being helpless, have their needs fulfilled for them. In the course of the fulfillment of these needs, the way in which the need is fulfilled comes to be almost as important as the fact of fulfillment. By the time a child is nearly adult enough to fulfill some of his own requirements for food and sleep, his habits are well established. These habits may be changed several times during the course of maturation, but even the need to change and the capacity to change are developed into habits. If it were not possible to change habits, any sort of "progress" or social change would be quite impossible.

The habits that are acquired by youngsters are part of the culture in accordance with which they are brought up. In one sense, the habits are the culture: if all the habits of all the people were changed, the culture would have changed.

There are, however, two ways in which culture can be "internalized." One is by habituation and the other by purposeful education. Western children are taught, rather systematically, to use a fork (a most clumsy instrument until you have mastered it); but they are not taught food preferences in the same purposeful way (although they may be taught, very purposefully indeed, what not to eat).

In habituation, human beings learn those aspects of culture that are not regarded in the culture as specifically learnable techniques. In education they are taught—specifically taught—the techniques. Education is usually defined as the directed learning process, either formally or informally carried out. The purpose here is not to make a pedantic distinction between these two aspects of education—many situations of human learning cannot be specifically set out as one or the other, but partake of both. It is merely to point out that human beings learn a great deal more than is specifically taught them: people pick up habits, without questioning them, because "that's the way it is done." Yet nobody picks up reading as a habit the way he picks up a taste for wheat bread and meat instead of millet porridge and fish.

Both of these processes—habituation and education—make it possible to live in the society in which we are born or in which we find ourselves. Neither stops, however, when the learner becomes a full-fledged member of adult society. Rather, he continues throughout his entire life to learn his culture—new culture or new fields of traditional culture. Education and habituation continue to the grave. There is no culture that it is possible completely to master, even though it is possible in some—but not in our own—to be "old and full of years," satiated with sufficient of one's culture that death is not an objectionable alternative to finishing the job.

Thus, as man's primary needs are cared for—those whose neglect would cause his death—he is habituated and educated. The habituation and education themselves set up a secondary set of needs for the primary needs to be cared for in certain ways. They may become as grave a need as the substantive needs.

Education may be carried on by any number of agencies. The family is probably the most important educating agency in every society. In some societies, a part of the job is taken over by professionals when the child is about six years old. Even in societies that lack any sort of formal schooling, the family may be assisted by other elements of the society when the child reaches about this age. Sometimes children are sent to their grandparents, because grandparents are thought in that culture, for one reason or another, to be the best formal instructors during certain periods of a child's life. In other societies, a child goes to his father's sister because it is thought that the parents themselves may be so fond of the child as to be too indulgent to insist on adequate training for coping with life and society. The father's sister, the evaluation in such a society runs, is a close kinswoman and hence will be kind and proffer some affection, but she is far enough removed that she will insist on the child's continuing education to the point of being strict if it is necessary. Some societies have formalized age associations that organize children to teach younger children.

Finally, the community as a whole may act as an habituating and educating agency simply by withholding its approval from people who do not behave "properly," or by rewarding behavior that is esteemed. The community may be to its members what Pavlov was to his dogs: in the end the individual learns to do what the community expects and even to like it, just as one of Pavlov's dogs told a peer who belonged to a different master: "I've got my guy trained to ring a bell every time he's about to feed me."

There are, of course, some failures. These are the people that the society brands neurotic, sick, criminal, or all three. Yet even these "failures" are habituated and to some degree educated: they rebel in terms of their own culture.

They speak the language, wear the clothes, eat the food of the society they are rebelling against. They sing songs written with the same scales and notes, and they recognize the same norms, even by valuing perversions of them.

Source:
From *Social Anthropology* by Paul Bohannan. Copyright © 1963 by Holt, Rinehart and Winston, Inc. Reprinted by permission of Holt, Rinehart and Winston, Inc.

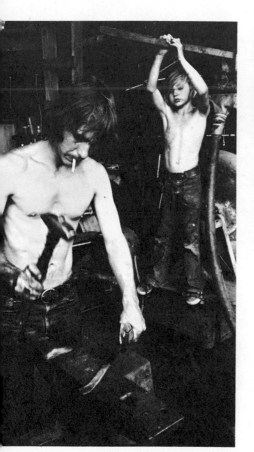

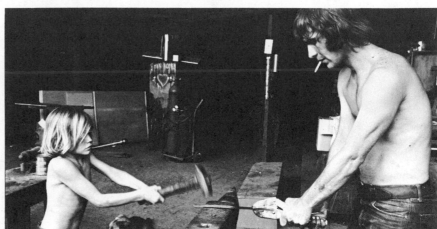

Figure 15-6. *A child in a California commune learns a skill by watching and helping adults.*

Summary

1.

Society to a great extent determines an individual's personality. Personality is formed through enculturation, the assimilation of a group's ways of thinking and acting. Every society operates according to a series of norms and ideals. Those who conform to these norms are rewarded; those who deviate are punished. The result is a "group personality," within which there is considerable variation.

2.

Ruth Benedict, in *Patterns of Culture,* saw cultures as conforming to two general types: the "Dionysian" and the "Apollonian." The "Dionysian" is characterized by ecstatic ritual, egocentrism, and extremely individualistic behavior; the "Apollonian" is characterized by avoidance of excess and distrust of individualism.

3.

Margaret Mead, in her studies of foreign cultures, emphasized the effects of culture on personality. Her Samoan studies indicate that a great deal of adolescent behavior is learned. A child learns through cultural transmission how society expects him to behave. Cultural transmission produces predictable patterns of behavior. These patterns provide a member of a society with a framework for interpreting the motivations and behavior of other members. On the other hand, Sigmund Freud emphasized the shaping effects of individual psychology on personality and culture. He used the Oedipus complex to explain the origins of culture and society. Most anthropologists today would not accept his conclusions, but the Oedipus complex is still valuable in the study of personality development.

4.

Abram Kardiner attempted to use both psychology and culture to explain personality. He held that personality structures, or cultural norms, vary widely within a society. Personalities differ because cultural institutions vary. He distinguished between primary and secondary institutions. Primary institutions arise to fill fundamental human needs and in turn give rise to secondary institutions. The interaction of the institutions with the personality shapes human culture. The most complete source of ethnopsychological data he analyzed was Cora Dubois' study of the Alorese culture of the South Pacific.

5.

One way to deduce individual character and personality is to observe the way different people react to the same situation. Anthropologists Whiting and Child have suggested that a society's child-rearing practices can reveal a group's personality.

6.

National character studies have focused on the modal characteristics of a people. They have then attempted to determine the child-rearing practices and education which shape such a modal personality. During World War II, investigators interviewed foreign-born nationals and analyzed newspapers, books, and photographs in attempts to portray national character. Many anthropologists believe that national character theories are based on unscientific and overgeneralized data.

7.

A culture determines the standards that determine normal behavior. Within the context of a given culture the concept of normal personality is meaningful. Abnormality involves developing a delusional system not accepted by culture. Culturally induced conflicts can not only produce psychosis but determine its form as well.

8.

Current culture and personality studies are combining traditional psychoanalytically based theories with biological and social factors to explain culture and cultural dynamics. Attention is also being given to the cognitive processes of the mind which are the mechanisms responsible for such cultural expressions as language, myth, and art.

Suggested readings

Barnouw, Victor *Culture and Personality*. Homewood, Ill.: Dorsey Press, 1963.
   Three approaches to personality determination form the background of this book: the childhood determinist, the situational, and the world view. The cultural and social determinants of personality are dealt with. Citing theories of such classic scholars as Benedict, Mead, and Malinowski, the author discusses some contemporary approaches as well as different methods of culture and personality research.

Hunt, Robert C., ed. *Personalities and Cultures: Readings in Psychological Anthropology*. Garden City, N.Y.: Natural History Press, 1967.
   The eighteen articles included in this book focus on various aspects of culture and personality. Attention is given to psychological and sociocultural variables and the relationships between them.

Norbeck, Edward, Douglas Price Williams, and William McCord, eds. *The Study of Personality: An Interdisciplinary Appraisal*. New York: Holt, Rinehart and Winston, 1968.
   The volume contains addresses given at Rice University in 1966. Its objective is to review and appraise knowledge and theories concerning personality in several scholarly fields (psychology, anthropology, sociology, philosophy of science, etc.). It also discusses factors that influence the formation of personality, and the personalities of social and psychiatric deviates.

Wallace, Anthony F. *Culture and Personality*. New York: Random House, 1970.
   The logical and methodological foundations of culture and personality as a science form the basis of this book. The study is guided by the assumptions that anthropology should develop a scientific theory about culture, and that a theory pretending to explain or predict cultural phenomena must reckon with noncultural phenomena (such as personality) as well.

Whiting, John W. M., and I. Child *Child Training and Personality: A Crosscultural Study*. New Haven: Yale University Press, 1953.
   How culture is integrated through the medium of personality processes is the main concern of this study. It covers both the influence of culture on personality and personality on culture. It is oriented toward testing general hypotheses about human behavior in any and all societies, rather than toward a detailed analysis of a particular society.

Patterns
of subsistence

Several times today you will interrupt your activities to eat or drink. You may take this very much for granted, but if you went totally without food for as long as a day, you would begin to feel the symptoms of starvation: weakness, fatigue, headache. After a month of starvation, your body would probably never repair the damage. A mere week to ten days without water would be enough to kill you.

All living beings, and man is obviously no exception, must satisfy certain basic needs in order to stay alive. Among these needs are food, water, and shelter. Man may not live by bread alone, but no man can live long without any bread at all; and no creature could long survive if its relations with its environment were random and chaotic. Living beings must have regular access to a supply of food and water and a reliable means of obtaining and using it. A lion might die if all its prey disappeared, if its teeth and claws grew soft, or if its digestive system failed. Although man faces these same problems, he has an overwhelming advantage over his fellow creatures; man has culture. If our meat supply dwindles, we can turn to some vegetable, like the soybean, and process it to taste like meat. When our tools fail, we replace them or invent better ones. Even when

our stomachs are incapable of digesting food, we can predigest food by boiling or pureeing. However, we are subject to the same needs and pressures as all living creatures, and it is important to understand human behavior from this point of view. The crucial concept that underlies such a perspective is **adaptation,** that is, how man manages to deal with the contingencies of daily life.

Adaptation

The process of adaptation establishes a moving balance between the needs of a population and the potential of its environment. One illustration of this process can be seen in the case of the Tsembaga, New Guinea highlanders who support themselves chiefly through slash-and-burn agriculture. Although they also raise pigs, they eat them only under conditions of illness, injury, warfare, or celebration. At such times the pigs are sacrificed to ancestor spirits, and their flesh is ritually consumed by those people involved in the crisis. (This guarantees a supply of high-quality protein when it is most needed.)

In precolonial times, the Tsembaga and their

Figure 16-1. *Throughout New Guinea, the killing of a wild pig is such an important event that it is surrounded by much ritual and symbolic action. The men of the Big Namba tribe turn out in their most elaborate costumes for the pig festival.*

neighbors were bound together in a unique cycle of pig sacrifices that served to mark the end of hostilities between groups. Frequent hostilities were set off by a number of ecological pressures in which pigs were a significant factor. Since very few pigs were normally slaughtered and their food requirements were great, they could very quickly literally eat a local group out of house and home. The need to expand food production in order to support the prestigious but hungry pigs put a strain on the land best suited for agriculture. Therefore, when one group had driven another off its land, hostilities ended and the new residents celebrated their victory with a pig festival. Many pigs were slaughtered, and the pork was widely shared between allied groups. Even without hostilities, festivals were held whenever the pig population became unmanageable, every five to ten years, depending on the groups' agricultural success. Thus the cycle of fighting and feasting kept the balance between men, land, and animals.

The term adaptation also refers to the process of interaction between changes made by an organism on its environment and changes made by the environment on the organism. The spread of the gene for sickle-cell trait is a case in point. Long ago, when central Africa was mostly covered by tropical forests, a genetic mutation appeared in the local human population, causing the manufacture of red blood cells that take on a sickle shape under conditions of low oxygen pressure. Since persons homozygous to this trait usually develop severe anemia and die in childhood, there was a selection pressure exerted against the spread of this gene in the local gene pool.

Then slash-and-burn agriculture was introduced into central Africa, creating a change in the natural environment that was conducive to the breeding of mosquitos that carry the parasite causing falciparum malaria. When transmitted to man, the parasites live in the red blood cells and cause a disease that is always debilitating and very often fatal. However, individuals who were heterozygous for sickle-cell trait turned out to have a specific natural defense against the parasite. Its presence in any red blood cell caused that cell to sickle; when that cell circulated through the spleen, which routinely screens out all damaged or worn red blood cells, the infected cell, and the parasite along with it, were destroyed. Since heterozygotes were therefore resistant to malaria, they were selected, and the sickling trait became more and more frequent in the population. Thus, while man changed his environment, his environment also changed him.

The unit of adaptation

The unit of adaptation includes both organism and environment: anthropologist Gregory Bateson calls it the "flexible organism-in-its-environment." By "flexible" is meant not just the flexibility of one individual, but the flexibility of a whole population to cope with variability and change within its environment. In biological terms, this means that different organisms within the population have somewhat differing genetic endowments. In cultural terms, it means that there is variation between individual skills, knowledge, and personalities. Organisms and environments form interacting systems. Men might as easily be farmers as fishermen; but we do not expect to find farmers in the Arctic Circle or fishermen in the Sahara Desert.

We might consider the example of a group of lakeside fishermen. The men live off the fish, which, in turn, live off smaller animals. Those animals, in turn, consume green plants; plants liberate minerals from water and mud, and, with energy from sunlight, transform them into proteins and carbohydrates. Dead plant and animal matter is decomposed by bacteria, and chemicals are returned to the soil and water. Some energy escapes from this system in the form of heat. Evaporation and rainfall constantly recirculate the water. Men add chemicals to the system in the form of their wastes, and, if they are judicious, help to regulate the balance of animals and plants.

Some anthropologists have borrowed the ecologists' term, **ecosystem.** An ecosystem is composed of both the physical environment and the organisms living within it. The system is bound by the activities of the organisms as well as by such physical processes as erosion and evaporation.

Human ecologists are generally concerned with detailed microstudies of particular human ecosystems; they emphasize that all aspects of human culture must be considered, not only the most obvious technological ones. The Tsembaga's attitude toward pigs and the cycle of sacrifices have important economic functions; we see them in this way, but the Tsembaga do not. They are motivated by their belief in the power and needs of their ancestral spirits. Although the pigs are consumed *by* men, they are sacrificed *for* ancestors. Human ecosystems must often be interpreted in cultural terms.

Evolutionary adaptation

Adaptation must also be understood from an historical point of view. In order for an organism to fit into an ecosystem, it must have the potential ability to adjust to or become a part of it. The Comanche, whose tribal history began in the harsh, arid plateau country of Montana, provide a good example. In their original home, they subsisted on wild plants, small animals, and occasionally large game. Their material culture was simple and limited to what could be transported by the women of the tribe. The size of their groups was restricted, and what little social power could develop was in the hands of the shaman, who was a combination of medicine man and spiritual guide.

At some point in their nomadic history, the Comanche reached the Great Plains, where buffalo were abundant and the Indians' potential as hunters could be fully developed. As larger groups could be supported by the new food supply, the need arose for a more complex political organization. Hunting ability thus became a means to acquire political power.

Figure 16-2. *Indian tribes of the American plains, such as the Sioux, Crow, Cree, Blackfoot, and Kiowa, share many culture traits because their means of subsistence are similar.*

Eventually the Comanche acquired the white man's horse and gun, which greatly extended their hunting prowess, and the great hunting chiefs became powerful indeed. The Comanche became raiders in order to get horses, for they were not horse breeders, and their hunting chiefs evolved into war chiefs. The once poor and peaceful hunter-gatherers of the plateau became wealthy pirates, dominating the Southwest from the borders of New Spain (Mexico) in the south, to those of New France (Louisiana) and the fledgling United States in the east and north. In passing from one environment to another, and in evolving from one way of life to a second, the Comanche made the best advantage of their developing potentials, or cultural **preadaptations.**

Many different societies develop independently, and some find similar solutions to similar

problems. The development of similar cultural adaptations to similar technoenvironmental conditions is called **parallel evolution.** To a large extent, the rise of great civilizations in China, northwest Mesopotamia, and Peru was made possible by the independent invention of irrigation agriculture in each of these areas. The problems of applying irrigation agriculture to making a living in similar environments—problems of labor and distribution—led to a number of parallels in the social and cultural development of those societies.

Culture areas

The Great Plains was an aboriginal **culture area,** a geographic region in which there existed a number of societies following a similar pattern of life. Thirty-one politically independent tribes faced a common environment, in which the buffalo was the most obvious and practical food source. Living close by each other, they were able to share new inventions and discoveries. They reached a common and shared adaptation to a particular ecological zone.

The Indian tribes of the Great Plains were, at the time of contact with the Europeans, invariably buffalo hunters, dependent upon this animal for food, clothing, shelter, and bone tools. The tribes were generally organized into a number of warrior societies, and prestige came from hunting and fighting skills. Their camps were typically arranged in a distinctive circular pattern. Many religious rituals, such as the Sun Dance, were practiced throughout the plains region.

Sometimes ecological zones are not uniform in climate and topography, and so new discoveries do not always diffuse from one group to another. Moreover, within a culture area, there are variations between local environments, and these variations favor variations in adaptation. The Great Basin of the southwestern United States is a case in point. The Great Basin Shoshone Indians were divided into a northern and a western group, both primarily migratory hunters and gatherers. In the north, a relative abundance of game animals favored the development of larger populations, requiring a great degree of cooperation between local groups. The western Shoshone, on the other hand, were almost entirely dependent upon the gathering of wild crops for a living, and as these varied considerably in their seasonal and local availability, the western Shoshone were forced to cover vast distances in search of food. Under such conditions, they could maintain groups of only a few families, only occasionally coming together with other groups, and not always with the same ones.

The Shoshone were not the only inhabitants of the Great Basin. To the south lived another closely related tribe, the Paiutes. They were also hunter-gatherers living under the same environmental conditions as the Shoshone, but the Paiute had discovered how to irrigate wild crops by diverting small streams. They did not plant and cultivate crops, but even without agriculture, the Paiute, unlike their northern neighbors, were able to secure a steady food supply. Hence, their populations were larger than those of the Shoshone and they led a settled existence.

In order to explain variations within culture areas, Julian Steward proposed the concept of **culture type,** a culture considered in terms of a particular technology and its relationship with the particular environmental features that technology is equipped to exploit. The example of the Great Plains shows how technology often decides just which environmental features will be useful. Those same prairies that once supported tribes of buffalo hunters now support grain farmers. The Indians were prevented from farming the plains not for environmental reasons, nor for lack of agricultural knowledge, since some of the plains tribes had been farmers before they came west. They did not farm because they lacked the steel-tipped plow that was needed to break up the compacted prairie sod. The farming potential of the Great Plains was simply not a relevant feature of the environment, given the available technology before the coming of the Europeans.

Culture core

Environment and technology are not the only factors that determine a society's way of subsistence; social and political organization also affect the application of technology to the problem of staying alive. In order to understand the rise of irrigation agriculture in the great centers of civilization, such as China and Mesopotamia, it is important to note, not only the technological and environmental factors that made possible the building of huge irrigation works, but also the social and political organization needed to mobilize large groups of workers to build and maintain the systems. It is necessary to examine the monarchies and priesthoods that organized the work and decided where the water would be used and how the agricultural products of this joint venture would be distributed.

Those features of a culture that play a part in the society's way of making its living are called its **culture core.** The culture core includes the society's productive techniques and its knowledge of the resources available to it. It encompasses the patterns of labor involved in applying those techniques to the local environment. For instance, do people work every day for a fixed number of hours, or is most work concentrated during certain times of the year? The culture core also includes other aspects of culture that bear on the production and distribution of food. An example of the way ideology can indirectly affect subsistence can be seen in a number of Moslem cultures. The religious beliefs of Moslems call for a four-week period of fasting during the spring;

no food can be eaten between sunrise and sunset. Because of the fasting, people can do very little heavy work. When the fast period coincides with the time crops should be planted, farmers plant less than they do normally and food is scarce for the next year.

A number of anthropologists, known as ethnoscientists, are actively attempting to understand the principles behind folk ideologies and the ways those principles help keep a people alive. The Tsembaga, for example, avoid certain lowlying, marshy areas because they believe these areas are inhabited by red spirits who punish trespassers. Modern Western science interprets those areas as the home of mosquitos, and the "punishment" as malaria. Whatever Westerners may think of the Tsembaga's belief in red spirits, it is a perfectly useful and reasonable one; it keeps them away from marshy areas just as surely as does a belief in malaria. If we want to understand why people in other cultures behave the way they do, we must understand their system of thought from their point of view as well as our own. Unfortunately, not all such beliefs are as easy to translate into our terms as is that of the Tsembaga red spirits.

The hunting-gathering life

At the present time, approximately three million people of a world population of three billion support themselves chiefly through hunting, fishing, and the gathering of wild fruits and vegetables. Although three million is a sizable figure, it comprises only .1 percent of the total world population. Yet, before men discovered agriculture and the domestication of animals ten thousand years ago, all men must have supported themselves through some combination of plant gathering, hunting, and/or fishing. Of all the men who have *ever* lived, 90 percent have been hunter-gatherers.

Because man developed as a hunter-gatherer, we owe many of the important features of human society and culture to this way of life. Early man implemented the division of labor, food-sharing, toolmaking, and language. It seems obvious then that if we would know who we are and how we came to be, if we would understand the relationship between environment and culture, and if we would comprehend the institutions of more complex societies that have arisen since the development of agriculture and animal husbandry, we should turn to the oldest and most basic of fully human life-styles, the hunter-gatherer adaptation.

When hunter-gatherers were dominant some ten thousand years ago, they had their pick of the best environments. These have long since been appropriated by farming and, more recently, industrial societies. Today, most hunter-gatherers have been left to their traditional life only in the world's marginal areas—frozen arctic tundra, deserts, inaccessible jungles. These habitats, although they may not support large or dense agricultural societies, provide adequate support for hunting and gathering peoples.

Until recently, it was assumed that these areas did not provide the best way of living. But one anthropologist, Marshall Sahlins, has gone so far as to describe hunter-gatherers as the "original affluent society." In his view, their diets are ample, they have plenty of leisure time, and if their material comforts are limited, so are their desires. The !Kung Bushmen of South Africa's Kalahari Desert obtain a better than subsistence diet in an average work week of twelve to nineteen hours. Others have observed that this is clearly not true for all hunting and gathering societies. Some people, like the Birhor of India, work very hard indeed and still often go hungry. It is probably true that ancient hunter-gatherers lived in better environments with more secure and plentiful sources of food than do their modern counterparts.

All modern hunter-gatherers have had some degree of exposure to more technologically advanced neighbors. Modern hunter-gatherers often have metal and firearms, and some have learned to do a little farming. Even the Kalahari Bushmen have been known to plant corn when rainfall has

Figure 16-3a. *This photo shows a dry season camp of the !Kung Bushmen of south central Africa. The hut walls are thatched but the roof is open.*

Figure 16-3b. *Two Bushmen dig into the dried clay soil at the end of the rainy season to obtain roots and bulbs, foods eaten only when other plants are scarce.*

Figure 16-3d. *Two Bushmen carefully fasten down with wooden stakes the hide of a hartebeest; when it is dried, the hide will be scraped and tanned.*

Figure 16-3e. *This hut is built for the rainy season; unlike the dry season hut in 16-3a, it has a roof but remains open to the air since there the winds are not strong.*

Figure 16-3c. *This photo shows a small band of Bushmen on the move to a new locale. They carry with them everything they own.*

Figure 16-3f. *These two Bushmen hunters carry with them the tools of their trade, virtually the only possessions they have— bow, arrows, digging stick, club, spear.*

been especially good. It also seems likely that some contemporary hunter-gatherers have only returned to this way of life after failing at agriculture. Such is thought to be the case of the Siriono of South America and the Veddas of Ceylon. Contact with other peoples has fundamentally changed, if not completely disrupted, the social organizations of many hunting and gathering societies. The Mbuti Pygmies of the Congolese Ituri rain forest live in a complex patron-client relationship with their agricultural neighbors, some Bantu and Sudani tribes. They exchange meat and military service for farm produce and manufactured goods. During part of the year, they live in their patron's village and are incorporated into his kin group, even to the point of allowing him to arrange their marriages.

Characteristics of the nomadic life

Hunter-gatherers are by definition people who do not practice animal husbandry or agriculture. Hence, they must accommodate their places of residence to naturally available food sources. This being the case, it is no wonder that they move about a great deal. Such movement is not aimless wandering but is done within a fixed territory or home range. Some, like the !Kung Bushmen who depend on the reliable and highly drought-resistant Mongongo nut, may keep to fairly fixed annual routes and cover only a restricted territory. Others, such as the Great Basin Shoshone, must cover a wider territory; their course is determined by the local availability of the erratically productive pine nut. A crucial factor in this mobility is the availability of water. The distance between the food supply and water must not be so great that more energy is required to fetch water than can be obtained from the food.

Another characteristic of the hunter-gatherer adaptation is the small size of local groups, twenty-five to fifty being the average number. Although no completely satisfactory explanation of group size has yet been offered, it seems certain that both ecological and social factors are involved. Among those suggested are the **carrying capacity** of the land, the number of people who can be supported by the available resources at a given level of food-getting techniques, and the **density of social relations,** roughly the number and intensity of interactions between camp members. More people means a higher social density, which, in turn, means more opportunities for conflict.

Both carrying capacity and social density are complex variables. Carrying capacity involves not only the immediate presence of food and water, but the tools and work necessary to secure them, as well as short- and long-term fluctuations in their availability. Social density involves not only the number of people and their interactions, but also the circumstances and quality of those interactions and the mechanisms for regulating them. A mob of a hundred angry strangers has a different social density than the same number of neighbors enjoying themselves at a block party.

Among hunter-gatherer populations, social density seems always to be in a state of flux, as people spend more or less time away from camp and as they move to other camps, either on visits or more permanently. This redistribution of people is an important mechanism for regulating social density as well as for assuring that the size and composition of local groups is suited to local variations in resources. Thus, cultural adaptations serve to help transcend the limitations of the physical environment.

In addition to seasonal or local adjustments, long-term adjustments to resources must be made. Most hunter-gatherer populations seem to stabilize in numbers well below the carrying capacity of their land. In fact, the territories of most hunter-gatherers can support from three to five times as many people as they typically do. In the long run, it may be more adaptive for a group to keep its numbers low, rather than to expand indefinitely and then suddenly be cut down by an unexpected disaster. It is not certain just how this stabilization is regulated, but among the population control methods used by hunting and gathering peoples are infanticide, abortion, prohibitions against sexual intercourse with nursing mothers, and various herbal drugs that interfere with fertility or conception. The population density of hunter-gatherer groups rarely exceeds one person per square mile, a very low density; yet, their resources could support greater numbers.

The impact of hunting on human society

Recently much has been written on the importance of hunting in shaping the supposedly competitive and aggressive nature of modern man. Although many anthropologists are unconvinced by these arguments, it does seem likely that three crucial elements of human social organization developed along with hunting. The first of these is the division of labor. Some form of division of labor by sex, however modified, has been observed in all human societies. There is some tendency in contemporary Western society to do away with such division. One may ask what the implications are for future cooperative relationships between men and women.

Hunting is universally a male occupation. This may be due to the fact that hunters must often travel long distances on foot, something which is not easily possible for nursing mothers and pregnant women. Women typically do the work of gathering; although it is often more arduous labor than hunting, it does not require long-distance travel.

Men, however, do not spend all or even the greatest part of their time in hunting. The amount of energy expended in hunting, especially in hot climates, is often greater than the energy return from the kill. Too much time spent at hunting might actually be counterproductive. A certain amount of meat in the diet guarantees high-quality protein that is not easily obtained from vegetable sources, but energy itself is derived primarily from plant carbohydrates; it is the female gatherer who brings in the bulk of the calories. Most modern hunting and gathering societies actually obtain 60 to 70 percent of their diets from vegetable foods, fish, and shellfish (a diet similar to that of prehuman primates); therefore, female food-getting activities are generally more important than male hunting.

Hunting, whether cooperative or not, seems to be correlated with food-sharing among adults, a very rare occurrence among nonhuman primates. Food-sharing is the second key feature of man's social organization. It is easy enough to see why sharing would be necessary if game is hunted cooperatively; but even individual hunters may find it in their interest to share what they cannot consume. Among the Hazda of northern Tanzania, a man will eat his fill at his killsite, then carry what he can back to camp. If the kill has been especially good, the camp may move to him. For the individual hunter, food-sharing is really a way of storing food for the future; his generosity gives him a claim on the future surpluses of other hunters. As a cultural trait, food-sharing has the obvious survival value of distributing resources needed for subsistence.

Although carnivores share food, the few examples of food-sharing among nonhuman primates all involve groups of male chimpanzees cooperating in a hunt and later sharing the spoils and even offering some to the females and infants. It is difficult to say how typical this behavior is for chimpanzees uninfluenced by human intruders, but it does suggest that the origins of food-sharing and the division of labor are related to a shift in food habits from rare meat-eating to a balance between hunting and gathering. This may have occurred among our earliest hominid ancestors.

Another distinctive feature of the hunting economy is the importance of the camp as the center of daily activity and the place where food-sharing actually occurs. Among nonhuman primates, activities tend to be divided between feeding areas and sleeping areas, and the latter tend to be shifted each evening. Hunting man, however, lives in camps of some permanence,

ranging from the dry-season camps of the Bushmen that serve for the entire winter, to the dry-season camps of the Hazda, oriented around the hunt and serving for several days or a week or two. Moreover, human camps are more than sleeping areas; people are in and out all day, eating, working, and socializing in camps to a greater extent than any other primates. It is thought that the first camps were primarily places where the spoils of the hunt were butchered and then consumed over a period of several days. It would seem that it is to these earliest hunters that we owe the very concept of home.

Cultural adaptations and material technology. The mobility of hunter-gatherer groups may depend on the availability of water, as in the case of the !Kung; of pine nuts, as in the Shoshone example; or of game animals, as in the Hazda example. Hunting styles and equipment may also play a role in determining population size and movement. Some Mbuti Pygmies hunt with nets. This requires the cooperation of seven to thirty families; consequently, their camps are relatively large. The camps of those who hunt with bow and arrow number from three to six families. Too many archers in the same locale means that each must travel a great distance daily to keep out of the other's way. Only during midsummer do the archers collect into larger camps for religious ceremonies, matrimonial bargains, and social exchange. At this time the bowmen turn to communal beat-hunts. Without nets they are less effective than their neighbors, so it is only when the net-hunters are widely dispersed in the pursuit of honey that the archers can come together.

Egalitarian society. An important characteristic of the hunter-gatherer society is its egalitarianism. Hunter-gatherers are highly mobile and, lacking animal or mechanical means of transportation, they must be able to travel without many encumbrances, especially on food-getting expeditions. Their material goods must be limited to the barest essentials, which include weapons that serve for

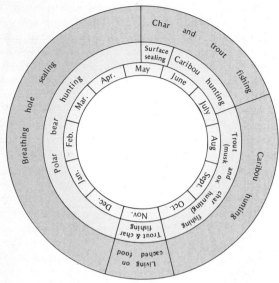

Figure 16-4. *The schematic diagram shows the cycle of subsistence activity among the Eskimo during the various seasons of the year.*

hunting, fighting, building, and toolmaking, and cooking utensils, traps, and nets. There is little chance for the accumulation of luxuries or surplus goods, and the fact that no one owns significantly more than another helps to limit status differences. Age and sex are usually the only sources of status differences in hunter-gatherer societies.

Hunter-gatherers make no attempt to accumulate surplus foodstuffs, often an important source of status in agricultural societies. To say that hunters do not accumulate food surpluses, however, is not to say that they live constantly on the verge of starvation. Their environment is their storehouse, and, except in the coldest climates, or in times of acute ecological disaster, there is always some food to be found in a hunter's territory. Because food resources are typically distributed equally throughout the group, no one achieves the wealth or status that hoarding might bring. In such a society, wealth is a sign of deviance rather than a desirable characteristic.

The hunter-gatherer's concept of territory contributes as much to social equality as it does to the equal distribution of resources. Most groups have territories or ranges which they exploit and within which access to resources is open to all members. If a Mbuti discovers a honey tree, he has first rights; but when he has taken his share, others have a turn. In the unlikely possibility that he does not take advantage of his discovery, others will. No one owns the tree; the system is first come, first served. Therefore knowledge of the existence of food resources circulates quickly throughout the entire group.

Families move easily from one group to another, settling in any group where they have a previous kinship tie. The composition of groups is always shifting. This loose attitude toward group membership promotes the widest access to resources and, at the same time, is a leveling device that promotes social equality.

The hunter-gatherer pattern of generalized exchange, or sharing without any expectation of a direct return, also serves the ends of resource distribution and social equality. A !Kung Bushman spends as much as two-thirds of his day visiting others or receiving guests; during this time, many exchanges of gifts take place. To refuse to share—to hoard—would be morally wrong. By sharing whatever is at hand, the !Kung achieve social leveling and assure their right to share in the windfalls of others.

The cold climate adaptation

The success of the hunter-gatherer adaptation depends on small, mobile groups, favoring the widest distribution of resources with considerable leeway for unexpected hard times. If the relationships we have been discussing were systematic, that is, were they interacting in consistent ways, we would expect that the replacement or addition of variables would have profound effects. This may have happened in some areas, when the discovery of animal husbandry and agriculture made available new sources of food and power.

Figure 16-5a. *A family of the Copper Eskimo tribe moves camp at the beginning of winter. The sled on which their possessions are loaded is so heavy that both dogs and people must pull to move it.*

Figure 16-5c. *When the group moves camp during the winter, a new village must be built in their new location. Men and women of all ages work at cutting and placing the blocks of ice that form the houses.*

Figure 16-5b. *When the water is completely frozen over, the Eskimo wait by holes in the ice for seals to surface for a breath. This photo was taken just ten years ago; many Eskimos still observe their traditional ways.*

Figure 16-5d. *During the summer, a shelter is constructed of caribou hides, then in plentiful supply as a result of the hunt. The warmer temperatures of the season permit more casual construction of shelters.*

This raised the carrying capacity of the environment, permitting larger, denser populations with new systems for producing and distributing materials and energy, and this, in turn, affected social relations and culture. Some of these changes can be found even among contemporary hunter-gatherers, particularly those of the cold climate adaptation. Examples of this type of society can be seen among many Eskimo tribes; some of the food-getting adaptations of the Eskimo are depicted in Color Portfolio 4, between pages 352 and 353. The Lapps and some of the inhabitants of northern Russia also typify the cold climate adaptation.

People may have come to live in cold climates as a result of a slow but steady population increase during the Paleolithic era. Consequently, man developed a series of cold climate adaptations that increased his cultural variabilities. In the extreme latitudes, in climates similar to those first inhabited by man about seventy thousand years ago, vegetable foods are only rarely or seasonally available, and animal protein is the staff of life. Furthermore, the extra energy expended in hunting and the digestion of animal protein is a source of body heat. A greater dependence on animal foods requires a more complex tool kit, game fences, and fish traps; cold climate living requires greater complexity in clothing and shelter as well. These kinds of possessions limit a group's mobility; it can be regained only through further material advances, such as the canoe, kayak, and dog sled. Still, the cold climate hunter is less fully nomadic than his warm climate brothers; long, cold winters further restrict his mobility and keep him close to his home base.

The fear of starvation plays an ominous role in the folklore of cold climate peoples. In most cold climates, populations often shuttle between feast and famine. This was especially true of the salmon fishermen of the northwest Pacific Coast. Even in the best of years, and with good preservation technology, winter often outlasted the food supply. The norms that required sharing of food caught by any hunter helped to ensure that existing food supplies were distributed throughout the entire community.

Figure 16-6. *This husband and wife model the clothes once worn by Copper Eskimos. These summer outfits are made almost entirely from caribou hide; warmer winter clothing utilizes sealskin and fur. Clothes of this type are no longer worn by the Eskimos.*

Culture and man ● part **4**

Cold climate peoples also had to solve the problems of intensive labor organization, redistribution of scarcer and less readily available resources, and redistribution of larger populations. There had to be some mechanism for motivating individuals to perform in a complex system. Among the solutions to these problems were the development of rich material cultures, complex systems of kinship and marriage, class systems, slavery, and chieftainships. One of the most dramatic solutions was the potlatch of the northwest Indians, a ceremony of conspicuous gift-giving, where giving was an honor and receiving a shame that could be resolved only by returning an even larger gift at a subsequent potlatch. (See the original study in Chapter 20 for a detailed description of a potlatch ceremony among the Kwakiutl Indians.) The potlatch is simply an extreme version of the obligation to share found in hunter-gatherer societies. Many of the "simple" hunters and fishermen of the cold latitudes, because of the pressures of their environment, were well on their way to the kinds of complex societies that developed in warmer areas only following the introduction of agriculture and the rise of urban civilizations.

□

Original study

THE TECHNOLOGY
OF THE GUAYAKI

The Guayaki Indians are purely nomadic hunters. Consequently, their technology is strictly adapted to a roving existence, in which moving is an almost daily affair. These journeys last the greater part of the year, with certain periods involving many hours of difficult walking, even for the Indians, because of the density of the vegetation. It therefore is immediately apparent that the quantity of goods and instruments the Guayaki can use is limited by what the women can carry. All the basic goods of each family are packed into the carrying basket, the capacity of which is only slightly limited by their great physical strength. In addition, the time spent in any one encampment is always so short that it is possible to devote only a little time to the fabrication of tools. Too, the Indians are continually exposed to diverse dangers such as the approach of another presumably hostile band, and more frequently, Paraguayans with clear intentions. All of this incites the Indians to remain ready to flee as soon as the danger has been spotted. Within only a few moments the women must assemble and pack up all the goods scattered around them in order to quickly disappear into the protection of the forest. This is another reason for owning only a few things and for never completely unpacking the basket.

If the Guayaki are poorly equipped, it is because they are nomads and their technology hinges on this form of life. Even if destitute, they are no less capable than any other tribe of satisfying the needs that their lives demand. And one could even say that, devoid of agriculture and wholly dependent as a result upon natural resources, the Guayaki, by surviving under such harsh conditions, show a remarkable capacity to adapt technically to the environment.

The principal activity of the men revolves almost entirely around hunting, and each Guayaki adult owns a bow and a set of eight to fifteen arrows. The dimensions of the bows and arrows are impressive. Without a doubt, there are few bows, at least in South America, that attain or surpass their height except those of the Siriono of Bolivia. The size of the bows varies from 6 feet, 4 inches to 7 feet, 8 inches, and it is a curious sight to see these small men manipulating gigantic weapons, which are sometimes as much as 3 feet taller than they are.

The arrows are as large as the bows, from 5 feet, 8 inches to 6 feet, 8 inches. They consist of two parts: the head, which is made of very hard wood, is between 2 and 4 feet long; it is joined to a reed shaft of between 1 foot, 8 inches and 4 feet long. A small cord of nettle fibers or a binding of tiana bark holds the head in the shaft. The feathering is tangential; the feathers are simply fastened into a tight binding of bark, which is itself then glued to the reed tube with wax. The exceptional length of these arrows is understandable, in that they must be in proportion to the bow in size and also because the head, even though it is of very hard wood, breaks frequently. Each time this happens the hunter resharpens the head and its length diminishes. When the head is too short for the initial shaft, it is fitted to a longer reed to obtain an arrow about the same length as the old one, causing the head and the shaft to vary inversely to their size. The making of arrows requires such patient labor that the head is used as long as possible; an arrow that goes astray or that is shot into the high branches of a tree is always salvaged.

Each Guayaki owns an average of twelve arrows, one of which is specially

Figure 16-7. *This Guayaki tribesman poses with his machete and a spear that he is making. The iron machete was probably mass-produced in a foreign factory.*

designed for small and middle-sized birds. It consists of a reed tube into which is stuck a piece of hard wood with a large rounded point. This makes it possible for the hunter to stun birds without tearing them to shreds.

[The stone hatchet] is the only tool used by the Guayaki for felling trees. For several decades, however, the Indians have known how to use iron stolen from the Paraguayans, and they use it more and more in place of the older stone hatchet. The Guayaki are probably the last people in South America to continue to use this neolithic hatchet. They find the stone in stream beds, and the polishing gives to this "diabase" a nearly cylindrical shape. One end is made thinner to use for cutting. Actually, this hatchet is not sharp; it mostly crushes the fibers of the tree to be felled. The other end is rounded off and embedded in a hollow area of the handle, which is made from the wood of the wild orange tree. No other fastening technique exists. The theory that the Guayaki fit handles to their hatchets by driving the stone into a stock that unites itself to this rock as it grows is pure legend.

The hatchet is used to cut down pindo palm, the wood of which serves as raw material for arrows. It is also used for widening the openings of beehives, which are hidden in the hollows of trees, in order to extract honey. Curiously, the women are the ones who polish the stone and attach it to the handle, the men being satisfied with cutting and hollowing out the wood. When traveling, it is the woman who carries this heavy hatchet. And so strong is this division of the sexes in carrying obligations that the modern metal hatchets, even though used only by the men, are always carried by the women.

Source:
From "The Guayaki" by Pierre Clastres in *Hunters and Gatherers Today: A Socioeconomic Study of Eleven Such Cultures in the Twentieth Century,* Edited by M. G. Bicchieri. Copyright © 1972 by Holt, Rinehart and Winston, Inc. Reprinted by permission of Holt, Rinehart and Winston, Inc.

Summary

1.

Needs and pressures force man to alter his behavior and adjust it to suit his environment. This adjustment is part of adaptation. Adaptation has two meanings. It means that there is a moving balance between the needs of organisms and the potential of their environment. It also means the process whereby the environment changes the organism and the organism changes the environment. The unit of adaptation includes both the organism and its environment. Adaptation takes place over long periods of time. To survive, organisms must be able to adjust to new environments and respond to changes in climate or biological environment.

2.

An ecological zone in which various societies follow similar patterns of life is known as a culture area. In culture areas, societies share inventions and discoveries. The climate and topography of an ecological zone often differ from area to area. Often each climate and topography require a different technology. As a result, in a diverse ecological zone, individual societies develop different technologies. A culture considered in terms of its technology and the ways it is applied to the environment is a culture type. Social and political organization also affect the application of technology to the problems of staying alive. Those features of a culture that play a part in the society's way of making its living are called its culture core. Anthropologists can trace direct relationships between types of culture cores and types of environment.

3.

Hunter-gatherers are people who do not practice animal husbandry or agriculture. They fish, hunt, and gather wild fruits and vegetables to sustain themselves. Although there are variations in hunter-gatherer activity, the consistency of the hunter-gatherer adaptation across cultures is a strong argument for subsistence activities as a determinant of social forms. There are two key features of the hunter-gatherer adaptation: (1) they move about a great deal to accommodate their living places to naturally available food sources, and (2) their groups are small. No completely satisfactory explanation for this has been given. One explanation contends small sizes fit land capacity to sustain the groups. Another contends the less people, the less chance of social conflict. Hunting styles and equipment may also play a role in determining population size and movement; efficiency of subsistence technology permits greater population size and stability.

4.

Ancient hunter-gatherers lacked animals or mechanical means of transportation. They traveled light, restricting themselves to the barest essentials. A territory belonged to all of its groups and group members were constantly shifting. Egalitarian societies developed. It is difficult to interpret modern hunter-gatherer activity. Today's hunter-gatherer has been exposed to at least some contact with more highly technological neighbors. He has been left to his traditional way of life only in the world's marginal areas—deserts, inaccessible jungles, and frozen arctic tundra. Hunting and gathering in frozen regions has led to cold climate adaptation, whereby man's cultural variabilities increased. This adaptation features redistribution of scarcer and less readily available resources and redistribution of larger populations.

5.
Three elements of human social organization developed along with hunting. First, the division of labor. In hunter-gatherer societies, men hunted and women gathered. Second, food sharing. Hunters who hunted in teams shared what they killed. One reason an individual hunter shared what he killed was to stake a moral claim on other hunters' future kills. Third, the camp as a center of daily activity. Hunters shared their food at a camp where they also worked, slept, and socialized. These features had important consequences for the continued evolution of patterns of social organization.

Suggested readings

Bicchieri, M. G. ed. *Hunters and Gatherers Today: A Socioeconomic Study of Eleven Such Cultures in the Twentieth Century.* New York: Holt, Rinehart and Winston, 1972.
Both ecological-historical reconstruction and participant-observer ethnographies are contained in this volume. Each chapter is preceded by a short introduction pointing out the specific character and basic features of each of the studies.

Oswalt, Wendell H. *Habitat and Technology.* New York: Holt, Rinehart and Winston, 1972.
The author develops a taxonomy which permits precise cross-cultural comparisons of the complexity of manufactures. The research is based on a systematic analysis of the known manufactures of non-Western peoples. Shelters, tools, clothing, implements, and cultivated foodstuffs are considered.

Rappaport, Roy *Pigs for the Ancestors.* New Haven: Yale University Press, 1968.
This is a study of the functions of ritual among the Maring, a primitive farming people of New Guinea.

Steward, Julian *Theory of Culture Change: The Methodology of Multilinear Evolution.* Urbana: University of Illinois Press, 1972.
The author discusses concepts and methods needed to develop a general methodology for determining regularities in the interrelationships of cultural patterns and culture change among different societies. The basic theory is illustrated with examples from selected cultures (Shoshone Indians, Bushmen, etc.).

Vayda, Andrew, ed. *Environment and Cultural Behavior: Ecological Studies in Cultural Anthropology.* New York: Natural History Press, 1969.
The focus of the studies collected here is the interrelationship between cultural behavior and environmental phenomena. The writers attempt to make cultural behavior intelligible by relating it to the material world in which it develops. This volume includes articles concerning population, divination, ritual, warfare, food production, climate, and diseases.

5

The formation
of groups

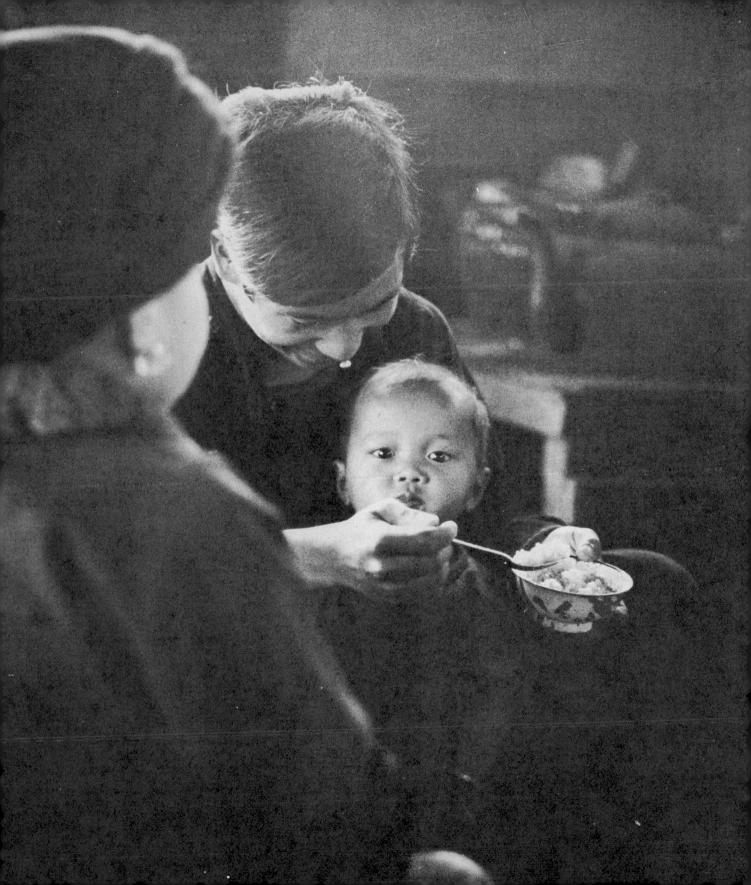

Seasons of the Eskimo

Of all the earth's regions, the Eskimos live in the harshest and most forbidding. Summers are short, cool and mosquito-plagued; winters long, dark, and cold. Yet despite the murderous climate and ever-present threat of famine, the Eskimo are gay, gregarious, good-natured, and amazingly contented. Innuit, the people, Eskimos proudly call themselves. Men, pre-eminent, the Original Men to whom earth herself gave birth.

Eskimo society in the past was one of equals. They acknowledged neither chiefs nor superiors; their language lacks the terms. The closest they can come is to call a man *ishumata*—he who thinks, a man whom others respect for his wisdom. But power he had none. What power there was lay within the community, in the rule of public opinion. The approval and esteem of other members of his group were a man's highest reward, ostracism his worst punishment.

The advent of the white man's culture destroyed the fragile fabric of this ancient way of life. Its concepts of master and servant, of material wealth as a measure of a man's worth, subordinated one man's wishes to another man's will and thus were alien and mystifying to the Eskimo mind. And as the Eskimo settled in permanent communities and adopted the white man's life, they lost touch with the cycle of the seasons. Their children no longer learn the lore of hunting and the ice and even sometimes do not learn their grandparents' language. In some smaller communities, however, the hunting-trapping life of the camps persists according to the

Winter camp in drifting snow.

Hunter wears slit-type bone goggles to protect his eyes from the intense glare of spring ice and snow.

Igloo for the night, built during a hunting trip.

Hunters with polar bear.

A hunter readies his harpoon; he has killed two seals already.

Eskimos gaff halibut that have floated up into a lead—a break in the thawing spring ice.

Hunter in a kayak.

Grandmother.

Drying caribou sinew; later it will be slit and used as thread to sew fur clothing.

Hanging split char (fish) to dry for preservation.

Women sew the sealskin cover onto a kayak frame.

Summer migration across the tundra with pack dogs.

immutable rules of old: to take from each season what each
season brings; to share your food with all members of the
group, as they will share theirs with you; to rise to
superhuman efforts when the hunt requires it, and to live
in quiet harmony with yourself and others when bad weather
imprisons you in your tent; to do as you like and let others
do as they like.

One of the last and largest camp areas in Canada,
(pictured on the preceding pages) is Bathhurst Inlet in the
Central Arctic, inhabited by fewer than ninety people living
in eleven widely scattered camps. In winter they hunt seal
at the breathing holes and fish through the ice. In spring,
the caribou come from the taiga in the south across the
vastness of the tundra to the Arctic shores. In summer, the
men fish; in fall, the seals are fat and float when shot, the
new clove-brown fur of the caribou is short and strong, ideal
for winter clothes, and the animals are heavy after
pasturing all summer on the Arctic meadows. Fat char ascend
the rivers and ground squirrels, ready for their eight month
winter sleep, look like plump, furred sausages with feet. It
is the time to collect meat and fish for the dark,
lean months of winter ahead.

Camp life is hard. It is an unpredictable life. One
year spring comes, but the caribou do not. The people travel
far, work hard, and find nothing. They may have to trap ground
squirrels to subsist. The dogs become weak; traveling is
curtailed. Another year, large numbers of caribou stay near
the camps all year, seals are plentiful, life is relatively
easy. To endure and succeed in such a life, a hunter must
be resourceful and hardy, he must have faith in himself, a
lot of optimism, a certain fatalism, and the ability to
live each day and enjoy the good it brings and not spoil
it with worry about the morrow. In the words of an Eskimo
song:
And yet, there is only
One great thing,
The only thing:
To live;
To see in huts and on journeys
The great day that dawns,
And the light that fills the world.

Photographs by Fred Breummer
Text adapted from "Seasons of the Eskimo" by Fred Breummer

Marriage and
the family

The family, regarded as an immutable social institution in American life, has surfaced as a matter for controversy and discussion. The women's movement, the new sexual freedom, and the soaring divorce and delinquency rates have raised questions about the functions of the American family and its ability to survive in a period of rapid social change. Evidence of the widespread interest in these questions can be seen in the popularity of books like *Open Marriage*, and television documentaries like *An American Family*.

Does the American family, as presently constituted, offer the best environment for bringing up children? Does it impose an inferior status on the woman, confined and isolated in the home, performing household and child-raising chores? Does the man, locked into an authoritarian role, suffer unduly in his personal development from bearing the sole responsibility of supporting the family? Are there adequate substitutes for people who have no family to care for them, such as old people and orphans? If the modern American family is found wanting, what are the alternatives?

Historical and cross-cultural studies of the family offer as many different family patterns as the fertile imagination of man can invent. These different family patterns are not just interesting products of human inventiveness; they are solutions to the different sorts of problems with which people must cope. Different family forms, at the same time, themselves present certain sets of problems which somehow must be dealt with. How men and women in other societies live together in families can be studied, not as bizarre and exotic forms of human behavior, but as evidence of the adaptive potential of culture.

Functions of the family

There is some disagreement among anthropologists as to the functions of the family unit, but all agree that the family in one form or another can be found in every known society. Our own notions of family are closely identified with marriage and romantic love. Thus we might conclude that the major function of the family is to control sexual behavior, limiting sexual access within the confines of the roles of husband and wife. Although this regulation is indeed one of the family's functions, it is safe to say that in human society the basic function of a family is the nurturance of children, which ensures the survival of society.

Nurturance of children

Primate babies are born helpless, and they remain dependent upon their parents for a longer time than any other animals. This dependence is not only for food and physical care but, as the studies of both Rhesus monkeys and human babies have revealed, for the physical nearness and response the mother provides.[1] Psychologist Harry Harlow separated baby Rhesus monkeys from their natural mothers and raised them with surrogate mothers—dummies made of wire or cloth. The baby monkeys preferred the soft dummies to the wire ones, whether or not the cloth ones were fitted out with baby bottles of milk—indicating the need for soft contact. More revealing, however, was the finding that monkeys who were nurtured only by surrogate mothers became emotionally disturbed; they were unable to interact with normally raised monkeys, cowered in a corner of the cage, and were unable to have sexual relations. After six months, this behavior became irreversible.

Another study, done in the early 1930s by Rene Spitz, compared four groups of human babies.[2] The study found that babies raised with parental affection were relatively healthy and hardy, even without any medical care. The babies raised in a clean, medically supervised orphan asylum were the most likely to sicken and die. These babies not only experienced the barest of human contact and interaction after they were weaned from the wet nurse, but there was nothing for them to look at but the ceiling, due to the arrangement of blankets hung on the sides of the cribs. Spitz concluded that human babies must have human contact and response, as well as some stimulation from the environment, for bare survival.

From such evidence it is apparent that children do not just "grow like Topsy" but that the care of at least a mother is essential to their growth. However, for the human infant, a mother alone

[1]Harry F. Harlow, "Social Deprivation in Monkeys," *Scientific American*, 206 (November, 1962), 1–10.
[2]Rene A. Spitz, "Hospitalism," in *The Psychoanalytic Study of the Child* (New York: International Universities Press), Vol. I (1945), pp. 53–72.

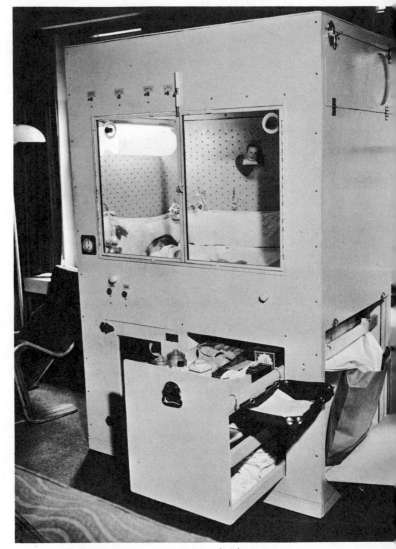

Figure 17-1. *These pictures implicitly contrast two different attitudes toward the raising of children. The photo on the left shows an American baby in a Skinner box, named after its designer, the famed behavioral psychologist B.F. Skinner. It is a mechanically controlled environment that keeps temperature and humidity constant in a sterile atmosphere. At right is a group of men on a New Guinea island; it is their responsibility to raise all male children.*

The formation of groups ● part **5**

is not sufficient. This is because, in all known societies, adult male and adult female roles differ to some degree, due to sexual division of labor. In order to function properly as an adult, a child needs to be closely associated with an adult of the same sex to serve as a model for the proper adult role. Moreover, the social division of labor common to all societies means that the presence of both adult males and females is necessary for the economic maintenance of the child-rearing unit.

The family is an effective grouping for the purposes of child-rearing. It provides for a close mother-child relationship, as well as for the presence of an adult male. This is not to say, however, that the family is the only unit capable of providing these conditions. Theoretically, other arrangements might be possible. For example, groups of children might be raised by paired teams of trained male and female specialists: the Israeli kibbutz was a step in the direction of such an arrangement. So the child-rearing function alone cannot account for the universality of the human family, even though the function itself is universal. Obviously, other factors must be involved.

Control of sexual relations

Another problem faced by all human societies is the constant sexual receptivity of the human female. In this, the human female goes the other primates one better. Although frequent receptivity is characteristic of all female primates, only the human female is continually receptive. On the basis of clues from the behavior of other primates, anthropologists have speculated about the nature of the evolutionary advantage this trait might have. Among the species of primates most closely related to man, sexual activity seems to reinforce social bonds, which themselves seem based on individual likes and dislikes. If indeed sexual activity helps to tie together a group of individuals of different sexes and ages, it seems possible that as the social life of early hominids became more crucial to survival, a selective advantage was enjoyed by those groups with the strongest cohesion. To the extent that constant sexuality reinforced this, natural selection worked to favor this attribute in females.

At the same time that sexual activity can reinforce group ties, it can also be disruptive. This is due to the basic primate characteristic of male dominance. It is based on the fact that, on the average, males are bigger and more muscular than females, although this differentiation is less noticeable in modern *Homo sapiens* than it probably was in the earliest hominids. Because of the males' larger size, they tend to dominate females when the latter are at the height of their sexuality; this trait can be seen among baboons, gorillas, and, to a lesser extent, chimpanzees. With the continual sexual receptiveness of early hominid females, the dominant males may have attempted to monopolize the females; an added inducement could have been the prowess of the female at food gathering. Such a tendency would introduce a competitive, combative element into hominid groupings. The establishment of the family unit to regulate sexual access would counteract this potentially disruptive force and help to provide the harmonious social relationships on which human survival depends.

Rules of sexual access. We find that everywhere societies have behavioral norms controlling sexual relations. In our society, many people marry to insure a partner for sexual relations, since marriage in America is a form of contract whereby a person establishes a continuing claim to the right of sexual access to another person. But marriage is not a prerequisite to family life; there can be families which are not established through marriage, as, for example, among the Nayars of India.

Actually, the United States is among a very small minority—about 5 percent—of all known societies whose formal codes of behavior prohibit any sexual involvement outside of marriage.[3] Among the Kaingang, a very small society of 109 people living on a reservation in the high jungles of Brazil, studied by Jules Henry in 1932, there was a bare minimum of restriction placed on sexual activity or physical contact between members of the community. "Brothers and sisters, brothers- and sisters-in-law and cousins, sleep next to one another. . . . Marriages and love affairs (exist) among all classes of relatives. . . ."[4] In the traditional culture of the Eskimos, the sexual favors of the wife are offered to a visitor as a means of expressing hospitality and, in fact, a rejection of this offer is considered insulting. Despite these exceptions, the family plays an important role in providing a means of satisfying sexual drives that otherwise might be socially disruptive.

[3] F. Ivan Nye and Felix M. Berardo, *The Family: Its Structure and Interaction* (New York: The Macmillan Company, 1973) p. 173.

[4] Jules Henry, *Jungle People* (Locust Valley, N.Y.: J. J. Augustin, Inc., 1941).

Figure 17-2. *A wood engraving from a newspaper of the 1870s shows a community of Shakers dancing; some suggest it was a way to release sexual energies.*

The incest taboo. All societies at all times in history have formulated a rule, called the **incest taboo,** that prohibits sexual relations between members of the same family. The rule's universality has fascinated anthropologists and other students of human behavior. In all known societies, sexual relations are prohibited between parent and child and (with only a few very specific exceptions) between siblings as well. It has become a matter of serious import for social anthropologists to explain why incest should always be regarded with such horror and loathing.

Many explanations have been given. The simplest and least satisfactory is based on "human nature"—that is, some instinctive horror of incest.

It is also said that human beings raised together have less sexual attraction for one another, but this argument really substitutes the result for the cause. The incest taboo ensures that children and their parents, who are constantly in intimate contact, avoid regarding one another as sexual objects.

Early students of genetics thought that the incest taboo precluded the deleterious effects of inbreeding. This theory has been abandoned to a great extent because, as with domestic animals, inbreeding can increase desired characteristics as well as deleterious ones. Sigmund Freud accounted for the incest taboo in his psychoanalytic theory of the unconscious. The son desires the mother, creating a rivalry with the father. (Freud called this the Oedipus complex.) He must suppress these feelings or earn the wrath of the father, who is far more powerful than he. The attraction of the daughter to the father, or the Electra complex, places her in rivalry with her mother. Freud's theory can be viewed as an elaboration of the reasons for a deep-seated aversion to sexual relations within the family.

A truly convincing explanation of the incest taboo has yet to be advanced. Some biologists believe that it may be due to an instinctual preference for a genetically different mate. Such an instinct has been demonstrated among other animals—the fruit fly, for example—and would have an obvious adaptive value in maintaining a high level of phenotypic diversity within a population. Another recent theory focuses on the protection of the young. Some psychologists endorse the belief that young children can be emotionally scarred by sexual experiences, which they may have interpreted as violent and frightening acts of aggression. The incest taboo thus protects children against sexual advances by older members of the family. A closely related theory is that the incest taboo helps prevent girls who are socially and emotionally too young for motherhood from becoming pregnant.

Endogamy and exogamy. Another way to explain the value of the incest taboo is to examine its effects on social structure. Closely related to the prohibitions against incest are the rules against **endogamy,** or marriage within a group of related individuals. If the group is defined as just one immediate family, then all societies prohibit endogamy and practice **exogamy,** or marriage outside the group. However, if the family group is enlarged to include more members—second and third cousins, for example—then we find that endogamy may be a common practice. For example, Scottish Highlanders traditionally married within the network of alliances of the family clan, strengthening its political and economic position.

Sir Edward Tylor, in fact, advanced the proposition that alternatives to inbreeding were either

Figure 17-3. A woman of the Big Namba tribe is making a new wig by sewing together strips of leaves from the pandanus, or breadfruit tree; she wears an older model of the same type of wig. The sole function of this hairpiece relates to a taboo against incest. Whenever a woman meets one of her brothers-in-law, she must immediately adjust the wig to cover her face, thus preventing these relatives of her husband from taking any sexual interest in her.

"marrying out or being killed."[5] Our ancestors, he suggested, discovered the advantage of inter-marriage to create bonds of friendship. Claude Lévi-Strauss elaborated on this premise. He made exogamy the basis of a distinction between early hominid life in isolated family groups and the life of *Homo sapiens* in a supportive society with an accumulating culture. The bonds with other groups, established and strengthened by marriage ties, make possible a sharing of culture.

In a roundabout way, exogamy also helps to explain the two exceptions to the incest taboo, that of brother and sister marriage within the royal family of ancient Egyptians, Incans, and Hawaiians. Members of such royal families were considered semidivine and their very sacredness usually kept them from marrying mere mortals. The brother and sister married to keep intact the godliness and purity of the royal line.[6]

Choice of mate

The institution of the family, and the rules that surround it, also regulate individual choice of a mate so as to promote and increase the social stability of the entire group. The American egal-itarian ideal that an individual should be free to marry whomever he or she chooses is an unusual arrangement, certainly not one that is universally embraced. Among the Arapesh, as described by Margaret Mead in *Sex and Temperament,* the father chooses his son's wife, who must be from another clan. Her brothers and her male cousins, who will be his son's brothers-in-law and his grandchildren's maternal uncles, must be "good hunters, successful gardeners, slow to anger, and wise in making decisions."[7] Rather than a neces-sary evil, the Arapesh regard marriage primarily as an opportunity to increase the warm family

circle within which one's descendants may then live.

In Gopalpur, a small village in southern India, marriage to any person related through the pa-ternal line is regarded as incest.[8] Marriage to relatives of a sister or a mother is looked for. Brides are usually brought in from another village and must be in the same caste.

The levirate and the sororate. If a husband dies, leaving a wife and children, it is often the custom that the wife marry one of the brothers of the dead man. This custom, called the **levirate,** not only provides social security for the widow and her children but also is a way for the hus-band's family to maintain their rights over her sexuality and her future children: it acts to pre-serve the bonds established. When a man marries the sister of his dead wife, it is called the **soro-rate.** In societies that have the levirate and soro-rate, the relationship between the two families is maintained ever after the death of a spouse; in essence, the family supplies another spouse to take the place of the member who died.

Monogamy and polygyny. Monogamy, or the taking of a single spouse, is the form of marriage with which we are most familiar. It is also the most common, primarily for economic rather than moral reasons. A man must be fairly wealthy to be able to afford polygyny, or marriage to more than one wife. Among the Gusii of Western Kenya,[9] four wives was the ideal; such an ideal was actually realized only by some of the older men. Wives were desirable because they worked in the fields and increased a man's wealth, but young men could not afford to purchase more than one wife. In our country, the rich Mormons practiced polygyny; they were hounded from state to state until they finally gave up the cus-tom, so repugnant was it to our moral code.

Polyandry, the custom of a woman having sev-

---

[5] Quoted in Roger M. Keesing and Felix M. Keesing, *New Per-spectives in Cultural Anthropology* (New York: Holt, Rinehart and Winston, 1971) p. 183.

[6] *Ibid.,* p. 182.

[7] Margaret Mead, *Sex and Temperament in Three Primitive So-cieties,* 3rd ed. (New York: William Morrow, 1963) p. 67.

[8] Alan R. Beals, *Gopalpur: a South Indian Village* (New York: Holt, Rinehart and Winston, 1972) p. 25.
[9] Wendell H. Oswalt, *Other Peoples, Other Customs* (New York: Holt, Rinehart and Winston, 1972) p. 120.

eral husbands, is far less common, because man's life expectancy is shorter and male infant mortality is high. Group marriage, in which several men and women have sexual access to one another, also occurs in very rare cases. Even in communal groups today, among young people seeking alternatives to modern marriage forms, group marriage seems to be a transitory phenomenon, despite the publicity it has been receiving.

Economic and political function of the family

In many societies, economic considerations are often the strongest motivation to marry. A man of New Guinea does not marry because of sexual needs, which he can readily satisfy out of wedlock, but because he needs a woman to make pots and cook his meals, to fabricate nets and weed his plantings.[10] A man without a wife among the Australian aborigines is in an unsatisfactory position since he has no one to supply him regularly with food or fire-wood. In all societies, the smallest economic unit is the family.[11]

In societies where the family is the most powerful institution exercising social control over individuals, marriages are arranged for the economic and political advantage of the family unit, as for example in feudal Europe, traditional China and India, and until most recent times, in Japan. The marriage of two individuals who must spend their whole lives together and raise their children together is only incidental to the serious matter of making allies of two families by means of the marriage bond. Marriage involves a transfer of rights between families, including rights to property and rights over the children, as well as sexual rights.

In many societies, marriage and the establishment of a family are considered far too important

[10] Robert Lowie, cited by Leslie White, *The Science of Culture: a Study of Man and Civilization* (Garden City, N.Y.: Doubleday, 1969)
[11] Charles W. Hart and Arnold R. Pilling, *Tiwi of North Australia* (New York: Holt, Rinehart and Winston, Inc., 1960)

362

Figure 17-4a-d. *Polygyny is quite common in many parts of the world. The photo at the upper right shows a Bakhtiari tribesman with his three wives and many children; the Bakhtiari are unusual in this part of the world because the women go unveiled. The other photos are of various African tribes.*

to be left to the whims of children. The function of marriage in such cases is often economic in nature and, for wealthy and powerful families, political. In our own upper class, the children of powerful families are segregated in private schools and carefully steered toward a "proper" marriage. A careful reading of announced engagements in the society pages of *The New York Times* provides clear evidence of such family alliances.

The family strengthens the bonds of an individual to a society. The web of relationships and the social control that is exerted by families over the individual is an important force in integrating a society and making it cohesive. The problems of child-rearing, the regulation of sex, the need for cooperation between the sexes, the formation of political and economic alliances, need not all be performed by the same institution. But they are interrelated functions. Child-rearing follows from sexual activity, and it requires cooperation between man and woman, who cooperate in other ways as well. At the same time that economic cooperation takes place between adult men and women, it also takes place between adults and children, as well as between larger bands of adults who form an extended family group. A reasonable and logical approach to this network of social needs is to deal with them together in the context of the family, and that is the way that most societies function.

Form of the family

Perhaps it would be useful at this juncture to define a family. Raymond Firth says a family is regarded as being incomplete unless the three elements—father, mother, child—are present.[12] Ashley Montagu adds that the union among them must be more or less permanent.[13] But most anthropologists define the family as a group com-

[12] Raymond Firth, *Human Types: an Introduction to Social Anthropology* (New York: The New American Library, Inc., 1958) p. 88.
[13] Ashley Montagu, M. F. A. (Ed.), *Culture: Man's Adaptive Dimension* (New York: Oxford University Press, 1968).

Figure 17-5. *The political and economic significance of marriage bonds is demonstrated by this picture taken at the wedding of Princess (now Queen) Elizabeth of England and Prince Philip of Greece.*

posed of a woman and her children and at least one adult male annexed through marriage or blood relationship. The American family is a conjugal one, formed on the basis of marital ties between a husband and a wife. The basic unit of mother, father, and dependent children is referred to as the **nuclear family;** other forms of conjugal families are polygamous and polyandrous families, which may be thought of as aggregates of nuclear families with one spouse in common.

An alternative of the conjugal family is the consanguine family, which consists of women and their brothers, and the dependent offspring of the women. In such societies, men and women get married, but do not live together as husbands and mates. Rather, they spend their lives in the households in which they grew up, with the men "commuting" for sexual activity with their wives. Consanguine families are rare; the classic case is that of the Nayar peoples of India.

The nuclear family

In our society, the nuclear family has become the ideal. It is not considered desirable for young people to live with their parents beyond a certain age, nor is it considered a moral responsibility for a couple to take their aged parents into their home when the old people are no longer able to care for themselves. Additional family members are no longer an economic asset but an expense.

The nuclear family as the sole family form is also found in societies that live in harsh environments, such as the Eskimos. The Eskimo mother and father each have their work to do. In the winter, these little families roam the vast arctic wilderness in search of food. The father hunts and makes shelters. The mother cooks, is responsible for the children, and makes and keeps the clothing in good repair. One of her chores is to chew her husband's boots to soften the leather for the next day, so that he can resume his search for game. The wife and her children could not survive without the husband, and life for a man is unimaginable without a wife. The Bushmen of the Kalahari Desert and the aborigines of the inhospitable Australian desert also have nuclear families.

Certain parallels can be drawn between the contemporary nuclear family in industrial societies and families living on the bare edge of survival. In both cases, the family is an independent unit that must fend for itself; this creates a strong dependence of individual members on one another. There is little help from outside in the event of emergencies or catastrophes. When their usefulness is at an end, the elderly are cared for only if it is feasible. In the event of death of the mother or father, life becomes precarious for the child. Yet this form of family is well adapted to a life that requires a high degree of mobility. For the Eskimo, this mobility permits the hunt for food; for Americans, it is probably the hunt for jobs and improved social status that requires a mobile form of family unit.

The extended family

The small nuclear family of industrialized societies was evolved from the larger extended farm family, a combination of conjugal and consanguineous families, which might include grandparents, mother and father, unmarried brothers and sisters, perhaps a spinster aunt, and a stray cousin or two. All these people, related by various ties of blood or marriage, lived and worked together.

Horace Miner described such families in his study of French Catholics on the St. Lawrence River in Quebec, Canada, where a unified family effort is necessary and a large family is essential to work the farms.[14] Children and unattached adults were an asset on the farm. The older children left to work their own farms or to find employment in the city and were usually assisted by

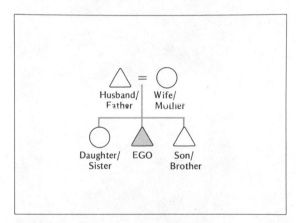

Figure 17-6. *Anthropologists use diagrams of this sort to illustrate the relationships formed through marriage. The diagram always begins with a hypothetical individual, called Ego, and then demonstrates the kinship and marital ties in his immediate family. This particular diagram shows the relationships in a nuclear family such as is found in our own society. Only two generations are represented, but all possible relationships between the various individuals can be determined from the diagram.*

---

[14] Horace Miner, *St. Denis: A French Canadian Parish* (Chicago: The University of Chicago Press, 1939).

a conjugal relationship is one that pertains to the husband and wife here).

the family until they were established. The land was capable of supporting a limited number of people, and even after the sons and daughters moved out of the immediate household, the relationship remained very strong.

The Tanala of Madagascar also formed extended families.[15] When the sons grew up and married,

[15] E. Adamson Hoebel, *Anthropology: The Study of Man* (New York: McGraw-Hill, 1966) p. 434.

they brought their wives to live in houses close to the parental home. The head of the family was the father, who made the important decisions concerning the agricultural activities of the family. If the sons worked on the outside, they gave their earnings to the father for the purchase of new cattle or for other family needs. The family worked together as a group and dealt with outsiders as a single unit.

Figure 17-6a. *A variant on the simple nuclear family is the extended family. All the members of this Kentucky family are descended from the couple at the back of the photo.*

The formation of groups ● part **5**

Extended families living together in a single household were the most important social unit among the Zuni Pueblo Indians of New Mexico.[16] Usually, the head of the household was an old woman; her married daughters, their husbands, and their children lived with her. The women of the household owned the land, but it was tilled by the men (usually their husbands). When extra help was needed during the harvest, for example, other male relatives, or friends, or persons designated by local religious organizations, formed work groups and turned the hard work into a party. The women performed household tasks, such as the making of pottery, together.

A different form of the extended family was practiced by the Chukchi people of northeastern Siberia, who lived by herding reindeer.[17] The family consisted of perhaps ten couples of about the same age. The group was formed by the males, who were not related by blood, and lived in separate camps. The marriages of the group were ritualized in a ceremony in which a reindeer was killed, and the males were annointed with the blood. The relationship among the males in the group was stronger than that of true blood relatives. The men of such a family were called "companions in wives" and protected each other in time of need. The wives did not rotate, but were offered to a companion if he was visiting. Occasionally, men might exchange wives. Sharing of women created a strong bond.

It is interesting to note that a form of extended family arrangement is currently being experimented with by young people today who have found the nuclear family inadequate for their needs. Their families are groups of nuclear families who own property in common and live together; hence, it is a form of the extended family. It is further noteworthy that the life-style of these modern families often emphasizes the kind of cooperative family ties to be found in the rural American extended family of old, where this family pattern provided a manpower pool for the many tasks required for economic survival.

[16]Oswalt, op. cit., p. 294.
[17]Ibid., p. 167.

Residence patterns. Where some form of conjugal or extended family is the norm, incest taboos require that at least the husband or wife must move to a new household upon marriage. There are four common patterns of residence that a newly married couple may adopt:

(1) A woman may live with her husband and his father. This is called **patrilocal** residence.
(2) A man may live with his wife and her mother. This is called **matrilocal** residence.
(3) A married couple may have the choice of living with the relatives of the husband or those of the wife. This arrangement is called **ambilocal** residence.
(4) A married couple may form a household in an independent location. This arrangement is referred to as **neolocal** residence.

Why do different societies practice different patterns of residence? The form of residence seems to be closely related to the nature of the economy.[18] Murdock proposed a direct correlation: matrilocal residence occurs where cooperation among women is crucial for subsistence; patrilocal residence occurs where men are the center of subsistence; and neolocal residence occurs where isolation of the nuclear family alone is emphasized. Ambilocality, on the other hand, allows for greater fluidity of social grouping, so that a population can move about in a way which optimizes the availability of resources and labor. The example of the !Kung Bushmen illustrates the way in which a hunting and gathering group can adjust itself to fluctuating resources.[19] The Bushmen typically live in one place for a few days until they have exhausted all available food resources. They then move as separate family units into camps where relatives with more abundant food resources are to be found. Ambilocality greatly enhances the Bushmen's opportunity to find food. For a people of low population density, ambilocality can be a crucial factor for survival.

[18]George P. Murdock, *Social Structure* (New York: The Macmillan Company, 1949).
[19]Lorna Marshall, "Sharing, Talking and Giving: Relief of Social Tensions among !Kung Bushman," *Africa*, Vol. 31 (1961).

By studying the differences between matrilocal and patrilocal societies, anthropologists have acquired further insight into the reasons that societies display the various patterns of residence. In patrilocal societies, both authority and lines of descent are centered on the male; consequently, males are responsible for and have authority in the communities within which they reside. In matrilocal societies, on the other hand, males retain the authority, but lines of descent are traced through the female. Thus, males live in the community of their mothers and sisters. Because they hold positions of responsibility in the community in which they are born, males cannot move too far away from their maternal communities. Furthermore, warfare is inconvenient in a matrilocal society. The question of residence involves not only economic factors but

Figure 17-7. *Some young Americans have attempted to recreate the extended family with an artificial family in a commune.*

The formation of groups ● part **5**

factors of social cohesion as well. The nuclear family's residence is determined largely by the best interests of society.

Serial marriage

Perhaps the most exotic and bizarre of marriage forms is our own serial marriage. In this form, the man or the woman either marries or lives with a series of partners. The term was used in the recent past by sociologists and anthropologists to describe the marital patterns of West Indians and lower class urban blacks. These black societies were matriarchal. A series of men fathered the children, who remained with the mother. An adult man's loyalties might be to his mother rather than his present wife, and he, too, might bring his children to his mother to care for. Usually, the grandmother was the head of the household (which amounted to a consanguine family); it was she who cared for all the children, while the daughters worked to support the whole group.

Middle class Americans have taken up a variant of this pattern. The children, born out of a series of marriages, remain with the mother. In a society such as ours, in which a major value is the well-being and happiness of the individual, divorce may not necessarily signal social disorganization, but, instead, a liberating of the individual. Serial marriage may be evolving as an alternative to the extreme form of the nuclear family as it exists in the United States.

Divorce

As with marriage, divorce in non-Western societies is a matter of great concern to the families of the couple. Since marriage is primarily not a religious but an economic matter, divorce arrangements can be made for a variety of reasons and with varying degrees of difficulty.

Among the Gusii of Kenya, sterility or impotence were grounds for a divorce. Among the Chenchu of Hyderabad and the Caribou Indians of Canada, divorce was discouraged after children were born, and a couple was usually urged by their families to adjust their differences. A Zuni woman might divorce her husband by placing his belongings outside the door to indicate he was no longer welcome in the household. Divorce was relatively common among the Yahgan, who lived at the southernmost tip of South America, and was considered justified if the husband was considered cruel or failed as a provider.

Divorce in these societies seems familiar and even sensible, considered in the light of our own entangled arrangements. In one way or another, the children are taken care of. An adult unmarried woman is almost unheard of in most non-Western societies; a divorced woman will soon remarry.

Sex roles

Margaret Mead was the first anthropologist to study sex roles in non-Western societies with the purpose of showing that the work, norms, and behavior of men and women is learned, not inherited, and varies from group to group. Other social scientists who have studied the personality and temperament of men and women tend to make the common characterization of women as nurturing, supportive, emotionally dependent, passive, and more verbal; whereas men are depicted as being dominant, competitive, positively sexed, innovative, and stronger. Mead wondered whether such stereotypes were universal.

Dr. Mead studied three tribes in New Guinea: the Arapesh, the Mundugumor, and the Tchambuli. She found the Arapesh men and women were trained to be "cooperative, unaggressive, responsive to the needs and demands of others."[20] Sex was not a powerful driving force for either men or women. The Mundugumor were totally unlike the Arapesh. Both men and women developed as "ruthless, aggressive, positively sexed . . . with the maternal cherishing aspects of the

---

[20] Margaret Mead, op. cit.

personality at a minimum." In the third tribe, the Tchambuli, she found a genuine reversal of the sex attitudes of our own culture. The woman was a "dominant, impersonal, managing partner," and the man the "less responsible and emotionally dependent" person.

Having carefully observed the different patterns of child-rearing in each of these societies, Dr. Mead concluded that "many, if not all, of the personality traits which we have called masculine or feminine are as lightly linked to sex as are the clothing, the manners, and the form of head-dress that a society at a given period assigns to either

sex." This statement still strikes many ears as a radical assertion.

Dr. Mead was interested in the cross-cultural variation in personality and temperament as related to the assigned sex roles. Sex roles are also closely linked to the work that is performed in a society. Men and women perform complementary economic roles within the family unit. There are few tasks which virtually every society assigns to only men or women, as there is a great deal of overlap for most jobs. What is defined as a woman's job in one society may well be classified as a man's job in another. Jo Freeman points

Figure 17-8. *The concept of "women's work" varies from society to society. At left is an Englishwoman at work in a munitions factory; at right is an Ivory Coast woman pounding millet in a wooden mortar.*

The formation of groups ● part **5**

out that in societies in which great physical strength was necessary for survival—where hunting and warfare played an important role—the male, as physically stronger, tended to dominate.[21] But even after the necessity for male strength ceases, the superiority of the male becomes incorporated into the value structure of the society, and maleness continues to confer a higher personal status than does femaleness.

It has been suggested that in modern societies as well the tasks which are assigned to males are defined as more honorific. If so, this would suggest that a division of labor based on sex in a family or society comes close to racial or caste distinction. The low ranking class, or sex, is kept from doing certain types of prestigious work. The corollary to this is that jobs that women do automatically are ranked as less important. But the sexual division of labor, of course, is an ancient primate trait; it remains to be seen whether there is any adaptive value in cultural regulations that attempt to counteract this trait.

☐

---

[21] Jo Freeman, "Growing up Girlish," *Transaction*, Vol. 8 (Nov./ Dec. 1970).

The Nambikwara have few children; childless couples are not uncommon, though one or two children constitute the norm, and it is quite exceptional for there to be more than three in one family. Sexual relations between parents are forbidden while their child remains unweaned: often, that is to say, until it is three years old. The mother carries her child astraddle on her thigh, and keeps it in place with a broad shoulder-strap of cotton or bark; as she also has to carry a large basket on her back, one child is clearly her maximum load. Living, as they do, a nomadic life in a very poor environment, the natives have to be very careful; and the women do not hesitate to resort to abortion of one kind or another—medicinal plants, or some mechanical device—in case of need.

They both feel and show, none the less, the liveliest affection for their children; and this affection is returned. Sometimes, however, this is masked by extreme nervousness; instability takes its toll. A little boy, for instance, is suffering from indigestion; between headache and vomiting he spends half his time groaning aloud and the other half in sleep. Nobody pays the slightest attention to him and he is left completely alone all day. But when evening comes his mother comes across to him, tenderly picks off all his lice as he falls asleep, signs to the others not to come near, and makes for him a kind of cradle with her arms.

Or, it may be, a young mother is playing with her baby. Playfully she gives him slap after little slap on the back; he loves it, and to make him laugh the louder she slaps harder and harder till he bursts into tears; then she stops and consoles him. . . .

When they are crossed, children often hit out at their mother, and their mother does nothing to stop it. The children are not punished, and I never saw one of them beaten—not even in pantomime—except by way of a tease. Sometimes a child cries because he's hurt himself, because he's hungry, because he's had a quarrel, or because he doesn't want to have his fleas picked off—but this last is rare: delousing seems to be as much fun for the patient as for the operator, and it is prized as a mark of interest and affection. A child—or husband—who feels in need of it will lay his head on the woman's knees, offering first one side and then the other. She will then part his hair, ridge by ridge, and peer through. A louse, once caught, is instantly eaten. Any child who cries during the proceedings is consoled by an older child or a member of his family.

And so there's a delightful gaiety in the spectacle of a mother with her child. Sometimes she dangles an object in front of him through the straw walls of their hut and whips it away just as he reaches out for it: "There—you missed it! Grab it at the front—or the back!" Or else she takes up the child and with great shouts of laughter threatens to throw him down to the ground. . . .

There's something correspondingly uneasy and exacting about the loving kindness with which the children surround their mother. They want to be quite sure that she gets her fair share of the spoils of the hunt. The child has lived very close to its mother. When they move camp she carries the child until it can walk; later, it hurries along at her side. It stays with her in their camp, or

Figure 17-9. *Young girls early learn the tasks that are allotted to their sex.*

their village, while its father goes hunting. Eventually, however, certain distinctions of sex may be remarked. A father is more interested in his son than in his daughter, because his son has to be taught the techniques of manhood; and the same is true of mother and daughter. But the relations between father and children are marked by tenderness and solicitude; a father will take his child for a walk on his shoulder and carve for him weapons appropriate to his tiny arm.

It's also the father's duty to tell his children the traditional legends of the tribe—transposing them down, of course, in terms acceptable to the infant mind: "Everyone was dead! No one left! Not one man! Nothing!" Thus begins the South American children's version of the Flood in which all humanity was once engulfed.

In cases of polygamy a special relationship exists between the children of the first union and their youthful stepmothers: a free-and-easy comradeship which is extended to all the other girls in the group. . . .

Another special relationship exists between those children whose degree of cousinage is such that they are allowed to call one another "Husband" and "Wife." Sometimes they behave like a real married couple and, at nightfall, they leave the family circle, take a few warm logs into a corner of the camp, and light a fire. After which they "set up house" and demonstrate their affections, in so far as they can, just as their elders do; the grown-ups glance their way in amusement.

Source:
Claude Lévi-Strauss, *Tristes Tropiques.* Newly translated by John and Doreen Weightman. Translated from the French *Tristes Tropiques* © 1955 by Librairie Plon. English translation © 1973 by Jonathan Cape Limited. Reprinted by permission of Atheneum Publishers, New York.

Summary

1.

There is considerable disagreement among anthropologists as to the functions of the family. One of its functions is to control sexual behavior. But it is fairly safe to say that the most basic function of the family is the nurturance of children to ensure the survival of the society. Studies of primate and human babies have revealed that a baby's physical nearness to his mother and constant affection and interaction with her are essential for his normal emotional development. Lack of human contact and response and some stimulation from the environment may lead to a baby's death. Parental care is essential for a baby's development.

2.

Everywhere societies have behavioral norms controlling sexual relations. In our society, many people marry to ensure a partner for sexual relations. By definition, marriage is a form of contract whereby a person establishes a claim to the right of sexual access with another person. But marriage is not a prerequisite to family life; there can be families without marriage, as among the Nayars of India.

3.

In most non-Western societies, economic considerations strongly motivate an individual to marry. The family arranges marriages in societies in which it is the most powerful social institution. Marriage serves to bind two families as allies. The family serves to supply a society with new members, ensuring its survival.

4.

In all known societies, sexual relations are prohibited between parent and child and usually between brother and sister. No one has advanced a convincing explanation of the incest taboo. Endogamy is marriage within a group of related individuals; exogamy is marriage outside the group. If the group is limited to the immediate family, all societies can be said to practice exogamy. The arrangement whereby an individual chooses his marriage partner is rare. The levirate provides that a widow marry her husband's brother; the sororate provides that a widower marry his wife's sister. Monogamy is the taking of a single spouse. It is more common than polygyny, in which a man takes two or more wives, and polyandry, in which a woman takes two or more husbands. Polygyny and polyandry are uncommon, primarily for economic reasons.

5.

Most anthropologists define a family as a group composed of a woman and her children and the relatives annexed through marriage or consanguinity. The basic unit of mother and/or father and their children is called the nuclear family. The nuclear family follows four basic residence patterns: patrilocal, matrilocal, ambilocal, and neolocal. Residence patterns seem closely related to the nature of a society's economy.

6.

The industrial society evolved the small nuclear family from the larger extended family. An extended family is a combination of conjugal and consanguineous families. All of an extended family's members might not be related by blood or marriage, but all live and work together. The joint family is a kind of extended family.

Suggested readings

Fox, Robin *Kinship and Marriage in an Anthropological Perspective*. New York: Penguin, 1968.

> Professor Fox starts his argument with the universal biological bond between mother and child and imagines a process in which the husband intrudes into the basic group.

Goode, William J. *World Revolution and Family Pattern*. Glencoe, Illinois: Free Press, 1963.

> Important changes in family patterns that have occured during the twentieth century in Japan, China, India, the West, sub-Saharan Africa, and the Arab countries are described and interpreted in an effort to relate the changes to transformations in other social processes, such as industrialization, social change, class stratifications.

Goodenough, Ward Hunt *Description and Comparison in Cultural Anthropology*. Chicago: Aldine, 1970.

> The book illustrates the difficulties anthropologists confront in describing and comparing social organization cross-culturally. The author examines marriage and family, kindred and clan, sibling and cousin, in relationship to social structure.

Goody, John *Comparative Studies in Kinship*. Palo Alto, California: Stanford University Press, 1969.

> Kinship and marriage are discussed in a cross-cultural context. There is a classification of double-descent, inheritance, and social change. Professor Goody relies heavily on empirical and statistical data.

Mair, Lucy *Marriage*. New York: Penguin, 1972.

> Dr. Mair traces the evolution of marriage and such alternative relationships as surrogates and protectors. Commenting upon marriage as an institution and drawing her examples from primitive cultures, Dr. Mair deals with the function, rules, symbolic rituals, and economic factors of marriage. She also cites the inferior status of women and discusses the self-determining behavior of "serious free women" as an important factor in social change.

Needham, Rodney, ed. *Rethinking Kinship and Marriage*. London: Tavistock, 1972.

> This collection of essays is concerned with a definition of kinship and the marriage procedure. It deals cross-culturally with the practices and rituals, and the relationship of marriage to the entire social structure. Contributors include Edmund Leach, Francis Korn, David McKnight.

Stephens, William N. *The Family in Cross-Cultural Perspective*. New York: Holt, Rinehart and Winston, 1963.

> This book describes the institution of the family in different societies. It reports on a wide range of topics, including plural and arranged marriage, kin groups, adultery, roles of wife and husband, and child-rearing.

Kinship
and descent

Human social groups have been classified in many different ways according to the function they perform in society; the family is one such social group. It is the chief organizational principle underlying every society—undoubtedly the primary human social group. The structural principle of the family may be further extended until it links every individual in a given society, placing all within a larger group of kinsmen called the kin group.

In small-scale or nonindustrial societies consisting typically of farmers, nomadic hunters, or pastoralists, a formal political system with administrative machinery and law courts does not usually exist. These societies lack the traditional chief to make and enforce laws, keep the peace, and perform other regulatory societal functions. Instead, the kinship system—the complex form of social organization which relates kinsmen and fulfills individual social and personal needs—is the organizing principle of society.

The importance of the kinship system in a non-Western society may be illustrated by the Ifugao of the Philippines. Among the Ifugao, the kin group consists of the descendants of an individual's four pairs of great-grandparents. It may include as many as 2,000 persons. In this case, prac-

tically the entire village is related in one way or another. In such a society, where the net of kinship, social, and political ties is very tight, it is extremely important that the individual know the exact nature of his relationship to each of his relatives—that he know, for example, who has the strongest claim on his loyalties, and to whom he may turn in time of need. This sorting out process is achieved through the society's kinship system, which lets an individual know exactly how he is related to others and what he can thus expect of them, and they of him. The kinship system structures the obligations and interests of its members: it dictates sharing economic and religious undertakings, provides psychological support in time of crisis, and legal help and defense when required. Among the Ila, a cattle-breeding people of Zambia studied by A. Tuden, for example, one's descent determines his rights in the use of farmland, his share in the distribution of grain and other goods, his place in the work force, and his treatment in disputes and quarrels.

An extreme example of the importance of the kinship system is found among the Jivaro Indians of South America. Among the Jivaro, a man's knowledge of his kin may be a matter of life and death. When an individual visits another tribe of

Jivaro, his host may casually question the visitor about his genealogy, attempting to ascertain whether the visitor belongs to a friendly or a hostile kin group. If the host determines the visitor is related to inimical kin, he may poison his beer or food, or ambush him when he leaves the village. Not surprisingly, Jivaro fathers drill their youngest sons in their genealogy for an hour before dawn each day.

Kinship studies also show that parts of a culture, such as political and economical spheres, are related to one another. For example, as societies grow larger, more mobile and dispersed, the importance of the kinship system as a social regulatory agency decreases, to be increasingly assumed by the state. Thus, in large-scale industrialized societies, such as our own, occupational specialization and complex systems of economic exchange are the rule, and business ceases to be confined to kinsfolk. Instead, relations with relative strangers—employer, doctor, merchant, teacher—become more important. ·

Rules of descent

The rules governing kinship and relationship among the members of a given society are known as rules of descent. Rules of descent arise because many societies must deal with problems which cannot be handled even by the largest of extended families. For example, it may be necessary for the members of one local group to be able to claim support and protection from individuals in another. Some way to share rights in means of production, such as farmland, is also essential. By application of a rule of descent, sets of kin are identified which can deal with such problems. Each individual can then trace a chain of parent-child links back to a common ancestor (who may be real or fictive) and, by so doing, establish his place in a descent group to which he has certain obligations and in which he has clearly defined rights and privileges.

To operate most efficiently, membership in a

Figure 18-1. *The society of the Jivaro, a South American tribe, illustrates an extreme dependence on kinship as a means of organization. The patrilineal family group, living under one roof, is the only existing social unit, except in times of war.*

descent group ought to be clearly defined. Otherwise, membership overlaps and it is not always clear where one's primary loyalty belongs. The most common determinant of kinship organization is sex. Instead of tracing membership back to the common ancestor, sometimes through men and sometimes through women, one does it exclusively through one sex. In this way, each individual is automatically assigned to his or her mother's or father's group, and that group only.

Unilineal descent

Unilineal descent (sometimes called unisexual or unilateral descent) establishes kinship exclusively through the male or the female line. In non-Western societies, unilineal descent groups are the most common form. The individual is assigned at birth to membership in a specific consanguineous—related by blood—kin group which may trace descent either **matrilineally,** through the female line, or **patrilineally,** through the male line. In patrilineal societies the males are far more important than the females, for it is they who are considered to be responsible for the perpetuation of the group. In matrilineal societies, the responsibility falls on the female members of the group.

There seems to be a close relationship between the descent system and the economy of a society. Generally, patrilineal descent predominates where the man is the breadwinner, as among pastoralists and full-time agriculturists. Matrilineal descent is important mainly among semi-agriculturists with societies in which female labor is a prime factor. Numerous matrilineal societies are found in South Asia, which may be a cradle of primitive agriculture in the Old World. Matrilineal systems exist in India, Ceylon, Indonesia, Sumatra, Tibet, South China, and many Indonesian islands.

It is now recognized that in all societies, the kin of both mother and father are important components of the social structure. In some societies, the relationship is quite clear; the membership in the descent group is traced through the mother, whereas succession to chieftainship is traced through the father's line. However, in most societies where unilineal descent prevails, there is a general overlapping of social responsibilities.

Patrilineal descent and organization. Patrilineal descent (sometimes called agnatic, or male, descent) is the more widespread of the two basic systems of unilineal descent. The male members of a patrilineage trace through the males their descent from a common ancestor. Ego and his sister belong to the descent group of their father's father, their father, their father's siblings, and their father's brother's children. Ego's son and daughter also trace their descent back through the male line to their common ancestor. In the typical patrilineal group, the power for training the children rests with the father or his elder brother. A female belongs to the same descent group as her father and his brothers, but her children cannot trace their descent through them. Ego's paternal aunt's children, for example, trace their descent through the patrilineal group of her husband.

The Tikopia: A typical patrilineal society. Among the Tikopia, a people of the western Pacific islands of Polynesia, studied extensively by anthropologist Raymond Firth, the patrilineal system prevails. The family, consisting of the father, mother, children, and usually the father's sister (if unmarried), lives near the house of the father's father. Residence, therefore, is patrilocal. As in most patrilineal societies, the father's brother and his sons exert a strong influence in the life of the father's male children. The children look upon their paternal uncle as a second father and behave toward him accordingly. The father's sister has a unique position among her brother's children. She is looked upon as a secondary mother, acting as nurse, protector, and mentor; her authority and ritual powers are akin to those of her brother.

Every individual Tikopian family belong to a larger group know as a *paito* (which means

Figure 18-2. *This diagram shows how patrilineal descent is traced. Only the individuals symbolized by a colored circle or triangle are in the same descent group as Ego. The abbreviation F stands for father, B for brother, H for husband, S for son, Si for sister.*

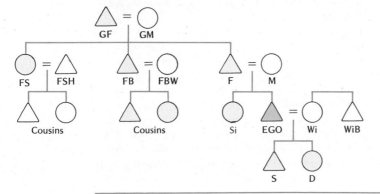

"house"). Each *paito* is composed of a number of families, the core members of which trace their descent through the male line to a common ancestor. The head of the *paito* is the senior living male descendant of this ancestor. A number of *paitos* combine to form the *kainana,* or clan, the largest social group on the island.

The position of an individual within the *paito* determines his social status. The kind of instruction he will receive as a child and his rights to the produce of the land depend on this. As an adult he will be entitled to a share in the land and other property, a house-site, and a given name when he marries. Membership in his family *paito* also entitles him to economic and ritual assistance when required, as well as use of religious formulae and certain prerogatives when he appeals to his principal ancestral deities. Moreover, the *paito* determines the individual's rank in the *kainana.*

The patrilineal system reaches throughout Tikopian social relations and determines legal matters of succession and inheritance. Succession to the position of *paito* head is solely in the male line; under no circumstances can a person belong to the *paito* of the mother rather than that of his father. On the death of an elder or chief, the kin group goes to the farthest limits of male descent and explores the collateral lines to the utmost to find an heir. The immediate sister's son is never even considered; he is excluded because his mother married into another patrilineage.

Each *paito* has its own economic organization. Its members are responsible for the production and consumption of food, the exchange of property, or ownership. Political activities of the *paito* involve the transmission of cultural goods, tradition, rank, and property as well as judicial matters such as the settling of disputes, both internal and external. The *paito* meets also on social and religious occasions, such as marriages, births, deaths, and initiation ceremonies. The patrilineal kinship group is indeed the backbone of Tikopian society.

Matrilineal descent and organization. In all respects but one, matrilineal descent is the exact

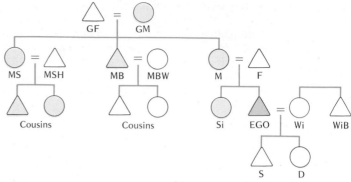

Figure 18-3. *This diagram, which traces descent through the matrilineal line, can be compared with Figure 18-2, showing patrilineal descent. The two patterns are virtually mirror images. Note that Ego cannot transmit his own descent.*

opposite of patrilineal descent: descent is reckoned through the female line and residence is matrilocal. The group resulting from the union of several matrilineages is the matriclan.

The matrilineal pattern differs from the patrilineal in that descent does not confer authority. Although descent passes through the female line, females do not exercise authority in the kin group; the males do. Apparently, the adaptive purpose of the matrilineal system is to provide continuous female solidarity within the female work group. Matrilineal systems are usually found in farming societies in which women perform most of the productive work. Because the food provided by the women is important to the subsistence of the society, matrilineal residence and descent prevail.

In the matrilineal system, Ego and his sister belong to the descent group of the mother's mother, the mother, the mother's siblings, and the mother's sister's children. Males belong to the same descent group as their mother and sister, but their children cannot trace their descent through them. For example, the children of Ego's maternal uncle are considered members of his wife's matrilineage. Similarly Ego's own children belong to his wife's, but not his, descent group.

The matrilineal system has one serious disad-

The formation of groups ● part 5

vantage: it is the source of a great deal of family tension and creates weak ties between husband and wife. The wife's brother, and not the husband-father, distributes goods, organizes work, settles disputes, administers inheritance and succession rules, and supervises rituals. The husband has legal authority not in his own household but in that of his sister. He is strongly tied to his natal household even though he and his wife may live elsewhere. Thus, brother-sister bonds are strengthened at the expense of husband-wife bonds. Moreover, family tension further arises from the fact that the father's property and status are not inherited by his own son but by his sister's son. It is not surprising that divorce, even though frowned upon, is often common in matrilineal societies.

Matrilineal organization among the Ashanti.
An example of a matrilineal system is found among the Ashanti, a horticultural people of Ghana. Among the Ashanti, a boy lives with his parents until he reaches adult status; then he moves to the house of his mother's brother, where his legal claims to a livelihood rest. After marriage, his wife lives with her mother and he lives with his father. In later years, the couple may establish their own household, usually on land that belongs to the wife's matrilineage.

In Ashanti society, the male head, chosen by consensus of both sexes in the lineage, governs the matrilineage. He may be assisted by a senior woman, called the Queen Mother, who oversees the conduct of the women in the lineage, administers the ritual matters of the females, and helps arbitrate family quarrels.

The male leader, with the further assistance of a kind of council of senior males, supervises the social, religious, and economic undertakings of the lineage. He also allocates the right to use property owned by the matrilineage, arbitrates quarrels, and approves all marriages, divorces, and remarriages. The male head also supervises funerals, enforces inheritance rules, and represents the matrilineage in its relations with other groups in the society.

Each segment of an Ashanti matrilineage is composed of the matrilineal descendants of an ancestress, and inheritance and mutual aid are generally restricted to this group, which owns its own land and other property. There is no legally recognized head within the segment, but the mother's brother is generally accepted as its voice or leader. The mother's brother, called the "house father," performs rituals for the family ancestors, arbitrates household disputes, and administers family property. One of the senior males who supervises the lineage's property is regarded as the leader of the entire lineage. Each lineage, in turn, belongs to one of the eight Ashanti clans.

In most matrilineal societies, the mother's brother has extensive legal authority over his nephews and nieces. He may bargain away or sell his nephews and nieces, he can deny them permission to marry, and, once they are married, he can deny them divorce should they seek it. Moreover, the children's father has no authority over them, nor can he transmit to them status or property. Among the Ashanti, however, the father's role in the family limits the influence of the mother's brother. The father-son relationship is very affectionate, and Ashanti fathers generally love their own sons more than the sons of their sisters. Thus, the role of the sister's brother, usually strong in a matrilineal society, is weak among the Ashanti.

Double descent

Double descent, or double unilineal descent, whereby descent is reckoned both patrilineally and matrilineally, is very rare. In this system, descent is matrilineal for some purposes and patrilineal for others. Generally, where double descent is reckoned, each lineage takes corporate action in different spheres of society.

For example, among the Yakö of eastern Nigeria, property is divided between patrilineal line possessions and matrilineal line possessions. The patrilineage owns perpetual productive resources, such as land, whereas the matrilineage owns consumable property, such as livestock. The legally weaker matrilineal line is somewhat more important in religious matters than the patrilineal line. Because of the existence of the double descent rule, a Yakö individual might inherit grazing lands from the father's patrilineal group and certain ritual privileges from the mother's matrilineal line.

Bilateral descent and the kindred

Bilateral descent, a characteristic of Western society, relates a person to other close relatives through both sexes; in other words, the individual traces descent through both parents simultaneously. Theoretically, all relatives on both the mother's and father's sides of the family are his relatives. Thus, this principle relates an individual lineally to all eight great-grandparents and laterally to all third and fourth cousins. Since such a huge group is too big to be socially practical, the group is usually reduced to a small circle of paternal and maternal relatives, called the kindred. The kindred may be defined as a group of people closely related to one individual through both parents. Unlike unilineal descent groups, the kindred is laterally rather than lineally organized. That is, Ego, or the focal person from whom the degree of each relationship is reckoned, is the center of the group. We are all familiar with the kindred; we simply call them "relatives." It includes the relatives on both sides of the family whom we see on social occasions, at family reunions, and at funerals. Most of us can identify the members of our kindred up to second cousins and grandparents. In our society, the limits of the kindred are variable and indefinite; no one is ever really certain which relatives to invite to a social function and which to exclude. The kindred is thus amorphous and vague, lacking the distinctiveness of the unilineal descent group. (It is also temporary, lasting only as long as the function it has been assembled to attend.)

The kindred possesses one feature which sets it apart from all other descent groups: because of its bilateral structure, a kindred is never the same for any two persons except siblings (brothers and sisters). Thus, no two people (except siblings) belong to the same descent group. Ego's father's kindred, for example, range lineally to the father's grandparents and laterally to cousins too distant for him to know; the same is true of his mother, and his maternal and paternal aunts and uncles. Thus, the kindred is not composed of people with an ancestor in common, but of people with a relative in common—Ego.

The Ego: Center of the kindred. Kindreds are referred to as "ego-centered" or "ego-focussed" groups because Ego, or the person viewing the group, is at its center. Even in relation to Ego, the membership of the group is constantly changing as Ego moves through life. When he is young, it consists of his parents, siblings, and other close consanguineous relatives, most of whom are usually older than he is. As Ego grows older and has children, the composition of his kindred changes; it consists of his descendants and the remaining relatives of his own generation. Thus, because of its vagueness, temporary nature, and changeable-

Figure 18-4. *Here the kinship pattern of the kindred is illustrated. These people are related not to a common ancestor but to a common relative, Ego. The squares represent persons of either sex; degree of relationship is not sexually determined.*

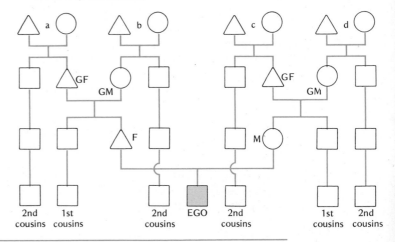

The formation of groups ● part **5**

ness, the kindred is a weaker social unit than other descent groups. For example, it cannot function as a group except in relation to Ego. Unlike other descent groups, it is not a self-perpetuating group—it ceases with Ego's death. It has no constant leader, nor can it hold, administer, or pass on property. In most cases, it cannot organize work, nor can it administer justice or assign status. In non-Western societies, for example, headhunting and trading parties are composed of kindred groups. The group is assembled, goes on the hunt, shares the spoils, then disbands. Thus, kindreds assemble only for a specific purpose.

Because of its shortcomings, the non-Western bilateral group usually exists side by side with more useful unilineal descent groups. Kindreds are found mostly in complex societies, such as our own, where mobility weakens contact with relatives. Individuality is emphasized in complex societies, and a strong kinship system is not as important as it is among non-Western peoples.

Cognatic descent

Unilineal descent provides an easy way of restricting descent group membership, so as to avoid problems of divided loyalty and the like. A number of societies, many of them in the Pacific and Southeast Asia, accomplish the same thing in other ways, though perhaps not quite so neatly. The resultant descent groups are known as nonunilineal, or cognatic, descent groups. Cognatic descent provides a measure of flexibility not normally found under unilineal descent; each individual has the option of affiliating with either the mother's or the father's descent group.

Cognatic descent among the Iban. An example of a cognatic society is found among the Iban of the Balek region of Sarawak, studied by J. D. Freeman. The Iban descent group is called the *bilek*. The husband and wife, when newly married, may affiliate with the *bilek* of either set of parents, depending on their choice of residence.

Thus, the land rights, ritual obligations, and other activities controlled by the *bilek* are decided at marriage. A couple that affiliates with one *bilek* relinquishes its claim on the other; there can be no overlapping membership. Their children can belong only to the *bilek* of their parents, and like the parents, when the children marry, they must decide with which *bilek* they will live. The distinctive trait of the cognatic descent group is the possibility of changing one's permanent affiliation by changing one's residence. A person can decide to his own advantage whether or not he will honor his original group obligation.

Among the Iban, an individual may belong at any one time to only one *bilek;* thus, Iban society is divided into discrete and separate groups of kin. However, other cognatic societies, such as the Samoans of the South Pacific and the Bella Coola and the southern branch of the Kwakiutl of the Pacific Northwest Coast, allow overlapping membership in a number of descent groups. As George Murdock notes, too great a range of individual choice interferes with the orderly functioning of any kin-oriented society:

An individual's plural membership almost inevitably becomes segregated into one primary membership, which is strongly activated by residence, and one or more secondary memberships in which participation is only partial or occasional.[1]

Generally, cognatic groups appear to be closer in structure to unilineal descent groups than they are to bilateral kindred groups.

Types of descent groups

In many parts of the world, a descent group is more than just a group of relatives providing warmth and a sense of belonging; it may be a

[1]George P. Murdock, "Cognatic Forms of Social Organization," in G. P. Murdock (ed.), *Social Stratification in Southeast Asia,* (Chicago: Quadrangle Books, 1960) p. 11.

tightly organized working unit providing security and services in the course of what is often a difficult, uncertain life. The tasks performed by descent groups are manifold. One of their most important social functions is generally the regulation of marriage by establishing which person a member of the group may marry. Since unilineal descent groups are usually exogamous, members of the group must look beyond its membership for eligible mates. In Truk society, in the western Pacific, for example, the largest group is the matriclan; therefore, a person cannot marry a member of his matrilineage or matriclan. Instead, he must go outside his descent group to seek a partner.

The descent group also acts as an economic unit providing mutual aid to its members; it may support the aged and infirm or help in case of marriage or death. But the unity of the descent group is perhaps most apparent on a political level, especially in time of war. The descent group also acts as a repository of religious traditions. Ancestor worship, for example, is a powerful force acting to reinforce group solidarity.

Lineage

A **lineage** is a corporate descent group composed of consanguineous kin who claim descent from a common ancestor and who are able to trace descent genealogically through known links. The term is usually employed where some form of unilineal descent is the rule, but there are similar cognatic groups.

The lineage is ancestor-centered; membership in the group is recognized only if relationship to a common ancestor can be traced and proven. In many societies, an individual has no legal or political status except as a member of the lineage. Since "citizenship" is derived from lineage membership and legal status depends on it, political and religious power are thus derived from it as well. Important religious and magical powers, such as those associated with the cults of gods and ancestors, may also be bound to the lineage.

Figure 18-5. *These photos show modern versions of the kindred. The top photo is a French family attending a wedding of one of its members; the bottom photo shows members of the family of Magnus McDonald in Marion, Illinois, enjoying their annual family reunion.*

The lineage, like General Motors or Polaroid, is a corporate group, because it continues after the death of members as new members are continually being born into it. This perpetual existence enables a lineage to take corporate actions such as owning property, organizing productive activities, distributing goods and manpower, assigning status, and regulating relations with other groups. Thus, the lineage is a strong, effective base of social organization.

Clan

A second type of descent group is the **clan.** The term clan, and its close relative, the term **sib,** have been used differently by different anthropologists, and a certain amount of confusion exists about their meaning. The clan (or sib) will here be defined as a noncorporate descent group in which each member assumes descent from a common ancestor (who may be real or fictive) but is unable to trace definite genealogical links back to the ancestor. A clan differs from a lineage in two respects: a clan cannot trace its descent links with certainty and it lacks the residential unity that tends to be characteristic of the lineage. As in the lineage, descent may be traced through either the male or female line exclusively.

The clan, unlike the lineage, does not usually hold property corporately. Rather, it acts more as a unit for ceremonial matters, assembles on certain occasions, and has a recognized head or leader. Moreover, clans often develop from splitting of lineages that have grown too large. Clans, like lineages, are usually exogamous.

Clans, lacking the residential unity of lineages, depend on symbols—of animals, plants, natural forces, and objects—to provide members with solidarity and a ready means of identification. These symbols, called **totems,** are often associated with the clan's mythical origin and provide clan members with a means of reinforcing the awareness of their common descent. The word "totem" comes from the Ojibwa American Indian word *ototeman,* meaning "he is a relative of mine."

Totemism has been defined by A. R. Radcliffe-Brown as a set of "customs and beliefs by which there is set up a special system of relations between the society and the plants, animals, and other natural objects that are important in the social life."[2] Creek Indian matriclans bear such totemic names as Alligator, Arrow, Bird, Corn, Deer, Red Paint, Spanish Moss, and Wind.

Totemism is a changing concept that varies from clan to clan. Evidence of totemism may even be found in our own society where baseball and football teams are given the names of such powerful wild animals as Bears, Tigers, and Wildcats. Totemism extends to the Democratic Party's donkey and the Republican Party's elephant, to the Elks, the Lions, and other fraternal and social organizations. Our animal emblems, however, do not involve the same notions of descent, nor are they associated with the various ritual observances associated with clan totems.

Phratries and moieties

A third type of descent group is the phratry or the moiety. A **phratry** is a unilineal descent group composed of two or more clans who are supposedly related, though they may not be. Like individuals of the clan, members of the phratry are unable to trace accurately their descent links to a common ancestor, though they believe such an ancestor exists.

If the entire society is divided into two and only two major descent groups, be they equivalent to clans or phratries, each group is called a **moiety** (after the French word for "half"). Members of the moiety believe themselves to share a common ancestor but are unable to prove it through definite biological links. As a rule, the feeling of kinship among members of lineages and clans is stronger than that felt among members of phratries and moieties. This may be due to the larger size of the latter groups.

[2]A. R. Radcliffe-Brown, "Social Organization of Australian Tribes." *Oceania Monographs,* No. 1. (Melbourne: Macmillan, 1931) p. 29.

Rise of the cognatic descent group

It appears that ambilocality, ecology, and the rise of cognatic descent groups are interrelated. Cognatic descent groups are often associated with ambilocality, in which the newlywed couple may live with either the wife's kinsmen or the husband's kinsmen. In the case of ambilocal families, two different relationships between cognatic descent groups and ecology have been pointed out in an effort to account for the rise of the cognatic group. Cognatic groups may have arisen as a result of pressure from overcrowding. An excellent example of this relationship is found on the Gilbert Islands of Micronesia. The cognatic extended family on the islands is the corporate landholding unit related to other social units through a series of cognatic kin ties and supported by ambilocal residence. This unit held title to certain garden plots which it cultivated; when the family cultivating a particular plot grew too large to share in the profits derived from the plot, the entire family, or some members, would leave the corporate unit to join similar units with which it had kin ties.

Another theory regarding the emergence of cognatic descent groups is that they act as a means of increasing populations where certain important resources are found in abundance. For example, anthropologist M. J. Harner found that among the Indians of the Northwest Pacific Coast, important resources such as salmon and sea mammals occurred in vast numbers, but only sporadically. The ambilocal residence pattern of the Indians' cognatic descent group allowed populations to adjust to the uncertainties of this situation by changing residences, so that these food sources could be exploited wherever and whenever they appeared.

Evolution of the descent group

Just as different types of families occur in different societies, so do different kinds of descent systems. Descent groups, for example, do not ap-

Figure 18-6. *These posts stand by the house of a Kwakiutl man; he believes his ancestors speak through the totem to advise him.*

pear at all in simple hunting and gathering societies, where marriage acts as the social mechanism for integrating individuals within the society. In horticultural, pastoral, or many intensive agricultural societies, however, the descent group provides the structural framework upon which the fabric of the society rests.

Lewis Morgan and other nineteenth century anthropologists believed that the descent group progressed in an evolutionary manner from promiscuity to matrilineal to patrilineal organization. In so-called promiscuous societies, paternity was never certain and descent could be traced only through the mother; hence the emergence of the matrilineal group. The accumulation of wealth, in the form of land and other valuable material possessions, was responsible for the rise of the patrilineal system, for wealth resided in the males. A means of passing wealth from male to male down the generations was required. Finally, civilization, with its complex patterns of individuality, specialization of labor, and greater mobility, brought with it the consideration of both paternal and maternal descent rules. This combination resulted in the bilineal or bilateral kinship system of modern Western civilization.

Morgan's evolutionary sequence was declared invalid by George Murdock, who found that the simplest of arctic hunter-gatherers practiced bilateral descent. Descent rules, according to Murdock, bore no relation to the level of technological or social development. Most scholars agree that Morgan's evolutionary thesis is incorrect. However, some relation between a society's technological level and its descent system does exist.

Kinship terminology

The ways in which kinship relationships are defined in any society are subject to elaborate cultural rules. Each society has a particular way of assigning the individual to his place in the descent group; a set of terms designates the individual's position within the groups to which he be-longs. These labels are called kinship terms, and the whole classificatory system is called the system of kinship terminology.

There are a number of factors at work in each system of kinship terminology that help differentiate one kin from another. These factors may be sex, generational differences, or genealogical differences. In the various kinship terminology systems, any one of these factors may be emphasized at the expense of others. But regardless of the factors emphasized, all kinship terminologies accomplish two important tasks. First, they group particular kinds of persons into single specific categories; secondly, they separate different kinds of persons into distinct categories. Generally, two or more kin are merged under the same term when similarity of status exists between the individuals. These similarities are then emphasized by the application of one term to both individuals.

Six different systems of kinship terminology result from the application of the above principles: the Hawaiian, Eskimo, Iroquois, Omaha, Crow, and Sudanese systems. Each of these six systems can be identified according to the way cousins are classified.

Hawaiian system

The Hawaiian system of kinship terminology, practiced mainly in Hawaii and other Malayo-Polynesian speaking areas, is the least complex system, in that it uses the least number of terms. The Hawaiian system is also called the generational system, since all relatives of the same generation and sex are referred to by the same term. For example, in one's father's generation, one's father, his brother, and one's mother's brother are all referred to by the single term "father." Similarly, one's mother, her sister, and one's father's sister are all called "mother." In Ego's generation, male and female cousins are distinguished by sex and are equated with his brother and sister.

The Hawaiian system reflects the absence of a strong unilineal descent group and is usually associated with cognatic descent. Because cognatic descent rules trace descent through both sides of the family, and members on both father's and mother's side of the family are looked upon as being more or less equal, a certain degree of similarity is created among the father's and the mother's siblings. Thus, they are all simultaneously recognized as being similar relations and are merged together under a single term. In like manner, the children of the mother's and father's siblings are considered related to oneself in the same way as one's brother and sister are.

Eskimo system

The Eskimo system of kinship terminology, comparatively rare among all the systems of the world, is the system used by Anglo-American cultures. It is also used by a number of hunting and gathering peoples. The Eskimo system, or lineal system, of terminology emphasizes the nuclear family by specifically identifying mother, father, brother, and sister, while merging together all other members such as maternal and paternal aunts, uncles, and cousins, without differentiating among them. For example, one's father is distinguished from his father's brother (uncle); but one's father's brother is not distinguished from his mother's brother (who is also called uncle). In addition, one calls all the sons and daughters of his aunts and uncles "cousin," without distinguishing their sex or the side of the family to which they belong.

Unlike other descent terminologies, the Eskimo system provides separate and distinct terms for each member of the nuclear family. Perhaps this is because the Eskimo system is generally found in societies where the dominant kin group is the bilateral kindred, in which only the closest members of the family are important. This is especially true of our society, in which the family is independent, living apart from, and not directly involved with, other kin except on ceremonial occasions. Thus, we distinguish between our closest kin (our parents and our siblings) but use the same terms (aunt, uncle, cousin) for other members on both sides of the family.

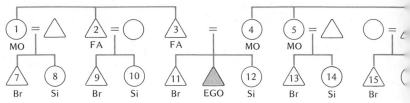

Figure 18-7. *The Hawaiian kinship system is shown in the diagram above. The men numbered 2, 3, and 6 are all called "father" by Ego; the women numbered 1, 4, and 5 are all called "mother." All cousins of the same generation (7–16) are considered brothers and sisters.*

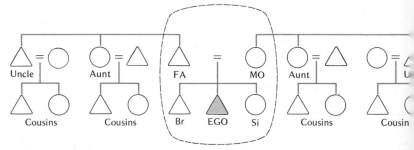

Figure 18-8. *The Eskimo system of kinship terminology emphasizes the nuclear family (here separated by the dotted circle). Ego's father and mother are distinguished from his aunts and uncles, and his siblings are distinguished from his cousins.*

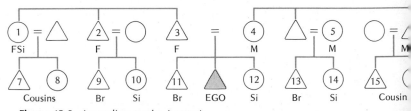

Figure 18-9. *According to the Iroquois system of kinship terminology, the people numbered 2 and 3 are called father; 4 and 5 are called mother; but 1 and 6 are aunt and uncle. 9–14 are all considered siblings, but 7, 8, 15, and 16 are called cousins.*

The formation of groups ● part **5**

Iroquois system

In the Iroquois system of kinship terminology, one's father and his father's brother are referred to by a single term (father), as are one's mother and one's mother's sister (mother); however, one's father's sister and one's mother's brother are given separate terms. In one's generation, brothers, sisters, and parallel cousins[3] of the same sex are referred to by a single term, whereas cross cousins are distinguished by separate terms.

Such a method of differentiating is called a bifurcate-merging system, a strange term which simply means some of the family members are separated (or bifurcated) and given different names, while other kin are combined (or merged) under a common term. The Omaha and the Crow systems are also examples of bifurcate-merging forms.

Iroquois terminology is very widespread and is usually found with unilineal descent groups, particularly in weak matrilineal systems of social organization. However, the Iroquois system has also been found among other types of descent groups as well.

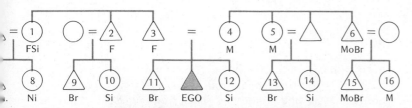

Figure 18-10. *In the Omaha system, 2 and 3 are father, 4 and 5 are mother, but 1 and 6 are aunt and uncle. In Ego's generation, the children 9-14 are all considered siblings, but 7, 8, 15, and 16 receive separate terms. 15 and 16 are equated with the older generation of the parents.*

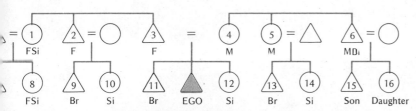

Figure 18-11. *The Crow Indians use a system that is the obverse of the Omaha system in Figure 18-10. 4 and 5 are merged under a single term, as are 2, 3, and 7. Ego's parallel cousins (9,10,13,14) are referred to in the same way as his brothers and sisters (11 and 12).*

Omaha system

In the preceding terminology systems, some relatives were grouped under common terms, while others of the same generation were separated and given different labels or terms. In the Omaha and Crow systems, another variable enters the picture: both systems ignore the distinction that occurs between generations among certain kinsmen.

The Omaha system, found in many parts of the world, is associated with a pattern of strong patrilineal descent and thus groups differently relations on the father's side and relations on the mother's side of the family. Cross cousins on the maternal side are merged with the parental gen-

[3] Parallel cousins are the offspring of parental siblings of the same sex. One's mother's sister's children and one's father's brother's children are one's parallel cousins. Cross cousins are the offspring of siblings of the opposite sex. One's mother's brother's children and one's father's sister's children are one's cross cousins.

eration (mother's sister or mother's brother), while those on the paternal side are merged with the generation of Ego's children. Otherwise, the system is much like the Iroquois system.

From our point of view, such a system is terribly complex and illogical. Why does it exist? The Omaha system is found where strong patrilineal descent is the rule. Thus, maternal cross cousins are terminologically merged with the lineage of Ego's mother, the lineage which, figuratively speaking, sired Ego. Ego's lineage, in turn, stands in the same relationship to the children of his father's sister and Ego's own sister; they are "sired" by Ego's lineage.

Crow system

The Crow system, named after the North American Indian tribe, is the matrilineal mirror image of the patrilineal system. Thus one's mother and one's mother's sister are called by the same term, whereas one's father and one's father's brother and father's sister's son are merged together under a common label, as are one's father's sister and one's father's sister's daughter. Similarly, one's male parallel cousins receive the same term as one's brother; one's female parallel cousins receive the same term as one's sister.

Sudanese system

In this relatively rare system, one's mother's brother is distinguished from one's father's brother, as is one's mother's sister from one's father's sister. Each cousin is distinguished from each other, as well as from siblings. It is therefore more precise than any of the other systems. This may be one reason why it is so rare. In few societies are all one's aunts, uncles, cousins, and siblings treated differently from one another.

Kinship behavior among the Western Pueblos may be comprehended most easily by a discussion of the extended matrilineal household where an individual receives his first and lasting cultural orientation. The household normally consists of a woman and her husband, married daughters and their husbands, unmarried sons, and children of the daughters. The women are the important members of the unit; they own the house, are responsible for the preparation and distribution of food, make all the important decisions, and care for the ritual possessions of the family. The oldest woman of the household enjoys the most respect, and the members of the unit look to her for instructions and seek her advice in times of trouble. Next in importance is her oldest daughter, who assumes the duties and responsibilities of the household when her mother is away. Men born into the household and lineage leave the house when they marry, although they return frequently, exercise considerable authority in religious matters, and may discipline their sister's children when asked. The husbands contribute to the economic support of the household, teach their children the techniques of making a livelihood, and provide warmth and affection toward their children; but in disciplinary matters and economic decisions, they defer to their wives and their wives' brothers and uncles.

Interaction with the father's relatives goes on almost simultaneously with those of the matrilineal household. These relatives, particularly father's mother and father's sisters, are frequent visitors and the child, in turn, frequently visits the home of his paternal grandparents and sisters. These relatives exert little authority and do not discipline, but they provide love, comfort, and aid during crucial and anxious periods of his life.

The Western Pueblo matrilineal extended household in the past occupied a series of adjacent rooms. With the increasing importance of wage work and livestock activities in recent years, this situation has changed. Families living on farms and ranches during the summer are now essentially of the elementary type: husband, wife, and children, and in some cases a widowed grandmother, a divorced daughter, or other relative. Off-reservation employment restricts the size of the household even more drastically. Although it is not uncommon to have one or even both parents of the wife living with a nuclear family on a farm or ranch, older people refuse to make their home with children who live in government quarters or rented houses in towns and cities. The large extended household of the Pueblos generally has thus tended to become a smaller and less integrated unit in recent years; nevertheless, there is keen awareness of all the relatives that comprise the household group. Modern forms of transportation afford resumptions of extended-household living. Frequent ceremonies draw members back to the village enabling close relatives to interact with one another and thus renew and strengthen the bonds of friendship.

The lineage is the living and functional representation of a particular clan; its members are in intimate contact with one another and bound together by deep loyalties. Marriages remove the men to the various households of their wives, but they renew lineage ties frequently to visit with maternal relatives and to attend ritual duties. Women of the lineage never permanently leave the village and constantly interact fulfilling household and clan responsibilities. An

older woman of one of the lineages is the head of the clan and her brother or maternal uncle usually performs the necessary rituals for the clan. Upon the death of the female head, the position goes to the next senior woman of the same household and lineage, but prominent members of the clan in the village may decide to designate as her successor a mature woman from another household and lineage. This is unlikely, however, for Pueblo custom tends to favor procedures deeply rooted in time and tradition. Among the Western Pueblos succession of important offices ordinarily remains within one household and lineage except where lineages have become extinct. The custom of having one household and/or lineage acting as the custodian of ritual paraphernalia and of providing the clan heads, both male and female, has tended to give a status ranking to lineages and clans. The village or town chief, an important official in all of these pueblos, although without the authority of his counterpart among the Eastern Pueblos, comes from a specific clan in most of the Western Pueblos: Bear clan, Hopi and Hano; Dogwood clan, Zuni; Antelope clan, Acoma, and perhaps Laguna.

Formerly, households of the lineage occupied a block of contiguous rooms, a pattern that has broken down in recent years, but the intimate bond of kinship remains even though the member households may be dispersed. Since each pueblo recognizes affiliation with other pueblo clans having the same name, lineages of equivalent clans in other pueblo villages are also considered legal kinfolk and the ordinary clan relations are extended to members of such lineages. Clans are land-holding units, each one having lands set aside for the use of its members. The control of ceremonies and their ritual paraphernalia are in the keeping of certain lineages. Adopted children retain the clan of their mothers; in most cases, however, children are adopted by members of their own clan. Marriage between members of the same clan is forbidden, as is marriage with a member of an equivalent Pueblo clan. In addition, marriage is disapproved with a member of father's clan. Violations of these latter restrictions occur, however, especially in recent years; but the rule that forbids marriage with a member of one's own clan is rarely violated.[1]

A Hano lineage is the living and functional representation of a particular clan; its members are in intimate contact with one another and bound together by deep loyalties. While marriages remove the men to the various households of their wives, they renew lineage ties frequently to exercise ceremonial responsibilities. Women of the lineage are, of course, constantly together. The lineages of the Hano are small and some are simply the matrilineal members of an extended household. A senior woman of one of the lineages is the head of the clan and her brother ordinarily performs the necessary rituals for the clan. Upon the death of the clan head, the position is usually assumed by the next senior woman of the same household and lineage, but prominent members of the clan in the village may decide to designate as her successor a mature woman from another household and lineage. Formerly households of the lineage occupied a block of houses adjacent to one another, a pattern that has broken down in recent years, but the intimate kinship bond remains even though the household members may be dispersed. Since the Tewa recognize affiliation with Hopi clans having the same name, lineages of equivalent clans in the Hopi villages are also considered lineal kinfolk and the ordinary clan relations are extended to members of these lineages.

Characteristics of Hano clan organization are revealed in the following statement by a Bear clansman:

I am of the Bear clan. Our mothers' mothers' mothers and our mothers' mothers' mothers' brothers were Bear clan people. They came a long, long, time ago from *Tsawadeh,* our home in the east. Our sisters' daughters' daughters' children, as long as women of my clan have children, will be of the Bear clan. These are our clan relatives, whom we trust, work with, and confide in. My mother's older sister guards the sacred fetish which is the power and guardian of our clan and which was brought in the migration from *Tsawadeh.* My mother's older sister feeds our fetish and sees that the feathers are always properly dressed. At important ceremonies, my mother's brother erects his altar and sets our fetish in a prominent place within the altar. My mother's older sister and my mother's brother make all the important decisions for our clan, and such decisions are accepted with respect and obedience by all Bear clan members. My mother's older sister and her brother are called upon to advise, to reprimand, and to make decisions on land and ritual affairs for all of us who are of the Bear clan. My mother's older sister's house is where our fetish is kept, and therefore it is a sacred house to us and there we go for all important matters that concern our clan.[2]

Sources:
[1] From *The Pueblo Indians of North America* by Edward P. Dozier. Copyright © 1970 by Holt, Rinehart and Winston, Inc. Adapted and reprinted by permission of Holt, Rinehart and Winston, Inc.
[2] From *Mano: A Tewa Indian Community in Arizona* by Edward P. Dozier. Copyright © 1966 by Holt, Rinehart and Winston, Inc. Reprinted by permission of Holt, Rinehart and Winston, Inc.

Summary

1.
The family is the chief organizational principle underlying every society, and is the primary human social group. Kinship is a powerful organizing principle in small or nonindustrial societies. As societies grow larger, more mobile and dispersed, the state increasingly assumes the function of kinship system.

2.
The rules governing kinship are called rules of descent. Unilineal descent establishes kinship exclusively through the male or female line. Patrilineal descent is traced through the male line; matrilineal, through the female. Generally, patrilineal descent predominates in societies in which the male is the breadwinner.

3.
The male members of a patrilineage trace through the males their descent from a common ancestor. A female belongs to the same descent group as her father and his brother; but her children cannot trace their descent through them. The Tikopia have a patrilineal system. The family is patrilocal, living near the house of the father's father. Individual Tikopian families belong to a *paito*. Each *paito* is made up of families whose members trace their descent through the male line to a common ancestor. The head of the *paito* is the senior living male descendant of this ancestor. A number of *paitos* form the *kainana,* or patriclan, the largest social group on the island.

4.
In all respects but one, matrilineal descent is the exact opposite of patrilineal. Matrilineal families are matrilocal and form matriclans. However, in a matrilineal society, though descent passes through the female line, males exercise authority in the kin group. The Ashanti have a matrilineal system. Segments of an Ashanti matrilineage are composed of the matrilineal descendants of an ancestress. The mother's brother is generally accepted as the leader of a segment.

5.
Double descent is reckoned patrilineally and matrilineally. Double descent is matrilineal for some purposes, and patrilineal for others. The Yako have a double descent system. Among the Yako, the patrilineage owns the land whereas the matrilineage owns the livestock.

6.
Bilateral descent is traced through both parents simultaneously. It is characteristic of Western society. An individual is lineally related to all eight grandparents and laterally to all third and fourth cousins. Such a large group is socially impractical. It is usually reduced to a small circle of paternal and maternal relatives, called the kindred, which is laterally organized. A kindred is never the same for any two persons except siblings.

7.
Cognatic descent is traced either matrilineally or patrilineally, according to the individual. The Iban have a cognatic descent system. The Iban descent group is the *bilek*. Upon marriage, a husband and wife select the *bilek* of one set of parents, relinquishing claims on the other. Children belong to the *bilek* of their parents until marriage.

8.

In many parts of the world, a descent group may be a tightly organized working unit providing security and services. A lineage is a corporate descent group made up of consanguineous kin who claim descent from a common ancestor and can prove it. A clan or sib is a noncorporate descent group, each member of which assumes descent from a common ancestor, but cannot prove it. The phratry or moiety is a unilineal descent group of two or more clans which are supposedly related.

9.

The rise of cognatic descent groups appears to be related to ambilocality and ecology. In the case of ambilocal families, cognatic groups may have arisen in response to overcrowding, or as a means of increasing populations where an abundance of natural resources called for it.

10.

Different types of descent systems occur in different societies. In hunter-gatherer societies, descent groups do not appear at all, whereas in intensive agricultural societies they provide a structural framework for society.

11.

Defining kinship relationships in a society is subject to elaborate cultural rules. Factors such as sex, generational differences, and genealogical differences help differentiate one kin from another. The Hawaiian system is the least complex of kinship systems. All relatives of the same generation and sex are referred to by the same name. The Sudanese system is the most complex. One's mother's brother is distinguished from one's father's brother, as is one's mother's sister from one's father's sister. Each cousin is distinguished from each other.

Suggested readings

Fox, Robin *Kinship and Marriage*. Baltimore: Penguin, 1968.
   An excellent introduction to the concepts of kinship and marriage, outlining some of the methods of analysis used in the anthropological treatment of kinship and marriage. Updates Radcliffe-Brown's *African Systems of Kinship and Marriage* and features a perspective focused on kinship groups and social organization.

Homans, George C. and Davis M. Schneider *Marriage, Authority and Final Causes: A Study of Unilateral Cross-Cousin Marriage*. Glencoe: Free Press, 1955.
   This is a study of "preferential marriage"—a system of unilateral cross-cousin marriage in which a male is expected to marry one specific female cousin. A discussion of the theories of Lévi-Strauss is included with examples from the Karienda.

Needham, Rodney, ed. *Rethinking Kinship and Marriage*. New York: Barnes and Noble, 1972.
   This is a collection of papers dealing with various aspects of the concept of kinship and marriage. Although fairly technical, it provides an introduction by the editor on present issues in theory and practice in the field of social anthropology.

Nimkoff, M. F. *Comparative Family Systems*. Boston: Houghton Mifflin, 1965.
   Major variations in the organization of the human family, such as what differences they make, what they are, what causes them are discussed. Verbal and quantitative, descriptive and analytical approaches are combined. The book examines comparative studies on family, analyzes family life in a particular society, and traces recent trends in family structure in industrializing and fully industrialized societies.

Radcliffe-Brown, A. R., ed. *African Systems of Kinship and Marriage*. London: Oxford University Press, 1950.
   The purpose of the volume is to present a general view of the nature and implications of kinship in Africa. It consists of a general introduction to kinship and marriage, and several chapters of detailed study of particular social systems (Swazi, Zulu, Lozi, Tswana, Bantu, Ashanti, etc.)

Schusky, Ernest L. *Manual for Kinship Analysis*. New York: Holt, Rinehart and Winston, 1965.
   A widely used book that discusses the elements of kinship, diagramming, systems, classification, descent and lineage with specific examples from American, Crow, and Omaha Indian societies.

Other forms
of social organization

As traditional ways are forced to vie with new ones, the importance of kinship diminishes to a great degree. One or more members of a family may be forced to leave their village for work in the cities or the mines, or are drawn away from home by a desire for adventure and excitement. The United States is not, after all, the only country faced with the problem of how to keep the young people down on the farm after they have read about the East Village, or Nairobi, or Johannesburg. Old ways may be abruptly dropped in such a move, or they may be snatched away, as under colonial rule or the coming of the missionaries.

Occasionally such changes, especially when they are involuntary, are catastrophic. Laurens van der Post, in a study of the lives and mythology of the Kalahari Bushmen, writes of the tragedy that results from the imprisonment of a Bushman for an act whose illegality he could not comprehend—hunting "out of season." Today the very survival of the Bushmen is threatened, in part because their social structure contains no mechanisms for cultural adaptation to their changing social environment.

Tribal or village organizations, initiation cults and other traditional groups help maintain stability at a time when the simplest as well as the most sophisticated institutions are challenged by rapid social change. The source of this strength may have been detected by A. R. Radcliffe-Brown in his work on *The Andaman Islanders:*

> A society depends for its existence on the presence in the minds of its members of a certain system of sentiments by which the conduct of the individual is regulated in conformity with the needs of the society. Every feature of the social system itself and every event or object that in any ways affects the wellbeing or the cohesion of the society becomes an object of this system of sentiments. In human society the sentiments in question are not innate but are developed in the individual by the action of the society upon him. The ceremonial customs of a society are a means by which the sentiments in question are given collective expression on appropriate occasions. The ceremonial (i.e. collective) expression of any sentiment serves both to maintain it at the requisite degree of intensity in the mind of the individual and to transmit it from one generation to another. Without such expression the sentiments involved could not exist.

Whether or not this explanation is sufficiently

comprehensive, observations do consistently show that where such functions are not served by kinship, other forms of association arise to take its place. Among these forms of nonkinship social organization we will examine age grouping, voluntary associations, and stratification.

Age grouping

Age grouping is so familiar and so important that one anthropologist calls it and sex the only two universal factors in social status. Our first friends generally are children our own age. Together we are sent off to school where together we remain until our late teens. At a certain age we become "legally adult," meaning that we can vote, should support ourselves and must, if required, go off to war if male or lend moral support if female. Until that time we cannot drink liquor, drive a car, or do any number of things reserved for our elders. We are "teenagers," "middle-aged," "senior citizens," whether we like it or not, and for no other reason than our age.

Age classification also plays a significant role in non-Western societies. There the term "coming of age" is possibly even more meaningful than in our own society, especially if it is associated with becoming a warrior. Old age too has profound significance, often bringing with it the period of greatest respect (for women it may mean the first social equality with men), although it may also in some cases mean abandonment—psychological, as in the United States, or literal, as in certain Eskimo tribes.

The institutionalization of age, as P. Gulliver points out, makes it clear that cultural rather than biological factors are of prime importance in determining social status. All human societies recognize a number of life stages; precisely how they are defined will vary from one culture to another. Out of this recognition they establish patterns of activity, attitudes, prohibitions, and obligations. In some instances, they are designed to help the transition from one age to another, to teach

Figure 19-1. *In many societies, it is common for children of the same age to play, eat, and learn together, like this group of African boys. Such a group forms the basis of age-set organization.*

needed skills, or to lend economic assistance. Often they are designed to help structure a society and to meet its particular needs.

Institutions of age grouping

An **age category** is a generalized role disposition into which specific roles may be built. Anthropologists recognize three such distinctions: age class, age grade, and age set. An **age grade** is generally defined as a category of persons who fall within a particular, culturally distinguished age range. The collection of people currently occupying an age grade form an **age class.** The term **age set** is used to describe a group of persons initiated into an age grade who move through some or all of life's stages together. Age-ascribed roles may be specific, defining and limiting the nature of relationships between persons in different age grades. The total range of age-defined roles may constitute a graded system that emphasizes the progressive movement from role to role.

A specific time is often ritually established for moving from a younger to an older grade. Although members of senior groups commonly expect deference from and acknowledge certain responsibilities to their juniors, all such age-grade levels imply ascribed rather than achieved status, since one grade is no "better" or "worse" or even more important than another, and no ranking is achieved through individual effort. There can be standardized competition (opposition) between

Figure 19-2. *Some forms of age-set organization can be found in American society, as illustrated here by the annual tug of war between the freshman and sophomore classes at Dartmouth.*

age grades, such as between sophomores and freshmen on American college campuses. One can, comparably, accept the realities of being a "teenager" without feeling the need to "prove anything."

Whether by age set, class, or group, all peoples in some way distinguish the main stages of individual development. Such divisions may be as simple as youngsters, mature adults, and elderly peoples, such as among the Kalahari Bushmen; or as complex as the system of the Kikuyu of Central Kenya, who have six age-categories for men and eight for women. Within the three grades for men of the Masai—uncircumcised boys, circumcised bachelors, and married men—there are an indefinite number of classes; for example, all boys circumcised during the same four-year period form a set whose solidarity continues for life. This latter instance is also an example of the way an elaborate classification can spring up spontaneously, requiring only a name or procedure, such as circumcision, to fix it into a definite bond.

In the face of such obvious distinctions, a certain amount of controversy has arisen over the relative strength, cohesiveness, and stability that go into an age grouping. To Gulliver in particular, the age-group notion implies strong feelings of loyalty and mutual support that emphasize a corporate nature. Because such groups may possess property, songs, shield designs, and rituals, and are internally organized for corporate decision-making and leadership, he calls for a distinction between them and simple age-grade groupings. Gulliver also distinguishes between transitory age groups, which initially concern younger men (sometimes women too) but become less important and disintegrate as the members grow older, and the comprehensive systems that affect people through the whole of their lives. Among his other distinctions are that entry into and transfer out of age grades may be accomplished individually, either by a biological distinction, such as puberty, or by a socially recognized status, such as marriage or childbirth. Whereas age-grade members may have much in common, engage in similar activities, cooperate with one another, and share the same orientation and aspirations, their membership may not be entirely parallel with physiological age. Other anthropologists do not generally make such a distinction, which is considered one of degree rather than kind.

Age groupings in African societies

An example of a simple, traditionally defined age class of a relatively unsophisticated kind is the Nuer of Kenya, as described by Edward Evans-Pritchard. Among the Nuer, the position of every male in relation to every other male Nuer is defined only in terms of seniority, equality, or juniority. Initiation has no educational or moral purpose. At initiation a boy receives a spear from his father or uncle and becomes a warrior; he is given an ox and becomes a herdsman. Once initiated, he remains in this grade for the rest of his life. His new status implies no administrative, judicial, or other political or military functions; other than a taboo against milking, his domestic duties remain largely unstructured until marriage. His membership does have certain definite ritual observations and avoidances; for example, a man may not marry or have sexual relations with the daughter of an age mate, for she is regarded as his "daughter" and he as her "father." In matters of etiquette and division of food, his behavior is carefully structured according to seniority. These distinctions have no connotation of privilege, but only of stratification, and are superseded only by kinship.

Embodying many of Gulliver's notions of age groupings are the Swazi of Swaziland and the Afikpo Ibo of Eastern Nigeria. In Swazi, men's age groups (*libutfo*) were formed roughly every five to seven years according to the need for a group of immature youths to be available for state rituals. Each group had its own name, insignia, songs, barracks, and officials; every Swazi male was automatically enrolled and remained a member of the same *libutfo* from its inception until his death. *Libutfos* were originally sufficiently powerful to cut across the boundaries of local chiefs

and the bonds of kinship, and incorporated individuals into a wider state unity. Although their primary activity was warfare, they took part in a number of civic functions and public works. Since their rituals and morality ran contrary to the teachings of the Christian missionaries, their influence ultimately waned, though they survive in attenuated forms.

The social organization of the Afikpo Ibo is well developed among both sexes. A village men's society, the *Ogo*, is found in every Afikpo village.

Figure 19-3. *Among the Pitjandara, a tribe of hunter-gatherers, the men in an age set undergo rituals together; these young men are participating in rather painful initiation rites. Such shared experiences create strong and lasting social bonds.*

The formation of groups • part **5**

Figure 19-4. *Graduation from one age grade to another is often marked by elaborate rites. The top photo shows a group of young girls from the Ivory Coast who are returning home from ceremonies initiating them into full adult status; judging from the things they are carrying, the rites must have lasted quite a while. The other photo shows a young Burmese boy on his way to a temple initiation.*

All initiated males perform religious, moral, and recreational functions involving the overall society, including the establishment of rules of conduct for all villagers. Also influential to a certain degree are age sets, which consist of persons living in one village born within approximately three years of one another. Men's and women's sets are paired and support one another in feasting and ceremonial activities. Age grades, composed of several contiguous age sets, form a larger body with important social and economic functions, strong feelings of loyalty, and mutual support. Age sets are formed on a village basis; age grades are organized on the basis of both the village and village group. Women's age sets and age grades exist at less highly organized levels and are subject to rulings of the men's age grades. Since the 1940s, village improvement associations and village group unions have also arisen.

Among the Afikpo, age grouping applies primarily to males. Girls' age groups sometimes occur, but the rights and obligations individually acquired in marriage and motherhood effectively curtail further relationships by age. Affairs purely for women are often organized by married women's groups, but age is an infrequent criterion, and the groups are weakly developed. Men's age grades determine the relationships for both men and women. In Swazi, even before the devitalization of traditional groups, a girl's marriage age had always been determined by her own parents rather than the rules of age grouping. Informal age groups do exist, but have flexible membership functions, and serve largely for temporary tasks. In contrast to this situation is the marked participation of women in voluntary associations.

The role of age groups varies considerably as these examples show; yet they are always of great importance in maintaining social continuity, in providing "performers" for various social roles from generation to generation, and in transmitting the social and cultural heritage of a society. This importance tends to increase in societies in which kinship fails to provide a workable solution to a society's need for functional divisions among its members. This may be, hypothesizes S. N. Eisen-

based on age. So strong is the force of age grouping that it is capable of cutting across and conflicting with both political and kinship ties, and with the possibilities of specialization and the achievement or privilege by effort and good fortune in a stratified society. In such instances, kinship dominates only where conflict might arise through antipathetic age roles.

Age, therefore, must be accepted as a force creating social units. Yet it may play only an indirect role in grouping; its influence is limited by sex division, and systems for social organization exist outside both age and kinship grouping.

Voluntary associations

The rise of voluntary associations, whether out of individual predilection or community need, is a theme intimately associated with world urbanization and its attendant social upheavals; our own society's fondness for joining is incontestably related to its complexity. This phenomenon poses a major threat to the inviolability of age and kinship grouping. An individual is often separated from his brother or age mate; he obviously cannot obtain their help in learning to cope with life in a new and bewildering environment, in learning a new language or mannerisms necessary for the change from village to city if they are not present. But such functions must somehow be met. Because voluntary associations are by nature quite flexible, they are increasingly, both in the cities and in the tribal villages, filling this gap in the social structure.

Kinds of voluntary associations

The diversity of voluntary associations is astonishing. Their goals may include the pursuit of friendship, recreation, and the expression and distinction of rank (usually among relatively small and technologically simple groups) as well as governing function and the pursuit or defense of

Figure 19-5. *This photo shows a "captain" of the warrior age class in the Aboure tribe of the Ivory Coast dancing with other members of the grade. Other villagers look on and cheer the dancers.*

stadt from his comparative study of African age sets, because age is a criterion that can be applied to all members of society in the allocation of roles. Moreover, since age relationships have no contractual bond to begin with, there is no obstruction to setting up standards of behavior

economic interests. Traditionally, associations have served for the preservation of tribal songs, history, language, and moral beliefs; the Tribal Unions of West Africa, for example, continue to serve this purpose. Similar organizations, often operating clandestinely, have kept traditions alive among American Indian tribes undergoing a resurgence of ethnic pride despite generations of reservation schooling. Also a significant force in the formation of associations is the supernatural experience common to all members; the Crow Tobacco Society, the secret associations of the Kwakiutl Indians of British Columbia with their cycles of secret rituals, and the Katchina Cults of the Pueblo Indians are well-known examples. Among other traditional forms of association are military, occupational, political, and entertainment groups that parallel such familiar groups as the American Legion, labor unions, block associations, and "co-ops" of every kind.

Such organizations are frequently exclusive, but a prevailing characteristic is their concern for the general well-being of an entire village or village group. Membership may connote prestige but never economic advantage. The rain that falls as a result of the work of Pueblo rainmakers nourishes the crops of members and nonmembers alike.

Men's and women's associations. Traditionally, women's contributions to voluntary associations have been regarded as less significant than men's. Although research, such as Phoebe Ottenberg's study of age grouping among the Afikpo Ibo, tends to support such an assumption, the thinking behind it is undergoing marked revision. Schurtz's theory that underlying the differentiation between kinship and associational groups is a profound difference in the psychology of the sexes was widely accepted for years. To Schurtz, women were eminently unsocial beings who preferred to remain in kinship groups based on sexual relations and the reproductive function, rather than form units on the basis of commonly held interests. Men, on the other hand, were said to view sexual relations as isolated episodes, an

attitude that fostered the purely social factor that makes "birds of a feather flock together."

Today, needless to say, this kind of thinking is being heatedly challenged by scholars of both sexes. It is suggested that women have not formed associations because of the demands of

Figure 19-6. *In American society, voluntary associations are a common form of social organization. These ladies are members of a church group, holding its annual Christmas bazaar to raise funds.*

raising a family and their daily activities. But given the plethora of women's clubs of all kinds in the United States for several generations, one wonders how this belief of women as unsocial survived as long as it did. Earlier, of course, when women had to stay at home in rural situations, with no near neighbors, they had no chance to participate in voluntary associations. Moreover, some functions of men's associations—like military duties—may be culturally defined as purely for men or simply repugnant to women.

But, as Robert Lowie and others clearly point out, women do play important roles in associations of their own and even in those in which men predominate. Among the Crow, women participate even in the secret Tobacco Society as well as in their own exclusive groups. Throughout Africa, women's social clubs complement the men's, and are concerned with educating women and with crafts and charitable activities. In Sierra Leone, where once-simple dancing societies have developed under urban conditions into complex organizations with a set of modern objectives, the dancing *compin* is made up of young women as well as men, who together perform plays based on traditional music and dancing and raise money for various mutual benefit causes. The Kpelle of Liberia maintain initiation of "bush" schools for both young men and women; women also alternate with men in ritual supremacy of a chiefdom. The cycle of instruction and rule (four years for males, three for females) that marks these periods derives from the Kpelle's association of the number four with maleness and three with femaleness rather than from a notion of sexual superiority.

Women's liberation organizations, consciousness-raising groups, and professional organizations for women are examples of some of the voluntary associations arising directly or indirectly out of today's social climate. These groups cover the entire range of association forming, from simple friendship and support groups to political, guildlike, and economic (the publication of magazines, groups designed to influence advertising) associations on a national scale. If an unresolved point does exist in the matter of women's participation, it is in determining why women are excluded from associations in some societies, whereas in others their participation is essentially equal with men.

Associations in the urban world

The importance of voluntary associations in areas of rapid social change is considerable. Increasingly such organizations assume the roles and functions formerly held by kinship or age groups; in many areas they hold the key both to individual adaptation to new circumstances and to group survival. Where once groups were organized to preserve tribal ways and structure against the intrusion of the modern world, urban associations accept the reality of such an intrusion and help their members to cope both socially and economically. Members may turn to such associations for support and sympathy while unemployed or sick; the groups may also provide education or socialization. An important need met by many of these associations is economic survival; to achieve such ends they may help raise capital, regulate prices, discourage competition, and organize cooperative activities.

Always the keynote of these groups is adaptation. As Kenneth Little observes, adaptation implies not only the modification of institutions but also the development of new ones to meet the demands of an industrial economy and urban way of life. Modern urbanism involves the rapid diffusion of entirely new ideas, habits, and technical procedures, as well as a considerable reconstruction of social relationships as a consequence of new technical roles and groups created. Age-old conventions yield to necessity, as women and young people in general gain new status in the urban economy. Women's participation, especially in associations with mixed membership, involves them in new kinds of social relationships with men, including companionship and the chance to choose a mate by oneself. Young persons on the whole become leaders for their less westernized and sophisticated counterparts. Even

in rural areas, such voluntary associations thrive, reflecting the increasing consciousness of the outer world. With an irony implicit in many former colonial situations, the European contact that so frequently shattered permanent age and kinship groups has, partly through the influence of education, helped remove restrictions in association membership both in age and sex.

In our own culture, voluntary associations such as women's clubs, Boy and Girl Scouts, Kiwanis, Rotary, and PTA abound. Elements of secret initiatory cults survive, to some extent, among the Masonic lodges, and fraternity and sorority initiations. Women's associations recently seem to have proliferated. Although we may think of our own groups as more complex and highly organized than those of primitive societies, many of the new urban voluntary associations in Africa, for example, are elaborately structured and rival many of our secular and religious organizations. Such traditional groups, with their antecedents reaching far back in history, may have served as models for associations familiar to us; now, in becoming westernized, they promise to outstrip our own in complexity, an interesting phenomenon to watch as the non-Western countries become "modernized."

Figure 19-7. *This pair of pictures furnishes implicit evidence of the value of voluntary associations in bringing benefit to the group members. Above is a turn-of-the-century factory scene; below is the meeting of a powerful modern labor union.*

Social stratification

The study of social stratification involves the examination of distinctions that may seem perplexing. But social stratification is a common and powerful phenomenon among many of the world's peoples and must, at least in part, be viewed dispassionately.

Basically a **stratified society** is one in which members of the same sex and equivalent status do not have equal access to the basic resources that sustain life (as opposed to unstratified societies that rank individuals merely on the basis of age, sex, and kinship). The possibility for nonstratification does exist within both the **egalitarian** society, characteristic of hunters-gatherers, in which as many positions for prestige exist in any given age/sex grade as there are persons capable of filling them, and the **rank society,** which sharply limits its positions of prestige without affecting the access of its entire community to the basic resources of life. Such societies, though, are rare. The Kalahari Bushmen is the best known example of an egalitarian society; the noncontemporary Nootka Indians of the American Northwest Coast are an example of a rank society.

One widely accepted definition of a stratified society contains the following elements: hierarchically ranked groups that maintain relatively permanent positions, have differential control of the sources of power relative to their ranking, are separated by cultural and individual distinctions, and have an overreaching ideology that provides the rationale for the entire system. Such societies can be distinguished by a relative degree of inequality of rewards and privileges.

Class and caste

Most persons, hearing the word "caste," automatically think of India. Many anthropologists, however, question whether caste—widely used to describe random groups within rigid systems of social stratification—and the caste system should be defined in terms of the Hindu system alone, or whether the structure should be broadened to include features also found in societies of Arabia, Polynesia, North and South Africa, Guatemala, Japan, aboriginal North America, and the contemporary Unites States. Gerald D. Berreman, for example, defines a caste as a network of status-equal interactions in a society characterized by a network of hierarchical interaction between birth-ascribed groups. His approach makes possible the inclusion of a broader range of systems under the term "caste" than is possible with concepts derived only from stratification theory. The essential attributes of his caste naming include birth-ascribed, hierarchically ranked, ordered and culturally distinct groups, differential evaluation, differential rewards, and differential associations.

The basic difference between class and caste is that in the latter (a special kind of class) mobility is severely restricted, and endogamy is particularly marked.

In a large society, the groups constituting a caste system are often economically interdependent and occupationally specialized. Their members view themselves and are viewed by others as relatively homogeneous elements in a system of different ranked component parts, rather than independent and mutually unranked self-contained systems. Members of each caste share such common characteristics as group name, skin color, language, occupation, dress, or place of residence. Individual attributes in a caste system are irrelevant; caste membership is birth-determined, universal, and lifelong. Individual mobility is impossible. Thus, although caste shares certain characteristics with age grouping, membership may be more subjective, containing such exalted notions as purity (as in India) or honor (as in Swat). Almost all social interaction—who may become one's friend, mate, neighbor, master, servant, client, or competitor—is largely a matter of caste. Taboos against interaction are strong.

The **plural society** is in essence a simplified variation of the caste system. Such a society is composed of cultural sections, each of which is really a little society in itself, with its own kinship, family, and socialization systems, recreational activities, religious beliefs and practices, values, and language variants. The whole system, while in many ways sounding like a collection of voluntary groups, is generally thought to be held together by the political domination of one section. However, in the view of the social scientist Talcott Parsons, consensual interests and values, rather than political domination, are the cohesive force.

Examples of pluralistic societies can be found in postcolonial Africa, where black Africans exercise control over Indians and Chinese, and in the class-color hierarchies of West Indian societies. In the latter cases, classes are separated not merely by color and status, wealth and power, but also by diverse cultural patterns and social frameworks

Figure 19-8. *Although India's once-rigid caste system has changed considerably, members of the lowest caste are still barred from many kinds of social opportunity. Rapid change in the system may benefit such individuals but it also creates much social confusion.*

involving legal, religious, educational, and family institutions. Dominating are upper class Creoles —of North European, African, and mixed descent—who rule over such groups as aboriginal American Indians, Portuguese, Chinese, East Indian, Javanese, and Syrian immigrants.

Determinants of stratification

Social stratification can be based on many criteria —wealth, cultural level, legal status, birth, personal qualities, ideology. The Natchez Indians used to maintain an elaborate system of social class based on three ranked groups of nobility and a single commoner class. Obligatory inter-class marriage kept the nobility small and re-plenished the commoners. The Aztec society at the time of the Spanish Conquest was divided into nobles and commoners, who in turn were divided into elaborate classes according to urban or rural settlement and occupation, from warriors through merchants and craftsmen. Three slave classes also existed. The entire scheme was ad-ministered by an elaborate bureaucracy of nobles and warriors.

Although economic determinists, such as Karl Marx, stress ownership of land and capital as the

Figure 19-9. *Evidence of social stratification in Nigeria can be seen in the homage paid by the kneeling village chief, an important man in his own right, to the turbaned king.*

determinant of social stratification, others, such as Max Weber, include the nature of the external standard of living. Hyman Rodman incorporates both objective and subjective working criteria. The expression of attitudes associated with difference in status and role show marked differences from one culture to another. Harold Driver notes that on the whole American Indian societies were far more democratic than those of Africa, but indicates that there were nevertheless marked differences in rank and status in some areas and true social classes in other areas. In all societies, as we have seen, each individual possesses a multiple number of statuses simultaneously, possibly ranked according to wealth, social heredity, proficiency, supernatural sanction, or any number of these factors in combination. Ideally, all statuses should be considered in giving an individual a place in a particular social class, but obviously this is rare. A point perhaps not as obvious is that for a society to be a "class" society at least two classes must exist; a one-class system is essentially classless.

The evils in social stratification of any kind may tend to overshadow the good; they at least appear to make life oppressive for large segments of a population. Often, the lower classes are placated by means of religion, which offers them a tolerable existence in the hereafter. If they have this to look forward to, they are more likely to accept the "here and now." In considering social stratification, we must, however, reckon with such deep-seated human drives as the desire to excel one's fellows. Although the impulse is suppressed by a few peoples, such as the Pueblo Indians, it is intense in most societies. Even in relatively democratic societies, certain goals stressed eventually become culturally fixed. Among the Winebago and Hopi Indians, the Sherente and Ugan-

dan peoples, clan superiority and kinship lineages are recognized in electing chiefs, performing sacred rituals, and other special tasks, whether or not membership entails any economic advantages. Even functions not related to class may contain within themselves the germ of class differentiation. Ethnic differences often lead to diverse classes and even castes, as members of our own society have experienced through the racial stereotyping that leads to social and economic disadvantages.

Classes perform an integrative function in society. They may cut across some or all lines of kinship, residence, occupation, and age group, depending on the particular society, thus counteracting potential tendencies for society to fragment into discreet entities. Stratification may also provide a means for an alien group to dominate large members of people. Those who dominate are aided by their acknowledged "upper class" status. They are respected by the lower classes, who "know their place" and let themselves be dominated.

☐

The Tiriki age group organization is directly borrowed from the Nilo-Hamitic Terik who border the Tiriki to the south. There are seven named aged groups (Kabalach, Golongolo, Jiminigayi, Nyonje, Mayina, Juma, and Sawe), each embracing approximately a fifteen-year age span. In addition, each age group passes successively through four distinctive age grades. The system is cyclical, each age group being reinstated with new initiates approximately every 105 years.

Perhaps the easiest way to grasp the difference in age groups and age grades is to review the nature of our college class system. Freshmen entering college in the autumn of 1958, for example, immediately become known as the Class of 1962—the year when they were due to graduate. Thenceforth, for as long as they live, they are known as the Class of 1962. While in college, however, members of the Class of 1962 must pass in successive years through four ranked grades: freshman, sophomore, junior, and senior.

In Tiriki each age group contains those men who were initiated over a fifteen-year age span, not simply during one year. The initiation rites, it will be recalled, traditionally extend over a six months' period, and are held every four years; thus each age group receives recruits from three or four successive initiations. The four traditional Tiriki age grades are *bandu bi lihe, balulu* (the warriors) *balulu basaxulu* (the elder warriors) *basaxulu bi biina, basaxulu bu luhya* (the judicial elders), and *basaxulu basaalisi* (the ritual elders). Before they were prohibited by the British about 1900, handing-over ceremonies were held at about fifteen-year intervals in conjunction with the closing of an age group to more initiates. At this time the age group just closed to initiates became formally instated in the warriors age grade, the age group that had just been the warriors' moved on to the elder warrior grade, the former elder warriors moved on to the judicial elder grade, and the former judicial elders moved on to the ritual eldership.

The cyclical aspect of Tiriki age groups can also be readily compared with the system of college classes, if one substitutes the Tiriki age group name for "Class of __," and remembers that each Tiriki age group embraces fifteen years. The Class of '62 at Harvard, for example, has been reinstated every 100 years for several centuries with a new group of college men, and thus can be viewed as part of a cyclical process. In Tiriki each cycle lasts 105 years instead of a century, because the seven age groups, *each* embracing fifteen years, cover a total span of 105 years. The Sawe age group, for example, open for initiates from 1948 to 1963, was previously instated and open to initiates from roughly 1843 to 1858.

The *warriors* were formally given the responsibility of guarding the country. They were said "to hold the land". An age group's lasting reputation was principally earned while it was occupying the warrior age grade. Similarly the reputation accompanying a man throughout the remainder of his life and then remembered by his posterity was primarily based on the leadership, courage, and good fortune he exhibited while a warrior.

The duties and perogatives of the *elder warriors* were neither as glorious nor as well defined as those of the warriors. They had relatively few specialized social tasks, but they gradually assumed an increasing share of administrative type activities in areas that were basically the responsibility of the elder age groups. For example, at public post-funeral gatherings held to settle property claims, usually a man of the elder warrior group was called upon to serve as chairman. His duty was to maintain order, to see that all the claims and counterclaims were heard, to initiate compromises, but always to seek and defer to the judgment of the elders in matters that were equivocal or a departure from tradition. Members of this age grade also served as couriers and envoys when important news needed to be transmitted between elders of different subtribes.

The age group occupying the *judicial elder* age grade fulfilled most of the tasks connected with the arbitration and settlement of local disputes. This included everything from delinquent or contested bridewealth payments to cases of assault or accidental injury. Any major disturbance or legitimate complaint by the head of a household served as sufficient reason for the community judicial elders to gather at the local meeting ground to hear the plaintiff and defendant, question witnesses, and give a judgment.

The *ritual elders* presided over the priestly functions of the homestead ancestral shrine observances, at subclan meetings concerning inheritance and the like, at semiannual community supplications, and at the initiation rites. Also, the ritual elders were accredited with having access to magical powers. They were the group who expelled or killed witches, or at least who were counted on to neutralize their evil powers, and they also were the group who underwrote the death through sorcery of anyone cursed by the community for violating the initiation secrets or for committing some other heinous crime. The advice of the ritual elders was sought in all situations that seemed to hold danger for or entail the general well-being of the community or the tribe. For example, the warriors solicited the auguries of the ritual elders before embarking on a major raid, and postponed the raid if the omens were bad.

Today, over sixty years after the last formal handing-over ceremony, the age group cycle still continues, kept alive by the regular performance of the initiation rites. The four graded statuses are still manifest in informal social behavior and in current social ideology and action, albeit in relatively informal and altered form. Young men whose age group according to traditional reckoning would now be warriors, are still occasionally called, or referred to as "warriors," but only in a spirit of friendliness and flattery. Today, instead of fighting, young men of this age grade find a modicum of excitement and adventure through extended employment away from the tribe. A fortunate few are pursuing secondary or advanced studies, teaching school, or holding clerical jobs; but in most cases they, too, are employed or are studying off-tribe. Members of the warrior age grade are no longer held in such esteem as formerly, and no one ever speaks of them as "holding the land." Their active participation, however, in the new and rapidly changing world beyond tribal boundaries still lends the warrior age grade a bit of glamour.

In contrast to that of the warriors, the relative status of those occupying the elder warrior age grade has increased dramatically during the last fifty years.

Men of this age grade have assumed nearly all the new administrative and executive roles created by the advent and growth of a centralized tribal administrative bureaucracy. With few exceptions they hold all the salaried offices in the tribal administration. It is quite in keeping with traditional age grade expectations that members of this age grade should occupy the executive and administrative positions, but pre-European conditions provided only a minimal number of such roles.

The judicial elders still serve as the local judiciary body, although their authority was somewhat altered and curtailed by the British colonial administration.

The ritual elders have suffered a severe diminution of their functions and powers. During the last twenty years, ancestor worship has declined until today the formal aspects of the cult are virtually extinct. They, like the warriors, have been deprived of a major part of their traditional age grade activity; but unlike the warriors, they have not found any substitute activity. The positions of leadership in the Christian church have been assumed by a small number of men, mostly of the elder warrior age grade. The ritual elders continue, however, to hold the most important positions in the initiation ceremonies, and their power as sorcerers and witchcraft expungers remains almost universally feared and respected.

Source:
From "The Bantu Tiriki of Western Kenya," by Walter H. Sangree, in *Peoples of Africa,* edited by James Gibbs, Jr. Copyright © 1965 by Holt, Rinehart and Winston, Inc. Reprinted by permission of Holt, Rinehart and Winston, Inc.

Summary

1.

Age groupings are important forms of nonkinship organizations. There are three age categories: age class, age grade, and age set. An age grade is a category of persons within a particular, culturally distinguished age range. The people currently occupying an age grade form an age class. An age set is a group of persons initiated into an age grade, who move together through some or all of life's stages. A specific time is often ritually established for moving from a younger to an older age grade. Anthropologists agree that all peoples distinguish the main stages of individual development. There is controversy, however, over the relative strength, cohesiveness, and stability of age groups; in many societies, they are relatively unimportant.

2.

An example of a simple, traditionally defined age class is found in the Nuer of Kenya. Among the Nuer, the position of each male is defined only in terms of seniority. More sophisticated age groupings are found in the Swazi of Swaziland and the Afikpo Ibo of Eastern Nigeria. Among the Swazi, men's age groups are formed roughly every five to seven years, depending on the need for immature youths to be available for state rituals. Each man remains a member of the same age group from its inception until his death. Among the Afikpo Ibo, age sets are made up of persons living in one village who are born within approximately three years of one another. Age grades, made up of several contiguous age sets, form a larger body with important social and economic functions in the context of the society at large.

3.

Voluntary associations are a form of nonkinship organization which has risen mostly as a result of world urbanization. Voluntary associations have traditionally served to preserve a society's cultural heritage. There is a current controversy over whether women have contributed as much to the development of voluntary associations as men. Women do play important roles in associations of their own and even in those in which men predominate. Among the Crow, women participate in the men's secret Tobacco Society, as well as in their own exclusive group.

4.

Voluntary associations are particularly important in areas of rapid social change. They are increasingly assuming the roles and functions formerly held by kinship or age groups. Urban associations help their members cope, both socially and economically, with the intrusions of the modern world. The keynote of these groups is always adaptation, implying not only the modification of institutions but also the development of new ones. Such groups are common in modern industrial societies.

5.

A socially stratified society is one in which members of the same sex and equivalent status do not have equal access to life-sustaining resources. The egalitarian society has as many positions in an age/sex grade as there are persons to fill them. The rank society sharply limits its positions to a selected few, but gives its entire community access to life-sustaining resources. Stratified societies contain hierarchically ranked groups. These groups maintain relatively permanent positions. Power is related to rank; it is conferred by the holding of certain social statuses.

6.

Caste is a kind of class in which mobility is severely restricted and endogamy is particularly marked. In a large society, the groups making up a caste system are often economically interdependent and occupationally specialized. Members of a caste system view only other members as equals. The plural society is essentially a simplified variation of the caste system. It is made up of cultural sections, each a society in itself. The whole system is generally thought by its members to be held together by a dominant group, but this need not be true in all cases.

7.

Social stratification can be based on many criteria, such as wealth, cultural level, legal status, birth, personal qualities, and ideology. A rigidly stratified society in which mobility is limited can make life oppressive for large segments of a popultion.

Suggested readings

Eisenstadt, S. N. *From Generation to Generation: Age Groups and Social Structure.* Glencoe, Illinois: Free Press, 1956.
Various social phenomena known as age-group and youth movements are analyzed to ascertain whether it is possible to specify the social conditions in which they occur. The analysis is based on a study of various societies—primitive, historical, and modern. The basic hypothesis of the book is that age groups exist in universalistic societies in which the family is not the basic unit of the social division of labor.

Friedenberg, Edgar *Coming of Age in America: Growth and Acquiescence.* New York: Random House, 1965.
A study of the effects of life in a mass society on the values of the people who share it. It is specifically an analysis of student values as these affect and are expressed in the choices made about school situations and attitudes toward secondary schools.

Lenski, Gerhard E. *Power and Privilege.* New York: McGraw-Hill, 1966.
Who gets what and why is explained by the distributive process and systems of social stratification in industrial nations: U.S., U.S.S.R., Sweden and Britain. Using a broadly comparative approach, the author makes heavy use of anthropological and historical material as well as the usual sociological materials on modern industrial societies. The basic approach is theoretical and analytical; the book builds on certain postulates about the nature of man and society, seeking to develop in a systematic manner an explanation of a variety of patterns of stratification. The theory presented is a synthesis of the two dominant theoretical traditions of the past and present, currently represented in both Marxian and functionalist theory.

Lowie, Robert H. *Social Organization.* New York: Holt, Rinehart and Winston, 1948.
This is a classic, though somewhat dated, study of social organization. The author discusses social organization on a cross-cultural basis, including age grading and voluntary associations.

part 6

Social integration

Economic
systems

It is perhaps in the study of the economy of non-literate peoples that we are most apt to fall prey to interpreting anthropological data in terms of our own technologies, our own values of work and property, and our own determination of what is rational. For example, many of us would say that certain West African people act like children in their seeming inability to plan ahead. These people conventionally and traditionally use up so much of their food feasting during the dry season that, when the wet season comes and they must break up the land for new planting, they do not have enough food. We might term the Kogi Indians superstitious because of the way they use their land. The Kogi, who inhabit the Sierra Nevada range of Colombia, are faced with a scarcity of land. In these mountain ranges, however, there are many terraces built by earlier inhabitants; using them as farm land would save the Kogi much moving from one place to another. Yet the Kogi will not use these terraces. "There are many spirits of the dead there," they say.[1]

In order to understand how the schedule of wants or demands of a given society is balanced against the supply of goods and services available,

[1]Melville Herskovits, *Economic Anthropology: A Study in Comparative Economics* (New York: Knopf, 1952) 2nd edition.

it is necessary to introduce a third variable—the anthropological variable of culture. In any given economic system, economic processes cannot be interpreted without culturally defining the demands and understanding the conventions that dictate how and when they are satisfied.

In the last thirty years, anthropologists have borrowed theory and concepts from the discipline of economics in an attempt to understand certain relationships of nonliterate people. Since economics is the study of the allocation of scarce goods and services in industrial society, it is a matter of controversy as to what modifications must be made in order for economic theory to be applicable to nonindustrial societies. Do nonindustrial societies have economic systems? Can we speak of the profit motive, savings, capital goods, and all the other concepts that economists use, in relation to nonindustrial societies?

There are anthropologists who adhere to the point of view that there is little to be learned from the study of market economies, where the principal motivation is profit, in studying people who do not exchange goods for gain. This position is called **substantivism.**

Other scholars, called **formalists,** take a different view. Formalists claim that economic theory really has to do with the ways people get the greatest personal satisfaction in saving things and in distributing scarce resources. If this is true, then economic theory is certainly general enough to apply to all societies.

An economic system may be defined as a set of institutions and regulations through which goods are produced and distributed within a given technology and social system. Almost every society produces a surplus, be it ever so minimal by our standards. Among nonindustrial peoples, the forms of production, distribution, and surplus may be so closely linked with institutions, such as religion and kinship obligations, that we scarcely discern them. Nevertheless, all societies produce a living and consume goods and at some times have leftovers.

Resources

In every society there are customs and rules governing the kinds of work that are done, which people do the work, who owns the land and tools, and how the work is accomplished. Land, labor, capital, and technology are the productive resources that a social group may use to produce desired goods and services. The rules surrounding the use of these resources are embedded in the culture and determine the way the economy operates.

Patterns of labor

Every society has rules to govern the allotment of work. There is always a division of labor along sex and age categories; such division is simply a further development of the patterns found in all higher primates. Whether men or women do a particular job varies from group to group, but much work is set apart as the work of either one sex or the other. The sexual division of labor in nonliterate societies has been studied extensively in anthropology, and some researchers have at-

Figure 20-1. *This Yanomamo woman is carrying a pack with all the possessions of her entire family. Here this task, which does require considerable physical strength, is considered women's work.*

tempted to make generalizations along physiological lines; for example, the women do the lighter work, the men hunt because they are stronger, the women stay nearer home because they feed and care for the children. Melville Herskovits, one of the first anthropologists to apply economics to anthropology, says, however, that a study of the work done by men and women in particular groups soon shows that "the specific forms taken by sex division of labor must be referred to the historical development of the particular body of traditions by which a particular people order their lives."[2] It is not possible to make such sweeping generalizations about the division of labor according to sex; rather each society must be studied to observe the assignment of work.

In Northern Australia, among the Tiwi, where the wealthier men usually had several wives, the women, with their baskets and perhaps a baby on their backs, spent the day gathering food—chiefly vegetables, grubs, and worms. Even the smallest household would contain at least one elder wife who knew the bush like the palm of her hand. These old women supervised and trained the younger women in the gathering and preparation of food for the household. The husband never interfered in matters concerning the work of the women. "If I had only one or two wives, I would starve," the head of a large household told a missionary who was preaching against plural marriage, "but with my present ten or twelve wives I can send them out in all directions in the morning and at least two or three of them are likely to bring back something at the end of the day; then we all can eat."[3] The vegetable foods obtained by the women gatherers were the everyday staples. The meat the men brought in was considered a dividend or extra. In such a culture, polygyny confers an adaptive advantage since it enables all members of the family unit to remain relatively well fed.

The men of the Copper Eskimos, who lived in the Northwest Territories in Canada, provided the food for the household.[4] In these northerly regions, there was scarcely any vegetable food. From May until November the men hunted caribou and fished. The rest of the year was devoted to hunting the ringed seal, except for a few weeks in early December, which were spent sewing clothes for the winter.

The entire community participated in caribou drives. Shouting women and children drove the caribou toward the bowmen, who lay in wait in pits behind stones and poles set up like scarecrows to resemble men. The men hunted the seal in groups, waiting for them at a blowhole. When a seal was speared through the hole, help from another man was needed to pull the heavy animal out of the water onto the ice.

The women devoted much of their time to taking care of the children. They also cooked, prepared skins for clothing, fished, and were expected to do such heavy work as pitching and breaking camp, pulling sledges with the dogs, and backpacking considerable loads in the summer. However, during the long winter days, when the men were hunting seal, they spent much of the day visiting and gossiping with the other women.

There may also be a division of labor according to age. Among the Tiwi, for example, the men who were too old to hunt manufactured the tools and artifacts of the tribe. The older men, those with large households and therefore a large labor force, had leisure time to develop skills in the manufacture of canoes, baskets, digging sticks, and beautifully made artistic creations, such as grave posts and ceremonial spears. These men also composed songs and dances.

Among the Copper Eskimos, old age was a difficult time because the harsh climate and migratory life were special hardships for the old. The cold and the damp accelerated aging, apparently, and the old suffered the most during famines. There was little work easy enough for the old of either sex to accomplish, so old people and children constituted more of a burden for the Eskimos than for people in a more salubrious climate. Eskimo boys began to make an economic contribution in their late teens, and a ceremonial event was made of the killing of their first seal.

In many nonliterate societies, both children and older people make a greater contribution to the economy in terms of work and responsibility than is common in our own. In South Vietnam, for example, young children not only look after

[2]Ibid., p. 132
[3]C. W. M. Hart and Arnold R. Pilling, The Tiwi of North Australia (New York: Holt, Rinehart and Winston, 1960) p. 34.
[4]M. G. Bicchieri (ed.), Hunters and Gatherers Today: A Socioeconomic Study of Eleven Such Cultures in the Twentieth Century (New York: Holt, Rinehart and Winston, 1972) pp. 12-19, 41-44.

their younger brothers and sisters but help with housework as well. "An American would be horrified to see a child, four or five years old, handling a chopping knife or lighting an oil lamp, but in Vietnam it is common."[5] Unlike the elderly Eskimos, old people in South Vietnam retain economic responsibilities. The grandmother, for example, holds the purse strings, markets, cooks, and cleans the house. A similar allocation of responsibility used to be common in rural American households, where the work load was heavy and the labor pool small.

Cooperation. Cooperative work groups can be found everywhere in nonliterate, nonindustrial, and nonpecuniary societies. Often, if the effort involves the whole community, there is a festive spirit to the work. Jomo Kenyatta described the time of enjoyment after a day's labor in Kenya. "If a stranger happens to pass by, he will have no idea that these people who are singing and dancing have completed their day's work. This is why most Europeans have erred by not realizing that the African in his own environment does not count hours or work by the movement of the clock, but works with good spirit and enthusiasm to complete the tasks before him."[6]

In Dahomey, the iron workers cooperate in the operation of their forges. Each man owns his own iron, and the members of the forge work on the iron of one man at a time. The product belongs to the man who provided the iron, and he is free to sell it in the market for personal gain, reinvesting his return in more iron. Meanwhile, he works at the forge for each other man until his turn comes again.[7]

Cooperative work is not necessarily voluntary. It may be part of fulfilling duties to in-laws; it may be performed for chiefs or priests, by command. The institutions of family, kinship, religion, and the state all may act as organizing elements that define the nature and condition of each worker's cooperative obligations.

[5] Randy Gellerman in *The New York Times*, July 24, 1973, p. 40.
[6] Herskovits, *op. cit.*, p. 103.
[7] *Ibid.*, p. 108.

Figure 20-2a. *The Danakil tribe in Ethiopia have a very narrow economic specialization; they obtain salt from the ground and sell it to neighboring tribesmen; this work, which calls for cooperative effort of all the men, supports the entire tribe.*

Social integration ● part **6**

Craft specialization.

In nonindustrial societies, where division of labor occurs along lines of age and sex, each person in the society has knowledge and competence in all aspects of work appropriate to his age and sex. Yet in every society there is some specialization of craft. Among the Trobriand Islanders, for example, the artisans of one village specialize in stone blades for adzes, whereas their neighbors may specialize in decorating pots or carving wooden handles for the stone blades.

An example of specialization can be seen among the Puluwats, who live in the Carolines: the most respected member of the society is the master mariner, a naval architect. He designs the frail *proas* that make long ocean voyages. He carves out logs into shapes as sophisticated as the limited technology will allow. He also makes the sails, blocks, and spars. During voyages, he is skipper of the craft and the navigator, finding his destination, perhaps three or four hundred miles away, across open water, to another tiny island like the one he came from. When asked by a European sea captain, "How did you find the island?" one master navigator is said to have replied, "I didn't find the island, sir. It has always been there."[8]

In Puluwat there are different schools of thought as to the best shape for a *proa,* and a young man desirous of becoming a navigator will apprentice himself for many years to a master navigator whose work he admires, in order to learn this specialty. An American anthropologist studied navigation for eighteen months with a master navigator in Puluwat and found that even after that length of time he scarcely began to understand the rudiments of *proa* building and of navigation. Specialties even in simple technologies are lifetime occupations and demand a high order of intelligence, knowledge, and skill.

Figure 20-2b,c. *Once the salt crust is broken up and removed (hard work in the hot sun and high temperatures), it is cut into smaller slabs that serve as the basic unit for trade. These slabs are then loaded on camels, and a caravan takes the salt across the desert to the coast and highlands to be sold.*

Land ownership

All societies have regulations that determine the

[8]Thomas Gladwin, *East is a Big Bird: Navigation and Logic on Puluwat Atoll* (Cambridge, Mass.: Harvard University Press, 1970).

way that valuable land resources will be allocated. Small-scale hunter-gatherer societies must determine who can hunt game and gather plants, and where these activities take place. Horticulturists or food growers must decide how their farmland is to be acquired, worked, and passed on. Pastoralists require a system that determines rights to watering places and grazing land, as well as the right of access to land over which they move their herds. Full-time or extensive agriculturists must have some means of determining title to land and access to water supplies for irrigation purposes. In our own industrialized Western society, the system of private ownership of land and the rights to natural resources prevails. Elaborate laws have been established to regulate the buying, owning, and selling of land and water resources.

In nonindustrialized societies, individual ownership of land is rare; generally it is owned by one lineage or tribe. For example, among the Tiwi, all land is owned by one of nine bands. Each band of about two to three hundred people lived on roughly 200 square miles of land which they considered to be their territory—their own country. The territorial boundaries between bands were well-known, although they might strike Westerners as vague and imprecise. Anthropologists Hart and Pilling comment:

> All pieces of country—clumps of jungle, stretches of grassland, sections of thick woods —had names. A thickly wooded area belonged to one band, while the more open country that began where the woods thinned out belonged to another; thus the boundary was not a sharp line but a transitional zone—perhaps several miles—where the change from trees to savannah became noticeable. The Tiwi thought of the landscape as a sort of spectrum where a man moved gradually out of one district into another as he passed from one type of landscape into another.[9]

The adaptive value of this attitude toward land ownership is clear; the size of the band territories,

[9] Hart and Pilling, op. cit., p. 12.

as well as the size of the bands themselves, can change in size to adjust to change in amount of resources in any given place. Such adjustment would be more difficult under a system of individual ownership of land.

Among some West African horticultural tribes, a feudal system of land ownership prevails, by which all land belongs to the head chief. He allocates it to various subchiefs, who in turn distribute it to lineages; lineage leaders then assign individual plots to each farmer. Just as in medieval Europe, the African people owe allegiance to the subchiefs (or nobles) and the principal chief (or king). The people who work the land must pay taxes and fight for the king when necessary. The people, in a sense, "own" the land and transmit their ownership to their heirs. However, an individual cannot give away, sell, or otherwise dispose of his plot of land without approval from the elder of his lineage. When an individual no longer needs the land allocated to him, the lineage head rescinds title to it and re-allocates it to someone else in the lineage. The important operative principle among such farmers is that such a system extends the right to the individual to use land for a certain period of time, and the land is not "owned" outright.

Capital

Economists use the term **capital** to describe any resource that is not used up in the process of producing goods. In our society, capital means steel furnaces, drill presses, and jigsaws, as well as the money that will buy such tools. But even nonindustrial societies have means of creating and allocating the tools and other artifacts used in the production of goods and passed on to succeeding generations. The number and kinds of tools that a society uses are limited by the life-styles of its members. Hunter-gatherers and nomads, who are frequently on the move, have fewer and simpler tools than the more sedentary agriculturist, because a great number of complex tools would decrease their mobility.

Figure 20-3. *A grandmother of the !Kung tribe supervises the cooking efforts of a young girl; both young and old contribute.*

Hunters and gatherers make and use a variety of weapons, many of which are ingenious in their effectiveness. (For an account of the tools of such a society, see "The Technology of the Gua-yaki" in Chapter 16.) They usually make for them-selves the tools they need and so have first rights to their use. They may give or lend tools to others in exchange for the products of their use. For example, a Bushman who gives his arrow to an-other hunter has a right to a share in any animals that the hunter may kill. Game is thought to "be-long" to the man whose arrow killed it.

Among horticulturists, the slashing knife and the digging stick or hoe are the primary tools. Since these tools are relatively easy to produce, every man can make them himself and thus has first rights to their use. When he is not using them, any member of his family may ask to use them and usually is granted permission to do so. To refuse would mean the tool-owner would be treated with scorn for his singular lack of concern for others. If another kinsman helps raise the crop that is traded for a particular tool, he becomes part owner of the implement, and it may not be traded or given away without his permission.

As tools and other productive goods become more complex, more difficult and costlier to make, individual ownership in them usually becomes more absolute, as do the conditions under which owners may borrow and use such equipment. It is easy to replace a knife lost by a kinsman during palm cultivation, but much more difficult to re-place an iron plow or a power-driven threshing machine. Rights to the ownership of complex tools are more rigidly applied; generally the man who has supplied the capital for the purchase of a complex piece of machinery is considered the sole owner and may decide how and by whom it will be used.

Technology

The economy of any society is dependent on the level of technological knowledge. In literate so-cieties, this knowledge is preserved in books; in nonliterate societies it is retained in the minds of the living members of the group.

The division of labor is a method by which much of the technology can be apportioned among the members so that it will not be lost and can even be improved. Knowledge of various plants, when they can be harvested, where they are found, which parts are edible, and how they should be prepared and cooked, is learned by the children as they watch the adults. Lévi-Strauss reports that small children may have a knowledge of the names and uses of hundreds of plants.[10] The behavior and habits of animals, how to track them, how to use their bones and skin, how to make arrows or spears for the hunt, all are bits and pieces of the technology of nonindustrial people. It is on this technology that their livelihood rests, and all of it must be learned and passed on to the next generation in order for the group to survive.

Production—the yearly economic cycle

In an agricultural society, the patterns of work involved in the production of farm goods follow the seasons. The yearly economic cycle in a small village in modern Greece is a good illustration of production in an economic system.

The crops of the village are grown both for home consumption and for the market. The first event of the agricultural year is the pruning of the grape vines, which is commenced at the end of the winter rains. Pruning, followed by deep hand-hoeing, is considered a man's occupation and must be completed quickly so that the men can turn to plowing the cotton fields. Cotton is a commercial crop, whereas the grapes are grown for the wine made and consumed by the household. Cotton is usually plowed by rented tractors; the planting is done by hand.

Once the cotton starts to grow, the hoeing be-

[10] Claude Lévi-Strauss, *The Savage Mind* (Chicago: The University of Chicago Press, 1966).

gins. This arduous labor is performed by the girls and women of the household. Other women from the village or even from neighboring villages may be hired if the crop is a large one. This work does not excuse the women from their regular housework.

In June the wheat which was planted in the late fall is harvested by machines that are owned and operated by people outside of the village. Payment is in kind, 8 percent of the amount of wheat threshed. The wheat, made into bread and consumed at home, is still, literally, the staff of life, the basic food for the people of the village. The chaff and straw are used for the animals.

In late June and early July the tobacco, which was planted at about the same time as the wheat, is ready to be picked and strung for drying—a task welcomed by the women after the hot, back-breaking work of hoeing the cotton. They can sit in the shade near their houses.

Irrigation work in the cotton fields starts for the men in July. Each field is irrigated about three times. In October and November the cotton is picked, which requires prolonged work by many hands as the cotton does not ripen uniformly. Women do this job and again may be hired if necessary. The farmer's problem is to get the cotton picked before the winter rains set in.

Meanwhile, the vines have ripened, and wine-making takes place in October. This is an occasion much enjoyed because the men, women, and children all pick the grapes together, talk and joke, and eat a little of the produce.

The round of productive activities starts again for the next year. The Greek farmer, like any peasant, is really running a household rather than a genuinely commercial enterprise. He is motivated by a desire to protect the welfare of his own family; and the family, as the economic unit, works as a group to maintain or improve its common position. The villagers measure prestige and honor by the degree to which a family succeeds in fulfilling its obligations. The natural environment, the technology, and the work roles of the family members each exert an influence on the success from year to year of the family efforts.

Figure 20-4. *An Australian hunter of the Walmadgeri tribe prepares to build a fire and cook a kangaroo. He will later supervise the customary distribution of the meat to members of his family group.*

Distribution and exchange

In our own money economy, there is a two-step process between labor and consumption. The money received for labor must be translated into something else before it is directly consumable. In societies with no medium of exchange, the rewards for labor are usually direct. The workers in a family group consume what they harvest; they eat what the hunter brings home; they use the tools that they make. But even where there is no formal medium of exchange, some distribution of goods takes place. Karl Polanyi, an economist, classified the cultural systems of distributing material goods into three modes: reciprocity, redistribution, and market exchange.

Reciprocity

Reciprocity refers to a transaction between groups within a community in the form of gifts and countergifts presented in a manner prescribed by ritual and ceremony. In non-Western societies, pure altruism in gift-giving is as rare as it is in our own society. The overriding motive is to fulfill social obligations and perhaps to gain a bit of social prestige in the process. It might best be compared in our society to a hostess who gives a dinner party. She may compete within her social circle in the gourmet food she prepares, the originality of her decorations, and the quality of wit and conversation of her guests. Her expectation is that she will be invited to similar parties by some, although perhaps not all, of the guests.

Social customs dictate the nature and occasion of gift-giving. When an animal is killed by a group of hunters in Australia, the meat is divided among the families of the hunters and other kinsmen. Each person in the camp gets a share, the size of which depends on his relationship to the hunters. The least desirable parts may be kept by the hunters themselves. When a kangaroo was killed, the left hind leg went to the brother of the hunter, the tail to his father's brother's son, the loins and the fat to his father-in-law, the ribs to his mother-in-law, the fore-legs to his father's younger sister, the head to his wife, and the entrails and the blood to the hunter. If there were arguments over the apportionment, it was because the principles of distribution were not being followed properly. The hunter and his family would seem to fare badly according to this arrangement, but they would have their turn when another man made the kill. The giving and receiving was obligatory, as was the particularity of the distribution. Such sharing of food reinforces community bonds and ensures that everyone eats. It might also be viewed as a way of saving perishable goods. By giving away part of his kill, the hunter gets a social IOU for a similar amount of food in the future. It is really quite similar to putting money in a time-deposit savings account.

Reciprocity in which neither the value of the gift is calculated nor the time of repayment specified is **generalized reciprocity. Balanced reciprocity** is not part of a long-term process. The giving and receiving, as well as the time involved, are more specific. Examples of balanced reciprocity among the Crow Indians are related by Robert Lowie.[11] A woman, skilled in the tanning of buffalo hides, might offer her services to a neighbor who needed a new cover for her tepee. It took an expert to design a tepee cover, which required from fourteen to twenty skins. The designer might need as many as twenty collaborators, whom she instructed in the sewing together of the skins and whom the tepee owner might remunerate with a feast. The designer herself would be given some kind of property by the tepee owner. In another example from the Crow, Lowie relates that if a married woman brought her brother a present of food, he might reciprocate with a present of ten arrows for her husband, which rated as the equivalent of a horse.

Negative reciprocity is a third form of gift-giving, in which the giver tries to get the better of the exchange. In Malekula, according to Her-

skovits, "a gift is at most a venture, a hopeful speculation."[12] At the very least, the gift-giver has placed the recipient under an obligation.

Giving, receiving, and sharing constitute a form of social security or insurance. A family contributes to others when they have the means and can count on receiving from others in time of need. A leveling mechanism is at work in the process of reciprocity. Social obligations compel a family to distribute their goods, and no one is permitted to accumulate too much more than the others. Greater wealth simply brings a greater obligation to give.

Barter and trade

Reciprocity in the form of obligatory gift-giving takes place within the group. When exchange takes place between two groups, there is apt to be greater hostility and competition. Such an exchange takes the form of trade, by which scarce items from one group are bartered for desirable goods from the other group. Relative value is calculated, and, despite an outward show of indifference, sharp trading is more the rule when compared to the reciprocal nature of the exchanges within the group.

An arrangement that partook partly of reciprocity and partly of trade existed between the Kota, in India, and three neighboring tribes who traded their surplus goods and certain services with the Kota. The Kota were the musicians and artisans for the area. They exchanged iron tools with the other three groups and provided the music essential for ceremonial occasions. The Toda furnished to the Kota ghee (a kind of butter) for certain ceremonies and buffalo for funerals; relations between the Kota and the Toda were friendly. The Badaga were agricultural and traded their grain for music and tools. Between the Kota and Badaga there was a feeling of great competition, which sometimes led to some unfair trading practices; it was usually the Kota who procured the advantage. The forest-dwelling Kurumba, who

[11] Robert Lowie, *Crow Indians* (New York: Holt, Rinehart and Winston, 1956, original edition 1935) p. 75.

[12] Herskovits, *op. cit.,* p. 157.

Social integration ● part **6**

were dreaded sorcerers, had honey, canes, and occasionally fruits to offer, but their main contribution was protection against the supernatural. The Kota feared the Kurumba, and the Kurumba took advantage of this fact in their trade dealings, so that they always got more than they gave. Thus there was great latent hostility between these two tribes.

Silent trade is a specialized form of barter in which no verbal communication takes place. The earliest and best-known description was given by Herodotus, who told of silent trade between the Carthaginians and the people who lived on the western coast of Africa, beyond the Pillars of Hercules. In California, an instance of silent trade occurred between the Tubatulabel and the other tribes with whom they had peaceful relations. They would trade piñon nuts and tobacco for lengths of white clamshell disks which passed for currency among all the tribes of that region. The reasons for silent trade can only be hypothesized, but perhaps trade was silent for lack of a common language, to avoid hostility, or because of problems of status which made verbal communication unthinkable. In any event, it provides for the exchange of goods between groups in spite of potential barriers.

The Kula ring

The classic example of trade among nonliterate people is the Kula of the Trobriand Islanders, first described by Malinowski.[13] The Kula is a trading system that involves the exchange of scarce goods, competition for prestige, and the all-important ceremonial exchange of highly-valued necklaces and armshells. Some of the first-class necklaces and armshells have names and histories, like Stradivarius violins, and, as Malinowski said, "always create a sensation when they appear in a district." The trade takes place throughout the islands, with the necklaces traveling in a clockwise fashion from island to island and the arm-

[13]Bronislaw Malinowski, *Argonauts of the Western Pacific* (New York: E. P. Dutton & Co., 1932).

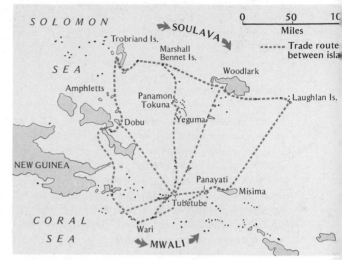

Figure 20-5. *The ceremonial trading of necklaces and armbands in the Kula ring encourages trade throughout Melanesia.*

shells traveling counterclockwise. No one man holds these valuables very long, and each employs strategies to improve his position. It is the Trobriand Island version of how to win without actually cheating. But a man cannot be too crafty or no one will trade with him.

A few men on each island participate in the Kula and have trading partners on the other islands. An important man may have as many as one hundred trading partners. These partnerships are lifetime relationships. Much ceremony and magic are attached to the Kula.

The Kula involves ocean voyages of fifty miles or more, and, as might be expected, more than necklaces and armshells are exchanged. A man may simply exchange necklaces and armshells with his Kula partner, but he is free to haggle and barter over other goods he has brought along on the trip for trading. In this way these island people have access to a whole range of material goods not found on their own islands.

The Kula is a most elaborate complex of ceremony, social relationships, economic exchange, travel, magic, and social integration. To see it only in its economic aspects is to misunderstand it completely. The Kula demonstrates once more the close interrelationship of cultural factors that is especially characteristic of non-Western societies.

Redistribution

In nonliterate groups, where there is a sufficient surplus to support a government, income will flow into the public coffers in the form of gifts, taxes, and the spoils of war; then it will be distributed again. The chief or king has two motives in disposing of this income: the first is to maintain his position of superiority by a display of wealth; the second is to assure those who support him an adequate standard of living.

The administration of the Inca empire in Peru was highly efficient both in the collection of taxes and methods of control. A census was kept of the population and resources. Tributes in goods and, more importantly, in services were levied. Each craftsman had to produce a specific quota of goods from materials supplied by overseers.

Forced labor might be used for agricultural work or work in the mines. Forced labor was also employed in a program of public works which included a remarkable system of roads and bridges throughout the mountainous terrain, aqueducts that guaranteed a supply of water, and storehouses that held surplus food for use in times of famine. Careful accounts were kept of the income and expenditures. A governmental bureaucracy had the responsibility of seeing that production was maintained and that commodities were distributed according to the regulations set forth by the ruling powers.

Through the activities of the government, **redistribution** took place. The ruling class lived in great luxury, but goods were redistributed to the common people when necessary. Redistribution then is a pattern of distribution by which the exchange is not between individuals or between groups, but, rather, by which a proportion of the products of labor is funneled into one source and is parceled out again as directed by a central administration. The progressive income tax in the United States is our method of redistribution;

Figure 20-6. *This frieze from the staircase of Persepolis illustrates the wealthy Persians bringing goods and livestock in tribute to the king; he redistributes the wealth to others.*

Social integration ● part **6**

Figure 20-7. *These great piles of yams are a sign of a good harvest in a New Guinea village. Many will not be eaten but rather displayed as a form of accumulated wealth.*

wealthy people theoretically pay relatively higher taxes and this money is redistributed through programs such as Social Security and aid to dependent children. For a process of redistribution to be possible, a society must have a fairly complex system of political organization and a substantial economic surplus.

Distribution of wealth

In nonliterate societies living barely above the subsistence level, gradations of wealth are small and systems of reciprocity serve to distribute in a fairly equitable fashion what little wealth exists.

Display for social prestige, what economist Thorstein Veblen called **conspicuous consumption,** is a strong motivating force for the distribution of wealth in societies where some substantial surplus is produced. These displays often take the form of feasts. The individual hosting the feast acquires status and prestige; his accumulated goods are dispersed throughout the group.

On Guadalcanal, one of the Solomon Islands, an ambitious young man plans a long-term strategic course to become an important person. His material goals are to have a fine, large house and to accumulate enough food to celebrate with a lavish feast. The building of the house may require as many as a hundred young men, all of whom have to be fed, along with his relatives who also assist in the work. His first move is to increase his gardens and accumulate livestock. The animals will require more labor, but they can be fed from the produce he has previously cultivated. After a few years, he lets it be known that he intends to erect his house. He is helped by all because of the excellent food they will get during the work and because they enjoy working together. Upon the completion of the house, a festival takes place which requires two weeks for preparation. An observer of one of these festivals counted 257 separate presentations of food.

In this instance, a surplus was created for the express purpose of gaining prestige by the display and the giving of food. Yet it also served as a levelling mechanism providing a distribution of wealth and preventing hoarding of goods that would make them unavailable for consumption. Conspicuous consumption in its most exaggerated form was exhibited in the nineteenth-century rivalry potlatch ceremonies of the Indians of the northwest United States and Canada. After a grandiose display of wealth by a person of high status, there was not only a great feast and generous gifts given to representatives of other groups, but a destruction of valuables such as canoes, blankets, and particularly European goods (including money), which had only recently been introduced into the society. There was competition for social prestige among chiefs and other persons of high status in the quantity of goods given away and destroyed.

Market exchange

The flow of goods passing from owner to owner in the marketplace, as a form of exchange, is familiar to Americans and is readily observable in foreign places. In fact, in the United States, there has been a revival and proliferation of "flea markets" where anyone, for a small fee, may display and sell handicrafts, second-hand items, farm produce, and paintings. There is excitement in the search for bargains, and an opportunity for

Figure 20-8a. *In nearly every society, the market is an important focus of social as well as economic activity. In our own society, going shopping is a popular weekend social occasion for groups of family and friends. The fact that many shoppers dress up in their best clothes emphasizes the social aspect of the excursion. This photo shows a Spanish market.*

Social integration ● part **6**

Figure 20-8b. *She sells sea snails by the sea shore of the Ivory Coast.*

Figure 20-8d. *This street in the bazaar of Marrakesh is devoted only to metalworkers.*

Figure 20-8c. *A bazaar in Delhi sells nuts and bolts and bicycle parts.*

Figure 20-8e. *This muddy food market is located in a Hong Kong slum.*

haggling. A carnival atmosphere prevails with eating, laughing, and conversation, and items may even be bartered without any cash passing hands. These flea markets, or farmers' markets, are similar to the markets of non-Western societies.

The first and most basic characteristic of the market in non-Western societies is that it always means a marketplace, a specific site where the actual goods are exchanged. In non-Western societies, the marketplace is totally different from what is known in modern economy as the principle of market exchange. The market principle involves the system of establishing prices by the powers of supply and demand, no matter where the transactions are made. Although some of our market transactions do take place in a specific identifiable location—much of the trade in cotton, for example, takes place in New Orleans' Cotton Exchange—it is also quite possible for an American to buy and sell goods without ever being on the same side of the continent.

This difference between "principle" and "place" clearly separates the market economy of modern industrial societies from the kind of marketing which prevails in traditional non-Western societies. When people talk about a market in today's world, the particular place where something is sold is often not important at all. For example, think of the way people speak of a "market" for certain types of automobiles, or for mouthwash.

The chief goods exchanged in non-Western markets are material items produced by the people. The people bring to the market the produce and animals they have grown and raised and the handicrafts they have made. These they sell or exchange for items they want and cannot produce themselves. Land, labor, and occupations are not bought and sold as they are through the Western market economy. In other words, what happens in the marketplace has nothing to do with the price of land, the amount paid for labor, or the cost of services. The market is local, specific, and contained. Some noneconomic aspects of marketplaces in nonindustrial societies overshadow the strictly economic aspects. Social relationships are as important in the marketplace as they are in other aspects of the economy. For example, dancers and other entertainers perform in the marketplace. It is customary for people to gather there to hear news. In ancient Mexico, under the Aztecs, people were required by law to go to market at specific intervals, in order to be informed as to what was going on. Chiefs held court and settled judicial disputes at the market. Above all, the market is a gathering place where people renew friendships, see relatives, gossip, and keep up with the world.

☐

Among the Kwakiutl Indians of British Columbia, the potlatch is the most important public ceremony for the announcement of significant events and the claiming of hierarchical names, hereditary rights, and privileges. Such announcements or claims are always accompanied by the giving of gifts from a host to all guests. The guests are invited to witness, and later to validate, a host's claims, and each receives gifts of varying worth according to his rank.

Potlatches are held to celebrate births, marriages, deaths, adoptions, or the coming of age of young people. They may also be given as a penalty for breaking a taboo, such as behaving frivolously or performing ineptly during a sacred winter dance. A potlatch to save face can be prompted by an accident even as trivial as the capsizing of a canoe or the birth of a deformed child. Among the most extravagant potlatches are those given for rivalry or vengeance.

All potlatches are public. The host, with the support of his family, numima (the next largest tribal subdivision), or tribe invites other families, numimas, or tribes. The size of the gathering reveals the affluence and prestige of the host. At the ceremony, he traces his line of descent and his rights to the claims he is making. Every name, dance or song used by the host must be acknowledged and legitimized by the guests. No announcement or claim is made without feasting and the distribution of gifts. Gifts are given to guests in the order of their tribal importance and of a value relative to this prestige. Clearly, high-ranking chiefs receive more gifts than lesser men. But the value and quantity of gifts distributed at a potlatch reflect less on the recipients than on the donor. The gifts he gives away—or in some cases the property he publicly destroys—are marks of his wealth, rank, generosity, and self-esteem. Over a period of time, they also measure the power and prestige that he will be able to maintain over others of high status. For, at a later potlatch, each high-ranking guest will try to return as much, or preferably more, than he received. To keep track of the gifts distributed and the precise hierarchy of guests, each donor has the assistance of a "potlatch secretary" whose records are needed to maintain correct social form and avoid offense.

Potlatch gifts vary widely, from money to property. They include boats, blankets, flour, kettles, fish oil, and, in former times, slaves. More recently, gifts have included sewing machines, furniture, even pool tables. Probably the most valuable potlatch material has little intrinsic worth but enormous symbolic value. These are coppers—large pieces of beaten sheet copper shaped like shields with a ridge running down the center of the lower half. They are painted with black lead and a design is incised through the paint. Each copper has a name and its potlatch history determines its value. One copper, called "All other coppers are ashamed to look at it," had been paid for with 7500 blankets; another known as "Making the house empty of wealth," was worth 5000 blankets.

During a potlatch, which can last several days and long into each night, speeches, songs, and dances are mixed with the giving of gifts, snacks and more lavish feasting. The host is not the only speaker; usually high-ranking guests also speak or supervise the singing, dancing, and drumming. Elaborate ceremonial costumes are worn by the speaker—who holds a "speaker's staff"—

by dancers and musicians; the hall where the potlatch is held is decorated with painted hangings and tribal insignia.

All potlatch ceremonies are marked by exacting standards of etiquette and behavior. Impropriety, whether intentional or accidental, requires an immediate response. Mistakes in procedure, public quarreling, or an accident witnessed by others brings a sense of shame and indignity on its perpetrator, who must immediately "cover (or wipe off) the shame," making a payment to re-establish his self-esteem. Often, blankets are torn into strips and each witness is given a piece.

The Kwakiutl respond similarly to insults. Potlatchers sometimes deliberately insult a guest by calling his name out of order, by spilling oil on him, by throwing him his gift, or by presenting him with an inappropriate portion of food. The offended guest retaliates immediately by giving gifts himself, or by destroying something valuable of his own while denouncing the potlatcher. Violence sometimes erupts. On some occasions the host ignores a face-saving

Figure 20-9. *The blankets given away at a potlatch often feature this type of totemistic design.*

gesture of a guest and this may precipitate a rivalry potlatch. If a host mistakenly offends, a guest restores his pride by giving the host a reprimand gift. Embarrassed by his carelessness, the correct host will make restitution in double the amount of the reprimand gift.

Rivalries also develop when two men compete for the same name, song, or other privilege. Each contestant recites his closest genealogical connection with the claim and tries to outdo his rival in the amount of property he can give away. In the heat of such rivalries, contestants sometimes break off a piece of copper, thereby destroying its value, and give the piece to their rival. The rival might then bring out his own copper of at least equal value, break it, and give both pieces back to the opponent. Great merit came to the man who threw his copper into the sea, "drowning it," thus showing his utter contempt for property and implying that his importance was such that what he destroyed was of little concern to him. At times this ostentatious destruction of property included canoes, house planks, blankets, and even slaves, in former days.

The witnesses to these dramatic acts of the potlatch act as judges to the claims; ultimately, they decide the victor. A powerful and prestigious man can sway public opinion by recognizing the claim of one contestant over another at a subsequent potlatch. Indeed, this is a basic principle of the potlatch; a successful potlatch in itself cannot legitimize a claim. It is the behavior of other hosts at later potlatches that validates a claim for once and for all.

Source:
From *The Kwakiutl: Indians of British Columbia* by Ronald P. Rohner and Evelyn C. Rohner. Copyright © 1970 by Holt, Rinehart and Winston, Inc. Adapted and reprinted by permission of Holt, Rinehart and Winston, Inc.

Summary

1.

The study of the economics of non-Western societies can be undertaken only in the context of the total culture of each society. Each society solves the problem of getting its living within the limitations of its resources of land, capital, and technology, and distributes its goods according to its own priorities.

2.

The work people do is a major productive resource and the allotment of work is always governed by rules according to sex and age. Few generalizations can be made covering the kinds of work performed by men and women. The cooperation of many people working together is a typical feature of non-Western peoples. Specialties requiring a great skill and knowledge are important even in societies with a very simple technology.

3.

Capital in non-Western economies is primarily in the form of land which is usually owned by the group—the family, the lineage, or the tribe—rather than by individuals. The technology of a people in the form of the tools they use, their knowledge of plants and animals, and their ability to control the environment determines the way they gain their livelihood.

4.

Production is dependent upon the natural environment. Hunters and gatherers will follow the migrations of animals and the seasonal occurrences of fruits and vegetables. The yearly cycle of planting and harvesting circumscribes the productive activities of horticulturists and agriculturists.

5.

Non-Western people consume most of what they themselves produce. But there is an exchange of goods. The processes of distribution which may be distinguished are reciprocity, redistribution, and market exchange. Reciprocity is the giving and receiving of gifts, not necessarily of equal value, according to rules fixing obligations.

6.

Barter and trade take place between groups. There are elements of reciprocity in trading exchanges but there is a greater calculation of the relative values of goods exchanged. A classic example of exchange between groups which partook of both reciprocity and sharp trading was the Kula ring of the Trobriand Islanders.

7.

A complex economic and political organization is necessary for redistribution to take place. The government assesses each citizen a tax or tribute, uses the proceeds to support the governmental and religious elite, and redistributes the rest in the form of public services.

8.

Exchange in the market place serves to distribute goods in a district. The market place also functions as a social gathering place and a news medium.

Suggested readings

Bohannan, Paul, and George Dalton, eds. *Markets in Africa.* Evanston, Ill.: Northwestern University Press, 1962.

Essays on the market system of African economic life. Studies economic activities ranging in complexity from aboriginal to present day marketing systems. Discusses the noneconomic function of African markets. One article deals with current changes in Africa as they affect markets.

Clark, J. G. D. *Prehistoric Europe: The Economic Basis.* Palo Alto, Calif.: Stanford University Press, 1962.

The book is concerned with the ways in which early man, in competition with other forms of life, maintained himself since the end of the Pleistocene Ice Age. It discusses how man managed to raise his standards from those of savages to those of peasants ready to support the full weight of urban civilization. Combines natural science and historical approaches.

Clough, S. B., and C. W. Cole *Economic History of Europe,* 3rd ed. Boston: Heath, 1952.

The authors have undertaken a study of economic developments to gain an understanding of the past. They use economic history as a thread which leads the student through important historical events and provides an understanding of human activity. They begin with the Middle Ages, convinced that most of the important elements of modern economic life had their roots then, and proceed with an analysis of European history to modern times, covering feudalism, guilds, commerce, capitalism, mercantilism, etc.

Heilbroner, Robert L. *The Making of Economic Society,* 4th ed. Englewood Cliffs, N.J.: Prentice-Hall, 1972.

This book attempts to present some of the basic content of economics in the light of theory and history. Emphasis is on the rise and development of the market system, the central theme of Western economic heritage. It begins with the premarket economy of antiquity and carries the study through the market society, industrial revolution and technology, to capitalism and modern economic society.

Nash, Manning *Primitive and Peasant Economic Systems.* San Francisco: Chandler Publishers, 1966.

This book studies the problems of economic anthropology, especially the dynamics of social and economic change, in terms of primitive and peasant economic systems. The book is heavily theoretical, but draws on field work done by the author in Guatemala, Mexico, and Burma.

Tuma, Elias H. *European Economic History: Theory and History of Economic Change.* New York: Harper & Row, 1971.

In the light of several competing theories of economic development and decline, this book examines the scale and methods of production and trade in Europe from the tenth century to the present. The medieval firm, living standards, territorial expansion, population growth, and technology are among the subjects that come in for extended discussion.

Vogt, Evon *The Zinacantecos of Mexico*. New York: Holt, Rinehart and Winston, 1970. A case study in anthropology concerning the Zinacantecos, a Maya tribe in Mexico who have a highly ceremonialized life-style. An interesting study of their society, culture, religion, economic system, and social structure.

Wolf, Eric R. *Peasants*. Englewood Cliffs, N.J.: Prentice-Hall, 1966. This book is concerned with the peasant stage in the evolution of human society—midway between primitive tribal and industrial society. The author discusses the economic and social aspects of peasantry, levels in religious traditions, and some peasant movements.

The Persian nomads

Among the last remaining nomads on earth are one of its oldest tribes—the Bakhtiari of Iran, who trace their lineage through 2500 years of Persian history to the most ancient Aryan peoples. Living on the fringes of the heartland of "civilization" near where the first cities of Sumer and Babylon flourished, they have resisted every attempt to change their way of life. In recent times, the father of the present Shah of Iran succeeded briefly in settling many Bakhtiari, but after his abdication in 1941, the tribesmen burned down their homes and went again to the mountains.

The Bakhtiari, or Lors as they are sometimes called, number nearly half a million in Iran today. They wander because they are herdsmen, and have always been. Spending the winter grazing their flocks of sheep and goats on the plains north of the Persian Gulf (where oil discoveries in 1908 made some of them very rich), the Bakhtiari drive their herds each spring some 250 miles into the high, lush pasturelands of the Zagros mountains, near Isfahan. Traditionally, the spring migration begins 14 days after Nowrouz, the Persian New Year, and at the time of the spring equinox. Leaving behind the increasingly sere plain, where temperatures reach 120 degrees in summer and grass withers to inedibility, the shepherds and their flocks climb almost 15,000 feet on a journey that may last over a month.

Such a journey is pictured on the following pages. Members of the Babadi, a subtribe of the Bakhtiari,

which consists of some 30,000 people subdivided into many clans, are led by their Kalantar (Chief) Jafar Qoli from Lali, their market town in the plains, to Kuh Rang, their summer quarters near Zardeh Kuh, the "Yellow Mountain."

By Bakhtiari standards, Jafar Qoli is a wealthy man. He has about a thousand sheep and goats, maintains several wives—one of whom, the shepherdess-wife, is seen in the center pages of this portfolio—employs three shepherds who earn about $1.25 per day, and owns some land. But it is the sheep that represent a Bakhtiari's wealth. Goats give milk and their hair is woven into tents, the black tents that are the nomads' trademarks; mules are valued pack animals, sure-footed and tough enough to survive the mountain journeys. The land yields wheat, which is planted in mountain valleys as the herdsmen travel upward, reaped some 40 days later and ground into flour in the autumn on the return journey. Sheep are the most valuable because the ewes bear lambs, which are sold for meat and wool. (Although Iran desperately needs protein for the nation's diet, the government has persisted in a policy of settlement for the Bakhtiari, a policy which would both destroy a way of life and waste a valuable resource. Some Bakhtiari, however, believe that the Shah himself is sympathetic to them and hope that they may maintain the old ways.)

On their migrations, the Bakhtiari travel in a maal, the smallest tribal unit consisting of from two to eight families. Each maal or Taefeh (clan) departs from its winter or summer quarters at a different time so that the migration route is not overgrazed. At various points along the journey, in valleys large enough to support them, the groups meet and the reunions are joyous. In the photograph on the opposite page, clan children enjoy a swing on the ropes used to tie down the pack burdens which the shepherds have thrown up into a tree. The life is hard, the way is treacherous, but the Bakhtiari prefer it to any other life they know.

Photographs by Anthony Howarth

Political organization

"I am the State," proclaimed Louis XIV. With this sweeping statement, the king declared absolute rule over France; he believed himself to be the law, the lawmaker, the courts, the judge, jailer and executioner—in short, the seat of all political organization in France.

Louis took a great deal of responsibility on his royal shoulders; had he actually performed each of these functions, he would have done the work of thousands of men, the number required to keep the machinery of a large political organization such as a state running at full steam. As a form of political organization, the state of seventeenth-century France was not much different from many that exist in modern times, including our own. All large states require rigid, elaborate, centralized structures involving hierarchies of executives, legislators, and judges who initiate, pass, and enforce laws for large numbers of people.

But such complex structures have not always been in existence, and even today, there are societies that depend on much less formal means of organization. In such small-scale societies, flexible and informal kinship systems with no designated leaders prevail. Social problems such as homicide and theft are perceived as serious "family quarrels" rather than affairs that affect the entire community. Between these two polarities of political organization lies a world of variety, including societies with chiefs, Big Men, or charismatic leaders, and segmented tribal societies with multicentric authority systems. Such disparity prompts the question, "What is political organization?"

The term "political organization" refers to those aspects of social organization specifically concerned with the management of the affairs of public policy of a society, whether it be organizing a giraffe hunt or raising an army. In other words, political organization is the system of social relationships that provides for the coordination and regulation of behavior insofar as that behavior is related to the maintenance of public order. Government, on the other hand, consists of an administrative system having specialized personnel which may or may not form a part of the political organization, depending on the complexity of the society. Some form of political organization exists in all societies, but it is not always a government.

The political organization of a society cannot be properly understood in isolation from its ecological and technoeconomic components; nor can it be meaningfully analyzed apart from its social and ideological context. Modern political anthropology, therefore, seeks to understand political systems not apart from, but rather in connection with, the other components of culture.

Kinds of political systems

Political organization is the means through which a society maintains social order and reduces social disorder. Such organization assumes a variety of forms among the peoples of the world, but scholars have simplified this complex subject by identifying four basic kinds of political systems. These are (in order of complexity) bands, tribes, chiefdoms, and states. The first two forms are uncentralized sociopolitical systems; the latter two are centralized systems.

Uncentralized political systems

Most non-Western peoples have neither chiefs with established rights and duties, nor any fixed form of government. The strong web of kinship forms the chief means of social organization among these peoples. The economies of these societies are of the subsistence type, so populations are typically very small. Leaders do not have real authority to enforce the society's customs or laws, and individual members conform out of fear that they will be ostracized or made the target of scorn and gossip. Important decisions are usually made in a democratic manner by a consensus among adult males; dissenting members may decide to act with the majority, or they may choose to adopt some other course of action if they are willing to risk the social consequences. This form of political organization provides great flexibility, which in many situations confers an adaptive advantage.

Band organization. The band is a small autonomous group; it is the least complicated form of political organization. Bands are usually found among hunter-gatherers and other nomadic societies in which there are factors that limit the size of the group. Bands are kin groups, composed of related men or women and their spouses and unmarried children; the closeness of the group is indicated by the fact that there are usually rules that prohibit marriage among band members. Bands may be characterized as associations of related nuclear families who occupy a common territory and who live together on it so long as environmental and subsistence circumstances are favorable. Some anthropologists believe that the band is the oldest form of political organization since all men were once nomadic hunters and gatherers, and remained so until the development of agriculture and pastoralism about 10,000 years ago.

Figure 21-1. *In the Ivory Coast, older tribal traditions of singing and dancing are mixed with the new custom of electioneering.*

Social integration ● part **6**

Since band members are typically hunter-gatherers who often must range far and wide to search for food sources, they are generally on the move most of the year, following herds and harvests. This migratory mode of existence is correlated with a second important feature of the band: its small size. Population density of the band is quite low, varying from a handful to a few hundred individuals; its size depends on the methods employed in gathering food. The more food the group is able to find, the more individuals it can support, and the larger the band. During seasons when food is scarce, the band may disperse over a broad area, perhaps dividing into several smaller groups.

Bands are generally quite democratic: no band member may tell another individual what to do, how to hunt, or whom to marry. There is no private ownership (except in the case of a few weapons or tools), and game and other foods are shared by all members of the group. Rank (other than age and sex status differentiation), the specialization of labor, and formal political organization are not found in this form of society. Generally, the band lacks the social techniques that would be necessary to integrate its members into larger political groups. Decisions in the band are usually made by a consensus of all adult members of the group, and so they require little formal implementation. The decision to undertake a hunting expedition or to begin a ritual celebration is reached after a meeting of the band's senior adult males.

Band leaders are usually older men whose courage, success in hunting, or ability to placate supernatural forces is recognized and admired by other members. The leader is followed not because he has coercive power, but because members know that in the past he has demonstrated good sense, skill and success; when he fails to lead well and make the right decisions, members will choose to follow another leader. The band leader is simply the first among equals, a leader with personal authority that stems from his abilities.

An example of the informal nature of leadership in the band is found among the !Kung Bushmen of the Kalahari Desert. Each !Kung band is comprised of a group of families who live together, linked to one another and to the headman through kinship. Although each band owns its territory and the resources within it, two or more !Kung bands may range over the same territory. The headman, called the *kxau* or owner, is the focal point for the band's ownership of the territory. The headman does not himself own the land or resources, but he symbolically personifies the rights of band members to them. If the headman leaves a territory to live elsewhere, he ceases to be headman, and some other member of the band takes his place.

The headman coordinates the band's movements when resources are no longer adequate for subsistence in a particular territory. His chief duty is to plan when and where the group will move; when the band moves, the headman's position is at the head of the line. He chooses the site for the new settlement, and he has the first choice of a spot for his own fire. He has no other rewards or duties. For example, the headman does not organize hunting parties, trading expeditions, the making of artifacts, or gift giving; nor does he make marriage arrangements. Individual band members instigate their own activities. The headman is not a judge, nor is he obligated to punish other band members. Wrongdoers are judged and regulated by public opinion, usually expressed by gossip among band members. If a headman is too young or too old or loses the desired qualities of leadership, band members will turn to another man to lead them.

Tribal organization. The second type of uncentralized or multicentric authority system is the tribe. Midway between the simple band and the more complex chiefdom or state, the tribe typically produces its goods through some form of agriculture or herding. Since these methods of production are more efficient and thus yield more food than those of the hunter-gatherer band, the tribe is able to support a greater number of individuals. The tribe has greater population density than the band; this brings a new set of problems to be solved at the same time that it permits new kinds of solutions.

Each tribe consists of one or more small autonomous units; these may then form alliances with one another for various purposes. As in the band, political organization in the tribe is informal and of temporary nature. Whenever a situation requiring political integration of all or several tribal groups arises, they join to deal with the situation in a cooperative manner. When the problem is satisfactorily solved, each group then returns to its autonomous state.

Leadership among tribes is also informal. Among the Navajo Indians, for example, the individual did not think of his government as something fixed and all-powerful, and leadership was not vested in a central authority. A local leader was a man respected for his age, integrity, and wisdom. His advice was therefore sought frequently, but he had no formal means of control and could not enforce any decision on those who asked for his help. Group decisions were made on the basis of public consensus, with the most influential man usually somewhat more responsible than others for the final decision. Among the social mechanisms that induced members to abide by group decisions were withdrawal of cooperation, gossip, criticism, and the belief that disease was caused by antisocial actions.[1]

The separate units of the tribe may be integrated by a number of pantribal factors. For example, organization can be based on membership in a kinship or descent group, an association or secret society, an age-set system, or territorial groups such as wards or towns.

Kinship organization. In many tribal societies, the organizing unit and seat of political authority is the clan, an association of kinsmen who trace descent from a common ancestor. Within the clan, elders or headmen are responsible for regulating the affairs of members and represent their kinship group in relations with other kinship

[1] Elman Service, *Profiles in Ethnology.* (New York: Harper & Row, 1958).

Figure 21-2a. *Sultan's palace in Cameroun.*

Figure 21-2b. *King's home in Cameroun.*

Figure 21-2c. *A tribal king in Dahomey wears traditional crown and French sunglasses.*
Figure 21-2d. *Another tribal king and crown.*

Figure 21-2e. *The royal family of an Ivory Coast tribal society.*
Figure 21-2f. *Dahomey king with noseguard to protect him against evil spirits.*

groups. As a group, the elders may form a council that acts within the tribe or for the tribe in dealings with outsiders. In some societies, the strategic and tactical planning for warfare rests in the hands of the clan.

Another form of tribal kinship bond that provides political organization is the segmentary lineage system. This system is similar in operation to the clan, but it is less extensive and is a relatively rare form of political organization. The economy of the segmentary tribe is generally just above subsistence level. Production is small-scale, and the tribe probably has a labor pool just large enough to provide necessities. Since each lineage group in the tribe produces the same goods, none depends on another for goods or services. Political organization among segmentary lineage societies is usually informal: there are neither political offices nor chiefs, although older tribal members may exercise some personal authority. In his study of the Tiv and the Nuer, Marshall Sahlins describes the way that the segmentary lineage form of political organization works.[2] According to Sahlins, segmentation is the normal process of tribal growth. It is also the social means of temporary unification of a fragmented tribal society to join in an action. The segmentary lineage may be viewed as a substitute for the fixed political structure which a tribe cannot maintain.

Among the Nuer, a tribe numbering some 200,000 people living in the swampland and savanna of the Sudan, there are at least twenty clans. Each clan is patrilineal and is segmented into lineages which are further segmented. A clan is separated into maximal lineages; maximal lineages are segmented into major lineages which are segmented into minor lineages, which in turn are segmented into minimal lineages. The minimal lineage is a group descending from one great grandfather or a greatgreat grandfather.

The lineage segments among the Nuer are all equal, and no real leadership or political organization at all exists above the level of the autonomous minimal or primary segments. The entire superstructure of the lineage is nothing more than an alliance, active only during conflicts between any of the minimal segments. In any serious dispute between members of different minimal lineage segments, members of all other segments take the side of the contestant to whom they are most closely related, and the issue is then joined between the higher order lineages involved. Such a system of political organization is known as complementary or balanced opposition.

Disputes among the Nuer are frequent, and under the segmentary lineage system, they can lead to widespread feuds. This possible source of social disruption is minimized by the actions of the "leopard skin chief," or holder of a ritual office of conciliation. The leopard skin chief has no political power and is looked on as standing outside the lineage network. All he can do is try to persuade feuding lineages to accept payment in "blood cattle" rather than taking another life. His mediation gives each side the chance to back down gracefully before too many people are killed; but if the participants are for some reason unwilling to compromise, the leopard skin chief has no authority to enforce a settlement.

Age-set organization.   Age-set systems provide a tribal society with the means of political organization beyond the kin group. Under this system, youths, usually at puberty, are initiated into the first age set. They then pass as a set from one age grade to another when they reach the proper age. Age sets cut across territorial and kin groupings and are the chief means of political organization.

Political matters of the tribe are in the hands of the age sets and their officers. An example of the age-set system as a form of political organization is found in A. Prins' study of the Kipsigis in his book *East-African Age-Set Systems.* Among the Kipsigis, there are two principal age sets: that of *murenik* or warrior, and that of *poysiek* or senior elder. Secondary age-set groups are the junior warriors (males below the age of puberty), junior elders, and retired elders. Young men are initiated into the warrior age class at puberty, at

[2]Marshall Sahlins, "The Segmentary Lineage: An Organization of Predatory Expansion" in *American Anthropologist* 63:322–343.

Social integration ● part **6**

which time they are taught tribal customs and religious codes. The tasks of the warriors are military and economic: they must defend the country and enrich and strengthen the tribe by begetting many children and capturing many cattle. The principal tasks of the elders are military, administrative, judicial, and religious. They may fight in defensive battles, and certain of them serve as chiefs of staff, organizing and advising the army.

Most political authority among the Kipsigis is vested in the age set of the elders who serve in the hamlet, village, and territorial group. In the hamlet, an elder versed in law mediates disputes. If the case cannot be resolved at the hamlet level, it is sent up to the village level, where a council of elders judges the case. Certain elders also preside at initiation ceremonies, and at those ceremonies where one age set is retiring and another rising to take its place.

Association organization. Sodalities, secret societies, and other associations that function as politically integrative systems within tribes are found in many areas of the world, including Africa, Melanesia, and India. Perhaps the best example of association organization may be found during the nineteenth century among the Indians of the Western plains of the United States, such as the Cheyenne. For these Indians, the basic territorial and political unit of the tribe was the band, but seven military societies, or warriors' clubs, were common to the entire tribe; the clubs functioned in several areas. A boy could join one of these societies when he achieved warrior status, whereupon he became familiar with the society's particular insignia, songs, and rituals. In addition to their military functions, the warriors' societies also had ceremonial and social functions. Among some plains Indians, notably the Arapaho, the warriors' societies were age-graded so that a man automatically passed from one society to another until he finally passed into the society of elders, which had great political and ceremonial importance.

The Cheyenne warriors' routine, daily tasks consisted of overseeing movements in the camp, protecting a moving column, and enforcing rules against individual hunting when the whole tribe was on a buffalo hunt. In addition, each of the warrior societies had a repertoire of dances that the members performed on special ceremonial occasions. Since identical military societies bearing identical names existed in each Cheyenne band, the societies thus served to integrate the entire tribe for military and political purposes.[3]

The Melanesian Big Man. Throughout much of Melanesia there appears a type of leader called the "Big Man." The Big Man combines a small amount of interest in his tribe's welfare with a great deal of self-interested cunning and calculation for his own personal gain. His authority is personal; he does not come to office nor is he elected. His status is the result of acts which raise him above most other tribe members and attract to him a band of loyal followers.

An example of this form of political organization can be seen among the Kapauku of West New Guinea. There the Big Man is called the *tonowi,* or "rich one." To achieve this status, one must be male, wealthy, generous, and eloquent; physical bravery and skills in dealing with the supernatural are also frequent characteristics of a *tonowi,* but they are not essential. The *tonowi* functions as the headman of the village unit.

The Kapauku culture places a high value on wealth, so it is not surprising that a wealthy individual is considered to be a successful and admirable man. Yet the possession of wealth must be coupled with the trait of generosity, which in this society means not gift-giving but the willingness to make loans. Wealthy men who refuse to lend money to other villagers may be ostracized, ridiculed, and, in extreme cases, actually executed by a group of warriors. Due to this social pressure, economic wealth is rarely hoarded, but is distributed throughout the group.

It is through the loans he makes that the *tonowi*

---

[3] E. A. Hoebel, *The Cheyennes: Indians of the Great Plains. Case Studies in Cultural Anthropology.* (New York: Holt, Rinehart and Winston, 1960).

Figure 21-3a. *The king of Akure holds court. His household consists of 156 wives and literally countless children; he rules over a large province of Nigeria and has about 230,000 subjects.*

Figure 21-3b. *The king of Akure is also a lawyer who was educated in England; here he wears the traditional wig and gown of the British barrister.*

Figure 21-3c,d. *The king drives up in his Chevrolet to his palace door; note the cement sculptures that decorate the palace, including the statue of a Nigerian in a British army uniform. The top photo shows the king stepping out of the palace with his retinue. The man on the far right, wearing Western dress, is the king's secretary; the man on the left is his page.*

Social integration ● part **6**

acquires his political power. The other villagers comply with his requests because they are in his debt (often without paying interest), and they do not want to have to repay their loans. Those who have not yet borrowed money from the *tonowi* are probably hoping to do so in the future, and so they too want to keep his goodwill.

The debtors of the *tonowi* are always his loyal supporters. This is in part due to their gratitude for his generosity; it is also due to the fact that debts can be inherited, and if anything happens to the *tonowi,* his heirs will probably ask for immediate repayment of all loans. Other sources of support for the *tonowi* are the apprentices whom he has taken into his household for training. They are fed, housed, given a chance to learn the *tonowi's* business wisdom, and given a loan to buy a wife when they leave; in return, they act as messengers and bodyguards. Even after they leave his household, these men are tied to the *tonowi* by bonds of affection and gratitude. Political support also comes from the *tonowi's* kinsmen, whose relationship brings with it varying obligations.

The *tonowi* functions as a leader in a wide variety of situations. He represents the group in dealing with outsiders and other villages; he acts as negotiator and/or judge when disputes break out among his followers. Leopold Pospisil, who studied the Kapauku extensively, notes:

> The multiple functions of a *tonowi* are not limited to the political and legal fields only. His word also carries weight in economic and social matters. He is especially influential in determining proper dates for pig feasts and pig markets, in inducing specific individuals to become co-sponsors at feasts, in sponsoring communal dance expeditions to other villages, and in initiating large projects, such as extensive drainage ditches and main fences or bridges, the completion of which requires a joint effort of the whole community.[4]

The *tonowi's* wealth comes from his success at

---

[4] Leopold Pospisil, *The Kapauku Papuans of West New Guinea* (New York: Holt, Rinehart and Winston, 1963). pp. 51–2.

pig breeding, for pigs are the focus of the entire Kapauku economy. Like all kinds of cultivation and domestication, raising pigs requires a certain amount of strength and skill, as well as some luck. It is not uncommon for a *tonowi* to lose his fortune rapidly, due to bad management or bad luck with his pigs. Thus the political structure of the Kapauku shifts frequently; as one man loses wealth and consequently power, another gains it and becomes a *tonowi*. These changes confer a degree of flexibility on the political organization, but prevent long-range planning and thus limit the scope of the *tonowi's* political power over the rest of the villagers.

Centralized political systems

Among bands and tribes, authority is uncentralized and each group is economically and politically autonomous. Political organization is vested in kinship groups and in other organizations. Populations are small, because the technological means of production permit no more. But as a society's social life becomes more complex, as population rises and technology becomes more complex, as the specialization of labor and trade networks produces surpluses of goods, the need for definite, stable permanent leadership becomes greater. In such societies, political authority and power are concentrated in a single individual—the chief—or in numerous groups of individuals—the state. The state form of organization is best suited to a complex heterogeneous society.

Chiefdoms. A chiefdom is a ranked society in which every member has a position in the hierarchy. An individual's status in such a community is determined by membership in a descent group: those in the uppermost levels, closest to the chief, are officially superior and receive deferential treatment from those in lower ranks.

The office of the chief may or may not be hereditary. Unlike the headmen of the band and lineage, the chief is generally a true authority figure, and his authority serves to unite his community in all affairs and at all times. For example, a chief can distribute land among his community and recruit members into his military service. In chiefdoms, there is a recognized hierarchy consisting of major and minor authorities who control major and minor subdivisions of the chiefdom. Such an arrangement is, in effect, a chain of command linking leaders at every level. It serves to bind tribal groups in the heartland to the chief's headquarters, be it a mud and dung hut or a marble palace.

On the economic level, a chief controls the productive activities of his people. Chiefdoms are typically redistributive economic systems; the chief has control over surplus goods and perhaps even the labor force of his community. Thus, the chief may demand a quota of rice from farmers which he will redistribute to the entire community. Similarly, he may recruit laborers to build an irrigation works, a palace, or a temple.

The chief may also amass a great amount of personal wealth and pass it on to his heirs. Land, cattle, and luxury goods produced by specialists can be collected by the chief and become part of his power base. Moreover, high ranking families of the chiefdom may engage in the same practice and use their possessions as evidence of status.

An example of this form of political organization was found in Hawaiian society. There was a class of nobles, rigidly differentiated in rank and specialized in occupation; they led the army and served as religious and political officials. Status was hereditary, and the gradations of status were so distinct that even children of the same parents were ranked in the order of their birth. The nobles near the top of the hierarchy were so important and powerful that ordinary people were required to throw themselves face down on the ground whenever one passed.

At the top of the hierarchy of nobles was the chief. It was believed that he was given the right to rule by the gods, to whom he was related. Around each chief was gathered a group of loyal nobles, who administered the affairs of politics, warfare, and religion. The nobles all paid some kind of tribute—goods and money—to the chief; they in turn collected tribute from inferior nobles, who collected tribute from the commoners. The chief's wealth gave him additional power and permitted him to undertake large-scale projects, such as wars of conquest. The chief had the right of life and death over all his subjects; he could also take away their property at will.

Although such a system would seem very stable, political power in Hawaiian society changed frequently. War was the way to gain territory and maintain power; great chiefs set out to conquer one another in an effort to become the paramount chief of all the islands. When one chief conquered another, the loser and all his nobles were dispossessed of all property and were lucky if they escaped alive. The new chief then appointed his own supporters to positions of political power. Thus there was very little continuity of governmental or religious administration.

State systems. The state, the most formal of political organizations, is one of the hallmarks of civilization. Inherent in the concept of the state is the idea of true, permanent government, public and sovereign, by which the state can use legitimized force to regulate the affairs of its citizens as well as its relations with other states. Found only in large, complex societies, the state has a central power and a formal rigid system of law and order administered by the central power.

An important aspect of the state is its delegation of authority to maintain order within and without its borders. Police, foreign ministries, war ministries, and other branches of the government function to control and punish such disruptive acts as crime, terror, and rebellion. By such agencies, authority is asserted impersonally and objectively in the state.

The state is found only in societies with numerous diverse groups, social classes, and associations; it brings together under a common rule many kinds of people. Typically, the state society is divided into social classes and strata, and economic functions and wealth are distributed unequally. A market economy involving money as

Figure 21-4. *One of the duties of the king of Akure is attending sessions of the House of Chiefs, a legislative body modelled on the House of Lords in Great Britain. The Nigerian government also consists of a trained bureaucracy, such as these officials of the Department of Health.*

a medium of exchange is an integral part of the state, as are vast surpluses of goods and services and the intense specialization of labor.[5]

Our form of government, of course, is a state government and its organization and workings are undoubtedly familiar to everyone. An example of a not so familiar state is found in Hilda Kuper's study, *The Swazi Of Swaziland.* The Swazi are a Bantu-speaking people who live in Southeast Africa. They are primarily agriculturists, but the activity of cattle raising is more highly valued than agriculture: the ritual, wealth, and power of their authority system are all intricately linked with cattle.

The Swazi authority system is characterized by a highly developed dual monarchy, a hereditary aristocracy, and elaborate rituals of kinship as well as by state-wide age sets. The king and his mother are the central figures of all national activity, linking all the people of the Swazi state: they preside over higher courts, summon national gatherings, control age classes, allocate land, disburse national wealth, take precedence in ritual, and help organize important social events.

Advising the king are the senior princes, who are usually his uncles and half brothers. Between the king and the princes are two specially-created *tinsila,* or blood brothers, who are chosen from certain common clans. These men are his shields, protecting him from evildoers and serving him in intimate personal situations. In addition, the king is guided by two *tindvuna,* or counselors, one civil and one military. The people of the state make their opinions known through two councils: the *liqoqo,* or privy council composed of senior princes; and the *libanda,* or council of state, composed of chiefs and headmen and open to all adult males of the state. The *liqoqo* may advise the king, make decisions, and execute them. For example, they may rule on such questions as land, education, traditional ritual, court procedure, and transport.

Government extends from the smallest local unit—the homestead—upwards to the central ad-

[5] L. Krader, *Formation of The State* (Englewood Cliffs, N.J.: Prentice-Hall, 1968).

ministration. The head of a homestead has legal and administrative powers: he is responsible for the crimes of those under him, controls their property, and speaks for them before his superiors. On the district level, political organization is similar to that of the central government. However, the relationship between a district chief and his subjects is personal and familiar; he knows all the families in his district. The main check on any autocratic tendencies he may exhibit rests in his subjects' ability to transfer their allegiance to a more responsive chief. Swazi officials hold their positions for life and are dismissed only for treason or witchcraft. Incompetence, drunkenness, and stupidity are frowned upon, but they are not considered to be good enough reasons for dismissal.

The functioning of the political unit

Whatever form the political organization of a society may take, it must solve certain problems in order to permit the smooth functioning of the group. Chief among these problems is the need to obtain the people's allegiance. In small, loosely organized groups, in which every member participates in the making of all decisions, loyalty and cooperation are freely given, since each person considers himself a part of the political system. But as the group grows larger, and the organization becomes more formal, the problems of obtaining and keeping public support become greater.

Elements of political organization

Many political theorists suggest that the political process is based on the use of some form of coercion to insure that decisions are carried out. This coercion may be a threat of force; it could just as easily be scorn, ridicule, or social neglect; in real life, names can often be as hurtful as sticks

Figure 21-5. *The legitimacy of any government rests on the consent of the people. This tribal ruler of Ghana is an Englishman who was once a colonial official; villagers asked him to assume the position of chief.*

Figure 21-6. *Legitimacy of political authority may be demonstrated by symbolic attire, such as this aged helmet.*

and stones. However, the reliance upon force as the most important instrument of political implementation tends to lessen the effectiveness of a political system. For example, the staff needed to apply force must often be large and may itself grow to be a political force. The emphasis on force often creates resentment on the parts of those to whom it is applied and so lessens cooperation. Thus police states are rare; most societies choose less extreme forms of social coercion.

Also basic to the political process is the concept of legitimacy, or the right of the political leaders to rule. Like force, legitimacy is a form of support for a political system; unlike force, legitimacy is based on the values which a particular society believes most important. Thus among the Kapauku, the legitimacy of the *tonowi's* power comes from his wealth; the kings of Hawaii, and England and France before their revolutions, were thought to have a divine right to rule; the chief of the Dahomey tribe of West Africa acquires legitimacy through his age, as he is always the oldest living male of the tribe.

Legitimacy grants the right to hold, use, and allocate power. Power based on legitimacy may be distinguished from power based on force: obedience to the former results from the belief that obedience is "right"; compliance to power based on force is the result of fear of the deprivation of liberty, physical well-being, life, material property. Thus, power based on legitimacy is symbolic and depends not upon any intrinsic value, but upon the positive expectations of those who recognize and accede to it. If the expectations are not met regularly (if the shaman fails too many times or the leader is continuously unsuccessful in preventing horse or camel theft), the legitimacy of the recognized power figure is minimized and may collapse altogether.

Religion and politics. Religion is intricately connected with politics. Religious beliefs are often the basis for the society's social and political goals. Religious beliefs may also influence laws: acts which people believe to be sinful, such as sodomy and incest, are often illegal. Fre-

quently, it is religion that legitimizes government.

In both small-scale and industrial societies, belief in the supernatural is important and is reflected in the governments of these peoples. The effect of religion on politics is perhaps best exemplified by medieval Europe. Holy wars were fought over the smallest matter; immense cathedrals were built in honor of the Virgin and other saints; kings and queens pledged allegiance to the Pope and asked his blessing in all important ventures, be they marital or martial. In the pre-Columbian Americas, the Aztec society was a religious state, or theocracy, that thrived as a result of the theological need for human sacrifices to assuage or please the gods. In Peru, the Inca emperor proclaimed absolute authority based on the proposition that he was descended from the sun god. In our own country, the Declaration of Independence, which is an expression of the social and political beliefs of the American people, stresses a belief in a Supreme Being. This document states that "all men are created (by God) equal," a tenet that gave rise to our own form of democracy because it implied that all men should participate in governing themselves. The fact that the American head of state takes his oath of office by swearing on a Bible is another instance of the use of religion to legitimize political power.

In many small-scale societies, religion is even more closely related to the political system. Among the Afikbo Ibo of Nigeria, for example, religion is a political force even though priests and diviners are not politically active and officials do not require supernatural approval to hold office. The political power of religion is vested in the Afikbo guardian *erosi*, the impersonal spirits connected with nature. These awesome spirits are instrumental in such important affairs as prosperity, fertility, and general welfare. Politically, the *erosi* reinforce the men's village society which is charged with maintaining order within the village. For example, if a person accused of a crime denies his guilt, he must swear his innocence on an *erosi* shrine. If he refuses, he is considered guilty; if he swears and is lying, the Afikbos believe the *erosi* will kill him or make him seriously ill within a short span of time.

War

One of the responsibilities of the state is the organization and execution of the activities of war. Throughout history, men have engaged in a seemingly endless chain of wars and intergroup hostilities. Why do wars occur? Is the need to wage war an instinctive feature of the human personality? What are the alternatives to violence as a means of settling disputes between societies?

Everyone shares certain fundamental needs. In order to survive, each of us requires sufficient food, water, and living space. Because these resources are available only in limited quantities, every society is faced with the problem of securing them for its members. Therefore, it is believed that a significant factor in human aggression is the stress related to population pressures. In societies with relatively efficient means of food production, it often happens that population increases faster than living standards improve. Obviously, a large population will need more food, water, and space than a small one. As population density rises, stress rises not only within a society, but between societies as well. War is one method of regulating and redistributing population.

There is reason to suppose that war has become a serious problem only in the last 10,000 years, since the improvement of food production techniques, the rise of the city, and the invention of centralized states. Among hunters and gatherers, warfare is not a common method of relieving population pressures; some sort of voluntary redistribution is much more likely. Because territorial boundaries and membership among hunting and gathering bands are usually fluid and ill-defined, a man who hunts with one band today may hunt with a neighboring band tomorrow. Warfare is further rendered impractical by the systematic interchange of women among hunting and gathering groups—it is likely that someone in each band will have a sister or a cousin in a

Figure 21-7. *The Pope's status in the political hierarcy of the church is supported by Catholics' religious faith. The Shah of Iran is considered both a political and a religious leader, so he is treated with great deference.*

neighboring band. Where property ownership is minimal and no state organization exists, the likelihood of warfare is greatly diminished.

Despite the traditional view of the agriculturist as a gentle tiller of the soil, it is among farming and pastoral populations that warfare is most prominent. As a result of the commitment to the land inherent in farming, agricultural societies tend to be far more centralized and stable in their membership than hunting and gathering societies. Moreover, these societies are often rigidly matrilocal or patrilocal, and each new generation is thus bound to the same territory.

The availibility of virgin land may not serve as a sufficient detriment to the outbreak of war. Among slash-and-burn agriculturalists, for example, competition for land cleared of virgin forest frequently leads to hostility and armed conflict. The centralization of political control and the possession of valuable property among agriculturalists provide much more stimuli for warfare.

On a broader scale, the difference between hunting and farming populations may be viewed as a difference in world view. As a general rule, hunters and gatherers tend to conceive of themselves as a part of nature and in balance with it. When a Bushman kills a giraffe, it is a serious and somber occasion, for the Bushman recognizes that the death of any creature upsets the balance of nature. This attitude may be referred to as a naturalistic world view.

The Bushman's respect for nature contrasts sharply with the world view prevalent among agriculturalists, who do not find their food in nature but take steps to produce it. The attitude that nature exists only to be used by man may be referred to as an exploitative world view. By extension, a society which adopts such a worldview may find nothing wrong with manipulating other societies in order to assure its own survival. The exploitative world view, prevalent among food-producing peoples, is an important prerequisite to intersocietal warfare.

A naturalistic world view is virtually nonexistent among modern industrial societies. Although technology and contraception have the potential to greatly reduce population pressures, the large populations of Western societies have created a great deal of stress both internal and external. Through the systematic exploitation of underdeveloped lands, European and American societies have largely overcome the need to fight for food and water and compete instead for power and influence. Despite the ability to control population, the elimination of war has yet to be achieved; value systems would therefore seem to be a crucial element in the existence of warfare.

War is not a universal phenomenon. Throughout the world, from the Bushmen of Africa to the Arapesh of New Guinea to the Hopi of North America, societies exist in which warfare as we know it is not practiced. Almost invariably, peaceful societies are those which have some form of naturalistic world view.

☐

TRIBAL ORGANIZATION OF THE BLACKFEET

A child born to Blackfeet parents began to learn the patterns of social interaction. He was first of all a member of a household—the occupants of a single tepee—which included the parents, unmarried brothers and sisters, and perhaps one or two other relatives as well, such as a grandparent, a maiden aunt, or other wives of the household head.

As the child grew older it learned that its family was the minimal economic unit of the Blackfeet society. The father was the decision maker, the one responsible for the protection and good behavior of its members; the first wife was the owner of the tepee, responsible for the other wives if any, for the care of the children, maintenance of the tepee and other duties within the women's realm. The child learned too about other kinsmen, that he had important relatives on both sides of the family—in other words, kin were recognized bilaterally.

As acquaintances were made beyond the household, he or she learned that there were other families that regularly lived near and traveled with one's own. These were members of the band, the day in and day out hunting and gathering group that was the basic economic and political unit of the Blackfeet. It was the band that moved according to the requirements of the yearly round, camped alone through the winter, joined with other bands in the summer for the tribal hunt. The child learned the band name and identified with it: he was a child of his parents and one of the Small Robes, Skunks, Lone Eaters or whatever his band might be. Over the years he learned too that the people who gathered during the summer hunt were fellow Piegan, and that among other people encountered on occasion were some who spoke his language, did things his way, were Blackfeet of the other divisions—the Siksika and the Kainah—who often came to the aid of the Piegan in times of conflict.

While kin ties were basic to band formation, friendship and self-interest played a part as well, and people changed bands when they felt it advantageous to do so. [Anthropologist John C.] Ewers believes that this shifting band allegiance had developed with the inequal distribution of wealth that followed the acquisition of the horse. Poor people became more dependent upon the generosity of the wealthy few and attached themselves to the bands of those men who could best provide for them.

Band membership then was based first of all upon kin ties, but with no absolute rule of descent. Wives usually joined the band of their husbands and children belonged to that of their father, but it was not unusual for a man to join his wife's group. A widow could choose to remain in her husband's band or to return to that of her parents. A man could change band affiliation "even in middle life . . ." (Wissler 1911). Other persons attached themselves to the band for various reasons, and long residence with a band, and acceptance by its members, was tantamount to band membership.

The tribe was a larger association of individual bands whose members recognized common ties of language, kinship and culture. It was an organized unit only during the few weeks of the summer hunt, and tribal discipline operated only at this time. Even here the bands retained their spatial and functional autonomy; each band had its habitual place in the camp circle and continued to operate as an economic and political unit with only a part of its powers surrendered to the tribal organization.

Like other Plains Indians, the Piegan had a series of men's organizations, or societies, of which there were three basic types: age-graded warrior societies, religious societies and cults, and the less formal dance association.

The named warrior societies (Mosquitoes, Pigeons, Braves, All-Crazy Dogs, etc.) were corporate groups, that is, they continued over time, surviving the individual members. Groups of young men of a similar age sometimes started a new society, or, more usually, got together and bought memberships in an ongoing society. Similarly the old members would in turn buy into the next age-rank. The transfer was between individuals and such purchases could occur at any time. It was customary, however, for several men to transfer at the same time. Periodic transfers of this kind made possible a progressive movement of membership from a lower to a higher ranking society as men grew older. The oldest society might continue as its ranks were renewed from below, or eventually die out as its members passed away.

These were the groups granted policing powers at the summer encampment. In addition they served to promote the military spirit of the members through war games and intersociety competition in races, dancing and games.

The medicine men's societies and related cults were less formally organized gatherings of men who owned important medicine bundles and powers. These men conferred together to aid in the organization and presentation of the Sun Dance and to promote the spiritual and material welfare of the tribe. The dance organizations were social clubs made up of young men who organized for the purpose of staging social dances during the time of the summer encampment.

Membership in one or more of these organizations created loyalties that cut across the ties of kinship and band affiliation, and helped to contribute to tribal solidarity. In other words, a person identified first with his kinsmen and with his band, but later established additional and potentially conflicting ties of loyalty by marrying someone from another band and by membership in a society that drew its members from many bands.

Band and tribal leadership was not inherited but open to all who could command a following. A band headman gained a position of influence by displaying the qualities valued in his society and by his continued exercise of these attributes. His influence depended upon his power to persuade others, and the support of many followers increased this ability. He conferred with family heads and all decisions were reached by mutual agreement.

Band leaders formed a council during the tribal encampment and one of them, by election or selection, came to be considered the chief of the tribe. The chief had no institutionalized authority and little disciplining power. His chiefly functions were to guide the council to agreement and to mediate in cases of conflict and uncertainty.

There were no formalized institutions for social control except for the policing duties of the associations under special regulations put into effect at the summer encampment. Conflict was first of all a matter between individuals, then a concern of the families and finally of the bands. The delinquent person was cautioned, ridiculed, gossiped about, and shamed into conformity. Ostracism and violence were the ultimate penalties within the band, but usually gossip and shame served to restore order. Boys and girls growing up in Piegan society were urged to achieve the ideals of that society. Boys were told to be brave, to be good fighters, able to defend themselves against their peers and to protect younger children. They were praised for skills and daring, even for sexual exploits. Girls were urged to be quiet, dutiful, sober, hard-working, and to protect their virginity. Both were rewarded with praise when they achieved, and punished with sarcasm and gossiped about when they misbehaved or failed. These sanctions contributed to a developing concern with their own identity and to a strong sense of shame, and such concerns in turn gave added force to these mechanisms of social control. Gossip and shame were also used to curb intratribal conflicts among adults. A cluster of tepees made an ideal setting for effective ridicule. Wissler describes a process of "formal ridicule" that was used to curb "mild persistent misconduct." When the people were quietly settled in of an evening, a headman would call out to a neighbor asking him if he had heard about that silly fellow two tepees down who had been mistreating his wife? Men in other tepees would join in telling what they thought of the man and his behavior, all to the discomfort of the victim and the enjoyment of everyone else. Sarcasm, ridicule, and the accompanying laughter, added up to an evening of entertainment for all but the victim, who was soon highly motivated to mend his ways.

In the more serious cases of adult disputes, force and physical punishment were employed if gossip failed. In cases of murder, a revenge killing might take place if a high payment was not offered in retribution and accepted. A person who disrupted the summer hunt might be beaten and have his clothing and weapons destroyed. An adulterous woman might have her nose cut off, or be put to death by the members of her husband's warrior society.

These forces contributed to the development of some general personality characteristics of the Blackfeet. [George Bird] Grinnell found them, like other Plains Indians, to be "talkative, merry, and lighthearted," and fond of joking, even though they appeared reserved and quiet when with strangers. Wissler commented on their fondness for jest and practical jokes. In addition, I get a picture of a brave, resourceful people, industrious and aggressive, yet much concerned with self, jealous, and easily shamed. These characteristics and their expression were further reinforced by the Blackfeet beliefs.

Source:
From *Modern Blackfeet: Montanans on a Reservation* by Malcolm McFee. Copyright © 1972 by Holt, Rinehart and Winston, Inc. Reprinted by permission of Holt, Rinehart and Winston, Inc.

Summary

1.

In all societies, social control and power is vested in a system of social relations or in a selected group for the purpose of maintaining social order. No group can live together without persuading or coercing its members to conform to the agreed upon rules of conduct. Political organization exists in every society to manage public affairs.

2.

In order of complexity, political organization ranges from the uncentralized bands and tribes to the centralized chiefdoms and states. The band is a small, autonomous group of hunters and gatherers made up of associated families or kin groups occupying a given territory. Political organization in bands is democratic and an informal social control is exerted by public opinion in the form of gossip. Leadership is transitory.

3.

The tribe, as a form of political organization, has an agricultural or livestock-raising economy with a larger population than the band, and the family units within the tribe are autonomous and egalitarian. Social control is informal but the authority of leadership is somewhat greater than in the band. Leadership within the clan may be based on kinship and is exercised by a group of elders. Another system of leadership which cuts across kinship and lineages is the authority vested in men in the group who shared the experience of initiation into the tribe at the same time. As these groups of men get older they become the effective leadership.

4.

Some tribes vest political authority in voluntary associations or men's clubs. A boy joins one or another men's club upon his initiation as a warrior. The men's organizations administer the affairs of the tribe. Another variant of authority in tribes is the Big Man, who privately builds up his wealth and political power until he must be reckoned with as a leader.

5.

Chiefdoms are centralized political systems in a hierarchical society in which rank is based on kinship membership.

6.

The state is a political unit which has a monopoly on the legitimate use of political force. States are permanent, with a large bureaucracy to administer the government, the authority to assess and collect taxes, to administer justice, and to make and enforce laws.

7.

Until quite recently political organization with a separation of church and state was rare. Religion is so intricately woven into the life of the people that its presence is inevitably felt in the political sphere. Fear of the supernatural is a form of social control and in the more complex chiefdoms and states, the head of state was often the head of the church or a demigod.

Suggested readings

Cohen, Ronald and John Middleton, eds. *Comparative Political Systems*. Garden City, New York: Natural History Press, 1967.
The editors have selected some twenty studies in the politics of nonindustrial societies by such well-known scholars as Lévi-Strauss, S. F. Nadel, Marshal Sahlins, and S. N. Eisenstadt.

Fortes, M. and E. E. Evans-Pritchard, eds. *African Political Systems*. New York: Oxford University Press, 1961.
This classic on comparative research on native African political systems focuses on areas formerly administered by the British. Among the peoples discussed are the Zulus of South Africa, the Bemba of Rhodesia, and the Nuer of southern Sudan. The editors' introduction outlines many of the fundamental issues of political anthropology.

Fried, Morton *The Evolution of Political Society*. New York: Random House, 1967.
The author attempts to trace the evolution of political society through a study of simple, egalitarian societies. The character of the state and the means whereby this form of organization takes shape is considered in terms of pristine and secondary states, formed because pre-existing states supplied the stimuli or models for organization.

Swartz, Marc J., Turner, Victor W. and Arthur Tuden *Political Anthropology*. Chicago: Aldine Press, 1966.
This reader in political anthropology attempts to trace the changes in the field since the publication in 1961 of Fortes and Evans-Pritchard's *African Political Systems*. The papers included illustrate the trend away from a classification of political structures and functions and toward an understanding of political processes.

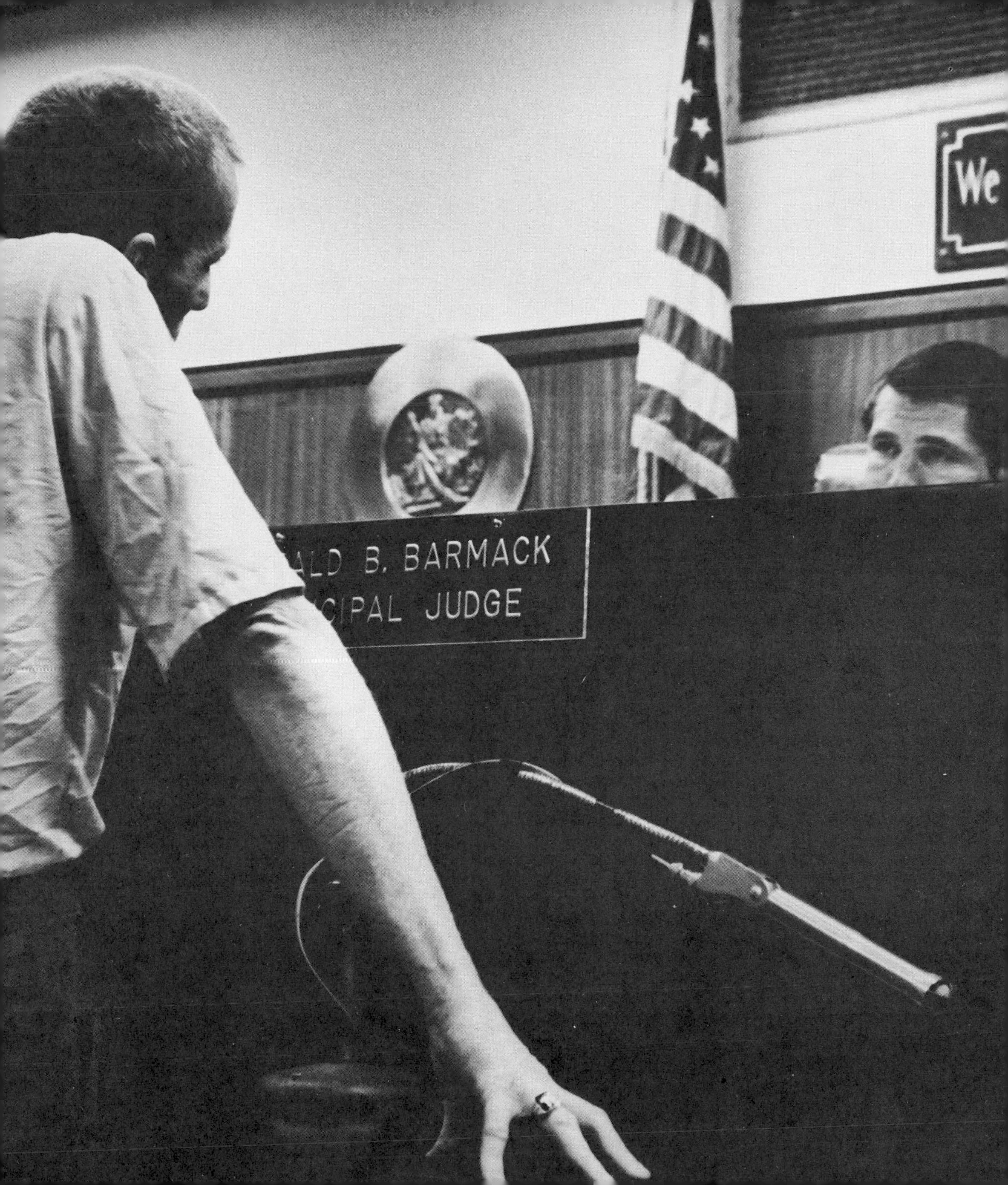
We
ALD B. BARMACK
CIPAL JUDGE

Social
control

Few of us would admit to blindly following the dictates of our society; indeed, we may purposely attempt to assert our nonconformity in the way we speak, look, act, and think. Yet as much as we may flaunt our individuality, most of our behavior is restricted to some degree by certain fundamental cultural guidelines. As members of a society, each of us is obliged to conform to certain rules and regulations.

Society determines not only the limits of acceptable behavior, but the penalties for exceeding those limits as well. Thus a society that forbids adultery will also have some means of punishing the adulterers. A Blackfoot who discovers that his wife has been unfaithful may either cut off the woman's nose or demand damages from the man who has offended him. An Eskimo in the same situation may kill his wife's lover, or he may prefer to challenge him to a song contest in which the two men will settle their dispute by competing in the composition of mutually abusive songs. Both the Blackfoot and the Eskimo are responding to a personal offense in a manner condoned by their societies.

In every society, institutions are developed to encourage members to behave in certain ways and not in others. Through social controls, a group of people encourages conformity to its norms and values, thereby perpetuating its culture and maintaining its system of social relations. Thus the group establishes a certain predictability of behavior, which is essential for social living. In this chapter, we shall examine some of the questions which arise in connection with the problem of social control.

The study of social control

The process of social control is probably older than culture itself. In other higher primate groups, dominant males seem to police the other individuals in certain ways. When fights break out, they rush to the scene of the quarrel; in most cases, their presence is enough to restore order.

Before the twentieth century, anthropologists based their concept of social control on the theories of the Victorian jurist, Sir Henry Maine. In *Ancient Law,* originally printed in 1861, Maine expressed the belief that, in "primitive" societies, interpersonal relationships are determined by ascribed social status, and not by contract, as they are in more "advanced" societies. That is, "primitive" people conform to the rules of society out of a blind obedience to custom and tradition. "Advanced" people, on the other hand, base their interpersonal relationships not on traditional beliefs but on mutually advantageous agreements; the model for this was Thomas Hobbe's social contract.

Émile Durkheim also focused on the supposedly different bases for social sanctions in Western and non-Western societies. In *The Division of Labor,* Durkheim argued that, in simple societies, everyone performs much the same kind of work and produces much the same kind of goods. In such circumstances, order is maintained by submission to certain universally acknowledged rules of behavior. As a society becomes more complex, and its work force more specialized, members become increasingly dependent upon one another for goods and services. The individual, no longer able to provide for all of his own needs, must contract with other producers and sellers. In such a society, relationships are determined by the exchange of goods and services, not by submission to an all-inclusive code of law. Contractual relationships, according to Durkheim, form the basis of civil law in complex societies.

This clear-cut distinction between social control in "primitive" and "advanced" societies was refuted in the early twentieth century largely through the work of Bronislaw Malinowski. In *Crime and Custom in Savage Society,* Malinowski described the maintenance of social order among the people of the Trobriand Islands. Malinowski argued that the factors which motivate conformity in more simple societies are the same factors which motivate conformity in more complex societies. According to Malinowski, the universal basis of social order is the principle of reciprocity. Each individual understands that if he behaves properly towards his neighbor, his neighbor will find it advantageous to behave properly towards him. On the other hand, if a man fails to cooperate with his neighbors, he realizes that they may withdraw their cooperation as well. Although Malinowski may have attributed undue importance to the reciprocal principle, his emphasis on the universality of this principle represented a major advance in our understanding of the mechanisms of social control. Much has since been written on social control—most notably by Hoebel in his study of the Cheyenne—but much research remains to be done on non-Western societies.

Internalized controls

People seem to behave as they are expected to mainly because of the implicit threat of the consequences of doing otherwise. Indeed, in all societies, the breaking of rules and laws is met with some kind of predictable counteraction. In some cases, the counteraction is visible and authoritative—a jail sentence, dismissal from an organization or club, the mark of the Scarlet Letter A, or a symbolic mutilation. Such punishment is imposed by the community, and the offender is properly shamed before his peers.

There are, however, forms of social control imposed on the guilty individual without the direct intervention of society. In such instances, controls have been so thoroughly built in to the individual that he provides his own punishment, and experiences a private shame. For example, in our society, people refrain from committing incest not so much from fear of legal punishment as from a deep abhorrence of the act and the shame they would feel in performing it. Built in or internalized controls rely on such deterrents as the fear of divine punishment, and magical retaliation. The individual expects that he will be punished by these forces even though no one in his community knows of his wrongdoing.

A society that strongly relied on internalized controls was that of the Penobscot Indians, a tribe that inhabited the northeastern part of North America. The Penobscots held a very strong belief in the effectiveness of magic. Every person was thought to have the potential for working magic—though some were more practiced than others. If a person secretly committed a crime, it was thought that sooner or later, the aggrieved party

Figure 22-1. *The top photo shows a group of Bakhtiari tribesmen holding a trial for one of their members who employed a professional thief to steal for him. The bottom photo is a trial of a !Kung Bushman accused of stealing a cow. The trial, held by the rival Tswana, is probably not a fair one, but it indicates an attempt to work within a legal system.*

would find out about it; he would then take some form of magical retribution. In fact the crime may have been of such a petty nature that it could never be discerned. Nevertheless, the wrong-doer's belief put him in a frame of mind wherein he expected to be discovered and punished. The first thing that happened out of the ordinary was therefore interpreted as retribution, and to escape worse punishment, the offender quickly took measures to rectify the wrong. Here equilibrium is achieved and social control effected not so much by direct legal processes of society but by the guilty party, acting alone.

Internalized controls as strong as these of the Penobscots tend to be reflected in, and supported by, other institutions in society. For example, the Penobscot religion posits a world inhabited by all sorts of spirits and superhumans. The tribe's mythology is rich with tales in which these super-humans punish people and other creatures for transgressions of the moral code. Myth-telling was a major recreational pastime, so the Penob-scot learned from earliest childhood exactly what happened to people who "didn't do right." Not only did the myths state a body of precedent for action, but they also presented the threat that, whatever else happened, an individual could at least expect divine retribution for any misdoing. A belief in magical and divine retribution achieved an internal control for crimes such as petty thievery and trespassing; only in more seri-ous instances were direct actions undertaken by society as a whole.

Externalized controls

Because internalized controls are not wholly sufficient even in a society like that of the Penob-scot, every society develops institutions designed to encourage conformity to social norms. These institutions are referred to as **sanctions;** they are externalized social controls. According to Radcliffe-Brown, "a sanction is a reaction on the part of a society or of a considerable number of its members to a mode of behavior which is thereby approved (positive sanctions) or disapproved (negative sanctions)." Furthermore, sanctions may be either formal or informal and may vary significantly within a given society.

Each group and subgroup within a society tends to develop its own distinctive pattern or usages and the means of maintaining them without necessary recourse to the municipal law. Sanctions there come to operate within every conceivable set of group relationships: they include not only the organized sanctions of the law but also the gossip of neighbors or the customs regulating norms of production that are spontaneously generated among workers on the factory floor. In small scale communities . . . informal sanctions may become more drastic than the penalties provided for in the legal code . . .[1]

Sanctions then operate within social groups of all sizes. As we shall see, they need not be enacted into law in order to play a significant role in social control. If a sanction is to be effective, it cannot be arbitrary. Quite the opposite: sanctions must be consistently applied, and their existence must be generally known by the members of the society.

Negative and positive sanctions. Social sanctions may be categorized as either positive or negative. Positive sanctions, by which we mean such incentives to conformity as awards, titles, and recognition by one's neighbors, seem generally to be of less significance in determining social behavior than negative sanctions. In most societies, the threats of imprisonment, corporal punishment, or ostracism from the community for violation of social norms are stressed far more heavily than are the advantages of social conformity. People are more willing to conform to society's rules than to accept the consequences of not doing so.

Formal and informal sanctions. Sanctions may also be categorized as either formal or informal,

[1] A. L. Epstein, "Sanctions" in *International Encyclopedia of Social Sciences*, 1968, Volume 14, p. 3.

Figure 22-2. *These Portuguese army officers seem satisfied with the positive sanctions— medals, honor, wealth—they have won.*

depending on whether or not a legal statute is involved. The man who wears tennis shorts to a church service may be subject to a variety of informal sanctions, ranging from the glances of the clergyman to the chuckling of nearby women. But if he were to show up without any trousers at all, he would be subject to the formal sanction of arrest for indecent exposure. Only in the second instance would he have been guilty of breaking the law.

Informal sanctions of the negative sort are very effective in enforcing a large number of seemingly unimportant customs. Because most people want to be totally accepted, they are willing to acquiesce to the rules that govern dress, eating, conversation, even in the absence of actual laws.

Organized and diffuse sanctions. According to Radcliffe-Brown, sanctions may further be classified either as organized or diffuse. Organized sanctions are those which reward or punish behavior through precisely regulated social procedure. Organized positive sanctions, such as military decorations or monetary awards, generally play a much smaller role in encouraging desirable behavior than do organized negative sanctions. This latter category of sanctions may include loss of status or rank, exclusion from social life and its privileges, seizure of property, imprisonment, and even bodily mutilation or death. When these sanctions are imposed by an authorized political body, they are referred to as **legal sanctions.** We shall have more to say about this special category of sanctions shortly.

Diffuse sanctions, defined by Radcliffe-Brown as "spontaneous expressions of approval or disapproval by members of the community acting as individuals," may assume a great many different forms. Often, diffuse sanctions involve patterns of behavior which, although they are enacted by no official authority, are, in fact, more or less institutionalized. In the *vito,* an old Spanish custom paralleled among various Mediterranean peoples, an individual who has offended community standards may be visited by a noisy delegation of his neighbors in the middle of the night. This unwelcome group of visitors may proceed to make such abusive noises or subject the offender to such inconveniences that he cannot possibly mistake or ignore his neighbors' disapproval of his behavior. The mockery of one's neighbors and the loss of honor act as powerful inducements to proper behavior. The *vito* exemplifies the **satirical sanction,** or the sanction of ridicule.

Witchcraft beliefs may also act as a powerful agent of social control in some societies. An individual would naturally hesitate to offend his neighbor when that neighbor might retaliate by resorting to black magic. Among the Azande of the Sudan, a man who thinks he has been bewitched may consult an oracle who, after performing the appropriate mystical rites, may then establish or confirm the identity of the offending witch. Confronted with this evidence, the "witch" will usually agree to cooperate in order to avoid any additional trouble. Should the victim die, his relatives may choose to make magic against the witch, ultimately accepting the death of some villager both as evidence of guilt and the efficacy of their magic. For the Azande, witchcraft provides not only a sanction against antisocial behavior but also a means of dealing with natural hostilities and death. No one wishes to be thought of as a witch, and surely no one wishes to be victimized by one. By institutionalizing their emotional responses, the Azande are able to successfully maintain social order.

Another important social control, and one that is likely to be internalized, is the religious sanction. Just as a devout Christian avoids sinning for fear of Hell, so do other worshippers tend to behave in a manner intended not to offend their powerful supernatural beings. The threat of punishment—either in this life or in the next—by gods, ancestral spirits, or ghosts is a strong incentive for proper behavior. In some societies, it is believed that ancestral spirits are very much concerned with the maintenance of good relations among the living members of their lineage. Death or illness in the lineage may be explained by reference to some violation of tradition or custom. Religious sanctions may thus serve not only to regulate behavior but to explain unexplainable phenomena as well.

Primary and secondary sanctions. According to Radcliffe-Brown, sanctions may be further classified either as primary or secondary. Primary sanctions involve direct community action against an individual; secondary sanctions are those which are directed at a person (or a group of people) by another person (or group of people) backed by the support of the community. The institution of the duel exemplifies the secondary sanction. In this case, the two involved parties settle their differences directly without the overt mediation of an official representative of the community. Secondary sanctions do not necessarily involve the use of physical force. Among the Trobriand Islanders, for example, a man may shout out his accusations against a neighbor in the middle of the night, informing the entire village of his complaint. So powerful is this sanction that people so accused have been known to commit suicide rather than face shame and dishonor.

Figure 22-3. *Secondary sanctions leave the individuals involved in a dispute to work out their own solution; this may lead to some form of regulated combat, as seen here in a picture of Mexican schoolboys settling a quarrel with boxing gloves.*

Function of sanctions

Sanctions are introduced in order to formalize the adherence to norms, including adherence to formal law. A society may be composed of many different groupings of individuals, each with its own needs and interests; yet despite these differences, all are bound by certain common norms and values. It is the function of sanctions to integrate the various social factions and to insure maximum harmony in the community. John Beat-

tie wrote about the sanctions found in Bunyoro, a kingdom in Africa:

> Thus in Bunyoro disputes between fellow-villagers are often settled by an informal group of neighbors who have the traditional right to impose a penalty on the party judged to be in the wrong, but lack any formal means of enforcing their judgements. The judgement is always a payment of meat and beer, which must be brought to the successful litigant's house on an appointed day. There it is consumed by both parties to the dispute, as well as by those neighbors who were concerned in the settlement.[2]

The object of such a procedure is not to administer punishment but rather to restore unity to a disrupted village. In most cases, sanctions are primarily intended not to restrict behavior but rather to prevent damage to the social fabric and to mend such damage when it occurs.

Law in non-Western societies

The Ifugaos are a tribe of head-hunters living in the mountains of Luzon. Among the Ifugaos, an individual who is unable to settle a dispute with another man through personal negotiations may enlist the aid of a professional go-between known as a *monkalun*. If a settlement cannot be agreed upon with the assistance of the *monkalun*, the plaintiff and his kinsmen may attempt to kill the defendant or his kinsmen. Among the Ifugaos, the alternative to peaceful negotiation is feud. Ultimately, there is no binding legal authority.

In Western society, on the other hand, a man who commits an offense against another man is subject to a series of complex legal proceedings. He will be arrested by the police; tried before a judge and, perhaps, a jury; and, if his crime is serious enough, he may be fined, imprisoned, or even executed. Throughout this chain of events,

[2]John Beattie, *Other Cultures: Aims, Methods and Achievements* (New York: The Free Press, 1964).

Figure 22-4. *In South Africa, law and custom intertwine to regulate racial behavior. The sign in the park (bottom photo) indicates the complexity of discriminatory rules. In most cases, blacks and whites remain separate.*

the accused party is dealt with by presumably disinterested policemen, judges, jurors, and jailers who may have no personal acquaintance whatsoever with the plaintiff or the defendant. How strange this would seem to the Ifugao! Clearly, the Westerner and the non-Westerner are operating under distinctly different assumptions.

Each society establishes institutions to encourage conformity to its norms and to define proper action in the event of breach of those norms. Through its sanctions, a society exercises a degree of control over the behavior of its members. An important part of a society's total system of social controls is that aspect referred to as law.

Definition of law

When two Eskimos settle a dispute by engaging in a song contest, the result of the contest is binding; that is, the affair is closed. No further action need be expected. Would we choose to describe the outcome of such a contest as a legal decision? If every law is a sanction, but not every sanction is a law, how are we to distinguish between social sanctions in general and those to which we will apply the label "law?"

The definition of law has been a lively point of contention among anthropologists in the twentieth century. In 1926, Malinowski argued that the rules of law are distinguished from the rules of custom in that "they are regarded as the obligation of one person and the rightful claim of another, sanctioned not by mere psychological motive, but by a definite social machinery of binding force based . . . upon mutual dependence." An example of one rule of custom might be seen in the dictate that guests at a dinner party should repay the host with entertainment in the future. A host who does not receive a return invitation may feel cheated of something he thought was owed to him, but he has no legal claim against his ungrateful guest for the $12.67 he spent on food. However, if he was cheated of the same sum by his grocer when he was shopping, he could invoke the law. Although Malin-

479

owski's definition introduced several important elements of law, his failure to adequately distinguish between legal and nonlegal sanctions left the problem of formulating a workable definition of law in the hands of later anthropologists.

An important pioneer in the study of primitive law was E. Adamson Hoebel. According to Hoebel, "a social norm is legal if its neglect or infraction is regularly met, in threat or in fact, by the application of physical force by an individual or group possessing the socially recognized privilege of so acting." In stressing the legitimate use of physical coercion, Hoebel de-emphasized the traditional association of law with a centralized court system. Although judge and jury are fundamental features of Western jurisprudence, they are not the universal backbone of human law.

In his study of the Kapauku Papuans, Leopold Pospisil defined law in terms of four basic attributes:[3]

1) A legal decision is backed by authority. Some individual or group of individuals must possess sufficient influence to insure the conformity of disputing parties to its decisions.

2) A legal decision is intended to have universal applicability; that is, it is expected that a legal decision made today will apply to comparable situations in the future.

3) A legal decision determines the rights of one party and the duties of the other. Law recognizes the two-sided nature of every dispute.

4) A legal decision determines the nature and degree of sanctions. Legal sanction may be physical—such as imprisonment or confiscation of property—or psychological—such as public ridicule or avoidance.

Some anthropologists have proposed that the precise definition of law is an impossible—and perhaps even undesirable—undertaking. When we speak of "the law," are we not inclined to fall back on our familiar Western conception of rules enacted by an authorized legislative body and enforced by the judicial mechanisms of the state? Can any concept of law be applied to such so-

[3] Leopold Pospisil, *The Kapauku Papuans* (New York: Holt, Rinehart and Winston, 1963).

Figure 22-5. *In a tribal society, such as that of the Akure in Nigeria, it is the king who acts as judge (bottom photo) in all questions of law. More complex societies, such as that of the nation of Zambia, require the creation of legal specialists, such as this Zambian lawyer who has just been elected to a seat on the nation's Supreme Court.*

cieties as the Nuer or the Ifugao for whom the notion of a centralized judiciary is virtually meaningless? How shall we categorize duels, song contests, and other socially condoned forms of self-help which seem to meet some but not all of the criteria of law?

Ultimately, it seems of greatest value to consider each case within its cultural context. That each society exercises a degree of control over its members by means of rules and sanctions, and that some of these sanctions are more formalized than others, is indisputable; yet, in distinguishing between legal and nonlegal sanctions, we should be careful not to allow questions of terminology to overshadow our efforts to understand individual situations as they arise.

Functions of law

In *The Law of Primitive Man* (1954), Hoebel writes of a time when the notion that private property should be generously shared was a fundamental precept of Cheyenne life. Subsequently, however, some men assumed the privilege of borrowing other men's horses without bothering to obtain permission. When Wolf Lies Down complained of such unauthorized borrowing to the members of the Elk Soldier Society, the Elk Soldiers not only had his horse returned to him but also secured an award for damages from the offender. The Elk Soldiers then announced that, to avoid such difficulties in the future, horses were no longer to be borrowed without permission. Furthermore, they declared their intention of retrieving any such property and administering a whipping to anyone who resisted their efforts to return improperly borrowed goods.

The case of Wolf Lies Down and the Elk Soldier Society clearly illustrates three basic functions of law. First, law defines relationships among the members of society, determining proper behavior under various circumstances. Knowledge of the law permits each member of society to know his rights and duties in respect to every other member of society. Second, law allocates the authority to employ coercion in the enforcement of sanctions. In most complex societies, such authority is generally vested in the government and its court system. In simpler societies, the authority to employ force may be allocated directly to the injured party. Third, law functions to redefine social relations and to insure social flexibility. As new situations arise, law must determine whether old rules and assumptions retain their validity and to what extent they must be altered. Law, if it is to operate efficiently, must allow room for change.

In actual practice, law is rarely the smooth and well-integrated system described above. In any given society, various legal sanctions may apply at various levels of society. Because each individual in a society is usually a member of numerous subgroups, he is subject to the various dictates of these diverse groups. The Kapauku individual is, simultaneously, a member of a family, a household, a sublineage, and a confederacy, and is subject to all the laws of each subgroup. In some cases, it may be impossible for an individual to submit to contradictory legal indications:

> In one of the confederacy's lineages, incestuous relations between members of the same sib were punished by execution of the culprits, and in another by severe beating, in the third constituent lineage such a relationship was not punishable and . . . was not regarded as incest at all. In one of the sublineages, it became even a preferred type of marriage![4]

Furthermore, the power to employ sanctions may vary from level to level within a given society. The head of a Kapauku household may punish a member of his household by means of slapping or beating, but the authority to confiscate property is vested exclusively in the headman of the lineage. An example of a similar dilemma in our own society occurred in Oklahoma, a state in which the sale of liquor by one drink is illegal. State officials arrested several passengers and workers on an Amtrak train passing through the state; these people knew their actions were legal

[4]Ibid., p. 36.

under federal law but were unaware that they could be prosecuted under state law. The complexity of legal jurisdiction within each society casts a shadow of doubt over any easy generalization about law.

Crime

As we have observed, an important function of sanctions, legal or otherwise, is to discourage the breach of social norms. A man contemplating theft is aware of the possibility that he will be captured and punished; yet, despite the severity of sanctions, individuals in every society sometimes violate the norms and subject themselves to the consequences of their behavior. What is the nature of crime in non-Western societies?

In Western society, a clear distinction can be made between offenses against the state and offenses against an individual. Henry Campbell Black said:

> The distinction between a crime and a tort or civil injury is that the former is a breach and violation of the public right and of duties due to the whole community considered as such, and in its social and aggregate capacity; whereas the latter is an infringement or privation of the civil rights of individual merely.[5]

Thus a reckless driver who crashes with another car may be guilty of a crime in endangering public safety; he may also be guilty of a tort, in causing damages to the other car, and he can be sued for their cost by the other driver.

In many non-Western societies, however, there is no conception of a central state. Consequently, all offenses are conceived of as offenses against individuals, rendering the distinction between crime and tort of little value. Indeed, a dispute between individuals may seriously disrupt the social order, especially in small groups where the number of disputants may be a relatively large proportion of the total population. Although the

[5] Henry Campbell Black, *Black's Law Dictionary* (St. Paul, Minn.: West Publishing Company, 1968).

Mbuti Pygmies have no effective domestic or economic unit beyond the family, a dispute between two tribesmen will disrupt the effectiveness of the hunt and is consequently a matter of community concern. The goal of judicial proceedings in most cases is to restore social harmony and not punish an offender. In distinguishing between offenses of concern to the community as a whole and those of concern only to a few individuals, we may refer to offenses as public or private rather than distinguishing between criminal and civil law. In this way, we may avoid values and assumptions which are irrelevant to a discussion of non-Western systems of law.

Perhaps the most fruitful path to understanding the nature of law lies in the thorough analysis of individual dispute cases, each within its own unique social context. Basically, a dispute may be settled in either of two ways. On the one hand, disputing parties may, by means of argument and compromise, voluntarily arrive at a mutually satisfactory agreement. This form of settlement, which may or may not involve the mediation of a third party, is referred to as **negotiation** or **mediation.** The Penobscot Indians sometimes used this technique. The mediator was a person who commanded personal respect and therefore wielded real authority. Generally the mediator was the tribal chief. Although he had no coercive power, he usually effected a settlement through his judgments.

On the other hand, an authorized third party may issue a binding decision which the disputing parties will be obligated to respect. This process is referred to as **adjudication.** The difference between negotiation and adjudication is basically a difference in authorization. In a dispute settled by negotiation, the disputing parties present their positions as convincingly as they can, but they do not participate in the ultimate decision making.

Although the adjudication process is not characteristic of all societies, every society employs some form of negotiation in the settlement of disputes. Often, negotiation acts as a prerequisite or an alternative to adjudication. For example, in the resolution of American labor disputes, striking workers may first negotiate with management, often with the mediation of a third party. If the state decides that the strike constitutes a threat to the public welfare, the disputing parties may be forced to submit to adjudication. In this case, the responsibility for resolving the dispute is transferred to a presumably impartial judge.

The work of the judge is difficult and complex. Not only must he sift through the evidence which is presented before him, but he must consider a wide range of norms, values, and earlier rulings in order to arrive at a decision which he hopes will be considered just not only by the disputing parties but by the public and other judges as well. In most tribal societies, a greater value is placed on reconciling disputing parties and resuming tribal harmony than on administering awards and punishments. Thus, "tribal courts may . . . work in ways more akin to Western marriage conciliators, lawyers, arbitrators, and industrial conciliators than to Western judges in court."[6]

In many societies, judgment is thought to be made by incorruptible supernatural powers, through a trial by ordeal. An example of such a trial was described by James L. Gibbs, Jr., who studied the Kpelle in Liberia:

> When there is some reason to doubt the testimony of a witness, or where the testimony of witnesses is in conflict, . . . a messenger is ordered to administer a spoonful of *katu* to the witness(es): *Katu* is a colorless liquid kept in a stoppered whiskey or wine bottle and is believed to have supernatural potency. In taking it, the witness swears over it, "If I bear false witness, then the *sale* [spirits] should kill me." It is believed that a person who breaks such an oath will be "caught" by the *katu*. His stomach will swell and he will die, or some other sickness will eventually strike. In the tropics, such a misfortune often occurs fairly soon, thereby supporting the belief in the efficacy of the liquid.[7]

[6] Max Gluckman, *The Judicial Process among the Barotse of Northern Rhodesia* (Glencoe, Ill.: The Free Press, 1955).
[7] James L. Gibbs, Jr., "The Kpelle of Liberia" in *Peoples of Africa* (Holt, Rinehart and Winston, 1965) p. 224-5.

Systems of social control

As we have seen, the mechanisms of social control are many and varied, and our societies utilize some combinations of internalized controls, which are part of the individual's enculturation, and externalized controls, which are administered by social institutions, such as the lineage or the state. It might be of interest here to compare two very different systems of social control. The Mbuti Pygmies and the Aztecs furnish a good comparison.

The Mbuti Pygmies

The Mbuti Pygmies are a tribe of hunters and gatherers situated in the Ituri forest of Central Africa. Although the Mbuti recognize no formal economic or political unit beyond the family and the band of which the family forms a part, the need for social cooperation binds the Mbuti into a closely knit community. Whether hunting with bows and arrows or with nets, the Mbuti are highly dependent upon each other for their day-to-day survival.

Despite the absence of any formal political structure, an informal hierarchy of social authority exists among the Pygmies. Leadership in various activities is determined largely by factors of age, sex, and marital status. Younger married men tend to lead the hunt, for example, while the younger married women generally assume responsibility for the gathering of mushrooms and nuts. Young unmarried men and women, on the other hand, tend to have little voice in group discussions. Nevertheless, every adult in the camp is free to express his point of view in reference to any situation.

Because the acquisition of food is a cooperative and communal activity, every individual understands that he is hunting for the band and not for himself. To be selfish or to withhold food from the band is a major offense among the Mbuti. Members of the band may noisily argue about their proper share of the day's food, but each claims only what is properly due him. Cooperation for the common good is the foundation of Mbuti society. Every man, woman, and child is made to understand that "a noisy camp is a hungry camp."

The Mbtui recognize no formal judicial process for the settling of disputes, and no such process seems to be necessary. Disputes between individuals are invariably harmful to the success of the band as a whole, and the Pygmy who jeopardizes the welfare of the group may find himself subject to public insult and ridicule. To be laughed at and humiliated may serve as a far more effective reprimand than a fine or a thrashing. After an offender has been appropriately chastised for his misbehavior, he is reunited with the band and quietly resumes his social role. There is no room in Mbuti

society for lingering punishments or for the bearing of grudges. The threat of social ostracism, however brief that ostracism may be, functions as a powerful instrument of social control among the Mbuti.

Resort to permanent exile is virtually unknown among the Pygmies. In most cases, disputes can be quickly resolved by an appeal to the common welfare. Although the mechanisms of punishment exist, the internal controls which are deeply instilled within each individual are usually sufficient to discourage any prolonged dispute. Conflicts are frequently resolved by the intervention of an impartial elder and the reminder that noise and hostility are harmful to the hunt and, consequently, to the welfare of the band. The maintenance of social control among the Pygmies is not achieved through any formal code of law; rather,

Figure 22-6a. *This photo shows the relative stature of Mbuti Pygmies and Europeans; the fellow primate on the right is a gorilla.*

Figure 22-6b. *These Mbuti men and boys are seated near the entrance of a leaf hut on the edge of the Ituri forest.*

it is understood that cooperation is a fundamental part of being Mbuti.

The Aztecs

The Aztec empire was a complex society which flourished in Mexico until the early sixteenth century. In contrast to the Mbuti, the Aztecs represented a highly structured and stratified society based on formally ritualized laws and customs. The Aztecs developed rigid and externalized mechanisms of social control, administered by the state.

Politically, the society of the Aztecs was a complex hierarchy including nobles, merchants, farmers, and slaves. Each individual had a clearly defined role to play within the civil and spiritual social structure. Church and state were tightly interwoven, and no distinction was made between the laws of the state and the laws of the gods. An offense against one was an offense against the other.

The Aztec court system was an elaborate and powerful instrument of law. Each town elected judges whose principal function was to settle minor disputes and to keep those disputes out of the two higher courts of appeal. Above the highest court was the emperor himself who, as Supreme Justice, was the final authority in all disputes. In addition to the regular courts, special courts for merchants and military leaders were established to serve the special needs of certain individuals.

Proper procedure in courts of law was carefully prescribed by law and custom. Judges were chosen from the ranks of respected nobles and warriors and served as intermediaries between the defendant and the gods. Lying under oath was punishable by death, as was the rendering of an unjust sentence due to partiality on the part of a judge. Aztec law was generally characterized by the swift and brutal administration of harsh penalties for violation of the law. Adulterers might be burned, thieves stoned, and homosexuals hanged. Strict laws governed every phase of Aztec

Figure 22-7. *This pair of pictures is from the Codex Florentino, a missionary book that attempted to explain the practices of the Aztecs.*

Figure 22-8. *This stone statue represents Coatlicue, mother of the Aztec gods. Her necklace is made of human hearts and hands; her skirt features writhing snakes.*

valued the prevention of conflict over its resolution. In order to insure conformity to social norms, Aztec culture was designed to continually re-enforce the values and standards of society.

> Crime was prevented by the system of domestic and public education, by constant vigilance of clan elders, by special inspectors and police, and by long speeches on all ceremonial occasions from the priests, the military leaders, and the ruler, which constantly reiterated the morals and ethics of the tribe.[8]

Characterized by self-discipline and obedience to authority, the social order of the Aztecs was maintained through a combination of continual reiteration of social standards and by the severe punishment of those who violated those standards. Unlike the Mbuti, the Aztecs were motivated to behave properly primarily by external controls.

life. The efficiency of Aztec justice rendered private vengeance unnecessary, nor could such vengeance be tolerated in a complex state with many interdependent parts.

Despite their detailed body of laws and elaborate system of enforcement, the Aztecs naturally

[8] Frederick A. Peterson, *Ancient Mexico* (New York: Putnam, 1959) p. 73.

INFORMAL SOCIAL CONTROL IN AN IRISH VILLAGE

The informal social control system of Inis Beag comprises the parish priest and curate, the headmaster of the school—chosen and strictly regulated by the parish priest, and a "king." The position of king is not hereditary and not supported by a majority of the population as in some other Irish islands, but is self-assumed and based on a number of factors to be considered shortly. Not only is king strictly a term of reference, but it is employed by the folk only when they are most critical of his actions; it also is used by certain outsiders who are frequent visitors to Inis Beag and are aware of the power structure there, but always out of earshot of the islanders.

The folk are devoutly Catholic, despite the fact that they are extremely critical of their priests and retain and reinterpret pagan religious forms. They are proud of their strength of belief, with its attendant morality, and of the sanctity of "Inis Beag of the Saints," and they look to the curate for spiritual comfort, as well as political guidance in several spheres, and are uncomfortable in his absence. His presence, it is believed, provides supernatural protection for the island, while his absence invites possible anti-social behavior, and harm to the soul of one who dies suddenly and is deprived of Extreme Unction at his deathbed. The compensatory rite performed later for the deceased who has been interred while the curate was away is thought to be less efficacious in shortening the stay of the soul in Purgatory.

The techniques of social control utilized by curates are many and mostly negative; they include weekly sermons, lectures to students in the school, talks with individuals who need guidance or reprimand, the use of informers and confessions, the allocation of indulgences, and, in extreme cases, the refusal of sacraments, and the placing of curses. It is difficult to overestimate the degree of fear of the clergy and anti-clericalism which have been inculcated among the folk by the more immoderate measures employed by priests during the last century. Sermons deal both with spiritual messages based on the scriptures and church pronouncements, and with instruction and censure directed toward past or anticipated actions of the islanders in concert or of particular persons. Talks with individuals may take place in their or the curate's home, and often result from information received by the priest from informers or the confessional. The informers, it is said, are usually the housekeeper of the curate and her family, and children who are intimidated by the priest to reveal talk and behavior of their parents and others; however, certain folk are known to bear tales to the clergy and are shunned for this reason. Well aware of the power that the confessional gives the priest over their lives, islanders are outspoken in its condemnation, and many will not confess particular sins, especially those of a sexual nature, to a curate known to assign severe penances and to carry matters beyond the confessional.

The awarding of indulgences represents a positive social control method and has been used frequently, I was told, to obtain needed monetary contributions and services from the folk. Although the priest cannot excommunicate a recalcitrant parishioner, he can achieve the same objective by forbidding confession and absolution and the other sacraments to him, and the islanders report its threat and use as a sanction several occasions in the past. Even more

feared is the "priest's curse," which in Co. Clare ". . . can bring ruin upon a prosperous house; can turn an unbeliever's head upon his shoulders; strike blindness . . ." (Arensberg 1937:28). In Inis Beag, it is called "reading the Gospel (or Bible) at," and can bring illness or death and ultimate damnation within a prescribed time; the folk reason that if a cleric can cure with prayer, he also can cause illness and death by its use.

It is difficult to ascertain today whether the headmaster or the king should be accorded the dominant position, after the curate, in the informal social control system of Inis Beag; for in recent years, the power and prestige of the former have been waxing and those of the latter waning. Headmasters were formerly older men with families whose tenure was long, who were much involved in local affairs and worked closely with the curate, who was politically active and backed candidates and tried to influence island voters, and who maintained social distance although considered "one of the people." For their teaching and other services, they were provided with food, given *curach* transportation without charge, and afforded other amenities by the folk. The house that they and their families occupied until recently is located in Castle Village, near both the old and new schools, and was owned by the diocese. Headmasters now are younger and often single, and are more independent of the curate (One in recent years quit his post, it is held, because he chafed at restrictions imposed on him by the priest.); also, they are apolitical and partici- pate less in the gamut of local affairs. The prestige of the headmaster derives from his having been selected by the parish priest who supports his actions, his status as a "scholar," and the discipline that he exerts in the school with its vestigial effects on those who have graduated. Few islanders will openly contest his decisions in school and civic matters.

The important nonacademic tasks performed by the headmaster are signing official forms—a duty that he shares with the bailiff, drawing up and witnessing the signing of wills, writing letters for the islanders, especially those directed to the county council and departments of the central government, and giving advice on such matters as the advisability of emigrating and of matrimonial matches. Like the curates, the headmasters seldom have tried to direct commu- nity projects and social affairs, other than dances and inter-island competitions. The present headmaster considers himself atypical in many respects, in that he is youthful, has exceptional skill in playing the accordian, likes compan- ionship and the festivities of party and pub, and has rapport with older boys and young men with whom he associates more than did his predecessors; as a result, he is the prime mover in social events—organizing dances and donating his musical talent. Older islanders often find him aloof and will apologize for "taking his time" when seeking favors of him.

Parents have little contact with the headmaster as regards the education of their children, and, although permitted and sometimes urged to do so, they seldom visit the school. They will consult with him about such matters as health problems of their children, but not about educational policies; nor do they complain to him of his role as pedagogue—"What the teacher does is right." Because of the severity of his discipline, and that of the other two teachers, and the fear that it arouses in his pupils, parents use him as a threat in disciplining their children at home.

Whereas the headmaster attracts the least amount of anti-authority sentiment of any other figure who regulates to a marked degree the lives of the folk, the king attracts the most. The latter is the senior of the two publicans, in age and role, whose home in Low Village accommodates guests as well as the shop and pub.

A personable man of great charm, the king has a measure of charisma which commands deference and respect, and it is said that had he chosen to become a priest or businessman on the mainland, he would now be a bishop or captain of industry. His business acumen is acclaimed, and many have become his customers because they believe him to be more "clever" than city merchants and well able to deal with them to the advantage of the islanders. The sources of his power are many. He began his career as a shopkeeper in the 1920s, with money provided him by a brother living in the United States (or, as claimed by some, with the insurance money that he received as a beneficiary when his brother was killed while serving in the armed forces of this country). Two brothers older than himself—the eldest the landholder—live in Inis Beag with large families, and he has their support and that of his many other kin. He gained a large following during the depression years of the 1930s by extending credit to customers for months without charging interest; many folk still show gratitude for this gesture by buying only from him and by acquiescing to many of his wishes, although covertly they may resent being in his debt and under his influence.

In Ireland, the term "gombeen" is used to demean the usurious shopkeeper, but this word is directed against the king only by those who most dislike him, and then to connote what they consider a combination of piety and avarice in his behavior rather than his economic practices. His role as moral guardian, with frequent instruction and reprimand as to manners and misdemeanors to men in the pub and children visiting the shop, is deeply resented by many. He does not care to have women make purchases in the shop, where they can observe men drinking and be observed in turn, ostensibly on moral grounds; he urges that children do the marketing instead, not for the convenience of their mothers, it is said, but because he can overcharge and shortchange them more easily. To dissuade women from shopping, he reads out their lists and talks with them about family affairs in a loud whisper, so that they have no privacy. The men complain not only of his alleged practice of overcharging and shortchanging them late at night when the pub is overcrowded with "light headed" drinkers, but also of his criticizing their actions in public, his frequent closing of the pub before midnight, and his refusal to serve those whom he feels have "taken too much" or those about to attend a party where more drinks will be proffered them.

Among the traits attributed to Inis Beag folk by nativists and primitivists are self-reliance, independence, and individualism. But the self-reliance of the islanders has become undermined increasingly since 1891 by a benevolent government; their independence is severely curtailed by restrictions imposed on them by curate, headmaster, king, and their fellows; and their individualism is a figment of literary imagination disguising a strict conformism. Inis Beag as much as any community is characterized by gossip, ridicule, and opprobrium, which gain their effectiveness as social control mechanisms from the deep concern of the folk with "saving face," and which serve to limit freedom of action and behavioral idiosyncracy. When asked to rank the major deficiencies of island life, the people almost without exception place the prevalence of malicious gossiping, along with poverty and the intrusion of the clergy into secular affairs, at the head of their list.

No matter how much the islanders detest gossiping when they are its victims, they nevertheless welcome every opportunity to engage in it. News of an event passes quickly by word of mouth from Low to Terrace Villages, and variations in the description of the event are usually numerous due to the distortions of rumor. In order to circumvent gossip, parties are organized at the last moment and invitations issued by small boys moving quietly from door to door in the night; persons will leave the island—sometimes to emigrate, visit the hospital with a serious illness, or enter an order—without previous announcement, running from their homes to the strand to board the last canoes for the steamer; and mail is posted just prior to the arrival of the steamer and picked up immediately after it is carried to the post office, for fear that the postmaster will open letters and talk publicly of their contents (or take money from them). It is customary for boys and young men to hide themselves in the darkness or behind fences in order to overhear conversations of passersby, or witness their misbehavior, which can be reported; this compels folk who move about after dark to conceal their faces and talk in whispers or low tones. When a person hidden in the darkness is accosted suddenly, he will vault a fence, run away, or crouch down and hide his face or draw a raincoat over his head and shoulders to avoid being recognized. Most social events and visiting take place after sundown, so that movements from one house to another will be unobserved.

Source:
From *Inis Beag: Isle of Ireland* by John C. Messenger. Copyright © 1969 by Holt, Rinehart and Winston, Inc. Adapted and reprinted by permission of Holt, Rinehart and Winston, Inc.

Summary

1.

Social controls enable a group of people to encourage conformity to group norms and values. Conformity to these norms and values perpetuates the group's culture and maintains its system of social relations. Social control is older than culture itself. Nonetheless, the anthropological study of social control in non-Western societies is a relatively recent development. The misconception that there is a basic difference between social control in "primitive" and "advanced" societies was refuted by Malinowski in the early twentieth century. Malinowski said that the universal basis for social order is the principle of reciprocity: if a man treats his neighbor well, his neighbor will treat him well.

2.

There are two kinds of social controls, internalized and externalized. Internalized controls are imposed by a guilty individual on himself. These built-in controls rely on such deterrents as the fear of God and the threat of magical retaliation. Internalized controls are insufficient. Every society develops externalized controls, called sanctions. Positive sanctions are societal reactions to a member's behavior which show approval; negative sanctions are societal reactions to a member's behavior which show disapproval. Societies stress negative sanctions more heavily than positive sanctions.

3.

Formal sanctions are codified in legal statutes: informal sanctions are not. Organized sanctions reward or punish behavior through a precisely regulated social procedure; diffuse sanctions are the immediate approving or disapproving reactions of individual community members to a fellow member's behavior. Primary sanctions are direct community actions against an individual; secondary sanctions are community-backed sanctions directed by one person or group of persons at another person or group of persons.

4.

Law is an important part of a society's social controls. Some anthropologists have proposed that to define law is impossible. E. Adamson Hoebel said that social norms are legal when they are regularly enforced by "socially recognized" enforcers. Leopold Pospisil said that the law has four basic attributes: the backing of authority; universal applicability; the recognition of rights and duties; determination of the nature and degree of sanctions.

5.

Law serves three basic functions: it defines relationships among the members of a society; it allocates the authority to employ coercion in the enforcement of sanctions; it redefines social relations and insures social flexibility.

6.

Western societies clearly distinguish offenses against the state, called crimes, from offenses against an individual, called torts. Crimes are public offenses; torts are private offenses. Many non-Western societies have no conception of a central state and conceive of all offenses as offenses against individuals. All societies use negotiation to settle individual disputes. Negotiation involves the parties to a dispute themselves reaching an agreement, with or without help. Adjudication, not found in some societies, involves an authorized third party issuing a binding decision.

Suggested readings

Bohannan, Paul, ed. *Law and Warfare: Studies in the Anthropology of Conflict.* New York: Natural History Press, 1967.
Examples of various ways in which conflict is evaluated and handled in different cultures are brought together in this book. It examines institutions and means of conflict resolution including courts, middlemen, self-help, wager of battle, contest, and ordeal. It also has a selection discussing war—raids, organization for aggression, tactics, and feuds.

Hoebel, E. Adamson *The Law of Primitive Man: A Study in Comparative Legal Dynamics.* Cambridge: Harvard University Press, 1954. Atheneum, 1968.
This book combines the study of law and anthropology to develop a setting of ideas and methods for the study of law in primitive society. It then analyzes seven primitive cultures (including Eskimo, Commanche, Trobriand Islanders, and Ashanti) with reference to the underlying legal forms which govern each. It ends with a discussion of the interrelationship between law and society.

Nader, Laura, ed. "The Ethnography of Law" in *American Anthropologist,* 1965, Vol. 67, Part II, No. 6.
This special publication is the result of a conference held in Stanford, California in 1964 on anthropologists and law. The discussion centered on problems and approaches to law in an anthropological context. It includes discussion on aspects of law, including "double institutionalization," law mechanisms, common law, and problems in cross-cultural comparisons of methodology.

Nader, Laura, ed. *Law in Culture and Society.* Chicago: Aldine Press, 1969.
This is a well-balanced and thorough collection of articles on law in different cultures and societies.

Religion
and magic

According to their origin myth, the Tewa Indians of New Mexico emerged from a lake far to the north of where they now live. Once on dry land, they divided into two groups, the Summer People and the Winter People, and migrated south down both sides of the Rio Grande. During their travels, they made twelve stops, before finally being reunited into a single community.

For the Tewa, all existence is divided into six categories, three human and three supernatural. Each of the human categories, which are arranged in a hierarchy, is matched by a spiritual category, so that when a man dies, he immediately passes into his proper spiritual role. Not only are the supernatural categories identified with human categories; they also correspond to divisions the Tewa make in the natural world.

From a Judeo-Christian vantage point, such a religion may seem, at best, irrational and arbitrary. It is neither—as has been shown by Alfonso Ortiz, a native-born Tewa anthropologist. Ortiz argues that his native religion is not only logical and socially functional, it is the very model of Tewa society.[1] The Tewa have one of the few extant "dual organization" societies in the world; it is

[1] Alfonso Ortiz, *The Tewa World* (Chicago: University of Chicago Press, 1969), p. 43.

divided into two independent moieties, each having its own economy, rituals, and authority. The individual is introduced into one of these moieties, which are not based on kinship, and his membership is regularly reinforced through a series of life-cycle rituals that correspond to the stops on the mythical tribal journey down the Rio Grande. The rites of birth and death are shared in by the whole community; other rites differ in the two moieties. The highest status of the human hierarchy belongs to the priests, who also help integrate this divided society; they not only mediate between the human and spiritual world, but also between the two moieties.

Tewa religion enters into virtually every aspect of Tewa life and society. It is the basis of the simultaneously dualistic/unified world view of the individual Tewa. It provides numerous points of mediation through which the two moieties can continue to exist as a single community. It sanctifies the community by providing a supernatural origin, and it offers divine sanction to those "rites of passage" that soften life's major transitions. In providing an afterworld that is the mirror image of human society, it answers the question of death in a manner that reinforces social structure. In short, Tewa religion, far from being arbitrary or illogical, gives a solid foundation to the stability and continuity of Tewa society.

All religions fulfill numerous social and psychological needs. Some of these needs—the need to confront and explain death, for example—appear to be universal; indeed, Malinowski has gone so far as to say that "there are no peoples, however primitive, without religion and magic."[2] Unbound by time, religion gives meaning to individual and group life, drawing power from the time of the gods in the Beginning, and offering continuity of existence beyond death. It can provide the path by which man transcends his arduous earthly existence and attains, if only momentarily, a spiritual selfhood. The social functions of religion are no less important than the psychological functions. A traditional religion reinforces group norms, provides moral sanctions for individual conduct, and furnishes the substratum of common purpose and values upon which the equilibrium of the community depends.

Because religion fulfills important psychological and social functions, it has survived the various onslaughts of anticlericalism, rationalism, science, and technology. Nineteenth century evolutionists believed that science would ultimately destroy religion by showing people the irrationality of their myths and rituals. But an opposite tendency has occurred, and traditional religious institutions continue to attract new members. And there are many new options: the fundamentalist, anti-rationalist cults, such as the so-called "Jesus freaks," who are trying to revive the mystical communion of earliest Christianity; the Eastern religions; astrology and occultism. Science, far from destroying religion, seems to have contributed to the creation of a veritable religious boom. It has done this by removing many traditional psychological props, while at the same time creating, in its technological applications, a host of new problems—pollution, atomic weapons, rapid travel and communications—which people must now deal with. In

[2]Bronislaw Malinowski, *Magic, Science and Religion* (Garden City, N.Y.: Anchor Books, 1954).

496

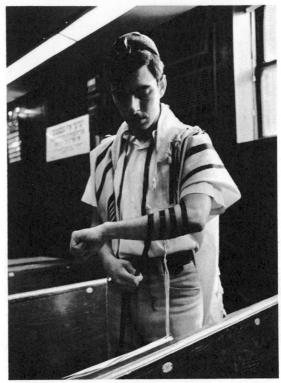

Figure 23-1. *This young Orthodox Jew is preparing to take part in an ancient rite.*

Figure 23-2a. *The Hare Krishna sect has attracted some young American believers.*

Figure 23-2b. *This shack is the church of a new fundamentalist sect in Georgia.*

Figure 23-2c. *An Indian guru speaks to his disciples, many from foreign countries.*

the face of these new anxieties, religion offers social and psychological support.

The persistence of religion in the face of Western rationalism clearly reveals that it is a powerful and dynamic force in society. Although the anthropologist is not qualified to pass judgment on the metaphysical truth of any particular religion, he can attempt to show how each religion embodies a number of "truths" about man and society.

The anthropological approach to religion

Melford E. Spiro defined religion as "an institution consisting of culturally patterned interaction with culturally postulated superhuman beings."[3] In other words, religion is that part of a group's cultural heritage that mediates between the profane world of everyday life and the sacred world of supernatural beings and powers. The interaction between these two worlds lies in a system of values, by which humans try to imitate the supposed values of the supernatural beings, and in a system of ritual consisting of symbolic activities which are designed to break down the barriers between the earthly and supernatural.

Talcott Parsons, a leading contemporary sociologist, has listed five factors which he believes all religions will be found to include. First, every religion encompasses a set of sacred entities which are set apart from ordinary objects and events of everyday life. Second, it has a system of expressive symbols, which are supposed to elicit sacred emotional states, and are typical of religions everywhere. Third, a religion always includes certain definite ritual activities, such as confession in Catholic Christianity, which are obligatory, or at least extremely important. Fourth, there is a feeling of collectivity or social solidarity among the religion's believers. Finally, there is a

[3] Melford E. Spiro, "Religion: Problems of Definition and Explanation" in Michael Bauton, ed., *Anthropological Approaches to the Study of Religion* (London: Tamstoch Publications, 1966), p. 96.

sense of some relationship between the supernatural world and the believer's moral values, goals, and rules of conduct.

These definitions of religion obviously differ from those one would expect from a theologian or a philosopher. The social scientist approaches religion from a particular point of view. The emphasis in anthropological definitions is on culture; religion is viewed not as an isolated institution existing within society, but as an integral part of society which affects and is affected by every other social institution, whether moral, economic, or political. According to Paul Radin:

> Religion is thus not a phenomenon apart and distinct from mundane life nor is it a philosophical inquiry into the nature of being and becoming. It only emphasizes and preserves those values accepted by the majority of a group at a given time. It is this close connection with the whole life of man that we find so characteristically developed among all primitive cultures. . . . Only when other means of emphasizing and maintaining the life-values are in the ascendant, does religion become divorced from the whole corporate life of the community.[4]

The early evolutionists

Nineteenth century anthropologists, struck by the seemingly universal practices of magic that existed without the benefit of intercultural contact, explained their observations through the theoretical perspective of cultural evolutionism. Unfortunately, this perspective was especially inappropriate to the study of religions. For one thing, most theorists approached religion from a distinctly Christian viewpoint, seeing all other religions as "lower" on the evolutionary scale. Neither anthropological research nor popular opinion today supports this assumption. Moreover, evolutionism automatically implied the search for the origins of religion—a search futile from the start—and for stages of development

[4]Paul Radin, *Primitive Religion* (New York: Dover Publications, 1937), pp. 5–6.

498

Figure 23-3. *The worship of holy animals is a feature of many religions. The Ainu keep bears captive in log cages and ritually kill the cubs with many apologies to the Bear Spirit. The Indian temple shown below is sacred to the worship of holy rats.*

leading, of course, to Christian monotheism. Despite these lapses, such "armchair anthropologists" as Sir Edward Tylor, R. R. Marett, and Sir James G. Frazer made some significant contributions to the study of religions.

Animism

In his search for the origin of all religious beliefs, Sir Edward Tylor came upon the concept of **animism.** Essentially, animism (from "anima" or "soul") is a belief in personal spirits which are thought to animate nature. Tylor, writing in 1873, noted many examples of animism. For example, the Dayaks of Borneo believed rice had a soul, and they held feasts to contain the soul securely in order to prevent crop failure. Fijian women, until the turn of the century, were expected to willingly submit to death when their husbands passed away, so they could remain at their husbands' sides in the other world. The Koriaks of Asia, after killing a bear, would flay the animal, dress one of their people in the skin, and dance around chanting that they were not really responsible for killing the bear, and that the Russians killed it.

Primitive men, Tylor suggested, were profoundly impressed by two groups of biological problems:

> In the first place, what is it that makes the difference between a living body and a dead one; what causes waking, sleep, trance, disease, death? In the second place, what are those human shapes which appear in dreams and visions? Looking at these two groups of phenomena, the ancient savage philosophers probably made their first step by the obvious inference that every man has two things belonging to him, namely, a life and a phantom.[5]

Thus is born the idea of soul, or anima. By extension, animals and plants are seen to embody

---

[5] Sir Edward B. Tylor, "Animism" in V. F. Calverton, ed., *The Making of Man: An Outline of Anthropology* (New York: The Modern Library, 1931), p. 635.

souls, for they also live and die. Through further analogy, stones, weapons, food, ornaments, and other objects are imbued with souls. Animism is, then, the minimum definition of religion and the basis upon which "higher" religions are founded.

Tylor's theory was widely accepted in his time, though few anthropologists would accept it today. The theory is essentially intellectualistic; that is, it claims that religion came into being through a process of reasoning, as a means of explaining otherwise unexplainable phenomena. Modern interpretations generally put the case the other way around: people tend to rationalize their beliefs only after they already hold them. Further, Tylor derives all spirits and gods from extensions of human personality, when actually many supernatural beings are not thought to resemble men. Thus it is not animism, but the more general **supernaturalism,** which is the minimum definition of religion. Criticism has also been directed against Tylor's theory of the evolution of modern monotheism in a series of stages from early animism. Such a sequence incorporates most of the evolutionary fallacies of Tylor's time: the idea that technologically primitive cultures are primitive in all other areas; the unawareness of hundreds of examples that may not fit the evolutionary scheme; the lack of fieldwork; and so forth. Yet, despite such valid criticism of Tylor's work, it remains undeniably true that animism is characteristic of hunter-gatherers, and therefore may well have been the first form of man's religion.

Animatism

One of the problems with Tylor's theory was that the concept of animism involves a personal soul, yet there are many cases where supernatural power is considered impersonal. The Melanesians, for example, think of *mana* as a force inherent in all objects. It is not in itself physical, but it can reveal itself physically. A warrior's success in fighting is not attributed to his own strength but to the *mana* contained in an amulet which hangs around his neck. Similarly, a farmer may know a great deal about agriculture, soil conditioning, and the correct time for sowing and reaping, but he nevertheless depends upon *mana* for a successful crop, often building a simple altar to this power at the end of his field. If the crop is good, it is a sign that he has in some way appropriated the *mana*. Far from being a personalized force, *mana* is abstract in the extreme, a power lying always just beyond reach of the senses. As R. H. Codrington described it:

> Virtue, prestige, authority, good fortune, influence, sanctity, luck are all words which, under certain conditions, give something near the meaning. . . . *mana* sometimes means a more than natural virtue or power attaching to some person or thing. . . .[6]

This concept of impersonal power was also widespread among American Indians. The Iroquois called it *orenda;* to the Sioux it was *wakonda;* to the Algonkins, *manitu.* However, though found on every continent, the concept is not necessarily universal.

R. R. Marett called this concept of impersonal power **animatism.** The two concepts, animism and animatism, are not mutually exclusive. They are often found in the same culture, as, for example, in Melanesia, and also in the Indian societies mentioned above.

Magic and religion

Among the most fascinating manifestations of religion is the belief that powers—whether forces, gods, demons, ghosts, spirits or other imagined forces—can be compelled to act in certain ways for good or evil purposes. This is a classical anthropological notion of magic. Many societies have magical rituals to ensure good crops, the replenishment of game and the fertility of domestic animals, the avoidance or cure of illness in humans. Although Western man, in seeking to objectify and demythologize his world, has largely suppressed (but not abolished) the existence of these fantastic notions in his own consciousness, they continue to hold him nevertheless—nowadays in novels about demonic possession or witchcraft that he half-guiltily devours and discusses. Non-Western man, on the other hand, quite freely endows his world with psychic properties; an African jungle dweller, for instance, sees a nocturnal creature by daylight and knows it is a medicine man who has temporarily taken its shape. A tree may have its own soul and voice. Some South American Indians *know* that they are a kind of parrot, though they are aware they lack feathers, wings, and beaks.

Sir James George Frazer made a strong distinction between religion and magic. Religion is "a propitiation or conciliation of powers superior to man which are believed to direct and control the course of nature and human life."[7] Magic, on the other hand, is an attempt to manipulate certain perceived "laws" of nature. The magician never doubts that the same causes will always produce the same effects. Thus Frazer saw magic as a sort of pseudo-science, differing from modern Western science only in its misconception of the nature of the particular laws which govern the succession of events.

Frazer differentiated between two fundamental principles of magic. The first principle, that "like produces like," he called the **law of similarity** or **sympathetic magic.** In Burma, for example, a rejected lover might engage a sorcerer to make an image of his scornful love. If this image was tossed in water, to the accompaniment of certain charms, the hapless girl would go mad. Thus the girl would suffer a fate similar to that of her image.

Frazer's second principle was the **law of contagion**—the concept that things or persons which have once been in contact can afterward influence one another. The most common example of contagious magic is the permanent relationship between an individual and any part of his body,

---

[6] As quoted by Godfrey Leinhardt in "Religion" in Harvey Shapiro, ed., *Man, Culture, and Society* (London: Oxford University Press, 1971), p. 368.

[7] Sir James G. Frazer, "Magic and Religion" in Calverton, *op. cit.,* p. 693.

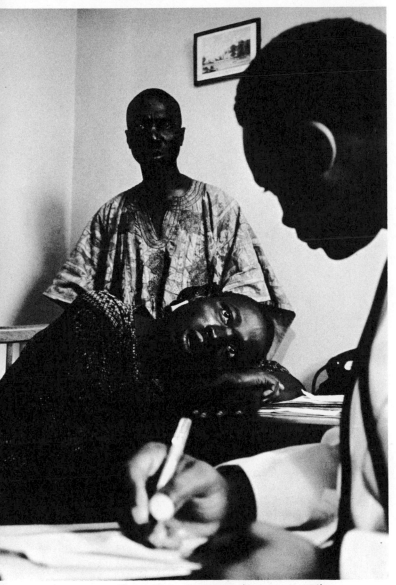

such as his hair, fingernails, or teeth. Frazer cites the Basutos, a tribe in South Africa, who were careful to conceal their extracted teeth, because these might fall into the hands of certain mythical beings who could harm the owner of the tooth by working magic on it.

The functions of religion

If early anthropological theories were dominated by evolutionary perspectives and assumptions, the twentieth century saw an increasing tendency to study religions not in terms of origins or sequential stages, but rather in terms of their psychological and social functions. What psychological, biological, and social needs does religion satisfy? In what ways does religion maintain the fabric of society? What is the relation between religion and other social institutions?

The twentieth century has also seen a growing rejection of vast generalizations and of attempts to reduce all religious phenomena to one "ism" or another, such as animism or animatism. Another significant feature of the more recent research is the emphasis on fieldwork; modern theorists are expected to have extensive first-hand knowledge of one or more non-Western cultures. Equally important, anthropologists tend not to see religion as having originated from attempts to explain the world through individual introspection, as Tylor and Frazer had suggested.

Society as "God"

Even the early anthropologists were led by their research to a realization of the social functions of religion. The study of totemism points up this tendency. Totemism is based on the division of the whole world into those things which are profane, or have no spiritual value for the clan or tribe, and those which are sacred. Not only gods and spirits are sacred; indeed, according to sociologist Émile Durkheim, "a rock, a tree, a spring,

Figure 23-4. *New ways do not necessarily displace the old; the two may coexist. The man at right is a Nigerian trained as a psychiatrist; helping him treat his patient is the local witch doctor, who has considerable skill in dealing with severe emotional upsets. He has been incorporated into the staff of the clinic under the title "native therapist."*

a pebble, a piece of wood, a house, in a word, anything can be sacred."[8] Among the tribes that practice totemism, such as the Australian aborigines, each clan is distinguished by its own totem—a particular animal, plant, or object which the clan is named after and which is considered extremely sacred. The clan's emblem is a pictorial representation of the totem. Plant and animal totems can be eaten only under rigidly prescribed conditions, and totemic objects must be approached only with the proper religious ritual. Each clan identifies with one totem, but this is merely the center of an ever-widening circle of specified sacred things. Blackwood trees, dogs, fire, and frost are assigned to the Pelican clan. The stars and the moon are classed as in the realm of the Black Cockatoo clan. In this way all of nature is classified and organized into one Great Tribe.

Durkheim, who believed totemism to be the basis from which all religions have developed, attempted to create a general theory of religion through a detailed analysis of the religion of the Australian Arunta. Like Tylor and Frazer, he was interested in the origins and evolution of religion, but unlike his precursors he did not find the answer in the individual. According to Durkheim, the individual is totally dependent on his society. Society holds such an awesome power over the individual's whole being that it is literally sacred to him. However, the clan itself is too complex and too abstract to be the recipient of this tremendous respect and awe, so these feelings are projected onto the totem, which stands for society. In turn, the organization and classification of nature is made to mirror the organization of the clan and tribe. In short, man deifies his own society, which becomes virtually God. Religion, then, is a vast symbolic system encompassing every aspect of society, and at the same time stabilizing and maintaining the continuity of society by constantly reinforcing its traditions and values.

Claude Lévi-Strauss has argued that totemism is not a valid concept, since it incorporates under

a single term a great number of phenomena that are not really alike. Another criticism of Durkheim's thesis is that many of the most profoundly religious experiences, whether among Arunta tribesmen or Western Christians, arise out of solitude. Although society may be the source of many religious beliefs and rituals, most theorists would agree that at least some religious phenomena directly arise from individual needs and emotions. Yet the Durkheim theory that saw society rather than the individual as central to explaining religious phenomena has held an integral place in anthropology.

Social function of religious customs

Looking at religious practices in terms of their functions for society enables us to make sense of seemingly bizarre customs. For example, one of the more gruesome (from our point of view) parts of the funerary rites of the Melanesians was the eating of the flesh of the dead person. This ritual cannibalism, witnessed by anthropologist Bronislaw Malinowski, was performed with "extreme repugnance and dread and usually followed by a violent vomiting fit. At the same time it is felt to be a supreme act of reverence, love and devotion."[9] This custom, and the emotions accompanying it, clearly reveal the ambiguous attitude of many people towards death: on the one hand, one longs to hold onto the dead person, and on the other hand, one feels disgust and fear at the transformation wrought by death. According to Malinowski, funeral ceremonies provide an approved collective means of expressing these individual feelings, while at the same time maintaining social cohesiveness and preventing disruption of society. Thus Malinowski attempted to reveal both the psychological and social functions of religious behavior.

Malinowski held that nontechnological people do not live in some prelogical dream world; rather they are extremely pragmatic and have a firm grasp of the workings of nature and of the practi-

[8] Émile Durkheim, *The Elementary Forms of the Religious Life* (New York: The Free Press, 1965), p. 52.

[9] Malinowski, *op, cit.,* p. 50.

cal aspects of survival. Religion and magic arise out of a need to reach beyond this practical knowledge in order to make the world acceptable and manageable. Religion and magic, then, can be viewed as the very foundations of culture and the basic integrative forces of society. Though Malinowski rejected Durkheim's theories almost totally, he shared with that great French sociologist the view that religion must be studied in terms of its functions.

A. R. Radcliffe-Brown went even farther than Durkheim in rejecting individual psychological interpretations of religion. He saw social phenomena as systems of adaptation, and society itself as a dynamic network of functionally interdependent elements. The function of religion is to celebrate and maintain the norms on which society depends. However, the need for social solidarity is not sufficient explanation for all religious phenomena. Deeper analysis, he believed, could show that objects selected for veneration are utilitarian; they either have practical social value or they have ritual value, the ability to fuse the natural and social orders. Thus, within any social system, those elements critical to social functioning will be made sacred.

Psychology and religion

Psychologists have generally followed Tylor and Frazer in tracing the source of religion to the needs and propensities of the individual. William James, for example, saw religion as developing, at least partly, from an intuitive individual awareness of a "More" just beyond consciousness. He claims "that our normal waking consciousness, rational consciousness as we call it, is but one special type of consciousness, whilst all about it, parted from it by the filmiest of screens, there lie potential forms of consciousness entirely different."[10] Although this postulates nothing about the objective truth of religion, it does suggest a subjective truth, namely the mystical experience.

[10]William James, *The Varieties of Religious Experience* (New York: Collier Books, 1961), p. 305.

Some later psychologists saw religion as the projection of the individual unconscious into the outer world. Chief among these were Sigmund Freud and Carl Jung. Although their theories of religion are accepted by very few anthropologists—and probably by only a minority of psychologists—they have had a subtle and far-reaching influence on the ways we view religion.

Religion as neurosis. As we saw in Chapter 15, Sigmund Freud believed that all culture originated in a sort of universal Oedipus complex. The primal father was killed by his sons, who ate him, because he was monopolizing their sisters and daughters. Expanding on this basic theory, Freud claims that sacrifice and feast were ritually practiced in order to assuage the sense of guilt over the murder of the father. God is simply the father projected into the heavens. According to Freud:

> The ordinary man cannot imagine this Providence in any other form but that of a greatly exalted father, for only such a one could understand the needs of the sons of men, or be softened by their prayers and placated by the signs of their remorse. The whole thing is so patently infantile, so incongruous with reality, that to one whose attitude to humanity is friendly, it is painful to think that the great majority of mortals will never be able to rise above this view of life.[11]

Classical psychoanalytic theory, then, sees religion as a system of defense mechanisms to relieve man of his burden of anxiety and guilt. Though Freud's evolutionary hypotheses are replete with logical and factual fallacies, many anthropologists have been influenced by his emphasis on anxiety-reduction as a primary function of religion and ritual. In many instances, religion seems to relieve the anxiety of the unknown by explaining it, or making it known.

Religion as therapy. Joseph Campbell notes that dawn and awakening from the world of

[11]Sigmund Freud, *Civilization and its Discontents* (Garden City, N.Y.: Anchor Books), p. 13.

dreams must always have been associated with the sun and sunrise. The night fears and charms are dispelled by light, which has always been experienced as coming from above and furnishing guidance and orientation. Darkness, weight, the pull of gravity, the dark interior of the earth, the jungle, the deep sea, must for untold ages have constituted a distinct and poignant area of human experience in contrast to the world of day. Thus a polarity of light and dark, above and below, guidance and the loss of bearings, confidence and fear may have arisen as a basic principle of human thought.

Part of the function of religion has been to dispel the fears of darkness. "In the morning, when the sun comes, we go out of the huts, spit into our hands, and hold them up to the sun." So was Carl Jung told of a simple ritual, performed almost unconsciously, by a native of Africa. However, though morning and day were celebrated, "From sunset on, it was a different world—the dark world of *ayik,* of evil, danger, fear." Jung, too, was impressed by the splendor of the African sunrise, and the brooding darkness of the African night. "It is the psychic primal night which is the same today as it has been for countless million years," he speculated. "The longing for light is the longing for consciousness."[12]

This interpretation of an African view of day and night epitomizes Jung's approach to religion. He believed that religion expresses the deepest truths of man's nature, that it draws these truths out of the dark night of man's unconscious and into the daylight of consciousness. For Jung, Freud's "subconscious" was merely the "personal unconscious," a concept of limited application. Beyond this lay the "collective unconscious"—a vast reservoir of inherited thought patterns called archetypes. These archetypes—abstract patterns which are universal to all mankind—are concretely projected into the outer world as symbols, such as the symbols of myth and religion.

For Jung, religion is not merely anxiety-reducing, but positively therapeutic. Religious

[12]Carl Jung, *Memories, Dreams, Reflections* (New York: Vintage Books, 1961), p. 266.

504

behavior is instrumental in helping the individual toward greater integration and maturity. Religion is not, as Freud would have it, infantile; rather it is a means by which the person can transcend his infantile fixations. Thus Jung and his school of analytic psychology emphasize positively transformative rituals and myths, such as those involving rebirth into a new selfhood and the magical journey of the hero.

The practice of religion

Much of the psychological and social value of religion comes from the activities called for by its practice. Participation in religious ceremonies may bring a sense of personal transcendence, a wave of reassurance and security, or a feeling of closeness to fellow participants. Although the rituals and practices of religions vary considerably, even those rites that seem to us most bizarrely exotic can be shown to serve the same basic social and psychological functions.

Rituals and ceremonies

Religious ritual is the means through which persons relate to the sacred; it is religion made overt. Not only is ritual the means by which the social bonds of a group are reinforced and tensions relieved, it is also one way that many important events are celebrated and crises, such as death, are made less socially disruptive and less difficult for the individuals to bear. Anthropologists have classified several different types of ritual, among them **rites of passage,** which pertain to crises in the life of the individual, and **rites of intensification,** which take place during a crisis in the life of the group, serving to bind individuals together.

Rites of passage. In one of anthropology's classic works, Arnold Van Gennep analyzed the rites of passage which usher individuals through the

Figure 23-5. *Another example of the ability of religion to integrate both old and new customs can be seen in the festival held in Chichicastenango, Guatemala. Ceremonies combine the worship of Christian saints and Mayan gods, in a carnival atmosphere of quite boisterous drinking.*

505

crucial crises of their lives; such as birth, puberty, marriage, parenthood, advancement to a higher class, occupational specialization, and death. He found that ceremonies for all of these life-crises could be subdivided into three stages: rites of **separation;** rites of **transition;** and rites of **incorporation.** The individual would first be ritually removed from the society as a whole, then he would be isolated for a period, and finally he would be incorporated back into the tribe in his new status.

Van Gennep described the initiation rites of Australian aborigines. When the time for the initiation is decided by the elders, the boys are taken from the village, while the women cry and make a ritual show of resistance. At a place distant from the camp, groups of men from many villages gather. The elders sing and dance while the initiates act as though they are dead. The climax of this part of the ritual is a bodily operation, such as circumcision or the knocking out of a tooth. Anthropologist A. P. Elkin says, "This is partly a continuation of the drama of death. The tooth-knocking, circumcision or other symbolical act 'killed' the novice; after this he does not return to the general camp and normally may not be seen by any woman. He is dead to the ordinary life of the tribe."[13] The novice may be shown secret ceremonies and receive some instruction during this period, but the most significant element is his complete removal from society. In the course of these Australian puberty rites, the initiate must learn the tribal lore; he is given, in effect, a "cram course." The trauma of the occasion is a pedagogical technique which ensures that he will learn and remember everything; in a nonliterate society, effective teaching methods of this sort are necessary for both individual and group survival.

On his return to society, the novice is welcomed with ceremonies as though he had returned from the dead. This alerts the society at large that the individual has a new status—that they can expect him to act in certain ways and

[13] A. P. Elkin, *The Australian Aborigines* (Garden City, N.Y.: Anchor Books, 1964).

Figure 23-6. *In Chichicastenango, a witch doctor pours an offering of firewater over an idol representing an ancient Mayan god. In the other photo, the king of Akure presides over a similar rite, in which a chicken is sacrificed to the tribal gods. The men performing the rites are tribal chiefs rather than specialized religious leaders.*

in return must act in the appropriate ways toward him. The individual's new rights and duties are thus clearly defined. He is spared, for example the problems of "American Teenage," a time when an individual is neither adult nor child but a person whose status is ill defined.

Sacrifice. Many societies engage in ritual sacrifice during rites of passage and intensification. Among the Nuer of Africa, when a boy is initiated his father gives him an ox. Through this ox, which represents oxen in general, the boy enters upon a new kind of relationship with god and with the ghosts of his ancestors. In effect, he identifies himself with his ox, which mediates between him and the supernatural world. When, as an adult, he sacrifices the ox, or a substitute animal, he is symbolically killing himself.

This custom is not so strange once we understand the nature of blood sacrifice. Sacrifice is a means of passing into the religious domain. Consecrated in death, the spirit of the sacrificial victim is released into the spiritual realm, and so far as the sacrificer himself is identified with the victim, he partakes of the sacred. Further, by eating the victim of the sacrifice, the participants in the ritual assimilate its sacred power.

One major reason for sacrifice is to avoid injury from supernatural forces by giving up something of value. For example, ritual "first-fruit" ceremonies, common among many agricultural peoples, are designed to protect the crops from the deity by appeasing him with the first vegetables or grains of harvest.

Rites of reversal. Another common kind of religious ritual is the rite of reversal, which involves an inversion of social rules or norms; it may take place during either rites of passage or of intensification. Among the Iatmul, a patrilineal society of New Guinea, the special relation between a man and his sister's son is expressed through a ritual called *naven*. The central feature of *naven*, which is performed to celebrate many of the important events in a boy's life, is the dressing of men in women's clothes and of women in men's clothes. As described by Gregory Bateson, the maternal uncles of the boy put on "the most filthy old tousled skirts such as only the ugliest and most decrepit widows might wear" and hobble about the village. Much to the amusement and teasing of the village children, these grotesque "mothers" search for their "child," namely, their nephew, who hides in shame, knowing that if he is found he will be further humiliated by them. In those *navens* in which women participate, they dress not in rags as the men do, but in the smartest male attire.[14]

Another rite involving sexual inversion is the widespread practice of the *couvade;* following the birth of a baby, the husband takes on the symptoms of postnatal illness and disability of the mother, while she goes about her daily affairs as usual. During the installation rites of a chief among the Ndembu of Africa, a different type of role reversal is manifest; the chief must sit in silent humility while he is reviled in the most blunt and vulgar terms by anyone who feels so inclined.

Such practices are not always "religious," but like some religious rituals, they function to stabilize society by releasing tensions generated by oppositions between sexes, roles, and classes.

Religious practitioners

In societies large and complex enough to support occupational specialists, the role of administering the mythologies, ceremonies, and ethical systems that hold a society together belongs to the **priest.** He is the socially initiated, ceremonially inducted member of a recognized religious organization with a rank and function that belongs to him as the tenant of an office held by others before him. His source of power is the society and the institution in which he functions.

Even in societies that lack occupational specialization, there have always been individuals who have acquired religious power individually, usu-

[14] Gregory Bateson, *Naven* (Stanford: Stanford University Press, 1958).

ally in solitude and isolation, when the Great
Spirit, the Power, the Great Mystery is revealed
to them. Such a man becomes the recipient of
certain special gifts, such as healing or divination;
when he returns to society he is frequently given
another kind of religious role, that of the **shaman.**
Joseph Campbell describes the shaman as "master
of his own initiation, the only valid expression of
the initiation archetype for the entire tribal group
to which he belongs."

Typicallly, one becomes a shaman by passing
through stages common to many religious myths,
often thought to involve torture and violent
dismemberment of the body; scraping away of
the flesh until the body is reduced to a skeleton;
substitution of the viscera and renewal of the
blood; a period spent in a nether region, such as
Hell, during which the shaman is taught by the
souls of the dead shamans and demons; and an
ascent to heaven. Among the Crow Indians, for
example, any man could become a shaman, since
there was no ecclesiastical organization that
handed down laws for the guidance of the religious consciousness. The search for shamanistic
visions was pursued by most adult Crow males,
who would engage in bodily deprivation, even
self-torture. The majority of the seekers would
not be granted a vision, but such failure carried
no social stigma. While those who claimed supernatural vision would be expected to manifest
some special power in battle or wealth, it was the
sincerity of the seeker that carried the essential
truth of the experience. Many of the elements of
shamanism such as transvestitism, trance-states,
and speaking in undecipherable languages can
just as easily be regarded as abnormalities, and
it has been frequently pointed out that those
regarded as specially gifted in some societies
would be outcasts or worse in others. The position of shaman provides a socially approved role
for otherwise unstable personalities.

The shaman is essentially a religious entre-
preneur. He acts for some human client, on
whose behalf he intervenes to influence or impose his will on supernatural powers. He can be
contrasted with the priest, whose "clients" are the

Figure 23-7a. *This sequence of photos
shows some events in the life of Buddhist
monks.*

Figure 23-7b. *Novices all eat together; their
food is donated by local worshippers.*

Figure 23-7c. *The monastery is one of the few sources of education for young boys.*

Figure 23-7d. *The higher status of the abbot is indicated by the decoration of his fan.*

Figure 23-7e. *A novice has his head shaved; all monks are shaved twice a month.*

Figure 23-7f. *A novice becomes a monk; his new name is written on the fan beside him.*

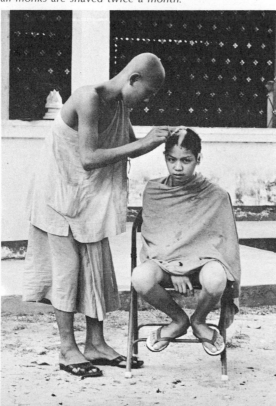

deities. The priest tells people what to do; the shaman tells supernaturals what to do. In return for his services, the shaman sometimes collects a fee—fresh meat, yams, a favorite possession. In some cases, the added prestige, authority, and social power attached to the status of shaman are reward enough.

Witchcraft

If blight seizes the groundnut crop it is witchcraft; if the bush is vainly scoured for game it is witchcraft; if termites do not rise when their swarming is due and a cold useless night is spent in waiting for their flight it is witchcraft; if a prince is cold and distant with his subjects it is witchcraft; if a magical rite fails to achieve its purpose it is witchcraft; if, in fact, any failure or misfortune falls upon anyone at any time and in relation to any of the manifold activities of his life it may be due to witchcraft.[15]

In this passage, E. E. Evans-Pritchard reveals the extent that witchcraft enters into the everyday life of the Azande, an African tribe. Although the Azande are not entirely typical in regard to witchcraft, since they believe that witches are simply ordinary persons who are born with a "substance" for witchcraft in their bodies, this list is an illustration of the widespread tendency on the part of some groups to explain many of the ordinary as well as extraordinary occurrences of life by reference to witchcraft.

The Azande and neighboring tribes distinguish between witchcraft or an inborn and often unconscious capacity to work evil, and sorcery, deliberate actions undertaken for the purpose of doing specific harm. Some anthropologists have attempted to generalize this distinction, but in many societies there is no division between the two types of evildoer. Perhaps a more practical classification is Lucy Mair's distinction between nightmare witches and everyday witches. The

[15]E. E. Evans-Pritchard, *Witchcraft, Oracles, and Magic Among the Azande* (London: Oxford University Press, 1950), pp. 63–66.

nightmare witch is the very embodiment of a society's conception of evil, a being that flouts the rules of sexual behavior and disregards every other standard of decency. Nightmare witches, being almost literally the product of dreams and repressed fantasies, have much in common wherever they appear: both the modern Navajo and the ancient Roman, for example, conceive of witches that can turn themselves into animals and gather to feast on corpses. Everyday witches are real people, often the social deviants of a group, those who are morose, who eat alone, who are arrogant and unfriendly. Such witches may be dangerous when offended and retaliate by causing sickness, death, crop failure, cattle disease, or any number of lesser ills; people thought to be witches are usually treated very courteously.

The functions of witchcraft

Why witchcraft? We might better ask, why not? As Mair aptly observed, in a world where there are few proven techniques for dealing with everyday crises, especially sickness, a belief in witches is not foolish, it is indispensable. No one wants to resign himself to illness, and if the malady is caused by a witch's hex, then magical countermeasures should cure it. Not only does the idea of personalized evil answer the problem of unmerited suffering, it also provides an explanation for many of those happenings for which no cause can be discovered. Witchcraft, then, cannot be refuted. Even if we could convince a person that his illness was due to natural causes, the victim would still ask, Why me? Why now? There is no room for pure chance in such a view; everything must be assigned a cause or meaning. Witchcraft provides the explanation, and in so doing, also provides both the basis and the means for taking counteraction. Moreover, the fact that certain kinds of antisocial behavior will result in an individual's being labelled a witch, and treated as such tends to deter people from such behavior. A belief in witchcraft thus serves a function of social control.

Figure 23-8. *In preparation for tribal religious rites, a Navajo man makes an elaborate sand painting of a god.*

Figure 23-9. *A witch doctor of the !Kung Bushmen chants a rite over his patient, whose leg was caught in a steel trap.*

Psychological functions of witchcraft among the Navajo. Though widely known as one of the more peaceable of American Indian tribes, the Navajo possess a detailed concept of witchcraft. Several types of witchcraft are distinguished. **Witchery** encompasses the practices of witches, who are said to meet at night to practice cannibalism and kill people at a distance. **Sorcery** is distinguished from witchery only by the methods used by the sorcerer, who casts spells on individuals, using the victim's fingernails, hair, or discarded clothing. **Wizardry** is not distinguished so much by its effects as by its manner of working; wizards kill by injecting a cursed substance, such as a tooth from a corpse, into the victim's body.

Whether or not a particular illness results from witchcraft is determined by divination, as is the identity of the witch. Once a person is charged with witchcraft, he is publically interrogated and possibly tortured until he confesses. It is believed that the witch's own curse will turn against him once he confesses, so it is expected that he will die within a year. Some confessed witches have been allowed to live in exile.

According to Clyde Kluckhohn, Navajo witchcraft served to channel anxieties, tensions, and frustrations that were caused by the pressures from the white man. The rigid rules of decorum among the Navajo allow little means of expression of hostility, which is released in witchcraft accusations. Such accusations funnel pent-up negative emotions against individuals, without upsetting the wider society. Another function of accusations of witchcraft is that they permit the direct expression of hostile feelings against people to whom one would ordinarily be unable to express anger or enmity.

Social functions of witchcraft among the Ndembu. Victor Turner described the use of sorcery in a struggle for political power in a small village of the Ndembu of Africa. Sandombu, a young man who had ambitions to the headmanship of Mukanza village, twice insulted the village headman, Kahali, in a challenge to his authority. This resulted in a fierce dispute, with each threatening the other with sorcery. Sandombu left for another village where a notorious sorcerer was supposed to live. A short time later, Kahali fell sick and died. There was no way to prove Sandombu's use of sorcery, but there was sufficient suspicion to prevent him from replacing Kahali as village headman. Instead, another man, not directly involved in the dispute, was chosen.

Turner shows that there is much more here than immediately meets the eye. Sandombu's insult to Kahali was a breach of the fundamental Ndembu principle that the older generation has authority over the younger. Further, Sandombu was of the same lineage as Kahali, and succession within the same lineage was looked upon with disfavor. Also, since Sandombu was sterile, and his sister barren, he had little basis for essential kin support. Though suspicion of sorcery was the ostensible cause of denying Sandombu headmanship, many other reasons lay beneath the surface.

This "social drama," as Turner calls it, shows how an accusation of sorcery was used to justify a political process and to effectively reaffirm such norms as the relationship between generations and the method of succession to authority. Belief in witchcraft, then, not only serves a number of psychological functions, it can also serve important social functions.

Religion and social change

In 1931, at Buka in the Solomon Islands, a native religious cult suddenly emerged, its prophets predicting that a deluge would soon engulf all whites. This would be followed by the arrival of a ship laden with European goods. The believers were to construct a storehouse for the goods, and to prepare themselves to repulse the colonial police. Because the ship would arrive only after the natives had used up all their own supplies, they ceased working in the fields. Although the leaders of the cult were arrested, the movement continued for some years.

This was not an isolated instance. Such "cargo

Figure 23-10. *Young New Guinea men parade with mock rifles made of bamboo in one of the rites of a cargo cult; note the letters USA on each man's chest. Many of the believers are also Christians, converted by missionaries; the people there see nothing contradictory in the two faiths.*

Social integration ● part **6**

cults"—and many other movements which have promised the resurrection of the dead, the destruction or enslavement of Europeans, and the coming of utopian riches—have sporadically appeared ever since the beginning of the century throughout Melanesia. Since these cults are widely separated in space and time, their similarities may well be due to similarities in social conditions. In these areas, the traditional cultures of the natives have been uprooted. Europeans, or European influenced natives, hold all political and economic power. Natives are employed in unloading and distributing Western-made goods, but have no practical knowledge of how to attain these goods. When cold reality offers no hope from the daily frustrations of cultural deterioration and economic deprivation, religion offers the solution.

Revitalization movements

From the 1890 Ghost Dance of the American Indians to the Mau Mau of Africa to the cargo cults of Melanesia, extreme and sometimes violent religious reactions to European domination are so common that many anthropologists have sought to formulate their underlying causes and general characteristics. It has been suggested that all such religious innovations may be considered revitalization movements.

A revitalization movement is a deliberate effort by members of a society to construct a more satisfying culture. The emphasis in this definition is on the reformation not just of one sphere of activity such as the religious, but of the entire cultural system. Such a drastic solution arises when a group's anxiety and frustration have reached such a degree that the only way to reduce the stress is to overturn the entire social system and replace it with a new one.

Anthropologist Anthony Wallace has suggested that there is a sequence common to all expressions of the revitalization process. First is the normal state of society, in which stress is not too great and in which there are sufficient cultural

means of satisfying needs. Under certain conditions, such as domination by a more powerful group, stress and frustration will be steadily amplified; this brings the second phase, or the period of increased individual stress. If there are no significant adaptive changes, the period of cultural distortion is ushered in, and stress becomes so chronic that the socially approved methods of releasing tension begin to break down. Steady deterioration of one culture may be checked at some point by a period of revitalization, during which a dynamic cult or religious movement grips a sizeable proportion of the population. Often the movement will be so out of touch with reality that it is doomed to failure from the beginning; this was the case with the Ghost Dance, which was supposed to make the participants impervious to the bullets of the white men's guns. More rarely, a movement may tap long dormant adaptive forces underlying a culture, and a longlasting religion may result. Wallace holds that all religions stem from revitalization movements.

Redemptive movements

Redemptive movements try to transform the individual, rather than the social order but in so doing, the social order may sometimes be changed. The Sun Dance of the Ute and Shoshone Indians of the Rocky Mountains is a true redemptive movement. In the early reservation period, around 1890, when misery and oppression were at their worst, the Sun Dance was introduced from the Great Plains tribes. The dance consists of a three-day, three-night ritual aimed at the acquisition of power. For the full period of the ritual, the dancers are forbidden food and water, and thus subject themselves to a long agony of hunger, thirst, and fatigue. With only brief rest periods during the long days, they charge and retreat from a pole in the center of a corral, concentrating intently on the power they are pursuing for their own health, for the health of their kin and of the whole community. Spectators, aware that the dancers are dancing for them, too, bring bundles of green plants to comfort and cool the dancers.

The Sun Dance flourished briefly after its introduction, then diminished, as the younger Indians drifted away from traditional ways of life and attempted more and more to identify with the white world. Then, in the 1960s, the Sun Dance sprang to vigorous life, to become again the religious center of Ute and Shoshone culture.

Why this resurgence of a tradition that one might reasonably have predicted would die out in the confrontation with modern technological culture? Joseph Jorgensen believes the Sun Dance of the Utes and Shoshones is a reaction to insoluble contradictions. The Indian is told that he must act like a white in order to be acceptable to whites, who hold economic and political power. But even when he does succeed in adopting white ways, he is still not acceptable. Since part of acting like a white means breaking tribal and kinship bonds and rejecting the values of Indian culture, he finds himself acceptable neither to whites nor to Indians. The Sun Dance offers a way out of this predicament. In reaffirming the Indian social ethic—as opposed to the individualistic and impersonal ethic of white culture—he regains his self-identity and esteem, a sense of belongingness, and brings an end to the impotence of trying to resolve a myriad of unresolvable contradictions. The Sun Dance provides both the subjective power and personal transformation of the religious experience, and the objective power of being a functional member of society.

Original study

THE SHAMAN

The stronghold of the shaman is among the reindeer herders and fishers of northeast Asia: the Yakuts and the Tungus, two widespread groups of tribes, and others living around the eastern shore of the Bering Sea: the Chuckchis, the Koryaks, the Gilyaks, and the Kamchadals of Kamchatka. Some of these live nomadically in felt tents and others in wooden villages, and in the long arctic nights of their bleak environment the comfort and entertainment that the shaman gives them is very well received. Typically it is believed that there are three realms of nature: an upper one, of light and of good spirits; a middle one, which is the world of men and of the spirits of the earth; and a lower one, for darkness and evil spirits. Men of the usual sort can move about the middle realm, and have some dealings with its spirits, but only a shaman can go above or below. A shaman also has the power of summoning spirits to come to him. Thus he can speak directly to spirits and ask what they want, which is his form of divining. Not only this, but a shaman deals with sickness in various ways through these same powers. If you have a disease spirit inside you, he can detect it and he knows how to send it off, perhaps by having a personal contest with it. Or you may have lost your soul—this explanation of illness turns up almost everywhere in the world—and the shaman gets it back. It has probably been enticed against its will by a stronger demon, and taken to the lower regions, and only the shaman can go after it, see, identify, and return it.

Both in Asia and America shamans, like witches, are generally believed to have familiar spirits, or animal souls, which are the things that gives them their peculiar qualities and powers. A Yakut shaman has two or three. One, called emekhet, is the shaman's own guardian angel, which is not only a sort of impersonal power like mana but also a definite spirit, usually that of a shaman already dead. This spirit hovers around its protégé, guiding and protecting him all the time, and comes at once when he calls for it, and gives him the advice he needs. Another spirit, the yekyua, has more character but is less accommodating. This one is an external soul, which belongs both to the shaman and to a living wild animal, which may be a stallion, a wolf, a dog, an eagle, a hairy bull, or some mythical creature, like a dragon. The yekyua is unruly and malevolent; it is dangerous and enables the shaman to do harm, rather like a witch, so that the people are in awe of him, but at the same time it has no consideration for the shaman himself and gives him continual trouble and anxiety, because his own fortunes are bound up with it. It is independent and lives far away, rather than upon the immediate tribal scene.

"Once a year, when the snow melts and the earth is black, the yekyua arise from their hiding places and begin to wander." When two of them meet, and fight, the human shamans to whom they are linked undergo the evil effects and feel badly. If such an animal dies or is killed, its shaman dies as well, so that a shaman whose yekyua is a bear or a bull can congratulate himself that his life expectancy is good. Of this phantasmal zoo the least desirable soul partners to have are carnivorous animals, especially dogs, because the shaman must keep them appeased, and if they go hungry they are not above taking advantage of their connection with the poor shaman to gnaw at his vitals to stay their appetites. When a person takes to shamanizing, the other shamans round about can tell whether a new yekyua has made its appearance far away, which will cause them to recognize the new shaman.

Siberian shamans all dress the part, as do so many shamans and medicine men of North America. The northeastern Asiatics wear clothing which is made of skin and tailored. A shaman has a cap and a mask, but it is his coat which distinguishes him like a collar turned around. It is a tunic made of hide—goat, elk, etc.—and usually comes down to his knees in front and to the ground behind, and is decorated to the point of being a textbook of shamanistic lore. On the front may be sewed metal plates which protect him from the blows of hostile spirits which he is always encountering. One of these plates represents his emekhet, and usually two others suggest a feminine appearance, since shamans have a hermaphroditic character, as we shall see. All over the tunic are embroidered or appliqued the figures of real and mythical animals, to represent those he must face on his travels in spirit realms, and from the back there hang numerous strips of skin falling clear to the ground, with small stuffed animals attached to some of them, all this alleged to be for attracting to the shaman any spiritual waifs of the vicinity, who might like to join his retinue. The whole getup would remind you of the unusual headdresses and paraphernalia in which medicine men are turned out among Indians of the Plains.

When a shaman goes into action the result is not a rite but a séance, which is full of drama and which the people enjoy immensely. A typical performance is a summoning of spirits, and is carried on in the dark (for the same reasons as among ourselves—i.e., to hide the shenanigans), in a house, a tent, or an Eskimo igloo. The people all gather, and the shaman says what he is going to do, after which he puts out the lamps and the fire, being sure that there is little or no light. Then he begins to sing. There may be a wait, and he beats his tambourine drum first of all, an immediate dramatic effect. The song starts softly. The sense of the song is of no consequence as far as the listeners are concerned; it is often incomprehensible, and may have no words at all. Jochelson knew a Tungus shaman who sang his songs in Koryak. He explained that his spirits were Koryak and said that he could not understand Koryak.

As the singing goes on, other sounds begin to make themselves heard, supposedly made by animal spirits and said to be remarkably good imitations. The shaman may announce to the audience that the spirits are approaching, but he is apt to be too absorbed or entranced himself to bother. Soon voices of all kinds are heard in the house, in the corners and up near the roof. The house now seems to have a number of independent spirits in it, all moving around, speaking in different voices, and all the time the drum is sounding, changing its tempo and its volume; the people are excited, and some of them who are old hands help the shaman out by making responses and shouting encouragement, and the shaman himself is usually possessed by a spirit or spirits, who are singing and beating the drum for him. The confusion of noises goes on increasing in intensity, with animal sounds and foreign tongues as well as understandable communications (among the Chuckchis, the wolf, the fox, and the raven can speak human language), until it finally dies down; the spirits give some message of farewell, the drumming ceases, and the lights are lit.

This is all a combination of expert showmanship and management and of autohypnosis, so that while the shaman knows perfectly well he is faking much of the performance he may at the same time work himself into a trance in which he does things he believes are beyond his merely human powers. He warns his audience strictly to keep their places and not try to touch the spirits, who would be angered and assault the offender, and perhaps even kill the shaman. When the show starts, the shaman produces his voices by moving around in the dark and by expert ventriloquism, getting the audience on his side and rapidly changing the nature and the force of the spirit sounds he is making.

A shaman need not perform only in the dark. He carries out some of his business in full view, especially when it is a matter of his going to the spirit world himself, rather than summoning the spirits to this world. The idea seems to be that he is in two places at once; i.e., his soul is traveling in spiritdom while he himself is going through the same actions before his watchers. He does a furious dramatic dance, rushing about, advancing and retreating, approaching the spirits, fighting them or wheedling them, all in a seeming trance. He may foam at the mouth and be so wild that he must be held for safety in leather thongs by some of the onlookers. After vivid adventures in the other realms, portrayed in his dance, he will accomplish his purpose, which may be to capture a wandering soul or to get some needed information from his spectral hosts. Then he becomes his normal self again.

After a death it is a regular thing for a Mongolian shaman to be called in to "purify" the yurt (felt hut) of the decreased's family, by getting rid of the soul of the dead, which of course cannot be allowed to hang around indefinitely. The mourners assemble late in the day, and at dusk the shaman himself comes, already drumming in the distance. He enters the yurt, still drumming, lowering the sound until it is only a murmur. Then he begins to converse with the soul of the newly departed, which pitifully implores to be allowed to stay in the yurt, because it cannot bear to leave the children or the scenes of its mortal days. The shaman, faithful to his trust, steels himself and pays no attention to this heartrending appeal. He goes for the soul and corners it by means of the power in his drum, until he can catch it between the drum itself and the drum stick. Then he starts off with it to the underworld, all in play acting. Here at the entrance he meets the soul of other dead members of the same family, to whom he announces the arrival of the new soul. They answer that they do not want it and refuse it admission. To multiply the difficulties, the homesick soul, which is slippery, generally makes its escape from the shaman as the two of them are on the way down, and comes rushing back to the yurt, with the shaman after it; he catches it all over again. It is lucky the people have a shaman! Back at the gate of the lower world he makes himself affable to the older souls and gives them vodka to drink, and in one way or another he manages to smuggle the new one in.

Source:
Excerpts from *The Heathens* by William Howells.
Copyright 1948 by William Howells.
Reprinted by permission of Doubleday and Company, Inc.

Summary

1.

Religion mediates between the profane, everyday world and the sacred world of supernatural powers and beings by means of values held in common by the group, and is made overt by ritual practices. Parsons postulates five components of every religion: sacred entities, expressive symbols, ritual activities, a sense of social solidarity in the group, and a relationship between the supernatural and the values, goals, and mores of the group.

2.

Early anthropologists sought an explanation for the origins of religion. Tylor explained the religious concepts of non-Western peoples by the concept of animism, in which humans, animals and even inanimate objects are thought to have a spirit or soul apart from their objective physical properties. Animatism as described by R. H. Codrington may be found with animism in the same culture. Animatism is a force or a power directed to a successful outcome which may make itself manifest in any object. Magic is a manipulation of natural laws. Frazer saw magic as a pseudo-science and found two principles of magic, "like produces like," or sympathetic magic, and the law of contagion.

3.

Durkheim introduced the idea of totemism and divided cultural life into the sacred and the profane. The totem is sacred and symbolic of the society and serves the function of stabilizing and binding the group together. On the other hand, Lévi-Strauss emphasizes the private and solitary functions of religion.

4.

The function of religion and magic for Malinowski was to allow the believer to have a sense of control over those areas of his experience which were beyond his practical knowledge. Radcliffe-Brown claimed that particular elements critical for social functioning were embued with religious significance and had adaptive value for the continuity of the social order.

5.

Individual needs as well as the capacity of the individual for mystical experience are psychological explanations of religion. Psychoanalysts like Jung and Freud explain religion in terms of man's unconscious. Freud sees religion as a system of defense mechanisms to relieve an individual of guilt. Jung went further and postulated a collective unconscious universal to mankind. These archetypes are projected onto the world as religious symbols and myths that have therapeutic value.

6.

Ritual is religion made manifest; through ritual social bonds are reinforced. Rites of passage are occasions for ritual. Van Gennep divided ceremonies for life-crises into rites of separation, transition, and incorporation. A ritual may consist of a sacrifice whose purpose is propitiation of the supernatural powers. A rite of reversal is a ritual in which there is a reversal of the normal values and customs. These may function as social safety valves.

7.

The priest is the religious expert and as part of the religious institution is a repository of the knowledge and practice of the religion. A shaman legitimates himself into the supernatural through a mystical experience and may practice healing or divination.

8.
Witchcraft functions much like science in offering an explanation for unwanted events. Sorcery is the practice of witchcraft for evil purposes and according to Kluckhohn serves as an expression of hostile emotions against individuals without disturbing the norms of the larger group.

9.
Domination by Western society has been the cause of certain religious manifestations in non-Western societies. In the islands of Melanesia the cargo cult has appeared spontaneously at different times since the beginning of the century. Wallace has interpreted certain religious reformations as revitalization movements in which an attempt is made, and sometimes successfully, to change the society. Redemptive movements, which try to change the individual, are a third method of coping with domination by a more powerful group by religious means. The "Sun Dance" of the Ute and Shoshone Indians is an example.

Suggested readings

Lessa, William A. and Evon Z. Vogt, eds. *Reader in Comparative Religion: An Anthropological Approach.* New York: Harper and Row, 1958.
The articles collected in the book discuss the universality of religion as it corresponds to deep and inescapable human needs. It discusses religion as a system of ethics, a response to the processes of nature, and an answer to the uncertainties of experience. The collection shows the relationship of religion to philosophy, theater, science, and ethics.

Malinowski, Bronislaw *Magic, Science and Religion, and Other Essays.* New York: Doubleday, 1954.
The articles collected here provide a discussion of a particular primitive people (the Trobriand Islanders) as illustration of conceptual and theoretical knowledge of mankind. The author covers such diversified topics as religion, life, death, character of primitive cults, magic, faith, and myth.

Norbeck, Edward *Religion in Human Life: Anthropological Views.* New York: Holt, Rinehart and Winston, 1974.
The author presents a comprehensive view of religion based on twin themes: the description of religious events, rituals, and states of mind and the nature of anthropological aims, views, procedures, and interpretations.

Wallace, Anthony F. C. *Religion, An Anthropological View.* New York: Random House, 1966.
This is a standard textbook treatment of religion by an anthropologist who has specialized in the study of revitalization movements.

The arts

Art is the product of a specialized kind of human behavior: the creative use of our imagination to help us interpret, understand, and enjoy life. Whether one is talking about a Chinese love song, a Navajo pot, a Balinese dance, or a Persian bracelet, it is clear that everyone involved in the activity we call art—the creator, the performer, the participant, the spectator—is making use of a uniquely human ability to use and comprehend symbols and to shape and interpret the physical world for something other than a practical or useful purpose.

What our other and perhaps "higher" purposes may be in what we call art will differ according to the specific kind of activity involved. Looking at a decorative wall-hanging will probably not serve precisely the same nonpractical purpose as singing a sea chanty or listening to a folktale. But the process in every case will require the same special combination of the symbolic representation of form and the expression of feeling that constitutes the creative imagination. Insofar as the creative use of the human ability to symbolize is universal and either expresses or is shaped by cultural values and concerns, it is properly and eminently an area of investigation for anthropology.

There appears to be no culture in the world without at least some kind of storytelling or a rudimentary kind of singing or dancing, if not a fully developed tradition of artistic expression. Reasoning backwards from effect to cause, some writers in recent times have consequently proposed the theory that humans may have an actual need or drive—either innate or acquired—to use their faculties of imagination. Just as we need food and shelter to survive, we may also need to nourish and exercise our active minds, which are not satisfied, except in times of crisis, with the mere business of solving the problems of daily existence. Without the free play of the imagination there is boredom, and boredom may lead to a lack of productivity, perhaps even in extreme cases to death. It is art that provides the means and the materials for our imaginative play and thus helps to sustain life. According to this way of thinking, art is therefore not a luxury to be afforded or appreciated by a minority of aesthetes or escapists, but a necessary kind of social behavior in which every normal and active human being participates.

As an activity or kind of behavior that contributes to well-being and helps give shape and significance to life, art must be at the same time related to and differentiated from religion. The dividing line between the two is not distinct: it is not easy to say, for example, precisely where art stops and religion begins in an elaborate tribal ceremony involving ornamentation, masks, costumes, songs, dances, effigies, and totems. Does religion inspire art, or is religion perhaps a higher kind of art in which the supernatural happens to be the central element?

This problem in semantics is not easy to solve, but it is often convenient to distinguish between secular and religious art, if not between art and religion. In what we call purely secular art, whether it is light or serious, it is clear that our imaginations are free to roam without any ulterior motives—creating and recreating patterns, plots, rhythms, and feelings at leisure and without any thought of consequence or aftermath. In religious art, on the other hand, the imagination is working still, but the whole activity is somehow aimed at assuring or establishing our past, present, or future through propitiation, celebration, and acknowledgment of forces beyond ourselves. Whether categorized as secular or religious, at any rate, art of all varieties can be expected to reflect the values and concerns of the people who create and enjoy it; the nature of the things reflected and expressed in art is the concern of the anthropologist.

In approaching art as a cultural phenomenon, the anthropologist has the pleasant task of cataloguing, photographing, recording, and describing all possible forms of imaginative activity in any particular culture. There is an enormous variety of forms and modes of artistic expression in the world. Because people everywhere continue to create and develop in new directions, there is no forseeable point of diminishing returns in the interesting process of collecting and describing the world's ornaments, body decorations, variations in clothing, blanket and rug designs, pottery and basket styles, architectural embellishments, monuments, ceremonial masks, legends, work songs, social dances, and other art forms. But the process of collecting must eventually lead to some kind of analysis, and then perhaps to some

Figure 24-1. *A young historian at the new university on the Ivory Coast is taping many tribal legends; this story-teller is accompanied by a drummer.*

illuminating generalizations about relationships between art and culture.

Probably the best way to begin a study of this problem of the relationships between art and culture is to examine critically some of the generalizations that have already been made about specific arts. In order to do this, we will look carefully at some facts and interpretations of verbal arts, music, and sculpture in a number of cultures, chiefly in West Africa.

Verbal arts

The term **folklore** was coined in the nineteenth century to denote the unwritten stories, beliefs, and customs of the European peasant as opposed to the "sophisticated" traditions of the educated elite. The subsequent study of folklore, concentrating on folktales, has become a discipline allied to, but somewhat independent of, anthropology, working on cross-cultural comparisons of themes, motifs, and structures, generally more from a literary than an ethnological point of view. In general, both linguists and anthropologists prefer to speak of the oral traditions and verbal arts of a culture rather than its folklore and folktales, recognizing that creative verbal expression takes many forms and that the implied distinction between folk and sophisticated art is valid only in the context of civilization.

The verbal arts include narrative, drama, poetry, incantations, proverbs, riddles, word games, and even naming procedures, compliments, and insults, when these take elaborate and special forms. The narrative seems to be one of the easiest kinds of verbal art to record or collect. Perhaps because it is also the most publishable, with popular appeal in our own culture, it has received the most study and attention. Generally, narratives have been divided into three basic and recurring categories: myth, legend, and tale.

Myth

The **myth** is basically religious, in that its subject matter is the ultimates of human existence: where we and the things in our world came from, why we are here, and where we are going. Any aspect of these very large questions may be called a myth. The myth has an explanatory function; it depicts and describes an orderly universe, which sets the stage for orderly behavior.

Here is a typical etiological, or origin-explaining, myth traditional with the Fon of Dahomey in West Africa:

> In the beginning the stars were visible both at night and in the daytime. The night stars were the children of the moon and the day stars were the children of the sun. One day the moon told the sun that their children were trying to outshine them. To prevent this they agreed to tie up the stars in sacks and throw them in the ocean. The sun went first and cleared the daytime sky of stars. The sly moon, however, did not keep her part of the bargain, but kept all of her children in the night sky. The sun's children became all of the brightly colored fish in the ocean, and from that time the sun has been the mortal enemy of the moon, pursuing her to try to get revenge for the loss of the stars to the sea. When there is an eclipse, the sun is trying to eat up the moon, and the people have to go out and beat on their drums to make the sun let her loose.

This myth may be encountered in a somewhat more elaborate form, with some more realistic and dramatic details, but the basic facts of the story will remain the same.

Such a myth, insofar as it is believed, accepted, and perpetuated in a culture, may be said to express a part of the **world view** of a people: the unexpressed but implicit conceptions of their place in nature and of the limits and workings of their world. The concepts of world view and science are intimately related, and it may be said that myth is the science of cultures which do not verify "truth" about nature by means of experiment. Extrapolating from the details of the Fon myth, for example, we might arrive at the conclusion that the Fon personify and respect the forces of nature, and that they believe they have both the ability and the duty to influence the behavior of these forces. In their protectiveness toward the moon in the myth, the Fon would seem to be approving either deceitfulness or cleverness. But other interpretations might be that the Fon simply accept a mixture of goodness and badness in the workings of nature, or that they fear any change in the balance of things already established. At any rate it is characteristic of an explanatory myth, such as this one, that the unknown will be simplified and explained in terms of the known. This myth accounts in human terms for the existence of fish and stars, for the movements of the sun and moon, and for the special phenomenon of the lunar eclipse. It is a product of creative imagination, and it is a work of art as well as a potentially religious statement.

The analysis and interpretation of myth have been carried to great lengths. The study of mythology has in fact become a science itself. It is certain that myth-making is an extremely important kind of human creativity, and the study of the myth-making process and its results can give some valuable clues to the way people perceive and think about their world. But the dangers and problems of interpretation are great. Several questions arise: Are the myths literally believed or perhaps accepted symbolically or emotionally as a different kind of truth? To what extent do myths actually determine or reflect human behavior? Can an outsider read into a myth the same meaning that it has in its culture? How do we account for contradictory myths in the same culture? New myths arise and old ones die: is it then the content or the structure of the myth that is important? All of these questions deserve, and are currently receiving, serious consideration.

Legend

Less problematical but perhaps more complex than myth is the legend. **Legends** are semihistorical narratives that account for the deeds of heroes, the movements of peoples, and the establishment of local customs, typically with a mixture of realism and the supernatural or extraordinary. As stories they are not necessarily believed or disbelieved, but they usually serve both to enter-

tain and to inspire or bolster pride in family, tribe, or nation.

The longer legends, sometimes in poetry or in rhythmic prose, are known as **epics.** In parts of West and Central Africa there are remarkably elaborate and formalized recitations of extremely long legends, lasting several hours, and even days. These long narratives have been described as veritable encyclopedias of the most diverse aspects of a culture, with direct and indirect statements about history, institutions, relationships, values, and ideas. Epics are typically found in nonliterate societies with a fairly complex form of state political organization; they serve to transmit and preserve a culture's legal and political precedents and practices. The Mwindo epic of the Nyanga people, the Lianja epic of the Mongo, and the Kambili epic of the Mande, for example, have been the subject of extensive and rewarding study by French, British, and American anthropologists in the last few years.

Legends may incorporate mythological details, especially when they make appeal to the supernatural, and are therefore not always clearly distinct from myth. The legend about Mwindo follows him through the earth, the atmosphere, the underworld, and the remote sky, and gives a complete picture of the Nyanga people's view of the organization and limits of the world. Legends may also incorporate proverbs and incidental tales, and thus be related to other forms of verbal art as well. A recitation of the legend of Kambili, for example, has been said to include as many as 150 proverbs.

For the anthropologist, the major significance of the secular and apparently realistic portions of legends, whether long or short, is probably in the clues they provide to what constitutes approved or model ethical behavior in a culture. The subject matter of legends is essentially problem-solving, and the content is likely to include combat, warfare, confrontations, and physical and psychological trials of many kinds. Certain questions may be answered explicitly or implicitly: Does the culture justify homicide? What kinds of behavior are considered to be brave or cowardly?

Figure 24-2. *A village elder of the Ivory Coast tells legends and tales to young boys of the tribe as part of their education.*

What is the etiquette of combat or warfare? Is there a concept of altruism or self-sacrifice? But here again there are pitfalls in the process of interpreting art in relation to life. It is always possible that certain kinds of behavior are acceptable or even admirable with the distance or objectivity afforded by art, but are not at all so approved in daily life. In our own culture, murderers, charlatans, and rakes have sometimes become popular "heroes" and the subjects of legends; we would object, however, to the inference of an outsider that we necessarily approved or wanted to emulate the morality of Billy the Kid or Jesse James.

Tale

The term **tale** is a nonspecific label for a third category of creative narratives, those which are purely secular, nonhistorical, and recognized as fiction for entertainment, though they sometimes draw a moral or teach a practical lesson. Here is a brief summary of a tale from Ghana, known as "Father, Son, and Donkey":

A father and his son farmed their corn, sold it, and spent part of the profit on a donkey. When the hot season came, they harvested their yams and prepared to take them to storage, using their donkey. The father mounted the donkey and they all three proceeded on their way until they met some people. "What? You lazy man!" the people said to the father. "You let your young son walk barefoot on this hot ground while you ride on a donkey? For shame!" The father yielded his place to the son, and they proceeded until they came to an old woman. "What? You useless boy!" said the old woman. "You ride on the donkey and let your poor father walk barefoot on this hot ground? For shame!" The son dismounted, and both father and son walked on the road, leading the donkey behind them until they came to an old man. "What? You foolish people!" said the old man. "You have a donkey and you walk barefoot on the hot ground instead of riding?" And so it goes. Listen: when you are doing something and other people come along, just keep on doing what you like.

This is precisely the kind of tale that is of special interest in traditional folklore studies. It is an internationally popular "numskull" tale; versions of it have been recorded in India, the Middle East, the Balkans, Italy, Spain, England, and the United States, as well as in West Africa. It is classified or catalogued as exhibiting a basic **motif** or story situation—father and son trying to please everyone—one of the many thousands that have been found to recur in world folktales. In spite of variations in detail, every version of the tale will be found to have about the same basic structure in the sequence of events, sometimes called the syntax of the tale; a peasant father and son work together, a beast of burden is purchased, the three set out on a short excursion, the father rides and is criticized, the son rides and is criticized, both walk and are criticized, and a conclusion is drawn.

Tales of this sort with an international distribution sometimes raise more problems than they solve: Which one is the original? What is the path of its migration? Could it be sheer coincidence that different cultures have come up with the same motif and syntax, or could it be a case of independent invention with similar tales developing in similar situations in responses to like causes? A surprisingly large number of motifs in European and African tales are traceable to ancient sources in India. Is this good evidence of a spread of culture from a "cradle" of civilization, or is it an example of diffusion of tales in contiguous areas? There are of course purely local tales, as well as tales with such a wide distribution. Within any particular culture, it will probably be found possible to categorize local types of tales: animal, human experience, trickster, dilemma, ghost, moral, scatological, nonsense, and so on. In West Africa there is a remarkable prevalence of animal stories, for example, with such creatures as the spider, the rabbit, and the hyena as the protagonists. Many were carried to the slave-holding areas of the New World; the Uncle Remus stories may be a survival of this tradition.

The significance of tales for the anthropologist rests partly in this matter of their distribution. They provide evidence for either cultural contacts or cultural isolation, and for limits of influence and cultural cohesion. It has been debated for decades now, for example, to what extent the culture of West Africa was transmitted to the Southern United States. So far as folktales are concerned, one school of folklorists has always found and insisted on European origins; another school, somewhat more recently, is pointing out African prototypes. But the anthropologist can be interested in more than these questions of distribution. Like the legends, tales very often illustrate local solutions to universal human ethical problems, and in some sense they state a moral philosophy. The anthropologist sees that whether the tale of the father, the son, and the donkey originated in West Africa or arrived there from Europe or the Middle East, the very fact that it has been accepted in West Africa suggests that it states something valid for that culture. The tale's lesson of a necessary degree of self-confidence in the face of arbitrary social criticism is therefore something that can be read into the culture's values and beliefs.

Other verbal arts

Myths, legends, and tales, prominent as they are in anthropological studies, turn out to be no more important than the other verbal arts in many cultures. In the Yoruba culture of Nigeria, for example, explanatory myths are now rare (the beliefs of Christianity and Islam have largely replaced them), but riddles, proverbs, figures of speech, poetry, and drama are all lively and active verbal arts that deserve and are beginning to receive more attention. Yoruba poetry, rich in both lyrical and dramatic elements, has only recently been studied and made available to the rest of the world, chiefly through the efforts of the new Nigerian institutes and local studies programs. Subjects of the poetry include alliances and conflicts with neighboring tribes; military and political triumphs and reverses; treaties, annexations, resettlements; the encroachment of the white man on the land of the Africans; and the undermining of the power of the chief by the missionary and the magistrate. Yoruba drama, previously not an especially popular verbal art, is being revived and cultivated and may be developing into a new and significant kind of creative activity.

In all cultures, the words for songs constitute a kind of poetry. Poetry and stories recited with gesture, movement, and props become drama. Drama combined with dance, music, and spectacle becomes a public celebration. The more we look at the individual arts, the clearer it becomes that that they are often interrelated and interdependent. The verbal arts are in fact simply differing manifestations of the same creative imagination that produces music and the plastic arts.

Figure 24-3. *A funeral is often an occasion for song and dance; men of the Mousgoum tribe blow horns and beat drums while relatives of the dead man dance.*

The art of music

The study of music in specific cultural settings, beginning in the nineteenth century with the collection of folksongs, has developed into a specialized field, called **ethnomusicology.** Like the study of folktales for its own sake, ethnomusicology is at the same time related to and somewhat independent of anthropology. Nevertheless, it is possible to sort out from the various concerns of the field several concepts that are of interest in general anthropology.

In order to talk intelligently about the verbal arts of a culture, it is of course desirable to know as much as possible about the language itself. In order to talk about the music of a culture, it is equally desirable to know the language of music—that is, its conventions. The way to approach a totally unfamiliar kind of musical expression is to learn first how it functions in respect to melody, rhythm, and form.

Elements of music

In general, human music is said to differ from natural music— the songs of birds, wolves, and whales, for example—in being almost everywhere perceived in terms of a repertory of tones at fixed or regular intervals from each other: in other words, a scale. We have made closed systems out of a formless range of possible sounds by dividing the distance between a tone and its first overtone or sympathetic vibration (which always has exactly twice as many vibrations as the basic tone) into a series of measured steps. In the Western or European system, the distance between the basic tone and the first overtone is called the octave; it consists of seven steps—five "whole" tones and two "semitones"—which are named with the letters A through G. The whole tones are further divided into semitones, for a total working scale of twelve tones. Westerners learn at an early age to recognize and imitate this arbitrary system and its conventions, and it comes to sound natural. Yet the overtone series, on which it is partially based, is the only part of it that can be considered a wholly natural phenomenon.

One of the most common alternatives to the semitonal system is the pentatonic system, which divides the octave into five nearly equidistant tones. In Japan there is a series of different pentatonic scales in which some semitones are employed. In Java there are scales of both five and seven equal steps, which have no relation to the intervals we hear as "natural" in our system. In Arabic and Persian music there are smaller units of a third of a tone (some of which we may accidentally produce on an out-of-tune piano) with scales of seventeen and twenty-four steps in the octave. There are even quarter-tone scales in India and subtleties of interval shading that are nearly indistinguishable to a Western ear. Small wonder, then, that even when we can hear what sounds like melody and rhythm in these systems, the total result may sound to us peculiar or out of tune. The anthropologist will need a very practiced ear to learn to appreciate—or perhaps even to tolerate—some of the music he hears, and only some of the most skilled folksong collectors have attempted to notate and analyze the music of nonsemitonal systems.

Scale systems and their modifications comprise what is known as **tonality** in music. Tonality determines the possibilities and limits of both melody and harmony. Not much less complex than tonality is the matter of rhythm. Rhythm, whether regular or irregular, is an organizing factor in music, sometimes more important than the melodic line. Traditional European music is rather neatly measured into recurrent patterns of two, three, and four beats, with combinations of weak and strong beats to mark the divisions and form patterns. Non-European music is likely to move also in patterns of five, seven, or eleven, with complex arrangements of internal beats and sometimes polyrhythms: one instrument or singer going in a pattern of three beats, for example while another is in a pattern of five or seven. Polyrhythms are frequent in the drum music of West Africa, which shows remarkable precision in the overlapping of rhythmic lines. In addition to polyrhythms, non-European music may also contain shifting rhythms: a pattern of three, for example, followed by a pattern of two, or five, with little or no regular recurrence or repetition of any one pattern, though the patterns themselves are fixed and identifiable as units.

Although it is not necessarily the concern of the anthropologist to untangle all these complicated technical matters, he will no doubt want to know enough to be aware of the degree of skill or artistry involved in a performance and to have some measure of the extent to which people in a culture have learned to practice and respond to this often important creative activity. Moreover, as with folklore, myths, and legends, the distribution of musical forms and intruments can reveal much about cultural contact or isolation.

Functions of music

Even without concern for technical matters, the anthropologist can profitably investigate the function music has in a society. First of all, it is rare that a culture has been reported to be without any kind of music. Even the Tasadays of the Philippines, the recently described nearly Stone Age forest dwellers, have adopted, if not invented, a bamboo jaw harp called a *kubing*. Kenneth MacLeish translates in these words the comments of the Tasaday *kubing* player: "If I play my kubing, it is because someone is listening. I really know how to play the *kubing*." Interestingly, these simple words seem to express the value music—in fact, all art—has in far more complex cultures: it is an individual creative skill which one can cultivate and be proud of, whether from a sense of accomplishment or the sheer pleasure of performing; and it is a form of social behavior through which there is a communication or sharing of feelings and life experience with other humans.

The social function of music is perhaps most obvious in song. Songs very often express as much as tales the values and concerns of the group, but they do so with the increased formalism which results from the restrictions of closed systems of tonality, rhythm, and musical form. Early investigators of non-European song were struck by the apparent simplicity of pentatonic scales and a seemingly endless repetition of phrases. They often did not give sufficient credit to the formal function of repetition in such music, confusing repetition with repetitiveness or lack of invention. A great deal of non-European music was dismissed as "primitive" and formless, and typically treated as trivial.

Repetition is nevertheless a fact of music, even European music, and a basic formal principle. Consider this little song from Nigeria:

> Ijangbon l'o ra,
> Ijangbon l'o ra,
> Eni r'asho Oshomalo,
> Ijangbon l'o ra.
> (He buys trouble,
> He buys trouble,
> He who buys Oshomalo cloth,
> He buys trouble)

Several decades ago, the Oshomalo were cloth-sellers in Egba villages who sold on credit, then harassed, intimidated, and even beat their customers to make them pay before the appointed day. The message of the song is simple, and both words and music are the same for three lines out of four; the whole song may be repeated many times at will. What is it that produces this kind of artistic expression and makes it more than primitive trivia? A single Egba undoubtedly improvised the song first, reacting to a personal experience or observation, lingering on one of its elements by repeating it. The repetition gives the observation not emphasis but symbolic form, and therefore a kind of concreteness or permanence. In this concrete form, made memorable and attractive with melody and rhythm, the song was taken up by other Egba, perhaps with some musical refinements or embellishments from more creative members of the group, including clapping or drumming to mark the rhythm. Thus a bit of social commentary was crystalized and preserved even after the situation had passed into history.

Whether the content of songs is didactic, satirical, inspirational, religious, political, or purely emotional, the important thing is that the formless has been given form and feelings are communicated in a symbolic and memorable way that can be repeated and shared. The group is consequently united and probably has the sense that their experience whatever it may be, has shape and meaning.

Musical instruments

The human voice, used in song, is of course the basic, universal musical instrument for melody; and the human body—stamping with the heels and toes, hitting the fleshy or bony parts with the hands—is the basic instrument for rhythm. Although it is quite possible to make music without artificial instruments, it is rare that a culture does so. Musical instruments are the artifacts of music, and the study of instruments is another adjunct of anthropology that can reveal a great deal about culture.

Rattle. Musical instruments are thought to have developed historically from experimentation with the augmentation of human sounds, perhaps first just for the sake of making audible our expressive body movements. The rattle, probably the simplest musical instrument, is a means of making audible the expressive body movement of shaking, suggesting fear, excitement, or perhaps anger. The simplest rattle is the strung rattle: a series of small hard objects such as shells or teeth strung on cords or tied in bunches and agitated vigorously in some regular rhythm. Because the objects used may be considered to have magical or supernatural value in some cultures, some anthropologists and musicologists have proposed a strong connection between magic or religion and music at this level of imaginative creativity. Nevertheless, it seems quite possible that the rattle could also have a secular origin.

The gourd rattle (a calabash filled usually with pebbles) is perhaps a higher refinement of the strung rattle. Countries where calabashes are not available have substituted wicker, clay, wood, and metal, achieving the same result. It has been observed that the rattle is often a woman's instrument; in East African cultures there are ceremonies or celebrations at which hundreds of women participate on the fringes of the action, all vigorously producing a rhythmic background with rattles. In our own culture the rather fanciful theory has been advanced that, as a woman's instrument,

Figure 24-4. *Kenyan dancers celebrate the independence of the nation. Their costumes and face paintings constitute another kind of expressive art. Note the modern addition of a flashlight for night-time dancing.*

the rattle has been preserved and introduced into the woman's part of the household, namely the nursery.

Stamper. The rattle makes audible an inaudible expressive movement of the body. Probably the simplest type of augmentation of an already audible expressive human movement, that of stamping, is through the use of the stamper. Especially as it is found in the South Pacific, this may take the form of a pit dug in the ground and covered with a rough lid of bark or curved board. The resounding cavity produces a dull, hollow sound when the cover is stamped on—again often by women—and it serves as a drumlike accompaniment for dancing. The term stamper is sometimes also applied to hand-stamping augmentations, such as sticks on gourds, bamboo tubes on mats, and pestles on mortars. It is almost impossible not to see a sexual symbolism in the process, and anthropologists have long proposed a connection between fertility and marriage rites and ceremonies, and the development of this kind of artistic expression. Again, however, it is not clear whether the cultural activity may have inspired the use of the instrument or the instrument may simply have found its way into ritual, with appropriate interpretations coming after the fact.

Drum. Stampers of more sophisticated types begin to show development in the augmentation of expressive movement in two directions: first there is the substitution of an artificial striking surface for a natural one, and second there is the use of an artifical striking device instead of the hands. The next stage of development seems to be the drum—the most versatile and varied of the percussion or rhythm instruments.

The drum represents various degrees in the perfection of the artificial striking surface. Technically a drum is any instrument in which the sound is produced by striking a stretched membrane covering the opening over any kind of frame or hollow body. The degree of technical perfection in a drum will be judged by the effective choice of a membrane, the skillful application of membrane to frame, and the invention or discovery of appropriate shapes and qualities in the resonating body. The various possibilities are numerous, and there are literally hundreds of different kinds of drums in the world.

The two main categories of drums are the cut wooden drums and the molded clay drums. Since woodworking usually antedates pottery making, the wooden drums are believed to be the older.

But clay drums are generally single-headed, and the double-headed wooden drum, with membranes on both ends of a cylinder, appears to be a more recent development of the wooden variety, postdating the earliest clay drums. Stick-drumming is likewise thought to be later than hand-drumming, but combinations of the two are not rare.

What is especially interesting about the drum for the anthropologist is perhaps not so much its functions and capabilities as a purely musical instrument, which are considerable, as its ritual value and even sacredness in many cultures. In East Africa, for example, the drum is so sacred that even criminals find sanctuary when they run to the safety of a drum-yard. Among the Wahinda, to see a drum by daylight is fatal; men must carry them by night only. Unlike rattles and stampers, drums often seem to be man's instruments. In Oceania a new drum is rendered useless if a woman sees it before it is completely finished.

As an augmentation of audible human expressive movements, the drum appears to go a step further than the stamper. It has been argued that in using rattles and stampers, people still have the feeling that they are wholly responsible for the sounds they are producing. But the drum, with its musical, mysterious, variable, and responsive sounds, requiring coaxing and heating and shrinking and pampering very much as a living creature, seems to have a voice of its own, perhaps from some strange force living inside it. Whatever the explanation, it is a fact that in many cultures drums are considered to have souls or to be the voices of spirits. This is particularly evident in animistic cultures in West Africa, the places of origin for the voodoo (properly *vodoun*) drums of the Caribbean. The mother drum, the father drum, and the baby drum have their respective voices and their individually appropriate roles in calling to or speaking for the spirits. Drummers may work themselves into a trance, during which the drum takes over and speaks in its own voice. Drums are also an important part of the shaman's equipment.

Friction instruments. Friction drums, found for example with the Ewe in Togo, produce sounds with rubbing rather than beating. The humming and squeaking noises that result are easily imaginable as superhuman sounds or voices. Friction instruments in general, the last major category of percussive or rhythmic musical instruments, are perhaps the least pleasant-sounding of all. The principle type is known generally as the scraper. Scrapers are resonating boxes or notched bones or sticks, scraped rapidly with a rigid object to produce a whirring or grumbling sound, perhaps like a mysterious voice or an animal. It is reported that among Cheyenne Indians, bone-scraping accompanying a dance was once considered to inspire love and to encourage marriage. Scrapers nevertheless also have a purely rhythmic function in some parts of the world, and interpretations involving too close a connection between rite and instrument may not always be wise or even possible.

Wind and string instruments. Wind and string instruments ordinarily carry melody more than they mark rhythm, and consequently they may be considered as providing an extension or modification of the human voice. This is particularly clear for the wind instruments—the flute and trumpet for example—in which the breath of the performer actually passes through the instrument and is transformed into a voice unlike his own. The new voice may be more beautiful or more powerful, or again it may be likened to a voice from the supernatural. Of curiously wide distribution throughout the world is a variety of instrument known as the nose flute, actually played by blowing through the nose. In Polynesia, where

nose flutes are especially widely used, it appears that breath from the nose is supposed to contain the soul (a notion that is by no means limited to Polynesia) and that it has more magical power than breath from the mouth. Therefore the curious method of playing this flute, probably an unacceptable one in our culture, would seem to have a reasonable explanation on cultural if not aesthetic grounds.

The enumeration and description of musical instruments as the artifacts of musical creativity and extensions of the basic human instrument, an intriguing and rewarding pursuit, can obviously be continued at considerable length; observations can lead to interesting theories and explanations, some of which can be supported with extra-musical details in various cultures. Art of all kinds is again seen to be demonstrably related to human sensibilities, and it should not suprise us to find also even more relationships between the arts themselves. Musical instruments, in their more complex, decorative, and symbolic shapes, bring us quite close to the third major kind of artistic activity to be considered here, namely sculpture.

The art of sculpture

In the broadest sense, sculpture is art in the round. Any three-dimensional product of the creative imagination may be called a piece of sculpture: a ceremonial knife, a decorative pot, a hand-crafted lute, an ornamental gate, a funerary monument, or a public building displays the same essential artistic process as a statue, a mask, or a figurine. All of these human creations represent an imaginative organization of materials in space. The artist has given tangible shape to his feelings and perceptions, creating or recreating symbolically meaningful form out of formlessness. In a narrower sense, sculpture means only those artifacts that serve no immediate utilitarian purpose and are fashioned from hard or semipermanent materials. But it is difficult to state unequivocally what may or may not qualify as a piece of sculpture, even with this limitation. Are the beautiful and highly imaginative tiny brass figurines of Ghana, for example, formerly used as weights for measuring out quantities of gold, not to be considered sculpture, even though the somewhat larger brass figurines of comparable design in Dahomey, which have never had a practical use, are obviously to be so considered? Or should we perhaps now call the Ghana figurines sculpture because they are no longer put to use?

Art and craft

Our use of the word sculpture in English seems to impose a distinction between types of creative activity where none may in fact exist. One solution is to substitute the more modern term plastic art, but the phenomenon remains the same. Objects that are obviously skillfully made but still do not quite qualify as sculpture by virtue of being somewhat trivial, low in symbolic content, or impermanent—by the standards of the culture—are generally known and considered as the products of craft (or, in modern times, industry). An automobile, for example, however beautifully it may be designed, however lovingly it may be displayed in front of the house as an object for admiration, and however cleverly we may interpret its parts and its functions as symbolic in our culture, is for us above all a mass-produced consumable, and to treat it as sculpture would be misrepresenting its *usual* value in our society. Furthermore, we must also consider the intention of the creator. What we call sculpture or plastic art is not ordinarily artistic by accident or through after-the-fact interpretation, but by design. Detroit does not intentionally produce sculpture.

As a type of symbolic expression, sculpture may be representational, imitating closely the forms of nature, or abstract, drawing from natural forms but representing only their basic patterns or arrangements. Representational sculpture is partly abstract to the extent that it generalizes from nature and abstracts patterns of ideal beauty, ug-

liness, or typical expressions of emotion. Michelangelo's "David" is representational sculpture, clearly depicting a human being; it is also abstract insofar as it generalizes an ideal of masculine beauty, quiet strength, and emotional calm, therefore functioning symbolically. Henry Moore's gigantic women with holes through their midsections are abstractions, using nature but exaggerating and deliberately transforming some of its shapes for the purpose of expressing a particular feeling toward them.

West African sculpture

West African sculpture, only comparatively recently studied and described in adequate detail, is an especially rich non-European tradition that may help illustrate some of the anthropological aspects of representational and abstract sculpture, its subjects, materials, and meanings.

Ancestor worship and reverence of royalty have found expression in a realistic or portrait-style sculpture throughout the region of the Niger and Congo River basins. Probably the most dramatically realistic are the so-called Benin bronzes: hundreds of finely detailed heads of ancestors, royalty, and important persons produced at the ancient Benin capital of Ife (in present-day Nigeria) around the beginning of the fifteenth century. Most of these heads were carried off to England at the end of the nineteenth century, and they have served as a forcible reminder to Europeans that the Mediterranean region is not the only source of fine realistic sculpture.

In addition to the Benin bronzes, the royal statues of the Bakuba kings in the Congo River region, the ancestor figures of the Guro in the Ivory Coast, the secular and satirical representations of Europeans by the Yoruba in Nigeria, and the small brasses depicting the royalty and animals of the Fon in Dahomey are also naturalistic in detail, and are obviously often intended to represent real persons or animals in characteristic moods or poses. Features and proportions may be somewhat stylized according to regional conventions of what is appropriate or possible in sculpture: heads may be disproportionately large, necks may be elongated, and sexual parts either exaggerated or minimized. It is interesting to note that most of these sculptures come from cultures in which subsistence techniques were efficient enough to produce a surplus, which was used to support a variety of occupational specialists. The artist was one such specialist; much of his work was commissioned by other specialists, such as priests and government officials.

The majority of West African sculpture is abstract or expressionistic—giving form to human feelings and attitudes toward gods, spirits, other humans, and animals. Generalizations about the nonrepresentational styles and purposes for the region are, however, almost impossible. Every West African culture that produces or has produced sculpture has its own identifiable styles, and this artistic cohesion undoubtedly reinforces the social unity of the group. A Fon recognizes a Yoruba mask, and disassociates himself from whatever symbolic significance it has for the Yoruba. Materials as well as styles differ in neighboring cultures. The most common material is wood, but there is also regional use of brass, iron, terra cotta, mud, and raffia. Sculpture may be rubbed with ash, smoked in banana leaves, oiled, waxed, painted, and adorned with cowrie shells, teeth, iron or brass nails, strips of metal, or cloth.

Symbolic content. The anthropologist is interested in exactly what is abstracted from nature, and why, in all these varieties of sculpture, whatever their style and material. He is also interested in the extent to which traditions are perpetuated, and what meanings may be developing or changing. It appears that any single piece of sculpture in West Africa may be interpreted in terms of its symbolic significance for the group, and that generally such significance is well known by the people who make and look at the sculpture. Consequently the anthropologist has only to ask.

A small wooden figure of a person, with a head, rudimentary limbs, and a large trunk purposely riddled with holes may be found among the

Balega of the northeast Congo region. The figure is known as a *katanda,* meaning the scattering of red ants when attacked; it is interpreted as symbolizing the bad effect of internal fighting on the unity of local descent groups. The *kanaga* mask of the Dogon in Upper Volta is an elongated head with triangular eyes, long pointed ears and nose, and a cap surmounted with an enormous crest, four or five times the size of the head, in the form of a double-armed cross; for young initiates the cross symbolizes a bird with out-stretched wings, the beginning of active flight into life, and for older initiates of high rank its structure symbo-

Figure 24-5. *This Nigerian house is decorated by a relief carved in wet cement; a bicycle and a car are prominent features.*

lizes a synthesis of contradictory or competing life forces. The *akua'ba* dolls of Ashanti in Ghana, flat disc-headed figures on a long, narrow, legless body with a simple cross-piece for arms, are said to symbolize an Ashanti ideal of beauty in the high, wide forehead; the dolls are tucked into the waist-cloths of young girls, who carry them like real babies, perhaps as talismans to assure their own physical development or that of their children.

Ritual masks. The widest variety of expression in African sculpture is certainly to be found in

Figure 24-6. *These tombs of Nigerian farmers are topped by statues showing them as whites dressed in European garb.*

the ritual mask. Styles range from the relatively realistic and serene faces made by the Baule in the Ivory Coast to the frightening, violent, and extroverted faces with protruding eyes produced by the neighboring Ngere of Liberia. Theories about the symbolism of the masks have arisen beside the explanations of local informants, particularly in cases where certain masks are no longer produced or known. One of the more interesting is the notion that the unnatural features of some of the masks representing spirits or the dead are made systematically unnatural in order to suggest that the other world, or the spirit world, is somehow an opposite of this one: noses are long instead of short, ears are large rather than small, eye cavities are hollow rather than filled, and so on. The mask, as well as other sculpture, therefore becomes as much as the myth an expression of world view. The sculptor again gives shape and meaning to that which is unknown.

As in musical expression, sculpture also crystalizes feeling in a form that can be shared and perpetuated. African sculpture is impermanent because of the impermanent nature of its materials (fifty years has been suggested as an average lifetime for a wooden figure exposed to weather), but it is generally considered a great shame when a mask or piece of sculpture disintegrates. An important piece of sculpture may be replaced by imitation, copied and perpetuated so that the traditions and beliefs may be preserved. There is often a ritual in mask-making, with great care taken to preserve and copy exactly the traditional specifications. Similarly, there is still in some places a special reverence in the process of sculpting in general, and the soul of the wood must be respected with attendant rituals and beliefs similar to what we have seen in relation to the drum. Traditional West African sculpture is currently in decline, but it is not by any means everywhere dead. An excursion beyond the major urban centers reveals continuing activity in this important kind of symbolic creativity.

Original study

THE ANTELOPE BOY OF SHONGOPOVI: A HOPI LEGEND

It was a time not at the beginning and not at the end, when the villages were standing there just as they are now. And in those days, it is remembered, there lived in Shongopovi a man and his wife and one daughter. The girl was old enough to marry, but she did not want it. She met with a certain young man of the village sometimes, but mostly she kept to herself. Her parents wondered about it. They said to each other sometimes, "She is really a young woman now. Why is she always alone? Does she want to live forever without a husband?"

One day the village crier went through Shongopovi announcing that there would be a rabbit hunt the next morning . . .

Early the following morning the young people began to gather at the edge of the village, and the girl's mother said to her, "Well, now, all the others are going out there to have a good time together, and you are staying behind like an old woman. This is not the way it should be."

The girl replied, "All right, I will go then." . . .

They arrived at the valley below. They began hunting. Whenever a boy saw a rabbit he chased it and tried to knock it down with his stick. If he found a rabbit hole he wet an end of his stick, poked it into the hole and twisted it to catch in the rabbit's fur. Each time a boy caught a rabbit he held it up by its hind legs, and the girls raced to see who could get there first. The boy gave the rabbit to the first girl to arrive, and she would give him somiviki [a corn meal paste] in exchange.

The girl who had been reluctant to participate in the rabbit hunt had won two rabbits and given away most of her somiviki. But she was not feeling well and was going along slowly. She fell behind the others. She could hear their voices in the distance but she could not see them. She stopped to rest. She felt pains in her stomach. She found a secluded place among the rocks and lay down. And while she was lying there she gave birth to a baby. She worried greatly. She thought, "I cannot take this baby home. My parents will be angry with me." And so, after staying there for a time, she arose, wrapped the infant in a piece of her clothing, and placed it in an abandoned badger hole. Then she returned to the village.

Now, after all the young people had finished with their hunting, a female coyote came out of hiding and began to look for food. Because she was old she could not run fast enough to catch game. She had watched the hunters, thinking that they might overlook some wounded rabbits and leave them behind. And so she went here and there where she had seen them using their sticks. She did not find any food. But she heard a sound coming from a badger hole. She approached the hole and looked inside. She saw the baby there and drew it out gently with her teeth. She thought, "This young one is hungry. If I were younger I would nurse it, but now I am dried up. I have no milk." She thought about the Antelope People living some distance north of Shongopovi. She thought, "Yes, I will bring it to them. They will take care of it."

Holding the baby carefully by its cloth wrapping, the old coyote went to the north. She came to the kiva of the Antelope People and set the baby down by the entrance. As was the custom, she stamped on the ground above the

kiva, calling out, "I am here. Is there someone below?"

An antelope person called back, "Yes, we are here."

The old coyote said, "Come up. I have brought something."

So the antelope person went up the ladder to where the coyote was waiting. The coyote said to him, "Here is a male child I found out there in a badger hole. He is hungry, but I have no milk to give him. So I have brought him to you. One of your young women can feed him."

. . . Because the baby drank antelope milk it grew as rapidly as an antelope. In four days he could walk a little. When he was four weeks old he was allowed to go out of the kiva to run with the antelope children. At first he was slow, but in time he could run as fast as the others. And thereafter he went out with the antelopes every day and did whatever they did. In the kiva the Antelope People resembled humans. But when it was time to go out they took their antelope skins from the wall, put them on and became antelopes. At night when they returned they removed their skins and hung them on the wall again. While the boy was an adopted son of the Antelope People he was not an antelope. He did not have a skin to put on when they went out together. He ran along on two legs.

A man of Shongopovi went out one morning to search for game. He went to the north. He saw antelopes grazing there. He approached them silently. He saw the older antelopes. He saw the young antelopes running together, and with them a young boy running as though he too were an antelope. The hunter did not hunt anymore, but returned to Shongopovi to tell what he had seen. He entered the kiva where other men were sitting and discussing things. He said, "Out there in the north, I was hunting. I came upon a herd of antelopes. The young ones were running together and among them was a human child."

The others answered in doubt, saying, "This is hard to believe. A human child running with the antelopes? The antelopes are swift. No human, large or small, could run with the antelopes."

The hunter said, "What I have told you is the truth. I was there and I saw it."

The next day another man went to the north to see if a boy was there with the antelopes. He came to where the antelopes were grazing. He saw the boy with the young antelopes. He saw them run together. He returned to the village to report what he had seen. He said, "It is true. There is a boy among them, and he runs as swiftly as the others."

. . . In the kivas the people discussed what to do. Some said, "Do nothing. If the boy chooses to live with the antelope, surely he has a reason." Others said, "No, it is not right for a boy to live among the antelopes. We must capture him and bring him to the village." So a hunt was organized to capture the antelope boy.

. . . The chief of the antelopes was the boy's ceremonial uncle because he had taught him the knowledge and secrets of the antelope kiva. That morning, while the villagers were taking their positions for the hunt, the antelope chief said, "Wait, let us not go out yet. Something is happening today and there is something that must be done." He called the boy to sit with him in the kiva.

The chief said, "My nephew. Today the villagers are having a great antelope hunt. But it is you they are looking for. They say it is not right for a boy to be living with the antelope. They mean to capture you and take you back with them. It is true, they are your people. Therefore you must return with them. Whoever captures you will take you as his own. So it is important for you to know who among them are your parents. When we go out today do not run with the young antelopes. Stay close to me. I will tell you who is your father and who is your mother. When the time comes I will let you know what to do."

The boy said, "My uncle, I do not want to go back to the village to live. The antelopes are my people."

The antelope chief said, "It is true, you are like one of our own. If things do not go well for you in the village, if they treat you badly, you can come back to us. But as for now, today you will have to go with your parents."

Then the Antelope People prepared the boy. They washed his hair and cut it above his eyes in the Hopi fashion. They put a fluffy white eagle feather in his hair. They powdered his face with white cornmeal and painted his legs yellow. Around his waist they wrapped a white kilt, and around his ankles they fastened ankle bands. When this was done the Antelope People took their antelope forms and set out to their usual grazing place.

The people of the villages were waiting. They surrounded the antelopes. They moved in closer, making the circle smaller. The antelopes sought to escape. But if they went one way, there were people there. If they went another way, there were people there also. So they kept going around in a circle, and as the people came closer the circle became smaller and smaller. And at last the antelopes were confined in a very small space.

The antelope chief said to the boy, "Look carefully. That young woman standing over there is your mother. And over there, that man by the rocks, he is your father. Do you see them?"

The boy said, "Yes, I see them."

The antelope chief said, "The next time we pass this way, go quickly to your mother. Otherwise someone else may take you."

. . . The boy left his place among the antelopes. He ran swiftly to his mother. He put his arms around her, saying, "My mother." People gathered around. He said again, "My mother."

At first the young woman said nothing. She was thinking, "How can this be? He is mistaken." But remembering at last how she had put her baby in the badger hole, she placed her arms around the boy, saying, "My son."

The young woman's uncle who had been standing nearby said to her, "Is it true? Is this boy your son?"

She answered, "Yes, he is my son."

Her uncle asked, "Where is the boy's father?"

The boy went to where his father was standing. He took his hand. He said, "My father."

His father replied, "My son."

The young woman's uncle was angry. He said, "Why have you deceived us?"

The young woman said, "I was afraid. I tied my belt tight so that no one would notice. I went on a rabbit hunt and the baby was born there. I was afraid to bring him home, so I wrapped him in some of my clothing and left him in a badger hole."

Her uncle said, "It was a bad thing you did. If the antelopes had not taken care of your son he would have died." He came forward. He pulled down the hair whorls from each side of her head. He straightened her hair and and tied it in a knot the way it is worn by married women. He said, "Take the boy home. His father will join you there."

She returned to her parents' house, taking the boy with her. After a while the boy's father came and lived with them there, as is the custom. They went on living. The mother loved the boy. The father loved him also, but he felt restless about the way things had happened. He scolded the boy and spoke to him sharply. He loved him but he could not manage to speak to him except in hard words. He neglected him as well. He did not provide him with moccasins like other boys had. He did not make a bow for him and teach him how to hunt.

The boy was unhappy. And one day after his father scolded him sharply he went out of the village and travelled north until he came again to the place of the Antelope People. He entered the kiva. He said to the antelope chief, "My uncle."

The chief said, "My nephew."

The boy said, "As you told me to do, I went to Shongopovi. But I cannot live there anymore. My father is angry with me. He does not want me. Therefore I have come back. You are my people. I will live here.

His antelope uncle said, "Yes, live here. From now on you are one of us."

The Antelope People washed his hair and fixed it in the antelope style. They dressed him in the antelope manner. His uncle gave him an antelope skin, and a name. He named him Yuteu. The boy became an antelope.

Back in Shongopovi they missed the boy and searched everywhere. His parents went to Shipaulovi and Mishongnovi to see if he was there. They looked in the fields on all sides of Shongopovi.

His mother said at last, "There is no use looking for him any more. He has returned to the Antelope People who were kind to him."

. . . The boy's father was filled with remorse. He wanted his boy. He went north to the antelope country. He watched the antelopes, hoping to catch sight of his son. But he did not see him. Day after day he went to watch the antelopes, forgetting to take care of his fields. But there was no boy there, only the antelopes, nothing more.

Source:
Harold Courlander, "The Antelope Boy of Shangopovi" in *The Fourth World of the Hopis.*
Copyright 1971 by Harold Courlander.
Reprinted by permission of Crown Publishers.

Summary

1.

The creative use of our imagination to help us interpret, understand, and enjoy life produces art. Art makes use of a uniquely human ability to use and comprehend symbols and to shape and interpret the physical world for something besides a practical or useful purpose. The creative use of our ability to symbolize either expresses or is shaped by cultural values and concerns. Anthropologists are interested in these values reflected by art.

2.

The verbal arts include narrative, drama, poetry, incantations, proverbs, riddles, and word games. Folklore denotes the unwritten stories, beliefs, and customs of the European peasant. The myth is basically religious; its subject matter includes where we and the things in our world came from, why we are here, and where we are going. A myth may be said to express part of a people's world view.

3.

Legends are semihistorical narratives relating the deeds of heroes, the movements of peoples, and the establishment of local customs. The longer legends, sometimes in poetry or in rhythmic prose, are called epics. Legends provide clues as to what constitutes ethical behavior in a culture. These clues give legends their major anthropological significance. Tales are purely secular, nonhistorical narratives. Although they are recognized as fiction for entertainment, tales sometimes draw morals or teach practical lessons.

4.

The study of music has developed into the field of ethnomusicology. Human music is almost everywhere perceived in terms of a scale. Scale systems and their modifications comprise tonality in music. Tonality determines the possibilities and limits of melody and harmony. Rhythm is an organizing factor in music. Traditional European music is measured into recurrent patterns of two, three, and four beats.

5.

The social function of music is most obvious in song. Songs often express a group's values and concerns as much as tales do. The closed systems of tonality, rhythm, and musical form place restrictions on songs, making their expression more formal. Musical instruments are thought to have developed historically from experimentation with the augmentation of human sounds. The development of the musical instrument has advanced in stages through instruments such as the rattle, stamper, drum, and scraper. Music enables people to communicate and share their feelings in a symbolic and memorable way.

6.

Sculpture is any three-dimensional product of the creative imagination. Sculpted objects, such as a ceremonial knife, or an ornamental gate, represent an imaginative organization of materials in space A more modern term for sculpture is plastic art. Certain objects, although skillfully made, do not qualify as sculpture. This may be because they are somewhat trivial, low in symbolic content, or impermanent. Sculpture may be representational or abstract. Representational sculpture closely imitates the forms of nature; abstract sculpture draws from natural forms, but represents only their basic patterns. The anthropologist is interested in what is extracted from nature, and why.

Suggested readings

Boas, Franz. *Primitive Art*. New York: Dover, 1955.
The book gives an analytical description of the basic traits of primitive art. Its treatment is based on two principles: the fundamental sameness of mental processes in all races and cultural forms of the present day, and the consideration of every cultural phenomenon in a historical context. It covers formal elements in art, symbolism, and style and has sections on primitive literature, music, and dance.

Fraser, Douglas. *Primitive Art*. Garden City, New York: Doubleday, 1962.
The book presents a systematic survey of primitive art, aiming to place each style studied in relation to both its local setting and to other styles near and far away. The author covers the three main geographical areas of Africa, Asia-Oceania, and America. Good color illustrations.

Kurath, Gertrude Probosch. "Panorama of Dance Ethnology" in *Current Anthropology*, May 1960, Vol. 1.
The article is a detailed survey of dance ethnomethodology, describing and analyzing dance throughout the world. It includes problems of choreography, form, relation to other fields, and recording of dances. It also discusses technological aids, and the training of ethnologists.

Nettl, Bruno. *Music in Primitive Culture*. Cambridge: Harvard University Press, 1956.
The book is designed as an introduction to primitive music, and attempts to show the kinds of phenomena that characterize it. It provides examples of types of primitive music, shows how they have been studied, and provides general conclusions which have been drawn from them.

Thompson, Stith. *The Folktale*. New York: Holt, Rinehart and Winston, 1960.
The book serves as a guide to the study of the folktale, in both written and oral form. It includes an account of well-known Western folktales and their history, and a section on the classical folktale as reconstructed from literary remains. North American Indian tales serve as examples of primitive culture tales. The final section provides some analysis of theory and methods in the field.

Wingert, Paul. *Primitive Art: It's Traditions and Styles*. London: Oxford University Press, 1962. World, 1965.
The book serves as an introduction to primitive art, defining that term and examining various prevailing attitudes and approaches toward it. The method of approach places art in a cultural context, and analyzes objects from Africa, Oceania, and North America.

The Indian's story

Paintings on the following pages by European
and American artists depict in brief the history of the
American Indian—from tribal ways and existence on
the land, to increasing encroachment by white settlers,
armed conflict, and tragedy. The following speech, abridged
only slightly, was made by the Seneca Chief Red Jacket in response to
an address by a white missionary at Buffalo, New York, in 1805:

Brother, listen to what we say. There was a time when our
forefathers owned this great island. Their seats extended
from the rising to the setting sun. The Great Spirit had
made it for the use of the Indians. He had created the
buffalo, the deer and other animals for food. He made the
bear and the beaver, and their skins served us for clothing.
. . . He had caused the earth to produce corn for bread. All
this he had done for his red children because he loved them.
If we had any disputes about hunting grounds, they were
generally settled without the shedding of much blood: but
an evil day came upon us; your forefathers crossed the great
waters and landed on this island. Their numbers were small;
they found friends, not enemies; they told us they had fled
from their own country for fear of wicked men, and come here
to enjoy their religion. They asked for a small seat; we
took pity on them, granted their request, and they sat down
among us; yet we did not fear them, we took them to be
friends; they called us brothers, we believed them and
gave them a larger seat. At length their number had greatly
increased; they wanted more land; they wanted our country.

Rosa Bonheur, *Buffalo Hunt*

George Catlin, *Indian Meeting*

Charles M. Russell, *The Wagons*   Jules Tavernier, *The White Man's Weapon*

Erneste Etienne Narjot, *Colonel J. C. Cremony Leading a Fight Against the Apaches*

Charles M. Russell, *"Her heart is on the ground"*

Our eyes were opened, and our minds became uneasy. Wars took place; Indians were hired to fight against Indians, and many of our people were destroyed.

Brother, our seats were once large, and yours were very small; you have now become a great people, and we have scarcely a place left to spread our blankets; you have got our country, but you are not satisfied; you want to force your religion upon us.

Brother, continue to listen. You say that you are sent to instruct us how to worship the Great Spirit . . . you say that you are right and we are lost; how do we know this to be true? We understand that your religion is written in a book; if it was intended for us as well as you, why has not the Great Spirit given it to us, and not only to us but why did he not give to our forefathers the knowledge of that book with the means of understanding it rightly? . . . We also have a religion which was given to our forefathers and has been handed down to us their children. . . . It teaches us to be thankful for all the favors we receive; to love each other and to be united. We never quarrel about religion.

Brother, the Great Spirit has made us all; but he has . . . given us a different complexion and different customs. . . . Since he has made so great a difference between us in other things, why may we not conclude that he has given us a different religion according to our understanding. . . . Brother, we do not wish to destroy your religion, or take it from you; we only want to enjoy our own.

Brother, we are told that you have been preaching to white people in this place; these people are our neighbors, we are acquainted with them; we will wait a little while and see what effect your preaching has upon them. If we find it does them good, makes them honest and less disposed to cheat Indians, we will then consider again what you have said. . . . As we are going to part, we will come and take you by the hand and hope the Great Spirit will protect you. . . .

The minister refused to join hands, insisting "that there was no fellowship between the religion of God and the works of the devil." And the Indians left politely.

From Samuel G. Drake, Biography and History of the Indians of North America, 1851: as found in "The Winged Serpent," an anthology edited by Margot Astrov.
Paintings courtesy Kennedy Galleries, New York

part 7

Change
and the future

Culture
change

Culture is the medium through which the human species adapts to its physical and social environment. Various cultural institutions, such as kinship and marriage, political and economic organization, and religion, mesh together to form one fully integrated cultural system. Because this system is adaptive, it is fairly stable and remains so unless the conditions to which it is adapted change. Archaeological studies have revealed how elements of a culture may persist for long periods of time. For example, the calendar used a thousand years ago by the Pre-Columbian Maya of Central America is still used by some modern Maya communities. Similarly, today's Maya live in houses resembling those built by their forbears during the height of Maya civilization (250 to 870 A.D.).

Although the most striking feature of most cultures is stability, cultural change does take place—we need only look at the incredible diversity of cultures today, all ultimately derived, in less than two million years, from a hunting-gathering base. Even more amazing is the fact that all nonhunting-gathering cultures have developed in the past 10,000 years. The causes of change are various. One common cause is change in the environment, which must be followed by an

adaptive change in culture; another is individual variation in the way people within a culture perceive its characteristics, which may lead to a change in the way society in general interprets the norms and values of its culture. A third source of change is contact with other groups, which introduces new ideas and ways of doing things, eventually producing change in the traditional values and behavior.

Change is characteristic of all cultures, but the rate and direction of change vary considerably. Among the factors that influence the way change will occur within a given culture are: the degree to which a culture encourages and approves flexibility; the particular needs of the culture at a specific time; and, perhaps most important of all, the degree of "fit" between the new trait and the existing cultural matrix.

Even when cultural changes are most beneficial and adaptive they may well be difficult for individuals within the culture to accept. Thus cultural change is considered a social problem even though it is part of the necessary process of adaptation. New ways of doing things not only feel wrong, they also require relearning. An example of this can be seen in the problems of Americans who move to England, where cars are driven on the left-hand side of the road rather than the right. In this case the individual's very body has become adjusted to certain patterns of behavior that bypass his presumed "openness" to change.

Mechanisms of change

Cultural change may be slow, occurring over long periods of time, or it may be rapid, occurring over relatively brief periods of time. The processes or mechanisms which determine cultural change are diffusion, invention, devolution, and accultura-tion. Diffusion is generally associated with slow rates of cultural change, while invention and acculturation are associated with rapid change. Devolution, or loss of a culture trait without replacement, may be either a slow or rapid change.

Invention

The term **invention** refers to the formation, by a single individual, of a new habit, tool, or principle that eventually gains the acceptance of others and thus becomes socially shared. It may be passed along through imitation by all members of society or by a subculture or subgroup such as an age-grade, status, or kinship group. The prestige of the inventor and imitating groups may influence the degree of social acceptance, while the invention's acceptance depends on how much better it is than the thing or idea it replaces.

The term "invention" can be further broken down into "primary" and "secondary" inventions. Primary inventions are the chance discoveries of new principles; secondary inventions are the improvements made by applying known principles. The bow may be considered the primary invention from which not only the bow and arrow but also the musical bow and the bow drill emerged; the latter, because it contained the principle of the shaft, gave rise ultimately to the potter's wheel and the wheel and axle. Another primary invention, the cooking oven, led to the

Figure 25-1. *Technological innovations require a leap forward in the imagination not only of the inventor but also of the beholder, as these pictures (the top is of the Wright Brothers' flight) show.*

pottery kiln, harder pottery, the discovery of ore smelting, and finally to the forced-draft furnace.

Primary inventions may set off rapid cultural change and stimulate other inventions. Indeed, cultural values and goals can themselves lead to inventions. There are many instances of an invention that had more than one discoverer: the theory of evolution, for example, was proposed by Wallace as well as Darwin; three men separately produced the telescope; and the steamboat had no less than four inventors—all of whom worked before Fulton's time. On the other hand, an invention's chance of acceptance is limited if it fails to fit into a society's pattern of established needs, values, and goals. Galileo's discovery of the rotation of the planets and Mendel's contribution to genetics are instances of genuine creative insights out of step with the needs of their times. In fact, Mendel's work remained obscure until 16 years after his death when it was "rediscovered" by three scientists working independently in 1900. Mendel's discovery thus is an example of an idea whose time had not yet come.

Diffusion

In cultural borrowing, or **diffusion,** the "inventor" is the introducer of a new cultural element from another society. Murdock[1] cites the colonial European-Americans, who borrowed not just the use of corn, squash, and beans but the entire Indian way of producing them. Borrowing is so common that Malinowski,[2] for instance, regarded it as being just as creative as other forms of cultural innovation, and Linton[3] suggested that borrowing accounts for 90 percent of any culture's content. People never borrow all available innovations but exercise a high degree of selectivity, limiting their selections to those compatible with

the existing culture. The Hopi, for example, have accepted the tin roofs, stoves, and glass of the white man but have resisted tractors and modern farm equipment. The Hopi religion, it seems, has certain rites essential to planting and harvesting with which machinery would interfere. Adoption would require far-reaching changes in Hopi religious practices.[4] On the whole, some areas, like technology, are highly prone to borrowing, and others, like social organization, far less likely to be borrowed. In all cases, the borrowed innovation must satisfy needs quicker and better than what has previously existed.

While the tendency toward borrowing is so great as to lead Robert Lowie to comment, "Culture is a thing of shreds and patches," the borrowed traits usually undergo sufficient modifications to make this wry comment more colorful than critical. Moreover, the borrowed trait may modify existing cultural traits. An awareness of the extent of borrowing can be eye-opening. Beals, for instance, points out the numerous things we have borrowed from the American Indians. Plants domesticated by the Indians— "Irish" potatoes, corn, beans, squash, and sweet potatoes—furnish nearly half the world's food supply. Among drugs and stimulants, tobacco is the best known, but others include coca in cocaine, ephedra in ephedrine, datura in pain relievers, and cascara in laxatives. Native American varieties of cotton cultivated by Indians supply much of the world's clothing needs, while the woolen poncho, the parka, and moccasins are universally familiar items. Not only has American literature been permanently shaped by such works as Longfellow's *Hiawatha* and James Fenimore Cooper's *Leather-Stocking Tales,* but American Indian music has contributed such ultramodern devices as unusual intervals, arbitrary scales, conflicting rhythms, and hypnotic monotony to world music. A further list of cultural borrowings can be seen in "Biases and Borrowings" in Chapter 13.

[1] George P. Murdock, "How Culture Changes," in *Man, Culture and Society,* Harry L. Shapiro, ed. (Chicago: University of Chicago Press, 1956).
[2] Bronislaw Malinowski, *The Dynamics of Culture Change* (New Haven: Yale University Press, 1945).
[3] Ralph Linton, *The Study of Man* (New York: Appleton-Century-Crofts, 1940).

[4] Alan R. Beals *et al., Culture in Process,* 2nd edition (New York: Holt, Rinehart and Winston, 1973) p. 298.

Devolution

Most often, we tend to think of change as an accumulation of innovations; new things being added to those already there. We do so because this seems so much a part of the way we live. A little reflection, however, leads to the realization that frequently the acceptance of a new innovation leads to the loss of an older one. This sort of replacement is not just a feature of Western civilization. For example, at one time the Indians of northeastern North America learned the art of making pottery, which then came into widespread use in the region. By the time Europeans arrived on the scene, this seemingly useful trait had been lost, and containers were made of basketry and birch bark instead. Actually, pottery is heavier and more breakable than baskets and birch bark containers, a serious drawback for peoples who move about from one campsite to another and must carry their belongings themselves. Basketry and birch bark were better adapted to their way of life than pottery.

Often overlooked is another facet of the loss of apparently useful traits: loss without replacement. This phenomenon we may call devolution, and it constitutes change just as surely as does the acceptance of a new innovation.

An example of devolution is the abandonment of an admittedly important ceremony by the Itza, a group of Indians living in the community of Soccotz, British Honduras (Belize). The ceremony, known as *primicias,* was a public ritual expression of gratitude to the deities. It was sponsored by an extended family in times of illness, with the object of overwhelming the deities by the quantity of offerings and the emotional intensity. For this, the utmost solemnity and propriety were mandatory for 24 hours. Moderation in all things, sexual restrictions, and achievement of a uniform feeling were essential. In short, a kind of mental paralysis through concentration was necessary to the success of the whole venture. The deities would tolerate no error, and the result of carelessness was death.

In 1942, the Itza became convinced that *pri-micias* presented an impossible task for human beings to accomplish, and so they abandoned it. This was the result of death apparently resulting from carelessness; the right attitudes were not maintained without exception for the 24-hour period. For example, in one case the wife of an ill person complained she was not rich enough. Following this, their food soured, the man died, and his wife followed soon afterwards. Shortly after that, a son died, and then the Ah-men who had conducted the ceremony died. As a result of this and other cases, public *primicias* are no longer given. As far as the Itza are concerned, it is better to have a sick man die than risk a wider calamity.

Acculturation

The process of **acculturation** demands special attention from anthropologists. Acculturation results when groups of individuals having different cultures come into intensive firsthand contact, with subsequent major changes in the original culture patterns of one or both groups. Its numerous variables include degree of cultural difference; circumstances, intensity, frequency, and amiability of contact; relative status of the agents of contact; who is dominant and who is submissive; and whether the nature of the flow is reciprocal or nonreciprocal.

Anthropologists use the following terms to describe what may happen during acculturation:

1) **Substitution,** in which a pre-existing trait or complex may be replaced by one that fills its function, involving minimal structural change;

2) **Syncretism,** in which old traits blend to form a new system, possibly resulting in considerable cultural change;

3) **Addition,** in which new traits or complexes may be added, and structural change may or may not occur;

4) **Deculturation,** in which part of a culture may be lost;

5) **Origination** of new traits to meet the needs of the changing situation;

Change and the future ● part **7**

Figure 25-2a. *A Tahitian woman cuts her grass with a gasoline-powered lawnmower.*

Figure 25-2b. *A Kenya television station broadcasts an American-style game show.*

Figure 25-2c. *A Camerounian schoolgirl does her homework on a typewriter.*

Figure 25-2d. *Mexican boys carry a portable radio styled to resemble a television set.*

25 chapter ● **Culture change**

6) **Rejection,** in which changes may be so rapid that a large number of persons cannot accept them, resulting in either total rejection, rebellion, or revitalization movements.

As a result of one or a number of these processes, acculturation may then develop along several lines. Merger or assimilation occurs when two cultures lose their separate identities and form a single culture. Incorporation takes place when one culture loses autonomy but retains its identity as a subculture, such as a caste, class, or ethnic group; this is typical of conquest or slavery situations. Extinction is the phenomenon in which one culture loses its individual members until it can no longer function, and members either die out or join other cultures. In adaptation, a new structure may develop in dynamic equilibrium. In this last instance change may continue, but in the slow, "melting pot" form.

It should be emphasized that acculturation and diffusion are totally disparate terms; one culture can borrow from another without being in the least acculturated.

Forcible change

Quite logically, instances of the acceptance of change are highest when the element of change results from a need within the society. This may represent a simple society's striving to economically adapt to the worldwide technological revolution, even though the ramifications of the change may be felt throughout the society. The changing roles of women in Africa, or, for that matter, right here, may be considered an example of such a change. However, changes are often imposed from outside a culture, usually by colonialism and conquest. We have examined in Chapter 23 two examples of societies attempting to deal with such intrusions: the cargo cults of Melanesia and the Ghost Dance of the American Indian. Here we will look at some of the anthropological theories that attempt to explain the dynamics of changes that are forcibly imposed.

Colonialism and conquest

One positive aspect of colonialism is the growth of applied anthropology and the use of anthropological techniques in helping a society improve itself in accordance with the goals it—and the anthropologists, too—sets up. British anthropology, for the most part, has often been considered the "handmaiden" of that country's intensive colonial policy. American applied anthropology began with World War II, and the first efforts at colonial administration, especially in the Pacific, were made by officers trained in anthropology. The rapid recovery of Japan was due in no small measure to the influence of anthropologists in structuring the American occupation. Other American experiments aimed at a full understanding of native culture so the colonial culture could fit into a native structure with the least possible disturbance also bore fruit. Although many of these studies were admittedly for purposes of military intelligence, they proved useful also in postwar programs.

On the other side of the coin, however, and reflected especially in the early literature of contact between Europeans or Americans with indigenous groups, is a complete lack of anthropological understanding, and often of humaneness. Such contacts frequently brought to many areas the decimation, misery, and community degeneration that is known colloquially as "culture crash." Severe disruption of the traditional community life, with indications of social chaos or discord and personal or individual malaise, often followed in the wake of colonial occupation. This by no means implies that traditional societies were frictionless before contact with "civilization" but rather that existing conflicts could be handled through established cultural institutions without prolonged disruptions of daily life. In these early cases, degeneration occurred because traditional institutions designed to deal with traditional stress or conflict could not cope with new and rapid change that did not fit into the context of the traditional system. Too rapid change in a value system, for example, leaves other parts of the

Figure 25-3. *These Indians are listening to a recorded speech made to them by President Wilson.*

culture to catch up. Beals points out the rather striking change brought to the Manus of the Admiralty Islands as studied by Margaret Mead:

> The anthropologist had left an isolated, nonliterate people twenty-five years earlier. She returned to find them moving rapidly and purposefully into the stream of modern world culture. She found them searching for education that would permit them and their children to participate more fully in the modern world. And this occurred in one lifetime![5]

Whereas most anthropologists had thought that rapid change was disruptive, Dr. Mead suggested the opposite: if change is desired by an entire group and if it affects all the culture and its parts simultaneously, there may be less social disorganization and personal maladjustment than if changes occur segmentally over a long period of time. The great danger, Beals observes, is that the Manus believed that by modelling themselves in the image of American society they could participate in a world dominated by the Western way of doing things and benefit from this participation. If they should find out, as many other peoples have discovered, that this is not necessarily the case, they too will become discouraged and demoralized. One way that the Manus manifested their faith in the American way of life was through the cargo cults.

The most extreme cases of acculturation usually occur as a result of military conquest and displacement of traditional political authority by the conquerors who know nothing about the culture they control. The indigenous people, unable to resist imposed changes and restricted in their traditional social, religious, and economic activities, may be forced into new activities that tend to isolate individuals and tear apart social integration. Slavery in the early years of the United States, possibly the best-known example to us, provides many explanations for racial problems once shrugged off as inferiority. It should be pointed out that slavery in early America was not confined to the United States. As part of the

[5] *Ibid.,* pp. 305-7.

prevailing economic system (known as "the plantation system") slavery was characteristic of the Caribbean Islands and coastal South America. The racial problems the United States inherited from the slavery era are shared by other areas in the Americas where slavery was practiced.

Rebellion and revolt

When the scale of forced acculturation reaches a certain level, the possibilities for rebellion and revolt—such as the Cuban Revolution or the Red Revolution on Mainland China—are high.

The question of why revolutions come into being, as well as why they frequently fail to live up to the expectations of the people initiating them, is a problem. It is clear, however, that the colonial policies of countries such as England, France, Spain, Portugal, and the United States during the nineteenth and early twentieth centuries have created a worldwide situation in which revolution has become nearly inevitable. In numerous technologically undeveloped lands which have been exploited by more powerful countries for their natural resources and cheap labor, a deep resentment of the foreign ruling classes prevails. Lack of responsiveness to this feeling makes revolution or rebellion in some emerging nations the only alternative. One historian who has examined four revolutions of the past—English, American, French, and Bolshevik—offers the following conditions that may precipitate rebellion and revolt:

1) Loss of prestige of established authority, often as a result of the failure of foreign policy, financial difficulties, dismissals of popular ministers, or alteration of popular policies.

2) Threat to recent economic improvement. In France and Russia, those sections of the population (professional classes and urban workers) whose economic fortunes had previously taken an upward swing, were "radicalized" by unexpected setbacks such as steeply rising food prices and unemployment.

3) Indecisiveness of government, as exempli-fied by lack of consistent policy; such governments appear to be controlled by, rather than in control of, events.

4) Loss of support of the intellectual class. Such a loss deprived the prerevolutionary governments of France and Russia of philosophical support, thus leading to their lack of popularity with the literate public.

5) A leader or group of leaders with charisma enough to mobilize a substantial part of the population against the establishment.

Apart from resistance to internal authority, such as in the English, French, and Russian Revolutions, many revolutions in modern times have been struggles against an externally imposed authority. Such resistance usually takes the form of independence movements that wage campaigns of armed defiance against colonial powers. The Algerian struggle for independence from France and the American Revolution are typical examples.

Revolts are not without their own problems. Hoebel quotes Max Gluckman writing of rebellion to oust the incumbents of offices without attempting to alter the nature of these offices. According to Gluckman, rebellions:

'throw the rascals out' and substitute another set, but there is no attempt to alter either the cultural ideology or the form of the social structure. In political revolution, attempts are made to seize the offices of power in order to change social structure, belief systems, and their symbolic representations. Political revolutions are usually turbulent, violent, and not long-lasting. A successful revolution soon moves to re-establish a stable, though changed, social structure; yet it has far-reaching political, social, and sometimes economic and cultural consequences.[6]

It should be pointed out, however, that revolution is a relatively recent phenomenon, occurring only during the last 5000 years. The reason for this is the fact that political rebellion requires a centralized political authority (or state) to rebel

[6]E. Adamson Hoebel, *Anthropology: The Study of Man,* 4th edition (New York: McGraw-Hill, 1972) p. 667.

against; the state has been in existence for only 5000 years. Obviously, then, in primitive societies, typified by tribes and bands and in other non-industrial societies lacking central authority, there could not have been rebellion or political revolution.

Hoebel characterizes as benign the cultural revolutions that move technologies and societies in a significant, though hardly discernible, direction while they are in progress. Through this kind of revolution alone can the quality of life be fundamentally and irrevocably altered. He cites as examples the development of Paleolithic culture when man developed toolmaking, the use of fire, speech, and symbolic systems; the Neolithic Revolution, which saw the development of food production; the Urban Revolution, during which cities and civilization emerged; and today's urbanization, that continues with the assimilation of the last of the earth's small-scale peoples within the cultural network of civilization.

Revitalization movements. One important aspect of rebellion and revolt as modes of forcible change is the revitalization process. Revitalization may be defined as a deliberate attempt by some members of a society to construct a more satisfactory culture by the rapid acceptance of a pattern of multiple innovations.[7] Once primary ties of culture, social relationships, and activities are broken, and meaningless activity imposed by force, individuals and groups characteristically react with fantasy, withdrawal, and escape.

Perhaps the most dramatic example of the revitalization theory is found in our own country, where today's youth turn to drugs in their attempt to deal with the imposed values of the American dream. Thus, many American youths have adopted lifestyles completely different from those of the preceding generation. Revolting against an overwhelming technology, they call for a return to the earth and simpler ways of living. Their revolt is expressed in their use of drugs, outlandish or "freaky" clothes, hair styles, music, speech,

[7]Anthony Wallace, *Culture and Personality* (New York: Random House, 1961).

and in their behavior toward authority and authority figures.

Investigators have pointed out that American youth is reacting not against the American dream, but against the fact that reality as they perceive it does not reflect the dream. These scholars believe that whenever the ideal and the real cultures are too disparate, revitalization movements are inevitable.

Clearly, when value systems get out of step with existing realities, a condition of cultural crisis is likely to build up that may breed some form of reactive movement. Not all suppressed, conquered, or colonialized people eventually rebel against established authority, although why they do not is still a debated issue. When they do, however, resistance may take one of the following forms, all of which are varieties of revitalization movements. A culture may seek to speed up the acculturation process in order to share more fully in the supposed benefits of the dominant cultures, as the cargo cults, in which case it is called **transitional.** It may attempt to resurrect a suppressed pariah group that has long suffered in an inferior social standing and that has its own special subcultural ideology, and is then referred to as **millenarism;** the most familiar examples of this are prophetic Judaism and early Christianity. If a movement tries to reconstitute a destroyed but not forgotten way of life, as did the Ghost Dance of the Plains Indians, it is known as **nativistic** or **revivalistic.** If the aim of the movement is directed primarily to the ideological system and the attendant social structure of a cultural system from within, it is then called **revolutionary.**

Modernization

Two of the most frequently used terms in describing social change as it occurs today through any of the aforementioned processes are urbanization and modernization. Urbanization implies the influence of western technology but need not be so limited. Modernization is a more general term that includes the less disruptive types of change.

One aspect of modernization, the technological explosion, has made it possible to transport human beings and ideas from one place to another with astounding speed and in great numbers. Formerly independent cultural systems have been brought into contact with others. Cultural systems that once served a multipolitical function have come to serve relatively few functions. Vast increases in population have multiplied the number of existing cultural systems. The cultural differences between New York and Pukapuka are declining, while the differences between fishermen and physicists are increasing. No one knows whether this implies a net gain or net loss in cultural diversity, but the worldwide spread of anything, whether it is DDT or a new idea, should be viewed with at least caution. That human beings as human cultural systems are different is the most exciting thing about them, yet the destruction of diversity is implicit in the worldwide spread of rock and roll, communism, capitalism, or anything else. When a song is forgotten or a ceremony ceases to be performed, a part of the human heritage is destroyed forever.

An examination of several small-scale cultures which have felt the impact of modernization or other cultural changes will be examined to pinpoint some of the problems these cultures have met. The cultures are the Pueblo Indians of the American Southwest, the Tanala of Madagascar, the Blackfeet Indians of Montana, and African tribal society in general.

The modern Pueblo Indians

An interesting example of an entire culture that has continuously undergone change in the last century are the Pueblo Indians of the American Southwest. The Pueblo, traditionally an agricultural people with a population of about 200,000, have been studied by Edward Dozier, himself a Tewa Indian, and others. Despite the influence of the Spanish and American conquest, basic Pueblo culture and society have endured. Dozier has

Figure 25-4. *Many European countries have sent technological "missionaries" to teach people in other countries new ways of doing old tasks.*

attributed this to the retention of the large extended family and the community as primary units of socialization and the persistence of indigenous languages. The traditional network of kin and community relations has not been disturbed. Thus, these factors have formed the same personality types over the years and have continued to reproduce individuals faithful to Pueblo beliefs. Pueblo social structure has remained virtually intact because the Indians have been able to retain their basic ethical and moral concepts.

However, outside influences, primarily those of the materialistic and technological American culture, have forced a number of cultural changes among the Pueblo. Not surprisingly, many of these changes have arisen as a result of modifications in the Pueblo's traditional agrarian economy.

As a result of their exposure to, and domination by, Americans, the Indians have abandoned their subsistence farming economy and have adopted the western credit system and cash economy. Thus, many facets of Pueblo life have changed. For example, the Pueblo village, or pueblo, has changed many of its communal characteristics. Isolated family adobe homes are replacing the traditional apartmentlike dwellings. Some of the more Americanized villages boast single-family dwellings similar to American houses, complete with garage, lawn, trees, yard, and shrubbery. Many villages also have electricity, running water, and inside plumbing.

Family possessions also reveal the increased economic status of many of the Pueblos: the furnishings found in a modern Pueblo home are quite similar to those found in many contemporary American homes. In the Santa Clara pueblo of New Mexico, television antennas are as numerous as in any small American town. Indeed, for many Pueblos, the television set has replaced the traditional gathering of the bilateral kin group to listen to Pueblo stories and legends. The formerly all-important corn-grinding equipment—*metates* and *manos*—is gone. Manufactured chairs and couches rest side by side with the trunk containing the ceremonial and dance

paraphernalia. In nearly all pueblos, the long pole suspended from the ceiling to hold the family's clothing and possessions has disappeared. While the Pueblos still wear their brightly colored dresses and shawls, they purchase these items from stores rather than manufacture them themselves as in the past. Refrigerators and pantries have taken the place of the small back room where melons were stored and corn was stacked. The busy activities of the annual harvest time have been replaced by weekend shopping trips to the local supermarket.

In most pueblos, automobiles and pickup trucks furnish the transport once provided by horses and wagons. Working for wages in nearby towns and cities is the new way of Pueblo life, and it does not seem probable that farming will ever return as the primary economic occupation. This is because Pueblo thinking remains communal and small scale; those Pueblos who still practice farming are no match for their profit-minded American counterparts. The Indians think only in terms of planting small plots of corn and garden crops rather than multi-acre cash crops. Similarly, investment in land, livestock, and machinery are beyond the Pueblo way of thinking.

In spite of all the outward materialistic and economic changes, the Pueblo remain a communal people, chiefly because of their social organization. Disagreements, which are common in every pueblo, are seen as family quarrels and have rarely broken up a village. In fact, most Pueblo communities occupy the same sites they have lived on for centuries before the Spanish came. One reason for the long life of the Pueblo community is found in the ways they deal with criminals: discipline is harsh, and eviction from the community is not a rare punishment for a persistent wrongdoer. Another more important reason for the survival of the Pueblo is the integration found in Pueblo lifestyles. Kroeber has described the integration of the Zuni; his description is just as applicable to the other Pueblos:

Four or five different planes of systemization crosscut each other and thus preserve for the whole society an integrity that would speedily be lost if the planes merged and thereby inclined to encourage segregation and fission. The clans (among the Tanoans, extended families and moieties), the fraternities, the priesthoods, the kivas, in a measure the gaming parties, are all dividing agencies. If they coincided, the rifts in the social structure would be deep; by countering each other they cause segmentations which produce an almost marvelous complexity, but can never break the national entity apart.[8]

Just as the central core of Pueblo life remains, so do their religion and ceremonials, despite the fact that the farming life around which they were built no longer exists. Pueblo religion still provides its members with recreational outlets and a strengthening of communal living and identity. Dozier theorizes that this may be sufficient to keep the religion alive and to maintain the positions required for the rich ceremonial and religious life. In the face of the American economic influence, it is surprising that among many Pueblos there appears to be a religious upsurge, and many ceremonies which have long been in disuse have been resurrected and reenacted in a number of pueblos. This may be due to a revitalistic movement among the Indians, or it may have something to do with the Pueblo agricultural background. Edward Spicer has observed that religion developed in an agricultural ethos may survive in other settings. For example, the Yaquis, who like the Pueblos work for wages in the city, still believe and practice the ancient ceremonies of their religion. The same holds true for the Pueblo; while many of them work in neighboring cities, they continue to practice their age-old ceremonies.

The Tanala of Madagascar

Despite the effects of modernization, the Pueblos have been able to maintain their own special cultural identity. What happens to a culture when

[8] Alfred L. Kroeber, quoted in Edward Dozier, *The Pueblo Indians of North America* (New York: Holt, Rinehart and Winston, 1970) p. 19.

it adopts a new method of food production because of a change in the natural environment? One such people, the Tanala of Madagascar, were forced to adapt to a new kind of environment. When dwindling land resources pressured the Tanala to change from dry rice cultivation to the newer technique of wet rice cultivation, an entirely new social system evolved. Under the traditional system, the Tanala moved their villages from one area to another as land was depleted. When they adopted the new cultivation technique, the Tanala were transformed from an individualistic, democratic society to a class-society with a king, a system of warfare, settled villages, and a less permissive family life.

The new cultivation techniques made available large tracts of land that previously had been unusable and hence undesirable. As a result, a new class of landowners emerged with a concomitant breakdown in the traditional Tanala extended family structure. The unity of the family was destroyed because the new cultivation technique required only a single family to tend it and not, as in the past, the cooperation of large numbers of people.

The new rice fields became the center of a permanent settlement because the new technique did not deplete the land. Some families, caught in a land squeeze as the permanent sites became occupied, had to move further and further into the jungle, thus becoming separated and isolated from the rest of the village. Each village was surrounded by a group of irrigation fields under private ownership and a constellation of "branch" or offshoot villages with a similar social organization.

Methods of warfare also changed because permanent settlements required permanent upkeep and defense. Extensive defensive systems requiring big investments had to be initiated and maintained to assure each village of adequate protection.

Religion, as practiced by the extended family, did not lose its importance in the culture of the Tanalans. Even after the households of the extended family had been dispersed, its members would come together on ceremonial occasions to venerate common ancestors. Intermarriage between different permanent villages occurred, and thus Tanala society moved from independent villages to tribal organization. Tribal organization gave rise to kingship. However, the kingdom ended before any adequate machinery of government could be brought into play.

The Blackfeet Indians of North America

Unlike the tightly-knit and communally-organized Pueblo Indians who resisted modernization, the Blackfeet Indians of Montana have uniquely adjusted to modernization. Among the Blackfeet, a bicultural community has evolved: the white-oriented group is organized around such values as work, individuality, acquisitiveness, and pursuit of future goals. The Indian-oriented group, on the other hand, attempts to retain its ethnic and cultural identity, staving off full economic integration with the encroaching American culture.

Anthropologist Malcolm McFee has described how this bicultural community functions in his study, *Modern Blackfeet Montanans on a Reservation.* According to McFee,

> The past events have not resulted in tribal disorganization, but in a reorganization that accommodates the simultaneous persistence of many traditional social and cultural characteristics from both interacting societies. A large part of the tribe has adopted the culture of the dominant (American) society and aspires to assimilate. A smaller number, for reasons already mentioned, retains more from the Blackfeet past and resists further change. The reservation social structure has changed to accommodate these contrasting points of view. The structure of a nonreservation community tends to be unilinear, with one general set of values, and one status hierarchy. But the physical and social boundaries of the reservation and the tribe incorporate two societies, and make possible a linear structure that offers a choice

of alternative limitations and possibilities for adoption. An individual, consciously or otherwise, can choose, and possibly choose again, which pattern he wishes to follow. His choice, and his acceptance and class assignment, depend upon what he brings to the situation in the way of aspirations, experiences, and capabilities.[9]

Changing tribal Africa

Colin Turnbull's concluding observations of his study of Africa in transition embody many of the essential features of the entire changing world: the removal of economic activities from the family-community setting; the altered structure of the family in the face of the changing labor market; the increased reliance of young children on parents for affection instead of on the extended family; the decline of general paternal authority; schools replacing the family as the primary educational unit; the discovery of the generation gap; and many others.

Among Turnbull's observations are many that reinforce some of the ideas that we have thus far discussed. For example:

> The Africa we have been looking at has been tribal Africa. The tribe still exists, and tribal ways still flourish in many parts of the continent. But change has come to other parts, and change is sweeping through everywhere. No tribes are untouched. Even when change comes, however, it cannot destroy everything it finds. It has to build on something. So the African tribal past is very important if we are to understand what is happening in Africa today. . . .
>
> Africa has seen many invasions from outside, just as it has seen continuous movement and invasions within. Greeks, Romans, Arabs, Southeast Asians, and Chinese have all at one time or another come to Africa and left their mark. Most recently of course came the Euro-

---

[9] Malcolm McFee, *Modern Blackfeet Montanans on a Reservation* (New York: Holt, Rinehart and Winston, 1972).

pean colonial powers, bringing change more drastic than anything that had been seen until then. These colonial powers brought with them a new and total way of life. They did not just bring change by being there, they did everything they could to force change. There was a conscious effort. They tried to bring change not to just one aspect of African life, but to the whole tribal way of life. . . The European colonial powers felt that the ideal would be for Africans to live and behave just like Europeans. Wherever schools were set up they were designed to bring this kind of change. It really amounted to an all-out attack on tribal life. On top of this, with the changes that colonialization brought in the way countries were governed, more and more Africans found that they were forced to abandon much of their traditional life. The tragedy is that it all happened so suddenly that there was no time for tribal society to adapt itself gradually, as it had always done in the past. It was as though the whole foundation had suddenly been swept away from beneath it. Yet tribal society is still far from dead, and in some ways it seems to be asserting itself again. . . .

As [the modern African child] grows up the change continues. Horizons begin to widen but again in a pattern quite unfamiliar in the tribe. Rather than learning about life by watching and being with parents and older relatives all the time, children are separated from their parents more and more, and spend their time at school. It is in school that they learn things that will help them in their future life. The break with their parents has already begun. Not only are they spending more time away from home, but they are learning things that will make them different from their parents. A boy whose father is a road worker may be learning to be an engineer. A boy whose father is a farmer may be learning to be a lawyer. No longer do children follow in the ways of their fathers, let alone their ancestors. . .[10]

[10] Colin M. Turnbull, *Tradition and Change in African Tribal Life* (New York: World Publishing Company, 1966).

Figure 25-5. *Slow change is coming to the Masai, a tribe of herdsmen. Young girls of the tribe are being taught agriculture, a skill needed for the adjustment to a settled way of life. The men of the tribe are being taught scientific methods of animal husbandry, such as vaccination against disease.*

Modernization:
Must it always be painful?

Although most anthropologists see the traditional acculturation process among primitive peoples caught up in the modern technological world as an ordeal, some scholars, like sociologist Alex Inkeles, see emerging from the process of modernization a new kind of man.[11] This man is kind of a prototype who, whether he comes from an African tribe, a South American village, or an American city, will be open to accept and benefit from the changes in the modern world. The first element in his definition of the modern man is a readiness for new experience and an openness to innovation and change. Here he is talking of a "state of mind, a psychological disposition, an inner readiness," rather than of specific techniques and skills a man or group may possess because of an attained level of technology. In this sense, therefore, a man working with a wooden plow may be more modern in spirit than someone in another part of the world who drives a tractor.

Secondly, a man is more "modern" if he "has a disposition to form or hold opinions over a large number of the problems and issues that arise not only in his immediate environment but also outside of it . . ." This man shows more awareness of the diversity of attitude and opinion around him rather than closing himself off in the belief that everyone thinks alike and, indeed, just like him. He is able to acknowledge differences of opinion without needing to deny differences out of fear that they will upset his own view of the world; he is also less likely to approach opinion in a strictly autocratic or hierarchical way.

Adaptation to cultural change. In the past mankind has survived periods of explosive cultural change similar to ours. Ten thousand years ago the invention of agriculture brought a period of rapidly increasing population, energy con-

[11] Alex Inkeles, "The Modernization of Man" in *Modernization: The Dynamics of Growth*, Myron Weiner, ed. (New York: Basic Books) pp. 141-44.

sumption, and invention. Self-limiting as this revolution proved once the potentials inherent in agriculture were worked out, it nevertheless witnessed environmental destruction and decline in population among numerous peoples in its wake. If civilizations such as these could destroy their own limited world, our worldwide civilization is certainly capable of far more destructive acts.

Whether or not the current cultural explosion proves to be self-limiting, however, certain scholars foresee that the systems caught up in it must adapt within the next few generations to a totally different and unprecedented set of environmental circumstances. If this adaptation is to be planned and systematic, it must, they say, make use of the experience and wisdom preserved in the existing variety of human cultural systems. The problem of unlimited population growth may perhaps be solved through the development of new techniques of contraception and abortion; but it also needs to be solved culturally through the introduction of new traditions, new forms of marriage, and new social arrangements.

The population explosion too can be regarded as a reflection of the rapid development of new ideas and ways of doing things. It would hardly have been possible without great increase in the production of food and other requirements for human existence. The numerous developments in technology have inevitably led to an explosive increase in man's capacity to exterminate himself or to alter the face of the earth. The threats of atomic warfare, bacteriological warfare, or chemical warfare are obvious and visible. Less visible are those threats posed by the introduction of new chemicals or by slow but massive changes in the seas, land masses, and atmosphere of earth, problems for physicists or marine biologists but also for human cultural traditions and human social arrangements.

Change in basic cultural units and the growing bureaucracy. As cultural traditions and cultural systems have become larger and more all-encompassing, the little traditions of neighborhood, community, and tribe have lost their uniqueness and their coherence. One hundred years ago most of the population of the earth lived in small communities, and in intimate relationship to their neighbors. Because the small community has been so general and pervasive for so many years, anthropologists have often drawn the conclusion that communities are essential to the preservation of human identity and well-being. In the modern world, it almost seems as if the small group and the small community have been declared enemies of the state. It is believed to be more efficient to have one large university with ten thousand students than ten small universities. The same principle holds true for factories and farms and all the other contexts within which people work, play, or live.

Modernization has also affected another basic cultural entity, the family. For example, Neil Smelser observes modernization's tendency to encourage "the development of a family unit that is formed on emotional attraction and built on a limited sexual-emotional basis." The family, he adds, removed from other major social spheres except for the segmental external ties of individual family members, impinges less on other social spheres, making nepotism an illegitimate basis for recruitment into roles and making the family a one-dimensional institution.[12]

In many modern societies, the life of the individual is governed not by small cultural units such as the family, or neighbors, or religious organization, but by faceless bureaucracies. In modern states and cities, such bureaucracies contend against each other for resources and seek to increase their size and influence. Whether seeking to grow or to control their clients, bureaucracies formulate new rules and employ more persons to enforce them. The individual is governed now, not by the cultural traditions of his community, but by the countless and inexplicable rules of the innumerable bureaucracies with which he must deal in order to survive. On the other hand, with the evolution of larger and larger cultural systems, and the increasing inclusion of mankind within a single world order, perhaps all of this is necessary, but perhaps it is time to consider what has been sacrificed upon the altars of modernity and efficiency.

Understanding cultural change. Since we cannot reverse the tide of this phenomenon for which we are at least in part responsible, the next best thing may be to continue our efforts to understand just where and how to apply our technological, sociological, psychological, and, above all, anthropolitical discoveries. For change will always be with us. In the words of Murdock:

> change is always uncomfortable and often painful, and people frequently get discouraged with its slowness or even despair of achieving any genuine improvement. Neither history nor anthropology, however, gives cause for pessimism. However halting or harsh it may appear to participants, cultural change is always adaptive and usually progressive. It is also inevitable and will endure as long as the earth can support human life. Nothing—not even an atomic war—can destroy civilization.[13]

As soon as such a statement goes into print it is challenged. Whether or not it is true, it is undeniably true that since this statement was issued the world as we know it has changed, in some areas beyond recognition, and in the face of numerous threats to civilization, we are still here.

☐

[12] Neil J. Smelser, "The Modernization of Social Relations" in Weiner, *op. cit.,* p. 119.

[13] Murdock, *op. cit.,* p. 260.

THE MODERNIZATION OF JAPAN

And what has happened since the end of the Tokugawa era to the family and other kin groups, the common-interest associations, the structure of Japanese society in general? Some of the major trends may be summarized as a decline in the size and functional importance of the family and other kin groups, a weakening of the bonds of kinlike personal ties with unrelated persons, a change in patterns of authority within the family and elsewhere, and the emergence or increased growth of many impersonal institutions that provide economic and social security. Social classes have taken form following occupational lines, and all indications point to the growth of a huge urban middle class.

The nuclear family is the prevailing form throughout the nation. At least until the young go out into the world as adults, however, ties between familial members remain intimate. When relatives beyond husband, wife, and their children live under one roof and form part of the familial unit, these are customarily the aged parents of the household head and the family is rural rather than urban. In the city a sentiment has grown against living with one's parent, parents-in-law, or mature children, and the idea is not a total stranger to rural residents. Father's voice has lost a good deal of authority and mother's has gained. Younger sons are often at no disadvantage as compared with the eldest son, and sisters and new brides have lost some of their meekness. To prepare them for an adult life that is likely to take them away from farming, younger sons and even daughters of rural families may receive more formal education than eldest sons, who are ordinarily expected to remain on the farm. The mother-in-law who attempts to dominate her son's bride is in danger of being branded as "feudal," a demeaning word. A common postwar saying is that two things have grown in strength since the war, stockings—now of tough nylon—and women.

The relationship between man and wife is both more nearly equal and more intimate than in former times. This trend of change is part of a group of alterations in familial relations, some of which represent complementary emphases and de-emphases. As other social devices have taken over various of the former roles of kinship, the familial continuity through the generations is both less important and more difficult to maintain. The status of the eldest son thus holds less eminence, and its loss of importance has been accompanied by a rise in the position of wife and mother. At the same time, the strict supervision of marriage has become less important. Conventions of former times discouraged intense bonds between men and women, for these endangered the position of preeminence of the eldest son. Relations of intimacy and equality between man and wife endangered familial continuity by detracting from the father-son relationship and by placing authority in the hands of women. The new bride was ideally the lowest member of the household. In her youth a woman was traditionally under the domination of her husband and in her old age under the authority of her eldest son. In their roles as bearers and rearers of children, women were necessary mechanical appurtenances to a scheme of social structure which had provisions for continuity that involved many people and which was made to seem far more important than the relations between

any two individuals. Proper men did not admit to romantic love for their wives; instead they spoke of them and to them as lowly creatures. Many other customs insured that women did not endanger the operations of the social machine.

Under the conditions of Tokugawa times, a low social position for females was congruous, and romantic love could find no approval either as a mode of selecting mates or as a desirable relationship between man and wife. It was only among people of lowest social classes, those lacking property and confined to egalitarian association with others of bottommost station, that men and women ordinarily married for love. Modern conditions of life provide increasing encouragement to romantic love and to lifelong attachments between spouses. The wife who walks some distance behind her husband on streets and roads has become a curiosity.

One of the many additional indications of the diminished importance of kinship is provided by present customs of using kin terms. Today they find less frequent use, especially for distant relatives and unrelated persons, and the use of personal names has grown. Kin terms long ago ceased to be appellations of respect and honor. The modern woman is often none too anxious to be called "aunt" or "grandmother," and it is of course possible deliberately to insult by choice of a kin term suggesting that the addressee has lost the premium of youth. In this matter, too, it seems reasonable to think that the changed culture of Japan offers an explanation. Where romantic love between husband and wife finds encouragement, a desire on the part of men and, especially, of women to appear attractively young seems congruous. The modern Japanese wife gives growing attention to her personal appearance, and the commercial beauty industry of Japan has become a vast network of establishments providing cosmetics and services that reaches down to the smallest community.

Fictive kinship has had an interesting career. In the earlier stages of the industrialization of Japan, the *oyabun-kobun* flourished as a social device transitional between the peasant and the industrial society. Young men and women migrating to cities entered this relationship with their employers or supervisors, and labor was often recruited on this basis. Today the *oyabun-kobun* relationship in its old form is common only at the fringes of society, in the world of professional criminals and prostitutes, where the economic innovations connected with legal employment have not penetrated. In the world of law-abiding citizens, the formal *oyabun-kobun* has generally been transmuted into milder forms of paternalism and these permeate Japanese society.

As compared with circumstances in the United States, Japanese society continues to give much importance to kinship and to personalized ties with unrelated people. Industrial and commercial concerns are heavily paternalistic, looking into and after the welfare of their personnel in ways that go far beyond the demand of coldly rational business. Small family enterprises remain very common and even the smallest shops and business concerns may provide living quarters for unrelated employees, especially the young and unmarried. Thus the firms take on many of the aspects of family enterprises. Large industrial firms frequently maintain apartments for married employees as well as dormitories for single people, and also often provide recreational facilities for their personnel. Labor unions are most frequently company unions. Nepotism in practices of employment is standard and often thoroughly approved. In the religious world priestly posts are customarily inherited. University professors are often still masters, and the students who become associated with them are their disciples. Leaders of gangs of criminals are also masters, who look after the welfare of their followers. No segment of Japanese society may be described as entirely free of familism, but even here continued trends of change are evident. The "progressive" inveigh publicly against paternalism, and the primary qualification for important positions in the worlds of industry and finance is personal ability. Commercial concerns have grown larger, rendering personalized relations more and more difficult to maintain, and the growth of the large business enterprises has been accompanied by the bankruptcy of many small concerns, which form the greatest strongholds of familism. The emphasis in employment shifts increasingly toward the recognition of talent and toward impersonality in employer-employee relations.

The functional substitutes for kinship that have emerged—institutions of social welfare, banks, labor unions, schools, courts of law, common-interest associations, and many other social and economic devices—continue to grow in importance. Among these, common-interest associations loom importantly in both city and county, and certain of them have assumed positions of vital importance to the rural resident. Any farming community of the nation includes among its residents members of twenty-five or more associations concerned with economic matters, community affairs, religion, and recreation. Of these, the agricultural cooperatives, in their postwar form, are the most important. These are the agency through which the farmer obtains machinery, tools, fertilizer, education in new techniques of agronomy, loans of money for farm improvement, insurance on crops and livestock, and much else. The cooperative is the farmer's bank for savings accounts as well as loans, the normal agency for sale of crops, and its social activities may provide much of the recreation available to the rural family. Under the circumstances of modern urban life—for the country as well as the city has become urbanized—common-interest associations offer a number of advantages. Their growth in Japan, as elsewhere, has marked a transition from strong reliance upon kinship and personal ties. Associations are highly elastic; kin groups are not. Associations may be formed, changed, or dissolved to meet altered circumstances, and their presence or absence does not disrupt family or community membership in any consequential way.

Various of the modern associations of Japan are modeled after American counterparts and bear English or English-derived names. The Parent-Teachers' Association (Pee-chee-eh) and 4-H (Yon-eichi) are examples introduced during the military occupation after World War II. Fraternal organizations stemming from the West that have high prestige in Japanese cities are the Rotary International and the Lions Club. Many other associations that have goals of social reform or humanitarian aims also resemble organizations of the Western world, especially of the United States, and have doubtless often been inspired by the foreign organizations. But here caution must be used. Common-interest associations are ancient in Japan as well as in the West, and they are a world-wide feature of human society, when circumstances encourage or allow their formation. When governmental control during the preceding century allowed the people of Japan to do so, they showed no reluctance to form their own common-interest associations, many of which had aims of social reform. Associations that appear to be entirely Japanese have sprung up thickly since the end of World War II, and their growth should not be interpreted as a mere copying of foreign social features. As an indication of the rising position of women, it is noteworthy that one of these is a large national organization called the Housewives' League (Shufuren) that seeks with considerable success to improve conditions of daily life and to combat social evils.

Source:
From *Changing Japan* by Edward Norbeck. Copyright © 1965 by Holt, Rinehart and Winston, Inc. Reprinted by permission of Holt, Rinehart and Winston, Inc.

Summary

1.
Because cultures are adapted to their environment, they are remarkably stable. And yet the diversity of the cultures in existence today attests to the amount of change that has actually taken place. Only 10,000 years ago all cultures were based on hunting and gathering. No culture escapes change altogether, not even those still based on hunting and gathering, but the rate and direction of change vary considerably. Individuals within a culture usually find change difficult to accept, beneficial though it may be.

2.
Cultural change by means of invention is originated by an individual within the culture who invents a new habit, tool, or principle. Other individuals adopt the invention and it becomes socially shared. Diffusion is the borrowing by one society of a cultural element from another. Acculturation is more than just borrowing. It stems from intensive first-hand contact of groups with different cultures and produces major changes in the culture patterns of one or both groups. Devolution is the loss of an important trait without replacement.

3.
Colonial administration guided by an understanding of the native culture can avoid causing serious disruption of the native culture. In many cases, however, colonialism has resulted in "culture crash": decimation, misery, and community degeneration. A struggle against externally imposed authority may be a rebellion, in which the aim is simply to oust the incumbents of offices, or it may be a revolution, in which attempts are made to change not only the incumbents but the nature of the offices, and to change belief systems and the social structure as well.

4.
When value systems diverge too widely from the realities in a culture, a condition of cultural crisis may develop and revitalization movements may appear. In a transitional revitalization movement, the culture tries to speed up the acculturation process in order to get more of the benefits it expects from the dominant culture. In millenarism it attempts to resurrect a pariah group with a subcultural ideology. Nativistic or revivalistic movements aim to reconstitute a destroyed but not forgotten way of life. Revolutionary movements try to reform the cultural system from within.

5.
An example of modernization is found in the Pueblo Indians, who have retained their extended families and indigenous languages but adopted the American economy and consumer goods. The Tanala of Madagascar have fared differently under modernization. Forced to adopt a new rice-growing technique that employs single families, the Tanala have suffered a breakdown of the extended family. The Blackfeet Indians have responded in yet another way. They have evolved a bicultural community with a white-oriented group and an Indian-oriented group.

6.
Modernization everywhere has tended to reduce the influence that the community and the family have over the individual. The trend is for the individual to be governed less by these small units and more by larger systems such as bureaucracies.

Suggested readings

Arensberg, Courod and Arthur H. Nieloff, *Introducing Social Change: A Manual for Americans Overseas* (Aldine, 1964).
This is an excellent "eye opener," showing the westerners that what appears to be bad or inefficient ways of doing things have purpose and meaning in the matrix of the particular culture, and that failure to understand such customs can lead to disaster when programs of change, no matter how well meaning, are introduced.

Barnett, Hower G. *Innovation: The Basis of Cultural Change* (McGraw-Hill, 1953).
This is the standard work on the subject, widely quoted by virtually everyone who writes about change.

Dalton, George (ed.) *Economic Development and Social Change: The Modernization of Village Communities* (Nat. Hist. Press, 1971).
The phenomenon known as modernization (it might almost be called westernization) is the subject of much anthropological attention these days, and this selection of writings is a good introduction to the subject.

A. L. Kroeber, *Anthropology* (see Suggested readings for Chapter 13 for complete reference). Several chapters of this work are given over to excellent discussions of innovation and diffusion. Particularly good are sections dealing with the histories of specific inventions.

Redfield, Robert; Ralph Linton, and Melville J. Herskovits Memorandum of the Study of Acculturation. *American Anthropologist* (38:149–152) (1936).
This article was the result of the growing interest of anthropologists in the effect of massive contact with western cultures on more traditional cultures. It was the first major attempt to specify what the phenomenon of acculturation was.

Tax, Sol, ed., The Forc Project. *Human Organization* (17:17–19) (1955).
A statement on a recent attempt by anthropologists to facilitate the kinds of changes desired by those who are to be affected by those changes.

The future

Anthropology is sometimes described as a backward-looking discipline. The work that we typically associate with anthropologists is the interpretation of the past and the description of the present. Yet anthropologists also have a special concern with the future and the changes it may bring. Like all residents of an industrialized culture, they wonder what the postindustrial society now being predicted will hold. More pressingly, they also wonder what changes the coming years will bring to non-Western cultures. As we saw in the preceding chapter, when non-Western pastoralists and hunter-gatherers are thrown into contact with Western industrialized peoples their culture is rapidly changed, often for the worse—it becomes both less supportive and less adaptive. How, then, can these threatened cultures adapt to the future?

The biological future of man

For all his culture, man remains an animal—and predictions of the future must take this into account. Is man still physically evolving? Though such questions are controversial, scientists have come up with plausible and tested theories. One thing is certain: it is not nature but culture which will be the major influence upon any adjustments that may take place in man's biological make-up.

The probability of alterations in man's biological make-up due to his culture raises a number of important questions. By trying to eliminate genes for balanced polymorphic traits, such as the sickle-cell trait, are we also removing genes which have survival value? Are we weakening the gene pool by allowing people with hereditary diseases and defects to reproduce? Are we reducing chances for genetic variation by controlling population size?

We are not sure of the answers to all of these questions. If we are able to wipe out sickle-cell anemia, we also may be able to wipe out malaria; thus we would have eliminated the condition that made the sickle-cell trait advantageous. Nor is it strictly true that medical science is weakening the gene pool by letting those with hereditary diseases, such as diabetes, reproduce. In the present environment, where medication is easily available, such people are as fit as anyone else. However, if production of medications ceased, such people would become unfit and die out.

The effects of culture in enabling individuals to reproduce even though they suffer from genetic diseases are familiar. Perhaps less familiar are the cases in which medical technology removes some individuals from the reproducing population. One example can be seen in the medical use of penicillin. Although its use saves many people who might otherwise have died from bacterial infections, it also kills some individuals who are allergic to some chemical in its composition. Another example of selective effects of culture can be seen in South Africa. About 1 percent of South Africans of Dutch descent have a dominant gene for a certain type of porphyria, a disease which renders the skin of its victims sensitive to light and causes skin abrasions. If the Afrikaners remain in their rustic, rural environment, they suffer only minor skin abrasions as a result of their condition. However, the gene has rendered them very sensitive to modern medical treatment, such as they would receive in a large cultural center like Johannesburg. If they are treated for some other problem with barbiturates or similar drugs, they suffer acute attacks and very often die. In their isolated environment, the Afrikaners with this peculiar condition are able to live normal lives; it is only when they come in contact with a culture in which modern medicine plays an important part that they may suffer physical impairment of loss of life. Thus culture, by saving some genetically maladapted individuals who would ordinarily die, and by injuring others who would ordinarily survive, is changing the human gene pool. It remains to be seen whether or not the change is deleterious to the species.

It is undeniably true that mutations are much more likely to be eliminated in small populations than they are in large ones, and thus population control may work to limit genetic diversity. Yet there is another aspect to this issue. The cultural activities of modern man have increased the amount of radiation in the environment, and they have exposed many people to the action of mutagenic chemicals. These two factors probably cause an increase in the normal rate of mutation—thereby increasing genetic variability.

The cultural future of man

Whatever man's biological future, culture remains his primary mode of adaptation. Yet some anthropologists have noted with concern what they interpret as a trend toward loss of adaptability in our culture. What can anthropologists tell us about what the culture of the future might be like?

One-world culture

Some anthropologists believe that the future world will be homogenized into a single culture. The concept that man is moving toward a "one-world culture" springs from the rapid developments in communication, transportation, and trade that link the great majority of today's people; the seeming Westernization of other countries (Japan, for example) exemplifies this trend. There can be little doubt that such a one-world culture would be a superculture, an outgrowth of modern industrial society where computers, cybernetics, and communications—in effect, technology—reign supreme. If this culture does develop, an American travelling in the year 2100 to Tierra del Fuego, Peking, or New Guinea will find that the inhabitants of these areas live in a manner identical or similar to him. They will eat the same kinds of food, read the same newspapers, go to the same kinds of churches, have the same kind of government.

Such a culture, many anthropologists believe, would be bland, lacking the richness and variety found in cultural diversity. They also believe that a standardized culture would lead to a loss of adaptability, should some future crisis arise. For example, suppose that the earth's supply of fossil fuels were to be totally exhausted by the start of the twenty-first century. What would happen to the people living in northern climates if they could no longer heat their homes artificially or buy gasoline for their piston-engine vehicles? If such a calamity were to occur today, while true

Figure 26-1. *Signs of the growing trend toward worldwide homogenization of culture include this supermarket in Mexico City that carries Bayer aspirin, Ritz crackers, and Nescafé, and these Zambian boys who earn their living by selling Coca-Cola.*

cultural diversity still exists, it is highly probable that Eskimos, Lapps, Siberians, and other peoples accustomed to a frigid, harsh environment would survive; these marginal cultures have the social organization and technology necessary to live, perhaps even to thrive, in this kind of ecosystem. Such cultures, being the only survivors of the human species in the north, would proliferate and carry on the human race. From these, other cultures would gradually develop and civilization would again emerge.

If the Eskimos had been assimilated into the single culture, they would all have traded in their dog sleds for snowmobiles, and their kayaks and umiaks for stainless steel boats powered by outboard motors. Thus their traditional techniques for survival would be lost and forgotten; the Eskimos would perish with everyone else, making *Homo sapiens* a species no longer found in northern climates.

The same applies to the world's small-scale agriculturists and pastoralists. If they had been assimilated into a one-world industrialized culture, they would have abandoned their old traditional agricultural and herding techniques for the West's complex power-driven machinery, chemical fertilizers, and pesticides. If a nuclear holocaust occurred or world energy became depleted, these cultures could not survive as they could have if they kept their traditional cultural technology. Thus, some anthropologists belive that fully developed cultures of great diversity, such as still exist in many parts of today's world, will be necessary in the future to provide options for human survival in the event of a global emergency.

Other anthropologists suggest that perhaps a generalized culture would be more desirable in the future, because certain fully developed cultures of today may be too specialized to survive in a changed environment. Examples of this situation abound in modern anthropology. When a traditional culture well adapted to a specific environment, such as the Indians of Brazil who are beautifully adapted to a life in a tropical rain forest, meets European-derived culture and the social environment changes suddenly and drastically, the traditional culture often collapses, because its traditions and its political and social organizations are not at all adapted to the new lifestyle. Usually, such societies adopt many of the cultural features of the Western societies to which they have been exposed. The apparently limited adaptability of non-Western cultures may be compared to some early hominid populations, such as *Australopithecus robustus,* who was physically less able to adapt to changing environmental conditions than were some other hominids, and so became extinct. The more generalized *Australopithecus africanus,* on the other hand, had the capacity to survive in the available environment; this group survived and evolved into what today is *Homo sapiens.*

Cultural pluralism

A second possibility for man's future may be the rise of cultural pluralism, in which more than one culture exists in a given society. Cultural pluralism is the social and political interaction within the same society of people with different ways of living and thinking. Ideally, cultural pluralism implies the rejection of bigotry, bias, and racism in favor of respect for the cultural traditions of other peoples. In reality, it has not always worked out that way.

An example of one form of cultural pluralism may be found in New York City where the Puerto Ricans, who have their own cultural traditions and values, exist side by side with other New Yorkers. The Puerto Ricans have their own language, music, religion, food; some live in their own *barrio* or neighborhood. This particular pluralism, however, is probably of a temporary nature, a stage in the process of integration into standard American culture. Thus, the Puerto Ricans, in four or five generations, like the Italians, Irish and Jews before them, may also become Americanized to the point where their lifestyle will be indistinguishable from others around them.

The United States, then, does not have a truly culturally pluralistic society where distinct cultures flourish. Rather, it has been a "melting pot" society where many cultures have been absorbed into the mainstream of American culture. There are, however, signs that a true pluralism may be emerging. Blacks, American Indians, Chicanos, and Puerto Ricans are proclaiming their intentions of retaining identifiable cultural characteristics. This could be the beginning of a trend away from the melting pot philosophy and toward real pluralism.

Other examples of cultural pluralism may be found in Switzerland where the Italian, German and French cultures exist side by side; in Belgium where the French Walloons and the Flemish each have different cultural heritages; and in Canada, where French and English-speaking Canadians live in a pluralistic society. An excellent example of a recently formed (1960) culturally pluralistic society is that of the Federal Republic of Nigeria, in West Africa.

Nigerian cultural pluralism. Nigeria, with a population in excess of 58 million, is very heterogeneous; it has a variety of culture groups and languages, nearly 100 of which have been recorded. The three chief languages are spoken by the country's three principal entities—the Ibo, Yoruba, and Hausa—each of which has its own customs, religion, and political organization.

For example, the Ibo, who live in southeast Nigeria, represent a combination of village groups related by a common language and culture. Their social organization is based on kinship groups, most of which practice ancestor worship and live on land containing spirit shrines. Ibo political organization is a form of democracy whose center is the village. Their religion is a combination of ancestor worship and belief in natural forces, but most Ibo have recently converted to Christianity.

Across Nigeria, the Yoruba live in southwestern Nigeria on the Guinea Coast, predominantly in large urban centers. These cities are basically communities of farmers and groups of people joined by kinship. Their political organization is stronger than that of the Ibo: they have powerful

Figure 26-2. *All large American cities contain pockets of immigrant cultures, such as this Spanish market in New York City.*

state governments, each with a king and bureaucracy. Traditional Yoruba religion had an elaborate pantheon; however, Christianity and Islam have made considerable inroads into the traditional beliefs.

In northern Nigeria live the Hausa and the pastoral Fulani peoples. The Hausa developed principles of kinship, chieftanship, and office in centralized emirates. A strong element of Islamic religion and social forms is found in Hausa society, and its members pride themselves on their unique tradition of literacy in Arabic.

In the last century, the pastoral Fulani settled in Hausaland and unseated the Hausas as the source of power in northern Nigeria. In Hausaland, many Fulani have given up their all-important cattle culture and have become assimilated

into the Hausa by marriage. Unlike the Hausa, the Fulani have an egalitarian form of political organization. The Fulani are Moslems; as pastoralist nomads, they have been largely responsible for the spread of Islam in West Africa.

Thus, in Nigeria, a number of ancient, fully integrated, fully developed separate cultures are trying to exist side by side, united politically and economically into a modern republic. Although, as the recent civil war has shown, such efforts are not always acceptable to all minorities, the policy of cultural pluralism is endorsed by many of the nation's diverse peoples. Similar pluralistic arrangements, some anthropologists say, will exist around the world in the future. They see cultural pluralism as the only true feasible instrument for global equilibrium and peace.

Ethnocentrism. An adjunct of cultural pluralism is the concept of ethnocentrism, or the belief that one's own culture is better than all others. In its natural form, ethnocentrism identifies the positive way an individual feels about his own culture; it serves to strengthen the individual's ego and his social ties to his own group. In many societies, this concept is important because it provides the individual with a world outlook and eases his social integration and adjustment as well. Ethnocentrism is stronger than patriotism or loyalty, because it assumes that every aspect of a culture—art, science, religion, politics, economics—is superior to all aspects of other cultures.

In its virulent form, ethnocentrism is a form of cultural evangelism that is often characterized by militaristic or aggressive tendencies on the part of one culture, as it tries to spread its beliefs to other cultures. Among large industrialized nations, ethnocentrism is often stretched to the point that the society may be blinded by its belief in its own "rightness." It is rationalized and made the basis for programs often detrimental to the wellbeing of other societies being influenced. This, of course, gives rise to social problems such as unrest, hostility, and even war.

Melville Herskovits believes that any culture that institutionalizes ethnocentrism is, in the end, basing its policy on a psychocultural unreality. No culture, he believes, is a commodity for export. No society can, by conquest or persuasion, influence another society to change its entire lifestyle. When such a practice is attempted, it must fail because the original culture is rarely entirely lost; some aspects of it always appear in some form.

Virulent ethnocentrism has been practiced by European countries, such as England, France, and Spain, in their colonial policies toward India, America, and Africa. The United States has also been guilty of a form of economic ethnocentrism. Interpreting through its own culture the Biblical injuction to help fellow man, the United States, convinced that its way of life is best, has attempted to spread democracy to certain so-called backward nations, by extending to them economic aid. In many cases, such aid led to the total destruction of the country's traditional cultures, resulting in power struggles and bloodshed, and the loss of economic and social welfare.

Perhaps the most memorable example of this form of ethnocentrism in recent history can be found in Nazi Germany. The Germans under Hitler thought themselves to be the master race who wished to rule the world. They wished to inflict their entire culture—art, politics, technology, language, religion—on the countries they conquered. Their ethnocentrism resulted in a devastating world war in which millions of people perished. Today, various degrees of institutionalized ethnocentrism can be seen in Russia, China, and other communist societies, as well as in some countries in Africa, the near east and mideast.

Although some anthropologists believe that traditional ethnocentrism may be replaced by one-world culture and cultural pluralism in the future, there can be little doubt that in the present, at least, ethnocentrism presents many problems that must be solved if mankind is to avoid further conflicts on an international scale.

Figure 26-3a. *The European idea that objects of daily use can be regarded as art has spread to Africa; this pottery museum is one result.*

Figure 26-3b. *The Nigerian government has instituted a program of conservation of its cultural heritage.*

Problems of the future

It seems that a currently popular amusement is the writing and reading of apocalyptic visions of the future. We have heard how the world will end with a bang, thanks to a nuclear holocaust; and how it will end with a whimper, from the effects of too many people and too much pollution. Biologists and sociologists have predicted many changes in man's physical and social environment; what can anthropologists tell us about the way that culture can help man adapt to these changes?

Population, urbanization, and crowding

One of the most critical problems facing mankind in the future is the so-called "population explosion." We are not sure yet whether urbanization and crowding themselves are serious problems, but there can be no doubt about the urgency of the crises which accompany rapid population increase, such as famine, poverty, social unrest, and psychological stress.

Because of such factors as increased longevity, improved agricultural techniques, and advances in medicine, population has grown at a dramatically increasing rate throughout recent history. For example, in 1974, world population reached four billion, thus doubling the two billion population of 1930.

Intricately connected with this astounding proliferation of human beings is the trend toward urbanization: each year, more and more people are crowding into the world's cities, causing a crisis certain to have far reaching consequences in the future. However, urbanization is only partly the effect of population growth; even more, it is the direct result of technology and the centralization of industry. Urbanization typically accompanies a shift from an agrarian to an industrial economy. As population increases, production demand also increases, making industrial jobs

Figure 26-4. *The fight against disease, carried on by such groups as the World Health Organization, has led to great increases in world population; this picture of a middle-class suburb in Nigeria typifies the problems of population growth and rising expectations.*

more plentiful. Simultaneously, automation in agriculture reduces the need for manpower. The result is a large-scale migration from rural to urban areas, as workers seek industrial jobs.

Our minds may suffer from overpopulation and urbanization long before our stomachs do. Such consequences of overcrowding as the loss of personal space and a surfeit of face-to-face encounters can give rise to a number of negative behavioral and physiological responses.

The effects of overcrowding on animals have been extensively studied by social and natural scientists. At the very least, overcrowding among animals results in the disturbance of normal social interactions, such as courtship, mating, and maternal behavior. Usual dominant-submissive relationships cease to function, with the result that a stable group organization can no longer be maintained. At the worst, the prolonged stress of overcrowding can stimulate extreme tension and hyperactivity, culminating in death.

Konrad Lorenz has suggested in his book, *Civilized Man's Eight Mortal Sins*,[1] that the earth may become so overpopulated that man will give vent to uncontrolled aggression, much like rats do when faced with overcrowding. But unlike rats, who always leave a few members alive for future breeding, man may destroy himself totally. Of course, men are not rats; their culture conditions them to accept a variety of personal space differences. But rats in crowded conditions behave very much like people in overpopulated human communities.

On the other hand, although man may react aggressively in an overcrowded environment, the flexibility of his cultural adaption has certainly extended his tolerance for human congestion. Stanley Milgram in a study entitled, "The Experience of Living in Cities,"[2] has observed the way New Yorkers have adapted to their overcrowded environment. Milgram believes overcrowding, or in his word, "overload," deforms urban life on several levels: it affects role performance, the

[1] Konrad Lorenz *Civilized Man's Eight Mortal Sins* (Munich: Pieper Verlag, 1974).
[2] Stanley Milgram, "The Experience of Living in Cities," in *Science*, 167:141–68.

evolution of social norms, cognitive functioning, and the use of facilities. This deformation leads to a number of adaptive mechanisms which create the distinct tone of the city life.

The first of these adaptive responses to overcrowding is a cutback in the amount of time spent with each acquaintance; this enables urbanites to conserve some of their psychic energy to perform necessary daily tasks. Second, the New Yorker invests his time and energy only with a few carefully selected friends and acquaintances. Thus, although he will go out of his way to keep a lunch date with an important business associate, he casually ignores a drunk lying sick in the street. Third, overcrowding causes a shift in function in some business exchanges and social transactions. For example bus drivers used to make change for passengers. Now, however, harried bus drivers are no longer able to do so, and this function must be assumed by the passenger. Fourth, there is a loss of receptivity on the part of New Yorkers to unannounced visitors. In some small towns, any citizen can drop into the Mayor's office unannounced for a chat. In New York, some people maintain unlisted phone numbers, others keep their phones off the hook to prevent incoming calls. Another manifestation of this "super-privacy" syndrome occurs when a New Yorker assumes an unfriendly face to discourage strangers from making contact.

The fifth adaptive mechanism ensures that relationships with friends remain on an entirely superficial level and never get very intimate. Sixth, specialized institutions are created to handle situations that would swamp the individual urbanite. For example, the welfare system prevents an army of beggars from roving the city besieging individuals for alms.

Can the problem of overpopulation and crowding be solved by disbanding the city and spreading the population more evenly throughout the country, as some have suggested? Probably not, because it is not population density by itself that creates problems. Sociological studies in New York, Chicago, and Los Angeles indicate that it is not population density that causes antisocial be-

havior, social breakdown, or breakdown of production. These are organizational and economic problems, deriving from society's chronic inability to provide optimal services; this inability is exacerbated in densely populated areas. Such problems result from overpopulation in general, not population density. Many of the troubles of the cities are found in equal proportion in rural areas. In the cities, they are amplified, because more people are involved. Moreover, spreading the population more sparsely would necessitate the use of more valuable agricultural land for housing and commercial purposes, thus causing serious problems of food production.

Food shortage

The foremost question deriving from the burgeoning world population is simply, "How can we feed so many people?" On a worldwide scale, many think man is faced with the prospect of possible exhaustion of his traditional food resources.

Most futurologists acknowledge that man has the technological capability to increase food production. The big question is: will he be able to do so? There have been major advances in agriculture and livestock breeding: powerful fertilizers, improved irrigation, genetical advances to yield bigger and better crops and animals, along with sea-harvesting techniques and even the chemical production of artificial foods. All of these developments augur the probability that man will be able to produce more food in the future. Some problems do exist. More intensive agriculture relies on one-crop cultivation; this increases the possibility that insects or diseases can decimate the crop. Moreover, the increased use of pesticides is producing genetically resistant species, larger and hardier. It remains debatable whether or not food supplies can be increased fast enough to keep up with population growth.

All his technological advances will be useless if man cannot change his cultural preferences for certain kinds of food. It is, and will continue to

Figure 26-5. *Technological advances, such as the development of harvesting machines, allow increased crop yield.*

be, difficult to change the eating habits of people. For example, in America, one of the world's largest producers of soybeans, most people refuse to eat soybeans and prefer beef instead. Soybeans are just as nutritional as beef; they are better for the health in that they contain less fats and cholestoral; they are much less expensive; and they are easier to grow. Further, an acre of land can feed many more people—about 50 times as many—if it is planted with soybeans rather than being used to graze cattle. In many East African societies, where cattle are considered a form of wealth rather than food, people live off such nutritional foods as ant larvae, insect grubs and locusts. Most Americans would find this type of food repulsive; nevertheless, like soybeans, such food is readily available in America.

On the other hand, many societies think that any food that comes from a can is unfit for human consumption. Totemic and religious taboos also affect the kinds of food people will eat. Beef is disgusting to Hindus, and pork is sinful to Mohammedans and Jews. If an individual of certain non-Western societies unwittingly eats his totemic animal, psychological vomiting may result when he discovers what he has done.

Another example of the difficulty of changing eating habits can be seen in the experiences of some American aid programs to countries with severe food shortages. The United States sent wheat to several countries—notably India—with severe food shortages. Wheat, especially American wheat, is very high in protein, higher than the poor grade of rice these people had subsisted on. But the people, who were accustomed to eating rice for centuries, had no idea how to prepare wheat and did not like its taste. Many Indians died of starvation because they were unable to switch to wheat as a substitute for rice.

This example also points to the importance of anthropology in helping solve some of the world's problems. If members of the American foreign aid program had consulted qualified anthropologists, such an error would not have occurred; anthropologists would have been familiar with the eating habits of the people who were

Figure 26-6. *Man continues to look for cultural adaptations that will permit him to extend his range and live in new environments. The National Aeronautics and Space Administration sponsored this research project in which small teams lived underwater for extended periods; it was designed to test man's ability to adapt to an environment of high stress. The technological problems of such a life are easier to solve than the social and emotional ones.*

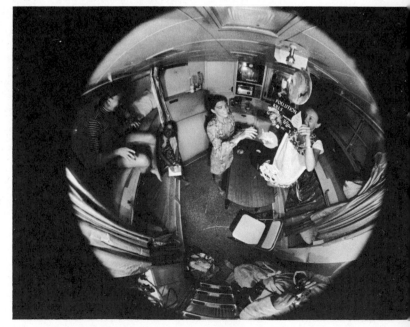

Change and the future ● part **7**

receiving the food and would have recommended another kind of food, or perhaps a program that taught Indians how to cook and eat wheat. Although it raises serious ethical problems, future anthropologists may be faced with the task of trying to change peoples' cultural tastes and customs to enable their survival. In this country, for example, anthropologists may have the exceedingly difficult task of advising the government about how to convince consumers that synthetic foods developed from single-cell organisms cultured on petroleum are nourishing.

Birth control

The primary method of meeting the population problem and the food crisis is to reduce the birth rate. The development of effective birth control methods has made this possible as never before; but whether or not these methods will be utilized on a vast enough scale depends on availability and cultural acceptance. Zero population growth goals have been adopted in many countries, and programs for dissemination of birth-control information have been developed.

However, in many societies, the chief problem is to convince individuals to use birth control devices and techniques. Many of the world's peoples adhere to cultural customs and beliefs which are totally antipathetic to the idea of birth control. For example, among the Kipsigis, a cattle-breeding people of East Africa, one of the primary duties of the young warrior is to enrich the tribe by begetting many children. In some societies, the number of children an individual has is a sign of prestige; if a man does not produce many children, he is looked down upon and thought a weakling. In other societies, particularly in the mideast, motherhood and fatherhood are respected and desirable institutions. A male is not thought of as a man nor a female a woman unless they bear a large number of children. Moreover, it is extremely difficult to convince a farmer to limit the size of his family when large families have been traditionally necessary to help with the

great amount of manual labor agriculture requires. The problem is compounded by the fact that minorities often view birth control programs as subtle plots by the majority to diminish their numbers.

Perhaps the solution to the problem of birth control will be brought about indirectly with the application of some other technological advance. For example, in parts of India, the introduction of electricity into some rural areas has been a more effective means of birth control than any of the devices and information offered by the government agencies. Apparently lighting gave the inhabitants of these areas other leisure time activities to engage in after dark. This connection is strengthened by the case of the events in New York City in 1965, when a power failure that crippled the city overnight caused an upsurge in births nine months later.

Figure 26-7. *In an effort to check the rapid rise in the population growth rate, many governments are sponsoring birth control programs; the Indian woman holds an IUD.*

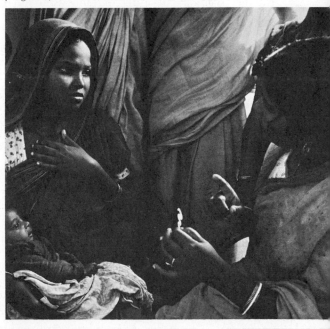

Pollution

Only recently has man come to realize the potentially disastrous consequences of overpopulation and unchecked industrialization on the environment for which humanity is completely dependent for life. Pollution has become a direct threat to human health—in the air we breathe, in the water we drink, in the food we eat. Less direct, but potentially as dangerous, are those pollutants, such as chemical pesticides and inorganic nitrogen fertilizers, that may upset the earth's fragile ecosystems.

Modern man knows the causes of pollution, and he realizes it is a danger to his future survival. Why then, can he not control this evil by which he fouls his own nest? The answer lies perhaps in his philosophical and theological traditions. As we saw in Chapter 22, Western industrialized societies, using the Bible as a guide, believe that they have dominion over all the creatures of the earth and all that grows and lives on it. This exploitative world view characteristic of civilization extends to all natural resources. Only when it has been of any advantage to him has Western man protected or replaced what his greed and acquisitiveness have prompted him to take from his environment. In recent years, recognizing the seriousness of the environmental crisis man was creating for himself, authorities have been forced to pass laws against such activities as hunting whales out of existence, dumping toxic wastes into streams and rivers, and poisoning the air with carbon monoxide fumes.

Members of many other societies see their environment in more symbiotic terms. They feel that the land and the forests are full of gods and ghosts who hold great power over them. Such people believe there is a special totemic relationship between themselves and their environment, including animals, plants, and natural forces. This kind of world view is particularly characteristic of hunter-gatherers. Hunters, for example, regard their game with respect, since their welfare depends on the animals. One avoids

Figure 26-8. *Two girls dramatize the problems of pollution. Yet many experts point out that pollution is only a resource in the wrong place; there may be constructive uses, such as the use of garbage for landfill.*

offending the animals, especially when their strength or cleverness make them dangerous. Among the Tupians and other South American tribes, the concept of the "Lord of the Game Animals" is common. After the hunt, the Gaboon Pygmies implore the slain "Father Elephant" not to avenge himself on his killers, and many tribes in the woodlands address the bear politely and apologetically before attacking him. The Ainu of Japan capture bear cubs and raise them for a year or two; they then kill and eat the animals during a special ceremony. They hope that the bear soul will return loaded with gifts to his master, the "Old Man of the Mountains" and convey to him man's wishes.

Among some agricultural people, plants are at the center of many totemic beliefs. For example, the Lamet, a tribe in Indochina, believe the soul of the rice is a kind of fluid that gradually collects at harvest time in a specific, consecrated part of the field; the crops harvested on that spot are used for sowing the following spring. The plant soul is also frequently visualized in animal or human form. Thus, the Indians in Peru believe in a Maize Mother and a Potato Mother. Similarly, in Indonesia, a Rice Mother is venerated, while the Grain Mother is likewise honored in parts of Europe.

Moreover, many non-Western societies stand in awe of natural forces, bestowing on them a special place in their religious system. For example, many people believe that rushing rapids, storms, the mountains and the jungles possess awful powers. This is also true of fire, which warms and destroys. For farmers, the sun, rain and thunder are important to their existence and are therefore often considered divine. Such world views prohibit the kind of environmental manipulation that causes severe pollution.

Scientific and technological expansion

If the future looks singularly bleak from the point of view of the social scientist, many physical sci-entists and medical researchers are relatively optimistic. Emmanuel Mesthene, director of the Harvard Program in Science and Technology, has summarized the reasons for this optimism:

> We have now, or know how to acquire, the technical capacity to do very nearly everything we want. Can we transplant human hearts, control personality, order the weather that suits us, travel to Mars or Venus? Of course we can. If not now or in five or ten years, then certainly in 25 or 50 or 100.

As knowledge in all areas grows, and technological society becomes increasingly complex, societies come more and more to rely on computers. According to futurologist Marshall McLuhan, it has been the computer, along with television, that has been responsible for what he calls "the Electronic Age" in which we now live. McLuhan's basic belief is that the form of communication drastically affects what is being communicated; similarly, the sensory apparatus alters the information it receives. Hence, McLuhan says, "the medium is the message."

Formerly, before the invention of typography and printing, man lived in a collective "tribal" world where his oral and aural orientation enabled him to perceive and experience many things at one time. In his small tightly-knit world, there was no written word, and man depended heavily on his ears to receive information about the world around him. His whole world of knowledge was contained in the "tribal encyclopedia"—a body of myths, religious tenets, moral and civil laws that was passed on by word of mouth by each generation. With the invention of printing, which is characterized by uniformity, continuity, and lineality, man was forced into a visual, sequentially logical way of perceiving and thinking. In his tribal state, man was accustomed to perceiving groups or patterns of sounds rather than one sound at a time. Unlike the man in the tribal society who heard and experienced many things simultaneously, visual man, accustomed to focussing his attention on specialized segments (letters and words), saw and perceived only one thing at a time. Such a way of organizing reality resulted in isolated individualism and contributed to the mechanical or industrial age where the environment (machines) was arranged in a series of lineally connected fragments, each following the other in orderly fashion like words on the printed page. Mechanization, then, was the fragmentation of a product or entity, followed by putting forth each of these fragments in a series. Thus the symbols of the mechanical age are the nut, bolt, wheel, gear and assembly line.

According to McLuhan, with the advent of the computer and television, man entered the electronic age and became tribal once more. Tribal man perceived patterns or groups of sounds as part of the entire whole or sentence. Now electronic technology has created an entirely new environment in which the old linear method of fragmentation and classification have yielded to computer methods where pattern recognition, or seeing relationships as part of an entire whole are once again important. With television, man becomes involved in the entire world and experiences more than one thing at a time. In effect, he is tribalized again; the electronic speed of computers and television causes everything to happen simultaneously, by compressing space and time. Man can experience a battle in the jungle of Vietnam, an election in Paris, a baseball game in Chicago, a strike in Tokyo, or a landing on the moon as soon as it happens via television. Television also provides the high involvement the tribe used to provide; it brings together men so they share experience collectively, not individually. The world has become, in McLuhan's words, "a global village," in which electronic speed brings all political and social functions together, impelling commitment and participation.

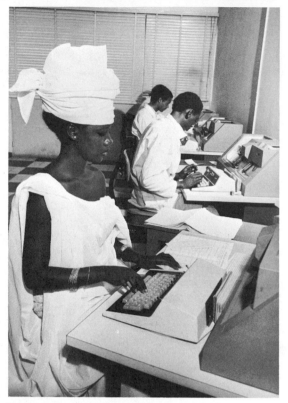

Figure 26-9. *Many suspect that the widespread use of the computer will change not just man's technology but also his world view. These users work for Senegal's Ministry of Finance.*

scribe small tribal groups, in out of the way places, which had not been "contaminated" by contact with Westerners. There are few such groups in the world today. Indeed, many classic ethnographies dealt with societies more affected by contact with Westerners than previously thought.

The work of the future

There can be no doubt that the role of the anthropologist is changing. The time is long past when the anthropologist could go out and de-

The disappearing past

At the same time that societies with which anthropologists have been traditionally concerned are fast disappearing, the need for information about them has become steadily more apparent. If we are ever to have a realistic understanding of that elusive thing called "human nature," we need lots of good data on all humans. We are confronted, then, with an urgent job of salvage. In spite of the fact that the societies traditionally studied by anthropologists are rapidly disappearing, anthropologists will continue to be concerned with them, gathering whatever data can still be obtained.

The need for salvage applies to archeological, as well as ethnological, data. Here, we are not confronted with societies which are rapidly being Westernized; rather, we are dealing with the remains of societies which are being drowned in reservoirs, covered by parking lots for shopping centers, or just plain bulldozed into oblivion. Archeological sites are being lost at an alarming rate, and this is a critical problem for two reasons. First, they are nonrenewable; second, they provide the essential data needed by anthropologists to understand the process of change over extended periods of time.

The archeological problem is not one of earthmoving alone. The last decade has seen the spectacular rise of an illicit international traffic in antiquities. So it is, for example, that ancient Maya monuments in the forests of Guatemala are broken up, smuggled out of the country, and reassembled to be purchased by art dealers and museums. Not only have prize pieces of Maya sculpture been destroyed, there has also been at least one murder connected with these operations. Although a number of museums and governments have acted to discourage such purchases, not nearly enough has been done to stem the flow of the illegal antiquities traffic.

Important though archeological and ethnological salvage work may be, anthropologists, as they must, are concerning themselves with the longer range future and are opening up new fields of research. More and more anthropologists are turning their attentions to studies of modernization, the process by which traditional, non-Western societies adopt such features as state governments, nationalism, and integration into industrial economies. This is a logical outcome of the traditional anthropological concern with the non-Western world, and it obviously involves anthropologists with problems of immediate concern. Some of these are: How should the so-called underdeveloped nations develop? What will be the effect of development on traditional ways? What traditional ways are worth preserving? How can this be done? How can a desired change be introduced into a traditional community with some chance of success?

Anthropologists are also becoming more concerned with the study of minority groups in their own countries. In part, this stems from the civil rights and related movements which became prominent in the United States in the 1960s. These created a new awareness of the problems of ethnic and other minorities. To a degree, such studies have brought anthropologists into an area of research which previously was the domain of sociologists. This opens up a new fruitful area for cooperation between the two fields, for the ethnographic techniques of the anthropologists offer a valuable supplement to the more traditional sociological techniques of census taking and administration of questionnaires.

Questions of ethics

The kinds of research outlined above raise a number of important questions concerning the ethics of scientific research. Who will make use of the findings of anthropologists, and for what purposes? In the case of a militant minority, for example, will others use anthropological data to suppress that minority? And what of traditional communities around the world—who is to decide what changes should, or should not, be introduced for community "betterment"? By whose definition is it "betterment," the community's or that of a remote national government? Not surprisingly, because of these and other questions, there has been a hot debate among anthropologists over the past decade on the subject of ethics. In 1967, the American Anthropological Association adopted a statement on problems of anthropological research and ethics. Among other things, this expressed concern about conditions that might threaten the ability of anthropology to contribute to the general interests of human welfare. What concerned the anthropologists was that their research findings might be used as a basis for policy formation, and that this policy might be to the detriment of the group from which those findings came.

This question has not always been a primary worry for anthropologists, although the anthropologists of the nineteenth and early twentieth centuries in the United States almost all felt a personal obligation to the people whom they studied. This sometimes involved them in fighting court battles on behalf of their informants, often at their personal expense.

In World War II, anthropologists were in great demand by the United States government, largely because of their familiarity with foreign cultures and the places where war operations were taking place. The anthropologists responded by preparing manuals for the troops, interpreting cultures for various agencies, and formulating policies for occupied areas. Perhaps the best-known by-product of these wartime activities was Ruth Benedict's *The Chrysanthemum and the Sword* (1946), an analysis of Japanese national character based on second-hand sources. Similar studies were made by Geoffrey Gorer and Weston LaBarre. Many of the conclusions of these studies have not stood up in the face of closer scrutiny based on first-hand observation.

Some of this wartime anthropological work was amazingly sound, but was not always listened to. A case in point is the work of the Foreign Morale Analysis Division of the Office of War Information. Headed up by an anthropologist-psychiatrist, it included several other anthropologists as well as psychiatrists and sociologists. This group correctly analyzed the deteriorating morale of Japanese soldiers and civilians as early as late 1944. Because it conflicted with the prevailing military view, it was largely ignored. In early 1945 the Division predicted a major blowup in Japan and, by spring, predicted a Japanese surrender between July and September 1945. Again they were ignored, but later it was learned that the Japanese, in May, 1945, before the atomic bombs were dropped, made a decision to surrender before November.

The current issue that has made anthropologists reexamine the ethics of their ties to the government was Project Camelot. This was a vast research project planned by the Department of Defense to find out the causes of social unrest leading to armed insurgency. From this data, ways of averting or suppressing armed rebellions could be found. Social scientists would thus be involved in the intervention of the United States government in the internal affairs of other nations. Project Camelot was cancelled while still in the planning stages. Anthropologists had reacted vigorously, both because other nations might react by refusing to allow United States anthropologists to conduct any research within their borders, and because of the larger ethical issues involved. The traditional concern of the anthropologist for the welfare of the people he studies, as *they* see it, has been reawakened.

CULTURE AND ADAPTATION

The intense crisis that threatens the world we live in seems to have come upon us so suddenly that it is understandable that we frantically search for immoralists to blame or scapegoats to sacrifice. When we were children and when some of us were young adults, we saw a disturbed world before us, but at that time the malady was focused so that it seemed to be the result of human error—we could still blame individuals, specific leaders, specific peoples. There was little to indicate to us, in our innocence, that civilization itself was threatened—that we were witness not merely to human moral weakness and error, but to an overwhelming evolutionary process. Yet today we know that civilization is threatened—threatened by itself.

But which civilization? We must repeatedly ask what civilization itself is. Not just our civilization, but civilization as a process: what it provides for us and what its future may be. To examine the crises of civilization one must go back to the idea of culture, and man's use of culture as his device for adapting to the world he lives in. Culture is the technical term, coined by anthropologists in the nineteenth century, to refer to the "artificial" extensions of the human being that allow him greater control over his own environment, over his social system, and ultimately, over himself. Culture is, to make an analogy, what the medical men call a prosthesis—an extension of the animal that makes it possible for him to do things he could not otherwise do. Artificial limbs, false teeth, and eyeglasses are common prostheses in the modern world. But by analogy all of culture can be seen as the prosthesis of the human being—an animal who specialized in brain and central nervous system and developed, through their use, extensions of himself that allowed him to remain an otherwise non-specialized animal, without built-in fighting equipment such as claws or horns or canine teeth; protective devices such as fur, natural camouflage, or fleetness; indeed, without any other form of physical specialization to give him any great advantages toward survival.

Culture, in other words, comprises all the things and devices—including the nonmaterial, such as myths and beliefs and stories—that human beings create to enhance, protect, or express themselves. Culture has, in the course of evolution, become the peculiar (but not unique) property of human beings, and human specialization in culture (like the specialization of tigers in saber teeth or of giraffes in long necks) has been the means by which man has survived and aggrandized himself on the planet. By it he must survive or perish.

Today we know that culture is a two-edged sword. The very while that it allows us to express ourselves more fully, to explore social organization more broadly, and to master our environment more thoroughly, it creates situations of alienation, tyranny, and ecological imbalance. It seems an irony when we realize that only by cultural means can man overcome the evil effects of culture and yet retain the good effects. Once he has started on this road man must learn more about how to get from himself the best and most enjoyable of lives; he must learn more about human social organization and how to control it without what we see as immoralities, even when we do them; and he must learn more about the physical world in which he lives so that his accomplishments will not so alter the earth as to make it uninhabitable.

Man, through several million years of evolution, is committed to living as a cultural being. Only in the last few decades have we realized that culture must be controlled by man himself, and his evolution altered to special kinds of cultural activities, if he is not to become extinct from overspecialization—from blind overspecialization in culture. There is, at this stage of the game, literally no answer except to treat the blindness, to have the courage to see.

The source of the human (and hence cultural) problem is an irony—man is born an *individual, social* animal. In that contradiction lies the basis of our neuroses, our social problems, our moralities. Since intelligence is brought to the survival of both the individual organism and the species, it is possible for the individual to act in what seem to be his own interests at the very time he is acting against the interests of the species. It is this irony that every society must, with one degree or another of success, organize itself to deal with.

But even the organization is ironic, for no two intelligences see it quite the same way. Since man is a social animal and has opted for a cultural mode of self-preservation, all human social groups consist of parties (sometimes individuals, sometimes small groups) interacting in terms of the available culture. Each social group—from the family to the nation, indeed, from the marriage or the mother-child relationship to the United Nations—has a cultural tradition. That tradition changes as new cultural items are invented by members of the group, or as members of the group come into contact with other people whose repertoires of cultural items are different from their own. Therefore, culture is not only handed on from generation to generation, it is also handed "sideways" from one social group to the next. In today's world, we live in a culturally privileged time because items from so many different cultural traditions are available to large numbers of people—indeed, prosperity can in one sense be gauged by the kind and amount of human culture available to a group. But so, obviously, can the potential for disaster. Culture grows as the group flourishes, and the group grows in size as culture flourishes. And then, suddenly—at least it always seems sudden—there is a vast disparity between the capacities of the available culture and the group it serves. The culture that was adequate for yesterday is inadequate for today and disastrous for tomorrow. If there is a law of culture, that is it.

And so it has always been. But today our ironic harvest seems particularly bitter because there is so much *good* culture, judged by our own inward awareness of what is good for us. And, worse, the bad culture is an epiphenomenon, or so its seems. Slowly we must realize that the problem of evil is with us again. In Roy Rappaport's words, it takes the form of the "evolution of maladaptation."

Actually, of course, the problem of evil was never absent, but for a while evil seemed to be attached to individuals, to institutions. And now, again, we see it as the other side of our natures—all our natures. In spite of villains, I too have an evil dimension. Existing culturally creates evil. Culture is, indeed, as the Genesis myth puts it, the knowledge of good and evil. We were thrown out of the garden we wish had once existed into a hell we wish did not.

For the dynamics of culture work in ways that are beyond the purposes of men, whatever they may be. Culture becomes something in itself, something beyond man. Ultimately, it becomes, in the inspired phrase of Jules Henry, culture against man. One's own prostheses turn on one's very self. That is the price one must always pay for prostheses, medicines, drugs, or even love.

When a small group of human beings adapts and successfully adjusts to its environment, the group survives. If its adaptation is unsuccessful, the group perishes: to survive, its members change and adapt in different groups, or they too will perish. If the cultural adaptation is successful, then the group is safe, its members perhaps comfortable. In response to the animality in us and to thousands of millions of years of evolution, the group, in its comfort, grows larger. As the group grows larger the available culture is "stretched"—it is like putting water in the soup to feed unexpected guests. Such diluted culture does not serve as it once did; the situation is no longer that for which it was designed and in accordance with which it evolved.

Three things can happen when culture is stretched too far: the population growth can be checked, either by a natural disaster of some sort or by a population policy; the group can break into two or more groups that separate, and each of them can begin again the process of achieving first optimum, then maximum, and finally destructive growth; the third choice is to invent new culture—new ways of coping with the environment, new ways of dealing with each other, of experiencing the human animalness of us.

Obviously, only those groups that choose the last way survive in the long run. Breaking into several groups, cell-fashion, works only so long as the ecological carrying capacity of the world is not seriously affected.

Thus the real problem arises because man is clever and can devise ways and means of beating the system—for short periods of time. The use of fire, the use of metals, the use of more complex hierarchies to achieve larger social organizations, all of these cultural discoveries and many others have allowed larger populations to survive and multiply, outgrowing the culture that spawned them, and in a sort of cultural Malthusianism, creating worse problems than they solved. Worse because so many more people are involved, and because they are more helpless the further they are removed from a simple ecological position in nature: man as a hunter and gatherer was just another animal.

Source:
Paul Bohannan, "Beyond Civilization,"
Natural History Special Supplement, February, 1971.

Summary

1.

Culture saves some genetically maladapted individuals who would ordinarily die and injures others who would ordinarily survive. By doing so, culture changes the human gene pool. Culture remains man's most adaptive mechanism.

2.

Some anthropologists believe that the future world will be homogenized into a single culture. Rapid developments in communication, transportation, and trade link the great majority of today's people. These developments gave rise to the idea of a "one-world culture." Many anthropologists believe a "one-world culture" would lack richness, variety, and the adaptability to handle a future crisis. Other anthropologists believe that certain cultures may be too specialized to survive in the future. Therefore, they find a generalized culture preferable to diverse cultures.

3.

Cultural pluralism is another possibility for man's future. Cultural pluralism is the social and political interaction within the same society of people with different ways of living and thinking. In its purest form, cultural pluralism rejects bigotry, bias, and racism and recognizes the cultural traditions of other people. Ethnocentrism, an adjunct of cultural pluralism, is the belief that one's own race or culture is better than all others. In its natural form, ethnocentrism identifies the positive way an individual feels about his culture. In its virulent form, it can lead to militaristic or aggressive behavior during attempts of one culture to spread its beliefs to other cultures.

4.

In the future, the "population explosion" will be one of man's most critical problems. A declining death rate, improved agricultural techniques, and advances in medicine have spurred rapid population growth. Urbanization has accompanied this growth. Urbanization is the direct result of tecnology and the centralization of industry. As population increases, production demand increases, making industrial jobs more plentiful; agricultural automation reduces the demand for farm workers. The result is large-scale migration from rural to urban areas.

5.

Overcrowding and food shortages have also accompanied population growth. Overcrowding causes a loss of personal space and too many face-to-face encounters. Such conditions can give rise to negative behavioral and physiological responses. Most futurologists believe that man has the technological capability to meet the nutritional needs of the future. This capability will prove useless unless man changes the cultural preferences of the world's peoples. A people's eating habits often exclude food that is plentiful and demand that which is scarce.

6.

The primary method of meeting the population problem is to reduce the birthrate. Effective birth control methods are now available. Whether or not these methods are used on a vast enough scale depends on their availability and acceptance. Many of the world's peoples adhere to cultural customs and beliefs that reject the idea of birth control.

7.
Pollution has become a direct threat to human health. Western man has protected his environment only when it was immediately advantageous to do so; he has felt no responsibilities toward the earth or its resources. Western man could learn much from non-Western societies which recognize themselves as integral parts of the earth.

8.
Marshall McLuhan believes that computers and television are making modern man tribal like early man. The electronic speed of computers and television compresses time and space, causing everything to happen simultaneously. All political and social functions are brought together, impelling participation. Modern man sees relationships as part of a whole and becomes highly involved just as early man did.

Suggested readings

Alland, Alexander, Jr. *Human Diversity*. New York: Columbia University Press, 1971.
Chapter 5 of this book, "Of Mice and Men: Behavioral Genetics and Human Variation" traces the implications of certain kinds of cultural change for man's biological future. Working from the supposition that man is relatively free of behavioral programming, the author examines one way this freedom has enabled man to cope with diverse environments and how these environments in turn have shaped him both culturally and biologically.

Kahn, Herman and Anthony J. Wiener *The Year 2000*. New York: The Macmillan Company, 1967.
To an anthropologist, the most interesting chapter of this book is Chapter 6, "Some Canonical Variations from the Standard World." It projects a number of possible cultural futures, including both a world of greater integration and one of greater disarray. Although there is much emphasis on technological factors throughout the book, this chapter focuses squarely on cultural alternatives.

McHale, John *The Future of the Future*. New York: George Braziller, Inc., 1969.
McHale's thesis is that the future of the future is in the present. Therefore much of his book is devoted to an analysis of present conditions, with a special emphasis on technological aspects of modern industrial culture. From this analysis, McHale then selects certain aspects that seem to foreshadow the future.

Credits

Chapter twelve

Chapter thirteen

Chapter fourteen

Chapter fifteen

Chapter sixteen

Chapter seventeen

Chapter eighteen

Chapter nineteen

Credits

22-7a, b. Courtesy of The American Museum Of Natural History

22-8   Lee Boltin

Chapter twenty-three

Figure 23-1   Photo by Steven Berkowitz

23-2a Photo by Cy Tetenman

23-2b Thomas Hopker from Woodfin Camp and Associates

23-2c Calogero Cascio from Rapho-Guillumette

23-3   Photo from Frederick Starr, The Ainu Group, Chicago: Open Court Publishing Company, 1904, from "The Ainu" by Hitoshi Watanabe, HUNTERS AND GATHERERS TODAY, M. G. Bicchieri Thomas Hopker from Woodfin Camp and Associates (bottom)

23-4   Marc & Evelyne Bernheim from Woodfin Camp and Associates

23-5   Marc & Evelyne Bernheim from Woodfin Camp and Associates

23-6   Marc & Evelyne Bernheim from Woodfin Camp and Associates

23-7a, b, c, d, e, f. Courtesy of Jane Hamilton-Merritt

23-8   Michal Heron from Woodfin Camp and Associates

23-9   From "The !Kung Bushman Of Botswana" by Richard Borshay Lee, HUNTERS AND GATHERERS TODAY, M. G. Bicchieri (ed.)

23-10 Kal Muller from Woodfin Camp and Associates

Chapter twenty-four

Figure 24-1, 2, 3, 4, 5, 6. Marc & Evelyne Bernheim from Woodfin Camp

Chapter twenty-five

Figure 25-1a Culver Pictures Inc.

25-1b Marc & Evelyne Bernheim from Woodfin Camp and Associates

25-2a Woodfin Camp and Associates

25-2b, c. Marc & Evelyne Bernheim from Woodfin Camp

25-2d Dan Budnik from Woodfin Camp and Associates

25-3   Courtesy of The American Museum Of Natural History

25-4a Marc & Evelyne Bernheim from Woodfin Camp and Associates

25-4b Courtesy of The Freelance Photographers Guild

25-5   Marc & Evelyne Bernheim from Woodfin Camp and Associates

Chapter twenty-six

Figure 26-1   Marc & Evelyne Bernheim from Woodfin Camp and Associates

26-2   Courtesy of United Press International

26-3, 4. Marc & Evelyne Bernheim from Woodfin Camp

26-5a, b. Ewing Galloway

26-6   Courtesy of NASA

26-7   Raghubin Singh from Woodfin Camp and Associates

26-8a Marc & Evelyne Bernheim from Woodfin Camp and Associates

26-8b Rick Winsor from Woodfin Camp and Associates

26-9   Marc & Evelyne Bernheim from Woodfin Camp and Associates

Glossary

absolute dates – in archeology, dates for archeological materials based on solar years, centuries, or other units of absolute time.

acculturation – the process that occurs when members of one society are brought into prolonged contact with another society and one group acquires cultural elements of the other group.

Acheulian tradition – tool making of *Homo erectus* in which the Chellean handax is further perfected and finished.

Adapis – early Eocene primate, lemur.

adaptation – the possession of anatomical, physiological, and behavioral characteristics that permit organisms to survive in the special environmental conditions in which they are generally found.

Aegyptopithecus – Egyptian ape of the Oligocene epoch.

age category – a generalized role disposition determined by age.

age-class – a collection of people occupying an age-grade.

age-grade – a category of persons who fall within a particular, culturally distinguished age range.

age-set – a group of persons initiated into an age-grade together who move through life's stages together.

akua'ba – dolls made by the Ashanti of Ghana.

allele – alternate forms of a gene located on paired chromosomes and coded for different versions of the same trait.

allomorphs – two varieties of the same morpheme occurring in different contexts but with no difference in meaning; a term in linguistics.

allophones – in linguistics, two different pronunciations of a sound having the same meaning.

ambilocal residence – a pattern in which a married couple have the choice of living with either the relatives of the wife or the husband.

animatism – a religious concept of impersonal power.

animism – a term used by Edward Tylor to describe a religious belief in personal spirits which are thought to animate nature.

anthropoids – higher primates; monkeys, apes, and man.

anthropology – the systematic study of man and his works, past and present.

anthropometry – the measurements of differences in human body size and form.

apartheid – a policy of segregation and discrimination against non-European groups in South Africa.

archeology – the study of extinct cultures through the recovery of their material remains.

Aterian culture – Upper Paleolithic culture found in northern Africa.

Aurignacian culture – dates from about 35,000 B.C. in Europe and Southwest Asia.

Australopithecus – a fossil with a mixture of simian and hominid characteristics; two species: *A. robustus* and *A. africanus*. A true hominid.

Azilian culture – Mesolithic culture found in southern France and Spain.

balanced reciprocity – refers to an exchange in which the giving and the receiving is specific as to goods and time.

band – a small group of related people occupying a single region.

berdache – an institutional arrangement among the Plains Indians in which a man may assume women's attire, perform women's work, and even marry another man.

bilateral descent – a system in which a person relates to close relatives on both the mother's and the father's side.

bound morpheme – a sound which can only occur in a language in combination with other sounds, as *s* in English to signify the plural.

brachiation – locomotion by using the arms to swing from branch to branch among the trees.

burins – stone tools of the Upper Paleolithic with a chisel-like edge used for carving bone and antlers.

capital – any resource that is not used up in the process of producing goods.

cargo cult – a religious belief in Melanesia that a deluge will engulf all the whites, following which a ship would arrive laden with European goods.

Capsian culture – a culture that flourished about 11,000 years ago in parts of North and East Africa.

caste – a special form of social class in which membership is determined by birth and remains fixed; the group is ranked in a hierarchy of groups in the system.

Chellean handax – more sophisticated all-purpose cutting tool developed from the Olduwan chopper; dates from about one million years ago.

chiefdom – a ranked society in which every member has a position in the hierarchy.

chromosomes – long strands of DNA found in the nucleus of each cell that transmit traits from one generation to the next.

clan – a noncorporate descent group with each member claiming descent from a common ancestor without actually being able to trace descent genealogically through known links.

class – a division of a society into groups which are ranked and have an unequal share of power, prestige, and worldly goods.

cognatic descent – a system of descent in which the individual has the option of affiliating with either the mother's or the father's side.

consanguine family – a family consisting of a woman and her brothers and the offspring of the woman.

conspicuous consumption – a term coined by Thorstein Veblen to describe a display of wealth for social prestige.

convergent evolution – a process in which two phylogenetically unrelated organisms develop greater similarities.

couvade – religious ritual in which the husband, following the birth of a baby, takes on the symptoms of postnatal illness and disability, while the wife goes about her usual daily routine.

cranium – the brain case in the skull.

Cro-Magnons – the first modern men.

cultural anthropology – the study of man as the animal of culture.

cultural ecology – the interaction of specific cultures with their environment.

cultural focus – an emphasis on a particular area of cultural activity.

cultural materialism – an approach to anthropology which studies the manner in which a culture adapts to its environment.

cultural preadaptations – characteristics within a culture that allow the group to survive in a different environment.

cultural relativism – the thesis that a culture be evaluated according to its own standards and values.

culture area – a geographic region where a number of different societies follow a similar pattern of life.

culture type – a relationship of a particular cultural technology to the environment exploited by that technology.

Dabban culture – a culture of the Upper Paleolithic found in Africa.

deep structure – in the theoretical linguistics of Noam Chomsky, a term based on the habits, conventions, and social adaptations of a culture on which a language is based.

dendrochronology – a method of absolute dating based on the number of rings of growth found in a tree trunk.

descriptive linguistics – a study of language concerned with registering and explaining all the features of a language at one point in history.

diffusion – a process by which culture traits or elements are borrowed from another culture as the result of contact, for example, trade.

diffusionism – the thesis that all cultures share a common origin.

divergent evolution – an evolutionary process in which an ancestral population gives rise to two or more descendant populations that differ from one another.

divination – a process of trying to contact the supernatural to foretell future events.

DNA – the genetic material: a complex molecule with information to direct the synthesis of proteins; DNA molecules have the unique property of being able to produce exact copies of themselves.

dominant genes – genes which can mask the presence of other genes.

double descent – descent established matrilineally for some purposes and patrilineally for others.

Dryopithecus – fossil ape of the Miocene and Pliocene epochs.

ecology – the study of the relationships between organisms and their environment.

ecosystem – an ecologists' term referring to a system composed of both the physical environment and the organisms living within it.

egalitarian society – one in which as many positions for prestige exist as there are persons capable of filling them.

enculturation – the process by which culture is transmitted from one generation to another in a society.

endogamy – the practice of marriage within a group of related individuals.

epics – long legends in oral tradition, sometimes in poetry or rhythmic prose that may last for several hours or even days.

erosi – a guardian spirit with political power among the Afkibo of Nigeria.

ethnocentrism – the belief that one's own culture is best.

ethnology – the study of contemporary cultures.

ethnomusicology – the study of music in a specific cultural setting.

ethnosemantics – an approach to anthropology which seeks to arrive at a description of a culture as a member of that culture expresses it verbally.

exogamy – the practice of marriage outside the group.

extended family – a large household group, related by ties of blood or marriage.

field linguistics – collecting raw data from speakers of a language, analyzing and describing it; primarily a descriptive process.

flotation – an archeological technique employed to recover very small objects.

fluorine test – a method for relative dating.

folklore – a nineteenth century term first used to refer to the oral traditions of the European peasant, later extended to those of all rural peoples.

foramen magnum – opening of the skull through which the spinal cord passes and connects to the brain; an important clue to evolutionary relationships among primates.

formalism – a school of thought which holds that the principles of economics are general enough to be applied usefully to all societies.

form classes – in linguistics, the parts of speech or categories of words that work the same way in all sentences.

fossil – the preserved remains of plants and animals that lived in the past.

fovea centralis – a shallow pit in the retina of the eye enabling an animal to focus on an object without losing visual contact with the surroundings.

free morpheme – in linguistics, a sound which has meaning and can occur unattached to another sound.

functionalism – a theory which explains culture and traits on the basis of their role in maintaining the integrity of the society.

gene flow – the exchange of genes between populations.

gene pool – the total number of different genes and alleles in a population.

generalized exchange – sharing without the expectation of a direct return.

generalized reciprocity – an exchange in which neither the value of the gift is calculated nor the time of repayment specified.

generative transformational grammar – Noam Chomsky's theory of linguistics.

genes – portions of molecules of DNA that direct the development of a single observable or identifiable trait.

genetic drift – the effect of chance events on the gene pool of small populations; an explanation for genetic change.

genotype – actual genetic composition of an organism.

Gigantopithecus – largest known primate fossil found in China; an extinct ape.

glottochronology – a method of dating divergence in branches of language families in linguistics.

grammar – in linguistics, the rules by which sounds are combined in a language to make meaningful statements.

Gravettian culture – dates from about 22,000 B.C. in Europe and southern Russia.

grid system – a system for recording data from an archeological "dig."

Hardy-Weinberg law – a genetic principle which demonstrates algebraically that the percentage of individuals that are homozygous for the dominant allele, homozygous for the recessive allele, and heterozygous, will remain constant from one generation to the next, given random mating in the population.

heterozygous – a chromosome pair which bears different alleles for a single gene.

historical linguistics – the study of language which investigates relationships between earlier and later forms of the same language.

historical particularism – the thesis that each culture is unique and that similarities between cultures are best explained by cultural exchange.

hominid – belonging to the family of man.

Homo erectus – earliest known members of the genus *Homo,* in the direct line of descent of Homo sapiens.

Homo habilis – fossil hominid discovered by the Leakeys in 1960. Transitional between A. africanus and H. erectus.

Homo sapiens – modern man.

homozygous – pair of chromosomes with identical genetic material.

horticulture – plant cultivation carried out with relatively simple tools.

hunter-gatherers – peoples who subsist on the collection of plants and animals which occur in nature.

hypothesis – a tentative assumption of the relationship between certain phenomena.

ideational order – the study of the symbols of a culture.

incest taboo – the prohibition of sexual relations between parent and child, or siblings.

independent invention – a process whereby cultures develop similar features without cultural exchange.

informant – a member of a society being studied with whom the anthropologist can communicate in a common language to learn the language and culture of the society.

integration – the tendency for all aspects of a culture to function as an interrelated whole.

isolation mechanisms – factors which separate breeding populations, creating divergent races and then divergent species.

kanaga – a variety of mask fashioned by the Dogon of Africa.

katanda – a small wooden sculpture found among the Balega in Africa.

kindred – a circle of the maternal and paternal relatives of a specific individual.

Kula ring – a trading system among the Trobriand Islanders first described by Malinowski.

kulturkreise school – a German school of anthropology which held that culture originated in several culture circles.

legends – semihistorical narratives that account for the deeds of heroes, the movements of peoples, and the establishment of local customs.

Levalloisian tradition – tool-making which produced flake tools from prepared cores about 200,000 years ago.

levirate – the custom that a widow marry one of the brothers of her dead husband.

lineage – a corporate group who claim descent from a common ancestor and can trace genealogy through known links to that ancestor.

linguistics – the study of language.

Magdalenian culture – dates from about 15,000 years ago in western Europe and as far east as Russia.

magic – an attempt to manipulate certain perceived laws of nature.

mana – a powerful force among the Melanesians, inherent in all objects.

matrilineal descent – descent traced through the female line for purposes of group membership.

matrilocal residence – a pattern in which a man lives in the locality associated with his wife's relatives.

meiosis – like mitosis except that the cell divides into four new cells with each new cell having half the number of chromosomes of the original cell. Human eggs and sperm are an example of cells formed by meiosis.

Mesolithic – the Middle Stone Age, occurring about 12,000 years ago.

microlith – a small flint blade characteristic of the Mesolithic; hafted in wooden handles to make tools.

mitosis – a kind of cell division which produces new cells which have exactly the same number of chromosome pairs as the parent cell.

moiety – a group which results from a division of a society into two halves on the basis of descent.

monogamy – the taking of a single spouse in marriage.

morphemes – in linguistics, the smallest units of sounds that have a meaning.

Mousterian tradition – tool-making of the Neanderthals which produced flake tools lighter and smaller than Levalloisian flake tools.

mutation – chemical alteration of a gene that produces a new allele.

myth – a religious narrative which explains ultimate questions of human existence.

Natufian culture – Mesolithic culture found in Israel, the Levant, and Jordan.

natural selection – the evolutionary process through which factors in the environment exert a pressure that favors some individuals over others to reproduce the next generation.

Neanderthal man – early representative of Homo sapiens; a true man.

negative reciprocity – a form of gift giving in which the giver tries to get the better of the exchange.

neo-evolutionism – an anthropological school of thought which seeks a revival of the search for universal laws of culture and cultural development.

Neolithic – the New Stone Age; marked the transition from hunting-gathering to a food-producing economy.

neolocal residence – a pattern in which a married couple forms a household in an independent location.

nomadism – having no fixed place of residence.

norm – a cultural value governing behavior.

Northarctus – early Eocene primate; a lemur.

nuclear family – a family unit consisting of a mother, father, and dependent children.

Olduwan chopper – pebble tool of the Lower Paleolithic.

Oligopithecus – small monkey of the Oligocene epoch.

Paleolithic – the Old Stone Age, characterized by chipped stone tools.

paleontology – study of past life by the examination of fossil remains.

palynology – a method of relative dating in archeology based on a study of pollen grains.

parallel evolution – the development of similar cultural adaptations to similar ecological conditions.

pastoralism – a subsistence pattern in which food production is based largely upon the maintenance of herds of animals.

Parapithecus – a near ape of the Oligocene epoch.

patrilineal descent – descent traced through the male line for purposes of group membership.

patrilocal residence – a pattern in which the woman goes to live with her husband in the locality associated with his father's relatives.

phenotype – the physical appearance of an organism which may or may not reflect its complete genetic constitution, or genotype, because it may carry recessive genes.

phenomenal order – that which can be actually observed by the anthropologist.

phonemes – in linguistics, the sounds that make a difference in meaning.

phratry – a unilineal descent group composed of two or more clans which claim to be related by kinship. If there are only two such groups, each is a moiety.

physical anthropology – the study of man as a biological organism.

Plesiadapis – a Paleocene primate, perhaps ancestral to more advanced forms.

Pliopithecus – small fossil ape of the Miocene epoch.

plural society – a society in which there exists a diversity of cultural patterns and social frameworks.

polyandry – the marriage custom of a woman having several husbands; a form of polygamy.

polygamy – marriage to more than one spouse simultaneously.

polymorphic species – a species with a gene pool with various alternative alleles.

polytypic species – a geographically widespread species with genetic variants unevenly distributed among local breeding populations.

pongid – belonging to the family of anthropoid apes.

population – concept in genetics referring to a group of similar individuals that interbreeds.

potassium-argon analysis – a method of absolute dating in archeology based on the ratio of potassium to argon in a volcanic rock.

Prosimians – the lower primates: tree shrews, lemurs, and tarsiers.

radio-carbon analysis – a method of dating the past in archeology based on the rate of decay of radio-carbon 14 in organic substances.

Ramapithecus – fossil primate of the Miocene epoch, probably ancestral to later hominids.

rank society – a society which limits its positions of prestige without affecting the access of the other members to the basic resources of life.

recessive genes – a gene which is masked by a dominant gene.

reciprocity – a transaction between groups within a community in the form of gifts and counter gifts prescribed by ritual and ceremony.

redemptive movements – religious movements with the purpose of transforming the individual.

redistribution – a form of exchange in which goods flow into a central place, such as a market, and are distributed again.

relative dating – the designation of an event or object as being younger or older than another in archeology.

revitalization movements – social movements of a religious nature with the purpose of a total reformation of the society.

rites of passage – religious ceremonies which mark important changes in the status of individuals, such as birth, marriage, and death.

Sangoan-Lupemban culture – Middle and Upper Paleolithic tradition found in the rain forest regions of Africa.

sedentarism – living in permanent settlements.

segmentary lineage system – a form of political organization in which a larger group is broken up into clans, which are segmented into lineages.

serial marriage – a form in which a man or a woman marries or lives with a series of partners in succession.

shaman – a person who has special religious power acquired through his own initiative and perhaps possesses certain special gifts such as healing or divination.

sib – see clan.

sign – a sound or gesture which has a natural or biological meaning.

silent trade – a form of barter in which no verbal communication takes place.

site – a place containing the archeological remains of previous human occupation.

social organization – same as social structure. The relationships that bind individuals together in a society.

social stratification – the ranking of people by socioeconomic class.

social structure – the relationships which hold a society together.

society – a group of people occupying the same territory, speaking the same language, and sharing the same cultural traditions.

sociolinguistics – a discipline concerned with the structure and use of language as it relates to society, culture, and human behavior.

soil-marks – stains that show up on the surface of recently plowed fields that reveal an archeological site.

Solutrean culture – dates from about 18,000 years ago in Spain and France.

sorcery – deliberate actions undertaken for the purpose of doing specific harm.

sororate – the custom that a widower marry the sister of his dead wife.

species – a population or group of populations, capable of interbreeding, that is reproductively isolated from other such groups.

status – prestige positions in a society. May be ranked or unranked.

stratified society – a society in which members do not have equal access to the basic resources which support life nor to social prestige.

stratigraphy – the most reliable relative method of dating the past in archeology, by means of geological strata.

structuralism – a theory of culture as an expression of the underlying structure of the mind.

subculture – a group sharing different standards within a larger culture.

symbol – any sound or gesture which stands for a meaning among a group of people.

syntax – in linguistics, parts of grammar which establish the rules or principles of phrase or sentence making.

tale – a creative narrative recognized as fiction for entertainment.

Tardenoisian culture – Mesolithic culture found in England, France, and Germany.

technology – objects made by men and the means of making them.

tells – great mounds revealing an archeological site.

theoretical linguistics – the study of language which makes a framework and a system for describing what happens in the whole encoding and sentence-making process for all languages.

theory – a system of validated hypotheses which explain phenomena systematically.

totem – a symbol, usually an animal but sometimes a plant, natural force or object, used by a clan as a means of identification, with religious significance.

totemism – a form of religion in which people are thought to be descended from animals, plants, or natural objects.

trade – a form of exchange between communities in which scarce items from one group are exchanged for desirable items from another group.

tribe – a group of bands which speak a common language, share a common culture, and occupy a specific region. The tribe may or may not be a unified political entity.

unilinear descent – establishes kinship exclusively through either the mother's or the father's line.

witchcraft – see *sorcery*. It is often seen as an inborn and often unconscious capacity to work evil.

world view – the unexpressed but implicit conceptions of a society or an individual of the limits and workings of their world.

Zinjanthropus – An australopithecine fossil found by Mary Leakey in Africa.

Bibliography

Aberle, David (1961) "Culture and Socialization" F. Hsu, ed. *Psychological Anthropology: Approaches to Culture and Personality.* Homewood, Ill.: Dorsey Press: 381–99.

Aberle, David F., Urie Bronfenbrenner, Eckhard H. Hess, Daniel R. Miller, David H. Schneider and James N. Spuhler (1963) "The Incest Taboo and the Mating Patterns of Animals" *American Anthropologist,* 65:253–65.

Adams, Robert McC. (1966) *The Evolution of Urban Society.* Chicago: Aldine.

Adams, Robert McC. (1960) "The Origin of Cities" *Scientific American,* 203:153–68.

Al-Issa, Ihsan and Wayne Dennis, eds. (1970) *Cross-Cultural Studies of Behavior.* New York: Holt, Rinehart and Winston.

Alland, Alexander (1970) *Adaptation in Cultural Evolution: An Approach to Medical Anthropology.* New York: Columbia University Press.

Anderson, Robert T. (1972) *Anthropology: A Perspective on Man.* Belmont, California: Wadsworth Publishing Co.

Ardrey, Robert (1961) *African Genesis: A Personal Investigation into the Animal Origins and Nature of Man.* New York: Atheneum.

Ardrey, Robert (1971) *The Social Contract.* New York: Dell.

Arensberg, Conrad (1961) "The Community as Object and Sample" *American Anthropologist,* 63:241-64.

Arensberg, Conrad M. and Arthur H. Niehoff (1964) *Introducing Social Change: A Manual for Americans Overseas.* Chicago: Aldine.

Bacon, Edward (1961) *Digging for History.* New York: John Day.

Bagby, P. (1953) "Culture and the Causes of Culture" *American Anthropologist,* 55:535–54.

Balandier, Georges (1971) *Political Anthropology.* New York: Pantheon.

Banton, Michael (1968) "Voluntary Association: Anthropological Aspects" *International Encyclopedia of the Social Sciences,* 16:357–62.

Barber, Bernard (1957) *Social Stratification.* New York: Harcourt Brace Jovanovich.

Barnett, H. G. (1953) *Innovation: The Basis of Cultural Change.* New York: McGraw-Hill.

Barnett, S. A. (1971) *The Human Species: A Biology of Man.* New York: Harper and Row.

Barnouw, Victor (1963) *Culture and Personality.* Homewood, Ill.: Dorsey Press.

Barth, Fredrick (1961) *Nomads of South Persia: The Basseri Tribe of the Khamseh Confederacy.* Boston: Little, Brown (Series in Anthropology).

Bascom, William (1965) "The Forms of Folklore-Prose Narratives" *Journal of American Folklore,* 78:3-20.

Bateson, Gregory (1958) *Naven.* Stanford, Calif.: Stanford University Press.

Beals, Ralph and Harry Hoijer (1971) *An Introduction to Anthropology.* New York: Macmillan (4th edition).

Beals, Alan R. with G. and L. Spindler (1973) *Culture in Process.* New York: Holt, Rinehart and Winston (2nd edition).

Beidelman, T. O., ed. (1971) *The Translation of Culture: Essays to E. E. Evans-Pritchard.* London: Tavistock.

Belshaw, Cyril S. (1958) "The Significance of Modern Cults in Melanesian Development" William Lessa and Evon Z. Vogt, eds., *Reader in Comparative Religion: An Anthropological Approach.* New York: Harper and Row.

Benedict, Ruth (1932) "Configurations of Culture in North America" *American Anthropologist,* 34:1-27.

Benedict, Ruth (1959) *Patterns of Culture.* New York: New American Library.

Bennett, John W. (1964) "Myth, Theory and Value in Cultural Anthropology" E. W. Caint and G. T. Bowles, eds., *Fact and Theory in Social Science.* Syracuse: Syracuse University Press.

Bernstein, Basin (1961) "Social Structure, Language and Learning" *Educational Research,* 3:163-76.

Berreman, Gerald D. (1962) *Behind Many Masks: Ethnography and Impression Management in a Himalayan Village.* Ithaca: Society for Applied Anthropology (Monograph No. 4).

Berreman, Gerald D. (1968) "Caste: The Concept of Caste" *International Encyclopedia of the Social Sciences,* 2:333-38.

Bidney, David (1953) *Theoretical Anthropology.* New York: Columbia University Press.

Binford, Lewis R. (1965) "Archaeological Systematics and the Study of Culture Process" *American Antiquity,* 31:203-10.

Binford, Lewis R. (1968) "Post-Pleistocene Adaptation" Sally and Lewis R. Binford, eds., *New Perspectives in Archeology.* Chicago: Aldine: 313-42.

Binford, Lewis R. (1967) "Smudge Pits and Hide Smoking: The Use of Analogy in Archaeological Reasoning" *American Antiquity,* 32:1-12.

Binford, Lewis R. and Sally R. (1972) *An Archaeological Perspective.* New York: Seminar Press (Studies in Archaeology).

Binford, Lewis R. and Sally R. (1966) "The Predatory Revolution: A Consideration of the Evidence for a New Subsistence Level" *American Anthropologist,* 68:508-12.

Birdwhistle, Ray L. (1970) *Kinesics and Content: Essays on Body Motion and Communication.* Philadelphia: University of Pennsylvania Press.

Bloch, Marc (1961) *Feudal Society.* Chicago: University of Chicago Press.

Blum, Harold F. (1961) "Does the Melanin Pigment of Human Skin Have Adaptive Value" *Quarterly Review of Biology,* 36:50-63.

Boas, Franz, ed. (1938) *General Anthropology.* New York: Heath.

Boas, Franz (1965) *The Mind of Primitive Man.* revised ed. New York: Free Press.

Boas, Franz (1962) *Primitive Art.* Gloucester, Mass.: Peter Smith.

Boas, Franz (1966) *Race, Language and Culture.* New York: Free Press.

Bock, Philip K. (1970) *Culture Shock: A Reader in Modern Cultural Anthropology.* New York: Random House-Alfred A. Knopf.

Bohannan, Paul (1966) *Social Anthropology.* New York: Holt, Rinehart and Winston.

Bohannan, Paul and George Dalton, eds. (1962) *Markets in Africa.* Evanston, Ill.: Northwestern University Press.

Bohannan, Paul and John Middleton, eds. (1968) *Kinship and Social Organization*. Garden City: Natural History Press (American Museum Source Books in Anthropology).

Bohannan, Paul and John Middleton, eds. (1968) *Marriage, Family, and Residence*. Garden City: Natural History Press (American Museum Source Books in Anthropology).

Bolinger, Dwight (1968) *Aspects of Language*. New York: Harcourt Brace Jovanovich.

Bordaz, Jacques (1970) *Tools of the Old and New Stone Age*. Garden City: Natural History Press.

Bordes, Francois (1968) *The Old Stone Age*. New York: McGraw-Hill.

Boserup, Ester (1965) *The Conditions of Agricultural Growth*. Chicago: Aldine.

Boyd, William C. (1963) "Four Achievements of the Genetical Method in Physical Anthropology" *American Anthropologist,* 65:243-52.

Boyd, William C. (1950) *Genetics and the Races of Man: An Introduction to Modern Physical Anthropology*. Boston: Little, Brown.

Brace, C. Loring (1971) *Atlas of Fossil Man*. New York: Holt, Rinehart and Winston.

Brace, C. Loring (1964) "A Consideration of Hominid Catastrophism" *Current Anthropology,* 5:3-45.

Brace, C. L. (1964) "A Nonracial Approach Towards the Understanding of Human Diversity" Ashley Montagu, ed., *The Concept of Race*. London: Free Press of Glencoe, Collier-Macmillan: 103-52.

Brace, C. Loring (1967) *The Stages of Human Evolution: Human and Cultural Origins*. Englewood Cliffs, N.J.: Prentice-Hall (Foundations of Modern Anthropology).

Braidwood, Robert J. (1960) "The Agricultural Revolution" *Scientific American,* 203:130-41.

Braidwood, Robert J. (1959) "Archaeology and the Evolutionary Theory" *Evolution and Anthropology: A Centennial Appraisal*. Washington, D.C.: Anthropological Society of Washington: 76-89.

Braidwood, Robert (1971) "The Earliest Village Communities of Southwestern Asia Reconsidered" Stuart Struever, ed., *Prehistoric Agriculture*. Garden City: Natural History Press: 236-51.

Braidwood, Robert J. (1952) *The Near East and the Foundations for Civilization*. Eugene: University of Oregon (Condon Lectures).

Braidwood, Robert J. (1967) *Prehistoric Men*. 7th ed. Glenview, Ill.: Scott, Foresman and Co.

Braidwood, Robert J. and Bruce Howe (1962) "Southwestern Asia Beyond the Lands of the Mediterranean Littoral" Robert Braidwood and Gordon Willey, eds., *Courses Towards Urban Life*. Viking Fund Publications in Anthropology, 32:132-46.

Braidwood, Robert J. and Gordon R. Willey (1962) *Courses Toward Urban Life: Archeological Consideration of Some Cultural Alternatives*. Chicago: Aldine (Publications in Anthropology Series, no. 32).

Breiul, Henri (1952) *Four Hundred Centuries of Cave Art*. Montignac: Centre d' Etudes et de Documentation Prehistoriques.

Brennan, Louis A. (1970) *American Dawn: A Model of American Prehistory*. London: Macmillan.

Brew, John O. (1968) *One Hundred Years of Anthropology*. Cambridge, Mass.: Harvard University Press.

Brinton, Crane (1953) *The Shaping of the Modern Mind*. New York: Mentor Books.

Bruner, Edward M. (1970) "Medan: The Role of Kinship in an Indonesian City" William Mangin, ed., *Peasants in Cities: Readings in the Anthropology of Urbanization*.

Buettner-Janusch, John (1959) "Natural Selection in Man: The ABO (H) Blood Group System" *American Anthropologist,* 61:437-56.

Buettner-Janusch, John (1973) *Physical Anthropology: A Perspective*. New York: John Wiley & Sons.

Burling, Robbins (1970) *Man's Many Voices.* New York: Holt, Rinehart and Winston.

Burling, Robbins (1969) "Linguistics and Ethnographic Description" *American Anthropologist,* 71:817–27.

Butzer, K. W. (1971) *Environment and Anthropology: An Ecological Approach to Prehistory.* 2nd ed. Chicago: Aldine-Atherton.

Calverton, V. F., ed. (1931) *The Making of Man: An Outline of Anthropology.* Westport, Conn.: Greenwood.

Campbell, Donald (1966) *Human Evolution: An Introduction to Man's Adaptations.* Chicago: Aldine.

Carneiro, Robert L. (1961) "Slash and Burn Cultivation among the Kuikuru and its Implications for Cultural Development in the Amazon Basin" J. Wilbert, ed. *The Evolution of Horticultural Systems in Native South America: Causes and Consequences.* Caracas: Sociedad de Ciencias Naturales La Salle: 47–68.

Carneiro, Robert L. (1970) "A Theory of the Origin of the State" *Science,* 169:733–38.

Chang, K.-C. (1967) *Rethinking Archaeology.* New York: Random House.

Chang, K.-C., ed. (1971) *Settlement Archaeology.* Palo Alto, Calif.: National Press.

Chapple, Eliot D. (1970) *Culture and Biological Man: Explorations in Behavioral Anthropology.* New York: Holt, Rinehart and Winston.

Chard, Chester S. (1969) *Man in Prehistory.* New York: McGraw-Hill.

Childe, V. Gordon (1968) *New Light on the Most Ancient Near East.* New York: Praeger.

Childe, V. Gordon (1958) "Retrospect" *Antiquity,* 32:69–74.

Childe, V. Gordon (1954) *What Happened in History.* Mammondsworth, Middlesex: Penguin Books.

Chomsky, Naom (1968) *Language and Mind.* New York: Harcourt Brace Jovanovich.

Clark, Grahame (1969) *World Prehistory: A New Outline.* Cambridge: Cambridge University Press.

Clark, Grahame and Stuart Piggott (1970) *Prehistoric Societies.* 2nd ed. Middlesex, Eng.: Penguin Books.

Clark, W. E. Le Gros (1963) *The Antecedents of Man.* New York: Harper and Row.

Clark, W. E. Le Gros (1973) *The Fossil Evidence for Human Evolution.* Chicago: University of Chicago Press.

Clark, W. E. Le Gros (1963) *Man-Apes or Ape-Men.* New York: Holt, Rinehart & Winston.

Clegg, E. J. (1968) *The Study of Man: An Introduction to Human Biology.* New York: American Elsevier Publishing Co.

Clifton, James A., ed. (1970) *Applied Anthropology: Readings in the Uses of the Science of Man.* Boston: Houghton Mifflin (Resources for the Study of Anthropology).

Codere, Helen (1950) *Fighting With Property.* Seattle: University of Washington Press (American Ethnological Society Monograph, 18).

Coe, M. D. and Kent V. Flannery (1966) "Microenvironments and Mesoamerican Prehistory" J. A. Graham, ed., *Ancient Mesoamerica.* Palo Alto: Peek Publications: 46–50.

Cohen, Myron L. (1968) "A Case Study of Chinese Family Economy and Development" *Journal of Asian and African Studies,* 3:161–80.

Cohen, Myron L. (1967) "Variations in Complexity Among Chinese Family Groups: The Impact of Modernization" *Transactions of the New York Academy of Sciences,* 29,5:638–47.

Cohen, Yehudi (1968) *Man in Adaptation: The Cultural Present.* Chicago: Aldine.

Coon, C. S. (1954) "Climate and Race" Harlow Shapley, ed., *Climatic Change.* Cambridge, Mass.: Harvard University Press: 13–34.

Coon, Carleton S. (1963) *The Origin of Races.* New York: Alfred A. Knopf.

Cottrell, Fred (1965) *Energy and Society. The Relation Between Energy, Social Change, and Economic Development.* New York: McGraw-Hill.

Cox, Oliver Cromwell (1959) *Caste, Class and Race: A Study in Dynamics.* New York: Monthly Review Press.

Dalton, George (1971) *Economic Anthropology and Development: Essays on Tribal and Peasant Economics.* New York: Basic Books.

Dalton, George, ed. (1967) *Tribal and Peasant Economies: Readings in Economic Anthropology.* Garden City: Natural History Press.

Daniel, Glyn E. (1950) *A Hundred Years of Archaeology.* London: Duckworth.

Darwin, Charles (1962 reissue) *The Origin of Species by Means of Natural Selection: Or, The Preservation of Favored Races in the Struggle for Life.* New York: Macmillan.

Davenport, W. (1959) "Linear Descent and Descent Groups" *American Anthropologist,* 61:557–73.

Davis, P. R. (1964) "Hominid Fossils from Bed I, Olduvai Gorge, Tankanyika" *Nature,* 201:967–68.

Deetz, James J. G. (1971) *Man's Imprint From the Past: A Reader in the Methods of Archaeology.* Boston: Little, Brown.

Deevy, Edward S., Jr. (1960) "The Human Population" *Scientific American,* 203:194–204.

Despres, Leo A. (1968) "Cultural Pluralism and the Study of Complex Societies" *Current Anthropology,* 9:3–26.

Dobyns, Henry F., Paul L. Doughty and Harold D. Lasswell, eds. (1971) *Peasants, Power, and Applied Social Change.* London: Sage.

Dobzhansky, Theodosius (1962) *Mankind Evolving: The Evolution of the Human Species.* New Haven: Yale University Press.

Douglas, Mary (1958) "Raffia Cloth Distribution in the Lele Economy" *Africa,* 28:109–22.

Downs, James F. and Herman K. Bleibtreu (1969) *Human Variation: An Introduction to Physical Anthropology.* Glencoe, Ill.: Glencoe Press.

Driver, Harold (1964) *Indians of North America.* Chicago: University of Chicago Press.

Dubos, Rene (1968) *So Human an Animal.* New York: Charles Scribner's Sons.

Durkheim, Émile (1965) *The Elementary Forms of the Religious Life.* New York: The Free Press.

Edmonson, Munro S. (1971) *Lore: An Introduction to the Science of Folklore.* New York: Holt, Rinehart and Winston.

Eggan, Fred (1954) "Social Anthropology and the Method of Controlled Comparison" *American Anthropologist,* 56:743–63.

Ehrlich, Paul R. and Anne H. (1970) *Population Resources, Environment: Issues in Human Ecology.* San Francisco: W. H. Freeman.

Eiseley, Loren C. (1958) *Darwin's Century: Evolution and the Man Who Discovered It.* Garden City: Doubleday.

Elkin, A. P. (1964) *The Australian Aborigines.* Garden City: Anchor Books.

Ember, Melvin and Carol R. Ember (1971) "The Conditions Favoring Matrilocal vs. Patrilocal Residence" *American Anthropologist,* 73:571–94.

Ember, Melvin (1967) "The Emergency of Neolocal Residence" *Transactions of the New York Academy of Sciences,* 30:391–402.

Emiliani, Casrae, et al. (1968) "The Pleistocene Epoch and the Evolution of Man" *Current Anthropology,* 9:27–47.

Erasmus, C. J. (1950) "Patolli, Pashisi, and the Limitation of Possibilities" *Southwestern Journal of Anthropology,* 6:369–81.

Erasmus, C. and W. Smith (1967) "Cultural Anthropology in the United States since 1900" *Southwestern Journal of Anthropology,* 23:11–40.

Ervin-Tripp, Susan M. (1973) *Language Acquisition and Communicative Choice.* Stanford: Stanford University Press.

Evans-Pritchard, Edward E. (1968) *The Nuer: A Description of the Modes of Livelihood and Political Institutions of a Nilotic People.* Oxford: Oxford University Press.

Evans-Pritchard, E. E. (1950) *Witchcraft, Oracles and Magic Among the Azande.* Oxford: Oxford University Press.

Farsoun Samih K. (1970) "Family Structure and Society in Modern Lebanon" Louise E. Sweet, ed., *Peoples and Cultures of the Middle East.* New York: Natural History Press, Vol. 2.

Firth, Raymond (1952) *Elements of Social Organization.* London: C. A. Watts and Company.

Firth, Raymond (1957) *Man and Culture: An Evaluation of Bronislaw Malinowski.* London: Routledge and Kegan Paul.

Firth, Raymond, ed. (1967) *Themes in Economic Anthropology.* London: Tavistock Publications.

Flannery, Kent (1965) "The Ecology of Early Food Production in Mesopotamia" *Science,* 147:1247–56.

Flannery, Kent (1971) "Origins and Ecological Effects of Early Domestication in Iran and the Near East" Stuart Struever, ed., *Prehistoric Agriculture.* Garden City: Natural History Press: 50–79.

Forde, Daryll (1968) "Double Descent Among the Yakö" Paul Bohannan and J. Middleton eds., *Marriage, Family and Residence.* Garden City: Natural History Press: 179–92.

Forde, C. Daryll (1963) *Habitat, Economy and Society.* New York: Dutton.

Forde, C. Daryll (1955) "The Nupe" Daryll Forde, ed. *Peoples of the Niger-Benue Confluence.* London: International African Institute (Ethnographic Survey of Africa. Western Africa, part 10): 17–52.

Fortes, Meyer (1969) *Kinship and the Social Order: The Legacy of Lewis Henry Morgan.* Chicago: Aldine.

Fortes, Meyer and E. E. Evans-Pritchard, eds. (1940) *African Political Systems.* Oxford: Oxford University Press.

Foster, G. M. (1955) "Peasant Society and the Image of the Limited Good" *American Anthropologist,* 67:293–315.

Frankfort, Henri (1959) *The Birth of Civilization in the Near East.* New York: Doubleday.

Fraser, Douglas, ed. (1966) *The Many Faces of Primitive Art: A Critical Anthology.* Englewood Cliffs, N.J.: Prentice-Hall.

Frazer, Sir James George (1931) "Magic and Religion" V. F. Calverton, ed. *The Making of Man: An Outline of Anthropology.* Westport, Conn.: Greenwood: 693–713.

Frazer, Sir James George (1961 reissue) *The New Golden Bough.* Garden City: Anchor Books.

Freud, Sigmund (n.d.) *Civilization and its Discontents.* Garden City: Anchor Books.

Fried, Morton (1960) "On the Evolution of Social Stratification and the State" S. Diamond, ed., *Culture in History: Essays in Honor of Paul Radin.* New York: Columbia University Press: 713–31.

Fried, Morton (1967) *The Evolution of Political Society: An Essay in Political Anthropology.* New York: Random House.

Fried, Morton (1972) *The Study of Anthropology.* New York: Thomas Y. Crowell.

Fried, Morton H., ed. (1968) *Readings in Anthropology.* 2nd ed. New York: Thomas Y. Crowell.

Garn, Stanley (1964) "The Absorption of Melanin in the Ultraviolet" *American Anthropologist,* 66:427.

Garn, Stanley M. (1954) "Cultural Factors Affecting the Study of Human Biology" *Human Biology,* 26:77–79.

Garn, Stanley M. (1961) *Human Races.* Springfield, Ill.: Charles C Thomas.

Geertz, Clifford (1963) *Agricultural Involution: The Process of Ecological Change in Indonesia.* Berkeley: University of California Press.

Geertz, Clifford (1965) "The Impact of the Concept of Culture on the Concept of Man" John R. Platt, ed., *New Views of Man.* Chicago: University of Chicago Press.

Geertz, Clifford (1968) "Religion: Anthropological Study" *International Encyclopedia of the Social Sciences,* 13. New York: Macmillan.

Gellner, Ernest (1969) *Saints of the Atlas.* Chicago: University of Chicago Press (The Nature of Human Society Series).

Gibbs, James L., Jr. (1965) "The Kpelle of Liberia" James L. Gibbs, ed., *Peoples of Africa.* New York: Holt, Rinehart & Winston.

Godlier, Maurice (1971) "Salt Currency and the Circulation of Commodities Among the Baruya of New Guinea" George Dalton, ed., *Studies in Economic Anthropology.* Washington, D.C.: American Anthropological Association (Anthropological Studies No. 7).

Goldschmidt, Walter (1971) *Exploring the Ways of Mankind.* New York: Holt, Rinehart and Winston, 2nd ed.

Goode, William J. (1963) *World Revolution and Family Patterns.* New York: Free Press.

Goodenough, Ward (1961) "Comment on Cultural Evolution" *Daedalus,* 90:521–28.

Goodenough, Ward (1956) "Componential Analysis and the Study of Meaning" *Language,* 32:195–216.

Goodenough, Ward (1970) *Description and Comparison in Cultural Anthropology.* Chicago: Aldine (Lewis H. Morgan Lecture Series).

Goodenough, Ward, ed. (1964) *Explorations in Cultural Anthropology: Essays in Honor of George Murdock,* New York: McGraw-Hill.

Goodenough, Ward (1956a) "Residence Rules" *Southwestern Journal of Anthropology,* 12:22–37.

Goodenough, Ward (1965) "Rethinking Status" and "Role: Toward a General Model of the Cultural Organization of Social Relationships" Michael Benton, ed., *The Relevance of Models for Social Anthropology, ASA Monographs 1.* New York: Praeger.

Goodfellow, D. M. (1973) *Principles of Economic Sociology: The Economics of Primitive Life As Illustrated from the Bantu Peoples of South and East Africa.* Westport, Conn.: Negro Universities Press (Reprint of 1939 edition).

Goodman, Mary Ellen (1967) *The Individual and Culture.* Homewood, Ill.: Dorsey Press.

Goody, Jack, ed. (1972) *Developmental Cycle in Domestic Groups.* New York: Cambridge University Press (Papers in Social Anthropology, No. 1).

Gough, E. Kathleen (1968) "The Nayars and the Definition of Marriage" Paul Bohannan and J. Middleton, eds., *Marriage, Family and Residence.* New York: Natural History Press: 49–71.

Graburn, Nelson H. (1971) *Readings in Kinship and Social Structure.* New York: Harper and Row.

Greene, John C. (1959) *The Death of Adam.* Ames, Iowa: Iowa State University Press.

Greenberg, Joseph H. (1968) *Anthropological Linguistics: An Introduction.* New York: Random House.

Gulliver, P. (1968) "Age Differentiation" *International Encyclopedia of the Social Sciences,* 1:157–62.

Hallowell, A. Irving (1955) *Culture and Experience*. Philadelphia: University of Pennsylvania Press.

Hammond, Peter B. (1971) *An Introduction to Cultural and Social Anthropology*. New York: Macmillan.

Harlan, J. R. and D. Zohary (1966) "Distribution of Wild Wheats and Barley" *Science*, 153:1074–80.

Harner, Michael J. (1970) "Population Pressure and the Social Evolution of Agriculturalists" *Southwestern Journal of Anthropology*, 26:67–86.

Harris, Marvin (1965) "The Cultural Ecology of India's Sacred Cattle" *Current Anthropology*, 7:51–66.

Harris, Marvin (1971) *Culture, Man, and Nature: An Introduction to General Anthropology*. New York: Thomas Y. Crowell Company.

Harris, Marvin (1968) *The Rise of Anthropological Theory*. New York: Thomas Y. Crowell.

Harrison, G. A., J. S. Weiner, J. M. Tanner, and N. A. Barnicot (1964) *Human Biology: An Introduction to Human Evolution, Variation and Growth*. New York: Oxford University Press.

Haviland, W. A. (1970) "Tikal, Guatemala and Mesomerican Urbanism" *World Archaeology*, 2:186–198.

Haviland, W. A. (1974) "Farming, Seafaring and Bilocal Residence on the Coast of Maine" *Man in the Northeast* (in press).

Hawkins, Gerald S. (1965) *Stonehenge Decoded*. Garden City: Doubleday.

Hays, H. R. (1965) *From Ape to Angel: An Informal History of Social Anthropology*. New York: Alfred A. Knopf.

Helm, Hune (1962) "The Ecological Approach in Anthropology" *American Journal of Sociology*, 67:630–49.

Herskovits, Melville (1952) *Economic Anthropology*. New York: Alfred A. Knopf.

Hewes, Gordon W. (1973) "Primate Communication and the Gestural Origin of Language" *Current Anthropology*, 14:5–24.

Hjelmslev, Louis (1970) *Language: An Introduction*. Francis J. Whitfield, trans., Madison: University of Wisconsin Press.

Hodges, Henry (1970) *Technology in the Ancient World*. New York: Alfred A. Knopf (Borzoi).

Hodges, Margaret (1964) *Early Anthropology in the Sixteenth and Seventeenth Centuries*. Philadelphia: University of Pennsylvania Press.

Hoebel, E. Adamson (1966) *Anthropology: The Study of Man*. New York: McGraw-Hill (3rd ed.).

Hoebel, E. Adamson (1954) *The Law of Primitive Man: A Study in Comparative Legal Dynamics*. Cambridge: Harvard University Press.

Hole, Frank, Kent Flannery and James A. Neely (1969) *Prehistory and Ecology of the Del Luran Plain*. Ann Arbor: University of Michigan, Museum of Anthropology (Memoirs, No. 1).

Hole, Frank and Robert Heizer (1973) *An Introduction to Prehistoric Archaeology*. New York: Holt, Rinehart and Winston. (3rd ed.).

Honigmann, J. (1954) *Culture and Personality*. New York: Harper and Row.

Hsu, Francis (1961) *Psychological Anthropology: Approaches to Culture and Personality*. Homewood, Ill.: Dorsey Press.

Hubert, Henri and Marcel Mauss (1964) *Sacrifice*. Chicago: University of Chicago Press.

Hulse, Frederick S. (1971) *The Human Species*. New York: Random House (2nd ed.).

Hulse, Frederick S. (1963) "Race as an Evolutionary Episode" F. S. Hulse, ed., *The Human Species: An Introduction to Physical Anthropology*. New York: Random House: 237–65.

Hymes, Dell (1964) *Language in Culture and Society: A Reader in Linguistics and Anthropology.* New York: Harper and Row.

Hymes, Dell, ed. (1972) *Reinventing Anthropology.* New York: Pantheon.

The Impact of the Natural Sciences on Archaeology (1970) London: Oxford University Press (contributions to a symposium held by the Royal Society and the British Academy, organized by a committee under the chairmanship of T. E. Allibone, 1969).

Inkeles, A. and D. J. Levinson (1954) "National Character: The Study of Modal Personality and Socio-Cultural Systems" in G. Lindzey (ed.) *Handbook of Social Psychology.* Cambridge: Addison-Wesley: 977–1020.

Jennings, Jesse D. (1968) *Prehistory of North America.* New York: McGraw-Hill.

Joffe, Julian A. (1970) *Studies in the History of Civilization.* New York: Philosophical Library.

Jolly, Alison (1972) *The Evolution of Primate Behavior.* New York: Macmillan.

Jopling, Carol F. (1971) *Art and Aesthetics in Primitive Societies: A Critical Anthology.* New York: E. P. Dutton.

Jorgensen, Joseph (1972) *The Sun Dance Religion.* Chicago: University of Chicago Press.

Jung, Carl (1961) *Memories, Dreams, Reflections.* New York: Vintage Books.

Kaplan, David (1972) *Culture Theory.* Englewood Cliffs, N.J.: Prentice-Hall (Foundations of Modern Anthropology).

Kaplan, David (1968) "The Superorganic: Science or Metaphysics" Robert Manners and David Kaplan, eds., *Theory in Anthropology: A Sourcebook.* Chicago: Aldine-Atherton.

Kaplan, Lawrence (1971) "Archaeology and Domestication in American Phaseolus (Beans)" Stuart Struever, ed., *Prehistoric Agriculture.* Garden City: Natural History Press: 516–33.

Kardiner, Abram and Edward Preble (1961) *They Studied Men.* New York: Mentor.

Keesing, R. M. and F. M. Keesing (1971) *New Perspectives in Cultural Anthropology.* New York: Holt, Rinehart and Winston.

Kelley, J. Charles and Carrol L. Riley, eds. (1969) *Pre-Columbian Contact Within Nuclear America.* Carbondale, Ill.: University Museum, Southern Illinois University (Mesoamerican Studies, 4. Research Records of the University Museum '69 MYA).

Kelso, Jack (1970) *Physical Anthropology.* Philadelphia: Lippincott.

Kenyon, Kathleen M. (1970) *Archaeology in the Holy Land.* New York: Praeger (3rd revised ed.).

King, Robert C. (1968) *A Dictionary of Genetics.* New York: Oxford University Press.

Klein, Richard (1969) *Man and Culture in the Late Pleistocene: A Case Study.* Scranton, Pa.: Chandler Publishing Co.

Klineberg, Otto (1951) "Race and Psychology" *The Race Question in Modern Science.* Paris: UNESCO:55–122.

Kluckhohn, Clyde (1949) *Mirror For Man.* New York: McGraw-Hill.

Krader, Lawrence (1965) *Formation of the State.* Englewood Cliffs, N.J.: Prentice-Hall (Foundation on Modern Anthropology).

Kroeber, Alfred (1948) *Anthropology: Race, Language, Culture, Psychology, Prehistory.* New York: Harcourt Brace Jovanovich.

Kroeber, A. L. and Clyde Kluckhohn (1952) *Culture: A Critical Review of Concepts and Definitions.* Harvard University (Papers of the Peabody Museum of American Archaeology and Ethnology, 47).

Kroeber, A. L. (1939) "Cultural and Natural Areas of Native North America." Berkeley, Calif.: University of California Pub. in *American Archaeology and Ethnology*, vol. 38.

Kroeber, Alfred (1958) "Totem and Taboo: An Ethnologic Psychoanalysis" William Lessa and Evon Z. Vogt, eds., *Reader in Comparative Religion: An Anthropological Approach*. New York: Harper and Row.

Kuhn, Thomas S. (1968) *The Structure of Scientific Revolutions*. Chicago: University of Chicago Press (International Encyclopedia of Unified Science, vol. 2, no. 2)

Kummer, Hans (1971) *Primate Societies: Group Techniques of Ecological Adaptation*. Chicago: Aldine.

Kuper, Hilda (1965) "The Swazi of Swaziland" James L. Gibbs, ed. *Peoples of Africa*. New York: Holt, Rinehart and Winston: 479-511.

Kushner, Gilibert (1969) *Anthropology of Complex Societies*. Stanford: Stanford University Press.

Laguna, Frederica de, ed. (1960) *Selected Papers From The American Anthropologist*. Evanston: Row, Peterson.

Laguna, Grace A. de (1966) *On Existence and the Human World*. New Haven: Yale University Press

Lanning, Edward P. (1967) *Peru Before the Incas*. Englewood Cliffs, N.J.: Prentice-Hall.

Lanternari, Vittorio (1963) *The Religions of the Oppressed*. New York: Mentor.

Lasler, Gabriel W. (1973) *Physical Anthropology*. New York: Holt, Rinehart and Winston.

Leach, Edmund (1962) "On Certain Unconsidered Aspects of Double Descent Systems" *Man*, 214:13-34.

Leach, Edmund (1962) "The Determinants of Differential Cross-Cousin Marriage" *Man*, 62:238.

Leach, Edmund (1963) "The Determinants of Differential Cross-Cousin Marriage" *Man*, 63:87.

Leach, Edmund (1965) *Political Systems of Highland Burma*. Boston: Beacon Press.

Leach, Edmund (1961) *Rethinking Anthropology*. London: Athione Press.

Leakey, Louis S. B. and V. N. Goodall (1969) *Unveiling Man's Origins*. Cambridge, Mass.: Schenkman.

Leakey, Louis S. B. and Jack and Stephanie Frost, eds. (1971) *Adam or Ape: A Sourcebook About Early Man*. Cambridge, Mass.: Schenkman.

LeClair, Edward and Harold K. Schneider, eds. (1968) *Economic Anthropology: Readings in Theory and Analysis*. New York: Holt, Rinehart and Winston.

Lee, Richard B. (1969) "!Kung Bushman Subsistence: An Input-Output Analysis" Andrew P. Vayda, ed., *Environment and Cultural Behavior*. Garden City: Natural History Press: 47-49.

Lee, Richard B. and Irven DeVore, eds. (1968) *Man the Hunter*. Chicago: Aldine.

Ledds, Anthony and Andrew P. Vayda, eds. (1965) *Man, Culture and Animals: The Role of Animals in Human Ecological Adjustments*. Washington, D.C.: American Association for the Advancement of Science.

Lenski, Garhard (1966) *Power and Privilege: A Theory of Social Stratification*. New York: McGraw-Hill.

Lerner, Michael (1968) *Heredity, Evolution, and Society*. San Francisco: W. H. Freeman and Company (Series of Books in Biology).

Lessa, William A. and Evon Z. Vogt, eds. (1972) *Reader in Comparative Religion: An Anthropological Approach*. New York: Harper and Row.

LeVine, Robert A. (1973) *Culture, Behavior and Personality*. Chicago: Aldine.

Lévi-Strauss, Claude (1969) *The Elementary Structures of Kinship*. Boston: Beacon Press.

Lévi-Strauss, Claude (1971) "The Family" Harry L. Shapiro, ed., *Man, Culture and Society*. London: Oxford University Press: 333-57.

Lévi-Strauss, Claude (1963) *Structural Anthropology*. New York: Basic Books.

Bibliography

Lévi-Strauss, Claude (1963) *Totemism*. Boston: Beacon Press.

Lewis, I. M. (1965) "Problems in the Comparative Study of Unilineal Descent" Michael Banton, ed., *The Relevance of Models for Social Organization* (A.S.A. Monograph No. 1).

Lieberman, Leonard (1968) "The Debate Over Race: A Study in the Sociology of Knowledge" *Phylon,* 29:127–41.

Lienhardt, Godfrey (1971) "Religion" Harry Shapiro, ed., *Man, Culture and Society*. London: Oxford University Press: 382–401.

Leinhardt, Godfrey (1964) *Social Anthropology*. London: Oxford University Press.

Linton, Ralph (1936) *The Study of Man*. New York: Appleton-Century-Crofts.

Lounsbury, F. (1964a) "The Structural Analysis of Kinship Semantics" Horace G. Lunt, ed., *Proceedings of the Ninth International Congress of Linguists*. The Hague: Mouton: 1073–93.

Lowie, Robert (1966) *Culture and Ethnology*. New York: Basic Books.

Lyons, John (1970) *Noam Chomsky*. New York: Viking Press.

MacNeish, Robert S. (1966) "Ancient Mesoamerican Civilization" J. A. Graham, ed., *Ancient Mesoamerica*. Palo Alto: Peek Publications: 39–45.

Mair, Lucy (1971) *Marriage,* Baltimore: Penguin.

Mair, Lucy (1969) *Witchcraft*. New York: McGraw-Hill.

Malefijt, Annemarie de Waal (1969) *Religion and Culture: An Introduction to Anthropology of Religion*. London: Macmillan.

Malinowski, Bronislaw (1922) *Argonauts of the Western Pacific*. New York: Dutton.

Maybury-Lewis, David (1960) "Parallel Descent and the Apinaye Anomaly" *Southwestern Journal of Anthropology,* 16:191–216.

Mayr, Ernst (1963) *Animal Species and Evolution*. Cambridge, Mass.: The Belknap Press of Harvard University Press.

McGrinsey, Charles R. (1972) *Public Archaeology*. New York: Seminar Press (Studies in Archaeology).

Mead, Margaret (1928) *Coming of Age in Samoa*. New York: Morrow.

Mead, Margaret (1970) *Culture and Commitment*. Garden City: Natural History Press.

Michaels, Joseph W. (1973) *Dating Methods in Archaeology*. New York: Seminar Press (Studies in Archaeology).

Middleton, John, ed. (1970) *From Child to Adult: Studies in the Anthropology of Education*. Garden City: Natural History Press (American Museum Source Books in Anthropology).

Montagu, Ashley (1964) *The Concept of Race*. London: Free Press of Glencoe, Collier-Macmillan.

Montagu, Ashley (1964) *Man's Most Dangerous Myth: The Fallacy of Race*. New York: The World Publishing Company, (4th ed.).

Murdock, George Peter (1965) *Social Structure*. New York: Free Press.

Murphy, Robert (1971) *The Dialectics of Social Life: Alarms and Excursions in Anthropological Theory*. New York: Basic Books.

Murphy, Robert and Leonard Kasdan (1959) "The Structure of Parallel Cousin Marriage" *American Anthropologist,* 61:17–29.

Nash, Manning (1966) *Primitive and Peasant Economic Systems*. San Francisco: Chandler Publishing Co.

Needham, Rodney (1973) *Belief, Language and Experience*. Chicago: University of Chicago Press.

Nimkoff, M. F. and Russell Middleton (1960–61) "Types of Family and Types of Economy" *The American Journal of Sociology,* 66,3:215–26.

Ortiz, Alfonso (1969) *The Tewa World*. Chicago: University of Chicago Press.

Osborne, Richard H., ed. (1971) *The Biological and Social Meaning of Race*. San Francisco: W. H. Freeman.

Oswalt, Wendell H. (1970) *Understanding Our Culture*. New York: Holt, Rinehart and Winston.

Oswalt, Wendell H. (1972) *Other Peoples Other Customs. World Ethnography and Its History*. New York: Holt, Rinehart and Winston.

Otten, Charlotte N. (1971) *Anthropology and Art: Reading in Cross-Cultural Aesthetics*. Garden City: Natural History Press (American Museum Sourcebooks in Anthropology).

Ottenberg, Phoebe (1965) "The Afikpo Ibo of Eastern Nigeria" James L. Gibbs, ed., *Peoples of Africa*. New York: Holt, Rinehart and Winston.

Ottenbein, Keith F. (1971) *The Evolution of War*. New Haven: HRAF Press.

Parsons, Talcott (1958) "Religious Perspectives in Sociology and Social Psychology" William Lessa and Evon Z. Vogt, eds., *Reader in Comparative Religion:* An Anthropological Approach. New York: Harper and Row.

Pelto, Tertti J. (1966) *The Nature of Anthropology*. Columbus: Charles E. Merrill (Social Science Perspectives).

Penniman, T. K. (1965) *A Hundred Years of Anthropology*. London: Ducksworth.

Pfeiffer, John (1972) *The Emergence of Man*. New York: Harper and Row (2nd ed.).

Piddocke, Stuart (1965) "The Potlatch System of the Southern Kwakiutl: A New Perspective" *Southwestern Journal of Anthropology*, 21:244-64.

Piggott, Stuart (1965) *Ancient Europe From the Beginnings of Agriculture to Classical Antiquity: A Survey*. Edinburgh: University Press.

Pilbeam, David (1972) *The Ascent of Man*. New York: Macmillan.

Pospisil, Leopold (1971) *Anthropology of Law: A Comparative Theory*. New York: Harper and Row.

Powdermaker, Hortense (1966) *Stranger and Friend: The Way of An Anthropologist*. New York: Norton.

Price-Williams, D. R., ed. (1970) *Cross-Cultural Studies: Selected Readings*. Baltimore: Penguin (Penguin Modern Psychology Readings).

Pumpelly, R. (1908) *Explorations in Turkestan: Expedition of 1904: Prehistoric Civilization of Anau*. Washington, D.C.: Publications of the Carnegie Institute, #73, Vol. 1.

Renfrew, Colin (1970) "The Treering Calibration of Radio-Carbon: An Archaeological Evaluation." *Proceedings of the Prehistoric Society*, 36:280-311.

Riley, Carroll L. (1972) *The Origins of Civilization*. Carbondale: Southern Illinois University Press.

Rodman, Hyman (1968) "Class Culture" *International Encyclopedia of the Social Sciences*, 15:332-37.

Sahlins, Marshall (1968) *Tribesmen*. Englewood Cliffs, N.J.: Prentice-Hall (Foundations of Modern Anthropology).

Sanders, William and Barbara Price (1968) *Mesoamerica: The Evolution of a Civilization*. New York: Random House.

Sapir, E. (1924) "Culture, Genuine or Spurious?" *American Journal of Sociology*, 29:401-29.

Sapir, E. (1917) "Do We Need a Superorganic?" *American Anthropologist*, 19:441-47.

Sapir, E. (1921) *Language*. New York: Harcourt Brace Jovanovich.

Sapir, E. (1916) *Time Perspective in Aboriginal American Culture: A Study in Method*. Ottawa: Geological Society of Canada (Memoir 90, Anthropological Series, no. 13).

Sauer, Carl O. (1971) "Planters of the Old World and Their Household Animals (excerpt)" Stuart Struever, ed., *Prehistoric Agriculture*. Garden City: Natural History Press: 407-14.

Schaller, George B. (1963) *The Mountain Gorilla.* Chicago: University of Chicago Press.

Service, Elman R. (1966) *The Hunters.* Englewood Cliffs, N.J.: Prentice-Hall (Foundations of Modern Anthropology)

Service, Elman R. (1971) *Primitive Social Organization: An Evolutionary Perspective.* New York: Random House (2nd ed.).

Shapiro, Harry, ed. (1960) *Man, Culture and Society.* New York: Oxford University Press.

Shinnie, Margaret (1970) *Ancient African Kingdoms.* New York: New American Library (Mentor).

Simons, Edwyn L. (1972) *Primate Evolution.* New York: Macmillan.

Simons, Edwyn L. (1963) "Some Fallacies In the Study of Hominoid Phylogeny" *Science,* 141:879–88.

Simpson, George G. (1949) *The Meaning of Evolution.* New Haven: Yale University Press.

Slobin, Dan I. (1971) *Psycholinguistics.* Glenview, Ill.: Scott, Foresman.

Smith, Raymond (1970) "Social Stratification in the Caribbean" Leonard Plotnicov and Arthur Tudin, ed., *Essays in Comparative Social Stratification.* Pittsburgh: University of Pittsburgh Press.

Solheim, William (1970) "Relics from Two Diggings Indicate Thais Were the First Agrarians" *New York Times,* Monday, January 12.

Speck, Frank G. (1920) "Penobscot Shamanism" *Memoirs of the American Anthropology Association.* VI:239–88.

Spiro, Melford E. (1954) "Is the Family Universal?" *American Anthropologist,* 56:839–46.

Spiro, Melford E. (1966) "Religion: Problems of Definition and Explanation" Michael Banton, ed., *Anthropological Approaches to the Study of Religion,* ASA Monograph #s. London: Tavistock Publications.

Stanner, W. E. H. (1968) "Radcliffe-Brown, A. R." *International Encyclopedia of the Social Sciences,* 13. New York: Macmillan.

Stephens, William N. (1963) *The Family in Cross-Cultural Perspective.* New York: Holt, Rinehart and Winston.

Steward, Julian H., et al. (1955) *Irrigation Civilizations: A Comparative Study.* Washington, D.C.: Pan American Union (Social Science Monographs, No. 1).

Steward, Julian H. (1972) *Theory of Culture Change: The Methodology of Multilinear Evolution.* Urbana, Ill.: University of Illinois Press.

Tattersall, Ian (1970) *Man's Ancestors: An Introduction to Primate and Human Evolution.* London: John Murray (Introductory Studies in Biology).

Tax, Sol, ed. (1962) *Anthropology Today: Selections.* Chicago: University of Chicago Press.

Thomas, W. L., ed. (1956) *Man's Role in Changing the Face of the Earth.* Chicago: University of Chicago Press.

Trigger, Bruce (1971) "Archaeology and Ecology" *World Archaeology,* 2:321–36.

Trigger, Bruce (1968) *Beyond History: The Methods of Prehistory.* New York: Holt, Rinehart and Winston (Studies in Anthropological Method).

Turnbull, Colin (1961) *The Forest People.* New York: Simon & Schuster.

Turner, V. W. (1969) *The Ritual Process.* Chicago: Aldine.

Turner, V. W. (1957) *Schism and Continuity in an African Society.* Manchester: The University Press.

Turnin, Melvin M. (1967) *Social Stratification: The Forms and Functions of Inequality.* Englewood Cliffs, N.J.: Prentice-Hall (Foundations of Modern Sociology).

Tylor, Sir Edward B. (1931) "Animism" V. F. Calverton, ed., *The Making of Man: An Outline of Anthropology.* New York: The Modern Library.

Tylor, Edward Burnett (1871) *Primitive Culture: Researches Into the Development of Mythology, Philosophy, Religion, Language, Art and Customs.* London: J. Murray.

Valentine, Charles A. (1968) *Culture and Poverty.* Chicago: University of Chicago Press.

Van Gennep, Arnold (1960) *The Rites of Passage.* Chicago: University of Chicago Press.

Van Lawick-Goodall, Jane (1972) *In the Shadow of Man.* Boston: Houghton-Mifflin.

Vansina, Jan (1965) *Oral Tradition: A Study in Historical Methodology,* translated by H. M. Wright. Chicago: Aldine.

Vayda, Andrew P. (1961) "A Re-Examination of Northwest Coast Economic Systems" *Transactions of the New York Academy of Sciences,* 2nd series, 23:618-24.

Vayda, Andrew P. (1961) "Expansion and Warfare Among Swidden Agriculturalists" *American Anthropologist,* 63:346-58.

Vernon, Philip E. (1960) "Race and Intelligence" *Man, Race and Darwin.* London: Oxford University Press.

Voget, F. W. (1960) "Man and Culture: An Essay in Changing Anthropological Interpretation" *American Anthropologist,* 62:943-65.

Wagner, Philip L. (1960) *The Human Use of the Earth.* Glencoe, Ill.: Free Press.

Wallace, Anthony F. C. (1970) *Culture and Personality.* New York: Random House (2nd ed.).

Wallace, Anthony F. C. (1965) "The Problem of the Psychological Validity of Componential Analysis" *American Anthropologist, Special Publication,* 67, no. 5, part 2:229-48.

Wallace, Anthony F. C. (1956) "Revitalization Movements" *American Anthropologist,* 58:264-81.

Wardhaugh, Ronald (1972) *Introduction to Linguistics.* New York: McGraw-Hill.

Washburn, Sherwood L. (1963) "The Study of Race" *American Anthropologist,* 65:521-31.

Washburn, Sherwood L. and Phyllis Dolhinow, eds. (1972) *Perspectives on Human Evolution, Vol. 2.* New York: Holt, Rinehart and Winston.

Washburn, Sherwood L. and C. S. Lancaster (1967) "The Evolution of Hunting" N. Korn and F. W Thompson, eds., *Human Evolution: Readings in Physical Anthropology.* New York: Holt, Rinehart and Winston: 67-83.

Watson, Patty Jo, Steven A. Leblanc and Charles L. Redman (1971) *Explanation in Archaeology.* New York: Columbia University Press.

Westermarck, Edward A. (1926) *A Short History of Marriage.* New York: Macmillan.

Wheeler, Martimer (1966) *Civilizations of the Indus Valley and Beyond.* New York: McGraw-Hill.

White, Leslie (1959) *The Evolution of Culture: The Development of Civilization to the Fall of Rome.* New York: McGraw-Hill.

White, Leslie (1949) *The Science of Culture: A Study of Man and Civilization.* New York: Farrar and Strauss.

White, Leslie (1940) "The Symbol: The Origin and Basis of Human Behavior" *Philosophy of Science,* 7:451-63.

Whiting, Beatrice B., ed. (1963) *Six Cultures: Studies of Child Rearing.* New York: Wiley.

Whiting, J. and J. Child (1953) *Child Training and Personality: A Cross-Cultural Study.* New York: McGraw-Hill.

Willey, Gordon R. (1966) *An Introduction to American Archaeology, Vol, 1, North and Middle America.* Englewood Cliffs, N.J.: Prentice-Hall.

Wolf, Eric (1966) *Peasants.* Englewood Cliffs, N.J.: Prentice-Hall (Foundations of Modern Anthropology).

Wolf, Eric (1959) *Sons of the Shaking Earth.* Chicago: University of Chicago press.

Index

Bella Coola, and cognatic descent, 385
Benedict, Ruth, 307–308, 590
　definition of culture, 306–308
　and individual personality, 310–311
Berdache, 316
Berreman, Gerald D., definition of caste, 410
Bifurcate-merging system, description of, 391
Bilateral descent, 384–385
Bilek, and cognatic descent, 385
Boas, Franz
　and American Indian culture, 15, 26
　reaction to evolutionism, 26–27
　study of Kwakiutl Indians, 306
Body type, 153–154
Bordes, François, and Lascaux caves, 210
Bow and arrow, 203
Boyd, William, definition of race, 159
Brace, Loring, and Neanderthal man, 139
Brachiation, definition of, 69
Brain
　of *Australopithecus africanus*, 115
　development in early hominids, 111–112, 124, 201
　of Neanderthal man, 135
　of primates, 68–69, 91–92

Chagnon, Napoleon A., and Yąnomamö people, 272–273
Chellean-Acheulian tradition, 197–200
Chenchu (Hyderabad), and divorce, 369
Cheyenne
　political organization of, 457, 481
　social control among, 474
Chiefdoms, 459–460
Child, I. L., and child-rearing, 312–313
Child-rearing, 356–358
　adolescence, 308–309
　of Alorese, 311–312
　and individual personality, 312–313
　of Japanese, 313, 315
　in New Guinea, 370
　of primates, 93–94
Chimpanzees
　description of, 74–76
　language of, 77
　learning abilities of, 79–80
Clothing
　history of, 277–278
　during Neolithic, 227–228
Code of Hammurabi, 246
Codrington, R. H., definition of mana, 500

Cognatic descent, 385
　and Hawaiian system, 389–390
　rise of, 388
Cro-Magnon man
　and art, 209
　description of, 132, 139–142
　origin of, 141–142
Crow Indians
　and reciprocity, 434
　kinship terminology, 392
　shaman of, 508
　Tobacco Society, associations of, 407–408
Chrysanthemum and the Sword, The (Benedict), 590
Cuban Revolution, 558
Cultural adaptation, 272–274
　and *Homo sapiens*, 150
　and hunting-gathering, 336
　in Lower Paleolithic, 197, 199–200
　during Stone Ages, 207
　in Upper Paleolithic, 203
　　See also Adaptation; cultural change
Cultural change, 274
　adaptation to, 565
　and African tribes, 563–564
　of Blackfeet Indians, 563
　in Japan, 567–570
　mechanisms of, 552–554, 556–559
　during Neolithic Age, 242–246
　of Pueblo Indians, 560–562
　and Tanala, 562–563
　　See also Adaptation; cultural adaptation
Cultural configuration, 306–308
Cultural ecology, definition of, 33–34
Cultural evolution, categories of, 195
Cultural fixations, 313
Cultural focus, definition of, 275
Cultural isolation mechanism, 150
Cultural materialism, definition of, 33
Cultural pluralism, 578–580
Cultural relativism, definition of, 27, 276
Cultural terminology, 293
Cultural traits, and natural selection, 53
Cultural transmission, 309
Culture
　and abnormal personality, 316–318
　and adaptation, 591–593
　and art, 524–525
　and biological change, 575
　characteristics of, 268–272
　concept of, 263–268
　definitions of, 8–9, 264

Malinowski, Bronislaw (*Continued*)
  and personality, 310–311
  and religion, 496
  social order in Trobriand Islands, 474
Marriage
  and choice of mate, 361–362
  in matrilineal descent group, 383
  and sexual access, 358
Marx, Karl, 22
  and social class system, 411–412
Masai and age-grouping, 403
Matrilineal descent, description of, 381–383
Matrilocal residence, 367–368
Maya
  loss of data on, 589
  religion of, 251
  in Tikal, 170, 172–175
Mbuti Pygmies (Congolese Ituri), 335, 338
  and crime, 482
  hunting style of, 337
  and social control, 483–485
Mead, Margaret, 361
  and individual personality, 310–311
  and Manus and cultural change, 567
  and Samoan adolescents, 13, 308–309
  and sexual roles, 369–371
Meiosis, definition of, 48
Melanesian Big Man, 457, 459
Melanesians and mana, 499
Mendel, Gregor, 553
  and heredity, 48
Mesolithic, 195, 206–207, 217
  cultivation and domestication during, 219–225
  cultures during, 218–219
  preagricultural villages during, 240–241
  trends during, 207–208
Mesopotamia
  diversification of labor in, 242
  emergence of culture, 241–242
  and farming methods, 242, 250–251
  internal stress, 250
  law in, 252–254
  social stratification in, 242, 244–245
  and urbanization, 231–232
  and writing, 247
Mexico
  emergence of civilization in, 242
  multicrop economy of, 251
    See also Aztec Indians
Microliths
  description of, 206–207

  during Mesolithic, 218
Middle Paleolithic, 195, 201–202
Milgram, Stanley, and overcrowding, 582
Miocene epoch and primates, 99
Missionaries and cultural change, 274
Mitosis, definition of, 48
Modal personality
  definition of, 312
  of Russians, 315
Modern Blackfeet Montanans (McFee), 563
Modernization and culture change, 559–570
Moiety, definition of, 387
Mongoloid, body type of, 154
Monogamy, 361
Montagu, Ashley
  definition of family, 363
  and Neanderthal man, 139
  and race, 159–160
Morgan, Lewis
  and descent groups, 389
  and social evolution, 25
Morphemes, definition, 291
Mousterian tradition, 201–202
Murdock, George
  and cultural change, 566
  and descent groups, 389
  and diffusion, 553
Music, 532–534
  diffusion of, 553
  elements of, 529–530
  functions of, 530–531
Musical instruments, 531–533
Mutations, description of, 50–51
Myth
  description of, 525–526
  etiological, 43
  among Penobscot Indians, 475

Nambikawa, family life of, 372–374
Natchez Indians, social class system of, 411–412
National character, 313, 315
  studies on, 316
Natufian culture, description of, 218
Natural selection
  and arboreal existence, 96
  and culture, 124–125, 273–274
  description of, 44–45
  and evolution, 51–53, 143–144
  and inheritance, 47
  and language, 298

Credits for Openers

ARCTIC OCEAN

Copper Eskimo

Caribou Eskimo

NORTH

Kwakiutl

Blackfoot

AMERICA

Iroquois

Cheyenne

Navajo

Pueblo

ATLANTIC

Hawaiian

Aztec

Maya

OCEAN

Yanomamo

PACIFIC OCEAN

Jivaro

SOUTH
AMERICA

Inca

Tikopia

OCEANIA

Guayaki

Location of the culture areas mentioned in the text book